International Encyclopedia of Communications

THE UNIVERSITY OF PENNSYLVANIA

The *International Encyclopedia of Communications*
was conceived, developed, and edited at
The Annenberg School of Communications,
University of Pennsylvania.

International Encyclopedia of Communications

ERIK BARNOUW
Editor in Chief

GEORGE GERBNER
Chair, Editorial Board

WILBUR SCHRAMM
Consulting Editor

TOBIA L. WORTH
Editorial Director

LARRY GROSS
Associate Editor

Volume 3

Published jointly with
THE ANNENBERG SCHOOL OF COMMUNICATIONS,
University of Pennsylvania

OXFORD UNIVERSITY PRESS
New York   Oxford

Oxford University Press

Oxford   New York   Toronto
Delhi   Bombay   Calcutta   Madras   Karachi
Petaling Jaya   Singapore   Hong Kong   Tokyo
Nairobi   Dar es Salaam   Cape Town
Melbourne   Auckland

and associated companies in
Berlin   Ibadan

Published jointly by
The Annenberg School of Communications,
University of Pennsylvania,
and Oxford University Press, Inc.,
200 Madison Avenue, New York, New York 10016

Library of Congress Cataloging-in-Publication Data

International encyclopedia of communications / Erik Barnouw, editor-in-chief . . . [et al.].
p.   cm.
Bibliography: p.
Includes index.
1. Communication—Dictionaries.   I. Barnouw, Erik, 1908–
P87.5.I5   1989   001.51′0321—dc19   88-18132   CIP
ISBN 0-19-504994-2 (set)
ISBN 0-19-505802-X (vol. 1)
ISBN 0-19-505803-8 (vol. 2)
ISBN 0-19-505804-6 (vol. 3)
ISBN 0-19-505805-4 (vol. 4)

2 4 6 8 9 7 5 3 1

Printed in the United States of America
on acid-free paper

Editorial Board

M

(continued)

MEANING

In any theory of communication the notion of meaning is bound to occupy a central place. Communication is achieved through the use of perceptible signs that carry a message between the participants (*see* SIGN). Thus words, gestures, and the like are said to mean something, and people who use them are able to mean something in doing so. These two aspects are interdependent: people can mean something because there are meaningful signs at their disposal, but these signs are meaningful because they are used to express what people mean to convey. Recent controversies about meaning turn on this distinction. *See also* GESTURE; MODE; SIGN SYSTEM.

The word *meaning* is but a derivative of the verb *to mean*. The scope of the latter, however, reaches beyond the domain of communication. In specifying the sense pertinent to this discussion, the theory of English philosopher H. Paul Grice, first proposed in his article "Meaning" (1957), will be examined.

Consider the contexts: "These spots mean measles" and "The murder of the crown prince means war." Notice first that in these cases nobody means anything by the spots or the murder. Notice second that it is the presence of the spots on a body that means measles, not the spots by themselves; spots, unlike words, have no meaning. Yet there is an element in these contexts that shows some similarity to meaning in the domain of communication. To the beholder the spots point beyond themselves; they warrant an inference to their cause, the measles. With the murder the inference goes the other way. The war is not its cause but its likely result.

Intention

Another use of the verb *to mean* is still not the one we are after. Consider, for example, "I meant to mail that letter today" and "I did not mean to hit you."

In these contexts *mean* is a near synonym of *intend*. Here, obviously, people mean something but not by employing a sign. Intentions play a crucial role in explaining meaning in communication too, but that is a more complex story.

The purpose of any communication is to influence the beliefs, ATTITUDES, and consequently the behavior of the recipient. Needless to say, such an influence can be exerted by other devices as well. Suppose A wants B to stop a car in front of a gate. One way of doing it is for A to cut down a tree and let it fall across the road. This obviously would not be an act of communication but physical interference. Another way is the following: A spreads some twenty-dollar bills on the roadway. Most likely B will stop but not because of any communication. Indeed, the tree and the bills do not mean anything.

There is a third way to achieve the same result. A may stand in front of the gate and raise a hand or even shout "Stop!" when B arrives. Whether or not B actually stops, communication will take place as soon as B understands what A meant by the gesture or the utterance, namely, that A wants B to stop. In this case both of the requirements mentioned above are fulfilled: that gesture and that word mean something, and A meant something in employing them. And B may understand A; that is to say, B may come to realize A's intention in using those signs, namely, that A wants B to stop because of recognizing that intention.

Contrast this with another case. A young man fakes a limp when appearing before the military draft board. His intention is clear: he wants them to come to believe that he is an invalid and send him home. Did he try to communicate? No, because he did not want his intention to be recognized.

Human communication takes many forms, in both the aims and the means employed. Consider the variety of such speech acts as statements, orders,

1

exhortations, promises, and apologies. Quite obviously the point of these utterances ranges from attempting to modify the listener's beliefs and attitudes to trying to influence conduct. Notice, however, that in all these cases communication is achieved once the addressee has understood the message; compliance is not required. Even if the speaker is not believed or obeyed, the force of the speech act and the listener's understanding of it will not be impaired. Meaning and understanding are not matters of behavior.

Since humans are not mind readers, the communicative intention of the sender has to be manifested in an observable fashion; that is, it has to be encoded in some tokens perceivable by the senses: signs, gestures, or words uttered or written down. These tokens, furthermore, must be recognizable by the recipient as expressions of that intention. The link between intentions and tokens, moreover, cannot be one established by nature, such as the causal relation between measles and the spots or between fire and smoke. Otherwise we would all speak the same LANGUAGE. Instead, in all human societies conventions connect tokens to intentions so that they can be used by the sender and understood by the addressee. Tokens satisfying this requirement are said to have meaning or to be meaningful, and the system of such (mainly verbal) tokens available to a given community is called a language.

The Nature of Meanings

A great deal of the philosophical discussion concerning language has centered on the problem of what kind of entities meanings are in themselves, that is, as distinct from their carriers. Are they mental or physical, concrete or abstract? The problem of language learning has provided a strong stimulus to seek meanings in the physical world. In the past decades, however, the futility of such a quest has been progressively acknowledged, mainly because of the work of Austrian philosopher LUDWIG WITTGENSTEIN.

In order to appreciate his approach, consider the notion of being valuable or having value. In Western societies bank notes, diamonds, and pieces of gold have value, but flies and common pebbles do not. Now the question What is value? is certainly not to be answered by looking for an entity in the physical world or out of it in which value would reside. The correct approach is to observe what we do with bank notes and contrast it with our treatment of pebbles. In Wittgenstein's terms, how do these things figure in our way of life? Roughly speaking, valuable objects play a role in the exchange of property. In a similar way the meaning of a word or a sign is to be established by observing its use in communication.

This approach spawned the slogan "Meaning is use," which is not quite right, as the slogan "Value is exchange" would not be. What is true is that as value is potential for exchange, meaning is potential for use in communication. Potentials, however, though distinct from their actualizations, have to be understood through these actualizations. The subtle lesson of Wittgenstein is this: Do not ask what meanings are, but look and see how words are used, how they are learned, and how their meanings are conveyed and codified, for example, in dictionaries—in short, what their place is in the life of society and CULTURE.

Meaning and Language Learning

Given the fact that the message to be transmitted is conventionally tied to the observable tokens, potential communicators have to learn which tokens are suitable for the encoding of various messages. In other words, they have to learn a language. *See also* LANGUAGE ACQUISITION.

There are two obvious difficulties involved in this endeavor. The first is that potential messages are infinite in number, but a learnable language must have a finite repertory. Accordingly, any possible message must be decomposable into elements for which the language provides means of encoding. Chemistry suggests an analogy: the number of possible compounds is without limit, yet the number of elements and the ways of combining them are finite. In language, too, the available words, grammatical structures, intonation patterns, and so forth form a finite, thus learnable, set. The adequacy of the language implies, then, that our thoughts, in which the messages are conceived, must have an analogous structure. This fact prompted some people to claim that we also think in a language, be it the natural language itself or an innate "language of thought" also capable of internalizing the rules of the natural language: its syntax (GRAMMAR), SEMANTICS (the meaning of words), and pragmatics (features of discourse). The first alternative would imply that infants and mutes have no thoughts, whereas the second leads to the conclusion that all natural languages must have the same basic structure mirroring the native endowment of the human mind. This claim, originally advanced by such rationalist philosophers as René Descartes and Gottfried Leibniz, has recently been revived by U.S. linguist Noam Chomsky and his followers, and it is the center of a lively controversy.

The other difficulty arises because words and structures are used to express the communicative intentions of the speaker. The language learner, however, has no direct access to these intentions. What elements of the public language correspond to what features of the message to be transmitted? The evidence has to be circumstantial. There are behavioral and circumstantial indications of what people intend to do and similar clues about what they intend to say. St. Augustine, who fully appreciated this problem, had this to say about his own progress in his *Confessions:*

My elders' . . . actions clearly showed what they meant, for there is a kind of universal language, consisting of expressions of the face and eyes, gestures and tone of voice, which can show whether a person means to ask for something and get it, or refuse it and have nothing to do with it. So, by hearing words arranged in various phrases and constantly repeated, I gradually pieced together what they stood for, and when my tongue had mastered the pronunciation, I began to express my wishes by means of them.

The need to include external situations in the process of language learning prompted philosophers throughout history to look for a word-to-world shortcut in the theory of meaning, bypassing unobservable intentions altogether. Two relations could qualify for this role: reference, linking names to things; and truth, connecting sentences to states of affairs.

The first approach, followed by thinkers from PLATO to English philosopher Bertrand Russell, equates meaning with denotation: as proper names denote individuals, so common names (and adjectives, verbs, etc.) denote such abstract entities as forms, universals, classes, properties, and relations. This account, however, is bound to become highly artificial when extended to adverbs, prepositions, and connectives, not to mention indexicals (*now, this, I*) or speech-act markers (*promise, censure*). Again, the paradigms of this approach, namely, proper names, are hardly meaningful: what does the word *Churchill* mean? One may ask, finally, what has been gained by eliminating unobservable intentions in favor of unobservable abstract entities?

More recently, particularly as a result of the work of Polish-born logician Alfred Tarski and U.S. philosopher Donald Davidson, the notion of truth is invoked to account for or to replace altogether the notion of meaning. This view is proposed in various forms, often with great sophistication. Roughly speaking, the claim is that knowing the meaning of a sentence is knowing its truth conditions—what has to obtain in the world to make it true. But since possible sentences form an infinite set, a further move is needed to keep the language learnable—a recursive procedure that derives the truth conditions of all sentences through their logical form from the satisfaction conditions of a finite number of predicates. A predicate is "satisfied" by all objects of which it is true. An extension of this approach accounts for the meaning of all sentences in terms of the set of possible worlds in which they are true.

The semantics based on truth is hardly less objectionable, however, than the one grounded in reference. First of all, the dimension of truth is applicable only to some speech acts (statements and the like) but not to others (orders, promises, and the like). Why, then, should the former domain be regarded as privileged with respect to meaning? Wittgenstein, for example, envisaged a language game consisting only of commands. Yet words in that language would have meaning, the absence of truth notwithstanding. Again, sentences containing such intentional words as *believe* and *want* cannot be viewed as logical products of their ingredients.

Finally, a recent development initiated by U.S. philosophers Hilary Putnam and Saul Kripke concerning the meaning of such "natural kind" words as *fish, water,* and *gold* casts doubt on the claim that knowing the meaning of such words amounts to knowing truth or satisfaction conditions. Only experts in the various scientific fields know these conditions, and they discovered them only recently (e.g., water is H_2O, gold is the element with atomic number 79). Yet for ages people used such terms effectively and thus knew their meanings. And the ancients who defined fire as "the hot and dry element" still knew what their word for it meant. The link tying these words to their referents seems to be historical, and people are able to use the words because of their familiarity with certain paradigms or stereotypes current in the culture, for example, "that heavy yellow metal used in making jewelry" for *gold*. Needless to say, the results of scientific progress may filter down and alter some of these stereotypes.

Thus the meaning of such terms reveals a social dimension: ordinary speakers defer to the experts, first, to discover the real nature of the referents of these terms and to determine thereby the extension of their applicability, and, second, to update and refine the stereotypes used in common practice. Quite obviously such a division of labor is not restricted to natural kind words but also applies to the terms of ART, technology, politics, RELIGION, and other social practices (think of such words as *sonata, radar, inflation, baptism*). Just as meaning is not "something in the world," it is not "something in the head" of individual speakers either. It may be the function of an interplay between speakers, experts, and even the features of the physical and human environment.

Lexicography

Lexicography, the art of compiling dictionaries, is the professional enterprise concerned with the meaning of words. Indeed, dictionaries can be viewed as instructions for using the words of a language. Bilingual dictionaries do this mainly by giving the equivalent word in the other language, with added remarks when necessary. Monolingual dictionaries may also use synonyms, but their basic move is to "define" the meaning of words. A careful look at dictionary entries teaches more about the notion of meaning than any philosophical speculation. Meaning is tied to use; dictionary entries describe that use in a systematic manner and thereby give the meaning. The fact that these descriptions are couched in the same language presents no difficulty; one has to use words to describe anything. *See also* LANGUAGE REFERENCE BOOK.

The lexicographer's work consists of two stages: first, find out what words mean, and, second, sum up the results in dictionary entries. The former task has two sources: observation of the circumstances in which people use a certain word and examination of the sentences in which the word is placed. The importance of these sources varies greatly. Such words as *ouch, hello,* and *hurrah* represent one extreme. They need not occur in sentences, and their meaning can be established entirely by the observation of speakers. Purely grammatical and logical words represent the other extreme. Words like *and, nevertheless,* and *almost* occur in any discourse, and their role is to give form to sentences regardless of their content.

Most words fall between these extremes. Although, no doubt, observation of speakers and circumstances may be helpful in discovering what such words as *cat, run, yellow,* or *good* mean, their meaning is more distinctly revealed by the regularities governing their use in sentences. These regularities indicate their grammatical role (noun, adjective, verb, etc.) and impose restrictions on possible co-occurrences with other words. Cats eat and sleep, but stones do not; stones crack and melt, but cats cannot. This kind of information is conveyed by saying that *cat,* for example, is an animate noun. Similarly, *yellow* and *good,* both adjectives, differ greatly, not only in their co-occurrences with other words (*good weather* but not *yellow weather*) but even in their grammar on a more sophisticated level. A person can be good at and a thing good for something or other but not yellow at or for anything. Verbs, too, differ significantly in their grammar: think of intransitives, transitives, or even more demanding verbs, such as *compare* and *assign.*

Thus grammar and co-occurrences represent a far more important source of lexical information than direct observation of speakers. Linguists have no great difficulty discovering the meaning of words in a dead language with no speakers, provided a large enough body of texts is available along with some information about some features: a few translated sentences, well-placed inscriptions, and similar clues.

The lexicographer's real art manifests itself in the second stage of work, in trying to convey the meaning of words in a concise and perspicuous fashion. Although attempts have been made to establish the general form of dictionary entries (particularly in the writings of U.S. philosopher Jerrold J. Katz), no such pattern can work in all cases because of the great variety of words. We can, however, list the most prominent devices used in compiling lexical entries.

1. *Discourse markers* indicate the special circumstances in which some words are used (like "greeting" or "apology") or the special field to which they belong (e.g., chemistry, law, tennis).
2. *Syntactic markers* give the word's grammatical status in terms of a detailed theory of syntax.
3. *Semantic markers* assign words to categories of increasing specificity. Indeed, the old-fashioned favorites genus and specific difference are but anticipations of a more advanced and detailed system. These markers correspond to and account for the co-occurrence restrictions mentioned above.
4. *Distinguishers* single out an individual item within the class defined by the semantic markers, for example, "large striped Asiatic feline quadruped" for *tiger,* "color of fresh blood" for *red,* "ingest food through mouth" for *eat,* and so forth. This is the place where the stereotypes mentioned above are to be given. In some dictionaries even pictures are used to generate a visual scheme for the recognition of a species of animal, plant, or garment. This represents a far echo of the old empiricist doctrine that meanings are something like pictures in the mind. If it is available the scientific definition or formula may be added: "H_2O" for *water* and "element with atomic number 79" for *gold,* for example.

In many, perhaps most, cases these devices will not be apt or sufficient. Thus it will be up to the lexicographer's ingenuity to convey the meaning by ad hoc definitions, the use of synonyms or near synonyms, and above all by giving examples of typical sentences in which the word is correctly used. The surprising thing is that a few such contexts are usually sufficient for the reader to gather the meaning and be able to use and understand the word in all contexts.

See also CLASSIFICATION; METAPHOR; SEMANTICS, GENERAL.

Bibliography. Donald Davidson, *Inquiries into Truth and Interpretation,* Oxford, 1984; Janet D. Fodor, *Semantics,* New York, 1977; Jerry A. Fodor, *The Language of Thought,*

New York, 1975; Jerrold J. Katz, *Semantic Theory,* New York, 1972; A. P. Martinich, ed., *The Philosophy of Language,* New York and Oxford, 1985; Hilary Putnam, *Mind, Language, and Reality,* New York and Cambridge, 1975; W. V. Quine, *Word and Object,* New York and London, 1960; Ludwig Wittgenstein, *Philosophical Investigations* (Philosophische Untersuchungen), trans. by G. E. M. Anscombe, New York, 1953, reprint Oxford, 1968; Paul Ziff, *Semantic Analysis,* Ithaca, N.Y., 1960.

ZENO VENDLER

MERGENTHALER, OTTMAR (1854–1899)

German-born U.S. inventor of the Linotype machine. The son of schoolteachers in Hachtel, Württemberg, Ottmar Mergenthaler showed great interest and skill in mechanics at an early age. Unable to afford engineering school, he was apprenticed at age fourteen to an uncle who was a watchmaker. He also took courses at night in mechanical drawing, blueprint reading, and electrical theory. In 1872 he emigrated to the United States and worked in his cousin's machine shop in Washington, D.C., and later in Baltimore, Maryland.

Printing-press technology had been dramatically advanced by this time, but type was still set by hand, piece by piece (*see* PRINTING). Scores of inventors had tried, with little practical success, to meet the need for mechanical composition. In 1876, while employed by his cousin in making models for patent applicants, Mergenthaler worked on a device for the lithographic transfer of typewriting for its inventor, Charles Moore, and Moore's financial backer, James O. Clephane. The device worked poorly, but it led Mergenthaler to a dedicated interest in typesetting.

Financed by Clephane and others, Mergenthaler experimented with several typesetting systems. Finally he produced a system of brass matrices (with one matrix for each character) notched for automatic sorting, stored in channels of a magazine, released by keyboard action, and (with spacebands between words) dropped into place to cast a lead-alloy line of type.

A group of publishers meanwhile became the machine's principal backers. Their leader, Whitelaw Reid of the *New York Tribune* (which first demonstrated the machine in July 1886), dubbed it the Linotype. Reid insisted that the machine be put into production immediately and would not let Mergenthaler perfect it. Sales, which were large at first, soon collapsed. The early backers regained control in 1888, enabling Mergenthaler to develop the greatly improved Simplex Linotype by 1890. Its use reduced printing costs

Figure 1. *(Mergenthaler, Ottmar)* Ottmar Mergenthaler demonstrating the operation of the "blower machine"— the first commercially successful Linotype—for Whitelaw Reid, in the plant of the *New York Tribune.* The Bettmann Archive, Inc.

and made major expansion possible in newspaper (*see* NEWSPAPER: HISTORY), MAGAZINE, and BOOK production.

See also TYPOGRAPHY.

Bibliography. Seán Jennett, *Pioneers in Printing,* London, 1958; I. E. Levine, *Miracle Man of Printing: Ottmar Mergenthaler,* New York, 1963; Willie Mengel, *Ottmar Mergenthaler and the Printing Revolution,* Brooklyn, N.Y., 1954; S. H. Steinberg, *Five Hundred Years of Printing,* 3d ed., Harmondsworth, Eng., and Baltimore, Md., 1974.

CHANDLER B. GRANNIS

MERTON, ROBERT K. (1910–)

U.S. sociologist whose theoretical framework for analyzing social phenomena has been usefully applied in communications research. Born in Philadelphia, Pennsylvania, Robert King Merton graduated from Temple University in 1931. In 1936 he earned a Ph.D. in sociology at Harvard University, where his thinking was influenced by his contact with such scholars as Talcott Parsons, Pitirim A. Sorokin, and George Sarton. From this intellectual experience Merton derived his theoretical framework for the analysis of social structure and functions, one of the foremost formulations of structural-functionalism in U.S. sociology (see FUNCTIONAL ANALYSIS). Merton taught sociology at Harvard from 1934 to 1940. In 1940 he moved to Tulane University and then in 1941 joined the faculty of Columbia University, where, after his retirement, he was appointed University Professor Emeritus and Special Service Professor. Among many honors, Merton was elected to the U.S. National Academy of Sciences.

Merton is best known in sociology for his seminal contributions to structural-functional theory and for studies in the sociology of medical education and the sociology of science. He has contributed directly to the study of communications through his own essays and research and indirectly through the application by others of his sociological concepts and theoretical framework. His appointment to the sociology department at Columbia began a lifelong friendship and working partnership with fellow sociologist PAUL F. LAZARSFELD, who succeeded in enlisting Merton's talents and interest in the department's research arm, Columbia's Bureau of Applied Social Research (BASR). Merton served as an associate director of the BASR, and in 1976 he became cochairman of the advisory board of the BASR's successor, the Center for the Social Sciences.

Among Merton's major works on mass communications is the now classic *Mass Persuasion: The Social Psychology of a War Bond Drive* (with Marjorie Fiske and Alberta Curtis, 1946). This intensive case study of a wartime RADIO marathon bond drive conducted by a popular entertainer of the time, Kate Smith, uncovers and analyzes the processes of mass PERSUASION through mass communication. The study's research design was unusual, combining a sample survey of PUBLIC OPINION, a CONTENT ANALYSIS of the broadcast messages, and detailed focused interviews with listeners.

The latter form of research interview, which focused on the subjective experiences of people known to have been exposed to some previously analyzed situation (e.g., a radio or television program), was a technique developed and promoted by the BASR. In 1946 Merton and Patricia Kendall formalized the procedure in a sociological journal article; in 1956 they, together with Marjorie Fiske, developed a fuller methodological exposition in *The Focused Interview*. Today the focused interview is a research technique used in commercial as well as academic communications research.

Merton and Lazarsfeld's participation in a series of lectures on problems of the communication of ideas in 1946 produced their sociologically critical essay "Mass Communication, Popular Taste, and Organized Social Action." This essay set forth their ideas on the social conditions that lead the mass media to play a conservative role in society. It introduces and conceptualizes such social consequences of mass communication as the status-conferral function ("The mass media *confer* status on public issues, persons, organizations and social movements"), the enforcement of social norms, and narcotizing dysfunctions (information overload may lead to apathy instead of action because one confuses *knowing* about current social and political problems with actually *doing* something about them). These concerns continue to interest communications researchers today. The essay also touches on the power of face-to-face communications to supplement mass communication, a point emerging from several communications studies at Columbia about that time (see also INTERACTION, FACE-TO-FACE).

Merton introduced the concepts of *local influential* and *cosmopolitan influential* into the ongoing research on mass communication and personal influence in "Patterns of Influence: A Study of Interpersonal Influence and of Communications Behavior in a Local Community" (1949). This study examines, among other issues, how these two types of influentials fit into the social system and what uses they make of mass-communicated news and information. The typology has been applied in communications studies and in other sociological works through the years.

Other works by Merton that address problems of communications include studies in the sociology of knowledge and of science, INTERPERSONAL COMMUNICATION and friendship formation (with Lazarsfeld), and radio and film PROPAGANDA (also with Lazarsfeld). Merton's work in the sociology of science has been particularly influential on studies of communication and information exchange among scientists. His study of friendship as social process coined the terms *homophily* and *heterophily* (the tendency for friendships to form among persons who are alike or who differ in certain characteristics or ATTITUDES), which found their way into communications research on the DIFFUSION of innovations. Earlier research on wartime propaganda (with Kendall) drew attention to the "boomerang effect" (unintended responses to propaganda).

In addition to these direct contributions to the field

Merton's general theoretical orientation and sociological concepts are relevant to contemporary communications theory and research. Some of these ideas have been explicitly applied to the field by other scholars. Three examples will be cited here. Merton's formulation of a structural-functionalist approach (1949) set the framework for the functional analysis of mass communications. His conceptualizations of role theory, reference group theory, and sociological ambivalence (1950, 1957, 1976) are relevant for research on mass communicators and audiences. Finally, Merton's theories of social structure and anomie (1938, 1957) relate both deviant and conformist behavior to social structure and are relevant for studies of the cultural values and social norms presented in mass communication content and for theoretical discussion of mass communication's role in socialization and social control.

Bibliography. Paul F. Lazarsfeld and Robert K. Merton, "Mass Communication, Popular Taste, and Organized Social Action," in *The Communication of Ideas,* ed. by Lyman Bryson, New York, 1948; Robert K. Merton, "Patterns of Influence: A Study of Interpersonal Influence and of Communications Behavior in a Local Community," in *Communications Research, 1948–1949,* ed. by Paul F. Lazarsfeld and Frank N. Stanton, New York, 1949; idem, "Social Structure and Anomie," *American Sociological Review* 3 (1938): 672–682; idem, *Social Theory and Social Structure* (1949), enl. ed., New York, 1957; idem, *Sociological Ambivalence and Other Essays,* New York, 1976; Robert K. Merton, Marjorie Fiske, and Alberta Curtis, *Mass Persuasion: The Social Psychology of a War Bond Drive,* New York and London, 1946; Robert K. Merton, Marjorie Fiske, and Patricia L. Kendall, *The Focused Interview: A Manual of Problems and Procedures,* rev. ed., Glencoe, Ill., 1956; Robert K. Merton and Patricia L. Kendall, "The Focused Interview," *American Journal of Sociology* 51 (1946): 541–557.

CHARLES R. WRIGHT

MESSAGE. *See* MODELS OF COMMUNICATION.

METAPHOR

Long regarded as a stylistic embellishment of interest only to specialists of RHETORIC and LITERARY CRITICISM, metaphor has come to be regarded as an essential tool of communication and COGNITION. Metaphors play a crucial role not only in POETRY but also in scientific, philosophical, and creative discourse of all sorts. And we have recently become cognizant of the extent to which metaphors pervade ordinary LANGUAGE.

Defining metaphor. ARISTOTLE provided the first systematic definition of metaphor in Western thought, stating in the *Poetics:* "Metaphor consists in giving the thing a name that belongs to something else: the transference being either from genus to species, or from species to genus, or from species to species, or on ground of analogy." Aristotle thought the most significant form of metaphor to be one based on analogy. Metaphor defined in this narrower sense is opposed not merely to literal language but also to other forms of figurative language.

Metaphor has been distinguished both from literal language and from many forms of figurative language in two ways. First, the transference of MEANING is marked by some sort of incongruity, often a semantic or conceptual deviance, or, when there is no deviance, conversational incongruity (e.g., Mao Zedong's "A revolution is not a dinner party"). Second, metaphor is characterized by the use of a single expression to convey two incompatible thoughts. One term, the vehicle, carries its usual meaning; the other, known as the topic, is the subject of the metaphor. For example, if we speak of a woman's beauty in terms of the beauty of a rose, *rose* (i.e., the word itself and what is usually expressed by the word *rose*) is the vehicle, and the woman's beauty is the topic.

One attempt to capture what has been called the double semantic import of metaphor is to suggest that metaphors have what Danish semiotician Louis Hjelmslev referred to as a connotative, in contrast to a denotative, semiotic (*see* SEMIOTICS). A SIGN used denotatively requires a level of expression and a level of content. In certain cases, as with dialect or jargon, the level of expression itself carries content, some information additional to the meaning of the word. The Hjelmslevian scheme is generalizable to other modes of communication (*see* MODE). One can say that metaphors are characterized by the fact that the expression level is itself a denotative sign, which is then used to convey an additional content. Thus in the sentence "It is trust that knits up the world" the expression *knits* carries, in addition to its denotative content, a content applicable to trust, one for which we have no easily identifiable term. ROLAND BARTHES, building on the work of Hjelmslev, speaks of myth as belonging to "a second-order semiological system." Eva Kittay argues that a second-order meaning with a connotative structure is particular to metaphor.

Theories of metaphor. A useful typology of metaphor is provided by linguistic philosopher Max Black, who contrasts his own interaction theory with the substitution and comparison theories. According to the substitution theory, metaphor is a figure of speech in which the vehicle is simply a more decorative or eloquent term substituted for a plainer term denoting the topic. In this view there is no cognitive gain in the use of metaphor, although one may exploit the emotive meaning of the substituted term.

In the comparison theory the topic is implicitly compared to the vehicle. The basis of the comparison appears to be some preestablished similarity between topic and vehicle. If metaphors are implicit comparisons, then they should be paraphrasable as statements of similarity. But because a metaphor does not normally state how the topic and vehicle are similar, and because there is always some sense in which any two given things can be said to be similar, it seems singularly uninformative to claim that a metaphor can be restated as a literal statement of comparison.

Black seems to think that the substitution and comparison views fit some metaphors but claims that the theories fail to do justice to the irreducible cognitive content of many others. His interaction theory holds that a metaphor is not the simple displacement or substitution of one term for another but that metaphor engages in an interaction between, in the words of I. A. RICHARDS, two contexts. The vehicle of the metaphor brings with it a set of associated beliefs that serve as a filter or lens through which we come to understand the topic. From this perspective some features of the topic are highlighted and some recede in importance. In the process our understanding of the vehicle is modified by its interaction with the topic. Thus a cognitive metaphor permits us to understand the world in a somewhat different manner from that which is put forward in a literal statement. The interaction of vehicle and topic produces a meaning distinctive to them and therefore irreducible to a literal paraphrase.

A more sophisticated version of the comparison view developed by U.S. philosopher Donald Davidson challenges the interaction theory. Davidson argues that although metaphors are not paraphrasable into literal comparison statements, they direct us to make comparisons and analogies. Their value comes not from what they mean—which, claims Davidson, is just the literal meaning of their words—but from what they suggest (e.g., that the reader explore the possible comparisons between the things brought together in the metaphor).

Brief History

Aristotle's treatment of metaphor found its way into classical and RENAISSANCE texts on the subject. The classical writers characteristically accepted a view akin to the substitution theory of metaphor, but they celebrated metaphor's decorative effect. Both CICERO and Quintilian esteemed the ornamental in language if it were fitting and appropriate to the subject at hand. Cicero noted that whereas some metaphors arise out of the poverty of language to communicate something requiring expression, others "do not indicate poverty but convey some degree of boldness of style." Quintilian made beauty in language a vir-

tue, writing that "the flash of the sword in itself strikes something of terror to the eye." In traditions devaluing the utilitarian, metaphor is praised for its ornamental effect, and its emotive and rhetorical efficacy is brought to the fore.

In the classical tradition rhetoric, along with dialectics or logic (see SYMBOLIC LOGIC), constituted the art of PERSUASION. The view of metaphor as mere ornament did not appear until rhetorical theory was fully fragmented by French philosopher Petrus Ramus in the sixteenth century. Rhetoric itself was reduced to elocution or style; invention, memory, and disposition were relegated to the art of disputation. Although Ramus's division initially had a beneficial effect on metaphor for the Elizabethan poets, the Renaissance call for plain speech otherwise diminished the stature of style and elocution (see STYLE, LITERARY). Metaphor as well as figurative language generally was devalued and thought to serve a sometimes trivial, sometimes pernicious function, distracting the reader from the serious, communicative function of plain PROSE. Seventeenth-century British philosopher JOHN LOCKE wrote: "All the artificial and figurative application of words eloquence hath invented, are for nothing else but to insinuate wrong *ideas,* move the passions, and thereby mislead the judgment." The study of metaphor was relegated to taxonomies of figurative language. Underlying this attitude toward metaphor is a conception of language as a conduit and the mind as a passive receptacle of perceptions. The mind, unencumbered by passions and interests, records the impressions of things as they are and collects these in the form of ideas that it is then the proper business of language to communicate in similarly unencumbered prose.

The romantics challenged this trivialization of metaphor (see ROMANTICISM), some drawing inspiration from Italian philosopher Giambattista Vico, who insisted on the intimate relation between thought and language and on the importance of poetry and metaphor in the shaping of language, and from German philosopher Immanuel Kant, for whom the mind actively contributes to the formation of the percepts and concepts by which we engage the world. French philosopher Jean-Jacques Rousseau, another early influence, maintained the thesis that language originated in metaphor and music. For English poet Samuel Taylor Coleridge, the imaginistic fusion of the symbol "produces that ultimate end of human thought and human feeling, unity" (see SYMBOLISM). Coleridge's views have been important in shaping those of Richards, whose work in turn has been central to the Anglo-American tradition.

The nineteenth-century German philosopher Friedrich Nietzsche spoke of the formation of the abstract concepts as an effacement and wearing away of metaphors until they are no longer recognized as such, just as continued use effaces the embossment on a coin until we no longer recognize the metal as a coin. He endeavored to show the metaphoric origin of language in order to emphasize the subjectivity of all linguistic utterances, his point being to show that there is no privileged discourse that expounds the truth; all discourse carries with it a perspectival, subjective stance born of our sensuous experience of the world. When we forget these metaphoric origins, which we do almost of necessity when we retreat to the security and stability of abstractions, we take refuge in the lie that these faded metaphors speak the truth.

Some Current Issues

Whereas contemporary European interest in metaphor has been shaped by the work of Nietzsche, recent Anglo-American interest in metaphor has emerged in large part as a reaction against the positivism that pervaded philosophy, psychology, and LINGUISTICS in the early twentieth century. In psychology, for example, which has turned away from behaviorism and toward cognitive theory, the challenge is to develop models of the mind that account for the predominance of metaphor in communication. That concern becomes a practical one in efforts to expand the capacities of ARTIFICIAL INTELLIGENCE. If machines are to communicate through natural language, they must be able to understand and produce metaphors. In attempting to provide a computational account of metaphor there is much to be learned about human communication; for example, how background assumptions function in both metaphorical and literal language.

Metaphor as semantics or pragmatics. In metaphor it appears that we are confronted with an utterance that says one thing and means another. Is this meaning that is not said really "meaning" at all? Black and others maintain that we can speak of metaphorical meaning and that consequently we should be able to give a satisfactory semantic account of metaphor (*see* SEMANTICS). Davidson counters that there is no puzzle about how we can say one thing and mean another, because there is no divergence between what a metaphor says and what it means. It is what an author has chosen to do with a sentence and how an audience construes it that gives rise to metaphor, but this is a matter of language use and not of meaning. A number of authors have taken seriously the proposal that metaphor belongs to the pragmatics of language and have suggested, with varied success, a speech-act approach to metaphor. Others have taken the position that because metaphor is not simply a linguistic phenomenon, because there are visual or even auditory metaphors, it cannot require any particular linguistic competences. More

general psychological competences, such as general propensities to analogy, are at play. Nonetheless, because each communicative mode entails its own competences and rules, it may be that unique capabilities are required to produce and comprehend metaphor in each mode. It seems most likely that metaphorical language is governed both by certain semantic rules—some of them for breaking the rules of literal, conventional language—and by pragmatic considerations that may be applicable to various communicative modes.

The interpretation of metaphor. If we agree that there is a distinctive metaphorical meaning, we need to ask how that meaning is arrived at, how metaphors are interpreted. A prevalent view, which may be called the predicate transfer thesis, claims that we interpret metaphors by projecting onto the topic those predicates or attributes generally taken to pertain to the vehicle of the metaphor. If we speak of marriage as a zero-sum game, then the predicates that apply to the concept "game"—that it is a contest, that there are contestants, that one wins at the expense of the other—may all be projected onto the topic, marriage. A related approach, the feature addition/deletion thesis (best exemplified by the work of U.S. linguist Samuel Levin), does not speak of transferred predicates but rather of transferred semantic features; that is, features that determine word meaning. This approach holds that when a term is used metaphorically the sentence will be semantically deviant, and the offending term(s) must be interpreted as losing certain features and/or adding certain others. For example, in the phrase "rosy-fingered dawn" the feature (human) would be transferred from "rosy-fingered" to "dawn." But these interpretive theories fail to consider the systematic interconnections between words and their importance in understanding metaphors.

Another approach to the interpretation of metaphors considers the systematicity of metaphor. Metaphors are readily extended. If we say that it is trust that knits up the world, then we can say of that world that it is a stuff peculiarly liable to fraying and raveling. Nelson Goodman spoke of an entire realm of labels that are transferred in the case of metaphor—if we speak of a picture as gay, then we can also speak of it as sad. Kittay, along with U.S. linguist Adrienne Lehrer, has used the notion of semantic fields to suggest that in metaphor what is transferred is a set of relations that a term (the vehicle) bears to other terms within its own semantic field. These relations reorder a portion of the semantic field of the topic. George Lakoff and Mark Johnson demonstrated the interconnectedness of many metaphors of everyday speech and showed that certain central metaphors structure how we consider whole areas of thought and action.

The deconstruction of metaphor. French philosopher Jacques Derrida, appropriating the Nietzschean view, attempted to show that metaphysical language is dominated by faded metaphors (words and concepts whose metaphorical origins have been forgotten), that the discussion of metaphor has itself been conducted in metaphorical terms, and that metaphor is grounded in a metaphysical (and metaphorical) distinction between words and their meanings. According to Derrida, metaphor self-destructs and does so in two senses. First, although metaphor is conceived of as a detour, a "provisional loss of meaning," as with all detours it must return to the "proper sense"; what is deviant and metaphorical is reappropriated by what is proper and literal. Second, the pervasiveness of metaphor in discourses that presumably are "proper" and nonmetaphorical explodes the distinction between what is metaphorical and what is literal. If we consistently find metaphor where we expect to find "proper" language, if the boundaries are so unclear, the distinction itself is misconceived. One may respond that without a distinction between the literal and the metaphorical we can make no sense of metaphor and that we can take into account some of Derrida's critique by relativizing the distinction.

Metaphor and Other Figures

Metaphor has at times been construed as including a host of other tropes, including metonymy, synecdoche, litotes, and hyperbole. Metonymy is a transfer based on contiguity, for example, as the name of an author is substituted for the author's work, a cause for an effect, a symbol for that which it symbolizes. Synecdoche, the substitution in expression of a part for the whole or the whole for a part, is often regarded as a special type of metonymy. Both involve transfers of meaning that come under Aristotle's definition of metaphor in the *Poetics*. Rather than accept metonymy as a species of metaphor, linguist ROMAN JAKOBSON suggested that metaphor and metonymy constitute two poles of linguistic competence and that studies of aphasia indicate that different pathologies affect a speaker's ability with relations based on either similarity (metaphor) or contiguity (metonymy). Litotes (understatement) and hyperbole (overstatement) again fall within the Aristotelian definition. In his discussion of metaphor Goodman includes not only litotes and hyperbole but also irony. Although all these shifts of meaning share with metaphor the transfer of meaning, in the more narrowly construed sense of metaphor the shift takes place across semantic fields or conceptual domains. In the other figures of speech shifts of meaning occur within one conceptual domain. One cannot fashion a metaphor using *knife* as a vehicle for fork or *chair* as a vehicle for table, because both terms are understood as belonging to the same semantic field. In the case of irony, terms with different values and positions within the same field are reversed. Irony can also be used very effectively with metaphor. The character Teiresias, the blind prophet with insight, embodies an ironical and metaphorical figure in which sightedness and blindness are reversed and then transferred from the field of perception to that of intellection.

The transfer of meaning in metaphor is often related to catachresis, defined as the misuse of language. Both catachresis and metaphor have been spoken of as transfers that occur when we lack a name for what we wish to speak of, as, for example, the "leg" of a chair. But catachresis may also be more like a genuine misnomer, as when a refrigerator is referred to as an "icebox" or a graphite pencil as a "lead pencil."

But the figure most closely associated with metaphor is simile. Metaphor has at times been spoken of as a condensed simile, and simile in turn has been considered an expanded metaphor. The comparison theory of metaphor has treated the two figures as one, whereas many proponents of the interaction theory have made a deliberate attempt to dissociate them. If simile is defined as merely a comparison of one thing with another announced by the words *like* or *as*, then the interactionists are right to distinguish metaphor and simile, for metaphor requires that the two things brought together be from distinctly different domains. But if we add the constraint that a simile must be a figurative and not a literal comparison, that the things compared come from two distinct domains (cf., "Richard is as tall as an elm" and "Richard is as tall as Harry"), then metaphor and simile are distinguished not by any conceptual feature but by the linguistic (or semiotic) feature that makes metaphor a connotative structure carrying a double semantic content. One could say that in a figurative comparison or simile the word *like* is itself metaphorical.

Bibliography. Max Black, *Models and Metaphors,* Ithaca, N.Y., 1962; David E. Cooper, *Metaphor,* Oxford, 1986; Donald Davidson, "What Metaphors Mean," in *Philosophical Perspectives on Metaphor,* ed. by Mark Johnson, Minneapolis, Minn., 1981; Jacques Derrida, "White Mythology: Metaphor in the Text of Philosophy" (La mythologie blanche), trans. by F. T. C. Moore, *New Literary History* 6 (1975): 5–74; Nelson Goodman, *Languages of Art,* 2d ed., Indianapolis, Ind., 1976; Eva F. Kittay, *Metaphor: Its Cognitive Force and Linguistic Structure,* Oxford, 1987; George Lakoff and Mark Johnson, *Metaphors We Live By,* Chicago, 1980; Samuel R. Levin, *The Semantics of Metaphor,* Baltimore, Md., 1977; Andrew Ortony, *Metaphor and Thought,* Cambridge, 1979; Paul Ricoeur, *The Rule of Metaphor: Multidisciplinary Studies of the*

Creation of Meaning in Language (La métaphor vive), trans. by Robert Czerny, Toronto, 1978.

EVA FEDER KITTAY

MICROELECTRONICS

Electronics and communications have, since the early days of this century, developed in a symbiotic relationship. Indeed we may think of wireless TELEGRAPHY and broadcasting as prime examples of a development in which the need to communicate over long distances was fulfilled by the application of electronics. In turn, early electronics were developed primarily to fulfill the need for communication. Other uses were, of course, found for the emerging technology of electronics, but various forms of communication always dominated the demand for electronics.

At the center of early electronics was the vacuum tube. Its invention is claimed by many, and indeed many diverse forms and aspects were invented by different individuals. The invention of the rectifying diode is usually ascribed to John Ambrose Fleming in 1904. The first amplifying tube, the triode, is ascribed to LEE DE FOREST in 1906. The first thirty years of tube development saw increasing use of electronic circuits in diverse applications such as broadcasting transmitters and receivers as well as a variety of electronic instruments.

Tubes became smaller and consumed less power; they also became more reliable and could be combined with resistors and capacitors into complex circuits. For mobile applications it became desirable to reduce the size and weight of communications equipment even further. Electronic equipment using tubes could be reduced in scale but remained too clumsy for many purposes. Particularly, airborne equipment and the so-called walkie-talkie communication system carried by infantry soldiers in World War II illustrated the need for further miniaturization.

Three developments eventually outmoded the vacuum tube: the need for very-high-frequency signal processing, especially in wartime radar applications; the construction and introduction of electronic computers; and the invention of a solid-state amplifying device—the transistor. The first two developments underlined the insoluble problems faced by electronics based on vacuum tubes, and the third represented the breakthrough that allowed a new electronics—microelectronics—to emerge and overcome the technical challenges.

The technologies affected by these innovations included radar, the computer (*see* COMPUTER: HISTORY), and a variety of telecommunications technologies. Radar is a device that transmits high-frequency electromagnetic radiation for the purpose of detecting and locating distant objects such as aircraft or ships. The objects reflect some of the radiation, and the reflected signal is detected. To achieve this, radar technology took a step backward in order to move forward and reintroduced the older crystal detector, popularly known as a cat's-whisker detector. A major research program aimed at improving radar detectors during World War II brought great advances in knowledge of the electrical properties of semiconductors.

The electronic programmable computer, an entirely separate development, though also speeded on its way by military support, first appeared in the immediate postwar period. The monster machine ENIAC, completed in 1946 at the University of Pennsylvania, used eighteen thousand tubes, weighed thirty tons, and consumed 140 kilowatts of power. Clearly computer development could not continue on these lines, and an alternative to tube electronics had to be found.

The need for an electronic amplifier with low power consumption, high reliability, low cost, and high-frequency capability had been articulated since the early 1930s. The obvious path to follow was to use solid-state devices, similar to the cat's-whisker detector or the familiar cuprous oxide rectifier. Many solid-state amplifiers were invented, many were patented, and none worked.

After World War II, Bell Laboratories in the United States set up a research team with the goal of investigating semiconductor materials to obtain devices useful to telecommunications. The device foremost in everybody's mind was, of course, a semiconductor amplifier. After a few unsuccessful attempts the development of the ancestral device of all microelectronics, the point contact transistor, was announced on June 30, 1948 (Figure 1). The first transistors were made of germanium and looked somewhat like two cat's-whisker detectors on a single tiny piece of crystal. The device was truly an amplifier, although not a particularly good one at first.

A period of rapid development was initiated by this first announcement. The point contact transistor was soon supplanted by the junction transistor, in which the two wire contacts to the crystal were replaced by two p (positive)-n (negative) junctions in close proximity to each other (Figure 2). The art and science of manufacturing transistors made rapid strides (Figure 3). Performance improved, prices fell, and increasing numbers of manufacturers offered their wares in a rapidly growing market. Three of the main inventors of the original transistor—John Bardeen, Walter Brattain, and William Shockley—were awarded the 1956 Nobel Prize in physics for this invention.

Interestingly, much of the rapid growth in transistor manufacture was carried by small, newly founded entrepreneurial firms that were well able to search

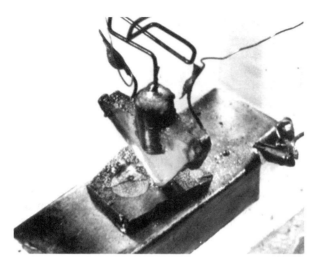

Figure 1. *(Microelectronics)* The point contact transistor, assembled in 1947. Courtesy of AT&T Bell Laboratories.

Figure 2. *(Microelectronics)* The junction transistor, assembled in 1947. Courtesy of AT&T Bell Laboratories.

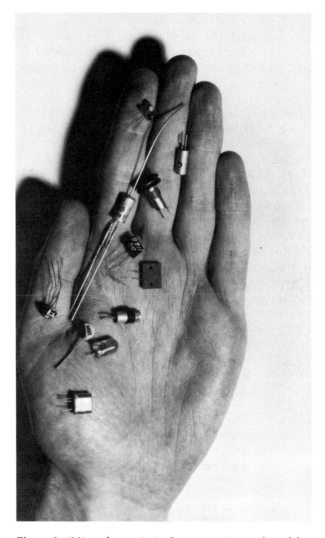

Figure 3. *(Microelectronics)* Some experimental models of the transistor, June 1953. Courtesy of AT&T Bell Laboratories.

out market opportunities. Transistors soon penetrated into all forms of traditional electronics but also opened up entirely new possibilities ranging from miniature hearing aids to light portable radios. TELEPHONE applications became as important as those in airborne communications, and these were soon joined by the first space ventures. A highly significant interrelationship was established between computers and semiconductor electronics. In fact, each successive generation of computers was based on new and better semiconductor electronics. The growth and improvement in computers and microelectronics are two inseparable aspects of technical progress and the capture of new markets.

The quality and performance of transistors were, to a considerable degree, determined by manufacturing methods. By about 1960 the so-called planar process began to dominate transistor manufacture.

The planar process is based on a photolithographic method of transferring desired patterns photographically onto the oxidized surface of a silicon chip, after which those parts of the oxide layer exposed to light are removed chemically. The previously important germanium was replaced by silicon, which became virtually the only raw material for microelectronics.

Very soon the question arose of why it was necessary to make single transistors and wire these together with resistors and other passive components to obtain electronic circuits when it might be possible to produce a complete circuit in a single chip by planar production techniques. This was easier said than done, but with a great deal of ingenuity the first integrated circuits were produced soon after the introduction of the planar process. Though the first attempts were only moderately successful and contained only a few components in each silicon chip, success nevertheless bred success. The number of transistors per chip grew inexorably from about 5 in 1962 to 150,000 in 1982, and the price per component fell with equal rapidity. By that time the separation between components within a chip had become an unbelievable five microns (0.005mm) or less.

One of the new products made possible by microelectronics was the pocket calculator. When the newly founded firm Intel was asked in 1969 to make several different integrated circuit chips for a range of calculators, it hit upon the idea that a single design for a chip could fulfill all the needs if it were programmable. Such a chip was designed and became known as a microprocessor. It is essentially the central part of a computer, and thus the vital functions of a digital computer had been concentrated on a single tiny chip of silicon. Microelectronics came of age, and an entirely new line of development started with improved generations of microprocessors following each other in rapid progression. The development has been termed the microelectronic revolution (Figure 4).

One further technical development deserves mention. Computers are helpless unless they can store information of all kinds: operating instructions (programs), data to be operated on, data to be accessed by the user when needed. Memory chips became established in the late 1960s and were also subject to rapid development in increasing capacity and de-

creasing price. In 1968 the state of the art was to put about one thousand bits of information on a single chip, and about twenty years later there were memory chips capable of holding one million bits of information. For longer-term storage, information is held on magnetic or optical disks.

So great has been the success of microprocessors and the whole gamut of microelectronic components that virtually all electronics is turning to digital signals and signal processing. Thus, instead of producing an electrical analog to some physical quantity, such as the pitch and amplitude of sound, we now tend to produce a numerical (digital) description of the same quantity (*see* SOUND RECORDING). This development has spread into communications, and in modern installations signals are transmitted and handled as streams of digits.

The combination of digital computers and digital signals has opened up many new possibilities for telecommunication services. Yet again the growth of microelectronics has been intimately linked with the provision of communications: microelectronics is the common base linking digital data processing with telecommunications. Computing and electronic data processing have become inseparably linked with both microelectronics and communications.

See also FIBER OPTICS; TELECOMMUNICATIONS NETWORKS.

Bibliography. Ernst Braun and Stuart Macdonald, *Revolution in Miniature: The History and Impact of Semiconductor Electronics Re-explored*, 2d ed., Cambridge, 1982; Tom Forester, ed., *The Microelectronics Revolution*, Oxford, 1980; Peter Large, *The Micro Revolution Revisited*, London and Totowa, N.J., 1984; F. F. Mazda, *Integrated Circuits*, Cambridge, 1978; R. M. Warner and B. L. Grung, *Transistors*, New York, 1983.

ERNST BRAUN

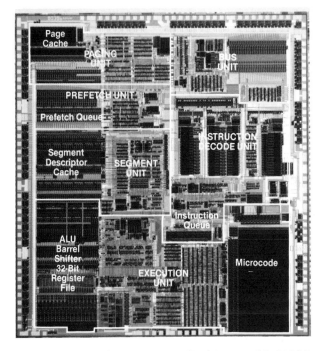

Figure 4. *(Microelectronics)* Intel's thirty-two-bit 80386 Microprocessor introduced in October 1985. Courtesy Intel Corporation.

MIDDLE AGES

The Middle Ages are delimited by two major transformations in the history of communications. At one end is the decline of the ROMAN EMPIRE, and with it the gradual disappearance of literate legal and administrative procedures in western Europe. At the other is the introduction of PRINTING using movable type invented by JOHANNES GUTENBERG and others in the 1430s.

We will probably never have a complete history of human interchange for the several hundred years that separate these two turning points. Medieval records are often poor in quality, discontinuous, and uninformative. Western Europe had profound regional variations, which resulted from accidents of geography, patterns of MIGRATION, and uneven eco-

Figure 1. *(Middle Ages)* The beginning of the Gospel of St. Luke. Early medieval codex in uncial script, probably from northern France. The Pierpont Morgan Library, New York. (m. 862, f. 93).

nomic development. There were different spoken languages and little agreement on the uses of LITERACY. A patchwork of laws, institutions, and kinship rules made feudal society—as it is often improperly termed—look less like an early modern state than a peasant society before the advent of science, technology, and industrialization. Only within the past two generations has the important role that the Middle Ages played in the history of communications come to be widely recognized. Much basic research remains to be done, and generalizations must be made with caution.

The Middle Ages are often pictured as a period of isolation, even darkness. But its techniques of communication grew naturally out of those of the ancient world. The linguistic background begins with the division of Latin into learned and popular forms, which was underway as early as the second half of the third century B.C.E. The major influence was Greek; the imitation of its syntax and rhetoric reinforced the separation of the written and spoken forms of Latin. More significantly, as Hellenism spread throughout the Mediterranean in the two centuries before and after the death of Christ, Latin authors gradually adopted and effectively transmitted to the West the notion of humanism based on allegedly higher and lower branches of the same LANGUAGE (*see* HELLENIC WORLD). Once established in the educational system, this pattern of interpretation was applied later in diverse linguistic and social situations. It drove a wedge between the official CULTURE, which was expressed in Latin, and the various unofficial cultures, which existed in spoken Latin or the early vernacular languages. During the RENAISSANCE a similar theory of high culture based on classical GRAMMAR helped to legitimize the use of literary Italian, French, and German. This perception of the differences between learned and popular culture is one of the chief legacies of medieval linguistic development and has been a source of inspiration as well as tension throughout subsequent social, political, and literary history.

Language and writing in transition. The major phase of transition took place roughly between 200 and 600 C.E. There were three fundamental changes: the emergence of a new cursive, the development of the codex, and the evolution of the Romance languages.

The new cursive, sometimes called *scripta latina rustica*, was in use everywhere but the imperial chancery by the mid-300s, and it gave novel vocabulary and syntax a permanent graphic form for the first time. An even more important transformation took place in book production, in which the papyrus roll was gradually replaced by the parchment or vellum codex, the forerunner of the modern BOOK (*see* WRITING MATERIALS). The triumph of the codex was complete by the late third or early fourth century. Its popularity is thought to have arisen chiefly from the Roman Christian habit of copying the Bible into parchment notebooks. The codex was more durable than the roll and easier to read and to store; it facilitated indexing, searching for facts, and the accumulation of knowledge characteristic of the much later age of print. But it owed its success less to technical than to political factors: the Bible, as transmitted by codex, became the official sacred book of ancient society after the imperial recognition of Christianity by Constantine I in 313 C.E. In addition to changes in WRITING habits and book production, the late Latin period witnessed the emergence of a new linguistic community in Europe, consisting of the speakers of present-day Italian, French, Provençal, Catalan, Spanish, Portuguese, and Romanian. The common Latin roots of these languages have given shape to much of the Romance cultural consciousness from the Middle Ages down to the present.

Diversification of language and writing continued throughout the later ancient world and the Middle Ages. The result was a large number of spoken and

Figure 2. *(Middle Ages)* Romanesque wall painting, Stories from the lives of St. Peter and St. Paul, eleventh century. Chiesa S. Piero in Grado, Pisa. Alinari/Art Resource, New York.

written languages whose internal histories can only be partially and indirectly reconstructed. By the time Charlemagne died in 814 a superficial imperial unity had been reimposed on northwestern Europe. But ordinary people in different regions who were ignorant of Latin could no longer understand one an-

other. A hiatus had developed not only between spoken and written languages but among the spoken languages themselves, which had begun to evolve grammatically distinct written forms. We do not know whether writing followed speaking, as Romance linguists often assume, or vice versa, as the

Carolingian revival of Latin studies would suggest. But by the ninth century there are a number of clear indications—for instance, the provision for vernacular preaching in the Council of Tours (813)—that the linguistic environment of Europe had been irrevocably altered. Latin remained the dominant vehicle of culture; it was the only language in which grammar could be taught (Greek having virtually disappeared in the West), and it was the only written language that was widely understood. Yet the various Romance and Germanic languages existed in substance if not in grammatical form, and each was independently evolving a colloquial as opposed to a literary dimension.

The "birth certificate" of the vernacular languages is normally thought to be the Strasbourg Oaths of 842, in which the armies of two of Charlemagne's grandsons swore oaths of alliance, each in its own vernacular. However, this was chiefly a symbolic event; only some decades after the millennium do we have evidence of a dramatic increase in the number of readers and writers (as well as visual representations of didactic material, which one finds in manuscript illustrations and Romanesque wall paintings). The textual fortunes of the vernacular languages varied considerably. For some, like Gothic, we possess only a handful of words and phrases, while for others, like Irish, Anglo-Saxon, and Old Norse, we have rich literatures. In the great works of medieval English, French, and Italian we observe Europe's earliest modern interaction among language, texts, and society.

Role of institutions. If we turn from language to the history of institutions, the clearest guide to the growth of communications is provided by the recordkeeping activities of the church (*see* RELIGION). Long before the Edict of Milan guaranteed the corporate freedom of the church, the popes had employed Roman notaries for recording the acts of martyrs, keeping the minutes of synods, and preparing transcripts of documents. The papal ARCHIVES became the official storehouse of ecclesiastical memory. Throughout the early Middle Ages the bureaucracy remained small, but from the eleventh century on the number of transactions greatly increased, and significant changes took place. During the papacy of Benedict VIII (1012–1024), papyrus was finally replaced by parchment. Later popes clarified the style of legislative letters, reorganized the systems of writing and dating, and supervised the adoption of a clear, legible script. From Gregory VII (1073–1085) on, the papacy was given direction by a distinguished series of lawyers, all of whom insisted on procedural regularity and the systematic accumulation of information, until under Innocent III (1198–1216) a consistent archival policy finally emerged.

During the same period the growth of the economy and of lay administration also required more ample documentation, particularly in the areas of commerce, property law, and contractual obligations. In southern Europe recordkeeping fell under the control of public scribes or notaries, whose cartularies, often astonishing in the completeness of their record of sales, debts, and contracts, first appeared in Italian towns, where secular and commercial instincts were the most highly developed. At first notaries were attached to the judiciary, but by the twelfth century they had begun to form guilds and to test prospective candidates. In the north, where customary law persisted longer, lay documentation accumulated in registers and archives and through the judiciary system. The age of bureaucracy had arrived, and along with it sophistication in the ancient art of forgery.

Role of oral traditions. The spread of writing tells only one part of the story of medieval communications. The other is related in oral traditions and by the manner in which they changed under the influence of literacy. This aspect of the question also requires some conceptual reorientation. In general, ORAL CULTURE has been viewed from the perspective of literates. This angle of vision greatly limits our appreciation of the Middle Ages, just as it restricts our understanding of how individuals communicate today in societies that carry on everyday activities by word of mouth. Such communities are not illiterate; they are nonliterate. In the Middle Ages the presence of texts is not always indicative of a high degree of functional literacy. On some occasions texts merely recorded oral legal transactions, just as written epic poems preserved oral performances, while the essen-

Figure 3. *(Middle Ages)* Bronze seal of Raimon de Mondragon, showing a vassal kneeling before his lord in the act of homage, twelfth century. Provence. Phot. Bibl. Nat., Paris.

Figure 4. *(Middle Ages)* Pilgrims witnessing the Last Judgment. Detail from the tympanum of Autun Cathedral, France, ca. 1130. Giraudon/Art Resource, New York.

tial act of communication was spoken, gestural, and ritualistic. On other occasions texts may have served a dispositive role, even though the signatories to a document were themselves unlettered. Most important, medieval oral discourse seldom if ever existed in isolation in the West. Like the spoken and written forms of language today, the aural and visual modes impinged on each other in a variety of ways. Whether communication took place by words or by letters is a matter for empirical investigation.

The starting point for such inquiries is the legacy of Germanic institutions in early medieval society. The clearest picture is found in law. The unwritten laws of the migratory peoples who increasingly settled on Roman soil after the second century were made up of words, rituals, and symbols. As time went on, the interaction of Roman and Germanic legal systems ultimately led to the codification of the customs of the various tribes. But scribal practices almost invariably preserved oral legal codes by imitating already functioning verbal institutions. For example, in place of signatures on a charter, one frequently had the ceremony of *manumissio,* the ritual placing of hands on the parchment. Again, witnesses did not normally record an act; Germanic

custom demanded that transactions actually be seen and heard. Twigs, branches, and pieces of sod were frequently sewn to medieval documents, and their physical presence rather than the inscribed words ratified the contract. The persistence of oral tradition is nowhere better illustrated than in the ceremony of *levatio cartae:* before the charter was written, the parchment, pen, and ink were placed on the land to be sold, from which, it was assumed, they acquired a special force. The final document was both a legal record and a quasi-magical object. Even a blank piece of parchment carried authority because of its potential associations.

The ambivalent role of texts is an aid to understanding the nature of what is called feudal society. The legal feudal bond originated as a spoken contractual arrangement between two individuals, normally a lord and a vassal, and included certain military obligations and property rights. This state of affairs persisted as late as the Carolingian age. Later, what had in principle arisen as a bond between people slowly but surely became enmeshed in the economic structures of a competitive agrarian society. Property and, consequently, the legal right to defend ownership became more important. As a result, the original oral features were either translated into written terms or, like the ceremony of investiture, retained as verbal RITUAL within an ever-widening network of written law.

By 1100 the conceptual apparatus of legalized feudalism was largely in place; by 1300 the customary laws for both secular and ecclesiastical estates were being systematically written down. Yet, despite changes in function, feudal rites were united by a number of common features throughout the Middle Ages. These included respect for the individual and his or her word, the belief in the concrete over the abstract, the formalization of obligations through ritual, and, lurking behind many ceremonies, the symbolic gestures of tribal warfare. The essential element was ritual. This, and not the written transcript of the proceedings, constituted the bond. The central ceremonies all blended the spoken, the symbolic, and the PERFORMANCE of rites. In homage, for example, the lord and the vassal stood facing each other. The vassal repeated a number of set phrases in response to statements by the lord. He then joined his hands and placed them inside the hands of his master, while the lord slowly closed his own hands over those of his dependent. The performance of such acts expressed the early medieval belief in the gift as the preferred form of material and social interchange.

Commercial expansion. From as early as the tenth century, this notion of reciprocal and redistributive exchange was effectively challenged by modern Europe's first prolonged commercial expansion. No other

Figure 5. *(Middle Ages)* Ambrogio Lorenzetti, *Allegory of Good Government: The Effects of Good Government in the City* (detail of fresco), 1338–1339. Palazzo Pubblico, Siena. Alinari/ Art Resource, New York.

upheaval had so great an impact on the world before the Industrial Revolution. The changes were many, affecting communications in a variety of ways, but the one constant was population increase. In the countryside, marshes were drained, rivers tamed, forests cleared, and land resettled after centuries of neglect. Isolated villages came into contact with one another, and entrepreneurial lords sponsored local markets. Cash crops and surpluses appeared as peasants introduced crop rotation, metal implements, deeper plowing, and foods that gradually spread northward from Islamic lands. Rents flowed to lords from water, wind, fulling, and tanning mills. A money economy surfaced as COINS began to circulate again via either Byzantium or royal mints. The once great Roman network of roads was refurbished to permit the flow of people and goods. Long-distance routes overcame the Alps, and rudimentary medieval navigators explored the Mediterranean (*see* EXPLORATION). Pilgrimages, which increased in number after the millennium, helped to create the demand for land routes free of brigands, while monasteries punctuated the pilgrimage roads to Rome, Compostela, and Jerusalem, along with hostels, which welcomed monks, entertainers, traders, and merchants, thereby creating a meeting place for the different orders of a once static society (*see* CRUSADES, THE).

The commercial revolution was created largely by the Italian city-states, and they derived the major benefits from it. By the twelfth century the wealth of Genoa, Pisa, and Venice surpassed the richest of business centers in the ancient world; by the early fourteenth the influence of Italian cities could be felt in England, Russia, the Middle East, India, and China. In the north the most active markets took place at the fairs of Champagne and Brie, but it was Italian merchants who created the demand for northern textiles, on which they flourished, and it was Italian financial arrangements that permitted long-distance transactions to take place in an atmosphere of confidence.

The replacement of barter by currency, the emergence of banking and credit, and, by the fourteenth century, the introduction of double-entry accounting were symptomatic of a new mentality that affected other areas of human exchange. From the end of the twelfth century Genoese money changers offered limited banking services. They accepted deposits withdrawable on demand, they transferred payments and made current account advances, and they settled debts with other nascent banks. Soon, larger houses sprang up in Piacenza, Pistoia, Siena, Lucca, and Florence. Close links were forged between centers of banking, market, and trade; many banks invested the deposits of individuals and the liquid assets of business firms, while the bigger banks engaged in international transactions such as ransom, military pay, and loans to cash-hungry rulers. A vast network of countinghouses and correspondents opened up. The Bardi, just one house, had some 350 employees and thirty branches in Italy, North Africa, and the Levant. Banking itself progressed as the older system of legal contracts gave way to private documents, correspondence, and account books. From about 1300 on, the contracts of exchange drawn up by notaries were superseded by simple letters of payment, the forerunners of bills of exchange.

Banking services were not only used by kings and the higher nobility; they also proved invaluable to bishops, abbeys, town corporations, burghers, and even peasants. What finally emerged from the medieval commercial revolution was nothing less than a primitive type of capitalism, involving the accumulation of capital and goods; the gradual separation of management from the ownership of capital and labor; the growth of money, credit, and impersonal market forces; and above all a ruthless spirit of competition, combined with a desire for profit, toward which the church more than occasionally turned a blind eye.

Twelfth-century renaissance in law. The commercial developments originating in the south took place about the same time as the large-scale reappearance of written culture in the north known as the twelfth-century renaissance. In continental Europe the legal revival established three fields of jurisprudence—Roman law, canon law, and the codification of feudal statutes—while a more precocious environment in England, dating from Anglo-Saxon times, led to the sealed writ and the institution of the royal courts, from which sprang other deputations such as the exchequer, the bench of common pleas, and the system of itinerant justices. During the twelfth century, in both Roman and common law, written documents replaced oral TESTIMONY, and objective methods of evaluating evidence challenged the role of duels, ordeals, and compurgations. The new method consisted essentially of taking evidence from witnesses, analyzing the various factors in a case, and scrutinizing the relevant written documents.

The legal renaissance went hand in hand with the growth of expertise in DIPLOMACY, textual criticism, and the authentication of acts. People began to think of facts not as recorded by texts but as embodied in texts, a transition of major importance in the rise of information retrieval and methods of CLASSIFICATION. The search for facts, which had hitherto been limited to memory, now shifted to the written text. The great codifications of the century—Peter Lombard's *Sentences,* Abelard's *Sic et Non,* and Gratian's *Decretum*—were inseparable from a changed attitude toward the organization and classification of knowledge.

Finally, at a more mundane level, the later twelfth century saw the definitive rise in northwest Europe of different types of written records for organizing and administering society. Some records, such as charters, testimonials, wills, and sealed memoranda, were kept by individuals. Other records were compiled by institutions as a permanent reminder of past practices and a set of guidelines for the future, such as surveys, court rolls, yearbooks, cartularies or registers, and chronicles.

Coexistence of written and oral evidence. The rebirth of literacy caused people everywhere to question the value of oral information. What resulted was a hybrid culture, in which the spoken word was rejected from some fields of knowledge and retained in others, or in which, as in the case of the Anglo-Saxon poem *Beowulf* (eighth to tenth century), oral traditions were written down in order to preserve them. Within historical writing one sees an increasing use of archival sources. Ordericus Vitalis, for instance, whose *Ecclesiastical History,* completed by 1141, is remarkable for its account of Norman life

Figure 6. *(Middle Ages)* Genoese banking scene. By permission of the British Library.

and institutions, exemplifies his age in lamenting the lack of written records for the period of the Scandinavian incursions, which, he says, he can only relate from "the oral traditions of old men." Yet within the same history, dreams, visions, and fantasies, none of which possessed records, are uncritically accepted as witnesses to events.

Another example of this ambivalence is found in the critical accounts of oral materials made for literate audiences. An example is the *Miracles of St. Foy*, by Bernard of Angers, in which the stories associated with the cult were gathered personally in the region around Conques sometime after 1010, and later sifted for inconsistencies. Perhaps the most radical critic of oral testimony was Guibert of Nogent, whose treatise questioning the validity of certain unauthenticated relics was completed by 1125. Guibert proposed a set of standards for assessing the claims of any holy object. He did not question that relics existed, but insisted that their claims be supported by textual proofs. He looked upon unwritten traditions as hearsay, by-products of local culture, or FOLKLORE.

Religious communication. The awakening of the critical spirit in communications is nowhere better reflected than in the history of medieval religious dissent and reform. Early reformers all championed literate standards, whether they were wandering preachers, Gregorian propagandists, or leaders of new religious orders. The impulse toward textual organization reached its apogee in the Cistercian order, in which ornament was reduced to a puritan minimum, the liturgy and prayer books standardized, and the economic planning of abbeys rationalized. But the literalistic biblical studies that supported reform also paved the way for diverse interpretations of religious texts, especially among the laity. Mass movements formed, attempted to institutionalize their messages, and inevitably came into conflict with the church.

The chief vehicle of communication utilized by such groups before the age of print was preaching. From the late eleventh century on, wandering preachers like Robert of Arbrissel and Bernard of Tiron roamed the countryside of northern France, while in Milan the Patarene movement organized rallies to harangue crowds about simony and clerical marriage. The most successful heterodox preacher of the time was perhaps Peter Waldo, founder of the Waldensians, whose life-style of apostolic poverty was imitated by the forerunners of St. Francis. Orthodox preaching received a stimulus from the tenth canon of the Fourth Lateran Council of 1215, which admonished bishops to preach publicly and encouraged the future antiheretical efforts of the Dominicans. *See also* HOMILETICS; PUBLIC SPEAKING.

The spread of heresy via the spoken word was

Figure 7. *(Middle Ages)* Gilded reliquary statue of St. Foy, late fifteenth century. Trésor Ancienne Abbaye, Conques. Giraudon/Art Resource, New York.

symptomatic of a breakthrough in medieval communications, the free circulation of ideas, which was destined to play a large role in developing a skeptical, scientific view of the world. But it also gave rise to the West's earliest successful instrument of repression, the papal Inquisition, which began its unfortunate history under Gregory IX in 1233–1234. What eventually defeated the church's monopoly of religious literacy was the introduction of vernacular translations of the Scriptures. In England the lay thirst for access to the Bible was satisfied in the fourteenth century by John Wycliffe's translation. Vernacular literacy subsequently became a major issue in the Lollard movement, first in England and later under Jan Hus in Bohemia. The Hussite wars terminated with the agreement at Jihlava in 1436; only seven decades later, in 1517, MARTIN LUTHER nailed up his theses in Wittenberg.

Implications of literacy. The Middle Ages have generally been thought to differ from modern times chiefly in the use of manuscripts as opposed to printed books. But in form, design, and function, later medieval manuscript culture is continuous with the age of print, and it is arguable that printing only succeeded as it did because a literate reading public already existed. Where the Middle Ages really differed from the modern age was in the type of transition that took place within its modes of perception. In the early Middle Ages, oral communication was well suited to a society that was regionalized and in which one's role, occupation, or status was often inherited. The continuity of culture depended on individuals who verbally transmitted mores, traditions, and kinship rules. Rulers, too, were individuals whose charisma and authority involved the spoken word. Knowledge was transferred in face-to-face encounters that united SPEECH and action and were rich in ritual and GESTURE. Society's only archive was human memory.

By contrast, in the period after the year 1000 medieval society became increasingly oriented around the scribe and the text. Written communication expanded economic and cultural horizons for some, but it also simplified a complex social environment. Through literacy, culture itself was externalized and objectified; it depended less on the individual voice than on the text by which it was recorded and transmitted. The knower was thereby separated from the known, with obvious consequences for logic, epistemology, and the birth of the scientific outlook. As the eye replaced the ear as the primary sense, and the written ALPHABET came to dominate the spoken phonetic system, social relations themselves became contextualized, and individuals, to paraphrase MAX WEBER, eventually found themselves suspended in webs of textual significance which they themselves had spun.

Bibliography. Erich Auerbach, *Literary Language and Its Public in Late Latin Antiquity and in the Middle Ages*, trans. by R. Manheim, London and New York, 1965; Franz H. Baüml, "Varieties and Consequences of Medieval Literacy and Illiteracy," *Speculum* 55 (1980): 237–265; Marc Bloch, *Feudal Society*, 2 vols., trans. by L. A. Manyon, London, 1961; Michael T. Clanchy, *From Memory to Written Record: England, 1066–1307*, London, 1979; Marcia L. Colish, *The Mirror of Language: A Study in the Medieval Theory of Language*, rev. ed., Lincoln, Neb., 1983; Ernst R. Curtius, *European Literature and the Latin Middle Ages*, trans. by W. R. Trask, Princeton, N.J., 1953, reprint 1973; Georges Duby, *Les trois ordres ou l'imaginaire du féodalisme* (*The Three Orders: Feudal Society Imagined*, trans. by A. Goldhammer, Chicago, 1980), Paris, 1978; Herbert Grundmann, "Litteratus-Illiteratus. Der Wandel einer Bildungsnorm vom Altertum zum Mittelalter," *Archiv für Kulturgeschichte* 37 (1955): 1–65; Jean Leclercq, *The Love of Learning and the Desire for God. A Study of Monastic Culture*, trans. by C. Misrahi, New York, 1961; Paul Saenger, "Silent Reading: Its Impact on Late Medieval Script and Society," *Viator* 13 (1982): 367–414; Brian Stock, *The Implications of Literacy: Written Language and Models of Interpretation in the Eleventh and Twelfth Centuries*, Princeton, N.J., 1983; J. W. Thompson, *The Literacy of the Laity in the Middle Ages*, Berkeley, Calif., 1939, reprint New York, 1960.

BRIAN STOCK

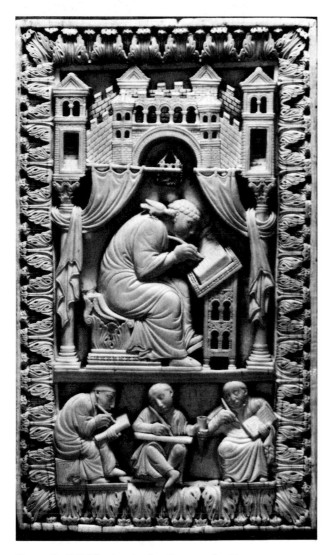

Figure 8. *(Middle Ages)* St. Gregory the Great as a scribe. Ivory panel, tenth century. Kunsthistorisches Museum, Vienna. Marburg/Art Resource, New York.

MIGRATION

In simple terms migration is a change in place of residence of an individual or a group of people, usually on a permanent or long-term basis. It is not otherwise easy to define migration because it includes so many different kinds of migrants and moves and so many reasons for moving. A migration may be as relatively minor a change as moving from city to city or from a rural region to a city, or as considerable as moving to a different country on a different continent. It may describe individuals moving to employment opportunities in a new industry or a large group resettling together, like the thousands of Mormons moving to establish a new home in Utah. It may be as temporary as students' periodic migration to college or the seasonal migration of laborers in response to needs for agricultural help, or as relatively permanent as the settlement of the American West in the nineteenth century.

Whatever the size and length of the migration, it is closely related to communication because communication ordinarily helps build the incentive and select the place for migration. Moreover, the migration ultimately encourages interest, continuing exchange of information, and further migration between the two places.

Who Migrates and Why They Move

Some people are more likely than others to migrate. Young adults, for example, are more likely than older ones to migrate because they are more likely to be seeking career opportunities. In middle age, people are less likely to move because they are already settled into a career and place of residence. If older people plan to move it is more often to a place of retirement than to a place offering employment opportunities.

The destinations of migrants are not randomly distributed. People are more likely to move to a larger than to a smaller community because more and better-paid employment will probably be available there. Furthermore, other things being equal, migrants are likely to move to a place they hear about frequently, and large places are more often in the news than small ones.

Voluntary and involuntary migration. A common distinction between types of migrants separates those who *want* to go and those who *have* to go. On the former side are those who follow a gold rush or a rich oil discovery, receive an offer of free land or more income, or simply want to start again in a more hopeful situation. On the other side are those who are compelled to migrate, like the African slaves brought in chains to Europe and the New World (*see* SLAVE TRADE, AFRICAN) and those driven by political or economic pressure or necessity. The partition of British India made it necessary for 8 to 9 million Hindus and Sikhs to be expelled from Pakistan, and 6 to 7 million Muslims from India. The revolution and civil war in Russia created a group of nearly 1.5 million international refugees. After the civil war in Spain some 300,000 Spaniards became refugees. Britain transferred 150,000 convicts to help settle Australia. Thus a large part of all migration has been involuntary.

Economic problems have also been responsible for some of the forced migrations of recent times. For example, the potato famine in Ireland in 1845 caused more than a million Irish citizens to migrate to the United States, and the economic hardships and political problems of Germany between 1848 and 1854 touched off an even larger migration from that country. It has been estimated that 80 percent of all immigrants to the United States between 1845 and 1855 came from either Germany or Ireland.

The answer to why people like these migrated is that they *had* to; they were forced out. But why did the voluntary migrants leave their homes?

The decision to migrate. Voluntary migration can generally be interpreted as a sum of individual or group responses to perceived inequalities in the distribution of opportunities. The elements appraised differ from case to case. Within a city the decision may depend on the standard and cost of housing; in deciding on longer moves, whole ways of life may be compared. In all these cases migrants are normally assumed to behave in a rational manner, evaluating the alternative locations and seeking to maximize the benefits to themselves of staying or moving. However, certain constraints are likely to intrude on any decision to change residence. One is the feasibility of moving, which requires consideration of the cost and effort, the relative cost of living, the housing allocation or financing policies of large corporations or public administration, or, on a wider scale, the immigration policies of nation-states.

Still another constraint is lack of information about opportunities and costs in the places to which one considers migrating. In the past and in less developed societies the sources of information have inevitably been highly personalized, often inaccurate and speculative. However, the efficacy even of RUMOR and informal DIFFUSION of information through a society can be seen in the large-scale migrations brought about when a climate of belief in the existence of better conditions elsewhere was created, as, for example, in European views of the limitless possibilities of life on the other side of the Atlantic (*see* COLONIZATION).

Personal experience has played an important role in providing the information on which a later decision to migrate could be based. Thus temporary migration or circulation has often given migrants an insight into the opportunities available elsewhere and has resulted in a permanent migration; indeed, it has been observed that temporary migration generally becomes permanent migration (if it is permitted to do so). It has also been observed that "active" or pioneer migrants establish a "trail" that is followed by relatives, friends, and persons from the same community, who become the "passive" migrants in a continuous stream of communication and movement. This is the phenomenon of "chain migration" whereby early migrants retain ties with their places of origin (e.g., through kinship links), write letters, make occasional visits, and thus create conditions in which others decide to make a similar move; when that happens, earlier migrants commonly help in the process of settling later arrivals. This process has created migration areas that become fashionable and comfortable for certain groups. Retirement migration is an interesting example.

The information sources on which a decision to migrate can be based have become more diffuse and have involved a whole series of elements, from picture postcards to mass media. Since a potential migrant makes a decision on the basis of a subjective view of what he or she is likely to find in a new location, it is the general image of places and opportunities that is important. In longer-distance migration, therefore, a potential migrant may put together such an image from a great variety of sources: personal educational background, radio (see RADIO, INTERNATIONAL) and television, newspaper reports, private evidence from friends and relatives, and such specific sources as advertisements designed to encourage the migration.

Transportation, communication, and migration. Transport systems have played a considerable role in influencing migration by affecting both the cost and the effort of moving and the amount of information available. Ernst Ravenstein first observed in the nineteenth century that a "distance decay" effect normally operates within any migration system: the amount of information about a particular place declines steadily with increasing distance from that place, although significant amounts of information about large places are likely to be available even at great distances. A "gravity model" relating the migration flow between any two places to the size of the places and to the distance between them has been proposed. Recent improvements in transportation as well as modern telecommunications (see TELECOMMUNICATIONS NETWORKS) have reduced these constraints on migration, but distance still has a frictional effect because the actual costs of moving plus the social costs of upheaval play a significant part in the potential migrant's appraisal of present versus other possible locations. While improvements in transportation and communication in the past certainly led to an increase in the amount of migration, that may be less true of the developed world at the end of the twentieth century. There are even some indications that the amount of migration in developed areas has

started to decline, possibly because the enhancement of modern telecommunications and transport means that there is less need for residential movement. Getting a job in a distant town no longer in every case necessitates moving there, for long-distance commuting is easier than it once was.

Three Scales of Migration

Although the basic decisions relevant to migration—the appraisal of relative opportunities and costs—enter into the majority of migration flows, the effects of migration, because of their complexity and diffuseness, can best be considered by illustrating the impact of migration on several scales.

Intercontinental migration. Migration has been the agency for diffusing humanity and peopling all parts of the world, as well as the process by which the present distribution of ethnic groups and nationalities has come about. Historically the role of migration has been immense, especially in the lands of the temperate zone settled by a process of colonization or other movements of large numbers of people from Europe. This latter effect has been especially noteworthy in countries like Canada, the United States, South Africa (the white population), Australia, New Zealand, and Argentina. Intercontinental migration has been less significant in creating the population distributions of many parts of the tropical world, where colonialism took the form of resource exploitation without settlement. However, the forced movement of large numbers of the initial populations of such tropical areas (for instance, as slaves or indentured laborers) has been of great significance in creating ethnic diversity within many receiving areas.

Although the term DIASPORA strictly speaking refers only to Jewish migration, the concept has been used increasingly as an analogy for the diffusion of other population groups such as the English (as a result of colonization), the Chinese, and the Indians. Some of the earlier patterns of long-distance migration have reversed, with large numbers of people moving from the Third World into the industrialized countries, to a large extent replacing the older movements that diffused population outward from these countries.

Interregional migration. This type of migration is generally associated with inequalities in the economic opportunities available within individual countries or subcontinents. A prime example is the massive wave of rural-urban migration that has affected almost all countries undergoing urban industrial growth. In these countries the agricultural sector has declined vis-à-vis industry, business, and services, thus creating a new spatial pattern of opportunities. However, in many other cases, particularly in the Third World, interregional movement has represented not so much a move to real opportunities in urban areas as an escape from a lack of opportunity in rural areas. Often the opportunities that are so desperately sought in the overcrowded cities are actually minimal.

Elsewhere many regional movements have occurred as a result of the opening of new lands and internal colonization. The opening of the western United States depended largely on interregional migration by those already settled farther east, although newly arrived intercontinental migrants also played a role. More recent examples of interregional migrations to "new lands," illustrating the role of governments in manipulating information flow, are the movements from west to east across the Urals in the USSR and the interisland migration from Java to Sumatra in Indonesia.

Local migration. Locally, migration within a city, such as residential relocation, appears normally to occur more often as a response to factors of the social environment than to economic considerations. The most common reason for intraurban movement is the household's need for new accommodations.

Constraints on movement often become very apparent at this scale. Real opportunities for change of residence are often limited by institutional or institutionalized processes restricting access of certain types of people to certain types of property. The result may be patterns of spatial segregation, with local migration streams confined to certain areas and restricted from transgressing the boundaries of the segregated areas. Socioeconomic class segregation normally occurs because potential housing occupants are separated on the basis of their ability to pay. Ethnic segregation, on the other hand, is generally a result of institutional processes, such as those embodied in the South African Group Areas Act. Local migration is therefore instrumental in setting up and maintaining urban social areas and thereby perpetuating the fragmentation of urban space into areas of distinctive population composition.

The Impact of Migration

The cumulative influence of all the types and acts of migration on the history and evolution of countries, regions, and cities has been immense. A single migration event can be seen in a systems framework to have effects on a wide range of phenomena. At the center of such a framework are the characteristics of the migrant. By being subtracted from the population of the place of origin and added to the population of the place of destination, the migrant affects the characteristics of both the sending and the receiving societies. Because it occurs in a context of perceived opportunities and operational constraints, the act of migration also has an effect on that context, modifying, strengthening, or weakening it in ways that vary from case to case. Migration is therefore at the heart of the process of evolution in human societies.

See also CRUSADES, THE; ISLAM, CLASSICAL AND MEDIEVAL ERAS; POSTAL SERVICE; SOUTH ASIA, ANCIENT.

Bibliography. Alan A. Brown and Egon Neuberger, eds., *Internal Migration,* New York, 1977; Murray Chapman and R. Mansell Prothero, eds., *Circulation in Third World Countries,* London, 1985; William H. McNeill and Ruth S. Adams, eds., *Human Migration: Patterns and Policies,* Bloomington, Ind., and London, 1978; Peter H. Rossi, *Why Families Move,* 2d ed., Beverly Hills, Calif., and London, 1980; Paul E. White and Robert I. Woods, eds., *The Geographical Impact of Migration,* London and New York, 1980.

PAUL WHITE AND ROBERT WOODS

MILTON, JOHN (1608–1674)

English poet best known for his *Paradise Lost* and *Paradise Regained,* John Milton also won a place in communications history with his *Areopagitica* (1644), an attack on press licensing and CENSORSHIP. For almost a century PRINTING in England, as in many parts of Europe, had been ruled by licensing procedures. The right to print in England was confined to the Master Printers of the Stationers Company, which maintained a register in which members were required to list books they wished to print. Official licensors reviewed all proposed publications. Printers were expected to assist in the suppression of unlicensed printing, which represented inroads on their MONOPOLY. Printers of unlicensed books were subject to severe penalties—fines, confiscation of property, imprisonment. In 1643 Milton wrote a PAMPHLET urging liberalization of divorce restrictions and was incensed by obstacles to its publication. This provoked his eloquent *Areopagitica.* Though its subtitle called it *A Speech for the Liberty of Unlicensed Printing,* it was printed as a pamphlet without the official imprimatur. Most widely quoted is the following passage:

. . . though all the winds of doctrine were let loose to play upon the earth, so Truth be in the field, we do injuriously by licensing and prohibiting to misdoubt her strength. Let her and falsehood grapple; who ever knew Truth put to the worse in a free and open encounter?

Milton's main theme was the invincibility of truth. He did not, in fact, advocate absolute freedom of expression, being mainly concerned with the stultifying effect of appointing censors ("a few illiterate and illiberal individuals") to review the works of better thinkers. He recognized the government prerogative to suppress "popish" views and indeed served as a censor of newsbooks in 1651.

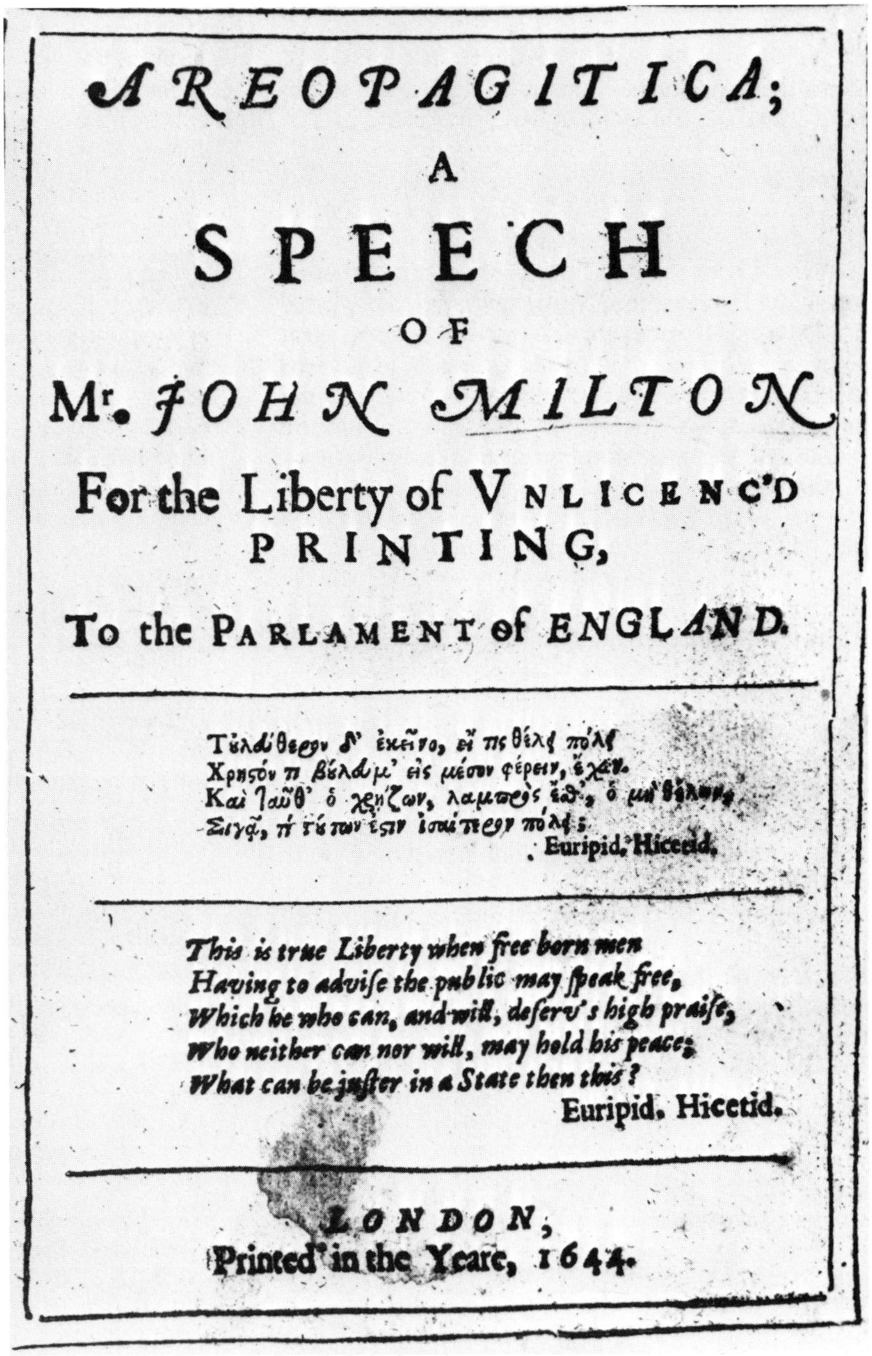

AREOPAGITICA;

A

SPEECH

OF

Mr. JOHN MILTON

For the Liberty of UNLICENC'D PRINTING,

To the PARLAMENT of ENGLAND.

Τοὐλεύθερον δ' ἐκεῖνο, εἴ τις θέλει πόλει
Χρηστόν τι βούλευμ' εἰς μέσον φέρειν, ἔχων.
Καὶ ταῦθ' ὁ χρῄζων, λαμπρὸς ἔσθ', ὁ μὴ θέλων
Σιγᾷ, τί τούτων ἐστὶν ἰσαίτερον πόλει;

Euripid. Hicetid.

This is true Liberty when free born men
Having to advise the public may speak free,
Which he who can, and will, deserv's high praise,
Who neither can nor will, may hold his peace;
What can be juster in a State then this?

Euripid. Hicetid.

LONDON,
Printed in the Yeare, 1644.

Figure 1. *(Milton, John)* John Milton, *Areopagitica*, 1644. The Bettmann Archive/BBC Hulton.

Areopagitica seems to have had little impact on government policy during Milton's time. When England finally abolished press licensing in 1694 it was apparently due less to philosophical objections than to mounting difficulties of enforcement. The insatiable demand for unlicensed works made enforcement almost impossible and increasingly coaxed the stationers into neglect of their enforcement duties. Milton's words, whatever their influence in his time, are today counted as classic statements in the long and recurring struggles against censorship.

For Milton's role in struggles for the establishment of authorship rights, *see* COPYRIGHT.

Bibliography. Fredrick S. Siebert, *Freedom of the Press in England 1476–1776: The Rise and Fall of Government Controls*, Urbana, Ill., 1952.

CHARLES M. FIRESTONE

MIME

A dramatic form that throughout its long history has portrayed the ordinary through extraordinary means, communicating through the use of GESTURE and movement rather than words. To do this mime has evolved a structure that conveys its message through the visual and tactile channels of expression and that is characterized by the features of NARRATIVE, time and space, and impulse and weight.

In a standard dictionary, definitions of mime refer to its usage both as a noun and as a verb. Moreover, in its noun form it refers to the person who mimes as well as to the GENRE. It is used in the sense of a number of theatrical forms as well as to mean imitation in general.

Throughout most of its history mime has been plagued by negative associations; decrees, licensing laws, and theater CENSORSHIP were designed, on the one hand, to contain mime within certain limits and, on the other, to guarantee the preserve of serious DRAMA (see THEATER). Yet mime continued and continues to be performed to full houses, precisely because it portrays the ordinary person in commonplace situations. It is a form of gesture and movement that has as its goal the presentation of the ordinary, but in evoking the everyday world it must use extraordinary means. Movement in mime is highly stylized, based on the principle of counterpoise, which frequently calls for the reverse of what one would normally do in a particular gesture in order to make it convincing to the viewer.

Moreover, mime communicates without the use of words. Mimes, audiences, critics, and scholars have frequently held up the primacy of gesture (in contrast to the potential of language) for deceit or, at best, for a secondhand portrayal of feelings and action. The theater of the absurd, for example, emphasizes gesture in the belief that gesture precedes the spoken word and is, in addition, the true expression of what we feel, whereas words only describe what we feel. These two characteristics of mime—the depiction of the commonplace and the reliance on gesture—have implications for the structure of the form.

Channels of expression. Of the possible channels of expression—kinesthetic, visual, aural, tactile—mime emphasizes the visual and the tactile. From its earliest open-air performances in the Sicilian countryside to today's performances by such artists as French mime Marcel Marceau, mime has used illusion, juxtaposition, exaggeration, masking (see MASK), and transformation to communicate. The mime works in a small space yet must create the illusion of a much larger world. Through the mechanism of illusion the empty space must be filled with objects, settings, and other people. Exaggeration makes the gestures meaningful to the spectator. CARICATURE is part of this

repertoire because the verbal channel cannot be used to fill out complex thoughts, characters, or actions. Juxtaposition and contrast again are ways of highlighting. Marceau's mime "The Maskmaker" is a good example. The maskmaker tries on a number of masks and is imprisoned in the happy mask. All his efforts to remove it fail; his body shows that he is exhausted and despairing at the same time that his FACE, in the happy mask, continues to smile. The use of masks in mime has characterized some periods, genres, and performers and has been rejected by as many others. Whiteface draws attention to facial gesture; masks generally lead to an emphasis on the body as the vehicle for communication and at the same time allow for an instantaneous recognition of a type. One of the best examples of the latter is the use of masks in the commedia dell'arte as a way of identifying stock characters.

Tactility in mime refers to the creation of a three-dimensional space and the relationship of the mime to that space. The mime moves as though space has weight and thickness. The impact of an imaginary object on the body of the mime has to be visible to the spectator.

Three structural features. Three features are fundamental to the structure of mime: narrative function, time and space, and impulse and weight. Every mime PERFORMANCE must have some narrative component. Narrative as used in mime includes storytelling, the elaboration of some universal truth, the portrayal of emotion, or a commentary on life. The task is to do this without the written or spoken word. Few mimes see the goal of their art as simply telling a story by substituting gestures for words. Even when one works from a standard literary text, as in the case of the Polish mime Henryk Tomaszewski's "Hamlet: Irony and Mourning," one is selective about the themes one chooses. Tomaszewski chose to emphasize the contrast between reality and fantasy that runs through Shakespeare's play. Marceau's mimedramas have used texts that can be distilled into fundamental human emotions: the poor man dreaming of riches in "The Overcoat," the downfall of a vain and selfish man in "Don Juan," the search for eternal youth in "Faust." The bulk of mime presents themes that are difficult, if not impossible, to express in any other way, as, for example, in "The Maskmaker."

For an audience to understand the narrative meaning of a mime certain structures of symbols and METAPHOR are necessary (see SYMBOLISM). In a solo mime performance that does not use props, words, or other actors, one sees an interaction of three kinds of symbols. The first is directly representative of objects, persons, animals, and behaviors—fish, birds, a snake, old people, children, painting a picture. Audiences recognize these kinds of representations

Figure 1. *(Mime)*   Marcel Marceau, Sadler's Wells Theatre, London, 1978. Photograph by Shuhei Iwamoto.

consciously and immediately. The second kind is more abstract, using metaphor and synecdoche, and usually conveys emotions or mood. Open and closed postures in the Western tradition, for example, convey beauty, good, and happiness in the case of the former and ugliness, evil, and sadness in the case of the latter. Likewise speed of movement is important: fast movements are associated with COMEDY and slow ones with TRAGEDY. Audiences are moved along in their understanding by this kind of symbol but usually at a subconscious level. The third category uses symbols that function like paragraph markers. They cue a change of scene or character or denote the passage of time. These include passing the hand down in front of the face, slowly closing and opening the EYES, and making one complete revolution in place. The timing and use of these three categories of symbols separate mimes who communicate successfully from those who do not.

Mime condenses time. Mime cannot take a long time to explain something; it has to be clear immediately. In addition mime consciously slows its movements and gestures because gestures executed at normal speeds are lost on an audience. Speeding up normal gestures, on the other hand, has a comic effect. Further, mime does not use the heightened rhythmical time that gives DANCE its ability to call forth a kinesthetic response. In this sense it is, even with its slowing and condensation, closer to ordinary rhythm than is dance.

Mime uses space in a condensed and economical manner as well. It creates the illusion of an expanded space that has volume, mass, and thickness. Space has tension and resistance as the body of the mime moves through it and shapes it. As Marceau has said, the mime sculpts the volume and size of what he or she portrays.

Impulse and weight, the last pair of features, are linked to time and space and are among the most important defining features of mime. Mimes begin each movement or gesture with a concentration of energy in the body and a quick release of that energy before the regular flow of the movement or gesture. This is impulse, and it gives definition and motivation to movement and gesture. It limns them, making them clear and sharp rather than undefined and shapeless. It focuses the audience's attention, although it is not a feature that most observers would notice except in its absence.

Mime succeeds in its illusions wherever the PERCEPTION of weight to the invisible is sensed. One example Marceau uses is that of the butterfly. We think of the butterfly as the epitome of lightness. If the mime is to make a convincing butterfly, however, there has to be a solidity about it. Mimes use such terms as "light-heaviness" and "feeling the weight," but there must be shadings depending on what is being portrayed. In Marceau's mime "The Tree" he metamorphoses from human to tree and back again. He is successful because he changes the density or weight of his body to match human and tree.

Bibliography. Étienne Decroux, *Paroles sur le mime,* Paris, 1963; David Mayer, *Harlequin in His Element: The English Pantomime 1806–1836,* Cambridge, Mass., 1969; Constant Mic [Konstantin Miklashevskiĭ], *La commedia dell'arte,* Paris, 1927, reprint 1980; Allardyce Nicoll, *Masks, Mimes, and Miracles: Studies in the Popular Theater,* New York, 1963; Bari Rolfe, ed., *Mimes on Miming,* Los Angeles, 1980; Anya Peterson Royce, *Movement and Meaning: Creativity and Interpretation in Ballet and Mime,* Bloomington, Ind., 1984; Franco Ruffini, *Semiotica del testo: L'esempio teatro,* Rome, 1978; Robert F. Storey, *Pierrot: A Critical History of a Mask,* Princeton, N.J., 1978.

ANYA PETERSON ROYCE

MINORITIES IN THE MEDIA

Media industries around the world, especially in countries with commercial mass media systems, are geared to provide services to broad, heterogeneous audiences. In consequence, the proportion of services specifically designed for social, ethnic, cultural, religious, or other minorities is generally quite small.

The degree and quality of coverage by the media of social "minority" groups such as women, CHILDREN, the elderly, the poor, and the handicapped have been criticized at several levels. First, inadequate or nonexistent coverage of minorities is considered severely damaging to vital processes of representative government. Second, the lack of fair treatment by the media and of full participation in them results in the diminution of minorities' rights and opportunities. Third, stereotyping has remained more persistent and persuasive than is acceptable to champions of equity at home and abroad. Participation by members of minority groups in communication industry organizations is often urged as a corrective measure, but the slow pace of such minority participation has been discouraging. As late as the mid-1980s, 61 percent of newspapers published in the United States employed no minority journalists (*see* MINORITY MEDIA). Minority employment opportunities were better on metropolitan newspapers than on local organs. At that time, out of a newspaper force of approximately forty-nine thousand, less than twenty-nine hundred were minority-group members.

All the news media are increasingly responsive to new commercial requirements useful to minorities. In the television industry, for example, modeling programming to certain audience segments—"narrowcasting"—has become more pronounced. Advertisers anxious about demographics are determined to reach specific segments of the potential audience. Minorities with a long history of communications distress find themselves appreciated as marketing opportunities (*see* CONSUMER RESEARCH). Broadcasting has become less commercially viable than narrowcasting. The collective wealth of minority groups has proven to be an unexpected boon. Segments of the general population according to sex, age, or geographic location are of great interest to those with products or ideas to sell, and politicians and government officials are also captivated by new promotional mixes.

Minority investment in and proprietorship of U.S. instruments of communication—newspapers, magazines, RADIO and television stations—is becoming significant, even in a communications world dominated by giant conglomerates. As of 1985 there were important radio station developments: 275 programmed to blacks, 2 to Japanese-Americans, 130 to Spanish speakers, 4 to Native Americans. In that year minority newspaper enterprises included 2 dailies and 159 weeklies directed to a black audience, 5 dailies and 24 weeklies in Spanish, 10 dailies and 2 weeklies in Chinese, 6 dailies and 4 weeklies in Japanese. These small beginnings have great social and political importance and indicate a possibility of sharp change by the turn of the century.

The people of the United States received a fair warning in 1968 from the National Commission on Civil Disorders, appointed by President Lyndon Johnson and chaired by then governor of Illinois Otto Kerner. The Kerner Commission had been charged with advising the president on means of reducing racial tensions after a long summer of rioting in major cities. The commission concluded:

The nation is rapidly moving toward two separate Americas . . . [which] threatens us with two perils. . . . [F]irst is the danger of sustained violence in our cities. . . . [S]econd is the danger of a conclusive repudiation of the traditional American ideals of individual dignity, freedom and equality of opportunity.

The Kerner Commission was concerned about how implicated the press was in the conditions that led to or away from the riots. Not surprisingly the commission found that there was a failure "to portray the Negro as a matter of routine and in the context of the total society." Results of this warning have been disappointing or ambiguous.

The Kerner Commission's advocacy of a single United States, served by a communications industry that would attempt to tell the story of commonly held dreams and aspirations, did not envision any other alternative to social disaster. Nevertheless, there are other scenarios. The Hispanics of the United

States follow several. As the largest bilingual collective in the population they subscribe to the majority media services and also, in significant numbers, to Spanish-language print and electronic media. Many have little choice, being primarily Spanish speakers on a daily basis or knowing little or no English. It is estimated that at least twelve million Hispanics watched Spanish-language television in the United States in any week of 1986. Newscasts, variety shows, sports events, and *telenovelas* came from Mexico and other Latin American sources (*see* SOAP OPERA; SPORTS). Audiences in sixty-two U.S. cities with large Hispanic populations were served by Spanish International Network (SIN). At that time almost twenty million Hispanics lived in the United States.

Proponents of bilingual communication stress that society as a whole could be enriched if the messages carried by the media bring people together. However, some critics allege that cultural affinity to special media could cause problems, charging that cultural preferences may have unacceptable political consequences. Bilingualism in public EDUCATION, and its effects on the necessary centrality of national identification, has become an increasingly heated subject, with controversy expected to remain intrinsic to national debates over what elemental requirements should be imposed on the citizenry as a whole.

The conflict between cultural pluralism and unification of political allegiances is central to international mass media issues in both developing and industrialized nations. Developing countries are concerned with the impact of Western (especially U.S.) media programming penetration, causing media consumers around the world to become expectant pursuers of materially unattainable or culturally irrelevant goals.

To stress internal planning and emphasize relationships between minorities and the politically or culturally dominant ethnic majority, many developing countries control domestic media programming one way or another. For example, Malaysia provides news in several languages, including Bahasa, Chinese, Indian languages, and English, through government-controlled electronic media. Whatever the language, there is tremendous sensitivity to divisive issues that could possibly inflame intergroup passions. The emphasis is on reporting culturally positive news. The commercial television channel that commenced operations in the mid-1980s also is careful about interethnic amity among Malays, Chinese, Indians, and others who are all Malaysians. However, its program schedules in that period reflect a heavy dependence on U.S. television productions. Such programs as "Webster," "The Night Stalker," "National Geographic," "Cutter to Houston," "Dynasty," "Cheers," "Knots Landing," "Star Trek," "Hill Street Blues," "Hardcastle and McCormick," and "Magnum P.I."

were all in a typical week's fare, and the precise impact of such a barrage can scarcely be assessed.

Malaysia is fairly representative of a general situation in the Third World. Productions of locally important television programs are in exceedingly short supply compared with the need to explain the peoples of the nations and region to one another. Educational and entertainment materials from far away, better suited to conditions in Chicago, New York, Boston, or Los Angeles (to the degree they are suited), shape new mental realities, myths, and expectations (*see* EDUCATIONAL TELEVISION). Local television services, governmental and private, have accepted the available in order to avoid the alternative—a void. To differing degrees such diverse nations as Zimbabwe, Kenya, Great Britain, Singapore, and Canada have suffered from cultural dilution by their absorption of foreign programming. Because each nation is really an amalgam of minorities, the result is that important internal problems are unresolved.

The objectives of media planners include much of import to minorities who require full, fair, representative, and honest depictions. Unfortunately, positive reporting has not been as evident as stereotyping, which seeds misunderstanding.

Bibliography. Samuel P. Huntington, *Political Order in Changing Societies*, New Haven, Conn., 1968; Elihu Katz and George Wedell, *Broadcasting in the Third World*, Cambridge, Mass., 1977; D. S. Mehta, *Mass Communication and Journalism in India*, New Delhi, 1979; Bernard Rubin, *Media, Politics, and Democracy*, New York, 1977; idem, ed., *Small Voices and Great Trumpets: Minorities and the Media*, New York, 1980; Anthony Smith, *The Geopolitics of Information: How Western Culture Dominates the World*, New York, 1980; Donald F. Ungurait, Thomas W. Bohn, and Ray E. Hiebert, eds., *Media Now*, New York, 1985.

BERNARD RUBIN

MINORITY MEDIA

The term *minority media* has been used since the late 1960s to include very diverse phenomena. It is based on the general concept of "minority" that evolved in the late 1960s as a result of the political revival of ethnic and other groups known as "awakening minorities." The term includes categories such as the immigrant press, the foreign-language press, the nationality press, and, more recently, the ethnic press. As other media joined newspapers in these areas, the term *minority media* became more accurate than *minority press*. Increasingly it is used also as a replacement for the term *special-interest* (or specialized) *media*, describing such different media as a newspaper published in a foreign or vernacular LAN-

GUAGE, a RADIO station serving a certain national or tribal group, a MAGAZINE published by a religious sect, or even publications by any culturally distinct group or movement that considers itself a minority, even if it is numerically a majority. In this sense the feminist press considers itself a minority press. Similarly other media representing or directed toward minority groups, be they prisoners, fans of special types of music, or gays and lesbians, are called minority media. Even political media, if they express dissent, are sometimes included in the category of minority media. Other terms for this phenomenon are *dissent media, alternative media,* or *radical media.*

The status of minorities. During the twentieth century sociologists have gradually removed the statistical connotation from the meaning of the word *minority.* Thus, although minorities generally are less

Figure 1. *(Minority Media)* Front page of the first Chinese newspaper published in New York, February 3, 1883. The Bettmann Archive, Inc.

than 50 percent of the population, the variable of size is itself not crucial; as the term is used by politicians and social scientists it is more important that a minority be subordinate to the dominant group within society. This politically subordinate position, rather than its being a numerical minority, is the basic defining characteristic of a minority group and, by consequence, of its media.

Minority media thus include those that are beyond the majority media system but at the same time are numerous enough to be important in the functioning of the whole social and political system. What is more, they are very important in the lives of significant segments of modern societies, especially in multinational countries. As groups relegated to subordinate positions in the status and power structure of a society, minorities traditionally have had limited access to communications media. However, mass education at the elementary level, developments in media technology, and political democracy all made it possible for media to develop that use modern, although usually more primitive and less expensive, technologies to communicate within minority groups and even to present their values to other audiences. In addition, because those media express the distinctiveness of minorities, they can serve to strengthen the identity of minorities.

The history of the minority media is long and complex and is closely related to the place each minority occupies in the larger society. Sometimes minorities exist in a society characterized by cultural pluralism, or "peaceful coexistence" of different minorities, in which differences are encouraged to a certain extent; other societies are characterized by assimilation, or the "melting pot" approach; and still others deal with their minorities through forced integration or the total suppression of minority groups.

History. The phenomenon of minority media is as old as media themselves. However, the minority media whose histories are best known are print media, especially the foreign-language press.

In the United States the first foreign-language newspaper, the German-language *Philadelphia Zeitung,* was established by Benjamin Franklin in 1732. The first U.S. daily in a foreign language was the *Courrier français,* published in Philadelphia between 1794 and 1798. Later, in the nineteenth century, almost a thousand newspapers and magazines were published in the United States for its newest immigrants, mainly of European origin. Those publications were either in the language of the immigrants or in both their language and English. Most of them were in German.

In the nineteenth century, blacks, Native Americans, Hispanics, and other ethnic minority groups on the North American continent established their own newspapers. The first Spanish-language newspaper in

the United States was *El misisipi,* printed in 1808 in New Orleans and partly in English. A few years later, in 1828, the Cherokee Nation founded the first American Indian newspaper, the *Cherokee Phoenix,* in Georgia; it too was a bilingual paper, published partly in English and partly in Cherokee.

In 1827 the first black newspaper in the United States was created as a tool to combat slavery. It was appropriately called *Freedom's Journal.* The explanation for creating such a newspaper was short and is valid for other minority media: "We wish to plead our own case. Too long have others spoken for us. Too long has the public been deceived by misrepresentation in the thing which concerns us dearly." In the case of *Freedom's Journal* this "thing" was obvious—the abolition of slavery. In other cases it was different but similar—fighting for the rights of the minority group represented.

The peak year for the foreign-language press in the United States was 1914. Subsequently the number of titles and the size of the circulation and readership of these newspapers steadily declined. In 1924 more than 140 foreign-language dailies were published; in the 1980s fewer than 40 dailies survived. The total number of foreign-language newspapers declined from approximately 1,000 to about 200 in some two dozen languages, the majority of them in Spanish, Yiddish, Polish, Irish, Italian, and Japanese. However, during the same period electronic media such as radio and television were used increasingly by minority groups. For example, although there were only 9 Spanish-language dailies in the 1980s, more than 120 radio stations aired their programs in Spanish, and more than 600 broadcast some Spanish programming. The newest immigrants, from Asia (Vietnamese, Koreans), were increasingly involved in radio programming in their languages.

The role of minority media. The two main functions of minority media are (1) fighting for the rights of the minority and (2) giving minority members a feeling of identity, increasing their social cohesiveness, and providing an escape from homesickness and the isolation of life in a strange or hostile environment. The print media better serve the first function; they are usually militant, advocacy media featuring a journalistic style that distinguishes itself from "objective reporting." Radio and television are better suited to the second function—serving the psychological and cultural needs of minorities.

In the second half of the twentieth century the number of minority media everywhere in the world substantially increased. In Western countries this was linked to market segmentation, a strategy of dividing the mass market into many easily identifiable segments of different groups of customers. Although minorities are ideal market segments, they were neglected by advertisers for years because of their lack of strong buying power (*see* ADVERTISING). Growing prosperity among the formerly most economically deprived minorities helped to support the media especially directed to them. This was especially true in the case of radio and television.

It is important to distinguish between minority media and minority-oriented media. The former comprise media that either are produced by minority groups or serve their cultural needs and help to fulfill their cultural, social, and political strategies. The latter comprise media that are produced not by the minority but by external groups—usually advertisers, sometimes political associations—that want to derive some advantage from the minority group. In practice the differences between media belonging to those two categories are not easy to define, but this distinction should be kept in mind when analyzing the role of different media in sustaining the cultural identity of minorities, directing their activities, and defining their relation to other minorities and to the majority. The growth in the number of minority media in Western countries is a result of the rapid increase in minority-oriented media rather than an increase in actual minority media.

In contrast there is a proliferation of minority media in Third World countries, mainly because of the political and cultural emancipation of formerly oppressed minorities and technological innovations that make it possible to employ mass media techniques even among very poor groups. This creates problems when minorities are secessionist, that is, are seeking both cultural and political independence. In the Soviet Union there has been a substantial increase in the number of minority media. However, these media are part of the centrally planned media system. Thus, while they serve certain cultural needs of minorities, especially in the sphere of language, customs, and FOLKLORE, at the same time they are used to integrate minorities into the larger political and ideological system, based on an assimilationist perspective.

The upheavals of World War II and the following years precipitated new waves of MIGRATION and new issues of minority needs and rights. The impact was felt in countries like the United States and Canada, which already had complex multiethnic societies, but also in Australia, where the population had been (except for its Aboriginal communities) predominantly of English descent. An immigration wave of the postwar years drastically altered the population pattern and gradually led to a profusion of multiethnic and multilanguage media. *See* AUSTRALASIA, TWENTIETH CENTURY.

Everywhere in the world the main problem with minority media is the issue of their independence from the whole society. Too much independence threatens the social order; too little can lead to resistance and potential revolt. The Western democracies usually resolve this dilemma by economic control, allowing only a certain degree of editorial freedom because the media are dependent on advertisers. The Third World countries most frequently use physical force to suppress the secessionist tendencies of minority media. And the Soviet Union uses the ideological concept of harmonious relations between nationalities and the political power of the Communist party to enforce cooperation among its different ethnic minorities.

British philosopher John Stuart Mill (1806–1873) wrote in his essay *On Liberty,* "If all mankind minus one, were of one opinion, and only one person were of the contrary opinion, mankind would be no more justified in silencing that one person than he, if he had the power, would be justified in silencing mankind." The spirit of this statement can be extended to argue that the real test of media freedom is the freedom of minority media and the extent to which minorities can openly express their goals and values, even if they strongly contradict majority aims and values. The history of the freedom of minority media is therefore the history of the freedom of the media.

See also AGENDA-SETTING; CITIZEN ACCESS; GOVERNMENT-MEDIA RELATIONS; MINORITIES IN THE MEDIA; RELIGIOUS BROADCASTING; TELEVISION NEWS.

Bibliography. *Burrelle's Special Groups Media Directory,* Livingston, N.J., 1980; Anthony Gary Dworkin and Rosalind J. Dworkin, eds., *The Minority Report: An Introduction to Racial, Ethnic, and Gender Relations,* 2d ed., New York, 1982; Lauren Kessler, *The Dissident Press: Alternative Journalism in American History,* Beverly Hills, Calif., 1984; James E. Murphy and Sharon M. Murphy, *Let My People Know: American Indian Journalism, 1828–1978,* Norman, Okla., 1981; Robert E. Park, *The Immigrant Press and Its Control,* New York, 1922, reprint Westport, Conn., 1970; Bernard Rubin, ed., *Small Voices and Great Trumpets: Minorities and the Media,* New York, 1980; Edward Sagarin, ed., *The Other Minorities: Nonethnic Collectivities Conceptualized as Minorities Groups,* Waltham, Mass., 1971; Clint C. Wilson and Felix Gutierrez, *Minorities and Media: Diversity and the End of Mass Communication,* Beverly Hills, Calif., 1985; Lubomyr R. Wynar and Anna T. Wynar, eds., *Encyclopedic Dictionary of Ethnic Newspapers and Periodicals in the United States,* 2d ed., Littleton, Colo., 1976; Donald Young, *American Minority Peoples,* New York, 1932.

TOMASZ GOBAN-KLAS

MODE

Thought and knowledge exist in a variety of distinct modes—symbolic systems dependent on our biological structures and physical environment that determine the kinds of information we perceive, manipulate, and communicate. MEANING can be understood or purposively communicated only within a symbolic mode, and some minimal level of competence is the precondition for the creation or comprehension of meaning within such a mode. Information is structured according to the principles of the mode within which it is perceived, comprehended, and communicated. Information coded within a mode is only partially susceptible to translation into other modes; thus competence in creating or comprehending meanings is acquired only through experience with a particular mode.

A mode of symbolic behavior is a system of internal and external actions and operations in terms of which objects and events are perceived, coded cognitively for long-term storage and retrieval (see COGNITION), subjected to transformations and orderings, and organized into forms that elicit meaningful inferences from the creator and others who possess competence in that mode. Modes of symbolic behavior are not identified with specific sensory systems. They may be organized largely within a single sensory system but may also blend and overlap. The same sensory system is capable of being utilized for PERFORMANCE in various modes of perceptual organization and symbolic communication.

Codes and modes. A CODE may be defined as an organized subset of the total range of elements, operations, and structural principles that are possible in a given mode. In the simplest sense any single LANGUAGE is a code existing within the lexical mode. We encounter symbolic modes in terms of particular native codes that then shape our perceptions, memories, and cognitive processes in that mode. Phenomenologically, the code, not the mode, is the primary level of analysis. Most people need never be aware that the code they know is not coextensive with the symbolic mode—for example, that the base-ten number system is but one of many possible mathematical codes for the symbolic expression of quantities, one code within the logico-mathematical mode.

Many symbolic codes have been formalized through the invention of notation systems such as the ALPHABET, numeric and mathematical signs (see MATHEMATICS; NUMBER), and musical notation (see MUSIC THEORIES—NOTATIONS AND LITERACY). These are powerful tools for the storage and transmission of symbolic messages. Skill in decoding a notation system and retrieving the information stored in the code frees one from dependence on immediate experience and allows wide access to the heritage of CULTURE. *See also* SIGN; SIGN SYSTEM.

Primary, derived, and technical modes. The primary symbolic modes are (1) the lexical, (2) the social-gestural, (3) the iconic, (4) the logico-mathematical, and (5) the musical. It should be noted that these modes are not all equally elaborated and formalized (or, possibly, equally formalizable), that they have many areas of interpenetration, and that they do not exhaust the total range of human symbolic activity.

Derived, or blended, modes build on one or more of the primary modes. DANCE may be the best example of this category because it combines significant elements and principles of the social-gestural and musical modes, creating a blend of NARRATIVE and expressive codes.

Technical modes of knowledge and action involve the application of competence in primary modes (e.g., the iconic, logico-mathematical, and lexical) to the understanding of physical and biological systems and structures and function as the basis of skills not primarily symbolic in nature. Such skills are involved in the production of material goods and the execution of complex nonsymbolic performances. These include the various sciences, engineering and the technologies, ARCHITECTURE, and so on, and are dependent on prior acquisition of competence in the appropriate symbolic modes.

The criteria that determine whether a mode is primary are independence and self-sufficiency. A primary mode is one that can be identified with (1) a range of objects and events or field of reference, (2) a distinctive perceptual/memory storage/retrieval capacity, (3) a set of operations and transformations, (4) principles of structuring that govern the formulation and communication of meaning, and (5) nontranslatability into other modes.

Information coded in one mode cannot be fully recoded in another. The essence of a symbolic message will only be understood within the code in which it was created. There is no adequate verbal translation of an equation in differential calculus, a Bach fugue, the smile of *La Gioconda*, or a *Śiva Naṭarāja*. Each of these conveys specific meanings with precision but only in the terms of the proper mode.

Acquiring symbolic competence. The ability to comprehend symbolic meaning depends on the acquisition of competence in the mode in which that meaning exists. Like all knowledge and skill, that competence can only be acquired through action. Activities that develop and extend our competence to deal effectively with the environment seem to be inherently satisfying and thus motivating. The learning process by which we develop competencies is self-sustaining once we reach the point of being able to produce desired effects and observe the incremental extensions of our abilities. The pleasures that attend such activities can be seen in the behavior of CHILDREN absorbed in the seemingly endless repetition of manipulations and movements.

The activities by which we acquire and extend competence in the comprehension and creation of symbolic forms, however, are a somewhat special case. In these activities we are interacting with and manipulating a social as well as a physical environment. The effects being produced and observed, as we learn to control and predict that social environment and the consequences of our actions, are not those of physical cause and effect. They are the responses of social beings, and the regularities governing them are not those of nature but of culture. A child can learn that fire burns through unambiguous physical contact but can only learn the meaning of symbolic actions and objects through interaction with other humans who respond in terms of a symbolic code. For example, SPEECH does not develop in the child as the inevitable unfolding of an innate ability; rather, it emerges through the interaction of a developing intelligence with responsive adults whose actions and reactions are consistent and ruled and who are eager to reward signs of consistency and purposiveness as they emerge in the vocalizations of the child.

The crucial aspect of the interactive learning process through which we acquire communicative competence in the symbolic modes is the recognition on the part of those who function as a source of feedback that we are engaging in behavior that is potentially meaningful. Only with such a response can we begin to identify the elements and organizational principles that determine the structuring of meanings within a symbolic mode.

Creative activity in a symbolic mode is deeply rooted in the process of comprehension in that mode. Meaning is defined by the conventions that govern the range of elements, operations, and organizational principles of a code. The ability to imply meaning intentionally is dependent on the ability to perceive and infer it. As U.S. musicologist Leonard Meyer stated, "It is because the composer is also a listener that he is able to control his inspiration with reference to the listener."

The tacitness of symbolic knowledge. In setting out to discuss the nature of science, U.S. philosopher Michael Polanyi insisted on the centrality and tacitness of skill: "The aim of a skillful performance is achieved by the observance of a set of rules which are not known as such to the person following them." Basic motor and perceptual-cognitive skills become increasingly less explicit and conscious as they become better known through practice. Skillful activity can be carried on efficiently only when we need not (or cannot) consciously attend to its ongoing physical, perceptual, and cognitive operations.

At least one reason for this often-noted tacitness of skillful action is that although we tend to conceive of conscious attention in terms of verbally coded information and thought, in fact much if not most of the physical, perceptual, and cognitive elements of skillful performance are not amenable to verbal coding and comprehension. We know much that cannot be expressed in words but that can be communicated in other symbolic forms. This is a second sense of the tacit nature of skill and derives from the essential nontranslatability of knowledge from a symbolic mode into some assumed verbal lingua franca of individual consciousness and social communication.

Symbolic codes become involuntary and transparent structurings of thought and action governing our constructions of reality. We assimilate the world via perceptual-cognitive schemata, which, although dependent on innate neurological structures, are developed, modified, and extended through interactions with and accommodations to the environment. Knowledge is acquired and expressed through performance in a mode, and the use of that mode becomes automatic and transparent. As we become competent native speakers, words and sentences in our native language become carriers of meanings, and we no longer need to pay—or can pay—conscious attention to their actual auditory or visual characteristics. We come to hear meanings rather than sounds and do so involuntarily.

Varieties of Symbolic Experience

Every person must acquire minimal competence in some of these modes in order to be defined as normal or even as human. In all cultures the lexical and the social-gestural modes form the basic complement of competence without which an individual is labeled deviant. Beyond that, however, cultures vary widely in terms of the symbolic competencies they require, reward, or even permit. In modern Western culture, at least, it is generally assumed that special attributes (best characterized by the concept of talent) are required in order for an individual to move beyond the basics of lexical and social-gestural competence to the development of competence in the iconic, logico-mathematical, or musical modes. As British ethnomusicologist John Blacking has argued in the case of music, other cultures make radically different assumptions about the symbolic capabilities of their members.

The lexical mode. The fundamental mode of symbolic thought and communication is that of verbal language. The lexical mode is so dominant an element of human consciousness that we tend to see it as *the* embodiment of intelligence and meaning. This is amplified by the fact that the lexical seems to be unique among symbolic modes in its reflexive capabilities, permitting users to engage in metalinguistic analyses of their own communicative behavior. Yet the lexical mode must also be seen in the context of the full variety of human symbolic experience.

The social-gestural mode. Most human behavior is determined by learned, culturally specific codes that communicate to others in that culture a great deal of information about the stable characteristics and present intentions of the actor. Usually one will become consciously aware of the fact that actions and gestures carry decodable information about one's background and intentions only when one is (1) placed in a foreign culture, (2) trained to observe deliberately such processes (e.g., in ethnographic or clinical training), or (3) attempting to control consciously the information being conveyed. In the last instance one can sometimes use books on etiquette in order to pass successfully in social circles in which one was not originally acculturated. Such code dictionaries are not written for native speakers, who often regard the use of such devices as a sign that the user does not belong.

Social-gestural coding extends from FACIAL EXPRESSION, bodily GESTURE, and the negotiation of personal space (*see* INTERPERSONAL DISTANCE) to the patterned messages of CLOTHING, housing style and furnishings, and even FOOD habits. The analyst's axiom that "nothing never happens" reflects the fact that we constantly signal our compliance with or defiance of social-gestural codes.

The iconic mode. Iconic images are uniquely suited for communicating about the spatial, topological nature of objects and about relations between objects in space, and they are among the most effective means of expressing and evoking emotions (*see* ICONOGRAPHY). Visual images and symbols can convey information that cannot be formulated in the lexical or indeed any other mode (*see* SYMBOLISM; VISUAL IMAGE). For one thing, as U.S. scholar William Ivins noted, words are essentially "conventional symbols for similarities" and are thus incapable of communicating the unique and singular aspects of objects and events that can be depicted visually.

The potential of visual images to convey precise information about particular objects and their spatial relationships was a prerequisite for the development of scientific and technological enterprises and the dissemination of their achievements. The invention of PRINTING and other means of precise GRAPHIC REPRODUCTION of images made possible the unprecedented and rapid growth of modern science and technology.

However, the particular power of the iconic mode probably resides in the impact of the singular visual image or object. Our relationship to the world is so tied to the sensory data of visual perception, providing us with the sense of space and volume through which we construct our environment (*see* PERCEPTION—STILL AND MOVING PICTURES), that we may intuitively assign an undue reality to visual images. Consequently human beings have often viewed the creators of visual works of ART—whether a two-dimensional visual image or a three-dimensional SCULPTURE—with awe for their ability to rival the creative powers appropriate to gods. In fact visual images and objects, like all symbolic constructions, are determined largely by conventions of selection, transformation, and organization that owe some allegiance to the facts of physical reality and the neuropsychology of perception yet are rooted in the historical processes of the negotiation of communicative meanings.

The logico-mathematical mode. Most adults are aware of the existence of the logico-mathematical mode as a strange and difficult terrain that they have traversed only as far as the foothills of simple arithmetic before being defeated by the demands of higher mathematics. Here, as with the iconic and musical modes, we have learned to quickly accept such defeats as proof that we lack the talent required to go further. Consequently it is difficult to appreciate the nature of thought in this mode; we must rely on the testimony of those who have mastered its challenge.

The eminent French mathematician Jacques Hadamard obtained statements from many mathematicians about their conceptions of the nature of logico-mathematical thought. The most consistent aspect of these reports was that mathematical thought is not performed in the linguistic mode. As Hadamard said of his own mathematical work, "I insist that words are totally absent from my mind when I really think." In describing logico-mathematical knowledge, Swiss psychologist JEAN PIAGET further clarifies its independence from language:

Logic . . . is not to be reduced, as some people would have it, to a system of notations inherent in speech or in any sort of language. It also consists of a system of operations (classifying, making series, making connections, making use of combinative or "transformation groups," etc.) and the source of these operations is to be found beyond language, in the general coordinations of action.

The musical mode. In every known human culture there exist musical codes of formally organized communication. As a culturally determined symbolic code, music, like mathematics, expresses and communicates specific but verbally ineffable meanings. The twentieth-century U.S. composer Roger Sessions described the musical experience in similar terms:

It seems to me quite clear that music, far from being in any sense vague or imprecise, is within its own sphere the most precise possible language. I have tried to imply this by saying that music embodies a certain type of movement rather than that it expresses it. All of the elements of this movement—rhythm, pitch, accent, dynamic shading, tone quality, and others sometimes even more subtle—are, in competent hands, kept under the most exquisite control, by composer and performer alike; the movement that is the stuff of music is given the most precise possible shape. . . . It achieves a meaning which can be achieved in no other way.

Cultures vary widely in the degree to which they expect, cultivate, and achieve widespread competence in musical creation and performance (see MUSIC COMPOSITION AND IMPROVISATION; MUSIC PERFORMANCE). In Western societies in particular it is generally assumed that only a gifted minority possesses the talent to produce music; most people are relegated to the role of audience member. But as Blacking has argued, this musical division of labor may reflect cultural assumptions and practices more than innate potentials: "Because there are some societies whose members are as competent in music as all people are in language, music may be a species-specific trait of man."

Even as listeners, however, members of all societies draw upon a tacit fluency in the specifics of the musical codes that they have heard since early childhood. In Meyer's words, "We perceive and think in terms of a specific musical language just as we think in terms of a specific vocabulary and grammar; and the possibilities presented to us by a particular musical vocabulary and grammar condition the operation of our mental processes and hence of the expectations which are entertained on the basis of those processes."

Bibliography. Rudolf Arnheim, *Visual Thinking*, Berkeley, Calif., 1969; John Blacking, *How Musical Is Man?* Seattle, Wash., 1973; Howard Gardner, *Frames of Mind: The Theory of Multiple Intelligences*, New York, 1983; Larry Gross, "Modes of Communication and the Acquisition of Symbolic Competence," in *Media and Symbols: The Forms of Expression, Communication, and Education* (Yearbook of the National Society for the Study of Education, Vol. 73, pt. 1), ed. by David R. Olson, Chicago, 1974; Jacques Hadamard, *An Essay on the Psychology of Invention in the Mathematical Field*, Princeton, N.J., 1945, reprint New York, 1954; Edward T. Hall, *The Silent Language*, New York, 1959, reprint 1973; William M. Ivins, *Prints and Visual Communication*, London, 1953, reprint Cambridge, Mass., 1969; Leonard B. Meyer, *Emotion and Meaning in Music*, Chicago, 1956; Michael Polanyi, *Personal Knowledge*, Chicago and London, 1958; Roger Sessions, *The Musical Experience of Composer, Performer, Listener*, Princeton, N.J., 1950, reprint 1971.

LARRY GROSS

MODELING. *See* SOCIAL COGNITIVE THEORY.

MODELS OF COMMUNICATION

Models simplify reality, select key elements, and indicate relationships. Communication models vary in the degree to which they are more dynamic (dealing with process and change) or more static (dealing with structure and relationship), although both aspects are present in all communication. Models also have potential disadvantages. Simplification involves selection and may mislead by omitting important features. The more general the model, the less true it will be to any one particular case. One should be aware of such limitations and of the fact that no model is suitable for all purposes or all levels of analysis.

The initial development of communication models in the late 1940s and early 1950s was associated with the emergence of a new science of communication and the search for a general framework for locating different kinds of communication phenomena. Initially the concept of *information* seemed to offer the basis for the new science, and information was conceived of mainly as "uncertainty reduction," following contemporary thinking about CYBERNETICS. The science of communication has developed somewhat differently, retaining a humanistic component and resisting efforts to treat the subject purely in a narrow, mechanistic way. *See also* INFORMATION THEORY.

Most communication models employ a small number of basic concepts: a sender; a process of encoding into signals or symbols; a message; a channel; a receiver; a relationship; a process of decoding; a range of things to which messages refer ("referents"); and an actual or probable effect, intended or not. Some models incorporate a feedback link from receiver to sender.

The development of communication models has reflected advances in understanding of how communication works. The most relevant points are (1) there is selectivity in attention, PERCEPTION, and retention of messages by the receiver; (2) communication is essentially transactional, with the receiver playing an active role in the course of any communication process; (3) communication does not always flow directly from one sender to one receiver but by way of intervening processes; (4) mass communication processes involve professional mediation between senders and receivers; and (5) communication takes place in complex social systems rather than in isolated acts of transmission and reception.

Early Models

In 1948 U.S. political scientist HAROLD D. LASSWELL presented his verbal model, which became known as the Lasswell formula: "Who says what in which channel to whom with what effect?" With its roots in Aristotelian (*see* ARISTOTLE) principles of RHETORIC, this model remains a useful way to split the communication process into basic components. Lasswell's own use of it is seen in Figure 1. The major

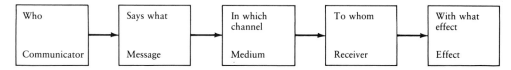

Figure 1. *(Models of Communication)* The Lasswell formula model. Redrawn after Harold D. Lasswell, "The Structure and Function of Communication in Society," in *The Communication of Ideas*, ed. by Lyman Bryson, New York: Institute for Religious and Social Studies, 1948.

value of this model lies in its use as a structuring device and in situations in which the sender has a clear intent to influence the receiver.

The mathematical model of communication was designed by CLAUDE SHANNON and WARREN WEAVER and was presented in 1949. It shows on the "sender" side the *source* and its *message,* which through the help of a *transmitter* is sent in the physical form of a *signal* to a *receiver,* which reconstructs the signal to another *message,* which ultimately reaches the *destination.* On its way the signal can be more or less distorted by interfering *noise,* which means that the signal received by the receiver is not necessarily identical to the one sent by the transmitter. The Shannon-Weaver model can be used on several different levels. Its original application was technical, but subsequently it was used as an analogy and was applied to different types of human communication.

The second stage in model building involved the elaboration of initial thinking to take into account the complications of human communication and the

development of devices for handling mass communication or communication in other fields. U.S. scholar George Gerbner's general model of communication (1956) has been especially influential and can be summed up in a single sentence that captures its main features: "Someone perceives an event/and reacts/ in a situation/through some means/ to make available materials/in some form/and context/conveying content/with some consequences." Figure 2 illustrates and elaborates on these features. The most important points are that Gerbner takes account of the context of communication situations and also of the participants' perception of and response to situations and communication processes. Communication situations include objective events and subjective perceptions. They are open and transactional. This model can incorporate machine as well as human processes in different combinations and at various stages.

In 1954 U.S. scholar WILBUR SCHRAMM drew on the work of CHARLES OSGOOD to emphasize the circularity of communication and to bring into the

Figure 2. *(Models of Communication)* George Gerbner's general model of communication. Redrawn after George Gerbner, "Toward a General Model of Communication," *Audio-Visual Communication Review* 4 (1956): 171–199.

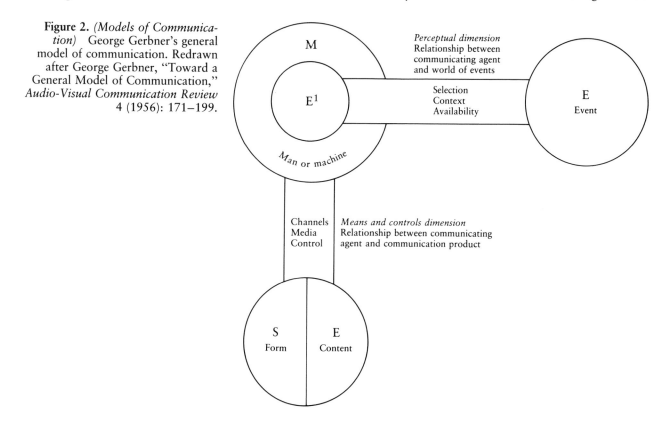

picture the processes of encoding and decoding, without which messages can have no MEANING. In doing so he laid the foundation for models dealing with essential aspects of mass communication. It was left to two mass media researchers, Bruce Westley and Malcolm MacLean, to incorporate further insights from social psychology into the portrayal of how communication works. These concerned the dynamics of communication as a process of information seeking and information giving. A central idea was that communication is the outcome of a search for balance and congruence between individuals on the one hand and their environment and other persons on the other. Westley and MacLean based their 1957 conceptual model for mass communications research on T. Newcomb's model of interpersonal relations (1953), in the form shown in Figure 3. The main elements labeled in the figure are as follows:

- X: an event or object in the environment
- A: the role of "advocate" or source wishing to present a particular view of event X
- C: a mass medium (or channel) role that selects among A's and X's for further transmission to an audience (B)
- B: the audience role—the eventual "destination" for information, views, and the like
- X': the choice made by C for access to the channel (modified into X'' on the way)
- fBA: feedback from audience to advocate (source)
- fBC: feedback from audience to mass medium (C)
- fCA: feedback from a medium (C) to an advocate (source)
- X_3C etc.: observations among X's made directly by a C (mass medium) without mediation by an A

The model is important for emphasizing several distinctive features of mass communication. (1) There is a long process of selection, with several distinct stages from event to reception. (2) Much of the communication process is nonpurposive, the role of a medium (C) being often that of neutral broker between audience interests and events or advocates and the audience itself rarely looking for specific information. (3) There are different kinds of, and variable opportunities for, feedback. (4) The whole process is open, self-adjusting, and dynamic, depending on the wider social environment and the number of alternative channels.

Models of Mass Communication and the Social System

Most of the earlier models tried to depict the communication process in a general way. Later several scholars in the field recognized the need for more specific models that would deal, for example, with mass communication.

One of sociology's contributions to mass communication model building has been to point to the relationships between the mass communication process and other processes in society. An example of this is the 1959 model of U.S. sociologists John W. Riley and Mathilda White Riley. In the graphic presentation of this model in Figure 4 one sees the exchange of messages between communicator and receiver, both of whom are tied to primary groups and find themselves in a larger social structure surrounded by an all-embracing social system. Communicating and receiving communications, the individual may find that this social web will mediate and influence the impact of the mass media.

That the mass communication system from a social-psychological standpoint may be quite complicated is shown in a model from 1963 by German communication researcher Gerhard Maletzke, whose "Schema des Feldes der Massenkommunikation"

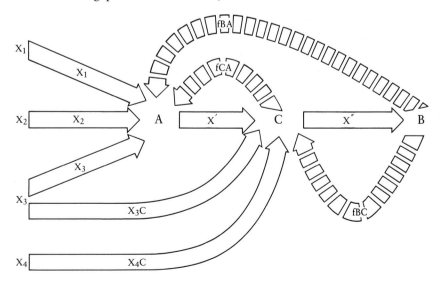

Figure 3. *(Models of Communication)* Bruce Westley and Malcolm MacLean's conceptual model of mass communication. Redrawn after Bruce H. Westley and Malcolm MacLean, "A Conceptual Model for Mass Communication Research," *Journalism Quarterly* 34 (1957): 31–38.

X_x

Figure 4. *(Models of Communication)* John W. Riley and Mathilda White Riley's communication system framed by a societal system. Redrawn after John W. Riley and Mathilda White Riley, "Mass Communication and the Social System," in *Sociology Today,* ed. by Robert K. Merton et al., New York: Basic Books, 1959.

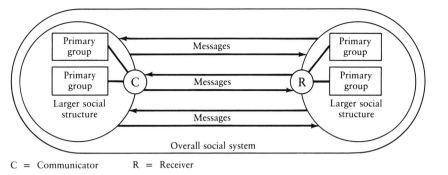

C = Communicator   R = Receiver

(Schema of the Field of Mass Communication) can be seen as an effort to summarize much of the research completed up to that time. The factors that have to be taken into account are shown in Figure 5. Maletzke's model has also proved useful as a structuring device for his comprehensive work *Psychologie der Massenkommunikation* (Psychology of Mass Communication), in which each factor and relationship is described and analyzed.

Communication Effects on Individuals

From the beginning a central issue about communication has been its effects on receivers. Despite the emphasis on intervening variables and social context, research on MASS MEDIA EFFECTS had too much

practical significance for the hypothesis of direct effect to be abandoned. Concern about the unintended, cumulative effects of television on CHILDREN was especially influential. In this connection a distillation of findings from a large amount of research by George Comstock and others (1978) led to a model to handle effects from television on individual behavior. This is presented schematically in Figure 6. The terms used in the model are as follows:

- TV act: any form of human behavior shown on television
- Inputs: messages from television and associated attributes
- TV arousal: extent to which a person is motivated to perform any act in a current situation

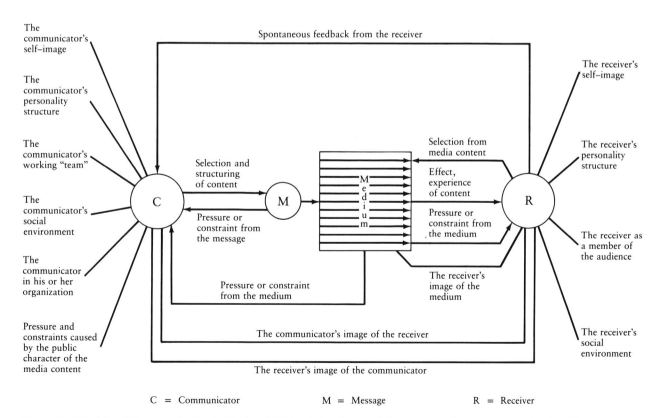

C = Communicator   M = Message   R = Receiver

Figure 5. *(Models of Communication)* Gerhard Maletzke's schema of the process of mass communication. Redrawn after Gerhard Maletzke, *Psychologie der Massenkommunikation,* Hamburg: Verlag Hans Bredow-Institut, 1963.

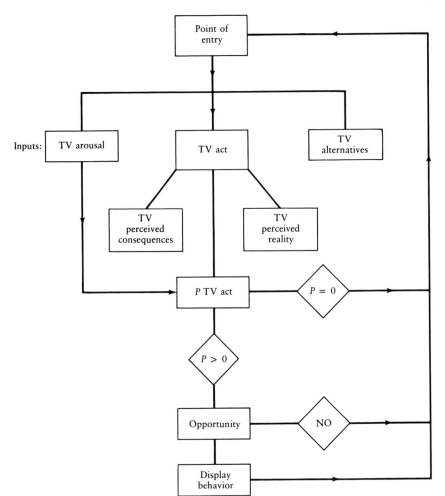

Figure 6. *(Models of Communication)* Model of television's effect on behavior. Redrawn after George Comstock et al., *Television and Human Behavior*, New York: Columbia University Press, 1978.

- TV-perceived consequences: sum of all positive minus all negative values that are learned from television and that go with a given act
- TV-perceived reality: degree to which a person perceives the television portrayal (TV act) to be true to life
- TV alternatives: other (relevant) social behaviors shown on television
- *p* TV act: probability of carrying out TV act
- Opportunity: real-life chance of putting TV act into practice
- Display behavior: observable performance of social behavior shown on television

This is a probability model in that no effect is intended, but more exposure is likely in general to lead to more effect. Higher probability of effect is associated with higher arousal (interest, excitement), behavior displayed with more positive than negative associations, greater relative prominence of displayed behavior, greater realism, and opportunities for putting behavior into practice (a necessary condition). The effects envisaged can be prosocial as well as antisocial, the process of effect being essentially the same in both cases.

The model treats behavioral effect as an outcome of a sequential learning process that may be repeated endlessly, with cumulative probabilities of change, depending on the factors mentioned. The underlying model remains that of stimulus-response. The model abstracts the television experience from the complex web of social life and the context of viewing, but it is a useful tool for experimental research and a guide to rational thought about unintended effect. Television is treated as the functional equivalent of any other experience or display from which a behavior might be learned, and the model could thus be used for other kinds of communication situations.

The two-step flow of information model by Elihu Katz and PAUL F. LAZARSFELD (1955) suggests that (1) mass media messages by and large reach people indirectly, that is, they are mediated through and influenced by social relationships; (2) knowledge and dissemination of media content often are transformed into personal influence; and (3) mass communication should be treated in connection with

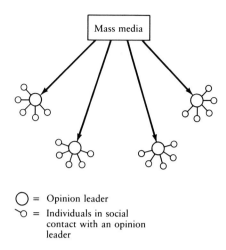

Figure 7. *(Models of Communication)* Elihu Katz and Paul Lazarsfeld's model of the two-step flow of information. Redrawn after Elihu Katz and Paul F. Lazarsfeld, *Personal Influence,* Glencoe, Ill.: Free Press, 1955.

INTERPERSONAL COMMUNICATION systems. According to this model, illustrated in Figure 7, an OPINION LEADER will often function as an interpreter and mediator between medium and individual. The mass-mediated information will now be spread within the interpersonal network around the opinion leader. Some have argued that there may be more than two steps in this process and have therefore proposed a multistep flow of information model. Of all models, the two-step flow of information model would be one of the most widely used—in areas as diverse as rural innovation, political campaigns, and marketing of new products.

A special aspect of communications research and theory deals with the DIFFUSION of innovations. To a considerable extent the important elements and relations in several traditional models of the communication process and those in a diffusion model are seen to be similar. In the diffusion version, however, the sources of messages are typically inventors, change agents, and opinion leaders; the message is the innovation and its perceived attributes; the channels may be mass media or interpersonal; and the receivers are members of social systems. In both types of model the effects are the same: knowledge, attitude change, and behavioral change. In the diffusion of innovations model, overt behavioral changes are especially emphasized.

Probably the most well-known diffusion model is that of U.S. scholars Everett Rogers and Floyd Shoemaker (1971), which describes the innovation-decision process in terms of four main stages: knowledge, PERSUASION, decision, and confirmation. In a later version Rogers (1983) adds a fifth element—implementation—between decision and confirmation. In real life, empirical evidence has shown that one or more stages may be skipped, or the stages may occur in a different order. Rogers himself has announced (1976) the passing of the paradigm represented by the model, stressing that change should not be superimposed from outside but can and should occur from below, that is, from those who seek it on their own behalf.

Using Communication

Whereas most other models take the sender as their starting point, those that deal with use of media and the gratifications they provide necessarily start with the individual member of the media audience and his or her more or less basic needs and motives for engaging in media use. A good example is the model by Olga Linné and Cecilia von Feilitzen (1972), which includes most of the elements and relations one finds in general descriptions of the theory. The actual model (see Figure 8) also gives the individual

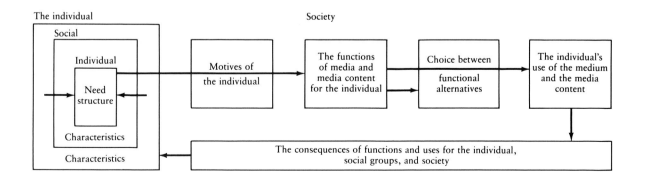

Figure 8. *(Models of Communication)* A model of media audience gratification. Redrawn after Olga Linné and Cecilia von Feilitzen, "Masskommunikationsteorier," in *Radio och TV Möter Publiken,* ed. by Rune Sjöden, Stockholm: Sveriges radio, 1972.

the choice of using media or turning to a functional alternative. The media use may or may not be functional—that is, fulfilling the individual's needs and thereby yielding the sought-for gratifications. It may also have other consequences and effects on the individual as well as on the social environment.

A more complex version of a uses-and-gratifications model was presented by Swedish scholar Karl Erik Rosengren (1974). A major characteristic of that model was its emphasis on gratifications as solutions to what an individual would regard as problematic.

An important motive in communication is the search for information. A model drawn by Lewis Donohew and Leonard Tipton (1973) describes how information is "sought, avoided and processed" by an individual. Graphically it is in the form of a flow chart, which illustrates that the nature of the process consists of a series of consecutive choices to be made. In the flow chart (see Figure 9) the process starts with the perception of a stimulus—a piece of information—that will then be tested in terms of relevance and consistency with the individual's image of reality. If the result is positive the next question deals with

whether action is to be taken. With a positive answer, level of priority is assigned, and after having assessed the situation, the individual can define the kind of sources for information that would be suitable. There will be a choice between a narrow and a broad focus. In the former case one decides immediately to use one specific source; in the latter the individual first reviews the sources at hand and then decides which to consult. With enough information the individual acts and evaluates the outcome and eventually ends up with a more or less changed image of reality.

Mass Media Systems: Production, Selection, and Flow

As already indicated, the process of mass communication has posed the greatest challenge to model builders because of its complexity. The main difficulties concern the representation of an elaborate institutional framework within which communication takes place and also the many factors that can intervene in organizations between the planning and

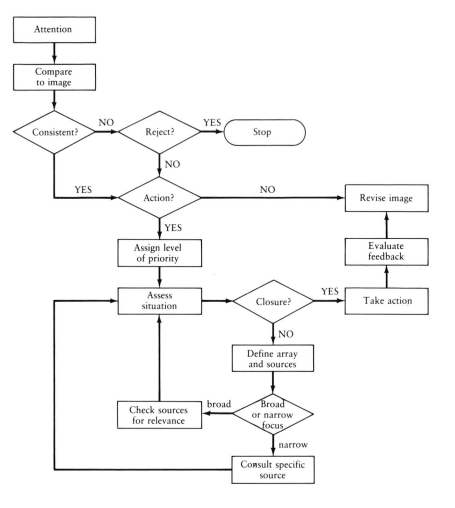

Figure 9. *(Models of Communication)* L. Donohew and L. Tipton's model of seeking, avoiding, and processing information. Redrawn after L. Donohew and L. Tipton, "A Conceptual Model of Information Seeking, Avoiding, and Processing," in *New Models for Communication*, ed. by Peter Clarke, Beverly Hills, Calif.: Sage, 1973.

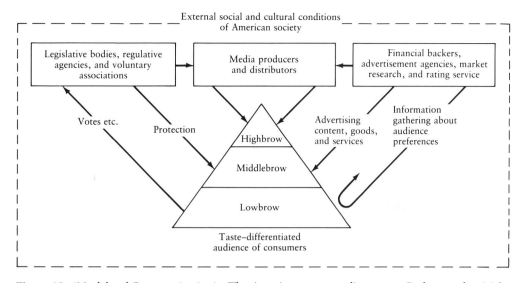

Figure 10. *(Models of Communication)* The American mass media system. Redrawn after Melvin L. DeFleur, *Theories of Mass Communication*, New York: D. McKay Co., 1966.

the realization of the message as sent. The institutional context of mass media activity varies from one national system to another, but a model depicting that of the United States (a free-market system) was drawn by U.S. scholar Melvin DeFleur (1966) and can be used for comparison with other national contexts (see Figure 10).

The drawing is a much simplified version of the original, designed to emphasize the following main points. First, the audience is assumed to be the prime mover (by its demands for media content) and can be stratified according to its tastes and interests in a way that closely corresponds to socioeconomic stratification. Second, financial support is provided to media producers by commercial agencies, whose task is to assess the size of different kinds of demand for content and to invest accordingly. Third, media organizations make and supply content, but usually not without some kind of regulation on legal, technical, social, or financial grounds, through agencies that may represent the interests of the state, the general public, or sections of the audience. The whole system thus works, driven by demand, fueled by finance, and guided by regulatory agencies. The maximization of audiences in such a system is crucial, but demand may be actively stimulated and managed as well as simply responded to. In practice several alternative organizations usually compete to meet or control demand.

The aspects of processing of content within media organizations that have attracted the most attention and that are amenable to treatment by models involve especially the selection and shaping of content. The general process of gatekeeping (*see* LEWIN, KURT) of media content was first described and investigated by David Manning White in 1950, using an implicit model of the kind shown in Figure 11.

This model simply shows that key figures in a media organization select from incoming material what to transmit further and what to reject at the "gates" of the organization, as it were (see the "channel role" in the Westley-MacLean model described above in Figure 3). Later researchers have drawn attention to significant additional features of this process. First, it has become clear that external sources (the advocates of Westley and MacLean) try to gain access through the gates by establishing collaborative relations with reporters, and there is a differential pressure behind such attempts. Second, in many cases of flow of news items from event to published report, several successive gates must be passed, such as local news agency, central agency editor, telegraph editor, or subeditor or chief editor of a news medium. Third, items pass gates only if they have certain favorable attributes or meet criteria of news value. Fourth, media content is usually processed to make it conform to technical and presentational criteria deployed by media organizations.

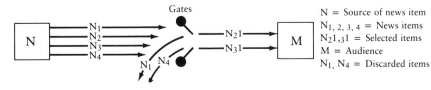

N = Source of news item
$N_{1, 2, 3, 4}$ = News items
$N_21, 31$ = Selected items
M = Audience
N_1, N_4 = Discarded items

Figure 11. *(Models of Communication)* The gatekeeper model. Redrawn after David Manning White, "The 'Gatekeepers': A Case Study in the Selection of News," *Journalism Quarterly* 27 (1950): 383–390.

Conclusion

The communication model is a useful general device rather than an instrument to be applied to one particular field or to one theory. It has its biases and limitations, especially its unsuitability for dealing with cultural matters and with communication as RITUAL or expression rather than as transmission. Many models are revised or supplemented to take into account new technologies of communication. They are likely to include information-search behavior initiated by the receiver, interactive exchanges, and central registration of communication activities connected in the same network. Different patterns will be associated with different forms and uses of the new technology, and models can play a role in describing and analyzing the changes under way.

Bibliography. George Comstock, Steven Chaffee, Nathan Katzman, Maxwell McCombs, and Donald Roberts, *Television and Human Behavior*, New York, 1978; Melvin DeFleur and Sandra Ball-Rokeach, *Theories of Mass Communication*, 4th ed., New York, 1982; Lewis Donohew and Leonard Tipton, "A Conceptual Model of Information Seeking, Avoiding, and Processing," in *New Models for Mass Communication Research*, ed. by Peter Clarke, Beverly Hills, Calif., 1973; Elihu Katz and Paul F. Lazarsfeld, *Personal Influence*, Glencoe, Ill., 1955; Harold D. Lasswell, "The Structure and Function of Communication in Society," in *The Communication of Ideas*, ed. by Lyman Bryson, New York, 1948; Olga Linné and Cecilia von Feilitzen, "Masskommunikationsteorier," in *Radio och TV Möter Publiken*, ed. by Rune Sjöden, Stockholm, 1972; Gerhard Maletzke, *Psychologie der Massenkommunikation: Theorie und Systematik*, Hamburg, 1963; Everett M. Rogers, "Communication and Development: The Passing of the Dominant Paradigm," *Communication Research* 3 (1976): 213–240; idem, *Diffusion of Innovations* (1962), 3d ed., New York, 1983; Everett M. Rogers and F. Floyd Shoemaker, *Communication of Innovations*, 2d ed., New York, 1971; Wilbur L. Schramm, "How Communication Works," in *Process and Effects of Mass Communication* (1954), rev. ed., ed. by Wilbur L. Schramm and Donald F. Roberts, Urbana, Ill., 1971; idem, *The Science of Human Communication*, New York, 1963; Bruce H. Westley and Malcolm S. MacLean, Jr., "A Conceptual Model for Communications Research," *Journalism Quarterly* 34 (1957): 31–38; David Manning White, " 'The Gatekeeper': A Case Study in the Selection of News," *Journalism Quarterly* 27 (1950): 383–390.

DENIS MCQUAIL AND SVEN WINDAHL

MONOPOLY

Monopolistic control over the mass media has become a subject of continuing controversy in the modern world. Modern societies, with their large, urban, interdependent communities and popular participation in politics, need newspapers, magazines, journals, radio, television, books, cinema, and other impersonal mechanisms to disseminate public information and political discourse. Since information and ideas help shape political values, monopoly or control over the mass media is closely associated with control over politics.

Literal monopoly exists where all media in a nation are owned and operated by governments or ruling parties of governments. Some governments do not directly operate their media but achieve a high degree of control by subsidy and favoritism for sympathetic media and CENSORSHIP and criminal sanctions against nonconforming ones. In other societies the media are mostly privately owned, protected by law or tradition against substantial government interference. But in some of these countries a small number of corporations develop such dominance in the media marketplace and have such similar political and economic values that they represent a potential for monopoly and for overwhelming influence over national information and ideas.

Whether through government operation or private economic dominance, monopolistic control confers powers of censorship. It has been estimated that in the last quarter of the twentieth century a third of the print media of the world and more than half of the electronic media are not free to disseminate content that offends government or private owners of the media.

Monopoly can exist in individual media, like newspapers, or it can affect sweeping infrastructures, like telecommunications or news distribution networks. For example, the global distribution of news is basically controlled by an oligopoly; five services distribute most news throughout the world. They are the Associated Press and United Press International, based in the United States and privately operated; Reuters, based in Great Britain and privately operated; Agence France Presse, based in France with significant government participation in its administration; and Tass, based in the Soviet Union and controlled by the government. In fifty other countries the domestic news service is controlled by the state, but in a majority of nations the five international services provide virtually all news from beyond each nation's borders and control worldwide news about those nations. This dominance created an international issue between the major powers and Third World or nonaligned countries. *See* NEWS AGENCIES.

National variations. Total control of all media within a society is represented in the last half of the twentieth century by such countries as the Soviet Union and China, where all media are produced either by the government or by the established political party. In such countries the nature of the media is determined by the underlying philosophy of government. In these countries the purpose of the media is not to provide a diversity of views or to produce a monetary profit, but to educate and encourage the citizens toward economic and social goals of the larger society. In a few places the goal is different, like the theological goal of *Osservatore Romano,* the monopoly newspaper of Vatican City.

In some countries the media are theoretically private enterprises but the government silences opposition media, as in South Africa and the Philippines during much of the latter part of the twentieth century. Similar monopolization over expression has been typical of military dictatorships. In many such countries the law guarantees freedom of expression, but there is an added provision, either in law or by fiat, prohibiting whatever may be deemed to undermine state power.

Where the media are free of government controls, problems of economic domination by oligopolies of private corporations have developed. In Australia, for example, there are more than 50 daily and 450 nondaily newspapers, but three corporations control every metropolitan paper and, through interlocking interests, most smaller newspapers as well as magazines, radio, and television. In Japan five companies control more than half of all national newspaper circulation, and in Canada two firms monopolize most of the media. In the United States, despite an extraordinarily high number of outlets in every medium, a few dozen corporations control most of the output of every mass medium.

Resistance to monopoly control. In most societies, including some with severe penalties for such activities, there are both open and covert attempts to resist the effects of government and private corporate control. When there is official government control, for example, there are often secret production and distribution of literature, art, and culture that depart from official norms. In the Soviet Union and Eastern bloc nations, for example, there is a tradition of samizdat, clandestine material distributed privately. Official punishment ranges from imprisonment to public denunciation.

In countries with media that are privately owned but operate under military or other stringent restrictions, there is also a high frequency of antiestablishment material, though offenders there, as elsewhere, may suffer harsh consequences. Newspapers have been closed or physically destroyed by semiofficial marauders, editors and journalists jailed or executed, and poets and other writers exiled or imprisoned. In South Africa, for example, producers of such matter can be banned under laws that, among other things, forbid future publication.

When there are private oligopolies, opposition comes in the form of smaller operations, though these seldom succeed in achieving widespread distribution because of their inability to compete against the economic power of the largest operators. Political opposition to monopoly often takes the form of agitation for restrictive laws against excessive size of media corporations, prohibitions against certain mergers, or actions to force large companies to divest portions of their holdings.

In private enterprise societies, opposition to corporate oligopolies often includes government itself, which may sympathize with laws or regulations against excessive corporate size. Government leaders may react to homogeneous printed media by resorting to broadcasting to reach the public, since broadcasting is regulated and tends to conform more readily to requests of government. *See* TELEVISION HISTORY—GLOBAL DEVELOPMENT.

Some democratic governments support competitive media. In the Netherlands and some other nations, the state has made low-interest loans and subsidies to failing newspapers or new ones. Governments may inhibit the homogenizing effects of private monopolies on political ideas by such devices as granting professional journalists a voice in media policies, creating independent trustees to limit mergers, or limiting acquisition of existing media properties to owners deemed likely to operate in the public interest.

Government actions to inhibit private monopolies in the media have had only partial success. In Great Britain, for example, the Monopolies and Merger Act of 1965 did not prevent continued consolidation of ownership. In the United States, antitrust law did not prevent the rapid growth of concentrated ownership in communications industries such as the TELEPHONE and the computer, as well as in the major mass media.

Occasional court decisions have had an immediate and significant impact on media monopolies, though later developments have often weakened that impact. For example, the Associated Press, long the major news service for the United States, is cooperatively owned by member newspapers. For decades members could veto service to their competitors. Other news services employed similar measures, and together these severely limited formation of new newspapers. In 1945 the U.S. Supreme Court, in *Associated Press* v. *United States,* ruled that the press could not take such actions that had the effect of preventing others from publishing. Nevertheless, oligopolistic trends continued, reinforced by economic factors. In the United States, as elsewhere, newspaper failures have resulted in many single-newspaper cities, and a growing number of papers have come under chain ownership. *See* NEWSPAPER: TRENDS.

Similarly, the 1948 U.S. Supreme Court decision in *United States* v. *Paramount et al.* forced a drastic reorganization of the film industry, requiring studio divestment of theater ownership, an end to block booking, and freer market access for independent producers. But the decision applied only to domestic operations. Foreign activities, increasingly important to the industry—in television as well as theatrical film—enabled the major studios to retain and even solidify their industry dominance. *See* HOLLYWOOD.

Similarly, the Federal Communications Commission, formed in 1934 with authority over the licensing of RADIO and television stations in the United States, adopted rules to limit the number of stations that could be owned by a single owner. But the economic power of the industry lay in networks and their growing ADVERTISING revenue, matters beyond FCC jurisdiction, and the FCC controls became increasingly ineffectual, particularly as network activities became increasingly international. In the 1970s and 1980s the rules were largely negated by a trend toward deregulation. *See* GOVERNMENT REGULATION.

In all these major media, leading companies were acquiring new power through ties to other industries and through transnational operations. This tended to move antimonopoly agitation from the national to the international scene.

International aspects. Internationally, all major media have posed control issues. Radio, while losing ground to television in many countries, acquired an increasingly significant international role. Because of relative ease of transmission over long distances and because the spoken word circumvents illiteracy, radio counters internal national monopolies. This can occur accidentally or by intention. It can be done for both commercial and propagandistic reasons. A lively global system of international radio broadcasting has developed in a great range of languages, often aimed at specific nations or groups within nations (*see* RADIO, INTERNATIONAL). The transistor revolution, introducing inexpensive hand-held receivers on a worldwide scale, added to the significance of this development. Television has also become an international medium in various ways, via transborder reception, cable and SATELLITE distribution, the marketing and exchange of telefilms, and videocassettes, often clandestinely distributed (*see* TELEVISION HISTORY—WORLD MARKET STRUGGLES).

Broadcasting that penetrates national borders has created tension even where there are no serious political differences, as between the United States and Canada, where most of the Canadian population lives within easy reception of U.S. radio and television stations. Such cultural and commercial differences occur also in adjacent states of Africa, Asia, Europe, and Latin America.

Though broadcasting almost everywhere is owned or regulated by government, some democratic countries have created a mechanism between government operation and private control. In those nations a substantial portion of all radio and television is placed under the control of a body of independent citizens designed to represent the public interest, as distinct from the government or private enterprise. This exists on a large scale in the Federal Republic of Germany, Japan, and the United Kingdom. In some countries, such as the Netherlands, citizen groups that achieve a given size may be granted a portion of time of their own in the national broadcast system. In the United States, a CITIZEN ACCESS movement achieved considerable momentum in the early years of CABLE TELEVISION. Nevertheless, despite occasional mechanisms to dilute centralized control of the mass media, monopolies continue to exercise significant control over information and culture among large portions of the world population.

Bibliography. Ben H. Bagdikian, *The Media Monopoly*, Boston, 1983; Jane Leftwich Curry and Joan R. Dassin, eds., *Press Control around the World*, New York, 1982; George T. Kurian, ed., *World Press Encyclopedia*, 2 vols., New York, 1982; Dan D. Nimmo and Michael W. Mansfield, *Government and the News Media: Comparative Dimensions*, Waco, Tex., 1982; Herbert I. Schiller, *Mass Communications and American Empire*, New York, 1969.

BEN H. BAGDIKIAN

MORRIS, CHARLES (1901–)

U.S. philosopher and semiotician. Born in Denver, Colorado, Charles William Morris obtained a B.S. in 1922 from Northwestern University and a Ph.D. in 1925 from the University of Chicago's Department of Philosophy, where he studied under GEORGE HERBERT MEAD. He taught philosophy at Rice University, the University of Chicago, and the University of Florida at Gainesville, retiring in 1971.

In *Foundations of the Theory of Signs* (1938) Morris began to develop his ideas about what came to be known as the general theory of signs, or SEMIOTICS (*see also* SIGN). Influenced by C. K. Ogden and I. A. RICHARDS's *The Meaning of Meaning* and following the theory of signs developed by CHARLES S. PEIRCE, Morris declared that semiosis—"the process in which something functions as a sign"—consists of three components: the *sign vehicle* ("that which acts as a sign"); the *designatum* ("that which the sign refers to"), or *denotatum* if the sign refers to an actual object; and the *interpretant* (the sign's "effect on some interpreter").

From the relations among the sign vehicle, the designatum, and the interpreter Morris abstracted three dimensions of semiosis: *syntactics*, which studies the formal relations of signs to one another; *semantics*, which is concerned with the relations of signs to their designata or denotata; and *pragmatics,* which studies the relations of signs to their interpreters. Each dimension is governed by its own rules, and any LANGUAGE or SIGN SYSTEM can be characterized by examining how these rules govern its usage of sign vehicles. Syntactical rules are divided into formation rules, which determine permissible sentences, and transformation rules, which determine the sentences that can be obtained from other sentences. Semantical rules determine under which conditions a sign can refer to an object or a situation. Pragmatical rules designate "the conditions in the interpreters under which the sign vehicle is a sign."

Morris emphasized the unity of the science of semiotics. Dividing the field into syntactics, semantics, and pragmatics enables various aspects of semiosis to be studied, much as various aspects of biology are studied under anatomy, ecology, and physiology. However, the three branches are interrelated (and themselves irreducible), and no sign-using process can be fully understood unless it is examined in terms of all three dimensions.

Semiotics, Morris believed, has important implications for other sciences, not only because "every science must embody its results in linguistic signs" and scientists must therefore be careful not to confuse linguistic and nonlinguistic problems, but also because semiotics could "play an important role in bridging the gap between the biological sciences, on the one hand, and the psychological and human social sciences, on the other, and in throwing new light upon the relation of the so-called 'formal' and 'empirical' sciences." Morris himself was associate editor of the *International Encyclopedia of Unified Science,* the project for which his *Foundations of the Theory of Signs* was written.

In his later work Morris explored sign use from a behaviorist perspective and attempted to develop a general theory of value. He examined the role of signs in such diverse areas as POETRY, music, DANCE, psychopathology, and morality.

See also LINGUISTICS; SEMANTICS.

Bibliography. Charles Morris, *Foundations of the Theory of Signs* (International Encyclopedia of Unified Science, Foundations of the Unity of Science, Vol. 1, no. 2), Chicago, 1938; idem, *Signs, Language, and Behavior,* New York, 1946, reprint 1955; idem, *Signification and Significance,* Cambridge, Mass., 1964; idem, *Writings on the General Theory of Signs,* The Hague and Paris, 1971.

ABRAHAM NOSNIK

MORSE, SAMUEL F. B. (1791–1872)

U.S. artist and inventor of the telegraph and the CODE used for telegraphic communication. The ca-

Figure 1. *(Morse, Samuel F. B.)* Matthew Brady (or assistant), *Samuel F. B. Morse.* Courtesy of the Library of Congress.

reer of Samuel Finley Breese Morse can be divided into two parts, the first as artist and the second as inventor of the telegraph. While attending Yale, Morse became interested both in painting and in the emerging field of electricity. After graduating in 1810 he first pursued a career in painting, achieving a measure of success in England and the United States. He helped establish the National Academy of the Arts of Design (now the National Academy of Design) in New York and served as its first president.

While returning from Europe in 1832, Morse overheard a conversation about André-Marie Ampère's experiments with the recently discovered electromagnet and considered the possibility of instantaneous communication by electricity. He spent much of the voyage in a fever of creativity, arriving in New York with a set of sketches for the first telegraph. This plan already embodied the three basic elements of the final system: a transmitting device that operated by opening and closing an electric circuit; a recording device at the other end actuated by an electromagnet; and a code that converted numbers and letters into dots, dashes, and spaces. Morse continued to paint, but his attention was increasingly taken up by his plans for TELEGRAPHY, and after 1837 he painted only one portrait. He was, however, instrumental in introducing the daguerreotype into the United States in 1839, lecturing on and teaching the new technique, which he had learned in Europe from LOUIS DAGUERRE.

Inventors in Germany, Great Britain, France, and the United States had laid the groundwork for various phases of the electric telegraph, but Morse worked with Leonard Gale, Joseph Henry, and Alfred Vail to perfect his own model. Morse encountered considerable difficulty in gaining acceptance for his telegraph, but in 1843 Congress finally voted thirty thousand dollars for construction of a telegraph line from Washington to Baltimore. On May 24, 1844, Morse sent the first message over the wire, his famous words "What hath God wrought!"

What followed was a series of legal battles pitting Morse against various other inventors and his former partners in a struggle over patent rights to the telegraph. In 1854 the U.S. Supreme Court granted Morse these rights, and he subsequently became a wealthy and successful businessman and promoter of telegraphy. Once the telegraph had proven itself, its possibilities were quickly realized, and transmission lines were pushed in every direction, linking distant parts of the United States in the first rapid communication network. Although the telegraph is now little used, Morse will be remembered as the developer of the first means for rapid distant communication.

Bibliography. Carleton Mabee, *The American Leonardo: A Life of Samuel F. B. Morse,* New York, 1943, reprint 1969; Edward Lind Morse, ed., *Samuel F. B. Morse: His Letters and Journals,* 2 vols., Boston, 1914, reprint New York, 1972.

ROBERT BALAY

MOTION PHOTOGRAPHY

Earliest photographic optics and chemistry prohibited the recording of moving subjects except for a few experiments under special circumstances. Anything that moved produced a blur on the photographic plate or paper, and this was seen as limiting the medium's inherent capacity for absolute REALISM (*see* PHOTOGRAPHY). The camera's inability to record motion, perceived as a problem similar to its inability to record color, was addressed almost immediately after the birth of the medium and solved step by step. The solution had widespread consequences: it made vulnerable the assumptions about the veracity of the medium, it produced a new graphic system to represent movement, and it led to the invention of MOTION PICTURES. It also furnished the basis for the study of ballistics, the training of athletes and soldiers, and the development of scientific labor management.

By the 1850s the advent of smaller cameras, faster lenses, and primitive shutter systems heralded the first widespread attempts at the photographic conquest of motion. The "snapshots" of this period showed pedestrians and horse-drawn carriages frozen into awkward postures. The attitudes fixed by the camera were quite different from anything seen by the naked eye or depicted by the artist, but because of the strength of the belief in the camera's objectivity and truth they were quickly accepted.

The use of photography to dissect a single action into its component parts was a valuable addition to the nineteenth century's ongoing investigation of the time-space relationships that constitute motion. This investigation would produce the railway, standard world time, and TELEGRAPHY, the TELEPHONE, and the phonograph.

The earliest of these photographic analyses was undertaken in 1872 in Sacramento, California, when the Anglo-American landscape photographer Eadweard Muybridge was hired by Leland Stanford to prove or disprove current theories pertaining to the gaits of the horse. Stanford, governor of California and builder of the American Central Pacific railway, hoped to apply the results of Muybridge's inventions to the training and breeding of his racehorses. Muybridge used a number of cameras (and the wet collodion process) in his attempt to get a single representative picture, but there exists no absolute proof of his success until 1878. That year, in Palo Alto, Muybridge was able to record the consecutive phases of a particular stride in exposure times ranging from 1/500th to 1/1,000th of a second. He set up a battery of cameras along the path traversed by the horse. Each camera shutter was tripped by an electrical release system devised by Stanford's railroad engineer, John D. Isaacs, and was put into action by the horse breaking wires stretched out at equal intervals along its path. Using a series of cameras to record movement had already been suggested by Thomas Rose in 1860 and Oscar Rejlander in 1873, but Isaacs's electrical installation made the Stanford-Muybridge project practicable.

The widespread publication of Muybridge's photographs caused a sensation in the United States and Europe. They were evidence that what had hitherto been established by visual perception as literal truth was mere convention; they contradicted the habitual perception of movement and revealed phases of locomotion that, being invisible, could not be validated by the unaided eye (Figure 1). In artistic circles in which direct observation was as important as interpretation, Muybridge's photographs caused a dispute over the relative merits of literal and aesthetic truthfulness. While academic artists struggled to incorporate into their work the stationary attitudes revealed by the camera, others (such as the French sculptor

Figure 1. *(Motion Photography)* Eadweard Muybridge, *Galloping Horse*, 1883–1885. Gernsheim Collection, Harry Ransom Humanities Research Center, The University of Texas at Austin.

Auguste Rodin) insisted that movement was customarily perceived as a fluid, ongoing effect and should be rendered as such. *See* PERCEPTION—STILL AND MOVING PICTURES.

An invitation from the University of Pennsylvania in 1883 allowed Muybridge to expand his study and to experiment with the new gelatine bromide (dry plate) process. The result of this work, *Animal Locomotion,* was published in eleven portfolios in 1887. The complete work contained 782 plates, each one composed of from twelve to thirty-six sequentially arranged images. *Animal Locomotion* is not scientific in the sense of a quantitative analysis of locomotion: there is no indication of time passing or space traversed, and many phases of the specific movements are missing, while some plates are no more than random assemblages of disparate images. Nevertheless, the volume is a treasure trove of figurative imagery, adopted by nineteenth-century academic painters such as Jean-Louis-Ernest Meissonier of France, by the U.S. painter Thomas Eakins (who worked with Muybridge at Pennsylvania but soon abandoned his system for one similar to Étienne-Jules Marey's), by the French painter Edgar Degas, and, in the twentieth century, by the Irish artist Francis Bacon.

Marey, an eminent French physiologist, saw Muybridge's photographs of horses in 1878. Marey's scientific career had been devoted to the foundation of the "graphic method": the invention and refinement of machines that transcribed motion and converted it into graphic form. With these machines—the predecessors of modern medical electronic graph-

ing devices like electrocardiographs—he had studied the widest possible examples of human and animal locomotion. Marey was quick to understand the advantage of photography: the subject need not be connected to, or supply any motive power to, the recording instrument. After meeting Muybridge in Paris in 1881 and seeing more of his results, Marey dismissed the serial camera system as prone to inaccuracy and developed a photographic gun based on a model that the French astronomer Pierre-Jules-César Janssen had made in 1874 to record the transit of Venus. Janssen's gun, which included a revolving circular plate intermittently exposed to light by a slotted disk acting as a shutter, was improved by Marey to yield an exposure time of 1/720th of a second and used to capture birds in flight. In 1882 Marey increased the number of slots in the disk shutter and incorporated it into a fixed-plate camera whose lens was left open while a figure dressed in white passed between it and a black background. The regular intermittent activity of the revolving slotted disk allowed each phase of the movement to be recorded in its correct spatial position relative to all the other phases on the plate. Marey's system became known as chronophotography.

To alleviate the confusion of superimposition that was produced on the plate by slow movements, Marey subsequently turned the figure into a measurable graphic notation by clothing it in black and marking the joints and bones with reflecting buttons and strips of metal. Pieces of white paper were attached to animals whose dark coats were deepened with lampblack. The resulting abstractions became the vocab-

Figure 2. *(Motion Photography)* Étienne-Jules Marey's arrangement for chronophotography at the Physiological Station, Bois de Boulogne, Paris, 1882. Gernsheim Collection, Harry Ransom Humanities Research Center, The University of Texas at Austin.

Figure 3. *(Motion Photography)*   Étienne-Jules Marey, chronophotograph, 1880s. National Film Archive, London.

ulary of a new language of motion in the twentieth century.

Chronophotography, with its insistence on a single unified point of view, produced a synthesis of movement in time and space rather than a sequential analysis as Muybridge had done (Figures 2 and 3). However, until 1888 Marey was limited to recording only those subjects that could pass in front of his black hangar. Then, after experimenting with a camera containing an oscillating mirror, he substituted a roll of sensitive paper for the glass plate. Although he synthesized the photographs made in this way on a Zoetrope, he did not succeed in projecting them until 1893. He did not envisage a commercial application for either machine; his primary interest was in recording what the eye could not grasp, not in replicating what it could normally see.

Muybridge and Ottomar Anschütz, who used an improved battery-of-cameras system in his photography for the Prussian military, also synthesized the images they had made. Muybridge's Zoopraxiscope (1879) illuminated and projected painted images made from his photographs. Anschütz succeeded in projecting photographs by means of his Electrotachyscope (1887). These were just two of the many instruments (or philosophical toys, as they were then called) based on the theory of the persistence of vision that synthesized phases of movement.

Other applications of motion photography included the study of hospital inmates by Albert Londe, a doctor at the Salpêtrière hospital in Paris, who studied rapid movement between 1883 and 1893 with a single camera incorporating a corona of six to twelve lenses. The Photophone (1892) of Georges Demeny, Marey's assistant, reproduced the movement of the lips in slow motion and was used in the teaching of deaf-mutes. The study of ballistics, aided by electric spark and flash photography (initiated by William Henry Fox Talbot in 1851), was carried out by Ernst Mach and P. Salcher (Prague, 1887), Charles Vernon Boys (London, 1892), and Lucien Bull (Paris, 1899). Frank B. Gilbreth's 1912 analysis of workers' movements by means of his Cyclograph (a modification of Marey's Chronophotograph) marked the beginning of scientific labor management.

In his manifesto, *Fotodinamismo futuristica* (1913), Anton Giulio Bragaglia declared the photography of movement to be an artistic and futurist enterprise and cited the French philosopher Henri-Louis Bergson as an authority for his method, a version of chronophotography that blurred the intermediate phases of the action. But, in an official proclamation, the futurist painters publicly disassociated their movement from Bragaglia's heresy, even though their own paintings incorporated the overlapping repetitive forms first revealed by the camera. Ironically, the futurists, who celebrated new technology in any

Figure 4. *(Motion Photography)* Harold Edgerton, *Milk Drop Coronet*, 1936. Gernsheim Collection, Harry Ransom Humanities Research Center, The University of Texas at Austin. Copyright Dr. Harold Edgerton, M.I.T., Cambridge, Mass.

form, could not accept the threat to the traditional hierarchy of the arts embodied by photography.

In the twentieth century, advances in the conquest of movement have evolved from further reductions in exposure times, either through high-speed shutter systems or by short-duration, single- and multiple-flash sources (stroboscopic photography). The pioneer of modern stroboscopic technology, Harold Edgerton, extended the work of both Muybridge and Marey (Figure 4), taking single exposures of events beyond the visual threshold at speeds up to one microsecond and recording successive phases of movement with electronic units capable of flashing up to a million times a second.

Bibliography. Harold E. Edgerton and James R. Killian, Jr., *Moments of Vision*, Cambridge, Mass., 1979; Helmut Gernsheim and Alison Gernsheim, *The History of Photography, 1685–1914*, 2d ed., New York, 1969; Stephen Kern, *The Culture of Time and Space, 1880–1918*, Cambridge, Mass., 1983; Anita Ventura Mozley, ed., *Eadweard Muybridge: The Stanford Years, 1872–1882*, Stanford, Calif., 1972; Aaron Scharf, *Art and Photography*, London, 1968, reprint Baltimore, Md., 1975.

MARTA BRAUN

MOTION PICTURES

The following three articles describe the rise of the motion picture:
1. Prehistory
2. Silent Era
3. Sound Film

1. PREHISTORY

In 1895 and 1896, when astonished audiences around the world had their first glimpse of motion pictures, it was both the beginning of an era and the culmination of a long, complex evolution. Diverse strands of development had come together in the invention of the motion picture.

The 1830s had seen the appearance of various popular-science novelties such as the Phenakistiscope ("deceitful view") created by the Belgian physicist Joseph Plateau, known for his studies of subjective visual phenomena. A series of painted images representing phases of a figure in motion was mounted on a disk that had slots along its rim. As the disk was revolved, a viewer saw the images in a mirror, through the slots. The sequence of images, each seen momentarily, seemed to merge into a moving figure (Figure 1). An essentially identical device, the Stroboskop ("whirling view") of Simon Ritter von Stampfer of Austria, was developed about the same time, apparently independently.

Soon afterward came the Zoetrope ("wheel of life"), in which a thin strip of pictures was mounted on the inside of a hollow cylinder. As it revolved, a viewer watched through slots in the cylinder. Again, the cycle of pictures, each momentarily glimpsed, merged into an illusion of motion. The Zoetrope remained popular for decades in homes, country fairs, and arcades (Figure 2).

These devices had used drawn or painted figures, but soon PHOTOGRAPHY became involved. In 1870 in Philadelphia, Henry R. Heyl photographed a man and a woman posed in six stages of a waltz. He mounted glass slides of the six poses around a disk, using each cycle three times. The disk was whirled in front of a light source, which projected the images onto a screen. A shutter moving in a contrary direction darkened the screen between images, so that each was seen only briefly, creating an illusion of the cyclical action of the waltz. Heyl called his device the Phasmatrope ("wheel of illusion").

A cycle of photographs was similarly used in a device unveiled in 1887 by the German Ottomar Anschütz, who used images of gymnasts and cavalry horses photographed by a series of cameras. The photographs were again mounted on a whirling disk. Because they were lit one by one by an electric spark, each momentarily, a shuttering device was not needed. The images were not projected but were observed directly by a small group of viewers through a rect-angular slot. Anschütz called his device an Electro-tachyscope ("electric rapid vision"; Figure 3).

Other experimenters, including French astronomer Pierre-Jules-César Janssen, French physiologist Étienne-Jules Marey, and photographer Eadweard Muybridge in the United States, were working in the same direction for different ends. These were scientists engaged in research who wanted to develop equipment with which some phenomenon or event could be documented (see MOTION PHOTOGRAPHY). Muybridge and Marey, who encouraged each other, learned to project their fragmentary image sequences, and Marey took a further important step. He switched from a revolving photographic plate to moving strips of photographic paper, and still later to celluloid strips. These permitted more extensive sequences not limited to cyclical motion.

U.S. inventor THOMAS ALVA EDISON observed the work of Muybridge and Marey at various stages and meanwhile undertook development of a device to serve popular ENTERTAINMENT rather than research purposes: the Kinetoscope, a coin-in-the-slot machine in which individuals would glimpse moving images in sequences. The development work was done almost entirely by William Kennedy Laurie Dickson, an Englishman in Edison's employ. Dickson's first working model, about 1887, placed the images on a cylinder similar to that used in early Edison phonographs, and there was thought of combining the two inventions. In later models Dickson, proceeding along the same lines as Marey, switched to strips of film, which were obtained from the Eastman Company. The Kinetoscope was demonstrated in 1893 and put on the market the following year. In penny arcades customers could now see short sequences of serpentine dancers, rope-twirling cowboys, and boxers in combat (Figure 4). Kinetoscopes were rushed to foreign markets and for a short time seemed headed for wide international success. Instead they served as catalysts for a different saga.

While Edison was intent on serving individual viewers, not group audiences (he said he did not want to "kill the goose that lays the golden eggs"), others had opposite thoughts. The idea of serving audiences had already engaged many experimenters, and others were joining in. At various times the quest involved such inventors as Louis A. A. Le Prince, William Friese-Greene, and Robert W. Paul in England; Max Skladanowsky and Oskar Messter in Germany; C. Francis Jenkins and Thomas Armat in the United States; the brothers LOUIS AND AUGUSTE LUMIÈRE in France; and others. Efforts were intensified by the discovery that Edison had failed to patent the Kinetoscope internationally—perhaps to avoid conflict over ideas derived from Marey. The race toward a "projecting Kinetoscope" thus seemed open to one and all.

Among entrepreneurs who watched the race with

Figure 2. *(Motion Pictures—Prehistory)* A Zoetrope, manufactured by Carpenter and Westley, London, ca. 1868. Gernsheim Collection, Harry Ransom Humanities Research Center, The University of Texas at Austin.

special anticipation were magicians, the master showmen of the time. They were headliners of vaudeville programs, and many had their own magic theaters, which in major cities provided a high point for family trips. Unknown to most people, projections from hidden magic lanterns played a crucial role in many magic illusions. It had been so since the 1790s,

when Paris audiences were awestruck and even terrified by *Phantasmagorie,* a show created by the Belgian Étienne Gaspard Robertson, who called up spirits of the dead and other spectral creatures, so impressively that some in the audience fell to their knees in prayer (Figure 5). The images came from slides projected onto smoke rising from braziers in the darkened room. The twisting smoke gave the shapes an unearthly motion. The effect, in countless variations, remained in use throughout the nineteenth century.

Meanwhile, the magic lantern acquired other sophisticated applications. Duplex lanterns made possible dissolves from one slide to another, and slides acquired movable parts operated by levers. Illusions involving the choreography of projections from multiple lanterns were in the repertoire of magic theaters like the Théâtre Robert-Houdin in Paris, famous since 1845. In 1888 it was purchased by rising young magician Georges Méliès, who began showing audiences trips to the moon, journeys to the bottom of the sea, and descents into hell (Figures 6 and 7). In London the Egyptian Hall, "England's Home of Mystery," featured similar illusions (Figure 8). Magicians realized that the projecting Kinetoscope would be able to carry such effects to new heights. They were determined to have it for their theaters. When the Lumière brothers announced that their cinematograph would make its commercial debut at the Grand Café in Paris on December 28, 1895, it was a suspenseful moment for magicians.

The Lumières had won the technology race. Louis Lumière, the main inventor of the cinematograph, said later that all details of the mechanism had suddenly become clear to him during one sleepless night late in 1894. A prototype was soon constructed, and private showings were held in March and June 1895. At the June showing during a convention, the astronomer Janssen and others were astonished to see a film of themselves arriving for the convention on the previous day. The cinematograph was ingenious: a portable camera that could be adapted into a machine for printing film and readjusted into a functioning projector—a whole system in one mechanism.

Louis Lumière made an unusual decision: he would not put the device on the market. Instead he arranged for the fabrication of dozens of additional machines

Figure 3. *(Motion Pictures—Prehistory)* Ottomar Anschütz, Electrotachyscope. From *Scientific American,* 1889.

and the training of *opérateurs* in their use. By the time of the premiere the company had quietly prepared for worldwide exploitation tours. In one capital after another, Lumière representatives would show "the miracle of the century, the wonder of the world," making additional films as they went—street scenes, royalty, parades.

The premiere fulfilled expectations. Within weeks other Lumière shows were running in Paris, and representatives were en route to foreign capitals. But the magicians were dismayed. Finding the Lumières unwilling to sell the miracle-making equipment, many converged on a close competitor, Robert Paul of London. Paul, having lost the race, was ready to sell to one and all (Figures 9 and 10). In a memoir he was to recall that "an extraordinary demand arose, first among conjurers," then among other show people. Paul's workshop labored to fill the demand. Thanks to him, films became part of the Méliès programs at the Théâtre Robert-Houdin within weeks after the cinematograph premiere. The Egyptian Hall acquired Robert Paul equipment and began featuring "animated pictures." U.S. magician Carl Hertz, embarking from England on a world tour in March 1896, left with a Paul projector and a few weeks later gave the first film showing in South Africa and, in August 1896, the first in Australia (Figure 11). Other magicians were racing the Lumière *opérateurs* across the globe. Audiences in many countries appear to have seen film first as part of a magic act and to have accepted it as such. They knew that world leaders and squadrons of soldiers had no business marching across a room before them; it was clearly magic.

Figure 4. *(Motion Pictures—Prehistory)* Kinetoscope (and phonograph) parlor, Detroit, 1894. Courtesy of Erik Barnouw.

Figure 5. *(Motion Pictures—Prehistory)* Étienne Gaspard Robertson, *Phantasmagorie*, Paris, 1790s. Courtesy of Erik Barnouw.

Figure 6. *(Motion Pictures—Prehistory)* Georges Méliès in *Le diable géant* (The Enormous Devil), 1902. National Film Archive, London. Copyright: Famille Méliès. All rights reserved.

Figure 7. *(Motion Pictures—Prehistory)* Georges Méliès, *À la conquête du pole* (The Conquest of the Pole), 1912. The Museum of Modern Art/Film Stills Archive.

Figure 8. *(Motion Pictures—Prehistory)* A poster from the Egyptian Hall introducing Nevil Maskelyne's Mutagraph, patented in 1897. State Historical Society of Wisconsin, Erik Barnouw Collection/Museum of London.

Figure 9. *(Motion Pictures—Prehistory)* Robert Paul's Kine-camera, on a revolving stand, 1896. Trustees of the Science Museum, London.

Figure 10. *(Motion Pictures—Prehistory)* Robert Paul ▷ operating his Kine-camera. From *Strand Magazine*, 1896, p. 134. Trustees of the Science Museum, London.

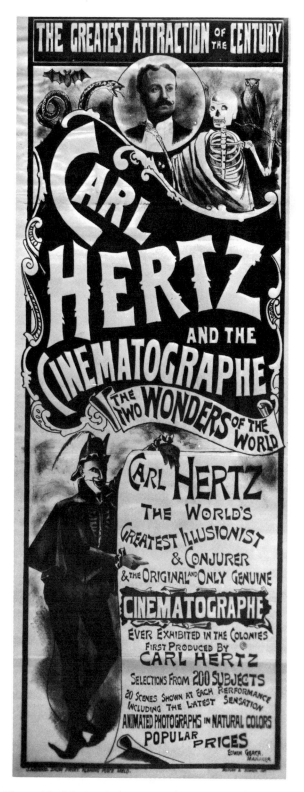

Figure 11. *(Motion Pictures—Prehistory)* Carl Hertz poster, Melbourne, Australia, 1896. State Historical Society of Wisconsin, Erik Barnouw Collection/Houdini Collection, Library of Congress.

For Edison, the rapid spread of the projected motion picture posed a crisis. His Kinetoscope was doomed. His agents hastily arranged to take over the projector developed by Jenkins and Armat and to present it as the Edison Vitascope, premiering it on April 23, 1896, at Koster and Bial's Music Hall in New York.

Toy makers, fairground impresarios, photographers, scientists, magicians, and others had all contributed to the invention, and all brought different ideas and traditions to the new medium. The motion picture, with this diverse heritage, readily adjusted itself to a world it would soon transform.

See also ANIMATION; CINEMATOGRAPHY; FILM EDITING; SPECIAL EFFECTS.

Bibliography. John Barnes, compl., *Precursors of the Cinema*, Part 1, *Barnes Museum of Cinematography, Catalog of the Collection*, St. Ives, Eng., 1970; Erik Barnouw, *The Magician and the Cinema*, New York, 1981; C. W. Ceram [Kurt Wilhelm Marek], *Archaeology of the Cinema*, New York, 1965; Jacques Deslandes, *Histoire comparée du cinéma*, Vol. 1, Tournai, 1966; John L. Fell, ed., *Film before Griffith*, Berkeley, Calif., 1983; Gordon Hendricks, *The Edison Motion Picture Myth*, Berkeley, Calif., 1961, reprint New York, 1972; Kenneth Macgowan, *Behind the Screen*, New York, 1965.

JOHN L. FELL

2. SILENT ERA

The motion picture era called silent is generally described as extending from the mid-1890s, when people in many countries had their first film experience, either via peepshow machine or an early projected screening, to the period 1928–1935, when most film industries switched over to production with sound. Films were, in fact, seldom silent; most were accompanied during projection by music, ranging from a single piano to a full orchestra.

It was a time of experiment. Films moved freely across borders. Since intertitles in different languages could be substituted, language was not a barrier, and influences spread rapidly, creating an international art form. Almost every aspect of film technique was pioneered by silent filmmakers, and many films of this era remain unsurpassed in their imaginative use of the medium.

Primitive Era: 1894–1908

Until 1903 a film generally consisted of a single shot and was usually less than a minute long. Various types were emerging: scenics were shots of interesting locales (*see* DOCUMENTARY); topicals showed newsworthy events (*see* NEWSREEL). Others recorded acts by famous performers, as when Annie Oakley showed off her skeet-shooting for the camera at THOMAS ALVA EDISON's studio. Nearly all films were shot in bright sunlight, either in real locations or on open-air stages with backdrops for scenery. The earliest studios, such as Edison's "Black Maria" and Georges Méliès's glass-walled studio in Montreuil (Figure 1), used sunlight exclusively. As the film industry grew more stable, more studios were built, usually on rooftops to catch daylight but occasionally enclosed to add electric light. After 1902 increasing numbers of NARRATIVE films were made.

In these early years filmmaking was mainly concentrated in France, England, and the United States, although camera operators from those countries traveled the entire world showing and making films. Distinctive filmmakers or groups emerged in each country. The brothers LOUIS AND AUGUSTE LUMIÈRE had been responsible for the first commercial showings of projected films, beginning in late 1895. Their touring projectionist-filmmakers soon built up a large catalog of brief films. Louis Lumière proved adept at varying his framing to suit the circumstances: a dynamic diagonal composition into depth for *Arrivée d'un train à La Ciotat* (The Arrival of a Train at La Ciotat Station); an intimate medium shot for *Le répas de bébé* (Feeding the Baby); a carefully balanced framing to keep the staged comic action of *L'arroseur arrosé* (Watering the Gardener) clear to the audience (all in 1895). Méliès initially copied such open-air filming, but by 1897 his talents as a magician and graphic artist had led him into the studio, where he began making fantasy films with elaborately painted scenery and skillful camera effects (Figure 2). Méliès made *Le voyage dans la lune* (A Trip to the Moon), *Cinderella,* and hundreds of others between 1896 and 1912, when increasing competition drove him out of filmmaking. In turn, Méliès's films were imitated by the powerful Pathé studio, which after the turn of the century rose to be the most successful film company in the world, a position it would hold until World War I (*see* PATHÉ, CHARLES).

Filmmaking in England began primarily with the work of Robert W. Paul, whose early films were brief scenics, topicals, and narrative scenes similar to those made in France (Figure 3). Around 1900, Paul, James Williamson, and G. A. Smith were working in a small group of studios in southern England known as the Brighton School. Their inventive use of close-ups, as in Smith's *Grandma's Reading Glass* (1900); trick effects, as in Williamson's *The Big Swallow* (1903); and skillful editing, as in Williamson's *Mary Jane's Mishap* (1903), were widely copied. Cecil Hepworth's 1905 *Rescued by Rover* assembled many shots of different locales, all joined by the movement of its canine hero; it was one of the most widely successful and imitated films of the primitive era. Faced with competition in world markets from French, U.S., and, increasingly, Danish and Italian films, the English cinema began to lose its prominence about 1907, until the Quota Act of 1927 bolstered British production once more.

In the United States the Edison Company tried to use its patents to gain MONOPOLY control. The American Mutoscope and Biograph Company, however, circumvented these efforts by inventing its own camera, and its main cinematographer-director, G. W. Bitzer, continued to make scenics, topicals (e.g., his coverage of the Galveston flood in 1900), and staged scenes. Biograph used the conventional rooftop studio but was inventive in its use of artificial lighting to film the Jeffries-Sharkey fight on location in Madison Square Garden in 1899 and in its early installation of electrical lighting in its indoor New York studio in 1903. Edison's main cinematographer-director was Edwin S. Porter, who kept abreast of European developments and added his own touches. His considerable influence began with the release early in 1903 of *The Life of an American Fireman* and continued that same year with *The Great Train Robbery.* Using a combination of single long shots for some scenes and brief series of shots for others, Porter built up relatively elaborate editing patterns, with characters moving from one space to another. The final scene in *The Life of an American Fireman* shows the rescue of a mother and child, first in a single shot inside their bedroom, then repeated from a vantage point outside. This use of overlapping time was an attempt to solve the problem of moving characters from place to place through a coherent line of action. Over the

Figure 1. *(Motion Pictures—Silent Era)* Georges Méliès's studio, Montreuil. National Film Archive, London. Copyright: Famille Méliès. All rights reserved.

Figure 2. *(Motion Pictures—Silent Era)* Georges Méliès, *Voyage à travers l'impossible* (The Impossible Voyage), 1904. The Museum of Modern Art/Film Stills Archive.

next fifteen years or so, filmmakers in various countries would devise other filmic strategies for handling this problem. Early Vitagraph films were consistently innovative; one of the earliest known instances of cross-cutting (editing back and forth between separate locales) occurs in its 1906 film *The Hundred-to-One Chance.*

Throughout the primitive era the popularity of films increased and production grew enormously. Distinct narrative genres began to emerge. The chase film, pioneered by the Brighton School—as in Williamson's *Stop, Thief!* (1901) and *Fire* (1902)—became the most common type of film after 1904. Pathé and American Mutoscope and Biograph became adept at long comic chases, and the genre encouraged film-

makers to string more shots together in increasingly elaborate ways. Slapstick comedies, crime thrillers, melodramas, and last-minute rescues were all common, early silent films being more oriented toward action than toward psychological drama.

As the primitive period drew to a close around 1908, the cinema was still expanding in every way. Films were longer. By 1909 the one-reel film (about fifteen minutes) with multiple shots had become standard. By the teens some companies, particularly in Europe, were making films of two or more reels, and these proved popular everywhere. More countries were now making films in significant numbers. By 1908 Danish and Italian films were becoming widely known, and the Italian industry was particularly

Figure 3. *(Motion Pictures—Silent Era)* Walter R. Booth for Robert W. Paul, *The Motorist,* 1905. National Film Archive, London.

Figure 4. *(Motion Pictures—Silent Era)* Giovanni Pastrone, *Cabiria*, 1913 (top and bottom). National Film Archive, London.

successful, growing to challenge the French films on world markets in the years before the war.

Transitional Period: 1909–1918

In the decade after the primitive period, filmmakers gradually formulated the "classical" narrative system of commercial filmmaking that has remained familiar to the present day. In the United States this transition lasted approximately from 1909 to 1916, with the traits of what we know as the HOLLYWOOD cinema being largely standardized by 1917.

Early in this era the lengthier feature film became dominant, spurred particularly by the success of Italian epics in the early teens. While the Italian industry had turned out its share of melodramas and comic

Figure 5. *(Motion Pictures—Silent Era)* Charlie Chaplin ▷ in *The Vagabond*, 1916. National Film Archive, London/ Black Ink Films.

one-reelers, its greatest popularity came with multiple-reel historical films using large sets and crowds of extras. *Quo Vadis?* (1912), *Gli ultima giorni di Pompei* (The Last Days of Pompeii, 1913), and *Cabiria* (1913; Figure 4) were widely imitated internationally. During the same years popular comedy STARS made series of films with continuing lead characters: Max Linder and Rigadin in France, Pimple in England, John Bunny and various Keystone comedians in the United States, including Mack Sennett and CHARLES CHAPLIN (Figure 5). U.S. westerns, too, became internationally popular and were copied in European countries (*see* WESTERN, THE). The increasing length of films permitted more character development, and psychological REALISM became a more prominent trait in films of the early teens. Denmark's major company, Nordisk, became noted for the realistic characterization of its dramas. Louis Feuillade, a prominent French director, made a number of naturalistic melodramas from 1911 to 1914, including a series called "La vie telle qu'elle est" (Life as It Is). Similarly, U.S. director D. W. GRIFFITH, already famous for last-minute-rescue films, turned increasingly to character studies. *The Painted Lady* (1912) and *The Mothering Heart* (1913) used subtle facial expressions to dwell on characters' reactions to their situations and were part of a trend to make character traits the wellspring of narrative action. In later years, however, he became better known for epic-sized features such as *The Birth of a Nation* (1915; Figure 6) and *Intolerance* (1916).

With the beginning of World War I and a sharp wartime decline in French and Italian filmmaking, U.S. films gradually came to dominate world screens. At the same time, the Hollywood studio system was emerging, and filmmakers were developing a standardized, efficient way of making popular narrative films, leading to what has come to be called the classical Hollywood cinema. All stylistic techniques were made to serve narrative functions. Plots concentrated on goal-oriented protagonists who came into conflict with other characters. The viewer's interest was ensured when one scene raised questions that the next scene answered. Cinematic techniques enhanced narrative action, maintaining clear spatial relations and emphasizing characters' states of mind. Early in a scene editing established a locale with a long shot, then presented closer views of significant facial expressions and details in order to intensify the drama. The camera could also follow the characters with tracking and panning movements. With quick pacing, happy endings, and popular stars, Hollywood films quickly became dominant in many

Figure 6. *(Motion Pictures—Silent Era)* D. W. Griffith, *The Birth of a Nation*, 1915. The Museum of Modern Art/Film Stills Archive.

countries, and such names as Mary Pickford, Douglas Fairbanks, and Dorothy and Lillian Gish were known worldwide. By the end of the war audiences in South America, much of Europe, and Australia were more likely to see Hollywood films than any other kind.

In Europe the war had widely varied effects in different countries. French filmmaking, after a nearly complete shutdown in 1914, began to recover slowly in late 1915. Patriotic war stories were common. Feuillade made films of this type but turned increasingly to the SERIAL form, in which he scored such popular successes as *Les vampires* (1915–1916), *Judex* (1916–1917), and *Tih Minh* (1918–1919). Production in Italy remained slow throughout the war, while U.S. competition chipped away at Italy's lucrative foreign markets. But the Russian and German industries benefited from the isolation caused by the war. Neither had been a significant producing force before 1914, having depended largely on imports. When commercial routes into Russia were blocked, small companies sprang up there and began producing films. The most notable were by Yakov Protazanov, whose literary adaptations—for example, *Pilovaya Dama* (The Queen of Spades, 1916) and *Otets Sergii* (Father Sergius, 1918)—were not innovative stylistically but were well acted and popular. Protazanov would remain the most popular director in Russia through the 1920s. In the first years of the war Germany continued to depend on U.S. and Danish imports. Gradually German production companies appeared, and the government fostered them for the PROPAGANDA value of film. Notable ENTERTAINMENT films appeared as well. Many of these were in the fantasy genre, such as Paul Wegener's *Der Rattenfänger von Hameln* (The Rat-Catcher of Hamlin, 1918) and Richard Oswald's *Hoffmanns Erzählungen* (Tales of Hoffmann, 1916). Fantasy and horror films would remain a staple of German production into the 1920s (*see* HORROR FILM).

During these years, the adventure serial became one of the most popular forms worldwide. It reached a peak with the Pearl White serials in the United States, including *The Exploits of Elaine* (1915) and *The Iron Claw* (1916), and a host of rival projects by others in every producing country. Concentrating on exotic villains and locales, fast action, and plots that carried over between episodes at high points of suspense, serials could involve anywhere from a few episodes to dozens. One serial, *The Hazards of Helen* (1914–1917), made in the United States, ran to 119 parts.

Postwar Era: 1918–1929

As the war ended countries around the world found themselves trying to compete, against formidable odds, with the popular Hollywood cinema. In some cases this meant imitation. In every national cinema, including the Soviet and the Japanese, features were made that closely resembled Hollywood films. However, there were also significant departures.

Scandinavia. The world became aware of a uniquely Swedish cinema. Its two major directors, Maurice Stiller and Victor Sjöström, often left the studio to film in the impressive scenery of the Swedish countryside, and landscape became a major part of the drama in such films as Stiller's *Herr Arnes pengar* (Sir Arne's Treasure, 1919; Figure 7) and Sjöström's *Berg-Ejvind och hans hustru* (The Outlaw and His Wife, 1918). Together these two directors created Sweden's brief golden era, which ended in the mid-1920s when they departed for jobs in Hollywood, where Sjöström became Seastrom.

In Denmark, Benjamin Christensen had established himself during the teens with *Det hemmelighedsfulde X* (The Mysterious X, 1913) and *Haevnens nat* (Blind Justice, 1915), melodramatic films with stark night lighting and skillful camera movement. After the war, he created one more major film, the bizarre *Häxan* (Witchcraft through the Ages, 1921), composed of startling satanic imagery. Christensen, too, departed for a brief career in Hollywood, but he was overshadowed by a man who soon became the most renowned Danish director, Carl Dreyer. Dreyer's Danish features, from *Praesidenten* (The President, 1919) to *Du skal aere din hustru* (Thou Shalt Honor Thy Wife, 1925), were sparse, restrained dramas, employing deliberately simple settings and camera techniques that eschewed the glamor of Hollywood. In the middle and late 1920s Dreyer worked in various European countries, becoming part of an international AVANT-GARDE FILM movement.

Germany. The German government bolstered the postwar film industry by restricting imports, and producers there found themselves in a strong position. They were interested in making films noticeably different from those of Hollywood in order to offer world markets a competitive alternative. One such alternative was the historical epic, which the Germans made in imitation of the prewar Italian successes. Under the skillful guidance of directors like Ernst Lubitsch and Oswald, such films did indeed succeed abroad. Lubitsch's lavish *Madame Dubarry* (1919), a story of the French Revolution, was the first German film to be widely shown abroad after the war, and it spawned a host of similar films. Lubitsch, however, was soon lured away to Hollywood.

Another, more distinctly German alternative emerged when, influenced by German EXPRESSIONISM in the visual arts and theater, a group of filmmakers made *Das Cabinet des Dr. Caligari* (The Cabinet of Dr. Caligari, 1920), directed by Robert

Figure 7. *(Motion Pictures—Silent Era)* Maurice Stiller, *Herr Arnes pengar* (Sir Arne's Treasure), 1919. National Film Archive, London/ Swedish Film Institute.

Wiene. Its sets, made of painted canvas, depicted buildings in the manner of an expressionist woodcut. The distortions were justified as rendering the subjective vision of a madman. The resulting film was a success at home and abroad. The German industry responded by producing more expressionist films, creating an avant-garde movement within a mainstream film industry.

France. A second distinct stylistic movement arose in France after the war. The major companies as well as the many small independent firms were willing to give young directors a chance to compete with Hollywood. The 1918 releases of *La dixième symphonie* (The Tenth Symphony), by Abel Gance, and *Rose France,* by Marcel L'Herbier, initiated the French impressionist film movement. Gance, L'Herbier, and the other directors of this movement were more theoretically inclined than their German counterparts, and they published their views on film in journals like *L'art cinématographique* and *Cinéa— Ciné pour tous* that supported the new avant-garde style. The editor of *Cinéa,* Louis Delluc, became a filmmaker and was a leader of the movement (*see* FILM THEORY). He fostered the early career of another impressionist, Jean Epstein, whose films include *Coeur fidèle* (Faithful Heart, 1923) and *Finis terrae* (The End of the World, 1929). Germaine Dulac, already established as a director, moved between conventional projects and impressionist films, the best known of which is *La souriante Madame Beudet* (The Smiling Madame Beudet, 1923; Figure 8).

The impressionists were all concerned with the depiction of mental states through SPECIAL EFFECTS.

Their films use point-of-view framings, out-of-focus shots, multiple exposures, filters, hand-held camera movements, and other devices to suggest events as experienced by the characters, especially in heightened emotional moments such as exhilaration, fear, drunkenness, and dreams. The impressionists also developed a rapid-editing technique for suggesting the rhythms of music or for conveying fleeting sensations. In elevating characterization and style above considerations of unified action, the impressionists created a recognizably French type of cinema. Despite their success with intellectual French audiences, however, few impressionist films fared well in larger

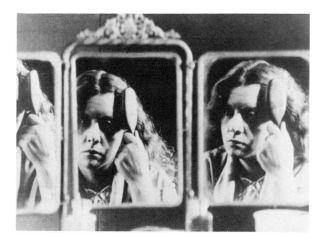

Figure 8. *(Motion Pictures—Silent Era)* Germaine Dulac, *La souriante Madame Beudet* (The Smiling Madame Beudet), 1923. National Film Archive, London.

markets. The costly failures of Gance's epic *Napoléon* in 1927 and L'Herbier's ambitious *L'argent* (Money) in 1928 signaled the movement's end. The directors found financing more difficult to obtain after sound raised production costs. Dulac had already turned to surrealist and abstract experimental shorts. Gance, L'Herbier, and others accepted more conventional projects, using occasional touches of impressionist style, and Epstein continued his early work on occasional modest films. But the techniques devised by the impressionists for suggesting characters' subjective reactions became staples of filmmaking. *See* CINEMATOGRAPHY.

Soviet Union. A third major stylistic alternative to Hollywood cinema emerged somewhat later in the Soviet Union. After the 1917 Revolution, many commercial filmmakers emigrated, taking much of the country's cinematic equipment with them. During the hardships of the years 1917–1924 those interested in building up the industry could do so only gradually. Still, many young people hoped to create a specifically socialist approach for the cinema, seeing it as a powerful medium for educating the population about the new social order. The government's control of filmmaking was strict, but because officials saw a need to develop a nonbourgeois cinema, for a brief period considerable experimentation was allowed. The movement called the Soviet montage style began with SERGEI EISENSTEIN's *Stachka* (Strike, 1925; Figure 9). Another central figure was Vsevolod Pudovkin, who made *Mat* (Mother, 1926) and *Konyets Sankt-Peterburga* (The End of St. Petersburg, 1927; Figure 10). The most prominent non-Russian Soviet director was Aleksandr Dovzhenko, whose highly poetic films on Ukrainian themes are among the classics of the period: *Zvenigora* (1928), *Arsenal* (1929), and *Zemlya* (Earth, 1930).

The Russians used the French term *montage* to designate dynamic FILM EDITING. The montage filmmakers created strong conflicts between shots, believing that this would arouse a strong response in the viewer. Rapid editing, strong conflicts of graphic qualities between shots, temporal overlapping or ellipses, and other vigorous cutting techniques characterized their films. Some films dispensed with a single protagonist to concentrate on groups forming a mass hero. Acting emphasized athletic gestures rather than psychological reaction, and casting often involved nonactors thought to look the part, an approach called typage. Montage filmmakers used a variety of camera angles to reinforce the dynamism of their cutting. Stories often dealt with the history of the revolutionary movement, as in Eisenstein's use of the 1905 uprising in *Bronenosets Potyomkin* (Battleship Potemkin, 1925). A few montage films were made with sound in the early 1930s, but by then the government had rejected the experimental traits of

Figure 9. *(Motion Pictures—Silent Era)* Sergei Eisenstein, *Stachka* (Strike), 1925. National Film Archive, London/Sovexport.

the montage style, putting pressure on filmmakers to produce films more comprehensible to the masses.

Japan. Although it lacked the unified group styles seen in Germany, France, and the Soviet Union, the Japanese cinema was notable in various ways, including its prolificacy; during the 1920s it produced more films than any other country. Japanese filmmakers quickly mastered Hollywood storytelling principles and took a vigorous eclectic attitude toward technique. Sword-fight films rendered combat in breathtakingly fast motion and galloping hand-held shots. Teinosuke Kinugasa's *Kurutta ippeiji* (A Page of Madness, 1926) pulled impressionist and expressionist devices into a kaleidoscopic vision of hallucination. Well into the 1930s major directors were making such silent masterworks as Kenji Mizoguchi's *Orizuru osen* (The Downfall of Osen, 1934) and YASUJIRŌ OZU's *Umarete wa mita keredo* (I Was Born, but . . . , 1932). Mizoguchi experimented with complex camera movements and unusually long takes, while Ozu relied on a consistently low camera position and rigorous editing patterns. An unusual feature of Japanese silent film was the BENSHI, a narrator who stood beside the screen, explaining, and achieved a unique status.

India. India had begun feature film production in 1914, when DHUNDIRAJ GOVIND PHALKE, the "father of Indian film," scored a spectacular success with *Harischandra* (1914), setting in motion an industry and at the same time creating the mythological film (*see* MYTHOLOGICAL FILM, ASIAN). Its subject matter was drawn from the ancient Indian epics, the Ramayana and the Mahabharata, known through much

Figure 10. *(Motion Pictures—Silent Era)* Vsevolod Pudovkin, *Konyets Sankt-Peterburga* (The End of St. Petersburg), 1927. National Film Archive, London/Sovexport.

of Asia. The tales seemed incomprehensible to British audiences but won for Indian filmmakers an immediate hold on Indian audiences, and showings through much of South Asia. Phalke, in dealing with the doings of gods and heroes, showed himself to be an early special effects genius. Mythologicals dominated Indian film production for a decade but were soon joined by social films, those dealing with modern subject matter. By the 1920s India was producing more films than Great Britain, but most theaters showed U.S. films.

United States. In Hollywood the studio system was pouring several hundred films a year into world markets. Its logic favored typecasting—from the star down. A Rudolph Valentino triumph in *The Sheik* (1921) quickly led to Valentino in *Blood and Sand* (1922); a Lon Chaney success in *The Hunchback of Notre Dame* (1923) led to Chaney in *The Phantom of the Opera* (1926); Buster Keaton as *The Navigator* (1924) led to Keaton as *The General* (1927); Greta Garbo in *Flesh and the Devil* (1927) led to Garbo's *The Mysterious Lady* (1928). Stars tended to become subgenres, as did producers and directors. There were many versatile talents among them, but the best known tended to be those who became identified with specific styles: Cecil B. DeMille and his erotic religious spectacles like *The Ten Commandments* (1924); Lubitsch of the continental touch, risqué and sumptuous, as in his first U.S. successes, *The Wedding Circle* and *Forbidden Paradise* (both 1924); Erich von Stroheim with his penchant for intense melodrama with bizarre detail, as in *Greed* (1924) and *The Wedding March* (1928).

An international avant-garde. The silent era also saw a constant avant-garde film activity, which began in Europe and often focused on short films. In Germany the movement started with an emphasis on abstract ANIMATION, as in Hans Richter's *Rhythmus 21* and *Rhythmus 23* (1921–1924). In France the impulse was toward dadaism and surrealism, as in René Clair's *Entr'acte* (1924) and LUIS BUÑUEL's *Un chien andalou* (1928). Documentary experiments were the focus of JORIS IVENS in the Netherlands, as in his *De Brug* (The Bridge, 1926) and *Regen* (Rain, 1929; Figure 11); and of Henri Storck in Belgium, as in his *Histoire du soldat inconnu* (History of the Unknown Soldier, 1930). Avant-garde artists tended to be mobile, holding joint screenings in cineclubs and film societies, and their films often merged influences from various places. Epstein's 1928 *La chute de la maison Usher* (The Fall of the House of Usher) exhibited a French impressionist style but combined it with German expressionist–inspired settings. Dreyer worked in France on *La passion de Jeanne d'Arc* (The Passion of Joan of Arc, 1928), but a German designer contributed quasi-expressionist sets, and there were moments of impressionist subjectivity and montage-style editing and camera angles. The advent of sound, with the new expenses it involved, brought a decline in independent experimentation, and many of these directors moved into other modes and activities.

Increasingly, however, the U.S. studios hired successful European directors, contributing to the decline of national stylistic movements. International avant-garde traits blended with the established clas-

Figure 11. *(Motion Pictures—Silent Era)* Joris Ivens, *Regen* (Rain), 1929. National Film Archive, London. Copyright Joris Ivens.

sical style of Hollywood, an influence evident in U.S. films into the 1940s. By the end of the silent era sophisticated explorations of the film medium had taken place and had been widely assimilated, and in spite of the static, "talky" quality of many early sound films, the achievements of the late silent era were only temporarily eclipsed. These films, like many that had gone before, made a permanent impact on the medium.

Bibliography. Richard Abel, *French Cinema: The First Wave, 1915–1929*, Princeton, N.J., 1984; David Bordwell, Kristin Thompson, and Janet Staiger, *The Classical Hollywood Cinema: Film Style and Mode of Production to 1960*, New York, 1985; Kevin Brownlow, *The Parade's Gone By*, New York, 1968; Jay Leyda, *Kino: A History of the Russian and Soviet Film*, New York and London, 1960, *With a New Postscript and a Filmography Brought up to Date* (rev. ed.), Princeton, N.J., 1983; Rachael Low, *The History of the British Film 1896–1939*, 7 vols. [Vol. 1 with Roger Manvell], London, 1948–1985; George Pratt, *Spellbound in Darkness*, rev. ed., Greenwich, Conn., 1973; Georges Sadoul, *Histoire générale du cinéma*, 6 vols., Paris, 1948–1975; Barry Salt, *Film Style and Technology: History and Analysis*, London, 1983; Friedrich von Zglinski [Friedrich Pruss von Zglinicki], *Der Weg des Films*, 2 vols., Berlin, 1956, reprint Hildesheim, FRG, 1979.

KRISTIN THOMPSON

3. SOUND FILM

The global diffusion of sound-recording technology in the period 1927–1932 decisively changed the structure of the film industry and the aesthetic dynamics of filmmaking. In one sense sound simply added a new dimension to an existing, if still evolving, medium. Yet it could also be seen as creating an entirely new medium. The former view dominated filmmaking in the transitional period, but it was the latter that ultimately made the change significant. *See* SOUND RECORDING.

Transition

The transition to sound was extraordinarily swift. Conversion of the U.S. industry, where the process began, took place in fewer than fifteen months, from late 1927 through 1929. During this time business was booming, but inside the theaters and studio soundstages it was a time of feverish adaptation. There were initially three competing systems: Western Electric's Vitaphone, a sound-on-disc process; Fox Movietone sound-on-film; and RCA Photophone sound-on-film, which ultimately became the industry standard. None of them was compatible with either of the others. Equipment for all three was so constantly modified and revamped that it was sometimes obsolete before it was uncrated.

Technical crises. It is often said, with some reason, that movies ceased to move when they began to talk. Microphones of the time had a limited range, so that actors had to speak directly into them to register on the track, and were largely immobilized. But the same microphones were omnidirectional within their range and would pick up every sound made near them on the set, including that of running cameras. Cameras, which had generally been hand-cranked in the silent era, were motorized in 1929 to run at a standard speed of twenty-four frames per second. Unvarying speed was essential to avoid distortion on the soundtrack. To prevent camera noise from being picked up by microphones, the cameras and their operators were at first enclosed in soundproof booths, six feet on a side, ironically dubbed iceboxes because they were so hot and stuffy. Thus the camera, too, was immobilized (Figure 1). It could pan about thirty degrees on its tripod but could neither tilt nor track. Several directors, including Rouben Mamoulian in the United States and ALFRED HITCHCOCK in England, experimented with putting their booths on

Figure 1. *(Motion Pictures—Sound Film)* Alfred Hitchcock on the set of *Blackmail*, 1929. National Film Archive, London. Courtesy of Weintraub Entertainment.

wheels, but this was hardly a permanent solution. Meanwhile lighting caused other problems. The carbon arc lamps of the silent era made a humming noise that plagued the soundtrack. Studios were converting to incandescent tungsten lamps, but they were less intense and posed a new set of problems for camera operators.

If acting and camerawork suffered, an even more serious regression overtook FILM EDITING. In both sound-on-disc and sound-on-film systems most early editing became transitional, since in general cuts could only be made (as the camera could only be moved) when no sound was being recorded synchronously on the set. Furthermore, U.S. studio executives felt that an absolute pairing of sound and image was necessary to avoid confusing literal-minded audiences. In the early sound era both practice and ideology dictated that everything heard on the soundtrack should be seen on the screen, and vice versa. Of course there were protests, especially from film editors, directors, and critics, who felt that the emphasis on synchronous sound was a threat to cinema as a creative form. In "Sound and Image," a famous manifesto issued in August 1928, Soviet filmmakers SERGEI EISENSTEIN, V. I. Pudovkin, and Grigori Alexandrov denounced synchronous sound in favor of asynchronous or contrapuntal sound, which would counterpoint the images it accompanied to become another dynamic element in the editing process or, as they called it, montage. Others, like French director René Clair and Austrian director G. W. Pabst,

supported this position, and soon there was a full-blown controversy on both sides of the Atlantic about the proper use of sound. *See* FILM THEORY.

Technical and theoretical dilemmas gradually gave way to solutions. As cameras were equipped with "blimps"—lightweight, soundproof housings that muffled the motor—camera operators escaped their prisons. They regained mobility with long-armed microphone booms and then with a wide range of cranes and steerable dollies, developed from 1930 on. Meanwhile microphones became more directional, lighting—both arc and incandescent—was improved, and track noise suppression devices came into use.

For the film editor an especially crucial change came with the innovation of postsynchronization, which took place after sound-on-film had become the industry standard. This called for image and sound to be printed on separate strips of film so that they could be manipulated independently. Postsynchronization seems to have been first used by U.S. director King Vidor in the all-black musical *Hallelujah!* (1929). Filmed on location in Memphis, Tennessee, the film contains a sequence of long tracking shots in which the hero is chased through swamplands. Vidor shot the sequence silent with a continuously moving camera and later added a separately recorded soundtrack that contained noises of the pursuit—breaking branches, screeching birds, heavy breathing—modulating them from the natural to the impressionistic. The following year Lewis Milestone used postsynchronization for the battle sequences in *All Quiet on the Western Front* (1930), shooting them mute on location with a moving camera and dubbing in the SOUND EFFECTS in the studio (Figure 2), a technique used simultaneously in Germany by Pabst in *Westfront 1918* (1930). These and other films of the time demonstrate a gradual shift in emphasis from production recording to rerecording, with increased importance given to the latter.

Still another important editing development was multiple-channel recording. Until 1932 the soundtrack for a sequence generally consisted of dialogue *or* music, rarely both together unless they had been recorded simultaneously on the set. By 1933 technology had been introduced to mix separately recorded tracks for background music, sound effects, and synchronized dialogue without audible distortion at the dubbing stage, and by the late 1930s it was possible in the RCA system to record music on multiple channels. Postsynchronization and the mixing of multiple recorded soundtracks quickly became standard industry procedure. Although postsynchronization was first developed for sound effects, it was soon applied in many productions to dialogue. Before long it was not uncommon for 90 percent of the dialogue in a film to be added in postproduction.

Human problems. Not all the transitional problems were technical; some were purely human. In the silent era it had been common for directors literally to direct their performers during a take, giving them instructions on how to move, emote, and interact while the cameras were rolling. Sound recording obviously eliminated this practice, depriving directors of a large measure of control. For performers the situation was worse. They were now required not only to have acceptable voices and clear articulation but also to work through long dialogue sequences without the direction they had come to expect. In the silent era actors were rarely expected to learn lines or to stick to the script. Many simply could not or would not do it. Others attempted to master the new methods but were defeated by heavy foreign accents (Emil Jannings, Pola Negri) or voices that did not match their screen images (Norma Talmadge, John Gilbert). Many silent STARS were displaced by actors with stage experience. British actors like Ronald Colman, Clive Brook, and Herbert Marshall were particularly valued in HOLLYWOOD for their low-pitched, well-modulated voices that registered with near perfection on the soundtrack.

Many producers assumed that the sound film would provide the perfect medium for photographing stage hits with their original casts, and between 1929 and 1931 much of U.S. cinema was "canned theater" in which Broadway plays were transferred from stage to screen with little or no adaptation. Audiences quickly tired of these static "all-talking" productions, derisively called teacup dramas because they seemed to feature interminable pouring of tea. But they brought into motion pictures many THEATER directors and players who remained on a more or less permanent basis. Similarly, the urgent need for dialogue scripts revolutionized the profession of screenwriting and caused studios to import literary talent from New York and elsewhere—playwrights, critics, editors, novelists—many of whom stayed on to make lasting contributions to the quality and sophistication of U.S. sound films.

Impact on the Medium

In the United States the conversion to sound had two major effects: it gave rise to important new genres that were to remain industry staples, and it consoli-

Figure 2. *(Motion Pictures—Sound Film)* Lewis Milestone, *All Quiet on the Western Front*, 1930. National Film Archive, London. Copyright © by Universal Pictures, a Division of Universal City Studios, Inc. Courtesy of MCA Publishing Rights, a Division of MCA, Inc.

Figure 3. *(Motion Pictures—Sound Film)* Al Jolson in *The Jazz Singer,* 1927. The Museum of Modern Art/ Film Stills Archive.

dated the studio system of production that had been forming since the teens. Probably the most significant new GENRE was the film musical, whose appearance and evolution obviously depended on sound (*see* MUSICAL, FILM). Photographed versions of Broadway musicals were among the first sound films made, and Warner Brothers' *The Jazz Singer* (1927)—a film long considered the catalyst for the conversion—was one of them (Figure 3). Concurrently, the ANIMATION field, notably in the work of WALT DISNEY, was pioneering a sound film genre that might be called the animated musical in shorts like *Steamboat Willie* (1928; Figure 4) and *The Three Little Pigs* (1933).

At the other extreme the new REALISM permitted by sound gave rise to a cycle of terse, topical urban gangster films that exploited tough vernacular speech and the audibly destructive power of the recently invented Thompson submachine gun. *Little Caesar* (1930), directed by Mervyn LeRoy, was the proto-type, and it soon inspired such subgenres as the prison film, exemplified by *The Big House* (1930), and the newspaper picture, for which *The Front Page* (1931) set the pattern. All these types relied on authentic-sounding dialogue for much of their effect. Another Hollywood genre dependent on seemingly realistic dialogue was the historical BIOGRAPHY or "biopic," represented by films like *House of Rothschild* (1934) and *The Story of Louis Pasteur* (1936).

In the COMEDY field, slapstick—a staple of the silent cinema and perhaps its most memorable genre—could not survive, owing to its entirely visual nature. But it was replaced by equally vital sound film types: the anarchic dialogue comedies of the Marx Brothers and W. C. Fields and the wisecracking, furiously paced screwball comedies of such directors as Frank

Figure 4. *(Motion Pictures—Sound Film)* Walt Disney, *Steamboat Willie,* 1928. The Museum of Modern Art/ Film Stills Archive.

Capra, Howard Hawks, and Leo McCarey. The HORROR FILM, with its roots in German EXPRESSION-ISM, was greatly enhanced by the possibilities of eerie music and sound. In fact, Universal Pictures' three celebrated horror classics—*Dracula* (1931), *Franken-stein* (1931), and *The Mummy* (1932)—were all early sound films.

But the most important shaping force of the U.S. sound film was economic, as the process of conver-sion caused corporate fortunes to be borrowed, won, and lost. By 1930 a series of mergers and takeovers had concentrated 95 percent of all U.S. production in the hands of an oligopoly of eight studios. Between 1930 and 1945 this system mass-produced some seventy-five hundred feature films in which every variable was carefully controlled, from scripting and filming through booking and exhibition. *See* MONOPOLY.

Nevertheless, the period was in many ways a golden age for American cinema, and at least four directors working within it—Josef von Sternberg, John Ford, Hawks, and Hitchcock—emerged as major figures of the sound film. All produced distinguished bodies of work during the studio era that have become part of cinema's classical heritage. It was also the era of *Gone with the Wind* (1939), a triumph of promotion as well as of opulent production. Yet by far the most extraordinary film to emerge from the studio system (albeit subversive *of* it), notable for its dynamic use of sound and its extreme deep-focus PHOTOGRAPHY, was ORSON WELLES's *Citizen Kane* (1941). This monumental and eccentric cryptobiography of WILLIAM RANDOLPH HEARST became the paradigm for the modern sound film and remains Hollywood's most audaciously experimental film of the era.

Spread of Sound Technology

The triumphant manufacturers of U.S. sound technology, Western Electric and RCA, having created large new markets for their product at home, were eager to do the same abroad, and the U.S. studios were similarly eager to extend their dominance of the international film world into the sound era. This expansion was briefly stalled by two factors: a hard-fought patent war with the German Tobis-Klangfilm group for world dominion of sound equipment, and language problems. The patent struggles were more or less resolved in a 1930 meeting in Paris, when German and U.S. interests agreed on a sweeping territorial division and a pooling of patents. The wiring of theaters then went forward rapidly, and new markets opened everywhere.

But language presented a troublesome barrier to many of these markets. Since dialogue dubbing was very difficult in the first years of sound, the alternative was to shoot films in several language versions using the same sets, shuffling actors as needed. In 1930 Paramount built a vast studio at Joinville in the suburbs of Paris to mass-produce films in many languages. Other Hollywood studios joined the project, and Joinville—soon christened Babel-sur-Seine—became a movie factory operating twenty-four hours a day to make films in as many as fifteen languages, including Rumanian, Lithuanian, Egyptian, and Greek—often in less than two weeks per feature. The quality of the Joinville product was predictably low. By the end of 1931 the technique of dubbing had been sufficiently improved to provide an inexpensive alternative to multilingual production. Paramount converted the Joinville studio into a dubbing center for all Europe and the Middle East. Dubbing—and,

less frequently, subtitling—became the basis for wide international distribution.

England. Conversion had moved rapidly in England. Almost two-thirds of its theaters were wired by the end of 1932. Most were showing Hollywood films, although American accents often baffled British audiences. Meanwhile the British industry's first important creative contribution to the new era was the work of Hitchcock, whose *Blackmail,* released in June 1929, marked the effective beginning of sound production in England. *Blackmail* was already in production as a silent film when word came down from British International Pictures executives to transform it into a "part-talkie" with some RCA Photophone equipment hastily imported from the United States. Characteristically, Hitchcock used the occasion to experiment with the new medium and produced what is surely one of the most innovative films of the early transitional period, notable for its fluid camera style and its expressive use of both naturalistic and nonnaturalistic sound. Other British filmmakers of note during the thirties were the Hungarian émigré brothers Alexander, Zoltán, and Vincent Korda, who founded London Films in 1934 and collaborated on some of Britain's most spectacular pre–World War II films, including *The Private Life of Henry VIII* (1933) and *The Four Feathers* (1939).

France. The French had evolved no marketable technology for sound recording, probably owing to the slow development of their electrical industry relative to that of the United States and of Germany. Thus, during the transition, producers and exhibitors alike were vulnerable to the Americans at Joinville and to the Germans, who had purchased large studios for Tobis-Klangfilm in the Paris suburb of Epinay as early as 1929. In the face of these threats the French industry regrouped itself into two mammoth consortia formed around the former giants of the 1910s, Pathé (*see* PATHÉ, CHARLES) and Gaumont. Sound created in French audiences an unprecedented demand for French-language films about French subjects, which French filmmakers naturally made better than anyone else. Between 1928 and 1938 French production almost doubled, going from 66 to 122 features annually; box-office receipts increased to the point that the French audience was considered second in size only to that in the United States; and by 1937–1938 French cinema had become the most critically acclaimed in the world, taking prizes and winning export markets in every industrial country, including the United States.

The French filmmakers who did most to achieve this eminence were Clair, Jean Vigo, and JEAN RENOIR. Clair was a former avant-gardist who experimented with asynchronous soundtracks in musical comedies, including *À nous la liberté* (Liberty Is Ours, 1931), a recognized classic of the early sound

Figure 5. *(Motion Pictures—Sound Film)* René Clair, *À nous la liberté* (Liberty Is Ours), 1931. The Museum of Modern Art/Film Stills Archive.

film (Figure 5). Though Vigo made only two feature films, *Zéro de conduit* (Zero for Conduct, 1933) and *L'Atalante* (1934), their intensely personal nature seems to have inspired the "poetic realist" style of 1934–1940, more popularly associated with the films of Jacques Feyder, Julien Duvivier, and Marcel Carné. But it is in the work of Renoir that French cinema of the thirties finds its most distinguished and passionate artist. Son of the famous impressionist painter,

Renoir experimented with both image depth and sound in a number of significant films during the decade, culminating in his two great masterworks, *La grande illusion* (Grand Illusion, 1937) and *La règle du jeu* (The Rules of the Game, 1939).

Germany. Ownership of the Tobis-Klangfilm patents placed the German film industry in a position of relative strength during the transitional period, and from it emerged several of the world's most significant early sound films. Von Sternberg made *Der blaue Engel* (The Blue Angel) in 1929 (Figure 6); G. W. Pabst contributed highly original work including his *Kameradschaft* (Comradeship), released in 1931; and Leontine Sagan's *Mädchen in Uniform* (Girls in Uniform) won international acclaim the same year. But probably the most influential work of the early German sound film was Fritz Lang's *M* (1930), scripted by Thea von Harbou (Lang's wife) and based on a famous series of Dusseldorf child-murders. Like Hitchcock, Lang used the soundtrack to create a dimension of aural imagery to counterpoint his visuals. After Adolf Hitler took power in 1933, with JOSEPH GOEBBELS as PROPAGANDA minister, technical experimentation of this sort virtually ceased—except in the DOCUMENTARY field, in which the virtuosity of Leni Riefenstahl, especially in her portrayal of a major Nazi party rally in *Triumph des Willens* (Triumph of the Will, 1935), won her worldwide attention and notoriety.

Italy. Sound came slowly to the Italian cinema because competition from the U.S. and German in-

Figure 6. *(Motion Pictures—Sound Film)* Josef von Sternberg, *Der blaue Engel* (The Blue Angel), 1929. National Film Archive, London/ Atlas International Film.

dustries during the 1920s had already pushed it to the brink of collapse. But the introduction of sound did draw Benito Mussolini's attention to the enormous propaganda value of film, and his regime successfully manipulated the Italian industry through the 1930s by encouraging its expansion and controlling its content. Economic incentives and subsidies caused production to rise, from seven features in 1930 to eighty-seven in 1939. As in Nazi Germany, Fascist CENSORSHIP determined the mix: along with romantic comedies (known as *telephono bianci,* or "white telephone" films, owing to their glamorous studio sets) came an assortment of nationalist films on heroic themes, such as Alessandro Blasetti's *1860* (1934) and Carmine Gallone's *Scipione l'Africano* (1937).

Soviet Union. Sound was also slow in coming to the Soviet Union. Two Soviet engineers, P. G. Tager and A. F. Shorin, had designed optical sound systems as early as 1926, but neither was workable until 1929. In fact, the first Soviet sound films, such as Yuli Raizman's *Zemlya zhazhdyot* (The Earth Thirsts, 1930), were recorded with German equipment. It is often argued that the Soviets' late start enabled them to profit from the mistakes of their Western counterparts. But sound and silent cinema continued to coexist in the USSR for nearly six years, the last silent production being released in 1936. Of all the industrialized nations, only Japan experienced a longer transitional period.

As in Germany and Italy, the arrival of sound reemphasized the value of film as an instrument of mass indoctrination, already an article of faith to the Bolsheviks, in whose interests V. I. Lenin had early nationalized the Soviet cinema and founded the VGIK (State Film School). Joseph Stalin further consolidated state control in 1930 by dissolving Sovkino, the state film trust supervised by the Ministry of Education, and replacing it with Soyuzkino, an organization directly responsible to the Supreme Council of the National Economy and thus to Stalin himself. Simultaneously the party promulgated the doctrine of "socialist realism," a blend of didacticism and propaganda informed by Stalin's own cult of personality. Its imposition by the Kremlin in 1932 as the official style of all Soviet art signaled a rejection of the earlier AVANT-GARDE experiments and ensured a stolid conformity of style and content in Soviet cinema that would last until the death of Stalin in 1953.

The filmmakers most affected, of course, were the great montage artists Lev Kuleshov, DZIGA VERTOV, Eisenstein, Pudovkin, and Aleksandr Dovzhenko. During the transitional period each had made admirable sound experiments that were ultimately suppressed or defamed by the party bureaucracy. It is one of film history's ironies that these five, who had brought international prestige to the Soviet cinema during the twenties, were virtually hounded out of

Figure 7. *(Motion Pictures—Sound Film)* Sergei Eisenstein, *Alexander Nevsky,* 1938. The Museum of Modern Art/Film Stills Archive.

the industry during the thirties and forties. Of them all, only Eisenstein was able to reassert his genius—in *Alexander Nevsky* (1938; Figure 7), whose contrapuntal soundtrack has become a textbook classic, and in the operatic, grandiose *Ivan Grozny* (Ivan the Terrible, Parts I and II, 1943–1946). The mainstream of the period featured glorification of national heroes, as in Vladimir Petrov's *Pyotr Pervyi* (Peter the Great, Parts I and II, 1937–1938); literary adaptations, including Mark Donskoi's Gorky trilogy *Detstvo Gorkovo* (The Childhood of Maxim Gorky, 1938); and pure escapism, as witnessed by the mid-1930s vogue for Hollywood-style musicals such as Grigori Alexandrov's *Vesyolye rebyata* (Jazz Comedy, 1934).

Japan. Japanese motion pictures had always "talked" through the mediation of the BENSHI, the commentator who stood to the side of the screen and explained the action. The arrival of synchronously recorded sound served to free Japanese cinema from subservience to a live narrator. Heinosuke Gosho's *Madamu to nyobo* (The Neighbor's Wife and Mine, 1931) was the nation's first successful talkie, and it ranked high in technical achievement among early sound films. But, as in the Soviet Union, the conversion to sound was a long process. Silent films were produced in large numbers until 1937. One sweeping consequence of the transition, however, was the vertical monopolization of the Japanese industry by a few major production companies. Paralleling developments in the United States, the Japanese majors of the time (Nikkatsu, founded 1914; Shochiku, founded 1920; and Toho, founded 1932) consolidated their positions by the aggressive absorption of smaller companies and organized their studios for mass production. Although there was hardly any export market for Japanese films until after World War II, the coming of sound enabled the Japanese industry to become one of the world's most productive, releasing an average of four hundred features annually to the nation's twenty-five hundred theaters. As Japan became increasingly xenophobic and militaristic in the late thirties, its most distinguished directors, including YASUJIRŌ OZU and Kenji Mizoguchi, turned to works of social criticism known as tendency films. In response to these dissident films the government imposed official censorship on the industry, which it maintained through the war years.

India. In India, which had a thriving silent film industry reaching Indians, Burmese, Ceylonese, and others, sound brought a confusion of tongues. Production, centered mainly in Bombay, Calcutta, and Madras, soon involved many languages—eventually more than two dozen. Even the majority Hindi-speaking market of 140 million people had regional variations. Under these conditions the first talking feature, the Hindi music drama *Alam ara* (Beauty of the World, 1931), by Ardeshir M. Irani, seemed a risky undertaking. But the film was a huge popular success (as indeed were nearly all early Indian sound films) and heralded a long-lasting boom. The reason was grounded deep in Indian culture: the sound film drew on a musical folk-drama tradition that went back many centuries and had always tended to be "all-singing, all-dancing" (*see* MUSIC THEATER—ASIAN TRADITIONS). Indeed, most Indian sound films seemed to exist mainly as an excuse for musical PERFORMANCE. The Indian film industry nevertheless became a powerful entity during the early sound era. From producing twenty-eight films in 1931—twenty-three in Hindi, three in Bengali, and one each in Tamil and Telegu—it was producing 233 in 1935 in ten different languages. A handful of these were social problem films like the Hindi *Achhut kanya* (Untouchable Girl, 1936), but the vast majority were "historicals" or held to the traditional mythological film genre (*see* MYTHOLOGICAL FILM, ASIAN).

Sound Film since World War II

In the devastation of World War II few film industries escaped havoc. Among areas of Europe that remained largely intact was neutral Sweden, where INGMAR BERGMAN began serving a film apprenticeship during the war years. After the war the Swedish film industry achieved international status and a distinct film personality as Bergman won worldwide attention.

Italy. Meanwhile a more influential renaissance was taking place in Italy. Because of its early surrender, it too had remained comparatively untouched, and quickly seized the world's film spotlight. It was with NEOREALISM—a movement exemplified by the work of Luchino Visconti, Roberto Rossellini, and Vittorio De Sica—that Italian film moved into a new and prominent role. As the first postwar cinema to reject Hollywood NARRATIVE conventions and the studio mode of production, Italian neorealism had enormous influence on film movements that succeeded it, such as British social realism and the French and Czechoslovakian NEW WAVE FILM movements and similar waves in a number of Third World countries. By extension neorealism announced the mode of production—on-location shooting, natural lighting, postsynchronized sound—that was to become the world standard several decades later. The movement also provided the training ground for two filmmakers whose work returned the Italian cinema to international renown in the 1960s: Federico Fellini and Michelangelo Antonioni. Their films offered an example that the Italian cinema's second postwar generation—Pier Paolo Pasolini, Bernardo Bertolucci, and Lina Wertmüller, among others—were quick to follow into the 1970s and beyond.

Latin America. The Italian example, turning its back on studio formula and stressing natural locales, held special meaning for Latin America and later for countries of Asia and Africa. Many of these countries had long histories of colonial oppression, and the evolving film mode seemed to serve their efforts to develop a national consciousness free of imposed foreign values. Latin America began to create distinct cinematic styles during the 1960s. In postrevolutionary Cuba, the government-subsidized Instituto Cubano del Arte y Industria Cinematográficos fostered a sophisticated cinema of ideological praxis (*cine liberación*) in the work of such directors as Tomás Gutiérrez Alea, known especially for his *Memorias del subdesarrollo* (Memories of Underdevelopment, 1969), and Humberto Solás and Sara Gómez. In Brazil, the indigenous *cinema nôvo* (new cinema) movement that included Ruy Guerra, who made *Os fuzis* (The Guns, 1963), and Glauber Rocha, maker of *Terra em transe* (Land in Anguish, 1967), seemed to ignite similar activities by filmmakers elsewhere: Fernando Solanas and Octavio Getino in Argentina; Jorge Sanjinés in Bolivia; Miguel Littin and others in Chile. Some were suppressed in their native countries during the 1970s but continued work in Europe as filmmakers in exile. Ironically, the Spaniard LUIS BUÑUEL, having found his sardonic work incompatible with censorship in his native land, was meanwhile finding a welcome in Mexico, which became his base of operation and which experienced a film awakening of its own (Figure 8). *See* LATIN AMERICA, TWENTIETH CENTURY.

United States. The postwar years began as the most lucrative in history for the Hollywood industry. In 1946 two-thirds of the U.S. population went to the movies each week, helping to create a mood of unprecedented confidence. But the tables turned

Figure 8. *(Motion Pictures—Sound Film)* Luis Buñuel, *Los olvidados* (The Young and the Damned), 1950, National Film Archive, London.

quickly. Important foreign markets began to be ringed by protectionist quota systems in a number of countries. At home the rise of television (*see* TELEVISION HISTORY) brought a disastrous box-office decline, which continued for a decade; half the audiences seemed to abandon moviegoing. Equally devastating, a 1948 Supreme Court decision in the federal antitrust suit against the five majors and three minors resulted in the "Paramount decrees," by which the companies were obliged to divest themselves of their theater chains. Loss of control over exhibition meant the beginning of the end for the studio system. Along with these events came a political witch-hunt, a hysteria over "un-American" activities, under which many leading artists were for years blacklisted. As production schedules were slashed, safe and sanitized subjects dominated. Only a director like Hitchcock, with his oblique approach, could thrive in such a climate; significantly, he produced some of his most impressive work, such as *Rear Window* (1954), *Vertigo* (1958), and *Psycho* (1960), during this period.

Hollywood meanwhile sought to confront television—still mainly black-and-white and small-screen—with cinema's advantages of size and color. Multiple-camera processes such as Cinerama, introduced in 1952, and three-dimensional (3-D) processes heralded by Arch Oboler's *Bwana Devil*, debuting the same year, enjoyed a limited vogue; but the process that brought about a wide-screen revolution was Cinemascope—sumptuously introduced in 1953 with *The Robe*—in which an anamorphic lens squeezed a wide-angle image onto standard 35-mm film stock and another anamorphic lens reversed the distortion in projection to produce a wide-screen image. This process became the industry standard, together with several wide-film systems (such as 70-mm Panavision) used for special spectacular showings. Like sound-recording technology, wide-screen produced an initial regression while filmmakers were learning how to compose and edit their shots to accommodate the horizontality of the new frame. And, as with sound, after several years of trial and error widescreen was understood to have added a new and permanent aesthetic dimension to the cinema. As an extra attraction, all the new wide-screen systems of the fifties featured multiple-track stereophonic sound (four to six tracks), which also became an industry standard. Moreover, by 1952 new color stocks had been perfected by Eastman Kodak that would permit the conversion to 94 percent color production over the next fifteen years (as opposed to 12 percent in 1947). *See* CINEMATOGRAPHY.

Despite these extravagant attempts to rebuild its old audience, the U.S. film industry was no longer the monolithic entity it had been, and its studios were already moving in other directions. In the mid-1950s mass production of television programs began, aiming not only at U.S. but also worldwide markets. Starting in the 1960s, the once-powerful companies allowed themselves to be absorbed progressively by conglomerates, which gave the studios new leverage in a difficult era. As corporate subsidiaries, the studios functioned mainly as distributors of independent

Figure 9. *(Motion Pictures—Sound Film)* Karel Reisz, *Saturday Night and Sunday Morning,* 1960. National Film Archive, London. © 1961 Woodfall Film Productions.

productions, which became the industry's mainstay. And Hollywood sought salvation increasingly in television, CABLE TELEVISION, videocassettes, and other new technologies.

England. In England the immediate postwar years produced a conservative, literary cinema in the work of such directors as Laurence Olivier and David Lean and a series of witty comedies made for Ealing Studios, including *The Lavender Hill Mob* (1951) and *Kind Hearts and Coronets* (1949). But a younger generation of filmmakers, represented by Lindsay Anderson, Karel Reisz, and Tony Richardson, organized the "free cinema" movement in the mid-1950s, whose ideals and practices were grounded in Italian neorealism. These same directors became leaders of the British "new cinema" or "social realist" movement, signaled by Reisz's *Saturday Night and Sunday Morning* (1960; Figure 9). Stylistically influenced by the French new wave, the social realist films were generally shot on location in the industrial Midlands and focused on rebellious working-class protagonists. These films brought such prestige to the British cinema that London briefly became the film center of the Western world, attracting directors from the United States (Stanley Kubrick), France (François Truffaut), Italy (Antonioni), and elsewhere. As England's economy declined during the 1970s, however, so did its cinema, and many of the most successful social realist directors relocated in Hollywood.

Australia. If the U.S. and British industries showed little innovation or promise in the 1970s, the English-language cinema announced itself to be alive and well in the remarkable rise to international prominence of the Australian film. Early in the decade the federal government established the Australian Film Commission to stimulate the development of an indigenous industry and founded a national film school to populate it with native Australian talent. (It recruited the Pole Jerzy Toeplitz, who had headed a celebrated Polish film school at Lodz, to guide the early organization.) With financing provided by the Australian Film Commission and such semiofficial bodies as the New South Wales Film Corporation, film school graduates like Peter Weir (*Picnic at Hanging Rock,* 1975; Figure 10), George Miller (*Mad Max,* 1978), and Gillian Armstrong (*My Brilliant Career,* 1979) were able to make their first features in Australia on Australian themes. Many of these directors went on to work in other countries, primarily in the United States, and Australian cinema in the 1980s was acknowledged to be among the most influential in the world. *See* AUSTRALASIA, TWENTIETH CENTURY.

France. Like the British, French cinema after the war seemed to many viewers excessively literary—the heritage, perhaps, of the Nazi occupation when literary subjects were the only relatively safe ones. It was against this academic "tradition of quality" that the filmmakers of the new wave (*la nouvelle vague*) rebelled. It is hardly possible to overestimate the influence of this movement on world cinema. In vindicating the concept of personal AUTHORSHIP its creators demonstrated that filmmakers were capable

Figure 10. *(Motion Pictures—Sound Film)* Peter Weir, *Picnic at Hanging Rock,* 1975. National Film Archive, London. Copyright: Picnic Productions Pty. Ltd.

of writing "novels" and "essays" in the audiovisual language of film, and by exploding the narrative conventions of the past they added dimensions to that language that could express a whole new range of internal and external states. In doing so the new wave helped to revitalize stylistically moribund cinemas like the U.S., British, and West German and created a succession of "second waves" in already flourishing cinemas like the Italian, Czech, and Japanese.

The Federal Republic of Germany. Defeat in the war and the subsequent partitioning of the country had virtually killed the German film industry. In 1962 a manifesto produced by twenty-six writers and filmmakers at Oberhausen (FRG) proclaimed the death of the old German cinema and called for the establishment of a *junger deutscher Film* (young German cinema) to replace it. This Oberhausen manifesto became the founding document of *das neue Kino* (new German cinema), which was created through the establishment of the Kuratorium Junger Deutscher Film (Young German Film Board, 1965), a Film Subsidies Board (1967), and a private distribution company, the Filmverlag der Autoren (literally, the Authors' Film-Publishing Group, 1971). These institutions financed the first features of Oberhausen originators Volker Schlöndorff and Alexander Kluge in the mid-1960s, as well as the major work of three younger filmmakers who brought the new German cinema to international prominence—Werner Herzog (Figure 11), Wim Wenders, and the astonishingly prolific Rainer Werner Fassbinder. State subsidies enabled these directors and literally hundreds of others to extend the exploration of audiovisual language in films that seriously confronted German social and psychological realities—for the first time in decades.

Japan. Japan's postwar experience was unique. Nearly half of its movie theaters had been destroyed by U.S. bombing, but most of the studios remained intact, and films continued to be produced in large numbers at the war's end. During the postwar U.S. occupation, many subjects endemic to Japanese cinema were frowned on as promoting feudalism, and filmmakers dealt mainly with contemporary themes. Yet AKIRA KUROSAWA's *Rashomon* (1950), which brought Japanese cinema to international attention by winning the Golden Lion at Venice in 1951, was set in the medieval past. Kurosawa became the most famous Japanese director in the West owing to a series of distinguished samurai films, including *Shichinin no samurai* (Seven Samurai, 1954; Figure 12), *Kumonosujo* (Throne of Blood, 1957), and *Yojimbo* (The Bodyguard, 1961), which raised a conventional genre form to the state of an art (*see* MARTIAL ARTS FILM). Between 1951 and 1965 the Japanese cinema experienced a renaissance unprecedented in the history of any national cinema, as vast new export markets opened in the West and Japanese films won prizes in festival after festival. Established figures like Mizoguchi and Ozu produced their greatest work during this period, and relatively new figures like Kurosawa, Kon Ichikawa, Kaneto Shindo, and Masaki Kobayashi all made films that stand among the classics of the international cinema.

In the 1960s and 1970s Japan experienced a new wave in the work of its third generation of postwar filmmakers: Hiroshi Teshigahara, Susumu Hani, and especially Nagisa Oshima. Simultaneously, the Jap-

Figure 11. *(Motion Pictures—Sound Film)* Werner Herzog, *Auch Zwerge haben klein angefangen* (Even Dwarfs Started Small), 1970. The Museum of Modern Art/Film Stills Archive.

Figure 12. *(Motion Pictures—Sound Film)* Akira Kurosawa, *Shichinin no samurai* (Seven Samurai), 1954. National Film Archive, London/Toho Co. Ltd., Japan.

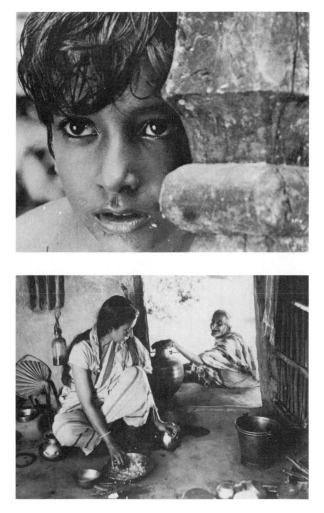

Figure 13. *(Motion Pictures—Sound Film)* Satyajit Ray, *Pather panchali,* 1955. The Museum of Modern Art/Film Stills Archive.

anese studio system began a precipitous decline in the face of growing independent production and the enormous popularity of television. By the mid-1970s the majority of industry production was given over to two domestic exploitation genres: the *yakuza-eiga,* or contemporary urban gangster film, and the sadoerotic "eroduction." In the decade following, serious directors like Kurosawa found it increasingly difficult to get industry funding for their projects, although Japan's annual film output continued to be one of the highest in the world.

India. For years the postwar Indian cinema was known to the world by the work of a single director, Satyajit Ray, whose Apu trilogy won many international awards and is among the great classics of world cinema (Figure 13). Partly as a result of Ray's prestige, several events of the 1960s contributed to a small but significant new wave within the world's largest, most aggressively commercial film industry.

In 1961 the government founded a national film school, the Film Institute of India; in 1962 an easing of censorship permitted the spread for the first time of serious film societies; and in 1964 the National Film Archive, which functioned for aspiring filmmakers as an Indian equivalent of the Cinémathèque Française, was established. The Film Finance Corporation (founded in 1960) made loans available to low-budget experimental projects, resulting in seminal first features by such directors as Mrinal Sen, Basu Chatterji, and M. S. Sathyu. These filmmakers worked primarily in the Bombay-based Hindi-language cinema, as did their more popular colleague, Shyam Benegal. But during the seventies the southwestern states of Kerala and Karnataka began extensive subsidy programs of their own that produced a southern new wave in the work of G. Aravindan, Girish Karnad, and others. Despite these harbingers of change, the Indian industry in the 1980s remained the world's most prolific producer of low-quality films (700 per year in sixteen languages), virtually all for domestic consumption.

Soviet Union. For the Soviet cinema the immediate postwar years were a time of stagnation. Under the increasingly constricting doctrine of socialist realism, its output fell from nineteen features in 1945 to five in 1952. Stalin's death in 1953 produced a loosening of ideological criteria, and by the middle of Nikita Khrushchev's "thaw" the Soviet industry had returned to a full production schedule of 120 films annually. During this period there was also a return to a cinema of individual expression in such award-winning films as Grigori Chukhrai's *Ballada o soldate* (Ballad of a Soldier, 1959), Mikhail Kalatozov's *Letyat zhuravli* (The Cranes Are Flying, 1957), and Sergei Bondarchuk's *Voina i mir* (War and Peace, 1965–1967). In the mid-1960s a new generation of directors emerged from the VGIK, many of whom were from the non-Russian republics of the Ukraine (Yuri Ilyenko, Larissa Shepitko), Georgia (Georgi Danelia, Georgi Shengelaya), Moldavia (Emil Lotyanu), Lithuania (Vitautas Zhalakevichius), Kirghizia (Bolotbek Shamshiev), and Uzbekistan (Ali Khamraev). Most prominent among the new directors were Sergei Paradzhanov (*Teni zabytykh predkov* [Shadows of Forgotten Ancestors, 1964]) and Andrei Tarkovsky (*Andrei Rublev,* 1966), both of whom were later persecuted as dissidents. The 1970s ushered in the doctrine of "pedagogic realism," a modified version of its socialist precursor, and two kinds of films dominated the industry: adaptations of literary classics—for example, Nikita Mikhalkov's *Oblomov* (1980)—and *bytovye,* films of everyday life, such as V. Menshov's *Moscow Does Not Believe in Tears* (1983).

Eastern Europe. In the eastern European nations in the early years following World War II, film schools

Figure 14. *(Motion Pictures—Sound Film)* Miklós Jancsó, *Csillagosok, katonák* (The Red and the White), 1968. Courtesy of the Amos Vogel Collection/Hungarofilm, Budapest.

were founded and industries nationalized according to the Soviet model. But, as in the USSR itself, Stalin's death produced a thaw, leading to the distinguished work of the "Polish School" in the fifties—Jerzy Kawalerowicz, Andrzej Munk, and, preeminently, Andrzej Wajda. Prominent figures in the Czech new wave of the 1960s (Miloš Forman, Jiří Menzel, Evald Schorm) and in the Yugoslav *novi film* or "new cinema" movement of 1961–1972 (Dušan Makavejev, Aleksandar Petrović) were officially repressed during the seventies. In Hungary an abortive revolution forestalled a postwar revival until the sixties, when Miklós Jancsó, whose films included *Még kér a nép* (Red Psalm, 1972), became one of the world cinema's major figures (Figure 14) and Hungarian cinema flourished nationally in the work of such younger filmmakers as István Szabó, Márta Mészáros, and Pál Gábor. The Czech new wave was crushed in the wake of the Warsaw Pact invasion of August 1968, and its major figures were forced into permanent exile. Many filmmakers of the "third Polish cinema" (Krzysztof Zanussi, Andrzej Zulawski, Grzegorz Krolikiewicz) faced a similar fate when martial law was imposed on the country in 1980. Though eastern European cinema has historically been among the most sophisticated and subtle in the world, since World War II it has become increasingly entangled with politics.

A Film World

In the decades before World War II film production had been the domain of·leading industrialized na-

tions, in most cases colonial powers. After the war countless other nations plunged into film production. Filmmaking began to seem a badge of nationhood, a means of national expression, sometimes fostered by subsidies and generating new energies at the international film festivals springing up on all continents. Every festival seemed to offer cause for astonishment in works from unexpected sources—such as those of Ousmane Sembène of Senegal, including *Mandabi* (The Money Order, 1970) and *Xala* (The Curse, 1974)—perceptive, witty, often moving reflections of a world in convulsive change. Segments of the film world no longer seemed to revolve around film industries and huge soundproof studios but around individuals—a Sembène in Senegal, a Ray in India, a Mohamed Lakhdar-Hamina in Algeria, a Lester James Peries in Sri Lanka, an Alexandro Jodorowsky (Chilean) in Mexico. In the medium of film a new kind of international dialogue seemed to be at work in the still-evolving medium of the motion picture. *See* AFRICA, TWENTIETH CENTURY; ASIA, TWENTIETH CENTURY.

Bibliography. Joseph L. Anderson and Donald Richie, *The Japanese Film: Art and Industry*, exp. ed., Princeton, N.J., 1982; Roy Armes, *French Cinema*, New York, 1985; Tino Balio, ed., *The American Film Industry*, 2d ed., rev., Madison, Wis., 1985; Erik Barnouw and S. Krishnaswamy, *Indian Film*, 2d ed., New York, 1980; Ernest Betts, *The Film Business: A History of British Cinema 1896–1972*, London, 1973; Peter Bondanella, *Italian Cinema: From Neorealism to the Present*, New York, 1983; Evan William

Cameron, ed., *Sound and Cinema: The Coming of Sound to American Film*, Pleasantville, N.Y., 1980; David A. Cook, *A History of Narrative Film*, 2d ed., New York, 1987; Timothy Corrigan, *New German Film: The Displaced Image*, Austin, Tex., 1983; Jay Leyda, *Kino: A History of the Russian and Soviet Film*, New York and London, 1960, *With a New Postscript and a Filmography Brought up to Date* (rev. ed.), Princeton, N.J., 1983; Mira Liehm and Antonín J. Liehm, *The Most Important Art: East European Film after 1945*, Berkeley, Calif., 1977; Alexander Walker, *The Shattered Silents: How the Talkies Came to Stay*, London, 1978.

DAVID A. COOK

MOTIVATION RESEARCH

A form of research aimed at understanding the psychological factors (conscious and unconscious) influencing human behavior. Such research has assumed special importance in ADVERTISING, in which it helps to guide decisions on product development, package design, and advertising appeals. As the field has expanded its techniques it has become known as *personality and motivation research*.

Although psychologists have been active in the advertising industry from the early 1900s on (e.g., John B. Watson and Edward K. Strong), it was not until after World War II that they began to direct their attention to consumer motivation. Best exemplified perhaps by Ernest Dichter, a Viennese who emigrated to the United States, they adapted the diagnostic techniques of the clinical psychologist in their efforts to probe the unconscious of the consumer.

Early developments. One of the techniques developed by this group is the depth interview. The questioning procedure and phrasing are left to the discretion of the interviewer, who is expected to probe into significant subject matter areas as they are revealed in the course of the dialogue between interviewer and respondent. As a result of this depth probing the analyst is expected to obtain a deeper understanding of the respondent's true underlying feelings toward the items or issues investigated.

Another technique is the projective test, consisting of ambiguous visual stimuli that are presented to an individual who is asked to interpret their meaning in his or her own terms. Many kinds of projective tests have been employed, among them the famous Rorschach Test (in which individuals are shown a standard series of ink blots and asked to describe what they see) and the Thematic Apperception Test (TAT), developed by Henry A. Murray (in which individuals

are shown a series of sketches and asked to interpret the depicted circumstances).

A third technique, employed by such early investigators as Arthur Koponen and Franklin B. Evans, is the paper-and-pencil personality inventory. These tests consist of a series of self-rating scales, the responses to which are scored according to some predesignated key to produce a personality profile.

Many early investigators simply employed these techniques without modification, believing that their routine application would be sufficient to understand why consumers behave as they do. A prime example of an attempt at such routine application was the study conducted by Evans in 1958. He administered the Edwards Personal Preference Schedule to a sample of seventy-one Ford owners and sixty-nine Chevrolet owners and found little difference between the two groups. He concluded that "personality needs, as measured in this study, are of little value in predicting whether an individual owns a Ford or a Chevrolet automobile." In other instances, however, measurement techniques were specially developed to suit the researcher's purpose and produced more positive results. One classic example is the study published in 1950 by Mason Haire in which he presented a sample of one hundred coffee drinkers with two seven-item shopping lists. Half the sample saw the first list, and the other half saw the second. The two lists were identical except for the way the coffee item was described. The first list specified "1 lb. Maxwell House Coffee (Drip Grind)," and the second list specified "Nescafé Instant Coffee." The subjects were asked to read the shopping list and then to write a brief description of the shopper's personality and character. By comparing the two sets of descriptions, Haire was able to contrast the different images projected by the two brands: 48 percent of the people described the Nescafé shopper as lazy, compared with 4 percent describing the Maxwell House shopper the same way.

Two other social scientists whose names are importantly associated with the motivation research movement are Burleigh Gardner, for his series of studies of the qualitative values of various print media, and Herta Herzog, a former advertising research executive, for her studies of broadcast programming and advertising.

A serious attack on the motivation research movement was published in 1957. Written in a nontechnical style and intended for the general public, Vance Packard's *The Hidden Persuaders* described the ways in which the advertising industry was allegedly using the techniques of motivation research to manipulate an unsuspecting public to act against its own best interests. Beyond Packard's claims of manipulation and invasion of PRIVACY, the problem of nonreplica-

Figure 1. *(Motivation Research)*   Lady Clairol billboard, 1964. Courtesy of Foster and Kleiser.

bility of research results, more than any other, caused the search for unconscious motivation gradually to wane.

From demographics to psychographics. Disenchantment with the methods of motivation researchers coupled with the rapid strides in computer development during the 1960s to bring about a new research movement called psychographics, to distinguish it from demographics. Emanuel Demby, the researcher who is generally credited with having coined the term, defined psychographics as

a quantitative research procedure which seeks to explain why people behave as they do and why they hold their current attitudes. It seeks to take quantitative research beyond demographics, socioeconomic and user/nonuser analysis, but also employs those variables in the research.

In the same way that the motivation researchers had borrowed the tools of the clinical psychologist and applied them to the solution of marketing problems, the psychographic researcher has borrowed the tools of the psychometrician and used them for the construction of paper-and-pencil personality inventories. The questionnaires employed in psycho-

graphic research most often involve long lists of statements or attributes that the respondent is asked to rate in terms of the extent to which they personally apply. Depending on the purpose of the research, the questions might include personality characteristics like self-confidence or irritability, ATTITUDES toward institutions like the government or organized religion, personal interests such as sports or cooking, or features desired in a new automobile.

Russell Haley believes that if the psychometric approach is to be useful it is important to select the items to be included in the questionnaire on the basis of their relevance to the product category under study. To this end he developed the concept of "benefit segmentation": respondents are classified into relatively homogeneous groups based on their ratings of the importance of a variety of possible benefits. With the knowledge of which attributes are more important to individual market segments, the advertiser can then decide how best to position the brand to have maximum appeal to the market segment to which the marketing efforts are directed. Although the popularity of benefit segmentation has continued into the mid-1980s, some researchers still hold to the notion that it is not always necessary to tailor the psychographic battery to individual product categories but, rather, that more generalized batteries of questions can serve a useful purpose as well.

Major studies. An early generalized psychographic study was completed in 1973 by the Newspaper Advertising Bureau, which defined sixteen different market segments and examined the product consumption and media usage behavior of each. Another early effort was the Yankelovich Monitor, a syndicated annual study of twenty-five hundred persons that seeks to track changes in life-style based on social trends. The original study, conducted in 1970, measured thirty-one such trends (e.g., Defocus on Money, Return to Nature, and Acceptance of Drugs); trends have been added and deleted over the fourteen-year period during which the survey has been conducted.

A later entry in the syndicated field is the Values and Life-styles (VALS) program of SRI International. Using a questionnaire, the scoring key for which is proprietary, SRI has developed a nine-category typology based on the hierarchy of human needs proposed by Abraham H. Maslow in the 1940s. Since the first VALS study in 1978, SRI has been publishing annual reports to subscribers exploring the implications of the VALS typology for business in the United States. Standardized approaches have proved useful as part of a large syndicated DATA BASE, but they have generally not been as useful when used in connection with proprietary research intended to deal with a particular brand or product category. The reason is that a syndicated data base contains information on hundreds of product categories and thousands of brands. Through the power of the computer one can quickly and inexpensively establish for any given product category the utility of the standardized measures in a particular application (*see* COMPUTER: IMPACT—IMPACT ON COMMERCE).

Personality and motivation research has enjoyed a period of over thirty years of increasing value to the advertising and communications industries. Over that period of time the pendulum has swung from using clinical psychological techniques, qualitative analyses, and small samples to the use of more quantitative psychometric procedures and large representative samples. The transition has been accompanied by much controversy, but in the process the methods that have emerged have contributed importantly to the development of advertising theory and practice.

Bibliography. Ernest Dichter, *The Strategy of Desire,* Garden City, N.Y., 1960; Robert Ferber and Hugh G. Wales, eds., *Motivation and Market Behavior,* Homewood, Ill., 1958; Harry Henry, *Motivation Research,* New York, 1958; Arnold Mitchell, *The Nine American Lifestyles,* New York, 1983; Vance Packard, *The Hidden Persuaders,* New York, 1957; Charles Ramond, *The Art of Using Science in Marketing,* New York, 1974; William D. Wells, *Lifestyles and Psychographics,* Chicago, 1974.

VALENTINE APPEL

MURAL

A large picture created directly on a wall or ceiling that is usually painted or rendered in mosaic, sometimes drawn or engraved. A mural is different from other two-dimensional images because it is intended as an integral and usually permanent part of its environment. This, together with the size of the mural, tends to make the wall an enhancement of the VISUAL IMAGE and the image the focus of its surroundings. Throughout history, murals have been a form of public ART intended to be seen by many people at one time. They become thereby a social art, repeatedly addressing people not merely as individuals but also as members of a group or community. Murals usually make explicit and advance the values, traditions, and purposes of a society. Typically they are utilized to assist in some important public function. Since prehistoric times murals have often been employed not only to represent reality but also to change it, either directly as by magic or indirectly by speaking to or about the gods, or by affecting human secular motives.

Prehistoric Rock Art

The earliest discovered example of visual communication, engravings on an ox rib, is well over two hundred thousand years old. In contrast, the oldest known graphic articulation on walls in the Eastern Hemisphere was created during the late Ice Age (ca. 30,000 B.C.E.) in southwestern France, then part of the most populous region of Europe. These wall markings consist of handprints and parallel finger tracings—some straight, others looping and crossing one another—made by many different hands in the clay sides and ceilings of caves at Gargas and Roufignac. Tracings in one cave may have been inspired by the adjacent markings of bear claws on the walls. Described as "macaronis" and "meanders," the finger tracings have been viewed as one of the oldest forms of symbol making, suggesting streams, thawing, freshet, and the availability of food. The image of a mammoth traced by a finger has been identified among one set of these lines.

In this region between 26,000 and 20,000 B.C.E. cave walls received more elaborate forms of art. There are negative silhouettes of hands made from pigment brushed or blown through tubes. Images of animals and nude women, probably fertility images,

Figure 1. *(Mural)* Spotted horses and negative hand imprints, Pech-Merle, ca. 15,000–13,000 B.C.E. Lot, France. From Paolo Graziozi, *Die Kunst der Altsteinzeit*, Florence: Sansoni, 1956, p. 192.

were incised and carved as bas-reliefs and still show traces of paint. Between 18,000 and 11,000 B.C.E. astonishingly lifelike images of mammoths, bison, deer, horses, and fish were painted on cave walls and ceilings, the best known of which were created at Lascaux in France and Altamira in northern Spain about 15,000 B.C.E. The images of animals reflect remarkable powers of observation and memory as well as the ability to invent realistic yet conventionalized symbols. Created by brushing or rubbing rock pigment on the walls, they were done unusually deep within caves, suggesting a RITUAL function. The images have been variously interpreted as instruments of magic used in hunting, in assisting the return of the seasons, or in rites of initiation.

The earliest known murals in the Western Hemisphere were discovered in 1985 at Boqueirao do Sitio da Pedra Furada in northeastern Brazil, in a rock shelter thought to be occupied in 30,000 B.C.E. Carbon dating indicates that the schematic images of men bending over what appear to be tortoises or turtles were painted at least by 15,000 B.C.E. North America abounds in petroglyphs carved in rock and pictographs painted on rock that picture humans, supernatural beings, and animals. Some images date from the fifth century C.E.; others go back much earlier. Those of Baja California, where larger-than-life-size images of men and deer overlay one another in a cave of the Sierra de San Francisco and a twelve-foot whale swims up an overhanging rock above the Arroyo de San Gregorio, are particularly impressive.

Scholars find a close resemblance among the rock paintings of France and Spain and those of Africa, where a great quantity have been found. The Tassili mountains in the Sahara offer the most abundant sites, with the earliest works dated about 5500 B.C.E. Here and at other sites in the Sahara and Nubian deserts can be found pictures of cattle painted by herders shortly after 5000 B.C.E., horsemen and chariots dating from the fourth millennium B.C.E., and from the first centuries C.E. camels that had been imported from Arabia. Most rock painting from Tanzania to South Africa is the work of the Bushmen, but some is attributed to the Bantu.

Finger-traced and incised meanders are also the earliest human markings on walls to be found in Australia. Those at the Koonalda Cave in the south were done at least by 18,000 B.C.E. The Aborigines had come to Australia by 40,000 B.C.E., and their descendants today believe that in the earliest era of Dream Time, which still parallels everyday life, their ancestors shaped the world and then turned themselves into the rock-shelter images that preserve their power. In the multitude of sites across the Australian continent these images vary from X-ray-like pictures exposing patterned skeletons to ghostlike beings without mouths but with haloed skulls. Some of the paintings may go back more than seven thousand years. The Aborigines continue to invoke the spirits in the images, but the practice of repainting them every year faded in the twentieth century.

The Ancient World

Among the earliest murals of urban civilization yet discovered are those at Çatal Hüyük in Asia Minor.

Figure 2. *(Mural)* Egyptian tomb painting depicting the sowing and harvesting of wheat. Giraudon/Art Resource, New York.

Dating from about 6000 B.C.E., they are inside shrines and show landscapes with houses, an erupting volcano, scenes of deer hunting, and, later, painted figures and high reliefs of cattle, suggesting herding. The distinction between murals and reliefs is blurred because wall painting often had incised lines and surfaces carved at different depths, whereas reliefs, like much SCULPTURE, often were painted. Thus the bas-reliefs of Mesopotamia of the first three millennia B.C.E., recording royal conquests, tribute bearers, and hunts, are close to murals.

The earliest known tomb murals of Egypt were done about 3500 B.C.E. at Hierakonpolis. Such murals depict kings officiating at ceremonies and at court entertainments while slaves provide for their needs. The images surrounding the mummies of the pharaohs were intended to ensure the royal afterlife. Painting was done on dry plaster, which permitted rigid but graceful formality. Figures were conceptually arranged in profile or frontally "on" the wall and in overlapping parallel planes "behind" it. This was the basis for the later Greek, Roman, and RE-NAISSANCE handling of space, a major source of the formal stability of classic styles.

In commercial contact with Egypt and Mesopotamia, the Minoan cities of Crete and the other Aegean islands of the fifteenth century B.C.E. adopted some of the rigor of Middle Eastern wall painting to their own lively art. Minoan murals such as those at the palace of Minos in Knossos provide the first known examples of true fresco painting, in which wet pigment is applied to wet plaster to dry and crystallize, thereby becoming part of the wall.

As early as the sixth and fifth centuries B.C.E. Etruscan tomb painters, seeking to entertain their dead with scenes of banqueting, music, sports, and lovemaking, adopted the simple but animated drawing style of archaic Greek art (*see* ART, FUNERARY). During the Hellenistic era in the fourth century B.C.E. Greek artists came to Italy to decorate the villas of Roman patricians and the middle class. Residences at Pompeii and at nearby Herculaneum during the early ROMAN EMPIRE of the first centuries B.C.E. and C.E. were embellished with fresco portraits of homeowners, still lifes of food, architectural fantasies, landscapes, and mythological scenes.

At Teotihuacán, a metropolis and religious center in the Valley of Mexico that reached its height about 350 C.E., wall paintings on pyramids and temples and along the streets depicted priests, gods, and scenes of a paradisal afterlife telling of a joy that could only be sustained by the sacrifice of human blood to the deities. About 650 C.E. Mayan artists at sites in the Yucatán and Guatemala painted stately scenes of ritual and battle.

The Asian murals best known in the West are in the sanctuaries carved into the cliffs of Ajanta in central India. There the meditation, compassion, and sensuous detachment of Buddha and his followers are offered as examples to the devout. Created between the first century B.C.E. and the seventh century C.E., the murals reflect a refined court tradition of painting. Buddhism, introduced into China during the first century C.E., brought with it mural painting in cave temples and in tombs, an art that reached its greatest sophistication during the T'ang dynasty in the eighth and ninth centuries.

Medieval art. Although the Second Commandment forbade graven images, the power of representation (*see* REPRESENTATION, PICTORIAL AND PHOTOGRAPHIC) to strengthen belief encouraged its adoption, especially by Christians. The first Christian murals were frescoes of Moses, Jesus, and the Apostles in the catacombs of Rome from the second to the fourth century. When Christianity became the state religion in the fifth century, the rich resources of mosaics and Roman three-dimensional naturalism were employed in religious art at Ravenna. In the sixth century, churches there were embellished with opulent mosaic murals in the style of Byzantium (Constantinople). Their flat incorporeal figures, rigidly formal, stood out against golden backgrounds symbolizing eternity.

The Romanesque monastic churches of Spain and France of the eleventh and twelfth centuries featured frescoes of flat but vigorous biblical figures inside and murallike reliefs on their facades. The Crusades (*see* CRUSADES, THE) and revival of trade in Venice made possible in the late twelfth and thirteenth centuries the most extensive mosaic embellishment of the walls and vaults of any European structure, that of the Church of San Marco, with its imagery of the Old and New Testaments against a background of gold. As town life revived in northern Europe in the twelfth to sixteenth centuries, church builders developed a new style, the Gothic, and sought to replace walls with stained glass, which transformed murals into more highly illuminated images. *See* MIDDLE AGES.

The Renaissance. Prosperous merchants and bankers became the patrons of murals in the urban churches of Italy. It was largely through Italian church murals that the Renaissance was firmly established in the pictorial arts. Masaccio, for example, in his frescoes of episodes from the ministry of St. Peter (1427) and the Crucifixion (1428), created natural, weighty figures modeled by shadow in a three-dimensional space deepened by atmosphere and geometric perspective.

The new systematic perspective provided the stationary viewer a geometrically intelligible scene, but it was a view available only to one person at a time. This perspective reshaped real objects to conform to their appearance from the observer's unique viewpoint (*see* PERCEPTION—STILL AND MOVING PIC-

Figure 3. *(Mural)* *Revelers,* wall painting from the Tomb of the Leopards, Tarquinia, ca. 470 B.C.E. Etruscan. Alinari/Art Resource, New York.

TURES). Because of such limitations this kind of perspective is more appropriate to easel painting than to murals, which usually are addressed to an audience of many viewers. This did not present a problem to most Renaissance murals, which consisted of an ensemble of panels, but later, when everything was incorporated into a single scene, muralists often evaded the constraints of the single focus.

The new commercial princes of the age utilized murals to embellish their residences, but religion continued to provide the principal subject of Renaissance murals. In the refectory of the Church of Santa Maria del Grazie in Milan, Leonardo da Vinci utilized the new perspective to concentrate the tense drama of his *Last Supper* (1498). The popes saw to it that the talent of the age ornamented the Vatican. There the murals of Raphael and Michelangelo provided the climax of the Renaissance synthesis of Christianity, Greco-Roman culture, and spatial construction.

The baroque. A new era in mural painting broke through the restraints of Renaissance CLASSICISM, reflecting the discovery of new lands in both hemispheres, the expansion of empires, and the battle of the Roman Catholic church to convert the heathen and reconvert the heretic. Baroque murals sweep viewers up into their grandiose drama, impressing on them the power of secular and religious authorities to bring order to the universe. Correggio, Andrea dal Pozzo, Titian, Tintoretto, Paolo Veronese, the Carraccis, Peter Paul Rubens, and Giovanni Battista Tiepolo were the chief practitioners of this art of the mural from the late sixteenth through the eighteenth century.

The Modern Mural

The nineteenth century's principal innovation in public art was the commercial graphic advertisement (*see* SIGNAGE), which took the form of billboards or signs (*see* POSTER), ephemeral murals in which images largely replaced words. They became a familiar and accepted part of the visual environment and powerful shapers of consumer consciousness. In contrast, the

Figure 4. *(Mural)   The Thousand Buddhas* (detail). Fresco from Cave 2, Ajanta, ca. 600 C.E. SEF/Art Resource, New York.

Figure 5. *(Mural) Christ Pantocrator,* apse mosaic, Cefalù Cathedral, Sicily, 1148. Lauros-Giraudon/Art Resource, New York.

mural gained new life in the twentieth century from the social and democratic concerns associated with the rise of the working classes. Socially conscious murals first appeared in Latin America and the United States as movements of working people became strong enough to press governments to provide walls and funding. Leadership was offered by artists who linked their ideas of expression to solidarity with the collective body of urban and rural workers. The muralists' conception of a democratic art called for adopting a REALISM with modern formal innovations designed to reach the broadest sectors of the population and to encourage their capacities for public deliberation, political action, and artistic creativity.

Mexico and Latin America. The main impulse for the new murals came from Mexican artists in 1922 in the aftermath of that country's partially successful war of national liberation. When the fighting ceased, the new government commissioned artists to disseminate ideas of reform and nationalism. The leading Mexican muralists, Diego Rivera, José Clemente Orozco, and David Siqueiros, called in their art for return of land to the peasants, industrialization under the workers' control, full social services, and an end to U.S. intervention in Mexico's economy and politics. At first the muralists adopted the fresco technique and forms of the Italian Renaissance and Mexico's indigenous peoples to dramatize their message, but increasingly they came to utilize vernacular and experimental means that would appeal to a broad public. Siqueiros, for example, pioneered outdoor murals and sought to depict motion with mul-

tiple images of the same object, a device learned from the Italian futurists. He also designed figures from different points of view so that to the moving spectator they seemed to move. This "integral art," as he called it, culminated in 1973 with the largest mural ever created, *The March of Humanity,* an enormous auditorium painted inside and out.

The United States. Although in Mexico it was the social and political revolution that painters responded to, U.S. artists reacted to the upheavals of the depression and were concerned with affirming workers' roles in industrial and agricultural production. For example, in the early 1930s Thomas Hart Benton created a montage of workers in mills, construction, transportation, and farming that he titled *America Today.* These subjects were to preoccupy muralists during that decade. Later, however, Benton turned his attention from urban industrial workers to agrarian laborers and became a spokesman for the regionalist and often nostalgic American Scene painters who produced much of the art of the period.

At the same time, the Mexican example helped persuade President Franklin D. Roosevelt to create federal art programs intended to "bring art to the people" through commissions for post offices, schools, and other public buildings and also to provide employment for artists made jobless by the depression. The work of Ben Shahn, who had painted with Rivera, is characteristic of this era. His squat, realistic, frequently portraitlike figures owe something to Rivera but also to the cartoons and comic strips (*see* COMICS) of the period. The New Deal art programs

Figure 6. *(Mural)* Giotto di Bondone, Arena Chapel, Padua, 1305–1306. Alinari/Art Resource, New York.

Figure 7. *(Mural)* David Siqueiros, *From Porfirio's Dictatorship to the Revolution,* 1958. Detail of the left wall in the second room showing the revolutionaries. Revolution Hall, National History Museum, Chapultepec Castle, Mexico City. From Mario de Micheli, *Siqueiros,* New York: Harry N. Abrams, 1968, plate 138.

advanced the careers of many artists who, because of poverty, race, or lack of patronage, had faced almost insuperable difficulties. This was especially the case with black painters such as Aaron Douglas, Charles Alston, Charles White, Hale Woodruff, and Romare Bearden, who during and after the 1930s produced important murals about black experience.

World War II ended both the depression and the federally funded programs of the New Deal. The socially conscious murals of the 1930s had brought artists under frequent criticism from conservative groups and politicians, criticism that intensified during the late 1940s and 1950s as a result of the cold war and the Communist witch-hunts. Not until the late 1960s did U.S. social murals reappear, and then in a different form.

The term *social realism,* applied to Latin American and U.S. murals of the period 1920–1960, refers not to a particular style but to the general approach that sought the empowerment of working people. Most of the artists who spread social realism throughout Latin America were influenced by Mexican and U.S. muralists. The drifting away from social realism toward murals that were increasingly patriotic, folklorist, or abstract was in part the result of rapid but uneven economic growth following World War II that brought with it a demand for murals by banks, movie theaters, office buildings, fashionable department stores, and luxury hotels. The departure from social realism was led by Mexican artist Rufino Tamayo, who treated folk themes in sophisticated expressionist ways.

Social realism had a rebirth in Cuba, however, after the revolution in 1959. In the early 1960s Orlando Suárez, who had painted with Siqueiros, coordinated an outpouring of murals in the streets and inside public buildings that memorialized a century of struggle. With the nationalization of all Cuban industry, billboards were replaced by murals that encouraged social responsibility and voluntary labor.

Liberation murals. The most important development in murals of the late twentieth century was the widespread effort of ordinary people to become involved in creating public art. People whose views and grievances had been denied access to the mainstream media—minority groups, workers, peasants, women, students, and dissenting professionals—initiated alternative forms of public communication (*see* CITIZEN ACCESS; MINORITY MEDIA). Murals were utilized by national liberation movements for decolonization and by the disadvantaged within the advanced industrialized nations. The principal aim of the new murals was to facilitate public dialogue by ordinary people on urgent issues. Because such murals were

Figure 8. *(Mural)* Ben Shahn, left portion of the *Jersey Homesteads Mural*, 1935–1938, Roosevelt, New Jersey. From the left, the mural shows immigrants, including Albert Einstein with a violin, landing at Ellis Island. In the upper left corner a storm trooper puts up an anti-Semitic poster in the old country. Sacco and Vanzetti lie in their coffins in the new country, having been convicted of murder by a jury swayed by their anarchist views and opposition to World War I. Toward the center are scenes of sweatshops. Scala/ Art Resource, New York.

Figure 9. *(Mural)* William Walker, *Black Love*, 1971, Cabrini Green Public Housing, Chicago. Photograph by Leo Tanenbaum.

Figure 10. *(Mural)* Alejandro Canales, mural, 1980. Luis Alfonso Velásquez School, Managua, Nicaragua. Detail showing a woman studying during the literacy crusade, which began after the Sandinista Revolution. Using the text, "The masses made the insurrection," she is shown how a word rich in significance, such as *masses*, can be broken into syllables with which to make new words. Photograph by Alan Barnett.

often critical of the establishment, they were frequently done on neighborhood walls contributed by local owners and used materials provided by the community. They were also done in labor union halls, secondary schools, and universities. Sometimes the work was clandestine and unauthorized.

Liberation artists borrowed techniques and styles from the Mexican muralists, from their own ethnic heritages, from popular art, and from contemporary ADVERTISING. These murals revealed the demand of ordinary people to participate in public communication and the capability of the untrained to produce art. Appreciation of their often self-taught creativity was encouraged by the challenge of modern art to stylistic standards.

Since the late 1960s, most notably in the United States, Mexico, Chile, Nicaragua, and western Europe but also elsewhere in the Third World, murals have been a popular instrument of social change and solidarity. In the midst of the electronic age the mural, one of the oldest art forms, has acquired new life as the result of the emergence of artists and activist groups who see it as a means of public expression and as a source of community.

See also ARTIST AND SOCIETY; AVANT-GARDE; DESIGN; ICONOGRAPHY.

Bibliography. Alan W. Barnett, *Community Murals: The People's Art*, Cranbury, N.J., 1983; Eva Cockcroft, John Weber, and James Cockcroft, *Towards a People's Art: The Contemporary Mural Movement*, New York, 1977; Alexander Marshack, *The Roots of Civilization*, London, 1972; Francis V. O'Connor, ed., *Art for the Millions*, Greenwich, Conn., 1973; "Paleo-African Cultures," and "Prehistory," *Encyclopedia of World Art*, Vol. 11, New York, 1960 ed.; Antonio Rodriguez, *A History of Mexican Mural Painting*, New York, 1969; Orlando S. Suárez, *Inventario del muralismo mexicano*, Mexico, D.F., 1972; Randall White, *Dark Caves, Bright Visions*, New York, 1986.

ALAN W. BARNETT

MUSEUM

The roots of the museum can be traced back to the great collections of treasure, relics, and objects of curiosity that the rich and powerful have amassed throughout history. At the same time the modern museum is a unique institution of middle-class, democratic CULTURE similar in structure to the public LIBRARY, the symphonic concert hall, and the UNIVERSITY. Like the modern university, in which the inventory of master texts and intellectual techniques of the society is available as an image of the culture itself, the museum is an ordered display of the material objects considered exemplary by the civilization. Just as concert halls present year after year the basic repertoire of classical music as an almost ritualized history of the arts of time, so too the museum displays a canonical, conservative sample of the spatial masterworks that define our current version of the past. Museum, university, and concert hall are aspects of a secular public world of culture that is an image of the state and nation while at the same time transcending them.

Origins

The museum in its modern form arose in tandem with the most aggressive and expansive moments of the nation-state. The museums of major cities are themselves expressions of the power of the state to

Figure 1. *(Museum)* Leo von Klenze, Glyptothek, Munich, 1830. Marburg/Art Resource, New York.

Figure 2. *(Museum)* Richard Rogers and Renzo Piano, Georges Pompidou National Center of Art and Culture ("Beaubourg"), Paris, 1977. TF/Art Resource, New York.

reach out and appropriate the culture of the past as its own and as an important symbol of the state's dignity, worth, and endurance. Wherever economic power reached, ART and artifacts flowed back, along with raw materials and other forms of wealth (*see* ARTIFACT). The close relations between the modern state and the museum are particularly visible in

Washington, D.C., a city that has often been called one large museum.

Within Western civilization the museum became a primary feature of civic space during the eighteenth-century Enlightenment, and in particular after the founding of the Louvre in Paris in 1893. The place of the museum can best be understood by contrasting it, on the one hand, with the earlier private princely collections and, on the other, with the modern factory. In its dedication to uniqueness, to preservation, and to those objects of the past whose useful life was in effect over, the museum came to celebrate just such values, in part because the mass production of objects under the factory system resulted in unlimited identical replications of objects made to be replaced as soon as they became obsolete. Museums became increasingly central in cultures touched most deeply by the modern system of mass production. The British Museum in London and the Metropolitan Museum in New York represent a new kind of institution. No longer do they provide a visible history of the culture itself—that is, a display of objects rich with local significance. Instead they are storage areas for authenticity and uniqueness per se, for irreplaceable objects from any culture or period.

Museums are counterinstitutions to the factory. As objects became more short-lived and geared to an ongoing series of inventions and improvements that produce obsolescence as one side effect, the museum became ever more skilled at preservation, at keeping selected things from deterioration or change. The modern factory system expanded during the same period that both political nationalism and democratization of access have dominated Western culture. What French scholar Germain Bazin has called the "museum age" began with the opening of existing princely and papal collections and the simultaneous ordering of such collections in a novel historical, intellectual way. With the climactic dislocation of art during the French Revolution and the Napoleonic Wars, the great European hoards were scattered, reassembled, and ultimately transferred from private to national ownership.

Structuring the Experience of Art

Museums locate for us one stage in the creation of new forms, both in terms of the assembly of objects and with respect to the role of the collective itself in social life. In the museum age, the new social aggregate—for which all future art would exist—was "the public." It is for the public that society in the new democratic age retraces in social space the amenities of LEISURE and privilege once held by the few within the private space of moneyed or aristocratic property. The game preserve becomes the public zoo; the collection of books, the public library; the pleasure grounds of large estates, the new public parks, forests, and recreation areas.

Once opened, the treasures became structured by the uses negotiated between the public and the objects now clearly identified as art. With the force of those new professional intermediaries, the critics and the historians, behind them, the museums explicitly converted the functions of art to educational goals. What had been riches became enrichment—became, that is, EDUCATION and consciousness.

Just as important as the democratization of treasure were two Enlightenment forces: the idea of systematic ordering, which came to be applied to many princely collections, and the use of spatial display as a form of education. Whereas sensory values once controlled the arrangement within the room of a palace so that pictures, ornate frames, mirrors, furniture, and the costumes of visitors completed a visually pleasing harmony, the new educational arrangement involved an instruction in history and cultures, periods and schools of art that in both order and combination was fundamentally pedagogic. Whereas earlier collections tended to include such ill-sorted combinations of objects as antiquities, cut stones, medals, COINS, and natural-history specimens, the newer national collections began with an essential definition of what is now familiar to us as the "work of art." Curious monsters, supposed unicorn horns, pieces of the true cross, historic battle souvenirs, and impressive gems part company from what can now be constructed as art.

Simultaneous with the opening of the galleries to the public and the clear distinction of works of art from other objects of value came the beginning of

Figure 3. *(Museum)* Charles Willson Peale, *The Artist in His Museum*, 1822. Courtesy of the Pennsylvania Academy of the Fine Arts, Philadelphia.

Figure 4. *(Museum)* Visitors to the Louvre surround the *Nike of Samothrace*. Sculpture ca. 190 B.C.E. Courtesy of the French Government Tourist Office.

historical work on the periods and styles of art that would lead to the ordered array lying at the heart of the museum. It is essential to see that the subject of the museum is not the individual work of art but rather relations between works of art, in terms of what they have in common (styles, periods, schools) and what most sharply clashes in their juxtaposition. When we walk past the works of art in a museum we recapitulate in our actions the motion of the history of art itself. It is the series, sequence, or juxtaposition—and not the work of art—that is the working unit of the museum.

The work of the eighteenth-century German archaeologist Johann Joachim Winckelmann on Greek art introduced modern conceptual history into the study and display of art (*see* HISTORIOGRAPHY). In the Belvedere Palace in the Vatican, the conceptions that Winckelmann had applied to ancient art were transferred to European paintings. The paintings were chronologically arranged within the three European schools: Germany, the Netherlands, and Italy. Lighter frames were used. The paintings were separated on the walls. No longer were they in floor-to-ceiling stacks; rather, they were displayed in the modern linear, isolated series that we call an exhibition.

The objects that the museum arranges into its intelligible sequences could more accurately be called fragments, parts of preexisting social and material structures that have been broken off to be resettled in the afterlife of the museum. As the French writer André Malraux has described it, the conversion of earlier objects of religious, familial, or patriotic use into works of art involved a certain violence to their nature. Images and objects from within the culture itself were removed from their settings of social practice and were rehoused in museums. A religious painting in a church and a family portrait on the wall of the house owned by descendants of those pictured are both objects within their original social worlds of practice and use (*see* PORTRAITURE). It is important to note that using the object appropriately in its natural setting does not necessarily involve looking at it, studying it closely, or having an experience of it. In fact, for many religious objects pious use requires lowering the head or closing the eyes in the presence of the object. Once removed from their social settings these objects were available to be experienced as works of art. To do so, the symbolic features had to be effaced or abstracted. What had been meanings or imperatives—as, for example, the look or bearing in an ancestral portrait is instructive or formative to the inhabitants of a house where for generations the ancestors look down from the walls at ongoing family life—became colors, shapes, styles, or indexes of period, or were referenced to the artist rather than to the subject or a system of belief.

Museums and the Creation of Value

Museums not only relocate objects from their earlier worlds of belief and use into the sequences and juxtapositions that make up art; they also exert the power to declare new wholes. The Elgin Marbles, as they are called under their museum name, are fragments of what was originally the pediment of a Greek temple. The Venus de Milo is a new whole without its arms. The famous archaic torso of Apollo is, as a work of art in the museum, a whole perhaps more powerful as a torso than it once was as a statue. No one repaints the once brightly decorated Greek statues; as museum art they are white. The presence of fragmentary wholes within the museum is a reminder of the violence with which every object has been seized from what was once its world. The unpainted, armless, headless torso has lost not only those details but its temple, its geography and climate, the light by which it was intended to be seen, and the beliefs and knowledge by which it once was instantly familiar. *See* SCULPTURE.

With the effacement of earlier works drawn from what the European cultural world considered its own classical and Judeo-Christian heritage, the first stage of the museum's work was complete. In the second stage European and U.S. museums began to include and exhibit objects from alien social and religious communities: African, Mayan, and Asian artifacts were converted into art by their presence in the museum. These traditions were not assimilated but rather were preserved in their differences. The new objects did not require effacement. Their contexts or possible social uses did not need to be forgotten by the average viewer, because they were unknown to begin with. These mute objects passed back along the trails of economic conquest; Asian objects in the second half of the nineteenth century, African objects in the first years of the twentieth.

After the stabilization of the museum as the place for art and after the historical definition of the past that sorts it into periods, developments, and sequences, a new and highly ambitious art object came to be produced, one with the destiny of the museum stamped on it from the start. The third stage of objects, joining the silenced images of our own culture and the mute images of cultures that we know only anthropologically, are the objects that have been produced in the museum age itself by artists whose primary goal is to see their works someday located within museums. We usually contrast these nonrepresentational objects, which are also nonuse objects, with what we call the realistic, utilitarian, or referential traditions of our own culture. In fact, these new works are the third and not the second sequence that we face, a sequence that intensifies and completes retroactively the silencing of the first group while confirming the proper place of the second, once alien, group. It is the group of abstract or preeffaced works that are, in certain ways, the goal of the museum structure itself.

This object that is at first a candidate for history, an applicant to the museum, is referred to as a part of modern art. The homes of major private collectors, in which such objects rest before finding final homes in public museums, often have been architecturally designed as miniature museums. The collector is an intermediary between the artist who first owns the work because he or she has made it and the public whose property the art will finally become. Like the Mellon or Frick collections, the Simon holdings, as we rightly call them, are destined for civic and educational use.

Unlike the commissions from patrons that provided an artist with a living, the price of modern works involves a complex speculation on the work's future as a past. Formerly, the amount of a commission reflected the value placed on the artist's time, craft, and level of skill, as well as the size of the work and the cost of materials. The modern price is based on some idea of how essential to any future series called art this particular type of object is likely to be. The price of a contemporary painting is a function of a prediction of its future, and for this future value to be determined, criticism must move closer and closer to a historicization of the present, determining on the spot the historical place of new

Figure 5. *(Museum)* Figures from the east pediment of the Parthenon, ca. 438–432 B.C.E. (examples of the "Elgin marbles"). Reproduced by courtesy of the Trustees of The British Museum.

candidates. Without this speculative, prophetic act of criticism, the object has no value as a commodity. The initial price is in effect a wager that in a reasonable time the object will come to be priceless, permanent, and among the few thousand objects protected from change until the end of the civilization itself.

In its climactic years the museum resettled the European religious, political, and social artifactual past into the system of art, accomplishing one phase of what the sociologist MAX WEBER has called *secularization*. What was in other contexts a demystification, a stripping away of the trappings of the sacred, became instead a remystification within one of the only remaining religions of the new middle class: the religion of art. At the same time the museum brought into a single system the diverse cultural traditions of the world, paralleling the growth of a world economy centered in the industrialized nations

of the West. Finally, the museum had created new specifications of the artwork of its own time. No longer would the artist produce either luxury goods for private owners or imagery for local familial, political, or spiritual systems. Instead he or she would now compete to add to what made up the self-image of an abstract and universalized civic past.

Although in its museums each major city has, in effect, a sample of the total history, an anthology of exemplary works, every collection still has its gaps. Malraux predicted that the museum of the future would be a "museum without walls," using the term to describe the art BOOK or compilation in which an intellectual comprehensiveness could be attained despite the physical location of various works in Rome, Paris, or New York. Malraux was incorrect only in his literal image of the book. Instead it is the photographic slide collection that has become the me-

a

b

Figure 6. (Museum) Robert Morris, *Labyrinth*, 1974. Created for the exhibition "Robert Morris/Projects." *(a)* Installation view; *(b)* the completed work. From *Robert Morris/Projects,* Institute of Contemporary Art, University of Pennsylvania, Philadelphia, 1974. Exhibition catalog.

dium of primary experience both for the study of the history of art and for the basic set of experiences of individual works that provides each viewer's frame of reference.

The slide, like the phonograph record that replaced the live concert or the paperback book that replaced the manuscript or the television PERFORMANCE that replaced the public THEATER, permits the experience of the work of art to occur at home, at a time of choice for the viewer. The domestication of all art, the process by which a relatively valueless copy makes available a book, musical performance, or film in the familial setting of the private home, carried even further the universalization that the museum had begun. At the same time it sacrificed the commitment to the eighteenth- and nineteenth-century ideal that important cultural experiences are a function of the public realm. The museum, then, played a decisive transitional role between a world of privately held treasure and a democratized, but once again private, world of universally available cultural experience.

See also AESTHETICS; ARTIST AND SOCIETY; VISUAL IMAGE.

Bibliography. Germain Bazin, *The Museum Age* (in French), trans. by Jane Cahill, New York, 1967; Niels Van Holst, *Creators, Collectors, and Connoisseurs* (in German), New York, 1967; André Malraux, *Voices of Silence* (Les voix du silence), trans. by Stuart Gilbert, Garden City, N.Y., 1953, reprint Princeton, N.J., 1978.

PHILIP FISHER

MUSIC, ELECTRONIC. *See* ELECTRONIC MUSIC.

MUSIC, FOLK AND TRADITIONAL

Generally speaking, folk music comprises traditional, orally transmitted, and regionally and ethnically based genres of music, often performed in small groups with a major everyday emphasis on face-to-face communication and social interaction (*see* INTERACTION, FACE-TO-FACE).

Early folklorists understood folk songs to differ both from popular music (tainted by professionalism, the profit motive, and mass media) and from art music (composed and performed for an urban, educated elite) (*see* MUSIC, POPULAR; MUSIC HISTORY; SONG). Folk songs, they thought, could be found only among an agrarian, illiterate peasantry; literacy, urbanization, and modernization were thought to work against folk tradition. This formulation meant that students of folk song were fated to preside over dying artifacts and that the nature and quality of folk song among descendants of settlers in the New World must be derivative and inferior. But as many

of those European peasant cultures disappeared during the twentieth century, folklorists observed that folk songs and folk processes were alive and well among European and American working classes and well-knit ethnic groups, whether in rural areas or in cities. In fact, for contemporary folklorists, process in folk music has become more important than ARTIFACT, and today a folk song is conceived of as a PERFORMANCE, not just a text with a tune. The MEANING of a folk song arises from its context, from what it communicates in the performance situation. *See* MUSIC PERFORMANCE.

Oral transmission in folk music means that most folk music is learned in person by imitation and example rather than through formal instruction and written notation. The result of this learning process is that folk songs exist in performance—that is, in several versions and variants rather than in a relatively more fixed, written text such as a Beethoven string quartet. Furthermore, in some folk-song traditions, such as Afro-American gospel music, variation and improvisation in performance are encouraged, making it even more difficult to locate the song as an artifact apart from performance. Catching music by ear rather than by sight from a score, the folk musician has a direct aural relationship to his or her art. Because music passes through the medium of print for the "paper-trained" musician, the relationship is both visual (spatial) and aural. Yet even the classical musician who plays from a score has learned style and expression aurally. *See* MUSIC COMPOSITION AND IMPROVISATION; ORAL CULTURE; ORAL POETRY.

Performance in face-to-face communication means that folk music reflects the informally shared experience of a folk group closely linked by occupation, neighborhood, social class, ethnic heritage, religious affiliation, dialect, race, age, political outlook, sex, and so on. Folk songs are shared among folk groups as events in the home or community gathering places in which most people take an active role, interacting as listeners, players, dancers, and singers. One of the more common settings for contemporary folk music in North America is an evening or weekend afternoon at a musician's home, where other local musicians and their families gather for music, socializing, and often FOOD. The music played may vary from old songs and ballads and traditional DANCE music to new and old hit tunes from RADIO and records, but in this context it is all folk music.

Like all folk arts, folk music possesses affect; that is, it has the power to reach people's feelings and to move them. Affect is constituted by performance, and performance is culture-specific and operates according to rules and principles understood by performers and audience in the folk group. Performances of folk music are intentional: performers (and folk groups) attach meaning to performances and intend meaning by performances.

Folk musicians do not perform naively and unreflectively; most can and do discuss and evaluate aspects of performance and repertoire among themselves, seldom relying on a professional class of music critics or a body of written music criticism. Memory plays an important role in folk music, not merely in recalling what was learned orally but also in associating certain music with certain people, events, emotions, symbols, and rituals from the past.

Cultural revitalization movements among various ethnic groups in the last hundred years or so have led to self-conscious efforts to preserve their heritage of folk music and dance, and often these movements adopted some of the methods of the conservatories—written notation, formal lessons, recitals—that characterize art music and tend to work against oral tradition. In Latin America and eastern Europe particularly, folk revivals, festivals, competitions, regional and national folk-song and dance troupes, and other such activities have tended to professionalize folk music and take it out of its local context. Irish music, undergoing a renaissance in Ireland and the United States, is very well organized, with a national music association, schools, clubs, and regional and national music contests. At the same time it must be recognized that within many folk groups, for example in eastern Europe and among Afro-Americans, professionals are the rule and carry some of the community's folk-song traditions.

In the twentieth century many regional and ethnically based folk music repertoires have been transmitted by the media—radio, recordings, television, MOTION PICTURES—and these media artifacts have sometimes acted as models for all musicians to imitate, thereby fixing tunes, texts, and styles and working against versions and variants. Prior to recordings, for example, blues song structure and length varied, but recordings and radio established the norm of the twelve-bar, *AAB* blues form and put song lengths at about three minutes, the most music that a 78-RPM record could hold.

Beginning in the 1920s U.S. commercial SOUND RECORDING companies featured special series for various ethnic groups: Polish, Irish, Jewish, and Afro-American, among others. At the same time, media transmission has brought local and regional repertoires to other regions, even to other nations, and the resulting musical cross-fertilization has created hybrid styles and genres, many of which are transmitted orally as well as by the media. A few of the many examples of such cross-fertilizations include salsa (a Puerto Rican blend of Latin music, African music, and jazz); *Zydeco* (a Louisiana Creole blend of Cajun music, Latin rhythms, and rhythm and blues); 1960s British rock (which drew on the traditions of early rock and roll, English music hall, Anglo-American folk music, and Afro-American blues from Chicago in the 1950s); African *highlife;* and Jamaican reggae. Since the mid-1960s inexpensive portable cassette tape recorders have democratized the media enormously, and now the "folk" make good use of the media, tape-recording performances chiefly to learn rather than to preserve them.

Many world cultures possessing folk music get along without a concept that distinguishes folk from other kinds of music. Indeed a few cultures have no word for music itself. But the idea of folk music has existed in Europe and the New World for at least two hundred years and has served to distinguish the music of ordinary people, "the folk," from the cultivated music of the courts, cities, and universities. The term is less useful outside the Euro-American context; even within that context some members of folk groups resent the term, thinking it demeans their music, while others embrace the term as a marker of ethnic or regional identity.

See also ETHNOMUSICOLOGY; FOLKLORE; FOLKTALE.

Bibliography. David Buchan, *The Ballad and the Folk,* Boston and London, 1972; David Evans, *Big Road Blues,* Berkeley, Calif., 1982; Henry Glassie, *Passing the Time in Ballymenone,* Philadelphia, 1982; Edward D. Ives, *Joe Scott: The Woodsman-Songmaker,* Urbana, Ill., 1978; Peter Kennedy, ed., *Folksongs of Britain and Ireland,* New York, 1975; Zoltán Kodály, *Folk Music of Hungary* (A magyar népzene), 2d ed., rev. and enl. by Lajos Vargyas, trans. by Ronald Tempest and Cynthia Jolly, London, 1971; J. Barre Toelken, *The Dynamics of Folklore,* Boston, 1979.

JEFF TODD TITON

MUSIC, POPULAR

Popular music is commonly understood to comprise different genres of music (e.g., the sentimental ballad, ragtime, blues, jazz, rhythm and blues, various types of rock and roll, punk and new wave, soul, reggae, country, country and western, folk, Broadway and Hollywood musicals) that have or have had a mass appeal; that are communicated and stored through mechanical or electronic means (e.g., sheet music, phonograph discs, compact discs, tape recordings, cassette recordings, film, videotapes, music videos); that are marketed for financial gain; that are conceived originally in a predominantly oral-aural rather than visual (notated) fashion; and whose principal function is to provide secular entertainment for consumption during LEISURE time. A majority, although by no means all, of this music has originated in the United States and since the closing decades of the nineteenth century has had a profound impact on the cultural lives of a majority of the people living in the Western world. *See* GENRE; SOUND RECORDING.

This common understanding requires qualification and expansion. Even within the Western world it is not possible to achieve a strict definition of popular music. Many criteria—for example, number of people involved, mass mechanical or electronic dissemination, production for financial gain, oral-aural rather than visual mode of conception, entertainment or leisure function—may indeed cover a sizable proportion of music commonly understood as popular, yet none covers all such music. Some "popular" music (e.g., AVANT-GARDE jazz) does not really have mass appeal; some (e.g., folk music) may be performed predominantly in live situations to which mechanical and electronic means of communication and storage are essentially peripheral; some (e.g., progressive rock) may be created for reasons that are primarily artistic rather than financial; some (e.g., the music of Broadway and Hollywood musicals) may be conceived in an overwhelmingly notated fashion; and some (e.g., protest music) conveys messages of social resistance that make any categorization as entertainment or leisure music questionable. *See* MUSIC, FOLK AND TRADITIONAL; MUSIC THEATER; MUSICAL, FILM.

Within the Western world, popular music may be thought of more usefully in terms of what it is not rather than what it is. The term *popular music* appears to be used to describe any "music of the people" that falls outside music traditionally performed in the Western concert tradition, and music having strong non-Western, traditional, and folk affiliations (e.g., Australian Aboriginal music, Asian high-culture music, and the traditional musics of Africa). Music of the Western concert tradition tends to constitute the subject matter of the academic discipline of historical musicology, and music from other traditions tends to constitute the subject matter of the academic discipline of ETHNOMUSICOLOGY. It should be stressed, however, that the distinctions between popular, classical, and traditional musics and the associated academic disciplines of popular music studies, historical musicology, and ethnomusicology are to a certain extent arbitrary. Popular music should not be thought of as a homogeneous entity but rather as a label of convenience that refers in a somewhat unsatisfactory manner to a wide variety of musical genres emerging from quite distinct social and historical circumstances.

Worldwide impact. In this context it is necessary to emphasize that popular music is a worldwide phenomenon with many roots quite independent of the mass-mediated Anglo-American genres that have made such an impact since the 1890s. In Great Britain, for example, there was significant resistance in the first half of the twentieth century to popular music that originated in the United States. Performers such as George Formby, Gracie Fields, and Vera Lynn owed much to the tradition of the British music hall, a tradition whose legacy can still be heard in the music of songwriters such as Paul McCartney. In many eastern European countries, musical genres that in the West might be considered traditional (e.g., the folk musics of Bulgaria) or dated (e.g., the *Schlager* of the German Democratic Republic and Hungary) form an integral part of the lives of older generations. Even in North America there are popular music genres such as the polka that both predate mass-mediated forms of Anglo-American popular music and remain to this day important to large segments of the population.

The worldwide impact of mass-mediated forms of Anglo-American popular music has nonetheless been staggering, particularly since the advent of the silicon chip, integrated circuitry, and the compact cassette. Multinational record companies have for many years attempted to establish markets wherever it has been politically and economically feasible. Such markets are more difficult to establish when countries are not members of the International Monetary Fund, when countries restrict the influx of Western cultural commodities for political reasons, and when record and cassette piracy is a common and uncontrolled practice. Yet there is scarcely a corner of the world in which mass-mediated Anglo-American genres of popular music are unknown. The advantage for multinational record companies lies not only in the money to be made through the establishing of new markets; it lies also in access to indigenous genres of music that can form the basis for new musical fashions in the Western world. Thus, although calypso became an internationally famous genre of music made popular on the RADIO during the 1950s and 1960s, it is to this day hardly heard on the radio in Trinidad outside of the carnival season. Radio in Trinidad is dominated by Anglo-American popular music.

The incursions of Western-based music industries seldom leave local musicians and their music unaffected. It is frequently difficult for local musicians to obtain royalties and so establish a secure financial basis from which to develop their own music alongside imported Anglo-American genres. In addition indigenous genres of music as disseminated within local communities frequently change under the impact of Western popular musics and their associated technologies. In Sri Lanka, for example, the impact of Western popular musics led, in the late 1960s, to the addition of the saxophone and electric guitar in the playing of traditional *baila* music. A boom in the Sri Lankan market for this music—itself a consequence of the introduction of the compact cassette—also resulted in the late 1970s in the original Afro-Portuguese language of *baila* music being totally replaced by Singhalese and, in the early 1980s, in the music being played to a limited extent on Sri Lankan radio, which before had considered it socially and morally unworthy of airtime. This airtime resulted in the emergence of a new, "clean" subgenre of *baila* music purged of "smutty" and topical political and social references.

Although the often questionable impact of Western music industries should not be underrated, it should also be emphasized that, in a context of increasing urbanization, many local Third World musicians have become more knowledgeable about royalties and COPYRIGHT laws and increasingly resourceful in their ability to maintain local recording companies and circulate recordings of local popular music (as in Sri Lanka). In addition many new genres of popular music have been created by local musicians through a cross-fertilization of indigenous and Anglo-American forms. *Highlife* music of Ghana and *juju* music of Nigeria provide good examples of such cross-fertilizations. In a very different context *Schlager* music in the German Democratic Republic has developed more hybrid forms influenced by Western rock music. And rock music in that country, although clearly influenced by many styles of Western rock, has its own particular sound and approach toward lyrics resulting from a concern to express the political and social experiences that underpin everyday life. Popular music, in other words, is a global phenomenon whose institutional arrangements and modes of production are varied and complex and, in addition, are marked historically by continual change, flux, and synthesis.

Modes of communication. If the institutional arrangements and modes of production of popular music are varied and complex, so too are the ways in which different genres of popular music communicate. Popular musics communicate primarily through SOUND, and questions of value in popular music (from the perspective of audiences) seem to be tied largely to the degree of "authenticity" of the sound, which is frequently focused on the unique characteristics of a particular singer's voice. In this, popular music differs appreciably from classical music, in which the stress in communication lies primarily with an extended harmonic and sometimes contrapuntal discourse to which the inherent qualities of the sound itself usually take second place. To the extent that few forms of popular music are now uninfluenced by mass-disseminated Anglo-American genres, and to the extent that these genres originally came into existence through a cross-fertilization of the musical heritages of black Africa and the European cultures of the United States, a majority of the world's popular musics now display some harmonic and rhythmic principles derived originally from European art music. However, such principles serve as little more than a framework within which other musical prin-

ciples such as the bending of pitches, the anticipating and delaying of beats, misplaced or syncopated metric stress patterns, an emphasis on individuated, "unpure" tone colors or timbres, and an emphasis on improvisation can all contribute to an authentic sound that, although mass-mediated, communicates powerfully, immediately, and on an individual basis to audience members.

Yet sound is not the sole channel of communication for popular music. There are four channels: sound, images, words, and DANCE. In many genres of popular music these channels are inseparable in presentation, yet each can contribute in different and sometimes contradictory ways to the overall impact of the music (or, perhaps more accurately, the music event).

If popular music communicates and is both created and produced in a complex and sometimes paradoxical fashion, then there exists a clear potential for individual popular music genres to be used and consumed by individual audience members in a wide variety of ways. However, above and beyond the question of the different meanings different groups of people may derive from various genres of popular music, there are two crucial issues at stake in attempting to understand the impact popular music may have on audiences and the role it may play in society. First, there is the question of the level of consciousness brought to popular music by audiences. Do audience members creatively negotiate a wide range of individual meanings from popular music, or do they accept the meanings invested in popular music by its producers in a largely passive and homogeneous fashion? Second, there is the tortuous question of the value of popular music, formulated not so much in terms of its authenticity as perceived by audiences but in terms of the positive or negative social effects a particular genre is perceived as having by commentators other than the audience. These questions are linked insomuch as audience members who bring a high level of consciousness to a particular genre of popular music may define the issue of authenticity to include the question of social desirability. On the other hand, critics may assess social desirability partially in terms of the degree of passive consumption perceived in a particular audience. It is consequently difficult to assess the different possible impacts of popular music independently of an understanding of the considerable range of interpretations brought to popular music by popular-music commentators. This range of interpretations results not only from the complex dialectics of communication through popular music but also from the variety of professional interests and ideological orientations of popular-music commentators.

Debates about meaning and function. The prevalent view of popular music is that it is a mass phenomenon. Those who see themselves as cultural guardians have argued consistently since the turn of the century that much popular music influences negatively a largely passive audience by leading them away from established social, moral, and aesthetic values. This view has been reinforced by musicologists unprepared and unable to understand the technical characteristics responsible for the expressive power of popular music. Although noting the ability of music to affirm the spiritual life of the individual, they have nonetheless understood "good" music to be a phenomenon essentially divorced from social processes and have engaged in formal modes of analysis that stress melody, harmony, and rhythm at the expense of timbre, improvisation, and inflectional devices. These latter characteristics have been interpreted as distortions of purer tonal values, tainted through the mass social processes of the industrial world. As a consequence of this interpretation, many genres of popular music have been viewed by musicologists as inferior.

This view of popular music as a mass phenomenon detrimental to the human spirit has found sympathy in a somewhat different quarter. THEODOR ADORNO, for example, has argued that popular music serves the interests not of those who might challenge the established social order but of those who would wish to preserve it. Popular music here becomes little more than an ideological device whose purpose is to desensitize consumers to the inequalities and ills of life in industrial capitalist societies. Marxist-influenced scholarship in popular music, however, has become rather more sophisticated since the mid-1970s. Few scholars in the critical tradition would deny the role of popular music as a cultural or ideological force supportive of existing class, ethnic, GENDER, and generational relationships, but there have been perceptible differences of opinion about the ability of individuals and groups to use popular music as a form of cultural resistance.

This tension in understanding processes of consumption is reproduced in work carried on outside an explicitly critical tradition and sometimes outside studies that place popular music in the context of massive social processes. One such trend, exemplified by French scholars such as Antoine Hennion, emphasizes the role of producers in defining cultural artifacts and meanings for consumers. A contrasting trend, exemplified by the U.S. ethnomusicologist Steven Feld, focuses on the rich linguistic discourses through which people make sense of and actively construct musical meanings.

Although popular music has long been established as a major force in the cultural lives of many people, an established field of study for its analysis has been slow to develop in comparison with fields of study for the analysis of other forms of mass-mediated communication precisely because of the varied professional interests and ideological orientations of popular-music commentators. In consequence there has been little common wisdom regarding either the effects of popular music or the social, ideological, or human implications of its modes of production and communication. To this uncertain but intriguing state of understanding there were signs in the late 1980s that feminist scholarship was starting to make a significant and lasting contribution in the realms of sexuality and gender relations as mediated through different genres of popular music. See FEMINIST THEORIES OF COMMUNICATION.

See also MUSIC COMPOSITION AND IMPROVISATION; MUZAK; SONG; TASTE CULTURES.

Bibliography. Steven Feld, "Communication, Music, and Speech about Music," *1984 Yearbook for Traditional Music* 16 (1984): 1–18; Simon Frith, *Sound Effects: Youth, Leisure, and the Politics of Rock 'n' Roll,* New York, 1981; Lawrence Grossberg, "Another Boring Day in Paradise: Rock and Roll and the Empowerment of Everyday Life," *Popular Music* 4 (1984): 225–258; David Harker, *One for the Money: Politics and Popular Song,* London, 1980; Antoine Hennion, *Les professionnels de disque,* Paris, 1981; Dave Laing, *One Chord Wonders: Power and Meaning in Punk Rock,* Milton Keynes, Eng., 1985; John Shepherd, "Definition as Mystification: A Consideration of Labels as a Hindrance to Understanding Significance in Music," *Popular Music Perspectives* 2 (1985): 84–98; Philip Tagg, *Kojak: 50 Seconds of Television Music: Toward the Analysis of Affect in Popular Music* (Kojak—50 sekunders tv-musik), Gothenburg, Sweden, 1979; Roger Wallis and Krister Malm, *Big Sounds from Small Peoples: The Music Industry in Small Countries,* London and Pendragon, N.Y., 1984.

JOHN SHEPHERD

MUSIC COMPOSITION AND IMPROVISATION

Music composition and improvisation are aspects of the same process: communicating in the music mode of discourse. The differences that do exist between them are ones of degree, not kind. However, their relationship is frequently misunderstood and has been reduced at times to a simplistic dichotomy. The assumptions used to support this dichotomy tend to reflect ignorance of non-Western musical traditions and a condescending attitude toward improvisation as a method of creating and communicating music. For example, the 1944 edition of the *Harvard Dictionary of Music* described improvisation as a "soap bubble phenomenon," an inspirational act that virtually defied rational description. This is a rather serious contention, since the majority of musical traditions in the world, particularly non-Western traditions, are based on improvisation. However, when the assumptions underlying this alleged dichotomy are examined, the lines between composition and improvisation soon become blurred.

The first assumption to question is that the written version of a piece of music is a composition, while the oral version is an improvisation. It has been said that Wolfgang Amadeus Mozart wrote a music manuscript as rapidly as someone might write a letter. When asked how he did it, he said that the composition was already in his head; he was simply copying it down. Was it any less a composition before it was a visual product on paper?

Furthermore, even when a musical composition has been written down in traditional Western notation, ambiguities in the notation present the performer with some degree of choice in the PERFORMANCE. A precise notation is one that uses monomial symbols: one symbol stands for only one thing. However, traditional Western notation also includes both binomial and polynomial symbols such as the trill, the mordent, and the appoggiatura as well as imprecise signs and indications such as the fermata, sforzando, ritardando, and accelerando. In addition, initial tempo markings and changes in tempo are often designated in terminology that allows considerable latitude in interpretation. Even metronome markings, when given, are not followed too accurately, because a given performer or conductor may question the judgment of the editor or even the composer, who made the designations from reading the score rather than from leading an orchestra. In other words, the written score is subject to variations in many basic elements such as tempo, dynamics, intonation, "interpretation," and so forth.

Because of these ambiguities, the proper realization of a traditional Western score continues to depend on the performers' and conductor's knowledge of the aural tradition surrounding it. Traditional Western notation, therefore, is prescriptive, not descriptive, and is subject to variable interpretations. In a very strict sense there is a degree of improvisation in every performance of musical compositions of the Western world.

Combinations of composition and improvisation. In the non-Western world, of course, the line between composition and improvisation is even more difficult to draw. A composition may be only partially written. For example, the notation of a composition for the Chinese *ch'in*, a six-string plucked zither, does not include the very essential element of rhythm. Part of the aesthetic in realizing a composition in this tradition includes a freedom of rhythmic choice on the part of the performer. It requires the musician to improvise one of the primary elements of music; and yet some of the famous compositions for *ch'in* have been part of the written musical tradition of China for many centuries.

In Java a musical composition written in one or another form of Javanese notation consists of a fixed melody (a nuclear theme used as the basis for improvisation), a structural part performed by different-sized gongs, and a standard drum pattern on which elaborations are improvised by the drummer. This "short score" may include a few directions for certain instruments regarding the desired octave in a given passage. The rest of the orchestra consists of a number of instruments performing—in individual idiomatic styles—improvisations based on the principal melody. To this are added female soloists and a male chorus, and possibly a narrator with DANCE or PUPPETRY, each engaged in a degree of improvisation. Although basic structures and movements are stereotyped in both the dance drama and the puppet play, artistic realization of them also demands individual improvisation. Until the late nineteenth century, several thousand Javanese musical compositions existed primarily in the oral tradition. Only about a century ago was the short score used as a means of preservation. (Performances today are not from the written score.) Are these major orchestral compositions, some of them lasting more than an hour, any the less compositions because they were written down, albeit in short score, rather recently?

But this blurring of composition and improvisation also occurs in the Western world. Charles Seeger was able to identify more than three hundred variants of the folk song "Barbara Allen." Some will argue that originally there must have been a single version of the piece and that variants of it developed as singers reshaped details according to individual preferences, usually with only an oral knowledge of the piece. Most of the three hundred variants were written down by collectors, not by folk performers, who knew them from hearing other performers. No one knows which, if any, of the extant variants is the original. But, like Mozart, the composer of the tune probably carried it in his or her head—and never bothered (probably was not able) to write it down. Is "Barbara Allen" any the less a composition for all this? It is erroneous to assume that successive performances of a folk song by the same singer show any greater or lesser degree of improvisation than the performances of standard works in the Western music literature performed by the best conductors. *See also* ORAL CULTURE; ORAL POETRY.

Similar examples abound in the Afro-American jazz idiom, in which improvisations based on well-known popular songs themselves often become codified as new compositions. For instance, the popular song "All the Things You Are," by Jerome Kern and Oscar Hammerstein, became a standard part of the repertoire of bebop jazz players in the 1950s, owing in part to the challenge of improvising upon its interesting chord cycle. An improvisation by trumpeter Kenny Dorham was developed into a new melody that could be played with the same chord changes; alto saxophonist Charlie "Bird" Parker is also credited with another improvisation that became a separate melody for these chords. Both have been recorded many times under the titles, respectively, "Prince Albert" and "Bird of Paradise"; Dorham and Parker are listed as the *composers* of these songs, which have copyrights in their names.

While "Prince Albert" and "Bird of Paradise" began as improvisations on the melody and chords of "All the Things You Are," today they are two distinct melodies to the same chord progression. Performers in the jazz idiom continue to create new improvisations on this same chord pattern, using any one of these three melodies as the opening or closing of the piece and often quoting from the others, thereby illustrating continuity and change, improvisation and composition as a continuing dialectic at the center of their art.

Possible criteria. It might be thought that composition and improvisation can be distinguished by criteria such as the relative simplicity or complexity of the music, the technological sophistication of the instruments used, the degree of formal training required to perform the music, or the professional (as opposed to amateur) status of the musicians involved. However, each criterion fails to provide a consistent and meaningful explanation for distinguishing between them.

For example, simplicity of expression, however it is defined, offers no clues, because some of the most beautiful examples of the bel canto line have been simple, whether in the lieder of Franz Schubert or in an anonymous folk song like "Greensleeves." Similarly, complexity is found in a wide range of musics, from the latest scores for ELECTRONIC MUSIC to the incredible sounds of the didgeridoo, a hollowed-out wooden tube lip-vibrated by aboriginal musicians in Australia.

Technological sophistication of the sound-producing instruments also offers no index either to the simplicity-complexity continuum or to the riddle of composition versus improvisation. For example, the didgeridoo produces sonic complexities that require sophisticated laboratory equipment to understand. Although the simple bamboo flute played in India lacks the pads, springs, and keys found on the Western flute, the practice of half-holing and forked fingering allows the Indian musician to perform a complicated melodic line that simply could not be duplicated by the Western musician on even the most technologically advanced flute. (Developments of the Western flute inhibit realization of the melodic subtleties essential to the unique character of Indian music.) Incidentally, Indian musicians improvise within the modal-melodic requirements and formulas of a particular raga, which includes some fixed compositional elements.

Sometimes the definition of musical composition is founded on the conviction that formal training in music is absolutely necessary to understand and perform the composition. In Western art music such a claim is reasonably defensible. From a cross-cultural perspective, however, this definition is severely flawed. Examples of informal training, or simply the absorption of musical norms by exposure, abound not only in folk and popular idioms of the Western world but also in musical traditions native to Africa, Asia, Oceania, Latin America, and elsewhere.

A related fallacy is the tendency to associate the act of composition with the professional musician, whether the music is art, pop, rock, country-western, or a hybrid. A professional musician is described in the West as someone who earns all or most of his or her livelihood from music. Of course, if such a definition is accepted, the finest musicians in much of the non-Western world—both composers and performers—would have to be classified as amateur, since their primary livelihoods often have nothing to do with music.

So far it would appear that composition and improvisation are hopelessly entwined. Another criterion, which is a little more helpful, is the concept of fixity versus flexibility in music, although here again the degree of fixity or flexibility is relative. For example, when a composition is printed (ignoring for the moment differences in interpretation from one performance to another), it would appear to be quite fixed. But subsequent editions of older compositions sometimes are known for the idiosyncratic interpretations of their different editors. In fact, some editions of a composition have become quite famous for their editorial differences. Of course, this kind of flexibility from edition to edition can hardly be called improvisation, but it weakens the argument that fixity is the hallmark of composition.

Musical composition on the island of Bali in Indonesia further challenges the fixity versus flexibility criterion. There is no improvisation at the time of a given performance by one of the large Balinese orchestras, in part because the instrumental practice called *kotekan*—extremely rapid interlocking parts—makes improvisation impossible. But traditional Balinese music is a kind of communal music, in which suggestions volunteered by the performers may alter a composition considerably in the course of numerous performances within even a few months. After some trials, the successive musical changes are judged by a consensus of performers in the gamelan orchestra. If the changes are considered an improvement they are incorporated into the original composition. This practice certainly stretches the usual meaning of improvisation, but it also rules out fixity as the sine qua non of composition.

True understanding of musical composition and improvisation requires complete rejection of the idea that these two forms of musical discourse represent a polarity. Far from being opposites, they are very similar in process. A composition is known by some kind of title and has a greater or lesser degree of fixity; perhaps it would not be contradictory in qualifying the statement to call it a flexible fixity. An improvisation has a greater or lesser degree of flexibility; perhaps it would not be contradictory in qualifying the statement to call it a fixed flexibility. These definitions are more than an exercise in the finesse of language. It is essential to grasp that while composition and improvisation are two different forms of musical utterance, they exist at related and mutually intelligible points along a continuum of the music mode of discourse.

See also ETHNOMUSICOLOGY; MUSIC, POPULAR; MUSIC HISTORY; MUSIC PERFORMANCE; MUSICAL INSTRUMENTS.

Bibliography. Derek Bailey, *Improvisation: Its Nature and Practice in Music*, Ashbourne, Eng., 1980; J. S. Brandts Buys-Van Zijp and A. Brandts Buys-Van Zijp, "Javaansche Gĕnding's bij Land en bij Seelig," *Djawa* 16 (1936): 230–243; idem, "Land's Transscripties van Gĕnding's," *Djawa* 15 (1935): 174–185; idem, "Omtrent Notaties en Transscripties en over de Constructie van Gamelanstukken," *Djawa* 14 (1934): 127–165; Mantle Hood, *The Ethnomusicologist*, new ed., Kent, Ohio, 1982; Bruno Nettl, "Thoughts on Improvisation: A Comparative Approach," *Musical Quarterly* 60 (1974): 1–19; Charles Seeger, *Studies in Musicology, 1935–1975*, Berkeley, Calif., 1977; Ernst Toch, *The Shaping Forces in Music: An Inquiry into the Nature of Harmony, Melody, Counterpoint, Form*, New York, 1948, reprint 1977.

MANTLE HOOD

MUSIC HISTORY

Music is a general term for many modes of human communication using movements that produce and reproduce sounds. The term designates not only "knowledge of moving well" (St. Augustine) but also the exercise of such knowledge and the results of the exercise, all three of which are interdependent. Musicians are human beings who communicate by "moving well" to produce and reproduce sounds, and each instance of such communication is a PERFORMANCE. *See also* MUSIC PERFORMANCE; SOUND.

The term *musical instrument* applies here to all tools and mechanisms used in transmitting, retaining, and exercising musical knowledge (*see* MUSICAL INSTRUMENTS). The instruments and agencies of musical communication include the following:

1. Objects and devices that transform into acoustic energy the nervous energy applied to these devices by musicians. The shoes of a tap dancer and the floor struck by the dancer's feet via the shoes constitute one instrument in this sense.

2. Sets of cues or instructions that musicians create and/or receive before and during performances. These are coded, stored, and named (SONG, tune, composition, etc.) in various ways, some of them partly dependent on use of graphic symbols (notations). *See* MUSIC THEORIES—NOTATIONS AND LITERACY.

3. Habits and strategies for evaluating cues and instructions. Some of these are commonly termed rules, modes of performance (*see* MODE), arts, theories, POETICS, and AESTHETICS. Musicians who employ sound-making devices are obliged to remember appropriate sequences of motions, and we may assume that handling the devices normally helps performers to recall typical orderings of cues and responses.

4. The self and others, as both agents and agencies of musical communication. Through clapping the hands, slapping a thigh, striking the vocal chords (see Figure 1), and similar gestures, a musician becomes an instrument of musical communication.

5. Extensions of these four types of agency, available in the twentieth century through electronic and computer technology (*see* ELECTRONIC MUSIC; SOUND RECORDING).

The study of musical communication is a study of how human beings communicate with spirits as well as with themselves and their instruments. Many musicians serve as mediums through whose motions the voices or sounds of others (spirits, humans of the same or a different time and place, animals, birds, inanimate objects) become present during performances. An instrument is often recognized as the voice, embodiment, or attribute of a spirit. Masks that alter the performer's voice and/or face are important in many modes of musical communication, especially in Africa and Asia (*see* MASK).

It is common for musical gestures to mark a change from one set of social circumstances and relationships to another. Partly by virtue of such gestures, the boundaries within which musical communication occurs usually differ in one or more respects from those that are essential to other modes of communication. Speakers of different languages, for example, often communicate successfully through music. In principle it is no more necessary to music than to SPEECH that all participants share a single standard for evaluating moves. Each such standard is an instrument in a sense, and many instruments may be employed in a single performance.

The history of musical communication is in large part the history of tools and skills developed and used in transmitting, retaining, and exercising musical knowledge. Human cultural diversity compels us to accept many answers to the questions, What have

Figure 1. *(Music History)* An Elamite boys' and women's choir. Detail of a relief from the Southwest Palace of Ashurbanipal at Nineveh, showing a court musician beating her throat to produce a vocal tremolo. Reproduced by courtesy of the Trustees of The British Museum.

been the instruments of musical communication? and What purposes have they served? Through comparative studies of the reproduction of musical knowledge in various civilizations and societies, music historians attempt to identify paths that have been followed by different populations in each region. Much of what every musician knows is implicit knowledge, reconstructed only in part during a given performance or sequence of actions. Thus interpretation of the archaeological and historical records of music is inevitably problematic, inasmuch as the evidence tells us little, at best, of what was known to those who produced it.

Early musical artifacts. Specialized flint tools developed in the Upper Paleolithic hunting cultures of Europe were used in shaping bird and animal bones into instruments, including bullroarers, scrapers, whistles, and flutes. The cognitive capacities and the intentions of those who made and used these instruments are an elusive subject of inquiry. We do not know why observations of the phases of the moon were marked on an eagle bone whistle from Le Placard, France, or why images of a masked and a naked dancer facing a bear's paw were engraved on opposite sides of a bone from Ariège. Nor do we understand the purposes served by the numerous rock and cave paintings in Europe and Africa that depict dancers and musicians holding various instruments (see Figure 2).

Possibly the earliest surviving sets of like instruments are Upper Paleolithic bone tubes of varying lengths, found with or without polished scrapers. Panpipes—several tuned tubes stopped at the lower ends and bound together in the form of a raft or bundle—may be a more ancient device for producing a set of distinct sounds than are single pipes with three or more finger holes. By the early first millennium B.C.E. there is evidence in Europe that pairs or sets of instruments (panpipes and horns) may have been "killed" before burial. Whatever their earliest uses, in recent centuries ensembles of like instruments (in Africa, for example, flutes and trumpets) have served to bind together several performers, each of whom may produce only one sound that complements those of the other players.

From the beginnings of farming and permanent settlement until the present, many human societies have been confronted with difficult choices between acceptance and rejection of innovations—among them innovations affecting musical communication. Excavation of the successive levels of early towns furnishes evidence of practices that were adopted, retained, modified, or abandoned at specific points in a town's history. At Çatal Hüyük in Anatolia (ca. 6250–5400 B.C.E.) wall paintings in (household?) shrines on levels V and III depict dances of hunters (see Figure 3), but the two more recent levels have no evidence of shrines devoted to hunters or even of

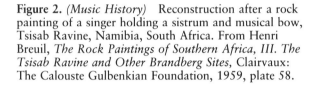

Figure 2. *(Music History)*   Reconstruction after a rock painting of a singer holding a sistrum and musical bow, Tsisab Ravine, Namibia, South Africa. From Henri Breuil, *The Rock Paintings of Southern Africa, III. The Tsisab Ravine and Other Brandberg Sites,* Clairvaux: The Calouste Gulbenkian Foundation, 1959, plate 58.

the hunters' obsidian spearheads. The bull, perhaps the most durable symbol of fertility in the ancient Near East, is represented in shrines on all levels at Çatal Hüyük. The sound boxes of the earliest surviving lyres (Mesopotamia, third millennium B.C.E.) seem to have been designed to represent the bull's body, the gut or sinew strings perhaps conceived as a means for a god's voice to be heard. A modern example of a similar idea is the *ngombi* harp of Central Africa, and anthropomorphic or zoomorphic designs are found on many lyres and harps of the ancient Near East and modern Africa (see Figure 4).

Historical records in written form, beginning in the third millennium B.C.E., provide evidence of some of the ways in which musical knowledge was codified and social life stratified in the cities of Egypt, Mesopotamia, and Anatolia. Of particular interest in the records of ancient Egyptian musical culture are the names, titles, and dates of prominent professional musicians and the large number of reliefs and paintings that depict musicians receiving and giving cues with hand signs. Names of specialists in hand clapping and foot stomping were deemed worthy of preservation, but not those of players on such "lesser"

instruments as the double clarinet. Modern historians are able to decipher certain of the hand signs, as the tomb artists apparently wished to represent the production of specific sounds (see Figure 5). Some of the same hand signs are still used in teaching Coptic chant; several other systems for teaching and guiding cantors through hand and head gestures were developed in the ancient Near East, India, Byzantium, and early medieval Europe. Written symbols appear to have been derived from the hand signs in some circumstances, but in others (including Egypt) the value of the gestural code may have made written cues seem unnecessary or undesirable. *See* SIGN LANGUAGE.

The CUNEIFORM writing developed in Mesopotamia was used as early as the mid-second millennium B.C.E. to record an extensive musical terminology in Sumerian and Akkadian, which names the pitches available on stringed instruments (lyres, harps, long-necked lutes), distinguishes several types of performers, and classifies songs according to musical type. One group of song catalogs from Ugarit, using the Akkadian terminology, contains detailed performance instructions that some historians regard as the

Figure 3. *(Music History)*   Wall painting of hunters' dances at Çatal Hüyük, Turkey. From James Mellaart, "Excavations at Çatal Hüyük, 1965. Fourth Preliminary Report," *Anatolian Studies. Journal of the British Institute of Archaeology at Ankara,* vol. 16, plate LXI *(a).*

oldest notated melodies. The use of WRITING to describe tone systems (with reference to stringed instruments) and to classify melodies became a major interest of scholars in West and South Asia, the Mediterranean, and, much later, northern Europe.

Identifying compositions and incantations by name made it possible to record detailed instructions for priests charged with carrying out particular ceremonies, such as the Akkadian RITUAL in which the hide of a newly killed bull was stretched over the temple kettledrum. Texts sometimes carry warnings against possible misuse. The tablets describing the kettledrum ritual are not to be shown to outsiders, and Ashurbanipal's hymn to the sun god concludes with the wish that a musician who disregards or alters the text will find his string playing rejected.

The literature of the ancient Near Eastern civilizations is rich in metaphors that describe and compare various agencies and purposes of musical communication. According to the instructions given by one Egyptian father to his son, singing, dancing, and incense are a god's food. An Akkadian song likens the throat of one newly recovered from illness to a wind instrument and notes that man as musician remains subject to sudden reversals of fortune: "One moment he sings a happy song/And in an instant he will moan like a mourner." Human societies alleviate the impact of such contingencies by prescribing or prohibiting certain genres (laments, praise songs) or behaviors at specific times of year. From the fund of names, metaphors, prescriptions, and prohibitions shared within a civilization or a society (and transmitted in writing and/or speech) historians and ethnographers can reconstruct and interpret that society's theory, poetics, and aesthetics of music.

Early theories of music. Relatively few of the world's five thousand or so languages, however, have one term for a discipline that systematizes several areas of musical knowledge in relation to other disciplines. Ideas developed in the Greek writings on *mousikē* and the Chinese writings on *yue* are of the greatest importance in music history, having been reinterpreted and adapted in many societies for more than two millennia. Although early work in both disciplines may have been indebted to the achievements of Babylonian mathematicians, the theories of *mousikē* and *yue* differ fundamentally in scope, purpose, and method. *See* MUSIC THEORIES—OVERVIEW.

Of major concern in Chinese musical thought were tuned sets of like instruments—detachable bamboo panpipes, bronze bells, and sonorous stones. Early correlations among material sources of sound, positioning of instruments in space, direction of winds, seasons, and DANCE movements were elaborated to serve the needs of ritual and ceremony. Because of their ceremonial uses, shields and battle-axes were classed among the instruments of music in the *Yue chi,* a work of the late Chou period that identified

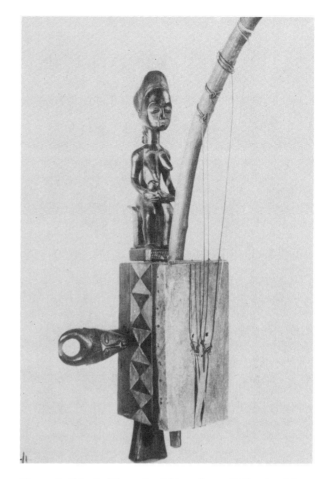

Figure 4. *(Music History)* African harp. Collection Musée de l'Homme, Paris. From Francis Bebey, *African Music: A People's Art,* Westport, Conn.: Lawrence Hill & Company, 1975, p. 118.

the purpose of music as being to harmonize responses from within and stimuli from outside the participants. Experience accumulated over many centuries by tuners of bells and sonorous stones provided a foundation for the subsequent development of theoretical and philosophical reflection, which articulated the need of the empire for accuracy in tuning (*see* MUSIC THEORIES—TUNING SYSTEMS). The Yue Fu (Ministry of Music), established in the second century B.C.E., employed more than one thousand musicians and dancers and supervised not only tuning standards and ceremonial music (including the melodies associated with Confucian POETRY) but also the several musics recognized as "exotic." The breadth of the ministry's responsibilities is perhaps the best indication of the scope of the Chinese concept of *yue* at the end of the first millennium B.C.E. *See* EAST ASIA, ANCIENT.

Metaphors that describe the singer as a divinely inspired artisan whose verses resemble well-built wagons occur in the poetry of several Indo-European peoples, as do formulaic expressions for the "imperishable glory" of heroes celebrated in song. In

Figure 5. *(Music History)* The Egyptian harpist Hekenu plays a fifth in response to a sign from the singer Iti. Relief from the tomb of Saqqarah. Egypt, fifth dynasty (2563–2423 B.C.E.). From Hans Hickmann, *Ägypten. Musikgeschichte in Bildern*, vol. 2, *Musik des Altertums*, Leipzig: VEB Deutscher Verlag für Musik, p. 143, plate 116.

addition to the verbal roots *tek's ("to build") and *kleu- ("to hear," "renowned"), two other reconstructed proto-Indo-European roots are of fundamental importance in the history of musical terminology: *ar- ("orderly arrangement") and *med- ("to measure by a tried-and-true standard"). Knowledge of ordering and measuring—given by the muses or *gāndharvas* to singers, instrumentalists, and dancers—was eventually codified in Greek writings on *mousikē* and Sanskrit treatises on *gāndharva* (later *sangīta*). Both theoretical traditions center on problems of "composing" a coherent whole by properly fitting together the several parts—pitches, units of duration, words. Musical communication is conceived mainly in terms of "voices," including instrumental analogues and extensions of human voices.

The Greek discipline of *mousikē*—and traditions developed with reference to ancient Greek thought in the Arab empires and the Latin West—had several divisions and subdivisions, classified in various ways. According to Aristoxenus (fourth century B.C.E.), a musician must know the sciences of harmonics, rhythmics, metrics, and organics (dealing with instruments). It was the intensive Greek concern with harmonics that most decisively shaped the subse-

quent music history of the Near East and Europe. Conceived as the primary and fundamental branch of musical knowledge, harmonics analyzed and enumerated—in the abstract—the elements of melody and their "harmonious" combinations. Rhythmics and metrics were similarly founded on analysis of parts and enumeration or description of appropriate combinations. The premise that musical knowledge is abstract as well as analytic is apparent in Aristoxenus's claim that "the essence and order of harmony depend not upon any of the properties of instruments." Through experience with lyres and other stringed instruments Greek theorists created a general science of harmonics, and the enduring distinction between theoretical and practical music corresponded to that between intellectual and manual labor.

The social and cultural role of music. No less enduring in European musical culture are the controversies, first recorded in the fifth century B.C.E., concerning the ethical power of music and the musical education appropriate to the freeborn. New versions of PLATO's question How may music become or remain an imitation of the manners of good men? have been debated in the most varied social circumstances, often marked (as in Plato's day) by conflicts between older and newer values.

The music history of every civilization involves changing relationships among practitioners of several arts and disciplines. Ritual, ceremony, dance, DRAMA, SPORTS, storytelling, and speech draw upon musical as well as nonmusical resources. The exercise of spiritual and temporal authority carries responsibilities for managing these resources, and the responsibilities themselves no less than the manner and circumstances in which they are met remain subject to change. Efforts to manage musical resources have created the documents and other sources of evidence that historians of music must interpret.

Some musical cultures have developed around the one or two types of instruments controlled by the ruling class and representing its authority. The advanced bronze-casting techniques of the Southeast Asian Dông Son culture (ca. 300 B.C.E.) produced large gongs in the shape of kettledrums (see Figure 6). These gongs may have been suspended and struck at the center by the player's right hand, at the rim by his left hand. Although some scholars now regard the kettledrum-shaped gongs as the prototype of numerous (forged rather than cast) gongs used in Southeast Asian ensembles, they have more in common with the suspended gongs of present-day ensembles than with gongs that are laid in a row. Of the thousands of different gamelan ensembles in Java and Bali, those with fewer and larger instruments are presumed to be older than those with a greater variety of smaller instruments in sets. The more elaborate court ensembles have also been simplified in villages.

Management of musical resources may give priority not to instrumental ensembles but to oral transmission and reproduction of a sacred Word. Provisions for recitation or cantillation of canonical texts in Jewish, Hindu, Buddhist, Christian, and Muslim religious life have allowed for various types and degrees of specialization, often thought to be independent of other musical and quasi-musical disciplines (particularly those associated with secular powers). At the center of many varieties of religious experience is the devotee's obligation to hear and repeat the sacred Word, to listen and then respond. Ideally the reciter is no less attentive than were the sages who received the Vedas from the god Brahma or the prophet Muhammad to whom the angel Gabriel revealed the Qur'an. Each of the great world religions has also nourished numerous genres (see GENRE) of nonliturgical or popular devotional music, many of them designed to create or strengthen links among different localities, milieus, classes, and castes. Musical behavior is vital to maintaining the bonds that join "little traditions" to a "great tradition," villages to temples and courts. See RELIGION.

At opposite ends of the Eurasian continent the organization and transmission of musical resources, concepts, and genres was profoundly affected by policies adopted in early medieval empires. What is perhaps the oldest secular repertoire of court music to survive in notation comprises about 130 pieces, preserved as a result of Japanese interest in Chinese court entertainment during the Tang dynasty (618–906). The entertainment of the cosmopolitan Tang court was organized around ten ensembles of musicians and dancers, named after genres (banquet mu-

Figure 6. *(Music History)* Kettledrum from the Dông Son culture, Thanh Hóa province, Vietnam. From Paul Collaer, *Südostasien. Musikgeschichte in Bildern,* vol. 1, *Musikethnologie,* Leipzig: VEB Deutscher Verlag für Musik, p. 11, plate 3.

sic, indigenous popular music) and regions (Korea; India and Indochina; the frontier town of Liang-chou; the oases of Turfan, Kucha, and Kashgar; and the Persian city-states of Samarkand and Bukhara). Although instruments, performers, and genres had long been exchanged as tribute or captured as spoils of war, the vast scope of Tang court entertainment was unprecedented. Among the more important consequences of the Tang cultivation of court music were the development of long orchestral suites with appropriate choreography and the elaboration of the tablature notations that enabled Japanese court musicians to learn and preserve portions of the Tang repertoire.

In Europe the policies of the Frankish king Pepin (752–768) and his son Charlemagne (768–814) conferred a new importance on plainchant, through efforts to standardize the liturgy and to propagate a "correct" melodic practice. Stabilization of the repertoire was furthered as the Carolingian clergy classified melodies according to a system of eight modes adopted from Byzantine sources and as models for oral performance were made available in notation.

Convergence and differentiation. Such cultural achievements as the cosmopolitan entertainment of the Tang court and the western European repertoire of plainchant result from countless acts of compromise among interested parties, including, of course, musicians as well as the temporal and spiritual authorities to whom they are subject. At the very heart of musical behavior lie capacities for synthesizing and reconciling impulses and ideas from many sources. As Béla Bartók and many other scholars have shown, "well assimilated foreign impulses" are no less evident in distinctive peasant idioms than in the musical legacies of courts and empires. Whatever their social status (generally higher for bards and skilled singers, lower for most instrumentalists and slaves), musicians have commonly acted as mediators between different milieus and behavioral norms—a role that has often entailed an itinerant way of life. In many situations, such as the singing contests held in various parts of medieval Eurasia, musicians have been expected to adapt rapidly to the unforeseen, to improvise responses. Whether diffused by word of mouth, in writing, or through the publicity mechanisms of the twentieth century, stories recounting the travels and exploits of exemplary figures have guided the conduct of a majority of musicians.

Music history over the long term involves the gradual working out of possibilities made available by cultural contact and conflict. As the great fourteenth-century historian Ibn Khaldūn observed, strong dynasties create the largest markets for sophisticated crafts, attracting musicians from less prosperous regions. Thus in the first three centuries of Islam, carriers of Persian, Arab, and other traditions came into close contact at the Umayyad and early 'Abbasid courts. Competition between "conservative" and "innovative" singers added to the luster of the ninth-century 'Abbasid court, but the ideal of synthesizing Persian and Arab practices may not have been realized until the thirteenth century, almost at the end of the long decline in the power of the 'Abbasid caliphate. Codification of a unified modal system by the thirteenth-century theorist Ṣafī od-Dīn formed a great bridge between ancient and modern musical theory in the Near East. The tendency of Near Eastern court music idioms toward "universality" has been complemented by strongly marked local differences in folk and popular music. Contact with the musical practices of various mystical brotherhoods and sects (many of them shaped by ideals of courtly behavior) enriched the court idioms of Ottoman Turkey and Safavid Persia beginning in the sixteenth century.

A very different history of exchange among regional musical practices is that of the hundreds of THEATER styles that have flourished in small districts or in large areas of China from the thirteenth century to the present. It is a history in which stylistic fusion and integration have been constantly offset by divergence and differentiation and in which court patronage has remained relatively unimportant. Many regional traditions of instrumental ensemble music, cultivated by amateurs, have centered on the elaboration of models drawn from vocal repertoires.

Polyphonic music in Europe. The development of multipart (or polyphonic) music in Europe over the past millennium required the efforts of successive generations of composers to solve technical problems born of various confrontations—including those between the melodic linearity of Mediterranean idioms and a northern emphasis on strong vertical sonorities; between the resources of Latin and the Romance languages, of German, and of many instrumental idioms; and between the regular stress patterns of dance music and melodic energies that resist rhythmic periodization. The eventual emergence of a strong historical consciousness among European musicians was inevitable, given the long-standing interest in "perfecting" the techniques of composition and achieving a greater control of musical resources. At several points in the history of polyphonic composition conceptions of "artificial" or "learned" music were challenged and ultimately enriched by appeals to various ideas of "natural" or "popular" music. In the polyphonic music cultures of late medieval, RENAISSANCE, and modern Europe the composer played the decisive role in directing the behavior of performers, who served as the composer's "instruments." Institutions of fundamental importance to the cultivation of polyphonic music were the chapel (salaried performers attached to a court, household, or church) and the academy (an association devoted to one or more of the arts and sciences).

From the Renaissance on, the art of composition grew closer to the art of RHETORIC. Like a speech or a CONVERSATION, a polyphonic composition had one or more "subjects" or "themes," and the composition was structured as a vehicle of expression. Beginning in the seventeenth century the techniques of polyphonic composition were differentiated by circumstances of performance, as church, chamber, and theater styles, and innovations in each of the latter two styles affected the others. The vitality of the more public forms of performance in the eighteenth and early nineteenth centuries was nourished by vigorous traditions of chamber music and domestic performance, allowing amateurs and connoisseurs to acquire and exercise the knowledge on which appreciation of polyphonic music depends.

Music-historical consciousness. The many instruments, channels, and levels of musical communication permit musicians to meet responsibilities toward their predecessors, their contemporaries, and themselves as individuals. Names of regional styles (in China) and names of composers and genres (in Europe) serve as "handles" that help musicians to grasp certain of their more important obligations in specific sociohistorical contexts. Another technique for binding present to past practitioners is the practice (highly developed in South Asia) of naming the chains of masters and pupils that constitute the "legitimate" lines of transmission. Still another mode of historical consciousness is apparent in the West African oral traditions that link particular instruments, ensembles, genres, and singing styles to political events of the past three or four centuries.

Reconstruction of many music histories has become a major task of twentieth-century musical scholarship. It is open to question whether or not this effort might lead to a unified "general history of music"—a project first attempted by late-eighteenth-century European writers such as Johann Nikolaus Forkel, Charles Burney, and John Hawkins. In contrast to the late-eighteenth-century historians we cannot interpret the history of "world music" as the history of one discipline. Countless arts and disciplines include "knowledge of moving well" to produce and reproduce sounds, and much of this knowledge is necessarily transmitted through person-to-person contact (using handles of many different kinds to activate the musical memory).

Modern music history, extending over the five centuries during which nearly all the world's peoples have been affected by European expansion and capitalist commercialization, is a history of extensive and intensive contacts and conflicts between peoples and between social classes. Challenges to human control of the instruments of musical communication

have occurred at an ever-increasing rate in most parts of the world. The transformation of African musical resources and concepts in the Americas may stand as the most significant development in the music history of the modern world, inasmuch as peoples of African descent in the Western Hemisphere have successfully retained, adapted, and synthesized so many modes of "moving well." The most urgent task for music historians at present is identification and evaluation of the strategies that have allowed many of the world's peoples to find solidarity and satisfaction through musical communication.

See also ETHNOMUSICOLOGY; MUSIC, FOLK AND TRADITIONAL; MUSIC, POPULAR.

Bibliography. Béla Bartók, *Essays,* ed. by Benjamin Suchoff, New York and London, 1976; Heinrich Besseler and Max Schneider, *Musikgeschichte in Bildern,* Leipzig, 1961–; Carl Dahlhaus, ed., *Neues Handbuch der Musikwissenschaft,* Wiesbaden, FRG, 1980–; Johann Nikolaus Forkel, *Allgemeine Geschichte der Musik,* Leipzig, 1788–1801, reprint Graz, Austria, 1967; Thrasybulos Georgiades, *Musik und Sprache,* Berlin, 1954; Erich M. von Hornbostel, *Opera Omnia,* ed. by Klaus P. Wachsmann, Dieter Christensen, and Hans-Peter Reinecke, The Hague, 1975–; Paul Henry Lang, *Music in Western Civilization,* New York, 1941; Bruno Nettl, *The Western Impact on World Music,* New York, 1985; J. H. K. Nketia, *The Music of Africa,* New York, 1974; L. E. R. Picken, ed., *Musica Asiatica,* London, 1977–; Gilbert Rouget, *La musique et la transe* (Music and Trance, trans. by Derek Coltman, Chicago, 1985), Paris, 1980; Curt Sachs, *The Wellsprings of Music,* ed. by Jaap Kunst, The Hague, 1961; Stanley Sadie, ed., *The New Grove Dictionary of Music and Musicians,* London, 1980; André Schaeffner, *Origine des instruments de musique* (1936), 2d ed., Paris and New York, 1980; William Oliver Strunk, comp., *Source Readings in Music History from Classical Antiquity through the Romantic Era,* New York, 1950; Bence Szabolcsi, *A History of Melody* (A melódia története, 2d ed.), trans. by Cynthia Jolly and Sara Karig, London, 1965; Klaus P. Wachsmann, ed., *Essays on Music and History in Africa,* Evanston, Ill., 1971; Max Weber, *Die rationalen und soziologischen Grundlagen der Musik,* Munich, 1921; Walter Wiora, *Die vier Weltalter der Musik* (The Four Ages of Music, trans. by M. D. Herter Norton, New York, 1965), Stuttgart, 1961.

STEPHEN BLUM

MUSIC MACHINES

There is a long history of human fascination with mechanical methods of creating sounds, particularly musical sounds. Records indicate that the Greeks perfected one of the earliest pipe organs, and by 1500 C.E. a number of automatic flute players and other mechanical curiosities were known in Europe.

During the industrial age, however, the manufacture of mechanical, self-playing MUSICAL INSTRUMENTS flourished. Between 1850 and 1925 there existed a very active market for various types of music machines designed for use in the home or in public places such as movie theaters, dance halls, and fairgrounds. Factories in the United States and Europe were able to mass-produce many types at affordable prices.

The earliest self-playing music machines were music boxes built in Switzerland and Germany around 1800; they played melodies by means of a steel comb brushing against pins on a rotating brass cylinder. Another form of music box using a large metal disc was developed in Germany around 1890 and soon swept the market because of its superior sound quality and the interchangeability of its program discs. In the United States the Regina company of Rahway, New Jersey, became the best-known U.S. manufacturer of disc music boxes. At the pinnacle of popularity, between 1892 and World War I, the Regina company offered machines with discs that could reproduce seven octaves and play for three minutes. A popular refinement was an automatic disc changer that could hold twelve discs, an idea later applied to the phonograph juke box.

Another popular music machine was the player piano, which employed a perforated roll of paper and a pneumatic mechanism to play music automatically on a piano (see Figure 1). The roll represented a piece of music, and each perforation represented a note to be played. A variation of the player piano was the reproducing piano, designed to reproduce not only the notes recorded on a paper roll but other characteristics of a performance as well. The actual touch of the performer could be reproduced to simulate the pressure applied to individual keys, the loudness of the notes, and other nuances. Ampico, Duo-Art, and Welte made reproducing pianos in the United States. The popularity of these machines was made possible by the availability of recordings of piano performances by major artists of the day.

Orchestrions were machines designed to imitate the sounds of a live orchestra. Most contained either a piano or a pipe organ as the primary voicing instrument, plus a wide variety of additional instruments such as xylophones, drums, cymbals, triangles, and mandolins. Orchestrions could be designed to play dance-hall numbers or entire symphonies, and during the height of their popularity dozens of companies in Europe and the United States were making orchestrions. While the earliest machines of this sort date back to the eighteenth century, they became most popular toward the end of the nineteenth century, when they could be mass-produced with pneumatic mechanisms and programmed by paper rolls. Prominent manufacturers included Hupfeld, Imhof

Figure 1. *(Music Machines)* Player piano-harmonium: Gally's autophone or self-playing musical instrument. The Bettmann Archive, Inc.

and Mukle, and Welte. Early motion picture theaters were sometimes equipped with a type of orchestrion called a photoplayer to provide music during a film. These machines could be designed to blend into the decor of a movie house and were placed in a visible location. Three U.S. companies dominated this short-lived market: Seeburg, Wurlitzer, and American Photo Player.

Another pneumatically operated machine applied the idea of the player piano to the violin. Called a violin player, it was programmed with paper rolls and usually employed a rotating horsehair bow to activate the strings (see Figure 2). The machines could have as many as three instruments; some were designed to combine a violin with another instrument such as a piano, cello, or xylophone. Prominent makers included the Mills Novelty Company and Hupfeld.

Although self-playing music machines had won considerable popularity, they were totally eclipsed by their descendants, a host of inventions offering an ever-growing range of experiences. The new inventions included the phonograph and the numerous

Figure 2. *(Music Machines)* The Violano-Virtuoso, ▷ made for the Smithsonian Institution in 1914 by Mills Novelty Company, Chicago. Smithsonian Institution, Washington, D.C. Photo no. 77,366.

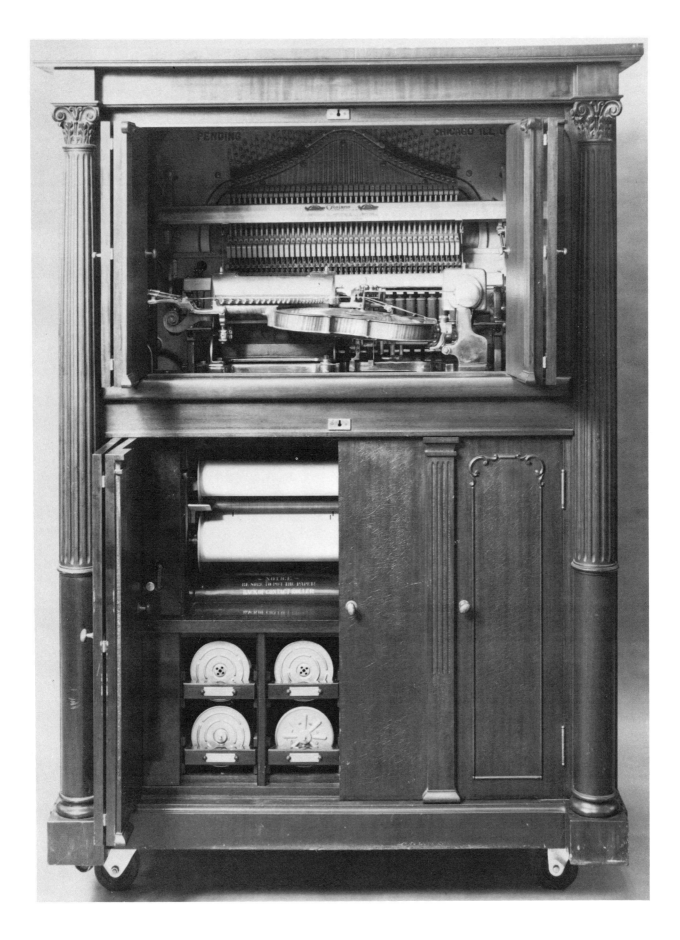

other products of SOUND RECORDING; broadcasting and its ramifications, including television; and the new specialized technologies that were developed in the field of ELECTRONIC MUSIC.

Bibliography. Q. David Bowers, *Encyclopedia of Automatic Musical Instruments,* New York, 1972; Pierre Schaeffer, *Traité des objets musicaux,* Paris, 1966.

THOMAS B. HOLMES

MUSIC PERCEPTION. *See* PERCEPTION—MUSIC.

MUSIC PERFORMANCE

The concept of PERFORMANCE practice *(Aufführungspraxis)* developed by musicologists has traditionally been limited to attempting to reconstruct the original SOUND of early European music by focusing on the written piece of music and by studying all sorts of literary, historical, and iconographic sources. The quest for historically authentic accounts of sound reproduction of early music led scholars to neglect or even to deny the role of performance contexts in modifying essential elements of a piece of music. Ethnomusicologists dealing primarily with non-Western or folk musics inherited the shortcomings of such an approach, limiting their study of performance to the idiosyncratic qualities of vocal and instrumental sound production in a given culture and in general applying Western concepts of sound *(see* ETHNOMUSICOLOGY; MUSIC, FOLK AND TRADITIONAL). Such studies, therefore, favored the musical text itself, whereas performance, like other aspects of context, was considered a secondary line of research, whether musical or extramusical.

Historians of western European music have traditionally considered the study of music performance as one way of interpreting early music (primarily prior to 1800) based on examples of written notation *(see* MUSIC HISTORY). The interpretations deal with speculation about the use of instruments in the performance of medieval music *(see* MUSICAL INSTRUMENTS), the intonation and tuning of early instruments, the proper execution of ornaments, thoroughbass, dynamics, and tempo, as well as the size of performing ensembles in music of the sixteenth to the eighteenth century. Although early music notations lack specificity because the oral tradition of performance was taken for granted, notations since about the mid-eighteenth century are generally considered more indicative of performance. However, problems of performance interpretation for nineteenth- and twentieth-century music remain, since notation, however specific, cannot fully explain all details of sound production. In folk, nonliterate, and urban popular cultures music exists more obviously in performance,

because notation as a prescriptive device of performance is absent or less related to the overall acoustic manifestation of the piece *(see* MUSIC, POPULAR). In the latter case the use of sheet music, lead sheets, chord charts, or "fake books" generally provides less performance prescription than the conventional score of art music (with the exception of aleatory, AVANT-GARDE, and experimental composition in twentieth-century music). However, behind all notational systems rests a dynamic oral tradition of performance subject to change in time and space. *See* MUSIC THEORIES—NOTATIONS AND LITERACY, TUNING SYSTEMS; ORAL CULTURE.

Most traditional notational systems have developed toward a higher degree of detail and precision in the visual indication of how sounds are to be produced. As expressed by Charles Seeger, the prescriptive method and use of music writing in the western European tradition "does not tell us as much about how music sounds as how to make it sound" and remains a subjective operation, allowing a relative margin of freedom of interpretation, particularly regarding timbre, tempo, phrasing, melodic articulation, and dynamics *(see* MUSIC COMPOSITION AND IMPROVISATION). To a great extent, notational ambiguities have represented the point of departure of creativity on the part of performers in their idiosyncratic understanding and rendition of a piece of music. In the twentieth century particularly, performer and audience interaction has consisted essentially in the fascination of listeners for the display of virtuosity and the reverence for special interpretive qualities of a given piece of music or style. The obvious fact that the audience plays an important part in the performance occasion has not been readily recognized because, as Roger Abrahams explained, "we come at performance from our highly Western sophisticated artistic conceptions, which have focused for so long on the virtuosic dimension of performance: the means by which the performer himself stuns everybody within the performance environment into silence."

The emphasis on sound-structure phenomena and the search for historical authenticity of sound production have thus limited the desirable broader conceptualization of performance. An all-inclusive approach to the study of performance must consider the various contextual factors affecting performance, the actual musical and extramusical behavior of participants (performers and audience), and the rules or codes of performance defined by the community for a specific context or occasion. As an organizing principle musical performance ends up being viewed as an event and a process fully integrated into the field of musical action as NONVERBAL COMMUNICATION.

Several concepts of the nature of performance articulated by anthropologist Milton Singer, folklorists

Abrahams and Richard Bauman, and ethnomusicologists Norma McLeod and Marcia Herndon have affected recent studies of music in and as performance. Singer defines the actual structure of what he calls "cultural performance" as consisting of "a definitely limited time span, or, at least, a beginning and an end, an organized program of activity, a set of performers, an audience and a place and occasion of performance." In addition Singer sees cultural performances as portions of activity thought by the members of a social group to be encapsulations of their culture "which they could exhibit to visitors and to themselves." Abrahams coined the term *pure performance* to name an "intensified (or stylized) behavioral system," including "an occasion, a time, places, codes, and patterns of expectation." Bauman suggests very pertinently the kind of "interpretive frame performance establishes or represents" and provides useful answers to the question "How is communication that constitutes performance to be interpreted?" For this purpose he discusses the patterning of performance in genres (*see* GENRE), roles, acts, and events and develops, with Abrahams, the concept of the "emergent quality of performance" and that of performance as a "display of communicative competence." Both advocate viewing the nature of performance as culture- and community-specific and the role of the folklorist and the ethnomusicologist in the study of performance as consisting primarily in elucidating ethnographically the extent of the domain of performance in a given community. Bauman sees performance as offering to the participants "a special enhancement of experience, bringing with it a heightened intensity of communicative interaction which binds the audience to the performer in a way that is specific to performance as a mode of communication" and that is part of the essence of performance. McLeod uses the term *musical occasion* in a contextual sense, that is, as a cultural performance of music. From her study of musical occasions on the Pacific island of Tikopia, she concluded that "there is a clear relationship between what we would call content, that is the performance item, and context, the occasion. As the general social texture of an occasion becomes thicker—with more forms of social structural principles present—music becomes more ordered."

At both social and musical levels of analysis, performance surely allows a clear view of the interplay of content and context. *Content* is understood here primarily as specific bodies of music with definable and identifiable styles. Prescribed sets of behavioral rules and dogmas determined by secular or sacred contexts frequently dictate the actual organization and internal contents of a given musical performance. The context itself in such cases calls for a more or less strict observance of performance contents. For example, in the Afro-Brazilian religious rituals known as *candomblé* in northeast Brazil, the sequence of songs and drum rhythms follows rigorously the specific progression of liturgical gestures related to the presence of certain gods within a specific ceremony, the ultimate RITUAL objectives of that ceremony, and the actual choreographed reenactment of certain myths to which pertinent SONG texts allude. The importance of the ritual sequence is thus paramount in the determination of the structure and contents of the music performance. Likewise the actual musical contents of, for example, a shamanic performance among numerous Native American cultures are determined by the specific purpose and nature of the performance (rites of puberty, therapy and curing, or the cult of the ancestors), the invocation of spirits or gods by natural or artificial means, the vision and eventual presence of such spirits, the interaction of the shaman as the main musical actor/performer with the spirits, and the like. Practices of performance, therefore, result from the relationship of context and content and involve numerous levels of possible analysis that reveal the multidimensionality of music.

The interactions between performers and audiences reflect the various meanings assigned to the performance event and process. The event itself dictates certain general expectations fashioned by tradition on the part of both performers and audiences. But the actual fulfillment of expectations depends on the specific elements present in a given performance occasion, some of which may be unpredictable. The ways nonmusical elements influence the musical outcome of a performance constitute an important part in assigning meanings to the various components of that performance. The various signs and symbols operating in the performer-audience interaction are subjected to collective and individual interpretation. Collective expectations and interpretations represent, to a great extent, the whole complex of conventions associated with a performance situation, such as "respectful" silence during the performance of an art-music composition in the western European great tradition, contrasted with "enthusiastic" applause at the end of the piece, or, conversely, the tradition of *gritos* ("shouts") during the performance of Mexican mariachi and other music genres as indications of approval and enjoyment. Audience expectations are also determined and conventionalized through the actual performance space, a significant part of the context itself, in that the nature of that space frequently determines and symbolizes types of behavior in terms of audience participation. The meanings of these various processes of interaction should be elicited primarily from the various ethnic views and evaluations of any musical situation.

Thus performance must be viewed as the occasion and event that fosters through social interaction and participation the collective consciousness and affirmation of group identity or ethnicity as well as the significant differences in musical styles and contents of songs that may exist within the stratified structure of the social group. It functions as a driving, crystallizing force in the enacting display of a given social group's AESTHETICS, that is, the value systems that validate the group's ethos. In addition music performance partakes of the system of symbols that is at the basis of cultural expression and appears fully integrated within that expression. In sum the process of performance is a central facet of musical communication. It brings together the historical and ethnographic concern with music as the enactment of prescriptions, plans, scores by specific social actors, and the sociological and psychological concern with modes of social participation that validate, reflect upon, and animate the interpretation of musical texts, styles, and genres.

See also MUSIC THEATER.

Bibliography. Richard Bauman, "Verbal Art as Performance," *American Anthropologist* 77 (1975): 290–311; Gerard Béhague, ed., *Performance Practice*, Westport, Conn., 1984; Marcia Herndon and Roger Brunyate, eds., *Symposium on Form in Performance: Hard-Core Ethnography* (Proceedings, University of Texas at Austin, April 17–19, 1975), Austin, Tex., 1975; Norma McLeod and Marcia Herndon, eds., *The Ethnography of Musical Performance*, Darby, Pa., 1979; Charles Seeger, *Studies in Musicology, 1935–1975*, Berkeley, Calif., 1977; Milton Singer, "The Cultural Pattern of Indian Civilization," *Journal of Asian Studies* (formerly *The Far Eastern Quarterly*, 1941–1956) 15 (1955): 23–36.

GERARD HENRI BÉHAGUE

MUSIC THEATER

This entry consists of two articles:
1. Western Traditions
2. Asian Traditions

1. WESTERN TRADITIONS

Since it is generally agreed that the dithyramb—a choral hymn in honor of Dionysus—was the wellspring of Greek DRAMA, it is clear that music and THEATER went hand in hand from the beginnings of drama in the West as they did elsewhere (see section 2, below). Of course, the hymn had words as well as music, so that dialogue, POETRY, and all other literary aspects that later came to dominate most plays stemmed in essentially equal measure from the same roots. As a rule, with notable exceptions to be discussed, although the story and poetry of a play—

its verbal aspects—soon attained a certain primacy, plays were rarely performed without some musical background or interludes until very recent times. Greek drama and COMEDY included not only choral odes but solo songs as well. Moreover, there was dancing in the plays, performed to appropriate music. Nevertheless, virtually from the start, there has been a feeling that the association of music and drama was not necessarily for the best. Music has been thought to distract from, cheapen, or in other ways vitiate the highest effects of good drama. Thus even the Greeks, who were aware of music's seminal importance to the drama, sometimes seemed to question the need for it in dramatic productions.

Early history. Livy suggested that Roman drama evolved out of SONG, but the Etruscan songs he referred to seem to have led rather to street shows, antecedents of later commedia dell'arte and punchinello entertainments. The extant canon of Roman TRAGEDY and comedy was modeled largely on Greek works. Roman tragedies retained the choral odes that had been a feature of Greek dramas, but their employment appears perfunctory and traditional. On the other hand, Plautus's comedies were rich in song and DANCE, often remarkably well integrated into the texts. Terence was more reserved, retreating conspicuously in his use of musical embellishments.

The theater of the late ROMAN EMPIRE and the early MIDDLE AGES consisted mainly of occasional bands of wandering entertainers who apparently presented songs, dances, magic acts, and other routines. The first signs of a theatrical renaissance, in which, once again, music played a crucial role, occurred when some musical elaborations were permitted in the Alleluia sequences in the celebration of the mass. By the ninth century musical embellishments had been added to other chants, and, more significantly, words were added to the music. These "worded" elaborations were called tropes. In time the tropes grew so lengthy and imposing that they put a strain on the mass, were cut from the service proper, and were banished from the church.

Two major changes were effected coincidentally, both significantly propelling the development of subsequent theater. First of all, freed from the mass, these short scenes were also freed from the necessity of employing church Latin. Vernacular speech was adopted, immediately making these sketches far more accessible to lay audiences. Moreover, the lines were no longer chanted. Music, the foundation of the new plays, was once again ripped away, so that it was no longer an integral part of the theatrical experience but served solely as an occasional ornament. The practice continued when medieval craft guilds took over the production of the plays (by then developing into extended cycles). Something of a festive holiday air crept into the presentation, with each playlet in a cycle being paraded from station to station in its city. That festive atmosphere—colorful costumes, brightly decorated pageant wagons, streets bedecked with flags and bunting—was consistent with the introduction of lighthearted songs and dances, and worldly rather than religious subjects became the rule.

The standard theater of Elizabethan and Jacobean times employed music for occasional flourishes as punctuation and momentary coloring. Songs were rarely injected into tragedies, much more frequently into comedies. These songs were generally solos with only the barest instrumental accompaniment. The masque, a form largely confined to court circles, was much more prodigal in its employment of music, using it throughout to underscore spectacle and pantomime passages as well as in choral and recitative passages (see Figure 1). In France the Senecan dramas of Robert Garnier established the fundamental pattern for Parisian theater that would be adhered to by seventeenth-century masters such as Pierre Corneille and Jean Racine. Here again comedy was far more generous in its use of song, and the music was never a truly integral part of the entertainment. In Italy during the same period, however, a conscious attempt was made by the Florentine Camerata "to reproduce as far as possible the combination of words and music which together made up the Greek theatre." The result marks the beginning of OPERA.

The spread of opera throughout Europe, and with it the need for a good-sized theatrical orchestra, coincided with the establishment of the proscenium arch and the development of a basic theatrical ARCHITECTURE that remained dominant until very recent times. Increasingly the auditoriums built during this period incorporated an orchestra pit in front of and just below the stage apron. The musicians who occupied the pit provided overtures, entr'actes, and incidental musical moments that were not necessarily related to the works being presented but were designed to amuse and pacify the often unruly audiences of the era. How long this practice persisted could be seen when in 1802 a U.S. magazine asked, "What would be Shakespeare's astonishment . . . to hear from the orchestra immediately after his inimitable dagger scene, the mysterious solemn strains of Yankee Doodle to please the gallery? Or after the mournful death of his Desdemona, a horn pipe or a country dance?" Orchestras resisted demands for this kind of musical entertainment at their own peril, sometimes being pelted or otherwise physically attacked for their stubbornness.

Ballad operas. Comedies and to a much lesser extent tragedies continued to insert musical numbers,

Figure 1. *(Music Theater—Western Traditions)* Inigo Jones, *Design for a Court Masque; Scene V. A Great City: In the Sky the Clouds with Deities.* Devonshire Collection, Chatsworth. Reproduced by permission of the Chatsworth Settlement Trustees, and the Courtauld Institute of Art, London.

and by the eighteenth century early genres of nonoperatic musical plays had begun to appear. In England these works were called *ballad operas*. The classic example, although it is not truly typical, is John Gay's *The Beggar's Opera* (1728). As a rule these ballad operas, especially at first, did not use original musical material but instead provided new and appropriate lyrics to be set to familiar airs. But within a short while composers were enlisted to write original scores for the librettos. From the start most composers attempted to write music reflecting the sentiments expressed in the lyrics. Complaints soon sprang up that the completed songs had little relationship to the mood or the story, whatever relationship the music of the song bore to its lyric. While such clumsy lack of integration mattered little to audiences out for an evening's entertainment, it bothered more discriminating playgoers, commentators, and writers. Thus by 1824 William Dimond in his preface to his *Native Land; or, The Return from Slavery* (for which Henry Rowley Bishop composed the music) observed, "[T]he MUSICAL SITUATIONS ought to spring with spontaneity out of the very necessities of the Scene; never betraying themselves to be labored introductions for the mere purpose of exhibiting vocal talent, but always to appear so many integral portions and indispensable continuations of the Story."

In many places in the early years of the nineteenth century, ballad operas, operas, and some other forms of musical theater were frequently presented not in auditoriums reserved exclusively for lyric theater but rather along with the dramas and comedies that were part of the regular repertoire of stock companies. This was readily achieved because, as mentioned, most theaters by then retained their own orchestras and because players in such ensembles were expected to "double in brass," demonstrating skill not only as actors but also as singers or sometimes even as dancers.

Melodramas. The same epoch witnessed the startlingly rapid rise and flourishing of another theatrical GENRE, one whose very name seemed to suggest the interaction between music and story: *melodrama*. In part melodrama arose as a response to the austerities and often rigid formalities of eighteenth-century CLASSICISM and to a theater that for all its excursions into bombast remained devoted to an artificial order and decorum. But in at least equal measure melodrama reflected heightened class distinctions in an era of industrial and social revolution. In England and in most important Continental theatrical capitals the few established playhouses enjoyed monopolies in exchange for a system of government licensing and control. With the growth of the population, especially in large cities, these theaters were unable to satisfy the growing demand for entertainment and in some instances were loath to offer the more bois-

terous diversions clearly favored by lower-class playgoers. As a result new, at first unlicensed, playhouses sprang up. However, they too soon came under some control: they were prohibited early on from presenting traditional plays and were confined to song and dance. They very quickly framed their musical numbers with stories, but to obey the letter of the law these so-called illegitimate theaters continued to emphasize the musical aspects of their performances.

In England, even as strictures were eased, the lord chamberlain still insisted that these pieces include no fewer than five songs. All such works were swept up loosely into a class known as burletta. In France a similar history gave rise to the comparable stage form of vaudeville. Although burletta, vaudeville, and other such genres came to be perceived as essentially lighthearted, another less playful branch developed simultaneously and soon monopolized the term melodrama. These plays had themes that purported to be more serious, often centering on blackguards' attempts to violate a maiden's purity. Such plays regularly featured spectacular scenes—a shipwreck, a fall from great heights, a burning building. Blaring musical passages served not merely to heighten the dramatic intensity of these moments but at the same time to cover up the noises made by the numerous stagehands working such effects (see Figure 2). While songs in serious dramas and even in comedies became fewer, a full musical accompaniment remained a part of melodrama into the early years of the twentieth century.

Almost inevitably, however, the popularity of ballad operas and other early forms of musical plays, the popularity of songs in legitimate dramas and comedies, and the requirement that songs be a part of any play in other theaters encouraged entertainments in which musical interest predominated. Several major genres emerged as a result: operetta, musical comedy, and the revue.

Operetta. At the risk of oversimplification this popular genre can be seen to have developed out of the traditions that had spawned such light operas as Charles-Simon Favart's *La chercheuse d'esprit* (1741), Daniel-Esprit Auber's *Fra Diavolo* (1830), and Adolphe Adam's *Le postillon de Longjumeau* (1836). Although the examples are French, similar ones could be culled from Italian, German, English, and other stages. However, it was in France that what can be accepted as the first modern operettas were created.

The earliest important pieces, mostly short works, were by Florimond Ronger, who wrote under the name Hervé. Despite Hervé's popularity in France, it was his contemporary, Jacques Offenbach, who composed full-length works that quickly attained international celebrity and are revived around the world to this day. His operettas are melodic, superbly orchestrated entertainments with richly comic libret-

Figure 2. *(Music Theater—Western Traditions)* The earthquake scene from *The Hope*, Drury Lane, 1911. The Mander and Mitchenson Theatre Collection.

tos. That much of the librettos' humor is based on local themes did not prevent the works from being received with acclaim outside France, for Offenbach's hummable songs gave the operettas instant vogue. Among his masterpieces are *Orphée aux enfers* (1858), *La belle Hélène* (1864), *La vie Parisienne* (1866; Figure 3), and *La grand-duchesse de Gérolstein* (1867). The early Viennese operetta is best represented by Franz von Suppé. His now-forgotten *Fatinitza* (1876) won worldwide acceptance, although he is better remembered today for *Die schöne Galatea (Galathée)* (1865) and *Boccaccio* (1879). Probably the most artistically well crafted of all comic operas are those by Gilbert and Sullivan. Their best works included *H.M.S. Pinafore* (1878), *The Pirates of Penzance* (1879; Figure 4), and *The Mikado* (1885). W. S. Gilbert's precise, brittle, often devastating wit has not translated well, but Arthur Sullivan's music has given these comic operas global recognition. His music was more varied than that of most of his predecessors but perhaps less theatrically flamboyant.

By the time Johann Strauss II, von Suppé's contemporary, came to be the preeminent figure among operetta composers, the comic side of operetta was giving way to a more romantic approach. Curiously, while some of Strauss's lesser operettas quickly achieved international popularity, his best works were

recognized only slowly. Thus his masterpiece, the 1874 *Die Fledermaus,* did not achieve widespread recognition for a quarter of a century or more in such supposedly knowing theater centers as Paris, London, and New York.

Other countries had their own operetta traditions, which remained popular where they had originated even if they did not achieve international renown. For example, the Spanish-speaking world embraced the zarzuela, which originated in the seventeenth century and whose golden age occurred in Madrid in the 1880s.

In 1905 the premiere of Franz Lehár's *Die lustige Witwe* (The Merry Widow) ushered in a new, softer, and more patently romantic school of operetta. Love stories rather than political satire and outlandish farce became the primary focus of the plots, while musically the newer works usually abandoned or minimized the pyrotechnical showpieces and swirling waltzes of the older school. A mellow, easy waltz became the signature of many of these operettas. *The Merry Widow,* with its popular waltz song, was the biggest success in the history of the popular musical stage and remains the most produced of all popular musicals. Other examples of the school are *Ein Walzertraum* (1907), *Die Dollarprinzessin* (1907), *Der Graf von Luxemburg* (1909), and *Grafin Mariza* (1924). U.S. examples, all slightly more stolid or

Figure 3. *(Music Theater—Western Traditions)* Jules Chéret, poster for *La vie Parisienne.* From Claude Dufresne, *Histoire de l'opérette,* Paris: Fernand Nathan, 1981, p. 25. Phot. Bibl. Nat., Paris.

earthbound in tone, include *Naughty Marietta* (1910), *Rose-Marie* (1924), and *The Student Prince* (1924).

Musical comedy. The second major genre, *musical comedy,* developed independently in a number of theatrical centers. London's burlettas and burlesques, Paris's vaudevilles, and New York's farce-comedies all evolved into markedly similar types of amusement that eventually interacted. The farce-comedy may serve as an example. The earliest farce-comedies were little more than specialized *variety* (the nineteenth-century term for what in the United States was later called vaudeville). *The Brook* (1879), assembled by Nate Salsbury, took four characters on a picnic, where they indulged in songs, dances, and other variety turns. The music was culled from popular songs of the time, much as music in the first ballad

operas had been. When farce-comedies finally did begin to employ original scores, they did not turn initially to writers of operetta. Instead they turned to "Tin Pan Alley"–style composers. As a rule these songwriters lacked the conventional musical training of operetta composers. They were essentially melodists and did not generally orchestrate their own compositions. The performers of these songs were not primarily singers. In the parlance of the time such performers were often branded "shouters." As a result these relatively slight musical comedy songs were often delivered in a quasi-spoken manner, while operetta numbers were likely to be sung in a full-throated, more operatic style.

In addition, while operetta composers traditionally looked to Europe for musical inspiration, farce-comedy

Figure 4. *(Music Theater—Western Traditions)* Poster for a D'Oyly Carte production of *The Pirates of Penzance*. The Bettmann Archive/BBC Hulton.

or musical comedy composers turned to popular U.S. traditions (*see* MUSIC, FOLK AND TRADITIONAL; MUSIC, POPULAR). U.S. musical comedy composers increasingly employed harmonies, rhythms, and structures from black music, first ragtime and later jazz. One of the best early examples of this trend was George Gershwin's *Lady, Be Good!* (1924), which established the pattern for jazz musical comedies. The music in these shows was not genuine jazz, part of whose essence is improvisation, but many other elements were there. A decade earlier Jerome Kern's song "They Didn't Believe Me," interpolated into the U.S. production of the English musical *The Girl from Utah,* began the vogue for contemporary 4/4 love ballads, at once breaking the hegemony of the waltz (in 3/4 time) and further

differentiating between operetta and musical comedy.

The revue. A third major genre, the *revue,* flourished from just before the turn of the century until about the time of World War II. However, its music was not distinctive, falling instead in line with traditional musical comedy composition.

In the late 1920s Kern's *Show Boat* (1927) broke from older operetta by employing many of the same native elements identified with musical comedy, such as black idioms and ballads in 4/4 time as principal songs (Figure 5). Nevertheless, *Show Boat* remained a largely isolated instance of this until Richard Rodgers's *Oklahoma!* (1943) launched a prolonged era of fundamentally U.S. operetta. Because by then the term *operetta* had pejorative connotations for many

Figure 5. *(Music Theater—Western Traditions)* "No Shoes" dance number from *Show Boat* at the Ziegfield Theatre, 1946. The New York Public Library at Lincoln Center, Astor, Lenox and Tilden Foundations. Billy Rose Theatre Collection.

critics and playgoers, these operettas were called musical plays, a term that, in fact, had been employed over the years to describe some of the earliest operettas.

Beset by competition from films and television as well as by crushing economic problems, musical shows have decreased in number, although their decline has not been as precipitous as that of nonmusicals, especially in the United States. The popular music of the 1930s and 1940s, such as swing, had only marginal influence on the theater, unlike ragtime and jazz in preceding decades. From the 1960s on, however, rock music proved popular among young theater composers. The most successful rock musicals were those of Englishman Andrew Lloyd Webber, especially the enormously popular *Cats* (1981).

A noteworthy and stimulating phenomenon in the United States has been the emergence of Stephen Sondheim. His musicals, such as *A Little Night Music* (1973), *Sweeney Todd* (1979), and *Sunday in the Park with George* (1984), combined elements of operetta, musical comedy, and opera in a fresh synthesis, which works more in terms of musically dramatic scenes than of isolated songs and is noted for its use of small motif-phrases and sentences that reappear frequently throughout a show.

See also MUSIC HISTORY; MUSICAL, FILM.

Bibliography. Gerald M. Bordman, *American Musical Theater: A Chronicle*, New York, 1978; Florian Bruyas, *Histoire de l'opérette en France, 1855–1965*, Lyon, France, 1974; Bernard Grün, *Kulturgeschichte der Operette*, Munich, 1961; Raymond Mander and Joe Mitchenson, *Musical Comedy*, London, 1969; idem, *Revue*, London, 1971; Richard Traubner, *Operetta: A Theatrical History*, Garden City, N.Y., 1983.

GERALD BORDMAN

2. ASIAN TRADITIONS

The cultural history of ancient Asia is the story of collisions and interactions among several religious and artistic traditions (*see* RELIGION). In particular the MIGRATION of Indian Buddhists from Hindu lands north to Tibet and China and eastward spread Indian manners, customs, and ways of thinking. As a result the dramatic traditions of ancient India had a profound influence on the development of all Asian arts, especially those of THEATER in its broad sense of music, DANCE, and dramatic narration or situation. *See* EAST ASIA, ANCIENT; SOUTH ASIA, ANCIENT.

Early Indian theater. DRAMA in India traces its origins to before the world began. According to the Vedas (holy books), Brahma, the breath of the world, commanded that the gods in heaven reenact in playful form for everyone's entertainment and edification their victory over the demons of evil. India's first dance as such, however, reveals the creation of the world. In it Lord Śiva stood atop a Himalayan peak, naked and alone with only a tiny hand drum for rhythm. Fire appeared in the palm of his hand, and the river Ganges flowed from his hair. By establishing a world of vibration through his movements, Śiva became Naṭarāja, king of dancers. Strict Hindus worship him in this guise, and dance as well as theater is part of temple worship (see Figure 1).

Sometime between 3 B.C.E. and 5 C.E. a massive

Figure 1. *(Music Theater—Asian Traditions) Śiva Naṭarāja, Lord of the Dance.* South Indian, eleventh century. The Cleveland Museum of Art, Purchased by Income J. H. Wade Fund.

manuscript appeared codifying the theory and practice of India's theater AESTHETICS. This was the *Nāṭyaśāstra*, a canonical work (sastra) of dance and drama (the word *natya* combines both) transmitted orally by the sage Bharata centuries before its actual transcription onto reed and palm leaves (*see* ORAL CULTURE; ORAL POETRY). So integral was theater to religion and the well-being of society as a whole that this sastra was named the fifth Veda. It listed an entire lexicon of gestures (*see* GESTURE), postures, poses, and movements for the dancer-actor, as well as systematic guidelines for staging, suitable themes, and appropriate plots. It clearly asserted the inseparability of dance, drama, and music (*see* MUSIC, FOLK AND TRADITIONAL) and the fusion within the one art of natya as religious expression. Its tenets continue to be the underlying principle of all Asian classical or traditional theater arts as we see them today.

Central to India's natya and illustrative of the sastra are the great and powerful epic poems Ramayana and Mahabharata. The Ramayana, with its intertwining love story of King Rama and his queen, Sita, and their army of monkeys combating Ravana, the ten-headed ogre of Sri Lanka, describes mythically the Aryanization of India around 5000 B.C.E. The Mahabharata annals of intrigue between competing court dynasties portray events occurring within India's earliest royal houses. Thus through theater commoners were permitted to peer into the mysteries of their temporal as well as their spiritual rulers.

Both epics provided—and still offer—an inexhaustible supply of characters, incidents, and plots for dramatization in SONG and dance. These were the materials, that is, instructive mythology disguised as entertainment, that early travelers and missionaries took with them and introduced to the indigenous populations abroad. By bringing the gods to earth and by presenting moral lessons as adventure tales, along with danced and mimed recountings of Buddha's life, theater served as powerful PROPAGANDA for the propagation of religious belief. On the one hand, theater fed faith, and on the other, by representing kings and queens, it also confirmed a political system of the *dava-raj* or god-king, the unity of church and state.

Among India's own various theater arts, most important is the South Indian dance form Bharata Natya. Bharata here refers not to the sage Bharata but to the original name for India. Of all India's multitudinous forms of theater Bharata Natya approximates most closely the ideals adumbrated in the sastra. By comparing today's living performances with the countless temple sculptures of dancers, one can easily see exactly how and where dance has preserved and at the same time evolved away from the sastra's orthodoxy. Such high-flown sentiments as "hands must be like fishes swimming, the body must have the suppleness of silk, and the feeling of the dance must be like the ecstasy of the peacock before his mate at sunset" can be verified even now at the best performances by the greatest artists.

Bharata Natya at present has become the sole province of women. A program lasting an hour or so of solo performances by a single dancer alternates between energetic, athletic, and abstract sections and more passive or interpretive *padas,* songs in which words are depicted in literal hand gesture and by FACIAL EXPRESSION. The themes of dance and drama in India are primarily devotional, directed toward the gods. However, since the pantheon of India's gods is depicted in human terms, there is sufficient room for realism, and even eroticism. In many of the accompanying songs the dancer's love for god is likened to that of a woman's love for a husband or other man. The PERFORMANCE can be aimed at one particular spectator in the audience rather than toward an invisible divinity. The spiritual ecstasy of these Hindu extravaganzas, it is said by initiates, is not unlike physical, earthly orgasm.

Kathakali from Malabar on the west coast of southern India is the masculine antithesis of Bharata Natya. Here all-male troupes perform stories from the Ramayana and Mahabharata in feature-obliterating makeups, enormous halolike head-dresses, and costumes that swathe the dancers' bodies in yards of cotton cloth. Side singers chant the dialogue to the beat of deafening drums. Actor-dancers interpret each word in mudras (hand gestures), a kind of mute SIGN LANGUAGE. These pictorial ideographs of flesh and bone formed by the fingers express complete ideas in a kind of miniature dance of the hands.

When India was crushed by the Moguls (Muslims) from Persia and Arabia, whose period of greatest power extended over the twelfth to eighteenth centuries, dance and drama declined. Bharata Natya became the province of devadasi (literally "servants of god" but in practice temple prostitutes). In the north, where Mogul power was centered, Nautch (a perversion of natya) and nautch girls became synonymous with prostitution. Gradually, as Muslim rulers became Hinduized, a new form of dance, Kathak, was encouraged and developed at court. In obedience to Islam, Kathak has little connection with religion as storytelling. It does not represent or depict those elements that Bharata found essential. Muslims found any portrayal of Allah and his messengers to be blasphemous. Kathak revels in abstraction, complicated footwork, dazzling body spins, and intricate musical patterns. Its mathematical precision becomes a kind of ecstatic, celestial astronomy. The dances seem like secular contests between drummer and dancer to determine who can play or stamp faster or which of them can invent surprises and syncopations that will trick the other virtuoso into missing a beat. Again because of Muslim predilection and inhibition, many Kathak dancers are men, some of whom dress as women in order to neutralize any obvious erotic content.

Modern revival. With the arrival of the British in the nineteenth century, dance and drama suffered further intrusion. To staid Victorians India's theater arts, already decimated by the Muslims, seemed vulgar and degenerate. It was not until 1929, when Anna Pavlova made her famous tour of Asia, that Indians were spurred into a reconsideration of their once sublime heritage. She merely asked everywhere in exasperation, "But where is your dance?" Before long a spate of pioneers, scholars, researchers, and Brahmin ladies of respectability took Indian dance seriously and encouraged its reemergence from the shadows of neglect.

After independence in 1947 dance in India was restored to a position of importance. Presidential awards honored those artists who had survived the vicissitudes and had contributed to art's resumption of its dignity in society as envisaged three thousand years earlier by Bharata. Uday Shankar (1900–1977) was a major force in spreading awareness of Indian dance in the West. In 1923 in Paris he met Pavlova, who wanted to choreograph a ballet on an Indian theme. He proposed the love story of Lord Krishna the cowherd and Radha the milkmaid, probably the most popular deities of modern India. This became *Le dieu bleu,* in which Shankar and Pavlova danced together. Shankar had no formal training as a dancer, but he was a miraculous showman with intuitive genius. His charming approximations of Indian traditional movements along with his hints and suggestions of classicism enchanted the world in the 1930s and finally brought him honor, belatedly, in his homeland.

India's gigantic movie industry keeps well in line with the sastra's dicta. Its films not only tell stories with devotional or supernatural inspiration, but also punctuate them with dances combining all the arts to delight the eye, ear, and heart. Advertisements for movies not only list favorite stars but often cite the number of dances the ticket buyer will see. *See* MO-TION PICTURES; MUSICAL, FILM—BOMBAY GENRE; MYTHOLOGICAL FILM, ASIAN.

It should also be noted that with the coming of electronic media in recent times, India in its larger cities has been quick to try its hand at innovations. AVANT-GARDE theaters step into the future with Western-style adaptations, all the while keeping half an eye cocked on India's rich past. *See also* AVANT-GARDE FILM.

South and Southeast Asia. India's cultural dominance two thousand years ago spread over Asia, but each country held to its own more primitive theater tastes. India's immediate neighbor to the south, Sri Lanka, is profoundly Buddhist. Despite this and its Hindu overlay, Sri Lanka has maintained its indigenous folk arts, notably the exorcistic devil dances and fire dances of animistic origin. The island's masked dramas can be traced directly to ancient India, but the dances performed annually on the occasion when Buddha's tooth is exhibited in a celebratory parade at Kandy, the cultural capital of Sri Lanka, are uniquely Singhalese. In certain respects they resemble katha-kali, but the mudras have been attenuated beyond recognition and only vaguely "speak words." Independent of dance, popular theater in Sri Lanka recites the island's history, and some plays even chronicle romantic episodes from its triple colonization, first by the Portuguese, then by the Dutch, and lastly by the British.

In Buddhist Burma the pwe (show) is a national entertainment of the people. It includes tales from the Ramayana, in which Ravana is sometimes presented as a clown, which is why Sita does not yield to his advances. The country also boasts a large number of "spirit dances," based on a pre-Hindu religion, that illustrate the thirty-seven nats (spirits) that inhabit Burma. They appear in an amalgam of music, dance, talk, MIME, and story and coexist with more sophisticated aspects of imported Hinduism and Buddhism. For example, in many areas of Southeast Asia spectators describe a play taken from the Ramayana in which the leading actor plays the role of King Rama as a "Buddha play." (In any event, they explain, Rama is a "future Buddha.") In certain areas Ravana is regarded as a hero because he does not violate Sita during the ten years she is his captive. And in Thailand, Kampuchea, and Laos, the very word for "dance" is *ram, rom,* or *lam,* taken directly from Rama, the god-king of legend.

Indonesia, a nation of some three thousand islands, is doubtless the richest country anywhere in variety of dance and drama forms. The ancient Hindu origins of theater were so entrenched by the time the Muslims invaded during the twelfth to fifteenth centuries and forcibly converted by the sword that dance and drama merely continued as they always had. Although thousands of miles from Mecca and the Middle East, Indonesia is the largest, most populous Islamic country in the world. Still, its Hindu and Buddhist operas, shadow plays, dances, and dramas hold its people in thrall in the cities, in the countryside, and above all in the palace courts of the sultans and *susunans* of central Java. Islam's injunctions against representative art were for the most part ignored.

One island, Bali, completely escaped Islam. Bali continues to be the only Hindu region outside the confines of India proper. Its theatrical vibrancy has astonished foreign viewers ever since the Dutch conquered it in 1908 (it was the last colony of Asia) and

Figure 2. *(Music Theater—Asian Traditions)* Balinese dancer and orchestra, Indonesia. U.N. photo 152,396/ Doranne Jacobson.

opened it to the outside world. Sir Rabindranath Tagore, the first Asian to receive the Nobel Prize for literature (1913), sadly noted on his visit to Bali some years later that "Lord Śiva left his dance to Bali, and his ashes to India." By this he meant that Indian dance had been more carefully preserved in that distant island, the farthest extent of India's erstwhile expansionism, than in India itself (see Figure 2).

China and Japan. In China even the lion associated with that country at New Year's time derives from India. There are no lions in China, and their likeness was introduced as the benevolent mascot of Manjusri, the bodhisattva disciple popularly known as the god of wisdom in the Buddhist pantheon. Among the most popular examples of *Jing hsi* or Peking opera, the country's national popular amusement, are those dealing with the Monkey King, a derivative of Hanuman from the Ramayana, with his army of monkeys fighting on the side of good and rectifying wrongs (see Figure 3).

Japan is where Indian influence might be expected to be weakest by reason of geographic distance and ethnic divergence. Such is not the case. Indian souvenirs from older times exist everywhere. The ICONOGRAPHY of esoteric Buddhism of the Shingon sect in particular retains mudras borrowed from Indian mysticism and dance theater. Also the practice of drawing magic patterns, or *mandaras* (mandala in Sanskrit), as a means to spiritual enlightenment persists in Japan. The paintings include Sanskrit words as part of their visual designs.

Fourteenth-century No dance dramas continue to be performed, making this exalted art not only the oldest professional theater extant but the most an-

cient theater of the world still approximating its original stagings (see Figure 4). This cannot be said for Greek or Shakespearean drama as we see them mounted today. In one No play, during a dance of longevity, the leading character Okina chants Sanskrit runes completely incomprehensible to contemporary audiences. Other No texts occasionally quote Sanskrit mantras or dharanis (magical formulas of mystical meaning) when the plot needs to exorcise ghosts or evil spirits. Such Sanskrit passages as "Namaku Samanda Bararada . . . ," which means "I dedicate myself to the Universal Diamond. Be this raging fury destroyed!" were left untranslated by Chinese Buddhists. It was thought that if sound were altered in favor of meaning it would forfeit their efficacy. These words exist in No transliterated as the deities were presumed to have uttered them originally.

At the time of No's beginnings plays had already begun to take on contemporary significance apart from religious purpose. Living persons of rank were not supposed to be represented, for fear of offending the high and mighty. Emperors dead or alive could be represented only by children, again to avoid verisimilitude. One category of No plays was called *Genzai mono* (plays of the present), in which events from real life were transported to the stage. By the time Kabuki, Japan's great classical theater form coeval with Shakespeare, developed in the seventeenth century, together with Bunraku, the realistic puppet theater (*see* PUPPETRY), drama in general had become independent of religious association. It then was something of a newspaper, a means of keeping the people at large informed of events happening in daily life. When two lovers committed suicide to-

Figure 3. *(Music Theater—Asian Traditions)* The Monkey King in a performance by the National Chinese Opera Theatre. Courtesy of the Information and Communication Division in New York, Coordination Council for North American Affairs.

Figure 4. *(Music Theater—Asian Traditions)*   Japanese No dance drama. Courtesy of Japan Air Lines.

gether, as was the custom in feudal Japan when society prevented them from marriage, the event was dramatized (and glamorized) within a matter of weeks. If a thief had his nose cut off for smuggling medicinal carrots from Korea the incident was sufficient for a playwright to weave a drama of five acts. Similarly, love affairs between famous courtesans and handsome commoners fed the dramatists of Kabuki as they themselves fed ever-increasing audiences. Above all, scandals in high places, when nobles vied for accession within ruling houses, when ambitions at court spilled over into treacheries or murder, and when heroic actions such as hara-kiri (seppuku) were committed by samurai—all such gossip became the stuff of great tragedies onstage. Theater in a way kept the public abreast of the news of the day. Although names and dates were disguised, every theatergoer understood exactly the factual truth within the unreality of the representation.

Most remarkable of all Japanese arts perhaps is Bugaku, dating back some fifteen hundred years, the world's oldest music and dance still in pristine form. It was imported from India and China in the seventh century as part of Buddhism's many miscellaneous advantages—tea, pickles, writing, red dyes, straw mats, and the like. It quickly became the elegant preserve of a succession of emperors who used it to entertain dignitaries on ceremonial occasions. It continues to be performed at the Imperial Palace in Tokyo and may be seen by special invitation. Bugaku's antiquity and historical authenticity are verifiable from ancient documents, but cave sculptures and temple bas-reliefs in China and India are all that is left of this art in those countries of its provenance.

With the airplane, TELEPHONE, RADIO, movies, television, and SATELLITE transmissions the world is growing more uniform theatrically. A Broadway success (see section 1, above) is very likely to be seen in translation in Tokyo within a year. Theatrical troupes from Asia constantly tour the United States and Europe and have clearly affected Western theater. Although the West marvels at the treasures of Asia's past, Asian theater is quick to adopt electronic innovations. In India's capital cities traditional religious and artistic forms are supplemented by slice-of-life stagings of contemporary themes. Fortunately governments are now sensitive to the loss of traditional arts. Efforts are being made in most regions to maintain the classics and to preserve the precious national heritages.

See also ACTING; MUSIC PERFORMANCE.

Bibliography. Faubion Bowers, *Theater in the East: A Survey of Asian Dance and Drama*, New York, 1956, reprint 1969; Balwant Gargi, *Folk Theater of India*, Seattle, Wash., and London, 1966; Zeami, *Kadensho*, trans. by Chûichi Sakurai and Lindley Hubbell, Kyoto, 1968.

FAUBION BOWERS

MUSIC THEORIES

This topic is discussed in three sections:
1. Overview
2. Notations and Literacy
3. Tuning Systems

1. OVERVIEW

Music theory normally refers to explicit knowledge of music, expressed in SPEECH, WRITING, notation, gestures, drawings, and occasionally in musical compositions and performances. Theories of music communicate (1) philosophical, scientific, and religious beliefs about the origins, meaning, value, and purpose of music and its relationship to other activities (often called AESTHETICS); (2) evaluations of pieces and performances of music (called criticism); and (3) the structural features of SOUND, musical systems, and individual compositions so that music can be understood, taught, remembered, and reproduced (called music theory proper). In this latter sense, music theory includes the study of acoustics, the structural principles of musical "languages" (e.g., tuning systems, rules for composition and improvisation), analyses of pieces and performances, guidelines for performance practice, instrumental instruction manuals, notation, and classification of MUSICAL INSTRUMENTS and genres.

Music theory as explicit knowledge should be distinguished from musical understanding or musical thought, which is implied and expressed completely and sufficiently—if tacitly—in every musical composition and performance and in the kinesthetic, aural, and intellectual experiences associated with them. Music cultures vary enormously in the amount and kind of musical understanding or thought captured explicitly in music theory and in the ways that theory is expressed. Until the 1970s scholars generally assumed that theories of music existed exclusively in the literate cultures of Europe and its colonies, the Middle East, and East Asia. Subsequent studies in ETHNOMUSICOLOGY, however, have demonstrated the existence of music theory in many nonliterate societies as well and continue to explore the nature of both tacit and explicit musical knowledge, understanding, and thought.

Content of Music Theories

In many cultures theories of music link human musical behavior to divine origins, supernatural purposes, or the laws of nature. In doing so they give to music the highest possible purpose and seriousness. This phenomenon is so widespread that the ethnomusicologist Bruno Nettl claimed that contact with the supernatural was probably music's fundamental purpose on a worldwide basis. In the ancient world from China through India and Babylon to Greece and in medieval Europe, the realization that music was governed by mathematical principles led to the belief that music was a manifestation of the laws of nature and that its proper performance ensured the "harmony of the spheres" and the stability of the state. Among the Flathead Indians songs are said to be given to men by spirits during vision quests. These songs then have the power to enlist the aid of the spirit when needed by the singer. In Java the gamelan gong orchestras are said to have originated among the gods as a means of sending messages and continue among humans to contain spirits and to affect the well-being of human life and society.

Theories of music also link musical behavior to other human behaviors. Common links include those to the emotions, to character, and to social behavior. Both PLATO and CONFUCIUS believed that music affected a person's character and decreed that only certain types of music were appropriate to the education of the ruling classes. Somewhat more widespread are beliefs that music affects, expresses, symbolizes, or evokes emotional states. Two of the more elaborate and systematic examples are the Indian theory of *nava rasa* ("nine sentiments") evoked by music and the seventeenth-century European "doctrine of the affections," in which it was believed that specific musical gestures epitomized specific emotional states. The emotional content of pieces or sections of music could thus be objectively encoded by the composer and decoded by the listener. In Arabic cultures effective musical performance evokes a state of *tarab* ("enchantment"), while in other societies it may lead to trance states. Theories of music often specify particular kinds of music for the appropriate social group—for example, men versus women, age groups, insiders versus outsiders.

Even when music theories do not specifically link music to human behavior and nonhuman phenomena, they are often linked by analogy and METAPHOR to other domains of thought, making music coherent within those domains or bringing musical behavior within the purview of some overarching, all-encompassing theory or pattern of explanation. In Europe from the sixteenth to the nineteenth century, music was analyzed using metaphors drawn from RHETORIC, an important subject in the curriculum during that period. Terms for musical form such as phrase, theme, exposition, and development are a legacy of this tradition and put the construction and analysis of music on the same footing as the construction and analysis of speech and writing. Rhetorical analysis also supported the belief that music, by analogy, had the same expressive and persuasive powers as speech. In the nineteenth century, reflecting the influence and prestige of the biological sciences, a piece of music came to be viewed as a "living organism" with a structure genetically determined by the particular melodic "cell" that began it. In the twentieth century MATHEMATICS, physics, INFORMATION THEORY, structural LINGUISTICS, and SEMIOTICS have all provided terms and ways of thinking that have influenced the writing of music theory. In addition, in Arabic theory geometry provides the basic analogies (points, lines) for attacks and durations in rhythmic theory. Among the Oglala Sioux music theory is not a separate domain. They verbalize about music in much the same way they talk about eating and other bodily functions. Among the Kaluli of Papua New Guinea melodic shape is described using water metaphors, linking human and natural sound domains, which are often perceived as existing together in counterpoint. Finally, ordinary speech about music often gains coherence by borrowing metaphors from other senses and experiences: hot, cool, jumps, wails, rocks, moves.

Theories of music often contain statements about the value of particular pieces and performances of music. In Europe music criticism developed during the nineteenth century, when it was considered important to identify works and composers of genius. Among the Navajo performances are evaluated according to their efficacy in effecting cures. In general, evaluations of music are probably the most common and widespread kind of verbalization about music. In many cultures everyone can ask or answer the question, "How did you like the concert?" Such speech about music is fragmentary and is used in particular social and musical circumstances to interpret and regulate musical experience and to integrate it into social experience. These casual speech events are sometimes based on systematic theories when they exist and are known by the speaker, and sometimes are a part of ordinary speech when no separate systematic theory of music exists, as among the Oglala Sioux.

Theories of music often codify or systematize musical knowledge for its own sake or as part of a general philosophical stance that seeks to order all phenomena in the world. The Arab al-Fārābī (878?–950?) and the Frenchman Jean-Jacques Rousseau (1712–1778), for example, included music within their systematic descriptions of all knowledge. Al-Fārābī lists nearly every type of melodic motion, ornament, and rhythmic cycle possible in Arabic music. The twentieth-century Indian theorist Nazir Jairazbhoy specifies the thirty-two possible ragas of North Indian classical music and their interrelationships. The German baroque composer J. S. Bach (1685–1750) demonstrated the viability of the new equal-tempered tuning system by systematically employing all the available keys in a set of pieces called *The Well-tempered Clavier* (see section 3, below).

Theories of music often divide up the cultural and natural sounds of the environment and assign meanings to them. Instrumental classification systems are a good example of this. In China instruments are classified according to the material used in their construction, so that an orchestra can be constructed to represent all the elements on earth. In India, where it is believed that one manifestation of God is vibration itself, instruments are classified according to the vibrating material. The Oglala Sioux, who view the world in terms of bodily actions, classify instruments according to how they are played.

Many cultures lack a unifying term for sounds considered musical in the West. In Bulgaria and in parts of Africa words for singing, drumming, playing instruments, and lamenting exist—but none for music. Instead, these musical behaviors are linked to other behaviors considered nonmusical in the West. For example, in Africa the word *ngoma* includes drumming, singing, clapping, dancing, and festive shouting and whistling. Among the Kaluli human and natural sounds are interwoven by theory into a single aesthetic soundscape in which it is possible to discuss weeping, singing, birdcalls, waterfalls, and other sounds from a unified perspective. In Islamic societies religious chanting, which sounds rather like secular singing, is excluded from music, which is regarded as the devil's attempt to seduce people from their proper devotion to God.

Theories of music sometimes contain analyses of particular pieces. The 'Are'are people of the Solomon Islands have an enormous vocabulary for distinguishing different types of melodic and harmonic intervals, melodic shapes, and the number and relationship between parts in a polyphonic texture. These descriptions are then used in teaching and distinguishing pieces of music. In the West analysis of pieces for its own sake seems to have developed in the nineteenth century in conjunction with the critical process designed to identify "works of genius." As part of a growing historical consciousness, analyses contributed to the construction of histories of musical style.

Theories of music can also contain instructions for practical musicians in the form of rules for composition and improvisation, guidelines for ornamentation and interpretation during performance, exercises and instructions in instrumental technique, and the rudiments of notation for beginners. Much of early European music theory seems to have arisen to teach otherwise untrained choristers how to sing from notation. During the RENAISSANCE and baroque periods of European music history much theory, written by and for composers, was devoted to rules of counterpoint, harmony, and improvisation at the keyboard. Today every instrument in the West has its "methods book" to introduce notation, technical exercises, and pieces of graded difficulty to learners.

Examples of instructional theory also occur in musical cultures that are primarily improvisatory.

Systematic technical exercises exist in India's aural tradition. In Java theory treats rules of improvisation in the context of partially fixed pieces. In the Middle East, North Africa, and India theory has tried to describe the rules for improvisation and the distinguishing features of each melodic mode.

Transmission of Theory

How theories of music are transmitted (who theorizes about music to whom, where, and using what media) varies enormously from culture to culture. In cultures in which music theory is a part of more general theories, music theorists are often religious figures or philosophers who interpret the meaning of music, as well as particular performances of it, to a general public. Theory is then communicated as part of religious instruction or general education in the form of myths, stories, and scholarly discourse. Since the primary purpose of this kind of theory is to link music to other domains of the natural and supernatural world, it is often divorced from details of musical practice and structure. In India the pandit or guru is a master of both musical and spiritual matters. Confucius, al-Fārābī, Plato, Boethius, Schopenhauer, and Rousseau are all examples of polymaths who wrote on every conceivable matter, including music. In American Indian tribes shamans, or medicine men, have the greatest knowledge of matters, such as music, with great powers in the spirit world.

Other than priests and philosophers, musicians form the main group who theorize about music. In the baroque period of Western music history composers were the main theorists, and as a consequence they wrote about matters of concern to them: compositional principles and proper performance practice. Instrument makers also participated in theory because they needed to know about acoustics in order to construct instruments containing the principles of the musical system. Among the 'Are'are, for example, the main bearer of music theory is the instrument maker.

While musicians and philosopher-priests usually create systematic, broad-ranging theories, knowledge of these theories is then distributed rather irregularly in society. In the West, for example, up until the beginning of the nineteenth century, music theory was taught as part of the seven liberal arts, and all educated people would have known parts of it. Today music theory is taught primarily to young musicians as part of their performance training and not as a part of general education. Among the 'Are'are knowledge of theory varies greatly, with only the instrument maker knowing it completely, some performers knowing a bit of it, and others knowing nothing at all.

Lack of knowledge of formal theory does not prevent ordinary people from speaking of music, however. Idiosyncratic as well as socially shared classifications of sound, genres, and musical instruments abound, and value judgments, ordinary metaphors, and self-reflection are expressed easily and naturally within a musical community.

Theory is usually transmitted within definable social groups. For example, when theory is tied to LITERACY, as in China, only the educated know theory, and knowledge of theory becomes a symbol of a certain social and intellectual standing. In nineteenth-century America country people who knew enough music theory to sing revival hymns in four-part harmony were known as *fasola* folk after the mnemonic solfège syllables used in their theory.

When and where theory is transmitted also varies with its centrality to the culture. When music is imbued with great power, as among American Indians, teaching of beliefs about music can occur at any time and from the earliest age. An Eskimo boy who is caught humming a powerful song will be admonished on the grounds that the song will lose its power and should properly be sung only by its composer. In other cases learning takes place at special times of life, such as in puberty rituals in parts of Africa or during formal schooling as in the West.

The media used to transmit theory also vary greatly. The most common form is speech. In some cases straightforward descriptive statements are made, as among the 'Are'are. In other cases theory is embedded in myths and legends that must be decoded. Some of the more intractable parts of the myths in Plato have been interpreted as containing detailed accounts of tuning systems. In nonliterate societies some aspects of theory are contained in speechlike mnemonic devices. In Africa, India, and most of the Middle East, for example, the many different types of drum strokes are encoded in spoken syllables that allow the patterns to be remembered and taught. One style of jazz—bebop—takes its name from spoken syllables that convey the rhythmic character of phrases. Many cultures have names for pitches, allowing them to be pointed to verbally.

In literate societies theory is conveyed in written texts and, in Europe and East Asia, in notation as well. Literacy then becomes a necessary precondition for acquiring knowledge of theory, and musical notation becomes one of the most important media for transmitting theory of music. Until the end of the nineteenth century, notation of music was important only in the West and in East Asia. In the twentieth century, contact with the West led to the application, at least in academic circles, of Western and some newly invented notations, as in Java, to many formerly nonliterate traditions. Typically notation contains the fixed aspects of the musical tradition, leaving other aspects to the discretion of performers. During the twentieth century composers in the West tried increasingly to fix every aspect of performance in notation, leaving virtually no room for performer discretion. In North India, on the other hand, with a highly evolved literary tradition of theory, notation is of virtually no importance because performances are primarily improvised. See section 2, below.

Finally, it might be argued that music itself transmits music theory, that theory is implicit in musical action. Bach, for example, is famous for sets of pieces such as the *Well-tempered Clavier* and *Art of the Fugue* that lay out systematically all the possibilities within a given framework. As a result these pieces, along with his set of chorale harmonizations, are still used to teach students the fundamental principles of tonal harmony and counterpoint.

The Relationship of Theory and Music

Theories can be classified as either prescriptive or descriptive. Prescriptive theory attempts to define how music should be performed. Descriptive theory attempts to categorize and encapsulate in words the practice of music. Prescriptive theory usually defines the behavior of composers and performers. For example, Arabic theory prescribes modulation from mode to mode and with ornamentation, the two most important features of good performance. Theory in the baroque period in Europe dealt with improvised keyboard accompaniments that embodied the harmonic system of the period. In medieval Europe and in nineteenth-century America theory contained the rudiments of music so that otherwise untrained singers could correctly perform the repertoire.

Prescriptive theory also exists on a modest scale in the West in the guise of music appreciation classes, given to high school and university students in order to guide their listening to music. Although musicians usually employ a combination of vast musical experience and knowledge of theory, listeners with less musical knowledge and experience can be taught to appreciate music with some knowledge of theory. The nineteenth-century composers Robert Schumann and Richard Wagner were early examples of music critics who sought to teach an emerging general public about the complicated music that formerly was meant only for a highly educated elite.

Prescriptive theory can also take the form of notation and verbal mnemonic devices that act as memory aids in the preservation of compositions. Notation in the West may have been developed to control the relationship between parts in a polyphonic texture. In China notations prescribe an extraordinarily elaborate playing technique. Notation can also affect performance practice; in both the West and Java, for example, notation seems to have curtailed improvisatory practices to a great extent.

Prescriptive theory often influences the precompositional plans from which composers work. The various "forms of music" are one such set of precompositional plans. In the European Renaissance period and in much of the Middle East poetic forms and scansions provide models for musical form and rhythm. During the Renaissance the solmization syllables of music theory were linked to syllables of the text or the title to create melodic motives.

Descriptive theory, in the form of analysis of pieces of music and characterization of musical systems, seems to have little direct effect on the practice of music, but rather to exist within intellectual and religious traditions that demand that the world be accounted for in some way. It often links the past with the present. References to historical practices lend prestige to modern ones, as in India. Modern composers in the West with a historical view can try to justify writing music not for the present but for an imaginary future audience.

In yet other cases musical systems are created to justify or rationalize musical practice, particularly practices that are new or revolutionary. In the twentieth century, composers such as Arnold Schoenberg, Edgard Varèse, Olivier Messiaen, and John Cage all wrote extensively about the new music they were creating. They obviously felt that revolutionary practices needed a theory to justify them, just as the older practice had its theory.

What begins as descriptive theory, however, often has a prescriptive effect when it is taught to music students. They come to understand through theory what music "ought to be like" and begin to compose and perform in accordance with this formerly descriptive theory. A. B. Marx, for example, first articulated the notion of sonata form in 1848 to describe the music of Wolfgang Amadeus Mozart, Joseph Haydn, and Ludwig van Beethoven, but his description influenced the form of compositions for decades. After the creation of a theoretical system of seventy-two possible scales in South India, composers set about composing pieces in all the theoretically possible scales.

While prescriptive theory often has a direct effect on the behavior of musicians, descriptive theory often takes on a life of its own. In this case music theorists are often able to exist in a social and economic role almost independent of musicians. Their knowledge of music theory and ability to verbalize about music, as opposed to musical ability, become their raison d'être and source of income, and they become teachers, scholars, and critics.

See also MUSIC, FOLK AND TRADITIONAL; MUSIC COMPOSITION AND IMPROVISATION; MUSIC HISTORY; MUSIC PERFORMANCE; SONG.

Bibliography. Judith C. Becker, *Traditional Music in Modern Java,* Honolulu, Hawaii, 1980; Steven Feld, *Sound and Sentiment: Birds, Weeping, Poetics, and Song in Kaluli Expression,* Philadelphia, 1982; Ernest G. McClain, *The Pythagorean Plato,* Stony Brook, N.Y., 1978; Hugo Riemann, *Geschichte der Musiktheorie im 9–19 Jahrhundert* (Theory of Harmony: A Study), 2d ed., Berlin, 1920; Hiromi Lorraine Sakata, *Music in the Mind: The Concept of Music and Musician in Afghanistan,* Kent, Ohio, 1983; Arnold Schoenberg, *Style and Idea,* New York, 1950, reprint (ed. by Leo Black) London, 1975; Charles Seeger, *Studies in Musicology, 1935–1975,* Berkeley, Calif., 1977; Ravi Shankar, *My Music, My Life,* New York, 1968; R. H. Van Gulik, *The Lore of the Chinese Lute,* Rutland, Vt., and Tokyo, 1940; Hugo Zemp, "Aspects of 'Are'are Musical Theory," *Ethnomusicology* 23 (1979): 6–48.

TIMOTHY RICE

2. NOTATIONS AND LITERACY

Notation is a transformation of musical sound, a system that sets music in visual forms using symbols, letters, and numbers. (An exception is notation for the blind, such as the Braille system, which is a tactile transformation of Western staff notation.) As such, notation represents one of the two important media for musical expression and communication, the other being oral. A people's concepts about music as well as about the world are illustrated in the types of notation and PERFORMANCE they use and in the balance between the two (*see* MUSIC PERFORMANCE). Some music exists only in notation, whereas in many societies with rich musical traditions notation has never been employed. Nonnotational societies should not be considered to be in a prenotational stage. Rather, they should be considered as not needing notation, probably because of the abilities that they have and that most notational societies tend to lack, such as the ability to memorize music without having recourse to any written material. See section 1, above.

Between the two extremes of notation and orality, however, there are intermediate systems that aid music learning and memorization. Two significant examples are body movement and oral notation (*see* BODY MOVEMENT NOTATION). The former includes chironomy (systematic use of hand movements in accordance with music) as well as the movements of modern conductors. The latter designates a variety of vocal activity that imitates music per se. Both methods—unlike written notation—are performed in real time, similar to actual music. However, as their performances are not the same as the music itself, they also are considered to be transformations of musical sounds. Once oral notation is written down, it becomes a form of written notation.

The functions of notations are generally considered to be the preservation and transmission of music that otherwise would be lost. It is true that the revival of early Western music was achieved mainly by the interpretation of notations. If there had been no notational systems available and if the composers and/or their copyists had not notated their works either in manuscript or in print, the barriers of time and space would have made it impossible to study and perform these works. In many cultures oral notation often augments this communicative function of written notation.

Types of notational systems. Apart from hypothetical notations in Babylonia (ca. 800 B.C.E.) and ancient Egypt, the history of notation can be traced back to about 500 B.C.E. in ancient Greece (*see* MUSIC HISTORY). Since then a wide variety of notational systems have developed. Although there are many methods of CLASSIFICATION, two are of special importance to the study of communications. The first classification is based on the relationship between notation and performance, and the second on the visual materials used in notational systems.

The first classification was proposed by U.S. musicologist Charles Seeger. He divided music writings into two categories: *prescriptive* and *descriptive*. The score of Beethoven's Fifth Symphony is typical of the prescriptive type: it was written and defined by the composer so that people could perform it according to his writing. In contrast, a musicologist's transcription of Eskimo songs is a descriptive notation: it describes the result of the performance rather than its origin. In prescriptive notation the flow of communication is composer → notation → music; in descriptive notation the flow is performer → music → notation. After Seeger's formulation another type of notation, generally called graph notation, was developed. This is neither prescriptive nor descriptive; it neither prescribes its performance in detail nor describes a certain preexisting performance. This notation is presented to performers as a visual stimulus to performance with many interpretive possibilities and could be termed *projective* notation (see Figure 1).

Notations can be classified in terms of visual materials according to the following categories: (1) onomatopoeic, (2) letter/character/number, (3) graphic, (4) terminological, and (5) hybrid. Pitches (absolute or relative), intervals, durations, timbres, dynamics, tempi, motives, chords, and playing techniques are represented either independently or jointly in each of these categories.

Onomatopoeic notations in Japan, for instance, are generally called *shôga*. Figure 2 is an example of the *shôga* for the samisen, a three-stringed plucked instrument. It is clear that the emphasis of this oral, or onomatopoeic, notation indicates the differentiation of timbre and playing techniques rather than pitches, because many different pitches are given the same name as long as they are played on the same string (e.g., several different pitches are called *tun*). Similar methods are found in such disparate places as Korea and Scotland.

Notations based on letters, characters, and/or numbers are widely distributed over time and around the world. Those symbols sometimes correspond to pitch names or to finger positions on instruments. Figure 1 can be rewritten by using different notational systems of this category. China has a long history of using this type, in which not only Chinese characters but also their abridged forms designate names of pitches, strings, holes of wind instruments, and so on. This type is dominant in Asian cultures, including India and Indonesia, and also in European tablatures for instruments in the RENAISSANCE and baroque eras. Tonic sol-fa is a relatively modern version of this system, as letters representing pitch names are used instead of ordinary staff notation.

Graphic notations include all the notations consisting of graphic symbols. The neumes notating Gregorian chant are typical of this type (see Figure 3). They represent not a series of independent pitches but patterns including these pitches. Figure 4 shows a notation for *shômyô* (Buddhist ritual song) in Japan. Directions of matchsticklike lines as well as curves refer to melodic movements to be sung. Notation of Tibetan Buddhist music has similar traits (see Figure 5).

Terminological notations include those that consist of verbal terms only. For example, if a long melody has a name, it is more convenient to write its name than to notate its music. For instance, Figure 1 denotes two specific melodic patterns of Bunraku that Bunraku musicians customarily refer to by the names *tsunagi* and *kei* instead of writing the notes themselves. These names function sufficiently as a notation, at least for those who have a solid memory of the melodies.

Hybrid notation is represented by modern Western staff notation, which uses the graphic category as well as other types of notation, including verbal (terminological) explanations. Korean mensural notation (*chŭnggan-po*) is also a hybrid type combining character and graphic notations (see Figure 6).

Whereas many systems of notations have developed in both Asia and Europe, a remarkable difference exists between the systems of these two cultures. In general, notations in Asia have a tendency to focus on minute expression of individual parts, vocal or instrumental. They emphasize the designation of timbre in oral notation as well as that of microtonal pitches. For instance, a difference of one-ninth of a whole tone can be notated in a Turkish system of staff notation (see Figure 7). At the same time, duration has not been indicated on notation directly but has been transmitted indirectly by the naming of rhythmic and/or poetic patterns. In other words, Asian notations tend to function more as aide-mémoire.

On the other hand, notation in the West has progressed from aide-mémoire to a medium for trans-

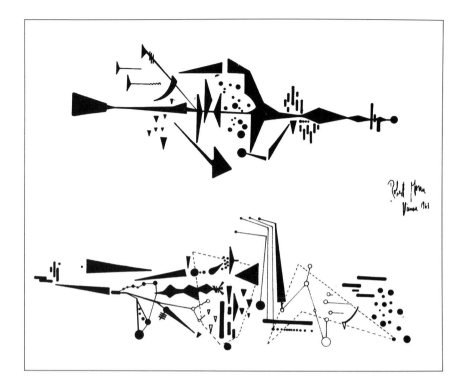

Figure 1. *(Music Theories—Notations and Literacy)* Graph notation: *(a)* Robert Moran, *Four Visions. Nos. 2 and 3.* Universal Edition A.G., Vienna. *(b)* Earle Brown, *Folio. December 1952.* Associated Music Publishers Inc., New York. From Erhard Karkoschka, *Notation in New Music,* New York: Praeger Publishers, 1972, pp. 131 and 91.

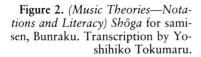

Figure 2. *(Music Theories—Notations and Literacy) Shôga* for sami-sen, Bunraku. Transcription by Yoshihiko Tokumaru.

Figure 3. *(Music Theories—Notations and Literacy)* Notation of a Gregorian chant: fifteenth-century gradual from the Abbey of La Cava. From the Benedictines of Stanbrook, *Gregorian Music: An Outline of Music Palaeography,* London: Benziger Brothers, 1897, plate 7.

mitting new information. Accordingly tablatures (notations that indicate fingering and other techniques rather than the pitch to be played), which are closely connected to specific instruments, have been replaced by more neutral systems, less connected to particular instruments. The emphasis of Western notations on indicating durations of notes and rests is also relevant to the formation of the new medium. The change from the medieval system of modal rhythm to Renaissance mensural notation (in which individual note values are clearly defined) and the attempt to establish an absolute unit for measuring time in terms of human pulses (*tactus*) are among the factors that contributed to development of a neutral method. Because of these developments Western music succeeded in formulating musical systems with vertical synchronization (polyphonic music since the late medieval and Renaissance periods, homophonic music since the baroque era). The idea of a musical score with synchronizing lines is a typical product of Western music. Western notations represent in detail the temporal relationships between different parts in a digital manner, with each symbol representing a distinct time-unit value. In contrast, Asian notations generally transmit such relationships orally as additional information rather than describing them overtly.

When they are notated, the symbols tend to indicate in an analog manner, with each symbol capable of encoding gradient temporal values, as seen in Figure 8. As MAX WEBER pointed out, the characteristics of Western notations have a strong connection with the formation of tonal harmony, the use of equal temperament (see section 3, below), and the mass production of MUSICAL INSTRUMENTS.

Notations, printing, and sound recording. Although notation has a long history, notational LITERACY is not nearly as widely diffused as literacy in the written word. Many musicians without knowledge of musical notation still actively work, even in Europe. The lack of use of notation among folk musicians in Europe has led to efforts by many music researchers to document musical traditions by transcribing orally transmitted music. Such researchers in Europe include Oskar Kolberg in Poland; A. N. F. von Zuccalmaglio, Wilhelm Erk, and Franz Magnus Böhme in nineteenth-century Germany; and two Hungarian musicologists, Béla Bartók and Zoltán Kodály, in the early twentieth century (*see* MUSIC, FOLK AND TRADITIONAL). Similar attempts to collect indigenous musical traditions have been carried out in various countries. All such works are classified as descriptive notations. In order to improve the preci-

Figure 4. *(Music Theories—Notations and Literacy)* *Shômyô (a)* Japan, and *(b)* equivalent in Western notation. From Kenji Hirano, ed., *Mieku nika hôyô*, p. 31. A booklet attached to the record album, CBS Sony, Tokyo, 1974.

Figure 5. *(Music Theories—Notations and Literacy)* *(a)* Tibetan notation, and *(b)* equivalent in Western notation. From Tsukamoto Atsuko, "The Music of Tibetan Buddhism in Ladakh: The Musical Structure of Tibetan Chant in the Ritual *bskaṅ-gso* of the *Dge-lugs-pa* Sect," *Yearbook for Traditional Music* 15 (1983): 132, 133.

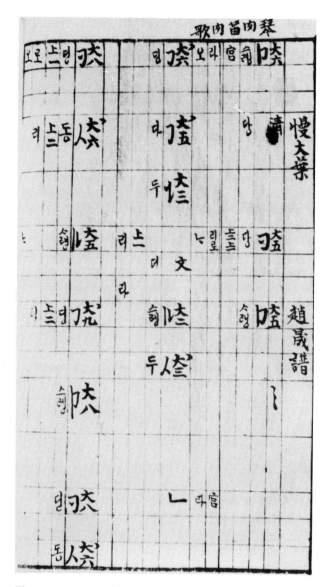

Figure 6. (*Music Theories—Notations and Literacy*) Korean notation. From Hye-Ku Lee, *Essays on Korean Traditional Music*, Seoul: Seoul Computer Press, 1981, p. 32. Copyright © 1981 by the Royal Asiatic Society, Korea Branch.

fazla	1/9	♯	♩
eksik bakiyye	3/9		♭
bakiyye	4/9	♯	♭
küçük mücennep	5/9	♯	♭
büyük mücennep	8/9	♯	♭
tanini (whole tone)	9/9	𝄪	♭♭

Figure 7. (*Music Theories—Notations and Literacy*) Suphi Ezgi's method for representing accidentals (Turkey). Redrawn after Suphi Ezgi, "Nagari ve Ameli," *Türk Musikisi* 1 (1933).

sion and comprehensiveness of this type of notation, various approaches and mechanical devices have been proposed. Seeger constructed a device called a melograph, which was designed to measure and graphically represent pitch, duration, and harmonics in a way that resolved certain problems of subjective measurement in transcription by ear. Recent advances in analog-to-digital conversion using computers have further improved the accuracy of description and measurement. Other questions, such as those concerning the musical consciousness of the people, however, will remain unsolved unless other, more humanistic, methods are used.

Apart from musical documentation by researchers, in the twentieth century bearers of orally transmitted musical styles often publish prescriptive notations of their own music. Their intentions are twofold: first, to stabilize the tradition, and second, to give a formal character to the music by making it comparable to other notated genres (*see* GENRE). In some cases the published notations define the performance in so much detail that they suppress other possible interpretations.

Publication of such notation is strongly influenced by the development of PRINTING technology. Music PUBLISHING has a long history, from the latter half of the fifteenth century in Europe (collections of religious music) and in Asia (collections of Buddhist music, for instance). It has enhanced the diffusion of musical works, especially after the seventeenth century. While specialists have been needed to supply musical writings and printings, the use of the computer in this field has diminished that need. At the same time, the function of printed notes themselves has diminished because of the invention of SOUND RECORDING. Popular songs in the United States have enjoyed wide print dissemination, later supplanted by the phonograph industry (*see* MUSIC, POPULAR).

In general the use of sound recording has changed the relationship between notation and oral/aural traditions. The communicative and preservative functions that notation has historically fulfilled tend to be replaced by a new form of orality (qualified as secondary orality by Walter Ong). The advantages and disadvantages of new media should not be evaluated in general terms without reference to specific contexts. In some cultures in which an oral tradition has been strongly maintained, however, dependence on recording machines has begun to weaken the tenacity of oral/aural learning and creating.

See also ETHNOMUSICOLOGY; MUSIC COMPOSITION AND IMPROVISATION.

Bibliography. Willi Apel, *The Notation of Polyphonic Music 900–1600*, 5th ed., rev., Cambridge, Mass., 1961; Erhard Karkoschka, *Das Schriftbild der neuen Musik* (Notation in New Music: A Critical Guide to Interpretation

a

b

Figure 8. *(Music Theories—Notations and Literacy)* Japanese notations: *(a)* numbers on the left: samisen part; numbers on the right: vocal part; *(b)* equivalent in Western notation. From Yoshihiko Tokumaru, "L'aspect mélodique de la musique de syamisen," Ph.D. diss., Université Laval, 1982, p. 166.

and Realization), Celle, FRG, 1966; Walter Kaufmann, *Musical Notations of the Orient*, Bloomington, Ind., 1967; Nippon Hōsō Kyōkai Symphony Orchestra, ed., *Gakufu no sekai* (The World of Notation), 3 vols., Tokyo, 1974; Walter J. Ong, *Orality and Literacy: The Technologizing of the Word*, London and New York, 1982; Charles Seeger, *Studies in Musicology 1935–1975*, Berkeley, Calif., 1977; Yoshihiko Tokumaru and Osamu Yamaguti, eds., *The Oral and the Literate in Music*, Tokyo, 1986.

YOSHIHIKO TOKUMARU

3. TUNING SYSTEMS

Tuning, in the West, usually connotes the setting of a musical instrument to abstract pitch standards in preparation for PERFORMANCE; the set or sets of pitches selected, adjusted, or available on a particular musical instrument; and the interaction of these settings or potentials with *intonation*, the auditory sensation that a musical performance is "in tune," that its pitches are inflected to a standard of consistency. In this sense tuning is usually a topic related specifically to discussion of MUSICAL INSTRUMENTS and to the interaction of specific adjustments (of tubes, slides, reeds, strings, etc.) with construction materials, environmental conditions, and patterns of physical use.

Of course this is far more complicated in practice, because instruments, ensembles, and musical genres have various norms and stylistic regularities of tuning. For example, some instruments are pretuned by a specialist other than the performer; nonetheless, because instrumentalists tune up alone and with one another just before a performance, they must develop procedures for mixing and matching instruments that are pretuned (like a piano) with those that can continually be retuned (like a violin). All instrumentalists are also aware of and use a variety of tuning and compensating techniques to adjust for subtleties of ensemble blending and also to adjust for the idiosyncrasies of their particular instruments during the course of a performance.

Tuning and intonation are also topics of a large body of oral lore that circulates among professional and amateur musicians. Topics include which make and style of specific instruments are "perfectly in tune" and which have certain pitches "out of tune" or require extensive compensation to achieve consistency in various keys. Tips and advice about how to negotiate the intonation of difficult musical passages often involve ideas about tuning. Many instrumentalists have several instruments of different age and manufacture or modifications for occasional use and choose accordingly for the tuning problems associated with certain pieces. With some instruments, like a harpsichord, instrumentalists choose the pieces for a performance so that the keys of each selection are related, lest the instrument sound as if it is going slightly in and out of tune from one piece to the next.

Although the Western dictionary sense of tuning usually refers to the procedures by which instruments are calibrated to preexisting standards and norms (usually described elsewhere as music theories), it is perhaps more accurate to say that tuning is the set of activities and ideas that interrelates the character of instruments, the conventions of pitch, and the norms of realization in a given musical tradition or practice. In this sense the Western musical traditions are no different from any other human musical tradition. The combination of acoustic, perceptual, material, and cultural factors has created extraordinary diversity in tuning systems known today, but it is also true that in all known human societies tuning can be counted as a fundamental dimension of musical communication. Were this not so, musical communication would not be characterized worldwide by the high degree of consistency and redundancy of pitch information and melodic type, performance techniques and styles, and instrument production and use. *See* MUSIC HISTORY.

It is important to realize that a tuning system is an imposition of musical order, culturally and acoustically rationalized, onto a larger perceptual framework that will permit many organizational possibilities. Human ears perceive tones from about sixteen hertz (Hz, cycles per second) to greater than sixteen kilohertz (kHz). In the Western musical sense this is a hearing range equivalent to about ten musical octaves, or a total of 120 chromatic tones in equal tuning. Actually, the Western tradition uses considerably fewer tones than these 120. For example, of the eighty-eight pitches on a piano, the highest is C^8 at 4,186.0 Hz, and the lowest is A^0 at 27.5 Hz; the human ear can hear upward at least two octaves (C^{10} would be 16.744 kHz) and downward a sixth (C^0 would be 16.3 Hz). *See* PERCEPTION—MUSIC.

But the fact that less of the ten-octave potential is utilized is not the only way in which a tuning system imposes an arbitrary order. The octave is a universal feature of human perception, but ways to organize the material—tonal spaces and the number of intervals—within the octave are highly variable. Westerners might think of that ten-octave expanse of human hearing as 120 semitones, but the human ear is capable of making about fourteen hundred discrete frequency discriminations within that expanse. This is not a linear process, however, with the ear being able to perceive some 140 distinctions to each octave; a greatly disproportionate number of those discriminations are in the area from one to four kilohertz (roughly the upper two octaves of a piano), and other factors such as loudness affect perceptual distinctions in the lowest hearing ranges.

To compare a familiar tuning system with twelve semitones to the octave (as in the Western chromatic scale intervals C-C♯-D-D♯-E-F-F♯-G-G♯-A-A♯-B-C) with other systems, it is useful to assign each semitone a mathematical value, for which we use the cent, one hundredth of a semitone. If we say that each semitone equals 100 cents, then each octave will equal 1,200 cents. The Western chromatic scale just listed corresponds to 1,200 cents, with a gap of 100 cents for each interval. The eight tones of the diatonic C major scale (C-D-E-F-G-A-B-C) are thus 0-200-400-500-700-900-1,100-1,200 cents, and this would be the numerical cents pattern for all Western major scales. These values are based on the system called equal temperament, the most typical Western system since 1850. Pythagorean tuning, with the same pitch set, was common in the West during the MIDDLE AGES. Based on the interval of a perfect fifth as the building block of tuning, it went out of favor because the thirds were too dissonant for chordal harmony, and a system for "tempering" the fifths developed. In the tempered system the intervals are the same in all keys.

Again taking the familiar Western chromatic or major scales as a reference point, a pentatonic system is a tuning of five divisions to the octave, and there are many different kinds of pentatonic tunings found throughout the world. That a musical culture favors pentatonic scales does not mean that other intervals cannot be heard; rather, it means that tuning each octave for five tones is the preferred system. To take two of the many possibilities, pentatonic tunings constructed as C-D-E-G-A (anhemitonic, without semitones) or C-D♭-F-G-A♭-C (hemitonic, with semitones) could use cents values close to Western ones and therefore be playable on a Western instrument.

Other pentatonics cannot be accommodated on a Western instrument, which is why we might think they are out of tune when we hear them. For example, a *slendro* tuning on a gamelan from Java might form a pentatonic this way: 0-246-487-706-960-1,206. It was once thought that *slendro* was an equipentatonic tuning, with the tones 240 cents apart, but in actual practice the tunings measured are all slightly different from that hypothetical abstraction, and different gamelan instrument sets are known for different tuning and timbre subtleties. The first pitch (see Table 1), at 246, is midway between chromatic D and D♯, producing a tone that is neither a major second nor a minor third away from the starting tone. The next tone, at 487 cents, is just slightly flat of chromatic F, and a Westerner will hear it as a

Table 1. Cents Values in Four Tuning Systems

fourth from the starting tone. Likewise the next tone, at 706, is so close to G at 700 that it would surely be heard as a fifth from the starting tone (differences of up to 8 to 10 cents may be barely heard by nontrained musicians; a trained musician might even be bothered by a difference of 2 or 3 cents). The next tone, at 960, is midway between chromatic A and A♯, neither a sixth nor a minor seventh from the starting tone. And the next tone, at 1,206, is extremely close to the octave. In sum the *slendro* sounds to a Westerner like a tuning system made up of a "normal" octave, fourth and fifth, bounded on each side by "out of tune" pitches, one between the major second and minor third, another between the sixth and minor seventh.

Some tuning systems divide the octave into equal equidistant intervals. An equal seven-tone, or equiheptatonic, tuning has been reported for places as geographically distant as Thailand and the Solomon Islands. In the latter area the 'Are'are people are well known for their four ensembles of bamboo panpipes. In a film and several articles Swiss ethnomusicologist Hugo Zemp has shown how the 'Are'are construct panpipes and tune them (*see* ETHNOMUSICOLOGY). A system of halving and doubling lengths of bamboo produces the intervals of octave, fifth, fourth, neutral third, and equiheptatonic second. The cents figures (see Table 1) for this tuning are 0-171-342-513-684-853-1,026-1,200. Again, comparing with the Western chromatic values, we find that the octaves and intervals of the fourth and fifth seem very close (513 cents and 684 cents, slightly sharp and flat, respectively, of the Western intervals). The two intervals on either side, between these tones and the octaves, are quite distinct. The first tone, at 171 cents, is midway between the Western chromatic diminished second and major second but more flat of the major second. The second tone, at 342 cents, is midway between the Western chromatic minor third and major third, hence the term *neutral third*. On the other side of the fifth the tone at 853 cents is midway between an augmented fifth and a sixth, and the tone at 1,026 cents sharp of a minor seventh.

The pelok, another tuning for the Javanese gamelan, is also heptatonic and provides quite a contrast to the equiheptatonic systems as well as to the previously described Javanese pentatonic *slendro*. As shown in Table 1, typical pelok cents values correspond closely to Western ones at the octave and at the minor third (294) and augmented fifth (803), far less closely at the minor seventh (976) and fifth (672), and not at all on the tones midway between diminished and major second (131) and perfect and augmented fourth (546). But this tells us relatively little; it makes far more sense to look at the cents distances between all the pelok intervals, where the pattern of 131-163-252-126-131-173-224 gives a clearer idea of the logic of the tuning pattern. It is also important

to recognize that these figures may not be exactly the same from octave to octave on a given instrument or the same for each instrument of the gamelan. This does not indicate a lack of concern with tuning, however, but rather an aesthetic preference found in Indonesian music for clashes of timbre and overtones created by slight internal pitch discrepancy.

Equally significant among tuning systems are ones that divide the octave into more than twelve segments, sometimes called microtonal systems. Microtonality can involve both fixed and relative dimensions of pitch. Systems of seventeen and nineteen fixed tones to the octave have been known in the Middle East; the modern Arabic quarter-tone system uses twenty-four fixed equal-tempered intervals, each 50 cents apart. Use of relative microtones involves inflectional conventions rather than specific constant pitches. This is shown by the variety of slides, bends, shakes, and oscillations in instrumental and vocal Afro-American idioms like blues, jazz, soul, and gospel music. The complex tuning system of India mixes several of these dimensions: a basic heptatonic structure; a theoretical division of these pitches into smaller intervals (22 sruti); and a performance tradition in which certain pitches are never altered, others may be flattened varying degrees according to the melodic context in the raga being performed, and yet one other pitch is raised a semitone—all yielding a sense of about twenty relative pitch positions to the octave.

Microtonality has also long been important to AVANT-GARDE composers and instrument inventors around the globe, for the expanded universe of sounds and harmonies that are available. Some important figures here include Harry Partch, a U.S. inventor who developed an ingenious mathematical figure of symmetrical pitches, the Tonality Diamond, and composed with a forty-three-tone octave system; Charles Ives, a U.S. composer who wrote quartertone pieces for two pianos, tuned a quarter tone apart; Adriaan Fokker, a Dutch acoustician who developed thirty-one-tone tuning emphasizing the purity of the major third and the minor seventh and built an organ for the performance of thirty-one-tone music; Ivan Vyshnegradsky, a Russian composer whose piece *Arc en ciel* was scored for six pianos, each tuned a twelfth of a tone higher than the last, and who designed a quarter-tone piano in the 1920s; George Secor, whose scalatron instrument allows the tuning of each key to any frequency; and Wajiha Abdul Haq, a Syrian inventor whose *kithara da damas* is a 440-stringed double-keyboard piano with back-to-back manuals tuned a quarter tone apart.

See also SOUND.

Bibliography. Donald H. Hall, *Musical Acoustics*, Belmont, Calif., 1980; Mantle Hood, "Sléndro and Pélog Redefined," *Selected Reports in Ethnomusicology* 1 (1966): 28–48; Mark Lindley, "Tuning," *New Grove Dictionary* *of Music and Musicians,* Vol. 19, New York, 1980 ed.; Tran Van Khe, "Is the Pentatonic Universal?" *World of Music* 19 (1977): 76–85; Hugo Zemp, " 'Are'are Classification of Musical Types and Jnstruments," *Ethnomusicology* 22 (1978): 37–67; idem, "Aspects of 'Are'are Musical Theory," *Ethnomusicology* 23 (1979): 6–48.

STEVEN FELD

MUSICAL, FILM

The musical is a GENRE that has become a part of film-making activity around the world, often drawing on regional music and THEATER traditions. This entry includes articles on the two most pervasive influences in the field:
1. Hollywood Genre
2. Bombay Genre

1. HOLLYWOOD GENRE

From their earliest days films have been accompanied by music, but the term *musical* has been reserved for films in which musical numbers play a significant role in conveying the dramatic NARRATIVE. The beginnings of the sound era in HOLLYWOOD in the late 1920s inevitably generated new genres, and among the most immediately successful was the musical, which became one of Hollywood's most distinctive contributions to the medium, with worldwide influence. The resources of the major studios enabled them to define the musical as a large-scale, often spectacular amalgam of SONG, DANCE, and DRAMA.

Origins

Although the film musical grew out of early talkie shorts and features produced at Warner Brothers in 1927–1928—notably *The Jazz Singer* (1927) with Al Jolson—a long tradition of musical theater and popular song predated and influenced the musical film. Among the influences was the Broadway revue, a mixture of (often satirical) sketches with performances of popular song and dance numbers. A variety format had also thrived in the U.S. theatrical forms known as vaudeville and, on an earthier level, burlesque. Loosely structured formats of this sort were used by Hollywood in MGM's *The Hollywood Revue of 1929,* *The Fox Movietone Follies* (1929), *Paramount on Parade* (1930), and Universal's *The King of Jazz* (1930), each displaying its studio's stable of musical talent in Broadway style, with emcees and curtained stages. MGM's *The Broadway Melody* (1929) inaugurated the tradition of the backstage musical. Here songs and dances were motivated by a plot about the preparation of a Broadway production. Another Broadway influence, which had been derived from Europe, was the operetta, in which no such pretext was sought, but song and dance were accepted as normal elements of dramatic narrative, motivated by situation or emotion. An early film example was *The Desert Song* (1929), a direct adaptation of the Sigmund Romberg–Oscar Hammerstein operetta.

Evolution

It was the backstage musical that first dominated the genre, largely due to a series of Warner Brothers productions directed in whole or part by a master of musical spectacle, Busby Berkeley. Among the Berkeley backstage musicals were *42nd Street* (1933), *Footlight Parade* (1933), *Gold Diggers of 1933,* *Dames* (1934; Figure 1), and *Gold Diggers of 1935.* These musicals were characterized by a radical separation of narrative and number, presenting naturalistic backstage dramas culminating in elaborate, often surrealistic production numbers. *Dames* was typical: the success of a young romance is linked to the success of the show in which the young couple is involved. The plot contrasts the Puritan ethic with the pleasure principle, lovemaking and show making are used as metaphors for each other, and the film ends with the celebration of their mutual success in the form of the extravagant Berkeleyan spectacle.

Contemporaneous with Berkeley's work at Warner Brothers were two other studio styles of the 1930s (categorized by Rick Altman as the "fairy-tale musical"): the Paramount operetta and the dance-centered, integrated musical comedies of Fred Astaire and Ginger Rogers produced at RKO. Operettas like *The Love Parade* (1929) and *The Merry Widow* (1934) showed the European influence of directors such as Ernst Lubitsch and Rouben Mamoulian. Set in mythical kingdoms, these fairy-tale musicals parallel the course of the romance with the need to maintain order in the kingdom. In the operetta tradition the musical numbers furthered the love interest, enabling the songs to be integrated with the stories. The operetta tradition continued through the 1930s at MGM in films starring Jeannette MacDonald and Nelson Eddy.

The integrating process continued with the Astaire-Rogers series of nine films, from *Flying Down to Rio* in 1933 to *Top Hat* in 1935 (Figure 2) to *The Story of Vernon and Irene Castle* in 1939. The RKO series of films continued the backstage tradition in that Astaire and Rogers frequently portrayed professional entertainers (archetypically in *Shall We Dance*) but seemed more in the fantasy spirit of the operetta films, sharing as well their tendency to integrate narrative and number. The Astaire-Rogers films differed from the operettas, however, in their use of contemporary popular music and in the emphasis on dance rather than song as the chief means for conveying plot and character relationships.

Figure 1. *(Musical, Film—Hollywood Genre)* Busby Berkeley, *Dames,* 1934. The Museum of Modern Art/Film Stills Archive.

What is often referred to as the golden age of the integrated musical came into being at MGM under the impetus of a group known as the Freed Unit (named for producer Arthur Freed). The Freed Unit functioned as a repertory company within the studio system, working out of a creative nucleus consisting of directors Vincente Minnelli, Gene Kelly and Stanley Donen, and Charles Walters; writers Betty Comden and Adolph Green; and performers Judy Garland, Gene Kelly, and Fred Astaire, among others. From the early 1940s until about 1955 (when MGM stopped mass-producing musicals) they were responsible for some of the best-known musical films, including *Meet Me in St. Louis, The Pirate, Easter Parade, On the*

◁ **Figure 2.** *(Musical, Film—Hollywood Genre)* Fred Astaire and Ginger Rogers in *Top Hat,* directed by Mark Sandrich, 1935. The Museum of Modern Art/Film Stills Archive.

Town, An American in Paris, Singin' in the Rain (Figure 3), *The Band Wagon,* and *It's Always Fair Weather.*

The Freed Unit was instrumental in developing a type of musical that has been labeled the folk musical. In this subgenre singing and dancing come not from professional entertainers performing for a paying audience but from ordinary people expressing a love of the land or the joys of everyday life. In these folk settings, usually involving a small town or otherwise rustic environment, performers such as Garland and Kelly could portray characters from whom singing and dancing appeared to rise spontaneously, lending to the MGM musical a folksy quality that belied the professionalism of its musical numbers. The Freed Unit, led by director Minnelli, also pioneered the "dream ballet," in which characters acted out their fantasies in stylized-dancing dream sequences. The dream sequence was typical of Minnelli's work, stressing the themes of art versus life and dream versus reality—themes that were so prevalent in the director's films and in the MGM musical as a genre.

The end of the golden age of Hollywood musicals coincided with the decline of the studio system, beginning in the mid-1950s. Musicals continued to be made, and some (e.g., *The Sound of Music,* 1965) were enormous financial successes. However, the energy and vitality that had previously driven the genre as a whole, as well as its glorification of entertainment, were increasingly replaced by a cynicism and self-examination that manifested itself in films like *All That Jazz* (1980).

The Hollywood musical has been studied as a film genre, a mass-produced formulaic narrative that gives the audience a ritualistic rather than a unique viewing experience. The value of the experience lies not so much in the artistic merit of a particular film but rather in the shared cultural meanings conveyed by the genre as a whole. The Hollywood musical—with its repeated confrontations between art and life, dream and reality, and entertainment and puritanism—has been described as a genre that mediates between the U.S. belief in the work ethic and its love of the carefree values of entertainment. In valuing entertainment the musical also promotes the virtues of the Hollywood studio system and of itself as a genre. Although we may think of the musical as pure entertainment, the genre also presents us with a ritual examination of the values of freedom, success, and love in the United States as they are realized over and over again in the utopian form of song and dance.

See also MOTION PICTURES.

Bibliography. Rick Altman, *The American Film Musical,* Bloomington, Ind., 1987; idem, ed., *Genre: The Musical,* London and Boston, 1981; Jane Feuer, *The Hollywood Musical,* London, 1982; Clive Hirschhorn, *The Hollywood Musical,* New York, 1981; John Kobal, *Gotta Sing, Gotta Dance: A Pictorial History of Film Musicals,* London and New York, 1971.

JANE FEUER

Figure 3. *(Musical, Film—Hollywood Genre)* Gene Kelly in *Singin' in the Rain,* directed by Gene Kelly and Stanley Donen, 1951. The Museum of Modern Art/Film Stills Archive. Courtesy of MGM/UA.

2. BOMBAY GENRE

When Universal's *Melody of Love,* the first sound film shown in India, made its appearance there in 1929, it seemed to India's young film industry a message of doom. HOLLYWOOD films already occupied 90 percent of Indian screen time. Could Indian filmmaking survive this new challenge? The conversion of existing facilities to sound production, requiring costly imported equipment and new kinds of expertise, seemed an overwhelming problem. In spite of this outlook, the Bombay exhibitor Ardeshir Irani managed to put together the musical *Alam ara* (Beauty of the World), made in the Hindi LANGUAGE and debuted in 1931—India's first sound film. Its reception was tumultuous. Police had to be brought in to control the surging crowds. Tickets disappeared into the black market. Twenty-two other Hindi films, all musicals, were released in 1931; all were similarly received. In Hollywood the musical had become one of several major genres (*see* GENRE); in India it became for a quarter of a century the *only* genre. Not until 1955 would any Indian producer venture to produce a film without songs or dances. By then, India's film industry had become one of the world's largest and one of the few to dominate its own screens. It turned out films—musicals, that is—in more than a score of Indian languages. *See* MOTION PICTURES—SOUND FILM.

Several factors help to explain the remarkable transition. In a land where foreign languages had for a thousand years dominated the councils and pleasures of the mighty, it was a startling and emotional experience to find one's own language issuing from the giant screen. To this was added another, equally powerful factor. *Alam ara* had a dozen songs (*see* SONG). Another early Hindi film is said to have had forty. All early Indian musicals had a profusion of songs, and most had dances (*see* DANCE). This was no accident: the industry was drawing on a tradition that went back some two thousand years.

In ancient India, in the golden age of Sanskrit THEATER—that of Śūdraka (fourth century C.E.) and Kālidāsa (fifth century C.E.)—DRAMA was always inseparable from music and dance. In the Muslim-dominated era, from about 1000 C.E., drama became an outcast, held in moral obloquy. But while it ceased to be an ornament of princely courts, it survived as folk drama performed by players traveling from village to village throughout India, always involving song and dance (*see* MUSIC THEATER—ASIAN TRADITIONS). In 1931 the Indian film world tapped this current, a mighty river of music that had flowed through millennia of tradition.

The Indian musical became more a way of drama than a genre: it comprised all genres. A musical could be a tale of love and sorrow, a mythological story (*see* MYTHOLOGICAL FILM, ASIAN), a historical spectacular, a farce, a mystery, a problem play, a TRAGEDY. In one of the most nostalgically revered of early musicals, *Devdas* (1935), whose songs are still heard on Indian radio, an intercaste romance is thwarted when the heroine obeys her father and accepts the suitable marriage he has arranged. But she never forgets her Devdas, who meanwhile takes to drink and at the end is found dead outside her home. For many young viewers the film unquestionably functioned as a vehicle of social protest. The Indian musical thus often reflects tensions of Indian society, in which many age-old customs are eroding. But, as in other film industries, the Indian musical more often reaches for a blockbuster impact with astounding action. In the film *Avvaiyar* (1951), made in the Tamil language by S. S. Vasan of Madras, a hero is held captive in an enemy fortress. In response to

prayers sung to the elephant god Gaṇeśa, a herd of elephants thunders across the landscape to his rescue and, pushing in unison, brings the fortress walls toppling to the ground.

Regardless of how spectacular the action, the obsessive loyalty belongs to the music. Film songs have become a constant Indian presence, accompanying weddings, funerals, state occasions, religious festivals, parades, parties, and political conventions. Their nature has evolved over decades. Originally drawn from Indian tradition, they have become highly eclectic, utilizing rhythms and instrumentation from all parts of the world. This has been denounced by some musicologists as a corruption of things Indian but has been enthusiastically welcomed by young audiences. It also seems to have helped the films win a growing export market, especially in other parts of South Asia and in East Africa. Many Indian musicals have won success in the Arab world, and some—notably films starring Raj Kapoor, such as *Awara* (The Vagabond, 1951) and *Shri 420* (Mr. 420, 1955)—have been well received in the Soviet Union.

In India the industry inevitably works in many languages. Some films are produced in several languages with a different cast for each. But most Indian musicals have from the start been made in Hindi. At the beginning of the sound era this language was spoken by some 140 million people, offering the most promising market. They were concentrated in a northern area, and the language was not understood in most of India—especially not in the South, which was dominated by languages having no relationship to Hindi. In spite of this, Hindi musicals have won an audience in these other areas, largely because of the music but also because song and dance and the NONVERBAL COMMUNICATION they involve perform so much of the storytelling function. Overt lovemaking has tended to be taboo on the Indian screen, but song and dance, often extremely sensual, provide functional dramatic equivalents of courtship and love. Thus the Hindi musical has transcended linguistic barriers. Like the Hollywood musical, it has also seemed to challenge a tradition of puritanism.

When India became independent in 1947 some leaders felt that Hindi should eventually become the national language, but political pressure toward this goal has aroused fierce opposition, especially in the South. Some observers speculate that if Hindi ever does become the national language it will be not because of government educational efforts but because of the penetration of the Hindi musical.

See also MUSIC, FOLK AND TRADITIONAL; MUSIC, POPULAR.

Bibliography. Erik Barnouw and S. Krishnaswamy, *Indian Film*, 2d ed., New York, Oxford, and New Delhi, 1980; Rani Burra, ed., *Film India: Looking Back, 1896–1960,*

New Delhi, 1981; Chidananda Das Gupta, *Talking about Films,* New Delhi, 1981.

ERIK BARNOUW AND S. KRISHNASWAMY

MUSICAL INSTRUMENTS

Musical instruments may be defined broadly as tools of musical communication, with the added qualification that certain body parts may be used in ways that form a musical instrument (such as blowing into the hollow formed by cupping the hands). The great number and diversity of musical instruments are nothing less than astonishing. That musical instruments have existed for a large part of human history is evidence of our need to rely on some artificial means of producing sound in order to convey the total spectrum of moods and emotions that motivate music making.

Musical instruments are relevant to communications in a number of ways. An instrument is a physical object with a recognizable form and timbre, both of which may acquire specific associations from the CULTURE in which the instrument is found. These may come to mind simply by seeing an instrument or hearing its SOUND. As a cultural ARTIFACT a musical instrument can provide information pertinent to the history of cultural interactions. Furthermore, it can offer concrete means of determining or at least confirming tuning systems in use in a particular music culture and can provide insight into the aesthetic preferences for particular sound qualities in a culture (*see* MUSIC THEORIES—TUNING SYSTEMS). The physical actions and behavior associated with playing musical instruments are instructive in understanding a system of music and the processes of socialization that maintain a tradition of music. Often particular social groups are associated with specific instruments or even instrument playing in general. Finally, the repertoires associated with musical instruments often acquire an independence that sets them apart from other modes of sound communication such as SPEECH and vocal music (*see* SONG). Some of these are closely allied to speech systems, even to the point of serving as surrogate speech systems (such as the talking drums of West Africa); others show greater affinity with vocal music sources; and yet another type appears to have little relation at all to a vocal system (such as Western symphonic literature). Studies of the SEMIOTICS of such systems contribute significantly to the general body of knowledge about human communication.

Systems of classification. Because of the great diversity of musical instruments and an underlying concern for determining genetic and cultural links, a prime aim of musicologists has been the development of a system of CLASSIFICATION. Actually the systematic classification of musical instruments has a long history. Writers on music in ancient India and China devised separate methods of grouping tools of musical sound. The Chinese system was based on the material of construction and included eight classes: earth, stone, metal, skin, wood, bamboo, gourd, and silk. The Indian system detailed in the *Nāṭyaśāstra,* the famous treatise on dramaturgy attributed to the sage Bharata (ca. 200–500 C.E.), provided the basis for the most widely accepted system of modern times, the Hornbostel-Sachs *Systematik,* named for its originators, Erich M. von Hornbostel and Curt Sachs. This system groups instruments into four main categories: those composed of rigid material sufficiently elastic to undergo periodic vibration (idiophones), those incorporating tightly stretched membranes (membranophones), those in which strings vibrate (chordophones), and those in which a column of air vibrates (aerophones). These categories are further refined with numerous subdivisions based on the physical characteristics of sound production (striking, rubbing, clapping, plucking, bowing, etc.) or the structural shape of the instruments (e.g., kettle-, tubular-, goblet-, or hourglass-shaped drums).

The primary usefulness of the Hornbostel-Sachs *Systematik* is that it provides a detailed and consis-

Figure 1. *(Musical Instruments)* Harpist invoking Horus. Egyptian-style painting, 1315. Louvre, Paris. Giraudon/Art Resource, New York.

tent vocabulary for discussing musical instruments. As a taxonomic system it has been criticized for its internal inconsistencies and its inability to classify all existing instruments satisfactorily. For example, the *cuíca* friction drum of Brazil, played by rubbing a wooden rod attached to the inner side of the membrane of a single-headed, open-ended cylindrical drum, has both idiophonic and membranophonic qualities, whereas the American banjo and the Indian *sārangī* and *sarod* combine chordophonic and membranophonic aspects. Even more interesting is the Indian *khamak*, an instrument associated with the unconventional Baul sect of Bengal. This instrument is similar in concept to the Brazilian friction drum but with the substitution of a tensed, plucked string for the rubbed stick. The *khamak* functions as a rhythm instrument but wonderfully combines percussive and melodic qualities into a synthetic whole. As ethnomusicologists have grown increasingly interested in developing culturally grounded explanations of the music systems they study, the *Systematik* has become less useful and more open to criticism because it contributes little to our knowledge of the cultural significance of a musical instrument (*see* ETHNOMUSICOLOGY). However, although many other systems of instrument classification have been proposed (e.g., André Schaeffner's two-part division of air and solid bodies as vibrating materials or Kurt Reinhard's system based on the number of sounding bodies and the means of pitch adjustment), none has gained the widespread acceptance of the Hornbostel-Sachs system.

Age of instruments. Musicologists attempting to ascertain the evolution of musical instruments often combine archaeology with geography, hypothesizing that an object's age is proportional to the extent of its DIFFUSION. These methods reveal that the existence of idiophones and aerophones extends at least to the first period of the Upper Paleolithic age (35,000–25,000 B.C.E.), with the use of idiophones probably occurring at a much earlier date, possibly as far back as the Middle Paleolithic (150,000 B.C.E.); chordophones and membranophones did not appear until the Neolithic period. In general we might also observe that musical instruments reflect the degree to which a culture has developed technology and control over its environment. Thus the earliest instruments in human history were rhythmic in function and idiophonic in structure, probably extensions of the use of the human body to produce slapping, clapping, and stamping sounds. Material prototypes of such instruments existed naturally (dried gourds, shells of crustaceans, etc.) and could fulfill a musical function with little or no preparation. That many such instruments continue to exist and command high cultural esteem among nonliterate tribes in many parts of the world lends support to this hypothesis.

Figure 2. *(Musical Instruments)*   Bolivian stone panpipe. Neg. Trans. No. 39583 (Photo by H. Millou). Courtesy Department of Library Services, American Museum of Natural History, New York.

Figure 3. *(Musical Instruments)*   Bronze figure of a trumpeter, Benin, Nigeria. Reproduced by courtesy of the Trustees of The British Museum.

Figure 4. *(Musical Instruments)* Hans Memling, organ shutter showing angel musicians. Flemish, fifteenth century. Giraudon/Art Resource, New York.

One such instrument is the slit-drum (sometimes called a gong), an idiophone formed from a section of a tree trunk by hollowing a cavity from a narrow longitudinal cut. Slit-drums are found among tribal peoples of the Pacific islands, South America, Africa, and Asia. Because of such wide distribution, we may assume that this instrument type is extremely old.

Tuning systems. Whether studying the music of a past age or the music in a contemporary society, musical instruments are often examined to gain an understanding of the tuning system(s) to which a given culture adheres. Often music theorists and musicians within a culture refer to particular musical instruments to articulate theories of tuning. In India theorists always have demonstrated the twenty-two sruti system of intonation with reference to string instruments, first on bow harps and later on long-necked lutes. And in ancient China an equivalent of the Western concert pitch was determined by the pitch produced by blowing across a bamboo tube (*lü*) of such a volume that it would contain a specified

number of dried peas. Other pitches of the Chinese tonal system were derived by a process based on the phenomenon of overblown fifths and the acoustical law stating that the ratio 3:2 will produce the interval of a perfect fifth. A tube two-thirds the length of the original tube thus emits a tone equivalent to the overblown fifth of the original. Furthermore, a tone an octave below the overblown fifth of this second tube can be produced on a third tube one-third greater in length than the second. By extending this process of producing fifths and their lower octaves the Chinese theorists constructed a scale based on the circle of fifths. The degree to which actual PER-FORMANCE practice adhered to such theoretically prescribed standards is altogether another matter.

Extramusical associations. Associations attached to particular instruments often tell us much about a music culture. For example, the Chinese board zither, *ch'in*, has always been associated with the literati. Thus, among other tools of the trade such as the special pens and brushes required for fine calligraphy,

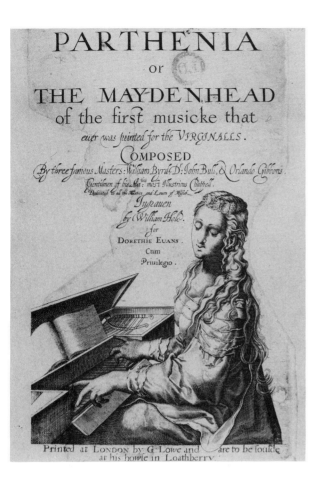

◁ **Figure 5.** *(Musical Instruments)*
The title page of *Parthenia*, published in London in 1611. This was the first collection of music engraved for keyboard instruments. By permission of the British Library.

the traditional Chinese scholar's study included a *ch'in* hanging on a wall, regardless of the owner's musicality. The folklore of the *ch'in* goes much deeper than this, though. Surrounding the performance practice of this instrument is a complex IDEOLOGY combining aspects of Confucianism and Taoism with Buddhist and yogic practices imported from India; playing the *ch'in* was an act bordering on a religious ritual of purification, not just an art.

Certain associations an instrument communicates to members of a culture may be tied ultimately to the materials from which it is constructed. Thus in Java bronze instruments are highly esteemed because bronze is considered to have religious significance. When the large *gong ageng* of a sophisticated gamelan is constructed, the blacksmith concludes the manufacturing process by distributing the water used in the final rinsing phase as a holy sacrament to members of his community. Material of construction becomes socially significant in Hindu India, a society

Figure 6. *(Musical Instruments)*   Jan Molenaer, *Children Making Music*, 1629. Reproduced by courtesy of the Trustees, The National Gallery, London.

Figure 7. *(Musical Instruments)* Hermitess with a tiger and playing the Indian lute (vīṇā). Indian, Golconda/Hyderabad, ca. 1750. Museum für Indische Kunst, Staatliche Museen Preussischer Kulturbesitz, Berlin (West), Sign: MIK I 5002/34. © Bildarchiv Preussischer Kulturbesitz, Berlin (West), 1975.

ordered by notions of purity and pollution, which relegates drummers to a less favorable status ranking because their profession requires that they contact the skins of dead animals. The exigencies of performance practice too appear to have been subsumed into the Hindu order, affecting the nature of the instruments represented in this culture. Thus, because wind instruments require close contact with the mouth, with the possible transfer of saliva (a polluting substance) to the mouthpiece, aerophones in general are less diverse and are not usually played by members of high castes. Paradoxically the sound of the *śahnāī*—a double-reed aerophone of conical bore—is believed to be especially auspicious, and *śahnāī* ensembles consisting of lower-caste or Muslim musicians are commonly enlisted to provide music at Hindu weddings to help ensure nuptial bliss and harmony.

Musical instruments throughout much of their his-

tory have been used to communicate information that borders on the nonmusical. The ivory horn, or oliphant, was a symbol of knighthood in medieval England and is said to have been used to signal a call of distress. The militaristic uses of the bugle are well known to Westerners as are the use of church bells to announce a call to service and the ringing of small hand-held bells to indicate particular points in the Catholic Mass. In Korea the *teuk-gyeong,* an idiophone consisting of a single stone slab suspended from a support, is used to signal the end of ceremonial court music.

More detailed signaling occurs in the drum languages of West Africa and the Congo area. The hourglass-shaped pressure drum, *dun dun,* of the Yoruba tribe of Nigeria and the slit-log drum, *bongungu,* of the Lokele tribe of Zaire are two types of drums commonly used to send rhythmically encoded messages. John Carrington has shown how these

Figure 8. *(Musical Instruments)* Masanobu, *Nakamuro Kiyozo as Yaoya Oshishi and Onoe Kikugoro I as Kichsaburo Dressed in the Costumes of Wandering Minstrels.* Early eighteenth-century Japanese print. Ross-Coomaraswamy Collection. 21.7226. Courtesy, Museum of Fine Arts, Boston.

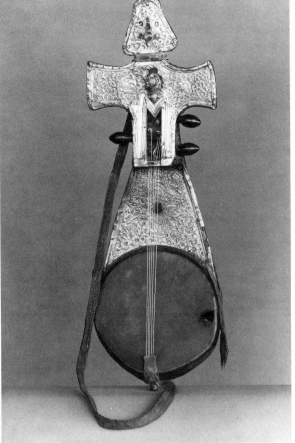

surrogate languages are tied closely to the tonal aspect of African languages in which the relative pitch of syllables acquires a phonemic function. The contrast of high and low pitches is produced on the *dun dun* by applying pressure to the laces that tie the heads together, creating a change in tension on the heads and a concomitant change in pitch. The contrasting tones are produced on slit-log-type signaling drums by shaving the "lips" of the slit to different thicknesses, resulting in one side's producing a tone higher in pitch than the other.

Possibly because of their capacity to produce sounds beyond the potential of the human vocal apparatus, musical instruments are often called upon to provide a means of communication with the spirit world. For example, Paul Berliner has explained the role of the *mbira dzavadzimu*, an idiophone with multiple manuals of plucked metal keys, in the spirit possession rituals of the Shona tribe of Zimbabwe. The Shona believe that the sound of this particular instrument has the power to penetrate the boundaries of the spirit world and call the ancestral spirits into the midst of the ritual activity.

Varied roles of musical instruments. In the course of their history instruments have evolved from ad-

◁ **Figure 9.** *(Musical Instruments)* Tibetan musical instrument. Wood overlaid with embossed silver and set with semiprecious stones. Courtesy of the Board of Trustees of the Victoria and Albert, London.

Figure 10. *(Musical Instruments)* Javanese metallophone. Reproduced by courtesy of the Trustees of The British Museum. Raffles Collection.

Figure 11. *(Musical Instruments)* Some of the unconventional musical instruments created by U.S. composer Harry Partch *(center front)*. Courtesy of the American Music Theater Festival.

junct functionaries keeping a beat for ritualistic or expressive purposes to complementary sources of melody supporting a vocal line, later to means of playing music conceived vocally, and finally to idioms of instrumentally conceived music. The music culture of India provides examples to elucidate the latter stages of this evolution. Certain instruments in the art music of North India function primarily as vocal support. These include the *sāraṅgī,* a bowed lute with a membrane-covered resonating cavity and numerous sympathetic resonating wires, and the harmonium, a small hand-pumped reed organ bequeathed by the British raj to Indian music culture. Both instruments function during a vocal performance of the raga-based improvisational music to fill in when the singer pauses to rest and to follow the melody line of the vocalist in a type of musical double talk, resulting in a heterophonic texture that is at times breathtaking in complexity and bewildering in execution. That the accompanists can be so adept in a process of music composition that is more akin to speech than to RHETORIC indicates the systematic nature of the music logic of these musicians, a talent obtained only after years of intensive training and practice.

Other Indian instruments are considered media for the performance of music originally conceived for vocal performance. These include the *sarasvatī vīṇā* (commonly called *bīn*) of North India, a fretted stick zither with two large gourd resonators, and the *Tañjori vīṇā* of South India, a fretted long-necked lute made from jackwood. Of the two, music of the South Indian *vīṇā* is more clearly modeled on vocal sources, as evidenced in the plucking patterns of the right hand. These are directly linked to the textual setting of the melody. Changes of syllable in a texted song are indicated in the instrumental rendition by articulations of the right hand.

Although the stroking patterns on the North Indian sitar may be recited vocally in a system of mnemonics, they usually are not tied to a preexistent vocal text. Because of their freedom from vocal sources these patterns have become conventionalized and form the basis for GENRE differentiation and improvisational forms in North Indian instrumental music. The basic patterns are constructed by linking together series of inward and outward strokes. Particular configurations of strokes in general tempo ranges are key determinants of genre in this system of music. Thus the *Masitkhānī gat* is based on a stroking pattern of sixteen beats played at a moderately slow tempo. The pattern begins on the twelfth beat of a sixteen-beat rhythm cycle maintained by a pair of drums, the tabla. The melodic and rhythmic cycles coincide on the first beat of the drum pattern. This also serves as a major point of closure for virtuosic flourishes departing from the set patterns played by either the sitarist or the tabla player.

The development of electronic musical instruments that incorporate digital sampling technologies poses interesting questions in the popular-music world of the West (*see* ELECTRONIC MUSIC; MUSIC, POPULAR). These instruments can sample the sound of any instrument and then reproduce that particular sound quality at any pitch, normally using a keyboard manual as a reference. Problems arise when the sound of a particular artist, cultivated through years of experimentation and hard practice, is sampled by another artist and used in a recording. In the United States the 1976 COPYRIGHT legislation may have to be revised to satisfy the demands of artists regarding the ownership of musical sound. That this issue arises amply demonstrates that musical instruments are just that—instruments. The final sound product produced on a musical instrument is a function of both the instrument's inherent acoustical potential and limitations and the artistry of its player.

See also MUSIC, FOLK AND TRADITIONAL; MUSIC HISTORY; MUSIC MACHINES; MUSIC PERFORMANCE; SOUND EFFECTS.

Bibliography. Paul Berliner, *The Soul of Mbira*, Berkeley, Calif., 1978; John F. Carrington, *Talking Drums of Africa*, London, 1949; B. Chaitanya Deva, *Musical Instruments of India*, Calcutta, 1978; Karl Geiringer, *Instruments in the History of Western Music*, 3d ed., New York, 1978; Mantle Hood, *The Ethnomusicologist*, new ed., Kent, Ohio, 1982; Percival R. Kirby, *The Musical Instruments of the Native Races of South Africa* (1934), 2d ed., Johannesburg, 1965; William P. Malm, *Japanese Music and Musical Instruments*, Rutland, Vt., 1959; Curt Sachs, *The History of Musical Instruments*, New York, 1940; R. H. Van Gulik, *The Lore of the Chinese Lute*, Rutland, Vt., and Tokyo, 1940.

STEPHEN M. SLAWEK

MUZAK

A trade name both for a corporation and for the patented music product and service it originated and sells worldwide. In the 1980s most people use the term to refer generically to a variety of musical contexts and forms, ranging from "easy-listening" RADIO and recordings to any form of taped or wired background music played at low volume in offices, restaurants, shopping areas, and other work or public places. Some people use the term to refer positively to any soft, soothing music; others use it to refer negatively to any "canned" commercial background music or SOUND EFFECTS. In effect, the term *Muzak* has come to mean both more and less than its owners intended.

The development of the Muzak style is related to changes in its contexts. On opening the New York operation in 1936, the Muzak Corporation sold a product characterized by orchestral strings playing long melodies in a style similar to film scores of the period. After 1940, when Muzak entered the workplace market of factories, banks, and offices, it began to hire arrangers to rearrange tunes in a style it considered more appropriate to its new settings. It was further encouraged in this direction by agreeing to conduct joint studies with the U.S. War Production Board to determine if the addition of music into the work setting could assist the war effort by increasing worker productivity. By 1950 Muzak had developed its notion of "stimulus progression." It no longer considered itself entertainment or background music, but "functional music," designed to be heard but not listened to, yet able to improve productivity. These ideas have persisted at Muzak, although the sound of Muzak has shifted as popular tastes have changed.

These changes in codes initially occurred at a time when the developing industrial economy had certain specific needs. First, the ongoing struggle for production efficiency was addressed by Muzak's idea of stimulus progression, in which each fifteen-minute segment contained five tunes, each one brighter and more stimulating in tempo and sound than the last. Muzak further claimed to assist efficient production by playing even faster and brighter arrangements during the predictable low daily productivity cycles. Second, it had become a common belief among employers that higher productivity occurred when workers were contented. Muzak was able to say that its music was very pleasant and gave workers a sense that the employer cared for them. Third, the growing consumer society wanted shopping to be a positive, pleasant experience. Muzak argued that shopping with music was more pleasing to customers than shopping in silence (*see* CONSUMER RESEARCH). Muzak was able not only to address these three broad trends in U.S. society but also to claim that its music was scientifically proven to produce desired results. Muzak's success can be attributed not only to being a part of the broad sweep of music throughout the culture made possible by the phonograph, radio, and jukebox, but also to addressing successfully these potent and ongoing ideologies.

What differentiates Muzak from its generic equivalents is an institutional framework of research, recording, and dissemination that provides an alleged scientific rationale for the efficacy of the final product. In addition to the stimulus progression idea, Muzak employs strict conventions for the orchestration and performance of its product in order to ensure a neutral, unaffecting quality that will not attract a listener's attention. In order for the product to have no entertainment or listening appeal, it should not engage the listener emotionally. The idea is to smooth out the rough edges of noisy environments by providing—in contrast to music—a constant sound that calls forth no emotions, no associations, no reflections, and no evaluations.

Some people interpret Muzak to be an insult, a devious mind-control plot to encourage buying or to anesthetize workers, or an extension of other forms of political and cultural hegemony. The International Music Council of UNESCO passed a resolution seeking a worldwide ban on specific and generic Muzak, calling it an assault on public PRIVACY. Others find it a far less ideologically charged product, even if they do not appreciate its intention or believe the scientific rationale for its effects. There have been many reports of contested control of the sound environment by workers in factory and other settings. Many managers today say that workers are most happy and efficient when they themselves control whether or not there is music in the workplace and when they control the variety and volume of the music. Others still use Muzak or similar services at the workplace but permit workers to use their own personal sound devices. Still others, workers and consumers alike, report that they like Muzak and even find themselves listening actively to it. There seems as little consensus about attitudes toward Muzak as about what it communicates.

See also IDEOLOGY; MOTIVATION RESEARCH; MUSIC, POPULAR; SOUND RECORDING.

JANE HULTING

MYSTERY AND DETECTIVE FICTION

Detective FICTION became an established GENRE in late-nineteenth-century Europe and the United States and has remained popular throughout the industrialized world. The NARRATIVE is typically concerned with the solution of a criminal mystery by a professional or inspired amateur detective. Usually the mysterious event is as opaque to the reader as it is to the characters, leading the reader to identify with the detective as the major source of information in the story. U.S. writer Edgar Allan Poe's short story "The Murders in the Rue Morgue" (1841) is the first to fit this description, and it contains all the major components of the genre: the subordination of narrative elements to detection, the insistence on the role of ratiocination, the infallible detective, the detective's admiring (and slow) friend, the preference for brutal murder as the crime to be solved, the slight shudder that accompanies its discovery.

The early to mid-nineteenth century also saw the beginnings of modern policing methods in Europe

and the United States, and the fictional figure of the detective is perhaps related to hopes of what the police force would be able to achieve. In 1828–1829 François-Eugène Vidocq, a French thief turned detective, published his memoirs, which launched the detective as a cult figure. The vogue for police memoirs lasted throughout the century (*see* AUTOBIOGRAPHY). This period also saw the beginnings of the emphasis on scientific knowledge that has characterized industrial society. The detective's emphasis on deductive reasoning reflects a fascination with the possibilities of the scientific method and especially of its application to social problems. Fascination with crime can also be found in literature of the time, particularly in the enormously successful, widely translated, and widely influential French novel *Les mystères de Paris* (1842–1843), by Eugène Sue. Sue's avenger hero, who rights the wrongs committed by Paris's criminal underclass against the poor and oppressed, anticipates later and equally popular fictional figures.

Writing about crime was not new; there is ample attention to the subject in preceding centuries, much of it in the form of protojournalism—tract and broadsheet accounts of individual crimes, biographies of famous criminals (*see* BIOGRAPHY), accounts of trials and executions, and gazettes announcing crimes and rewards for the return of stolen property. Various tendencies can be seen in this literature: insistence on the disruptive and horrific aspects of crime, overt moralizing about the inevitability of retribution, and enjoyment of the exploits of plausible rogues, a theme that entered the novel in the form of the picaresque. During the period of the Industrial Revolution there was increasing separation

Figure 1. *(Mystery and Detective Fiction)* Illustration from Eugène Sue, *Les mystères de Paris*, part 2, Paris: Librairie de Charles Gosselin, 1844, p. 152.

ment of evidence and culminating in a devastating display of deductive power that reveals the guilt of someone it is hoped was never suspected by the reader, were widely imitated. Successful early epigones include Freeman Wills Crofts and G. K. Chesterton in Britain, and Anna Katharine Green and Mary Roberts Rinehart in the United States.

The golden age of the detective story was the period between the two world wars. These years saw the emergence of the most successful Western writers in the genre. In Britain Agatha Christie, Margery Allingham, Ngaio Marsh, and Dorothy Sayers established themselves during this period. In the United States the style was imitated by the pseudonymous S. S. Van Dine and Ellery Queen. In France Georges Simenon began his Inspector Maigret series in 1933. At this time detective stories started to acquire the gamelike quality now associated with them. Rules of the genre were formulated, and novelists were encouraged to play fair by giving the reader a reasonable chance to work out the solution to the mystery independently of the deductions of the detective.

Figure 2. *(Mystery and Detective Fiction)* Cover of *New Nick Carter Weekly*, New York, 1905. The Bettmann Archive, Inc.

between writing condemning crime and writing expressing ambiguous fascination, and a strand emerged that increasingly glamorized the hero—who might be a bandit or outlaw—as a rebel against an unjust social order. Detective stories made use of this established fascination with criminality, but within the perspective of law and order, for they usually adopted the point of view of the detective and thereby excluded that of the criminal.

Poe's invention of the "formula" of the detective story did not lead to its immediate exploitation as a form of commercial storytelling. Despite writers such as Émile Gaboriau in France and Wilkie Collins in Britain (whose 1860 novel, *The Moonstone,* adopted some of Poe's procedures), it was not until after the 1870s that the formula was widely used, largely owing to the extraordinary success of Arthur Conan Doyle's Sherlock Holmes stories. These stories became the model for detective fiction for the next half-century and firmly established it as a primarily British genre. Sherlock Holmes himself was the model for the detective as hero—an inspired, isolated eccentric—and Doyle's plots, based on the detailed assess-

Figure 3. *(Mystery and Detective Fiction)* Alexander Rodchenko, cover design for a detective story, 1924. From S. Bojko, *New Graphic Design in Revolutionary Russia,* New York: Praeger Publishers, 1972.

Figure 4. *(Mystery and Detective Fiction)* Basil Rathbone as Sherlock Holmes. The Bettmann Archive, Inc.

These stories usually restricted their settings to the English provincial middle and upper classes, partly, no doubt, because that was presumed to be the world of their readers and partly because these environments plausibly provide the closed setting (the country house, for example) and the restricted cast of characters that the puzzlelike structure of these novels demands.

British domination of the genre was eclipsed in the 1930s by the U.S. "hard-boiled school," whose best representatives included Raymond Chandler and Dashiell Hammett, though its most commercially successful author was to be Mickey Spillane two decades later. The distinctive features of this style center on the nature of the hero, who is now as much a man of action as of ratiocination and who fights as much as reasons his way to a conclusion. Although the basic structure of the narrative still consists of the successful solution of a mystery, the presence of a man of action at the center of the story ensures that less of the narrative is concerned with the detailed evaluation of evidence than is the case in the traditional English detective story. Whereas the traditional detective relates to others primarily through the logical evaluation of evidence, the man of action also decides on moral and intuitive grounds whether he trusts others or not, which considerably widens the emotional scope of the stories. Heroes with these characteristics may be found in other stories about crime that have no mystery in them, which has led some critics to postulate the existence of a separate genre whose defining characteristic is the nature of the tough-guy hero. Those who see the two traditions as continuous point to a common function and regard both as "thrillers"—texts whose pleasure derives from mystery, suspense, and enjoyment of the skills of the main character.

The origin of the hard-boiled detective lies in the pulp MAGAZINE of the early 1920s. Named after the cheap paper on which they were printed, these periodicals published short stories and sometimes serialized novels (*see* SERIAL) in the general area of mystery, action, detection, and sensation. *Black Mask,* edited by Captain Joseph Shaw, evolved a style based on minimal PROSE and maximum action and published the major authors of the hard-boiled school, most notably Hammett and Carroll John Daly.

Explanations of the origin of this style vary, but factors cited include the literary influence of U.S. novelist Ernest Hemingway, in terms of both his minimal prose and the tough-guy ethos he espoused; the popularity of police memoirs and the memoirs of tramps and hobos, who also cultivated the image of the tough loner; changes in the social structure of the United States, particularly rising criminality in the rapidly expanding conurbations; the increasing working-class readership for inexpensive printed material (*see* LITERACY; PUBLISHING); and glamorous film portrayals of the gangster, especially the cycle of films launched by *Little Caesar* (1931). The theme also became a staple of comic strips such as "Dick Tracy" and, later, of popular comic books featuring superheroes like Batman and the Green Hornet (*see* COMICS).

The centrality of dialogue to the discussion of evidence virtually excluded detective stories from silent cinema. The introduction of sound in 1928–1929 (*see* MOTION PICTURES—SOUND FILM) largely coincided with the birth of the hard-boiled school, and such novels translated more easily to the screen than those in the British style, although Sherlock Holmes was incarnated on film in a successful series by British actor Basil Rathbone. Successful detective-novel heroes such as Hammett's Sam Spade and Chandler's Philip Marlowe provided star vehicles for actors like Humphrey Bogart. HOLLYWOOD's domination of world cinema combined with the international success of the hard-boiled school to largely Americanize detective stories after 1945. The rise of television in the 1950s transferred these stories from the large screen to the small and reinforced the tendency to create series heroes, or recurrent central characters, by programming stories in weekly series (*see* TELEVISION HISTORY). Screen versions of detective stories have increasingly favored action over deduction as the usual modus operandi of the hero and have increasingly revealed the identity of the villain to the viewer. Thus the solution of a criminal mystery as the central narrative device of these stories has tended to give way to the resolution of a conflict between law and crime, usually in favor of the law. Popular U.S. television series such as "Starsky and Hutch" and "Kojak" (mid-1970s), "Miami Vice" and "Cagney and Lacey" (early to mid-1980s), and the British program "The Sweeney" (early to mid-1970s) have increasingly focused on the personal characteristics and relationships of the central characters and have systematically reduced the importance of the traditional form of plot. *See* FICTION, PORTRAYAL OF CHARACTER IN.

Detective fiction's great commercial success and formulaic stability have led literary critics to dismiss the genre as popular literature and to regard its only functions as escapism and relaxation (*see* LITERARY CRITICISM; LITERATURE, POPULAR). Such judgments are based on criteria of literary value deriving from the romantic conception of the place of the arts in the social structure (*see* ART; ROMANTICISM). Some modernist critics, on the other hand, value detective stories for their rejection of the psychological analysis of character.

Sociological descriptions of the genre's communicative function focus on the links between the conceptions of character and action to be found in these stories and other features of the IDEOLOGY of industrial society. For example, it has been postulated that the tendency for many fictional detectives to be male and to espouse values of assertiveness and competitiveness reflects the cultural importance placed upon such qualities. The reader's vicarious enjoyment of assertive action may also be seen as implying a social definition of the ideal of (male) individuality. On a different level, the validation of law and order

in the stories has led U.S. critic Howard Haycraft to see a connection between the genre and political structure. He points to the popularity of detective fiction in democratic societies and to the banning of such stories in Nazi Germany and in the Soviet Union under Joseph Stalin. Alternative views suggest that these bans were caused by a fear of sensationalism and point to the ready availability of such fiction in the post-Stalinist Soviet Union. Other explanations of the success of detective stories refer to their representation of crime. The exclusion of the point of view of the criminal identifies that person as excluded from the social order and thus depicts crime as a form of social pathology, implicitly exonerating the social order from any responsibility for criminal acts. These various theories continue to fuel debate about the significance and function of a genre in which social transgression and individual retribution play central roles.

See also SPY FICTION; VIOLENCE.

Bibliography. John G. Cawelti, *Adventure, Mystery, and Romance*, Chicago, 1976; Michael F. Gilbert, ed., *Crime in Good Company*, London, 1959; Howard Haycraft, *Murder for Pleasure*, New York, 1968; H. R. F. Keating, ed., *Whodunit? A Guide to Crime, Suspense, and Spy Fiction*, New York and London, 1982; Jerry Palmer, *Thrillers: Genesis and Structure of a Popular Genre*, London and New York, 1978; Julian Symons, *Bloody Murder*, London, 1972; Colin Watson, *Snobbery with Violence*, London, 1971.

JERRY PALMER

MYTH. *See* FOLKTALE; ORAL HISTORY.

MYTHOLOGICAL FILM, ASIAN

The profuse traditional lore of South Asia associated with the Hindus, Buddhists, Jains, Sikhs, and other

Figure 1. *(Mythological Film, Asian)* Shantaram, *Ayodhyecha Raja* (The King of Ayodhya), 1932, with Durga Khote. State Historical Society of Wisconsin, Erik Barnouw Collection.

religious groups has come down to us via numerous epic-sized ancient narratives (*see* NARRATIVE), of which the most widely influential have been the Indian Mahabharata and Ramayana (*see* SOUTH ASIA, ANCIENT). Their content is reflected in the DANCE, SCULPTURE, painting, literature, songs (*see* SONG), and theatrical arts of an area extending from India to Indonesia and has also penetrated into East Asia, always with local and regional variations (*see* DRAMA). Inevitably this content dominated the thoughts of those who in 1913 embarked on production of the first Indian feature film, *Raja Harishchandra* (*see* PHALKE, DHUNDIRAJ GOVIND), and in so doing inaugurated the mythological film GENRE. The spectacular success of the film made the mythological the dominant genre of the first decade of Indian feature production, and it has remained a continuing factor. *See* MOTION PICTURES.

The genre earmarked for Indian filmmakers a subject area of their own on which the Western film world was unlikely to intrude and also gave them control of a segment of the film market in the Indian subcontinent and adjoining regions. Because the films could be equipped with subtitles in diverse languages, these silent films were able to penetrate many South Asian language areas. Within India the filmmakers became catalysts in the freedom movement, at first by merely evoking national awareness and pride, later by subtly introducing nationalist sentiments and Gandhian ideals into the mythologicals (*see* GANDHI, MOHANDAS). To British colonial officials the content of the films seemed generally bizarre and their popularity baffling.

Raja Harishchandra, based on a tale from the Mahabharata about a king who sacrificed all, including his loved ones, in dedication to the truth, is said to have been a story beloved by Gandhi as a child. The Mahabharata, reputedly the longest poem in existence (ninety thousand Sanskrit stanzas, most in thirty-two-syllable form), has a central theme with hundreds of substories branching out from it. The climax depicts a clan war such as historians believe may have taken place about 1000 B.C.E. The Bhagavad Gita, which has become the central SCRIPTURE of Hinduism, is placed dramatically within this battle sequence. The Mahabharata is peopled by polygamous gods and goddesses, heroes and heroines. The god-hero Krishna, the dominant figure of this epic, had two wives, a special consort, and sixty thousand gopikas, or girlfriends. In sharp contrast Rama, the hero of the somewhat later Ramayana—a far more unified epic with a beginning, middle, and end—was passionately devoted to his only wife and preached and practiced monogamy. A major Ramayana sequence concerns the rescue of the wife, Sita, from imprisonment on the island of Lanka (Sri Lanka) after she had been kidnapped by a many-headed demon. The rescue, depicted in many spectacular mythological films, is achieved when Rama, with the aid of an army of monkeys, builds a causeway from India to the island. Both Rama and Krishna were incarnations (avatars) of the same god, Vishnu, one of the three gods of the Hindu trinity. As in other religious lore, the dividing line between the saintly and the savage, the absurd and the sublime, the beautifully wise and the dangerously silly is often thin.

The mythological genre, having given Indian films a potent start, gradually lost its central role to films of more modern content. The mythological has persisted in the form of increasingly gaudy SPECIAL EFFECTS extravaganzas. The early devotional innocence appears lost as filmmakers expand the original matter with their own mythological innovations, intent on ever more astounding crises and miracles.

See also MUSIC THEATER—ASIAN TRADITIONS; MUSICAL, FILM—BOMBAY GENRE.

Bibliography. Erik Barnouw and S. Krishnaswamy, *Indian Film,* 2d ed., New York, Oxford, and New Delhi, 1980.

S. KRISHNASWAMY

(en), the fourteenth letter of the modern and thirteenth of the ancient Roman alphabet, represents historically the Greek *nū* and the Semitic *nun*. The earlier Greek forms were N and И, corresponding to the Phœnician Ϟ. The sound usually denoted by the letter is a voiced nasal consonant with front closure. . . .

NAKAHAMA MANJIRO (1828–1898)

Japanese fisherman and later diplomat who was influential in the opening of Japan to the West. In 1841 five Japanese fishermen in a small boat, including thirteen-year-old Nakahama Manjiro, were driven by a storm into the western Pacific and shipwrecked on an uncharted island. After a six-month ordeal they were rescued by a passing whaler out of Fairhaven, Massachusetts, and dropped off in Hawaii, except for young Manjiro. The captain of the whaler, William H. Whitfield, took him home to Fairhaven, where Manjiro became the first Japanese to reside and be educated in the United States. Under the name John Mung he avidly studied English, mathematics, navigation, and surveying. Not everyone in town welcomed him; the Congregational church attended by the Whitfields refused to allow the youth to be enrolled in its Sunday school because he was not white, which led Whitfield to transfer to the Unitarian church.

Manjiro occasionally shipped out on whalers and even took part in the California gold rush. In 1850 he made the perilous decision to return to his native land. He was joined in Hawaii by two of his fellow castaways, and they were dropped in a small boat near Japan. Under laws of the Tokugawa era (*see* TOKUGAWA ERA: SECLUSION POLICY), repatriates were subject to severe punishment (including decapitation) for having been contaminated by foreign contact. Yet officials were under increasing pressure to open Japan to the outside world and found in occasional returnees an indispensable source of intelligence. Manjiro was subjected to a series of judicial proceedings and interrogations, during which he was pressed for information about his life abroad, and his words were set down minutely. Manjiro's comments on daily life in the United States were well circulated among officials, his account of the Mexican War and his assertion that the United States had no malevolent designs on Asia making a deep impression—though some considered them treasonous. When the foreboding ships of Commodore Matthew Calbraith Perry, belching black smoke, appeared in Japanese waters in 1853–1854 to "open" Japan, Manjiro was summoned from his home on the island of Shikoku, where he had been banished, and brought before the Tokugawa rulers in Edo. Again he was questioned—by various government officials—about his knowledge of the foreigners. Although he was excluded from the negotiations with Perry (he was kept miles away from the discussions and under close guard), Manjiro provided valuable information to the shogunate; he also translated U.S. documents during the talks. After a treaty with the United States was concluded in 1854, Manjiro remained an important source of explanations and information about the West. He seemed to know all about the exhibits—including the telegraph and a miniature railway—that Perry had brought to demonstrate Western wonders.

Manjiro's influence continued in later years. He became a prominent figure, serving on foreign diplomatic missions, producing a manual on English conversation that became standard, teaching ocean navigation, and aiding in the planning of a Japanese oceangoing fleet along U.S. lines. Thus, with the passing of the Tokugawa era he contributed to the changes that came over Japan, bringing it into closer communication with the rest of the world. His unusual career has been the subject of several biographies and Stephen Sondheim's musical drama *Pacific Overtures* (1976).

See also ASIA, TWENTIETH CENTURY.

Bibliography. Henry F. Graff, ed., *Bluejackets with Perry in Japan*, New York, 1952; Hisakazu Kaneko, *Manjiro, the Man Who Discovered America*, Boston, 1956; Samuel Eliot Morison, *"Old Bruin": Commodore Matthew C. Perry, 1794–1858*, Boston, 1967; Toichiro Nakahama, *Nakahama Manjiro-den*, Tokyo, 1936; Arthur Walworth, *Black Ships off Japan*, New York, 1946, reprint Hamden, Conn., 1966; Emily V. Warinner, *Voyager to Destiny: The Amazing Adventures of Manjiro, the Man Who Changed Worlds Twice*, Indianapolis, Ind., and New York, 1956.

HENRY F. GRAFF

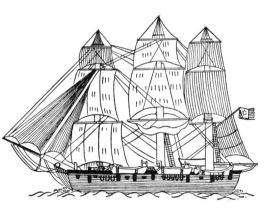

Figure 1. (*Nakahama Manjiro*) Drawing of a U.S. whaling ship by Manjiro. From Hisakazu Kaneko, *Manjiro, the Man Who Discovered America*, Boston: Houghton Mifflin, 1956, frontispiece.

NARRATIVE

The recounting of one or more real or fictional events by someone (a narrator) to someone else (a narratee). According to this most general of characterizations, even such texts as "The woman closed the window,"

"The canary died," or "The bottle fell on the floor" constitute narratives. They give an account of one event, one change in a state of affairs. On the other hand, a poem like "Roses are red / Violets are blue / Sugar is sweet / And so are you," a syllogism like "All men are mortal; Socrates is a man; Socrates is mortal," or a statement like "Tigers are large carnivorous mammals of the cat family" do not constitute narratives—they do not recount an event. A dramatic PERFORMANCE does not constitute a narrative either, even though it may represent many fascinating state changes. Rather than being recounted, these changes occur directly onstage.

Narratives are found in various media: oral and written LANGUAGE, in PROSE or verse (*see* POETRY), of course; but also SIGN LANGUAGE, still or moving pictures (as in narrative paintings, stained-glass windows, or films), gestures, music, or a combination of vehicles (as in comic strips). Indeed, any and all vehicles allowing for the reporting of events (as opposed to their realization or enactment) can be used in narrating. The forms narrative can take are even more varied: in the verbal domain alone are the novel and the short story, history, BIOGRAPHY and AUTO-BIOGRAPHY, epics, myths, folktales, legends and ballads, news reports, spontaneous accounts in everyday CONVERSATION, and many other possibilities. As for its distribution, it is probable that the origins of narrative coincide with the origins of human signifying practices. Moreover, it is certain that narratives appear in every human society discussed by history and anthropology and that the average human being knows how to produce and process them at a very early age. This universality no doubt accounts in part for the considerable interest narrative has evoked among literary analysts, folklorists, and anthropologists as well as linguists, philosophers, psychologists, historians, semioticians, computer scientists, and students of the arts, media, and communication. It also partly accounts for the remarkable growth since the 1960s of narratology—the systematic study of the nature, form, and functioning of narrative and of the singularly human competence they imply.

Elements of the narrative. Narrative can be viewed as a structure or product (the text—in the broad sense of signifying matter—that comprises the recounting of one or more events) and as a communicative act (the practice involving the production and reception of the text). As product, narrative is said to have two parts. One part is the story, the events recounted and the existents participating in them or constituting the setting in which they occur. The other part is the discourse, the way in which the story, its narrator, its narratee, and its very narration are represented.

By definition, a story consists of n events (where $n > 1$). More specifically, it consists of at least one transformation of a state of affairs obtaining at time t_0 into another state of affairs obtaining at time t_n (where $n \neq 0$). A story thus always involves temporal sequence, and this constitutes its most distinctive feature. Clearly, given a story made up of a number of situations and events, some of these may be simultaneous rather than successive: "The woman closed the window, and at the same time the man opened the door. Then they both sat down and settled their differences." Clearly, too, time relations are not the only ones possible between situations and events. Events may be causally related, for instance, with the causal link being explicit ("John lost weight, and as a result he went to see a doctor") or implicit and inferable on logical, necessary grounds ("All travelers waste fortunes; Susan was an inveterate traveler, and she squandered a lot of money") or on pragmatic, probable grounds: should an event e_2 temporally follow an event e_1 and be plausibly relatable to it, e_2 is taken to be caused by e_1 unless the narrative specifies otherwise ("Peter ate a rotten apple and got sick"). So important is this relation of probable causality that, according to the French structuralist critic ROLAND BARTHES, the confusion between consecutiveness and consequence represents one of the most powerful motors of narrativity. Narrative can be seen as the systematic exploitation of the *post hoc ergo propter hoc* fallacy, whereby what comes after x is interpreted as what is caused by x.

Though temporal succession (accompanied or not by causality) is a necessary condition of story and therefore of narrative, it is not quite a sufficient condition. The situations and events recounted must also make up a whole with a continuant subject, a sequence the first and last major terms of which are partial repetitions of each other, an autonomous structure having (in Aristotelian terminology) a beginning, a middle, and an end. Such a structure can itself result from the simple linking of two (or more) other story structures, from the embedding of one structure into another, from the alternation of units from one structure with units from another one, or from an ordered mixture of these modes of combination. Furthermore, and following the insight of the Russian formalists, some of the situations and events making up the story are essential to it and cannot be eliminated without destroying its causal-chronological coherence, while others are not and can. This sheds some light on the capacity of most stories to be summarized. It also sheds light on their capacity for (indefinite) expansion: any number of situations and events not fundamental or threatening to their coherence can be incorporated into them.

If ARISTOTLE's general account of story structure has proved exceedingly influential, the most seminal characterization of that structure in modern narratology is that of the Russian scholar Vladimir Propp.

He developed the notion of function or category of events considered from the point of view of their fundamental meaning in the story in which they appear, he characterized thirty-one functions that constitute the basic story elements of any (Russian) fairy tale, and he argued that tales always contain the function Lack or Villainy and proceed from it to another function that can be used as a denouement (e.g., Liquidation of the Lack or Villainy, Rescue, or Wedding).

Just as events can be grouped into fundamental classes, participants in them can be categorized in terms of the fundamental roles they may assume. Six roles or actants have been isolated by the French linguist and semiotician Algirdas Julien Greimas in his classic actantial model: any story involves a Subject looking for a certain Object; canonical stories further involve a Sender (of the Subject on its quest for the Object) and a Receiver (a beneficiary of the quest) as well as a Helper and an Opponent of the Subject. The same participant or actor can play more than one role, and, conversely, the same role can be played by more than one actor.

Further exploration into the nature of functions and actants would yield the following informal account of canonical story structure: after a contract between Sender and Subject whereby the Subject undertakes to attain an Object (to liquidate a Lack, for example, or to eliminate a Villainy), the Subject goes on its quest and, as a result of a series of tests, fulfills or fails to fulfill the contract and is (justly) rewarded or (unjustly) punished.

The "same" story can be recounted differently in different narratives adopting different modalities of discourse. Conversely, different stories can be conveyed in terms of the same discourse modalities. Thus, following the Russian formalist distinction between *fabula* and *sjužet* (analogous to that between story and plot), the situations and events can be presented in the order of their (supposed) occurrence or in a different order. Compare, for example, "John ate, then he went to sleep" and "John went to sleep after he ate." In addition, they can be presented in more or less detail and can be accompanied by more or less narratorial commentary. Furthermore, if they occur several times they can be recounted only once (iterative narrative), and if they occur once they can be recounted several times (repetitive narrative), only one time (singulative narrative), or not at all (in elliptical narrative they are inferable rather than stated explicitly). Finally, they can be conveyed according to different points of view: that of a narrator who is not in the world of the story and who is not subject to any perceptual or conceptual restrictions, for instance, or that of one or more participants in the story. To adopt the widely used terminology of the French narratologist Gérard Genette, the point of view may then be fixed (the perspective of one and only one character is used), variable (the perspective of several characters is used in turn to present different sequences of events), or multiple (different perspectives are used in turn to present the same sequence of events). The angle of vision employed can thus vary; so can the physical, intellectual, and/or emotional distance between the point-of-view holder and the story participants. The nature of the information explicitly provided can vary as well; it may, for example, pertain only to the participants' appearance, their external behavior, and the setting against which they come to the fore, or it may include their thoughts and feelings.

The role of the narrator. The narrator's role in the narrative text depends on the discursive modalities exploited. For instance, the narrator may be more or less intrusive (given to commenting on the narrating act itself or on the situations and events recounted, their meaning, and their importance), may have played no role in the story (third-person or heterodiegetic narrative), or may have been a (major) participant in it (first-person or homodiegetic narrative). Similarly, the narratee can be depicted in more or less detail, and so can the spatiotemporal context of the act of narration or narrating instance. Of course, a given narrative text may have several narrators, each addressing the same or different narratees, and the various narrating instances may be combined through simple concatenation (A recounts a sequence of events, then B recounts one), embedding (A recounts a sequence in which B recounts one), or alternation (A and B take turns recounting a series of sequences).

The very representation of a narrator telling a story to a narratee underlines the fact that narrative is not only an object or structure but also an act that, like other acts, occurs in a certain context because of any number of reasons and with any number of functions to fulfill (entertaining, informing, persuading, diverting attention, etc.). More specifically, narrative is a situation-bound transaction between two parties, an exchange resulting from the desire of at least one of these parties; further, the "same" story can have a different value in different circumstances (A wants to know what happened at time t, whereas B does not; A takes an account to mean one thing, and B takes it to mean another thing). This illuminates the tendency of many narrative texts to emphasize the contract between narrator and narratee, the contract on which the very existence of the narrative depends: I will tell you a story if you promise to be good; I will listen to you if you make it worthwhile; or, to use more literary examples, a tale for a day of survival as in *Arabian Nights*, a story for a night of love as in Honoré de Balzac's *Sarrasine*, a diary for redemption as in François Mauriac's *Vipers' Tangle*. This also explains why unsolicited narratives in particular must awaken and maintain desire in the receiver by relying on the dynamics of suspense and surprise; why—as the U.S. linguist William Labov underscored—narrators try to make clear that their narrative has a point, that it is worth telling, that it represents, illustrates, or accounts for something unusual and interesting; and why the very form of a narrative is affected by the context in which it occurs and the purpose it presumably serves. The sender of the message provides a certain kind of information, arranges it in a certain order, exploits one point of view as opposed to another, and evaluates certain details as particularly remarkable, important, or crucial, so that the receiver can better process the information in terms of certain imperatives and ends.

Significant functions of narrative. If narrative can have any number of functions, there are some that it excels at or is unique in fulfilling. Narrative always reports one or more changes of state, but, as etymology indicates (the term *narrative* is related to the Latin *gnārus*—"knowing," "expert," "acquainted with"—which itself derives from the Indo-European root *gnâ*, "to know"), narrative is also a particular mode of knowledge. It does not merely reflect what happens; it discovers and invents what can happen. It does not simply record events; it constitutes and interprets them as meaningful parts of meaningful wholes, whether the latter are situations, practices, persons, or societies. As such, narrative can provide an explanation of individual fate as well as group destiny, the unity of a self as well as the nature of a collectivity. By showing that disparate situations and events can compose one signifying structure (or vice versa) and, more specifically, by giving its own form of order and coherence to a possible reality, narrative supplies models for its transformation or redescription and mediates between the law of what is and the human desire for what may be. Above all, perhaps, by instituting different moments in time and establishing links between them, by finding significant patterns in temporal sequences, by pointing to an end already partly contained in the beginning and to a beginning already partly containing the end, by exposing the meaning of time and imposing meaning on it, narrative reads time and teaches how to read it. In short, it is the structure and practice that illuminate temporality and human beings as temporal beings.

See also FOLKTALE; MUSIC, FOLK AND TRADITIONAL.

Bibliography. Roland Barthes, *S/Z,* trans. by Richard Miller, New York, 1974; Wayne C. Booth, *The Rhetoric of Fiction,* 2d ed., Chicago, 1983; Seymour Chatman, *Story and Discourse: Narrative Structure in Fiction and Film,* Ithaca, N.Y., 1978; Gérard Genette, *Narrative Discourse: An Essay in Method,* trans. by Jane E. Lewin, Ithaca, N.Y., 1980; William Labov, *Language in the Inner City,* Phila-

delphia, 1972; Ladislav Matejka and Krystyna Pomorska, eds., *Readings in Russian Poetics,* Cambridge, Mass., 1971; W. J. T. Mitchell, ed., *On Narrative,* Chicago, 1981; Gerald Prince, *Narratology: The Form and Functioning of Narrative,* Berlin, New York, and Amsterdam, 1982; Vladimir Propp, *Morphology of the Folktale,* 2d ed., rev., trans. by Laurence Scott, Austin, Tex., 1968; Robert Scholes and Robert Kellogg, *The Nature of Narrative,* New York, 1966.

GERALD PRINCE

NEGOTIATION. *See* BARGAINING; INTERNATIONAL ORGANIZATIONS.

NEOREALISM

A period in Italian film history (roughly the decade from the end of World War II to the mid-1950s) distinguished by its emphasis on social issues (the war, the Resistance, poverty, unemployment); its rejection of both traditional dramatic and cinematic conventions, especially those of the HOLLYWOOD studio system; its use of on-location shooting and nonprofessional actors; and its DOCUMENTARY photographic style. In addition, the seminal essays of French film theoretician André Bazin popularized the view that Italian neorealism continued the long-take, deep-focus techniques of ORSON WELLES and JEAN RENOIR, rejecting the ideological montage of SERGEI EISENSTEIN and respecting the ontological wholeness of the reality being filmed. *See* FILM EDITING; FILM THEORY.

Film historians have unfortunately tended to speak of neorealism as if it were an authentic movement with universally agreed-upon stylistic or thematic principles. But the best neorealist films never completely denied cinematic conventions, nor did they entirely reject Hollywood codes. The basis for the fundamental change in cinematic history marked by the advent of Italian neorealism was less an agreement on a single, unified cinematic style than a common aspiration to view Italian life without preconceptions and to employ a more honest, ethical, but poetic cinematic language in the process.

The first major film in this tradition was Roberto Rossellini's *Roma, città aperta* (Rome, Open City, 1945). This work so completely reflected the moral and psychological atmosphere of the immediate postwar period that its international critical success alerted the world to the rebirth of Italian cinema from the rubble of the war. With a daring combination of styles and moods, Rossellini captured the tension and tragedy of Italian life under the German occupation and the partisan struggle out of which was born the new Italian republic (Figure 1). Although initially praised for its REALISM, *Roma, città aperta* is closer to traditional film melodrama than to a pure documentary cinema.

Figure 1. *(Neorealism)* Roberto Rossellini, *Roma, città aperta* (Rome, Open City), 1945. National Film Archive, London.

Rossellini's *Paisà* (Paisan, 1946) reflected to a far greater extent the conventions of NEWSREEL documentary. Tracing in six separate episodes the Allied invasion of Italy and its slow process up the boot of the peninsula, this film is characterized by a brilliant use of nonprofessional actors and an original merger of fact and fiction. Vittorio De Sica's 1948 film *Ladri di biciclette* (The Bicycle Thief) also employs nonprofessional actors, on-location shooting, and the social themes typical of many neorealist films, although the film cannot, in view of its mythic structure, be convincingly described as having a realistic style (Figure 2). That same year saw the release of

Luchino Visconti's *La terra trema* (The Earth Trembles). A more traditionally neorealist work, it employed no studio sets or sound stages; the cast was selected from a Sicilian fishing village and speaks the local dialect (necessitating Italian subtitles even for Italian audiences). The film's message is Marxist in tone, a call to resist human oppression and exploitation.

These four masterpieces captured the spirit of Italian culture in the immediate postwar period and made original contributions to film language. Italian directors had conclusively demonstrated that great art could be produced with a poverty of cinematic

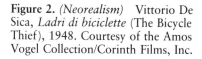

Figure 2. *(Neorealism)* Vittorio De Sica, *Ladri di biciclette* (The Bicycle Thief), 1948. Courtesy of the Amos Vogel Collection/Corinth Films, Inc.

Figure 3. *(Neorealism)* Federico Fellini, *Satyricon*, 1969. Courtesy of the Amos Vogel Collection/United Artists.

means. This lesson was important to the French new wave, which idolized Rossellini (*see* NEW WAVE FILM), to a number of Third World directors (especially Satyajit Ray), and to the next generation of Italian filmmakers (Pier Paolo Pasolini, Bernardo Bertolucci, Gillo Pontecorvo, the Taviani brothers, and many others). Yet, with the exception of *Roma, città aperta*, Italian neorealist films were relatively unpopular within Italy and achieved critical success primarily among Italian leftists and foreign critics. One of the paradoxes of the neorealist era in Italian cinema is that the very masses of ordinary people such films set out to portray were relatively uninterested in their self-image on the screen. Of the approximately eight hundred films produced in Italy between 1945 and 1953, only about 10 percent can be called neorealist, and most were box-office failures.

However, a number of neorealist works achieved greater success by means of an artistic compromise, occupying a position somewhere between strict documentary realism and Hollywood cinematic codes. In *Vivere in pace* (To Live in Peace, 1946), director Luigi Zampa turned the tragic thematic material of Rossellini's war films into a comic farce. Alberto Lattuada employed the traditional narrative structure of the U.S. gangster film to study the effects of the U.S. occupation of postwar Livorno in *Senza pietà* (Without Pity, 1948). In *Il cammino della speranza* (The Path of Hope, 1950) Pietro Germi borrowed John Ford's style of epic photography to film a plot set in Sicily but indebted to Ford's westerns (*see* WESTERN, THE). Giuseppe de Santis combined Marxist ideology with Hollywood cheesecake and eroticism in *Riso amaro* (Bitter Rice), a surprising 1948 box-office smash.

Critics of Italian neorealism have often viewed its departures from the canons of cinematic realism as part of a "betrayal" of neorealism. Yet it is misleading to see the progressive rapprochement of Italian cinema to Hollywood genres or cinematic styles as a betrayal of a movement, since no such programmatic set of theoretical principles ever united neorealist directors. In spite of the fact that Italian leftists preferred a revolutionary cinematic stance, the Italian public clearly preferred ENTERTAINMENT, and Italian directors themselves felt the critical preference for social realism was a constraint on their desire to explore different cinematic styles and psychological rather than social problems. The resulting ideological debate over the direction Italian cinema should take—a choice between artistic freedom on the one hand or programmatic Marxist ideology on the other—centered on critical reaction to *La strada* (1954), by Federico Fellini. Praised by Catholics for its religious message and damned by Communists for its spirituality, Fellini's film, as well as a number of lesser-known works by Rossellini and Michelangelo

Antonioni, introduced an entirely new kind of poetic film into the Italian cinema, one that transcended the predominantly social themes typical of Italian neorealism and moved toward a cinema of psychological introspection and personal imagery (Figure 3).

See also AVANT-GARDE FILM; MOTION PICTURES—SOUND FILM.

Bibliography. Peter Bondanella, *Italian Cinema: From Neorealism to the Present*, New York, 1983; Gian Piero Brunetta, *Storia del cinema italiano 1895–1945*, Rome, 1979; Franca Faldini and Goffredo Fofi, eds., *L'avventurosa storia del cinema italiano raccontata dai suoi protagonisti, 1939–1959*, Milan, 1979; Mira Liehm, *Passion and Defiance: Film in Italy from 1942 to the Present*, Berkeley, Calif., 1984; Lino Micciché, ed., *Il neorealismo cinematographico italiano*, Venice, 1975.

PETER BONDANELLA

NETWORK ANALYSIS

A method of research for identifying the communication structure in a system, in which relational data about communication flows are analyzed using some type of interpersonal relationships as the units of analysis. A *communication network* consists of interconnected individuals who are linked by patterned communication flows. The usual procedures of communication network analysis consist of (1) identifying cliques within the system, (2) identifying specialized communication roles (liaisons, bridges, and isolates) in the communication structure, and (3) measuring various indexes of communication structure (e.g., connectedness) for individuals, personal networks, cliques, or systems. This research approach entails a search for the regularized patterns of relationships that often lie beneath the surface.

Structure—the patterned arrangement of the parts of a system—provides stability and regularity to human behavior in a system. Social scientists are interested in various types of structure—social structure, organizational structure, and political structure, for example. Researchers using this framework investigate the *communication structure* of a system, defined as the differentiated elements that can be recognized in the patterned communication flows in a system. Considerable research evidence shows that the behavior of an individual is partly a function of the communication networks in which the individual is a member. Thus the communication structure of a system is one predictor of the behavior of the members of that system—voting in an ELECTION, purchasing a consumer product, adopting a new idea, and becoming integrated into a new social setting, for example.

Historically the German sociologist GEORG SIMMEL

provided the original theoretical stimulus for network analysis, but U.S. psychotherapist Jacob Moreno's *sociometry* was the main methodological contribution. Sociometry is a means of obtaining and analyzing quantitative data about communication patterns among the individuals in a system by asking each respondent to whom he or she is linked (*see* GROUP COMMUNICATION). Sociometry was a popular analytical tool during the 1940s and 1950s, but the rise of computers in social research led to the abandonment of Moreno's approach. However, the development of computer techniques for large-scale network analysis resulted in a resurgence of interest in networks in the 1970s and 1980s. Network analysis is a theoretical framework for understanding behavior, more than just a set of research techniques.

Features

A *link* is a communication relationship (an exchange of information) between two units (usually individuals) in a system. It is the basic datum in any type of network analysis. Such links are often measured by sociometric questions that ask a respondent to indicate the other individuals with whom communication links exist. Other alternatives are (1) observation, in which the researcher identifies and records the communication behavior in a system, and (2) unobtrusive methods, in which the method of measurement removes the observer from the events being studied (an example is the computer-recorded data obtained about who interacts with whom via an electronic messaging system). A combination of two or more measurements in a multimethod design is usually superior to the use of any single method.

Five main types of units of analysis can be utilized in network analysis: individuals, dyads, personal networks, cliques, and systems (networks). Individuals can be the units of analysis when network variables like opinion leadership are measured at the individual level (*see* OPINION LEADER). A dyad is composed of two individuals connected by a communication link. The personal network consists of individuals who are linked by patterned communication flows to a focal individual. In a *radial* personal network an individual interacts with a set of dyadic partners who do not interact with each other. In an *interlocking* personal network an individual interacts with a set of dyadic partners who interact with each other. *Individual integration* is the degree to which the members of an individual's personal communication network are linked to one another. A *clique* is a subsystem whose elements interact with one another relatively more frequently than with other members of the communication system. A network consists of all the individual and aggregate units in a system.

One particular method of network analysis, William D. Richards's *Negopy* computer program, has been widely utilized by communication scholars, but several alternatives such as factor analysis and other clustering techniques are also appropriate. All network analysis techniques rely fundamentally on their measure of *proximity,* the relative nearness of a pair of individuals to each other in a communication sense. Network data are almost always handled in the form of a who-to-whom matrix rather than as a sociogram. Matrix-ordered data fit naturally with computer data analysis methods.

Perspective

Viewing human communication in a network perspective leads to a redefinition of *communication* as a process in which participants create and share information with one another in order to reach a mutual understanding (rather than viewing communication as a one-way, linear flow intended to influence the receiver). *Information*—defined here as a difference in matter-energy that affects uncertainty in a situation in which a choice exists among a set of alternatives—varies according to the meanings that individuals give to the messages that are exchanged. The network conception of communication can be represented by a series of converging circles of information exchange between two or more participants who approach but never arrive at exactly the same point of understanding. *Convergence* may be defined as the tendency for two or more individuals to move toward a common interest or focus. The increasing attention that communication scholars are giving to the new interactive communication technologies (*see* INTERACTIVE MEDIA) is leading to greater interest in network analysis and to the convergence model of communication.

See also DIFFUSION; MODELS OF COMMUNICATION.

Bibliography. Everett M. Rogers and D. Lawrence Kincaid, *Communication Networks: Toward a New Paradigm for Research,* New York, 1981; Barry Wellman, "Network Analysis: Some Basic Principles," in *Sociological Theory 1983,* ed. by Randall Collins, San Francisco, 1983.

EVERETT M. ROGERS

NEW INTERNATIONAL INFORMATION ORDER

Resolutions, meetings, and manifestos calling for a "new order" in international information structures and policies became a feature of the world scene in the early 1970s and often generated intense dispute. The original impulse came from the nonaligned nations, many of which had gained independence in the postwar years. To many the euphoria of independence was turning to a sense of disillusionment. In spite of international assistance programs, the economic situation in many developing countries had not improved, and in some it had actually deteriorated. For certain countries foreign trade earnings could not cover interest due on foreign loans. These same years witnessed the rapid development of new communications media, and the era was constantly characterized as the Information Age—one in which information would be a key to power and affluence. To the developing countries it was increasingly clear that the "flow of information" (a term that seemed to subsume ideas and attitudes and followed a one-way direction from rich to poor countries) was dominated by multinational entities based in the most powerful nations. The resulting disparities tended to set the framework for discussion even within developing countries. Clearly political independence was not matched by independence in the economic and sociocultural spheres. A number of nonaligned countries saw themselves as victims of "cultural colonialism." The imbalances it involved, and what might be done about them, became the focus of debate for the nonaligned countries.

Evolution of the Debate

The nonaligned nations movement took form in 1955 at a meeting in Bandung, Indonesia, that brought together world leaders from Asia and Africa. Subsequent meetings—in some cases, summit meetings of nonaligned leaders—were held in Bangkok, Algiers, Tunis, Havana, and elsewhere. During the 1970s the membership grew to more than ninety countries plus several regional groups (see Table 1) and represented a majority in various United Nations bodies, with strong influence over their agendas. These UN agencies embraced a "development ideology," meaning that high priority would be given to the development needs of the Third World (*see* DEVELOPMENT COMMUNICATION).

A nonaligned summit held in Algiers in 1973 adopted a resolution calling for a "new international economic order," which was endorsed the following year by the UN General Assembly. This served as precedent and model for a similar resolution focusing on information, which was articulated at a 1976 nonaligned news symposium in Tunis. A leading figure at this meeting was Mustapha Masmoudi, Tunisian secretary of state for information, who demanded a "reorganization of existing communication channels that are a legacy of the colonial past." This "decolonization" of information, he said, must lead to a "new order in information matters." In subsequent meetings this phrase evolved into a *new international information order* and, at a later stage, into a *new world information and communication order*.

Table 1. Members of the Nonaligned Nations Movement (1979)

Afghanistan	Ethiopia	Mali	Senegal
Algeria	Gabon	Malta	Seychelles
Angola	Gambia	Mauritania	Sierra Leone
Argentina	Ghana	Mauritius	Singapore
Bahrain	Grenada	Morocco	Somalia
Bangladesh	Guinea	Mozambique	South Yemen
Benin	Guinea-Bissau	Nepal	Sri Lanka
Bhutan	Guyana	Nicaragua	Sudan
Bolivia	India	Niger	Surinam
Botswana	Indonesia	Nigeria	Southwest Africa People's
Burma (withdrew	Iran	North Korea	Organization (SWAPO)
September 1979)	Iraq	North Yemen	Swaziland
Burundi	Ivory Coast	Oman	Syria
Cambodia	Jamaica	Pakistan	Tanzania
Cameroon	Jordan	Palestine Liberation	Togo
Cape Verde	Kenya	Organization (PLO)	Trinidad and Tobago
Central African Empire	Kuwait	Panama	Tunisia
Chad	Laos	Patriotic Front	Uganda
Comoros	Lebanon	(Zimbabwe Rhodesia)	United Arab Emirates
Congo	Liberia	Peru	Upper Volta
Cuba	Libya	Qatar	Vietnam
Cyprus	Malagasy Republic	Rwanda	Yugoslavia
Djibouti	Malawi	Sao Tome and Principe	Zaire
Egypt	Malaysia	Saudi Arabia	Zambia
Equatorial Guinea	Maldives		

Source: 1979 News Dictionary, Facts on File (1980).

That same year UNESCO's General Conference in Nairobi also discussed information issues, in a context that produced sharp confrontation between the interests of developed and developing countries. The focus was on the free-flow-of-information doctrine. UNESCO's mandate in the area of communications is explicit in its constitution, adopted in 1946, which enjoined the agency to "collaborate in the work of advancing the mutual knowledge and understanding of peoples, through all means of mass communication and to that end recommend the free-flow of ideas by word and image." The free-flow doctrine was developed by the United States and other Western nations after World War II. As viewed by supporters, the unhampered flow of information would be a means of promoting peace and understanding and spreading technical advances. The doctrine had ties with other Western libertarian principles such as freedom of the press. However, critics of the doctrine came to view it as part of a global strategy for domination of communication markets and for ideological control by the industrialized nations. They saw it as serving the interests of the most powerful countries and transnational corporations and helping them secure economic and cultural domination of less powerful nations. A rewording of the doctrine was urged by nonaligned spokespersons calling for a free *and balanced* flow of information. The suggestion stirred deep suspicion in developed countries. If it meant that Third World nations would ordain a proper balance, and control or limit the flow, this would be—according to Western spokespersons—the very antithesis of a free flow. "Free and balanced flow" and "free flow" seemed at this meeting to be irreconcilable concepts.

An important outcome of this 1976 UNESCO meeting was the appointment by Amadou-Mahtar M'Bow, Director-General of UNESCO, of a sixteen-person commission—broadly representative of the world's economic and geographic spectrum and headed by Sean MacBride of Ireland—to study "the totality of communication problems in modern societies." Its members held different opinions about what sort of new order was needed, but all were in agreement that the existing information order was far from satisfactory. They began their work late in 1977 and, after two years of fact-gathering, committee hearings, and debate, submitted their final report—known as the MacBride Report—to the 1980 UNESCO General Conference in Belgrade. Published in English as *Many Voices, One World,* it has been translated into many languages. Along with a resolution adopted at the same conference confirming UNESCO's support for a *new world information and communication order* (see Table 2), the report became the focus of debate during the following years—a rallying point as well as a target for attack.

Themes

The debate had at first centered on the news-flow question. The major Western international news services—AP and UPI of the United States, the French Agence France-Presse, and Reuters of the United

Table 2. Resolution 4/19 Adopted by the Twenty-first Session of the UNESCO General Conference, Belgrade, 1980

The General Conference considers that
a) this new world information and communication order could be based, among other considerations, on:
    i) elimination of the imbalances and inequalities which characterize the present situation;
    ii) elimination of the negative effects of certain monopolies, public or private, and excessive concentrations;
    iii) removal of the internal and external obstacles to a free flow and wider and better balanced dissemination of information and ideas;
    iv) plurality of sources and channels of information;
    v) freedom of the press and of information;
    vi) the freedom of journalists and all professionals in the communication media, a freedom inseparable from responsibility;
    vii) the capacity of developing countries to achieve improvement of their own situations, notably by providing their own equipment, by training their personnel, by improving their infrastructures and making their information and communication media suitable to their needs and aspirations;
    viii) the sincere will of developed countries to help them attain these objectives;
    ix) respect for each people's cultural identity and for the right of each nation to inform the world about its interests, its aspirations and its social and cultural values;
    x) respect for the right of all peoples to participate in international exchanges of information on the basis of equality, justice and mutual benefit;
    xi) respect for right of the public, of ethnic and social groups and of individuals to have access to information sources and to participate actively in the communication process;
b) this new world information and communication order should be based on the fundamental principles of international law, as laid down in the Charter of the United Nations;
c) diverse solutions to information and communication problems are required because social, political, cultural and economic problems differ from one country to another and, within a given country, from one group to another.

Kingdom—were consistently described as having MONOPOLY control over the flow of news to and from developing countries, and exercising it from a limited perspective reflecting the economic and cultural interests of the industrialized nations. Expressions such as "coups and earthquakes" were frequently used to describe reporting of Third World events. In 1976 Indira Gandhi, the prime minister of India, expressed the prevailing view: "We want to hear Africans on events in Africa. You should similarly be able to get an Indian explanation of events in India. It is astonishing that we know so little about leading poets, novelists, historians, and editors of various Asian, African, and Latin American countries while we are familiar with minor authors and columnists of Europe and America." The need for policies and structures to develop communications between developing nations (sometimes referred to as "South-South dialogue") was constantly stressed. *See also* NEWS AGENCIES.

The flow of television programming, including ENTERTAINMENT programming, was soon incorporated into the debate, in large measure owing to a study conducted by two Finnish researchers, Kaarle Nordenstreng and Tapio Varis, and published by UNESCO in 1974. The study demonstrated that a few Western nations controlled the international flow of television programs, with the United States, the United Kingdom, France, and the Federal Republic of Germany accounting for the largest shares. The implications of this domination, in both financial and ideological terms, received increasing attention. *See also* TELEVISION HISTORY—WORLD MARKET STRUGGLES.

The integration of television with new technologies such as the communications SATELLITE—including direct broadcast satellites—and telecommunications networks that were channels for an increasing volume of transborder data flow difficult or impossible to control, extended the range of topics covered in the debate. Here the questions also included imbalances in the assignment of spectrum frequencies and of orbital slots for future satellites. *See also* COMPUTER: IMPACT—IMPACT ON THE WORLD ECONOMY.

The international flow of ADVERTISING, under similar multinational controls, was another issue that entered the debate. It was described by many as furthering not only products and services but also a way of life, generally centered on the acquisition of consumer goods. Some saw this as diverting attention from necessities to luxuries, and others saw it as a serious threat to indigenous culture. *See also* COMMERCIALS; SPONSOR.

In 1978 a new element was added to the debates with the passage of a UNESCO Declaration on the Mass Media. It was the result of six years of negotiation to achieve a consensus text, which finally carried the title *The Declaration of Fundamental*

Principles concerning the Contribution of the Mass Media to Strengthening Peace and International Understanding, to the Promotion of Human Rights and to Countering Racialism, Apartheid and Incitement to War. Regarded by the nonaligned nations as furthering the *new order* movement, it was the first international instrument referring directly to moral, social, and professional responsibilities of mass media in the context of "the universally recognized principles of freedom of expression, information, and opinion." Hovering over the debate once again was the issue of the role of government. The final version of the resolution did not include—because of Western demands—proposals to make national governments responsible for the actions of communications companies working within their jurisdictions.

Collision Course

In the early 1980s the nature of the debate underwent decisive changes. Nonaligned nations were no longer as unified as they had been; amid a widespread economic recession some leaned toward a more militant, others toward a more conciliatory, stance. Differences in political systems came more sharply into focus. In the developed nations a trend toward *deregulation* of information media and privatization of public-sector enterprises was gaining momentum (*see* GOVERNMENT REGULATION). The industrialized nations were increasingly attentive to information markets, including those in the Third World. Because the continued growth of the private sector seemed vital to this strategy, "government-controlled media" were viewed as particularly ominous.

The importance of this issue was evident at a 1981 UNESCO-sponsored meeting on the protection of journalists. For two decades attempts had been made by international organizations of journalists and publishers—such as the International Federation of Journalists, the International Federation of Newspaper Editors, and the International Press Institute—to draft and have adopted an international convention for the protection of journalists. At the UNESCO meeting the concerns of the journalists' organizations were quickly obscured by the recurring issue of the role of governments, this time revolving around licensing. Most governments were prepared to recognize the importance of safeguarding journalists, even though few seemed to cherish the activities of "investigative reporters." The status of journalists and the special protections proposed for them would presumably be based on professional credentials—but issued by whom? In raising this issue, Third World leaders were accused of wishing to license journalists, an idea that was anathema to Western nations.

Nonetheless, attempts were made during the early

1980s to steer the *new order* debates away from such divisive issues. This was especially evident in the creation of a new organization based on an earlier initiative of the United States: the International Program for the Development of Communication (IPDC). The IPDC was designed to be a key instrument for organizing international technical cooperation, helping in the creation and implementation of operational projects, and mobilizing the resources needed for those purposes. Although officially launched in 1980, its first meeting was not held until June 1981. It soon became apparent, however, that contributions from donor countries were much more limited than had been expected. The IPDC was faced with the same dilemma confronting a number of international development agencies: a necessary curtailment of expectations and plans.

The 1982 and 1983 UNESCO General Conferences, held in Paris, did not witness the heated polemics of similar meetings held in 1978 and 1980. At the 1983 conference the call for a new information and communication order was formally designated as "an evolving and continuous process"—a concession to Western interests intent on ensuring that the new order should not be viewed as requiring a sudden and radical transformation of existing communication structures.

A 1983 United Nations–UNESCO Round Table on a New World Information and Communication Order held in Igls, Austria, was another promising sign of dialogue. As the first official United Nations–UNESCO meeting on the issue, the Austrian round table was noteworthy for the absence of political rhetoric and the determination of participants to establish specific mechanisms for assisting the developing countries. Communications technology, rather than news flow alone, was now the primary concern of developing countries.

The year 1983 was to end with two paradoxical but not unrelated events. In early December the nonaligned nations movement held in New Delhi its first Media Conference. It opened with a call to intensify efforts to promote the proposed new order. Weeks later, as December came to a close, Secretary of State George P. Schultz of the United States sent a letter to the director-general of UNESCO informing him that, after the required one-year notification period, in December of 1984 the United States would withdraw from UNESCO. An indirect reference to the *new order* campaign was evident in a passage referring to the necessity of maintaining "such goals as individual human rights and the free flow of information." The U.S. decision to withdraw from UNESCO surprised observers who had taken note of the apparent absence of conflict in 1982 and 1983. However, it was clear that throughout the early 1980s there was significant bipartisan congressional

opposition to UNESCO, not only because of its efforts to promote a new information order but also because of disputes relating to Israel, UNESCO's examination of the issues of peace and disarmament, and a new generation of "people's rights," as well as various financial and organizational reasons. This opposition was widely backed by the U.S. press and other groups.

Challenges

Two decades of debates and resolutions had done little to solve underlying problems of the international flow of information, although they had made the world community more aware of the issues involved. Those issues would be a continuing presence, posing a diversity of challenges many of which had been spelled out in the MacBride Commission's report. A notable aspect of the report was that it went beyond immediate needs and brought to the fore the overall significance of communications in modern society and the implications of media policies for the world's future.

Meanings of technology. The commission noted that technological needs had been a central concern at many meetings but urged that they not be allowed to overshadow the social, political, and economic implications. The importance of the new communications technologies was seen to lie to a large extent in the fundamental transformations they impose on society. Governments and private companies alike have long been inclined to think of technology as a means available to serve their particular needs without consideration of the impact on humanity at large. Use of technical developments cannot and should not be slowed, in the view of the commission, but their implications should be constantly assessed. Technology "is seldom neutral; its use is even less so"—for use is influenced by political, financial, and other considerations. Therefore decisions about communications policies and priorities should not be made solely by technocrats but should involve wide public participation and discussion. "We must beware of the temptation to regard technology as an all-purpose tool capable of superseding social action." The commission noticed a widespread feeling that "technological progress is running ahead of man's capacity to interpret its implications and direct it into the most desirable channels," and cited the fear expressed by Albert Schweitzer that humankind has "lost the capacity to foresee and forestall the consequences" of its actions.

Ways of freedom. The commission noted the perilous status of freedom of expression around the world. The fact "that there is said to be freedom of expression in a country does not guarantee its existence in practice." The commission further noted that "even where freedom is not openly attacked by authority, it may be limited by self-censorship on the part of communicators themselves. Journalists may fail to publish facts which have come into their possession for several reasons: sheer timidity, an excessive respect for the power structure or in some instances lest they give offence to officialdom and thus risk losing access to their sources of information." Self-censorship, like censorship itself, was seen by the commission as a constantly distorting factor in the flow of communication.

The commission emphasized its view that the exercise of freedom in the communications field involves responsibilities. "We need to ask, moreover, on what grounds a claim for freedom is being made. The freedom of a citizen or social group to have access to communication, both as recipients and contributors, cannot be compared to the freedom of an investor to derive profits from the media. One protects a fundamental human right, the other permits the commercialization of a social need."

The report observed that because of the overwhelming importance of communication today, the state imposes some degree of regulation in virtually all societies. It can intervene in many diverse ways—through the allocation of broadcast licenses and newsprint and through visa policies, import restrictions, and many other procedures. "Some governments find it natural to assume total control over the content of information, justifying themselves by the ideology in which they believe. Even on purely pragmatic standards, it is doubtful if this system can be called realistic."

Democratization of communication. Surveying the "spectrum of communication in modern society," the commission found that it almost defies description because of its immense variety. Barriers could readily be seen: monopolistic controls, technical disparities, restrictive media practices, exclusion of disadvantaged groups, blacklists, censorship. Nevertheless, a tendency toward democratization seemed to be taking place—for example, in the growing role of public opinion. Governments throughout the world were becoming increasingly aware that they must take into account not only national opinion but "world public opinion," because today's media are capable of diffusing "information on international questions to every part of the world." Occasionally opinion crystallizes on some issue with enough force to compel action. This happened, as the commission saw it, on the issues of colonialism, apartheid, and nuclear proliferation. But a meaningful process of opinion formation will in the long run require richer media fare, development of widespread "critical awareness," assertion of the "right to reply," the establishment of "alternative channels of communication," and public participation in decision making on media policies. The goal, the commission felt, should be that everyone would be both "producer and consumer of communication."

"Communication can be an instrument of power, a revolutionary weapon, a commercial product, or a means of education; it can serve the ends of either liberation or of oppression, of either the growth of the individual personality or the drilling of human beings into uniformity." Each society and each communication system necessarily makes its choices.

World on edge. The commission looked at the communication challenges in the context of an uneasy world. "The whole human race is threatened by the arms race and by the persistence of unacceptable global inequalities, both of which generate tensions and which jeopardize its future and even its survival." The commission saw the sense of danger "heightened by intolerance, national chauvinism, and a failure to understand varying points of view" as well as by "the fragility of the ecosystem." The report observed: "Today the human race has no choice but to adapt itself to the natural conditions and resources of the planet"—a challenge requiring "enormous transformations in our attitudes and behavior patterns."

The commission saw the media as capable of a steadying role in these transitions, helping men and women "to understand and solve the inescapable problems of our age." This called for something beyond "crisis journalism." The report spoke frequently of responsibility. It seemed to the commission that the information order envisioned for the future would also require, as an essential dimension, a new moral and ethical order.

Bibliography. Cees Hamelink, *Finance and Information,* Norwood, N.J., 1983; International Commission for the Study of Communication Problems (UNESCO), *Many Voices, One World: Communication and Society, Today and Tomorrow,* Paris and New York, 1980; Dinker Rao Mankekar, *Whose Freedom? Whose Order?* New Delhi, 1981; Mustapha Masmoudi, "The New World Information Order," in *World Communications: A Handbook,* ed. by George Gerbner and Marsha Siefert, New York, 1984; Hamid Mowlana, *Global Information and World Communication: New Frontiers in International Relations,* White Plains, N.Y., 1986; Kaarle Nordenstreng, *The Mass Media Declaration of UNESCO,* Norwood, N.J., 1984; Kaarle Nordenstreng and Tapio Varis, *TV Traffic—A One-Way Street?* Paris, 1974; Fernando Reyes Matta, *La información en el nuevo orden internacional,* Mexico, D.F., 1977; Rosemary Righter, *Whose News? Politics, the Press, and the Third World,* London and New York, 1978; Colleen Roach, "Select Annotated Bibliography on a New World Information and Communication Order (NWICO)," in *Communication for All: New World Information and Communication Order,* ed. by Philip Lee, Maryknoll, N.Y.,

1986; Herbert I. Schiller, *Communication and Cultural Domination*, White Plains, N.Y., 1976; Robert L. Stevenson and Donald Lewis Shaw, eds., *Foreign News and the New World Information Order*, Ames, Iowa, 1984.

SEAN MACBRIDE AND COLLEEN ROACH

NEW WAVE FILM

"New wave" (*nouvelle vague*) is a label invented by the French press to designate a pronounced shift in styles, subjects, and modes of film production in France that first became evident in the 1958–1959 film season, although the changes had been in the making for some time. Pre-1958 French cinema was known to its admirers for its "tradition of quality," although its young critics called it the *cinéma de papa*—the old fogies' cinema. Quality cinema was dominated by a group of established artists and technicians and offered young aspiring directors virtually no entry into the profession. It was a cinema of big budgets and international coproductions, explicitly modeled on the HOLLYWOOD A picture that was its most formidable competition. Its critics charged that it favored craftsmanship over personal expression and that it unthinkingly refought old political battles (e.g., against the Catholic church, against the bourgeoisie) irrelevant to postwar Europe.

The quality tradition seems to have suited the tastes of most of the French public until the mid-1950s. But its appeal did not extend to many younger moviegoers, who inevitably made up an increasingly large portion of its market. By middecade box-office returns for big-budget domestic pictures had begun

to drop, whereas a small number of independent low-budget pictures had been produced that fared reasonably well. Suggestive of the later new wave, in subject and style, was Roger Leenhardt's *Les dernières vacances* (The Last Vacation, 1947). More idiosyncratic but also influential were works by Agnès Varda, Alexandre Astruc, and Roger Vadim.

Inspired by the successes of these and other, similar works, several aspiring young directors completed features for release in 1958–1959, many with money from family and friends rather than from traditional industry sources. Released in quick succession, their films seemed a veritable flood of critical and box-office hits, beginning with Louis Malle's *L'ascenseur à l'échafaud* (Frantic) and including *Le beau Serge* and *Les cousins* (both by Claude Chabrol), *Hiroshima mon amour* (Alain Resnais, script by Marguerite Duras), and *Les quatre cents coups* (The Four Hundred Blows, François Truffaut). The success of these works emboldened industry insiders to finance these and other new directors, and by the 1959–1960 film season the wave of first films became a deluge.

The new wave was actually composed of several relatively distinct components. Most important was probably the *Cahiers du cinéma* group of young film critics: Truffaut, Chabrol, Jean-Luc Godard, Eric Rohmer, Jacques Rivette, and a few others. But emerging at the same time was another group frequently called the Left Bank school, including Varda, Resnais, Georges Franju, and later Alain Robbe-Grillet. These people came to feature filmmaking not from criticism but from DOCUMENTARY cinema and

Figure 1. *(New Wave Film)* Alain Resnais, *L'année dernière à Marienbad* (Last Year at Marienbad), 1961. National Film Archive, London/Argos Films.

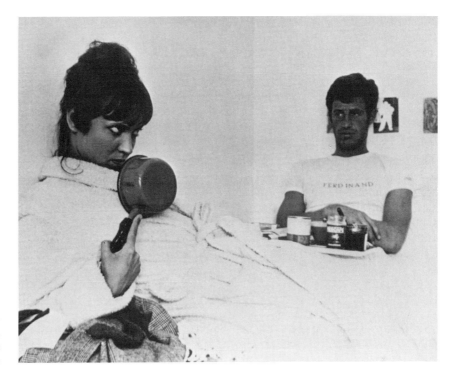

Figure 2. *(New Wave Film)* Jean-Luc Godard, *Pierrot le fou, 1965.* The Museum of Modern Art/Film Stills Archive.

from experimental prose FICTION. A third group, less important in retrospect but more feted at the time, had worked its way up through the dominant industry hierarchy; it included Malle, Michel Deville, and others. What these groups had in common was a rejection of the forms and subjects of the tradition of quality. Whereas the tradition made big-budget, mass-audience films from high- or middlebrow literary sources, films with big STARS, elaborate sets, and carefully crafted and witty dialogue, the new wave produced low-budget, personal films with little-known actors that were shot on location, as in Italy's NEOREALISM movement. Scripts were often improvised and frequently used remarkably vulgar, unliterary language. Along with their striking emphasis on real spaces (mostly in Paris), the new works often examined the tone and texture of everyday life—rituals of lighting cigarettes, saying hello and goodbye, telling jokes, going to the movies. A favorite subject was young people and their unhappy relations with established society. Stylistically the films abandoned the smooth textures of quality cinema in favor of jagged editing, hand-held cameras, direct address to the spectator, and sudden shifts of tone or cinematic means. The new wave filmmakers were devoted film buffs, schooled by long hours of screenings and talk at the Cinémathèque Française under its guiding spirit, Henri Langlois. They laced their works with references to films old and new, including Hollywood B pictures. Godard's *À bout de souffle* (Breathless) was perhaps the most radical work of the 1959–1960 season, but it carried admiring echoes of Humphrey Bogart.

For all its apparent momentum and diversity, the movement had dissipated in all but name by the mid-1960s. It is convenient to continue to speak of the new wave period after 1965 or 1966, but the old norms had reasserted themselves. Budgets crept back up; elaborate costumes and studio shooting came back in vogue; scripts were written, rewritten, polished. The producers were back in charge. Only a few rebels, such as Godard, resisted the pressure to conform. Many new wave innovations survived, such as the hand-held camera and dialogue featuring vulgar language, but in codified, standardized form. Nonetheless, the movement did not so much die out as leave the country of its birth. The French example inspired other waves in Europe and in the Third World; it even had some brief influence on the U.S. film industry. But the later waves seem to have survived best in relatively small, marginal markets; the Federal Republic of Germany's *junger deutscher Film* and Brazil's *cinema nôvo* are two examples. Elsewhere the movement's influence survives mainly in critical opinion and in FILM THEORY. Films continue to be judged and conceptualized in the terms developed by the pre-1959 proto–new wave critics (the *Cahiers du cinéma* group) and by later critics and theorists for whom the *nouvelle vague* was the very essence of what cinema ought to be able to do.

See also AVANT-GARDE FILM; MOTION PICTURES—SOUND FILM.

Bibliography. Claire Clouzot, *Le cinéma français depuis la nouvelle vague,* Paris, 1972; Francis Courtade, *Les malédictions du cinéma français,* Paris, 1978; Jean-Luc Douin, ed., *La nouvelle vague 25 ans après,* Paris, 1983; Peter Graham, ed., *The New Wave,* Garden City, N.Y., 1968; James Monaco, *The New Wave,* New York, 1976; René Prédal, *Le cinéma français contemporain,* Paris, 1984; William F. Van Wert, *The Theory and Practice of the Ciné-Roman,* New York, 1978.

ALAN WILLIAMS

NEWS, TELEVISION. *See* TELEVISION NEWS.

NEWS AGENCIES

In the process of providing the news and information that newspaper readers, radio listeners, and television watchers all around the world expect on a daily basis, the news agency plays a major and often determining role. It is the first link in a chain of news production that transforms unannounced happenings into reported events. News agencies are the primary selectors of which events to cover and thus play a crucial role in creating the pictures of the world that subsequently become current knowledge.

Nineteenth-century origins. The rise during the nineteenth century of an international network of communications, in which the production of news came to be dominated by a handful of international news agencies located in a few major industrialized countries, was inextricably related to the internationalization of European economic interests. As an adjunct of colonialism, the international network of communications radiated outward, supporting the conduct of financial, commercial, and trade relations and offering services to settlers of the colonial territories. *See* COLONIZATION.

In 1835 French businessman Charles Havas set up the world's first news agency, Havas of Paris, to collect information from the major European financial and commercial centers for distribution to a network of subscribers throughout France. By the mid-1840s the spread of telegraph facilities enabled Havas to include other European subscribers within his network (*see* TELEGRAPHY). Impressed by the success of the venture, two of Havas's employees, Bernhard Wolff and Paul Julius Reuter, left the agency, determined to capture a portion of the growing market for themselves. Wolff set up a similar agency in Germany. Reuter, after trying to do the same in France and Germany, established his agency in England.

The entrepreneurial efforts of the founders of these three European agencies succeeded primarily because they met the business world's increasing demands for financial and commercial information. In fact, the first major service established by Havas was the daily supply of European exchange rates to the French Bourse, and all three news agency pioneers found it profitable to supply bankers and merchants with financial information.

As the various provincial presses grew, demand increased for news that was both informative and entertaining. However, the networks through which such news was collected remained the same as those through which commercial information had been and continued to be gathered. News agency correspondents thus had to supply a news service articulated for two different audiences: the commercial audience, with its demands for information essential to the expansion of commerce and trade; and the public audience, avid for various other types of news. The broader demands being placed on the news agencies reflected not merely an expansion in general interest but also the expansion of the political and economic stakes involved.

However, as the different agencies continued to broaden their networks of correspondents and subscribers, the growing rivalry among European powers was paralleled increasingly by the competition among the European news agencies. Furthermore, the accommodation arrived at by the news agencies foreshadowed and paralleled the kinds of accommodation being developed by the major powers in the division of the world into "spheres of influence." The agencies mapped out areas that would belong exclusively to one or another. Within this framework they agreed to assist each other and share information. Thus, in 1856, in the first of a series of agreements among Reuter, Havas, and Wolff, the three agencies agreed on the mutual exchange of stock-market quotations and market prices. Through a supplementary agreement in 1859 they agreed to the reciprocal exchange of political news. And in 1869 the first of a series of "agency treaties" designated clear spheres of influence that would be allocated to each agency. In this treaty Wolff's agency obtained the right to markets in Austria, Scandinavia, and Russia; Havas's agency operated in the French Empire, Italy, Spain, and Portugal; and Reuter's agency was assigned the British Empire and the Far East.

Expanding markets. By the early years of the twentieth century the competition among the agencies to consolidate and expand their operations made them look increasingly to the Americas, and particularly to the United States. Here a battle was in progress between two domestic U.S. agencies: the Associated Press (AP), established in 1848 and owned by a newspaper consortium; and the privately owned United Press (UP), established in 1907. With London entrenched as the center of world communications—and the center of world commerce and trade—a contract for Reuter's services became a trump card in the AP-UP struggle. An exclusive Reuter contract was finally awarded to Associated Press, allying it with the cartel.

In Europe itself suspicion among the agencies continued, exacerbated by the growing subordination of the Wolff agency to the demands of the German government, which had started providing the agency with large-scale financial backing. The growing conflicts reflected tension at the international level, the climax of which was the outbreak of war in 1914.

The most important event in the development of international news and communications, however, was the post–World War I entry of the two domestic U.S. agencies into the international communications network. Until this time the scope of the U.S. agencies had reflected the isolationist worldview prevalent in the United States. With the end of the war, growing U.S. interests in the Far East and increased interagency competition within the United States encouraged U.S. agencies to expand into the international communications system.

At the same time, the exclusive contract that Associated Press had negotiated with Reuter was being weakened by continued assertions from the U.S. agency that Reuter, Havas, and Wolff were nothing more than government agencies. Both AP and UP had begun moving toward independent action, competing for clients in South America. These moves challenged cartel agreements, causing considerable tension within the cartel and eventually leading to AP withdrawal from it. Along with other developments, this altered the international news system. A second factor, particularly in South America, had been the wartime blockades on news from Europe, which had made it possible for the two U.S. agencies to move in and capitalize on the absence of European competition. At the same time, the growth of U.S. interests in East Asia led to increased U.S. news agency activity in that region. Both U.S. agencies were aware of the advantages to be gained from expansion into East Asia but found their paths blocked by the cartel. By 1926 pressure from the U.S. agencies had forced Reuter to amend the cartel arrangements so that Associated Press could make a direct agreement with the Reuter-allied Japanese news agency, Kokusai. By 1933 Reuter had no alternative but to give formal notification of the dissolution of the existing four-party treaty among the three European agencies and Associated Press. The termination of the cartel became effective in 1934, with Reuter and AP signing an agreement giving both agencies the freedom to collect and issue news anywhere in the world.

Although the concept of spheres of influence was no longer official policy, its legacy continued to affect news agency markets. The agencies tended to focus their efforts in markets that had already been secured and developed.

World War II and after. World War II further strained the news agencies, whose wartime function was increasingly the dissemination of ethnocentric news and information. Havas disappeared during the Vichy government and resurfaced in 1943 as Agence France Presse, the fusion of two Free French agencies. It employed the former Havas staff network. Reuter

was given British government support to transmit purely British news, emerging from the war as a cooperative owned by its newspaper subscribers in Britain. Both Associated Press and United Press International (UPI) found themselves better able to operate during the war without the restrictions that the cartel had forced on them during World War I.

The most important factors in the overall evolution of news agencies at the international level have been their outward expansion from Europe (and later the United States) and the establishment of worldwide markets for the services they provided. In fact, in the 1980s the structure of the international news media network was still based on the old cartel patterns—news agencies followed the economic interests of their original bases into overseas territories. In other words, the news flow patterns continued to reflect a world structure dominated by the Western capitalist economies. Although, in contrast to other forms of news media, news agencies have tended to be relatively invisible, their anonymity was challenged as pressure built up (particularly from the countries of the Third World) against what was seen as a MONOPOLY of a few world-level news agencies controlling international flows of news and information. As a result, in the 1970s and 1980s Third World countries found that their relatively recently won political independence was not often accompanied by similar independence in the field of communications. News agencies became the focus of criticism about the origins and dissemination of international and national news, and Third World countries began to explore ways of achieving sovereignty and autonomy in the production of news and information. *See* NEW INTERNATIONAL INFORMATION ORDER.

See also GOVERNMENT REGULATION; NEWSPAPER: HISTORY; TELEVISION NEWS.

Bibliography. Oliver Boyd-Barrett, *The International News Agencies,* London, 1980; Kaarle Nordenstreng and Herbert I. Schiller, eds., *National Sovereignty and International Communication,* Norwood, N.J., 1979; Jim Richstad and Michael H. Anderson, eds., *Crisis in International News: Policies and Prospects,* New York, 1981; Jeremy Tunstall, *The Media Are American,* London, 1977.

PHIL HARRIS

NEWSLETTER

Specialized periodical publication, usually concerned with only one topic. The origins of newsletters are obscured by a lack of documentary evidence. Few of the early ones have survived, because they were handwritten and often clandestine. It is thought that they originated in Germany during the sixteenth century to report international activities for bankers and traders.

As precursors of newspapers, newsletters were the most important news medium in Europe after the MIDDLE AGES. In England newsletters multiplied during the seventeenth century, in part because of the crown's strict control of PRINTING. Domestic CENSORSHIP of news only prompted the production of more newsletters, which required no printing presses, offices, or distribution networks, because their circulation was facilitated by "coffee-house society" and other informal channels (*see* NEWSPAPER: HISTORY).

Distinctions between early newsletters and newspapers are frequently blurred; for example, the first newspaper in the British North American colonies was called the *Boston News-Letter* (1704). Unlike newsletters, newspapers were intended for a larger, wider audience and accepted advertising (*see* ADVERTISING—HISTORY OF ADVERTISING). Developments in printing technology enabled the newspaper and the MAGAZINE to become the dominant print media for several centuries. Not until the twentieth century did newsletters flourish again. They filled a need for more specialized and timely information for specific groups. The concurrent development of sophisticated DIRECT RESPONSE MARKETING techniques to sell subscriptions and of low-cost word processors and personal computers for composition contributed to their growth. Many newsletters became available in the form of on-line services (*see* COMPUTER: IMPACT).

The first modern newsletter in the United States was the *Whaley-Eaton Letter* (1918), intended for diplomats, financiers, corporate lawyers, and other professionals. It was later acquired by the *Kiplinger Washington Letter* (1923), which by the 1980s had five hundred thousand subscribers at forty-eight dollars per year and was the oldest continuously published newsletter in the United States.

Types. Modern newsletters have generally been typewritten, offset publications of one to sixteen pages, printed on letter-size (8½ by 11 inches, or 216 by 279 mm) paper. Subjects covered range from accounting to zoology, and they are either acquired by subscription or received free of charge. Commercial, for-profit newsletters addressed to the business market generally have high subscription prices and small circulations (usually less than two thousand). The most expensive on record in the United States is *Access,* a daily intelligencer delivered by hand for eighteen thousand dollars per year. Consumer newsletters in areas like travel, health, and investment, however, have much lower subscription prices and may have circulations in the tens or hundreds of thousands. Some offer supplementary services, such as directories, proprietary reports, loose-leaf services, and seminars, for additional revenue. If the information reported is time-sensitive or in high-risk areas, electronic transmission increases its usefulness (*see* DATA BASE).

Not-for-profit newsletters are perhaps more numerous than commercial ones and serve to inform and unite association members, company employees, special-interest groups, school alumni, donors, family members, and so on. In Canada and the United States alone there are more than a hundred thousand of these newsletters, of which approximately six thousand are subscription letters. In other parts of the world newsletters are less popular, though many U.S. newsletters are sold in foreign countries, and vice versa. A trade publication to serve the U.S. newsletter industry, *Newsletter on Newsletters,* was founded in 1964.

See also PUBLISHING—PUBLISHING INDUSTRY.

PATRICIA HAGOOD

NEWSMAGAZINE

Periodical (usually weekly) publication devoted to news summaries and analysis in a MAGAZINE format. The first attempts to combine a newspaper and a magazine date from the early eighteenth century in England, where Daniel Defoe wrote and published *The Review* from 1704 to 1713 and Richard Steele brought forth an imitation, *The Tatler*, in 1709 (*see* NEWSPAPER: HISTORY).

Throughout the eighteenth and nineteenth centuries the predecessors of the contemporary newsmagazine were more often "magazines with news," as they served broader information and entertainment purposes (*see* PUBLISHING). The emphasis on news was first tried in 1923, when Briton Hadden and HENRY LUCE published *Time.* In an eighteen-page prospectus they noted: "People are uninformed because no publication has adapted itself to the time which busy men are able to spend simply keeping informed." Their publication, they pledged, would (1) organize the news, (2) interpret it, and (3) focus on individuals as newsmakers rather than on governments or other institutions. The idea was for writers and editors to take a closer, more penetrating look at stories and reflect on the flow of events to produce reports both *timeless* (i.e., not easily dated) and *timely* (i.e., keeping up with current events). The newsmagazine's primary purpose was not to shape PUBLIC OPINION but to present the news in a more lasting and literate manner than daily newspapers.

Although *Time* did not turn a profit until 1928, the idea of an entertaining journey through current affairs caught on. A peculiar literary style evolved (*see* STYLE, LITERARY), characterized by heavy use of adjectives (e.g., "shaggy-maned, beetle-browed John L. Lewis"), coined words (like "cinemaddict"), and inverted sentences (satirist Wolcott Gibbs wrote in *The New Yorker* magazine that "backward ran sentences until reeled the mind"). Readers received the product of writer-researcher teams and editors who compiled reports from *Time* correspondents and bureaus, other newspapers and periodicals, stories by NEWS AGENCIES, and books.

In 1933 two newsmagazines were launched to compete with *Time*. Thomas J. C. Martyn, *Time*'s first foreign-news editor, started *News-Week* (it soon became *Newsweek*), and political reporter David Lawrence inaugurated *U.S. News* (merged in 1948 with a companion publication to become *U.S. News and World Report*). To distinguish itself from *Time*, *Newsweek* maintained a calm and moderate tone, and its editors also attempted to split news coverage from opinion by reserving space for signed columns. In the 1960s *Newsweek* also led *Time* into an era of bylined coverage and the development of extended, in-depth cover reports and special issues on such problems as "The Negro in America—What Must Be Done" (1967). In turn, *Newsweek* followed *Time* in expanding readership overseas through three English-language editions with altered content. In 1986 *Newsweek* introduced an edition in Japanese in an effort to increase its reach and tap an important market.

Media competition and growth. After World War II, when television began to make inroads on the printed news media (*see* TELEVISION HISTORY), several magazine publishers sought to retaliate with digestlike, pocket-size newsmagazines. In the United States, Cowles Publications issued *Quick* in 1949, a miniature that was copied widely but most notably by *Jet*. By the late 1950s all other competitors had disappeared, but *Jet* continued to serve black readers (*see* MINORITY MEDIA).

A trend toward increased specialization of coverage started in the 1970s. The highly successful *Business Week* is aimed at the financial and business community in the United States. The old and respected British periodical *The Economist* was redesigned in the 1970s into a news-oriented publication for an economically upscale Anglo-American audience. Newsmagazines with a similar focus and target audience have appeared in many countries, among them Israel (*Israel Economist*) and Sweden (*Veckans affärer*). Specialized newsmagazines covering a wide range of topics (e.g., SPORTS, health, special interests, and advocacies) have become increasingly common.

Around the world. The concept of newsmagazines has spread to all continents. *East* started in 1933 in Shanghai, and *News Review* began to appear in Great Britain in 1937. Mexico gained *Tiempo* in 1942, France *L'express* in 1957, and Italy *Panorama* and Argentina *Primera plana* in 1962. In Africa *Jeune Afrique* is published in French and *AfricAsia* in English. Australia has the *Bulletin*, and Asia *India Today* and *Asahi* (the latter in Japan). *Veja* is published in Brazil, *Profil* in Austria, and *Cambio 16* in Spain.

European newsmagazines tended to develop as suppliers of more sensational material along with the customary coverage. For instance, the Federal Re-public of Germany's popular and influential *Der Spiegel*, established in 1946, spices its coverage of news with commentary, informed GOSSIP, and "exclusives" such as interviews with notorious criminals. In line with other European newsmagazines, its tone tends to be more abrasive than that of U.S. publications, and government and other institutions are likely to get negative, even cynical coverage.

Outlook for the future. Although newsmagazines remain primarily reliant on text, GRAPHICS and other design elements have been increasingly used to help the reader "make sense of the world" (as an advertisement for *Newsweek* claimed in 1985). Newsmagazines no longer merely merge newspaper and magazine in format. They serve national and international markets with selective, often subjective, compacted, digested, literary, and entertaining packages of current history, politics, government, the economy, sports, arts, sciences, and so on. The newsmagazines serve their readers by sifting and sorting the news, conveniently compartmentalizing it and spicing it with imagery-laden language to keep the readers interested. In the age of television the newsmagazine has found its place as journalism more substantial than that of television and radio, broader—and yet occasionally more specialized—than newspapers, and quicker than the history book (*see also* TELEVISION NEWS).

Bibliography. Robert T. Elson, *Time, Inc.: The Intimate History of a Publishing Enterprise*, ed. by Duncan Norton-Taylor, 2 vols., New York, 1968, 1969; Theodore Peterson, *Magazines in the Twentieth Century*, 2d ed., Urbana, Ill., 1964; William H. Taft, *American Magazines for the 1980s*, New York, 1982.

PETER P. JACOBI

NEWSPAPER: HISTORY

The newspaper can initially be defined as a written (not necessarily printed) means of conveying current information. In this sense the first organized attempt to provide such a service occurred in ancient Rome, where newsletters conveyed what was going on in the capital to the farther reaches of the ROMAN EMPIRE. In Julius Caesar's time there were also the *acta diurna,* daily announcements of government and other activities that were posted in the capital's public places.

The earliest printed news bulletins probably appeared in China, with a court gazette issued during the T'ang dynasty (618–906 C.E.) and read primarily by government officials, although scholars were later added to its readership. A later significant development often cited by historians was the issuing of newsletters by the Fugger family of Germany, a powerful clan of merchants and bankers in the fifteenth and sixteenth centuries. Their agents operated in nearly every part of the known world and sent in reports of business and other affairs from their posts. The reports were combined and circulated by means of the newsletters to all the units in the Fugger organization.

Newsletter to newspaper. But the newspaper as we know it is a relatively modern invention. The Fugger idea, in various forms, spread through Europe and England, resulting in the publication in September 1621 in London of *Corante, or, Weekely News from Italy, Germany, Hungarie, Spaine and France,* generally credited with being the first English newspaper. Other beginnings of the modern newspaper took place in European countries at about the same time, and Mexico recorded the Western Hemisphere's first printed news in 1541.

In Britain's American colonies a transplanted English bookseller named Benjamin Harris published his *Publick Occurrences, Both Forreign and Domestick* in 1690. Unfortunately Harris was a free spirit who was frequently in trouble with the law in both London and the colonies. He offended the authorities with two items in his gazette (besides printing it without a license), and the first issue of his newspaper was also the last. It had taken seventy years of colonizing to produce Harris's paper, and fourteen years more went by before the Boston postmaster, John Campbell, issued his *Boston News-Letter,* the second newspaper to appear in the colonies.

Although newspapers had common origins—that is, they were initially more newsletters and bulletins—they quickly developed along different lines in various parts of the world. The newspapers of England and the United States had much in common at first, but they acquired more differences as time went on. The French meanwhile devised their own style, and newspapers in other parts of Europe assimilated characteristics of all three. As the British and French colonial empires spread around the world they took their newspaper styles with them and implanted them firmly on the journalism of the countries they occupied. Even after the colonial empires ended, new styles were slow to appear, and today the newspapers of Africa, India, South and Central America, and parts of Asia reflect broadly the general techniques of France and England, with substantially less influence from the United States.

These varying styles have their roots in both the geographical and cultural characters of the nations involved. Because the United Kingdom is a relatively small, homogeneous nation its main newspapers, based in London, are national papers, supplemented by a provincial press that is local in character. In contrast the United States did not have papers meant to cover the whole country until the late twentieth century, when electronic transmission systems made it possible to publish the *Wall Street Journal,* the *Christian*

Figure 1. *(Newspaper: History)* Frontispiece of a Dutch newspaper, 1653. The Bettmann Archive, Inc.

Science Monitor, Gannett's *USA Today,* and to a lesser extent the *New York Times* simultaneously across the country. Similarly the Soviet Union covers its vast territory by using facsimile transmission to print its two major Moscow papers, *Pravda* and *Izvestia,* simultaneously from Leningrad to Vladivostok. Japan too uses the same system to print simultaneously in Tokyo and the northern islands.

Major lines of development. The two major developments in the history of the world press have been the struggle for control between government and the press in every country, from the beginning to the present, and the growth of mass circulations resulting from technological advances (*see* GOVERNMENT-MEDIA RELATIONS; GOVERNMENT REGULATION). At the beginning the idea of a free press did not exist. Governments everywhere saw the newspaper as an instrument to be used in their own interests, an idea that persists in much of the world today. Sometimes newspapers were licensed—that is, certain owners of PRINTING presses were permitted to print papers, books, or magazines—as occurred in the American colonies. In other places the press was simply controlled by the state.

Freedom from government control began to emerge in the Massachusetts Bay Colony in America about

1725, when two young Boston printers, Benjamin Edes and John Gill, having taken over the *Boston Gazette,* defied the authorities and led the slowly growing revolt against the crown, battling the authorities in the process. In New York JOHN PETER ZENGER is popularly celebrated as the father of a free press because as proprietor of the *New-York Weekly Journal* he was tried on a LIBEL charge and acquitted. However, this decision represented only the jury's defiance of local authority and was contrary to English common law, under which the case was tried. Truth as a libel defense, the basis on which Zenger's lawyer, Andrew Hamilton, pleaded the case, was not established in law in New York State until 1804, after which it was incorporated into the statutes of other states.

By the time the American Revolution had ended, the press in the new nation was not only free but had become a quarrelsome, vituperative ideological instrument in the hands of contending political parties. It was not until 1835, when JAMES GORDON BENNETT founded the *New York Herald,* that newspapers began to report news (or at least some of it) with a measure of impartiality. The modern U.S. newspaper was born with the *Herald,* which was organized in much the same way as papers are today. Bennett faced competition from other nineteenth-century giants: HORACE GREELEY and his *New York Tribune* (1841); BENJAMIN H. DAY's New York *Sun* (1833), the first successful penny paper; and Henry J. Raymond's *New York Times* (1851).

In New York, Boston, and Philadelphia, and later in the remainder of the nation, newspapers were operated by powerful editors and publishers who practiced a kind of personal journalism, political but independent, and supported primarily by circulation. The arrival in New York in 1883 of the Hungarian-born immigrant JOSEPH PULITZER and in 1896 of WILLIAM RANDOLPH HEARST, who had already made a success with his San Francisco *Examiner,* revolutionized journalism in New York and elsewhere. Pulitzer's *World* and Hearst's *Journal* set the pattern with a formula of sensational news stories; editorial crusades against "the interests," both business and political; Sunday papers designed for entertainment; and the introduction of the comic cartoon, followed by the modern comic strip (*see* COMICS).

The circulation wars between these papers foreshadowed the great change in newspaper PUBLISHING in the United States that began about the turn of the twentieth century, when ADVERTISING began to replace circulation as a newspaper's chief source of revenue. In order to attract advertisers, however, it was necessary to offer as much circulation as possible, so the competition for both readers and advertising dollars continued in tandem. Thus was born the concept of delivering audiences to advertisers, a practice that later became common to all the media.

In the late-twentieth-century United States, the newspaper became a big-business institution. The individual giants in the nineteenth-century sense disappeared and were replaced by entrepreneurs, only a scant few known to the public, who owned large groups of newspapers, the end result of consolidations and the deaths of numerous big-city dailies. The International Thomson Organization, a worldwide media conglomerate based in Toronto, was the largest owner of newspapers in the United States by 1987, but none of them was a major daily.

Journalism in Great Britain took a different turn, although there were a few similarities. Newspapers in the eighteenth century were almost exclusively political, but this kind of paper also produced such notable essayists as Sir Richard Steele and Joseph Addison, whose *Spectator,* begun in 1711, was a model of the type, as were, of course, SAMUEL JOHNSON's *Rambler* (1750) and the *Idler* (1758). In the early nineteenth century newspapers in England became much more scandalous, as they did later in the United States, and even blasphemous, which did not happen in the United States. In both countries journalism was more political than otherwise.

Modern journalism in Britain began in the nineteenth century with the rise of the London *Times,* which had been launched in 1785 by John Walter as the *Daily Universal Register* but changed its name at the beginning of 1788. By 1829 it had become so powerful and authoritative by virtue of such editors as Thomas Barnes and Edward Sterling that the rival *Morning Chronicle* coined the descriptive phrase, "The Thunderer," by which it is still sometimes called.

Other notable newspaper beginnings were the *Manchester Guardian* (1821), a provincial newspaper that dropped the "Manchester" from its title in 1860 and two years later began to publish as a national newspaper; the *Daily Mail,* begun in 1896 by Alfred and Harold Harmsworth; the *Daily Express,* founded in 1900 by C. Arthur Pearson; and the *Daily Mirror,* which was begun by Alfred Harmsworth as a women's paper in 1903 but which soon became the first illustrated tabloid.

The Harmsworths, in company with Kennedy Jones, also acquired an evening paper in London, the *Evening News* (1881), and their rival, Lord Beaverbrook (*see* BEAVERBROOK, 1ST BARON), came into the same field in 1923 with the *Evening Standard,* launched in the 1870s. Great Britain also has a newspaper published only on Sunday, until recently unique in the business, the *Observer,* founded in 1791. Its principal rival has been the *Sunday Times,* begun in 1822. These, with the *Sunday Telegraph,* became known as "quality" papers.

The London press has been transformed in many

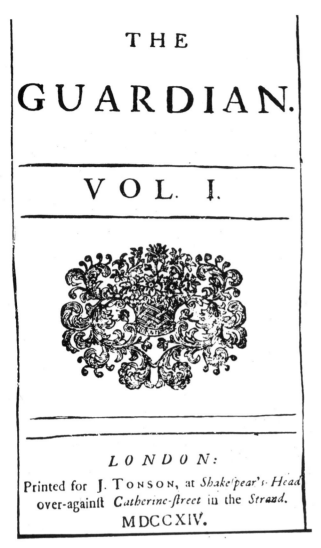

THE

GUARDIAN.

VOL. I.

LONDON:

Printed for J. T O N S O N, at *Shakespear's Head*
over-against *Catherine-street* in the *Strand.*

MDCCXIV.

Figure 2. *(Newspaper: History)* Title page of *The Guardian*, published in London, 1714. The Bettmann Archive, Inc.

respects by new owners and new technologies, resulting in the creation of such new, nearly fully automated papers as *Today* and the *Independent.* The *Times,* whose prestige has faded, became part of the empire controlled by the Australian media magnate Rupert Murdoch, who owned newspapers in Australia, the United States, and elsewhere. In London his tabloid daily, the *Sun,* and his Sunday paper, *The People,* practiced the kind of sensational journalism common in the United States during the 1920s but almost nonexistent today except for Murdoch's tabloid, the *Post,* in New York.

There are obvious physical differences between the U.S. press and the British press. In the United States TYPOGRAPHY is more or less standard and in general conservative, whereas in Britain headline styles and the writing itself are much more personal and idiosyncratic. The use by reporters of the personal pronoun *I* in some stories, virtually unknown in the

United States, represents this marked difference. The British press as a whole appears more personal than its U.S. counterparts.

Although those who read the scandalous London tabloids may believe that freedom of the press is greater there than it is in the United States (British papers, for example, sometimes use obscene words never seen in the U.S. press), the opposite is true. British newspapers are more tightly controlled than those in the United States because the libel laws are much more harsh and because there is no First Amendment and Supreme Court to enforce it, however ambiguously. Great Britain also has the Official Secrets Act, which gives the government legal means to preserve its traditional secrecy about its operations. The Watergate exposures of the Nixon administration in the United States, for instance, would not have been possible in England.

In the landmass of the USSR, by contrast with both England and the United States, there has never been anything but strict control of the press by government since the first newspaper appeared in 1703. Both the czars and the Communist government instituted after the Revolution have prevented the press from growing and developing as it has in other major nations. As V. I. Lenin enunciated it in 1919, the press is considered the instrument of the people, and since the government theoretically *is* the people, the press is part of the government. Newspapers are not dependent on either advertising or circulation revenue but are subsidized by the state.

In other European countries press developments have generally resembled those in Great Britain and the United States, with periodic shifts and variations. Germany, where JOHANNES GUTENBERG first introduced movable type, has known newspapers since 1609. One of its greatest, the *Allgemeine Zeitung,* was begun in 1798. After the German Republic was established in 1919 the press grew so rapidly that by 1932 there were forty-seven hundred newspapers in Germany, nearly three-fourths of them dailies. Adolf Hitler's rise to chancellor in 1933 interrupted both freedom and growth for a time, as press freedom was revoked and newspapers became propaganda organs for the state. After World War II the Federal Republic of Germany had such notable papers as *Die Welt* of Hamburg, and the more popular press boasts the large-circulation *Bild Zeitung,* also of Hamburg, as well as the *Frankfurter Allgemeine* and the *Berliner Morgenpost.*

The French press has been more literary than news oriented from the beginning. Editorial practices common elsewhere are less observed, and writers for newspapers are often professors, political scientists, philosophers, or other intellectuals rather than reporters. The general pattern of the essay rather than the traditional news story is followed, although not exclusively. French journalism also has deep roots, going back to 1631, but modern newspapers began in the nineteenth century and divided themselves into political, popular, and literary journals. *Le monde,* a product of the post–World War II reorganization of the press, remains the prestige daily. During the Nazi occupation the twenty-five Paris dailies were reduced to six, and after liberation only the four that had refused to collaborate were permitted to resume. *Le figaro* has long been the leading voice of the middle and upper classes; *France-soir* is the popular afternoon paper.

Middle Eastern journals are largely political and controlled, and Africa has a press as varied as the continent itself. Francophone countries there tend to have newspapers modeled somewhat after the Parisian papers, and those with a legacy of British colonial rule are more like the English press, as are South Africa's journals. All of the African press is primarily political and controlled in one degree or another. Most Indian newspapers of consequence are printed in English, the common language of the subcontinent. The *Times of India,* published in Bombay and New Delhi, has long been regarded as the country's principal paper, although the *Indian Express,* published simultaneously in five cities, has the largest circulation.

Mexico has a large and active press that has always played a political role, as have the newspapers of Central and South America. *La prensa* of Buenos Aires has long been regarded as one of the world's great papers. Japan has by far the most active press in Asia, concentrated mostly in Tokyo and Osaka. Its three leading journals, *Asahi shimbun, Mainichi shimbun,* and *Yomiuri shimbun,* are among the world's leaders. In the late 1980s China was beginning to develop a free and more modern press after years of repression. *See also* NEWSPAPER: TRENDS.

The role of newspapers. As a medium of communication newspapers have been most notable as purveyors of information, whereas books and magazines have been the dominant medium for ideas (*see* BOOK; MAGAZINE). Readers around the world, however, are dependent on newspapers for information about events affecting their daily lives. In earlier times, when the newspaper was the only medium for conveying information, it was an obvious source of power for state and church, and the press was controlled by one or the other or both.

In the United States particularly no factor was more important than the printing press in defining the country as the printers moved westward, carrying their equipment with them. But it was the advent of the steam-powered cylinder press early in the nineteenth century that profoundly influenced life and society, in the United States and in every country in which it was introduced. Combined with the use of

Figure 3. *(Newspaper: History)* *The New-England Courant,* February 11, 1723. The Bettmann Archive, Inc.

Figure 4. *(Newspaper: History)* Honoré Daumier, *Louis Philippe Threatening the Free Press*, ca. 1836. The Bettmann Archive, Inc.

stereotyped plates and cheaper methods of making paper, it opened wide the door to the mass market, and the subsequent flow of information was so profuse and difficult to control that the sources of power became multiple. The mass market for information and ideas thus created has been increasing ever since.

Experiments to develop the cylinder press began in England as early as 1790. The idea of such a press grew until the English-born inventor Robert Hoe and his associates took prototypes of the French Napier cylinder presses in 1825 and improved on them until they had produced the press that dispensed with the old flatbed entirely, carrying the type forms on the cylinders while other cylinders made the impression. The first true cylinder press, developed by Hoe's son Richard, did not appear in a newspaper office until 1847, when the Philadelphia *Public Ledger* installed a four-cylinder machine into which four boys fed the paper. It printed eight thousand sheets an hour on one side, and it revolutionized the newspaper business.

With this advance, coupled with the growth of public education, a market for information and entertainment was created for all the media. Later technological developments only served to make the basic process easier. In the late twentieth century the use of computers and photo-offset printing combined to produce a chain of automation from the reporter to the delivery room. Electronics, as noted, made possible the simultaneous printing of newspapers across such vast areas as the USSR and the United States as well as in small, homogeneous countries like Japan. There has been some human cost; not all technologically displaced workers can be retrained, and the typographical unions everywhere have fought a long and losing rear-guard action against these changes.

In the United States the second most important change has been the replacement of circulation as the chief source of income. In no other country has advertising become such a dominant factor as in the United States. Advertising has come to be not only commercial but ideological, encompassing corporate institutional advertising and presenting company viewpoints, in addition to pleas for support and statements of purpose from all kinds of organizations. CLASSIFIED ADVERTISING too offers a vast marketplace for individuals and business interests alike.

In its evolution from political medium to news medium to a news and entertainment format, the newspaper has come closer to the magazine in the late twentieth century, as the periodicals themselves have become more and more informational. Feature materials in both are often interchangeable. As the spectrum of information has broadened, major newspapers offer not only international, national, and local news but also information covering MOTION PICTURES, television, RADIO, books, music, ART, SPORTS, finance, science, home maintenance, and even personal problems. Smaller newspapers tend to concentrate on local news and to act as community bulletin boards.

Wars and revolutions have had major and continuing effects on newspapers. Since the Civil War in the United States, and even earlier in Europe, people relied on newspapers for coverage of hostilities, and in earlier days for the printing of casualty lists. It is significant that when revolutionary changes of government occur, with only a few exceptions the first act of a new government is to control the press and make it subservient to the new regime. If the controls are relaxed later, they are tightened again immediately if the chief source of political power is threatened. In countries in which the press is free, or relatively so, newspapers become major battlegrounds for conflicting political ideas. In both Great Britain and the United States, for example, large questions of foreign and domestic policy, particularly war and events leading to possible war, are debated in the newspapers, and presumably the press influences public support for government policies, or the reverse. Uniquely in the United States newspapers can be a major factor in exposing political corruption to the extent of bringing down public officials, including presidents, in a way not considered possible in countries with other forms of government.

Challenges to newspapers. Newspapers everywhere are in a constant struggle to maintain their

Figure 5. *(Newspaper: History)*
New York Times advertising poster,
ca. 1905. The Bettmann Archive, Inc.

integrity and independence, if they have it to begin with, and their economic viability as well, in the face of increasing competition from other media. They and the other print media have been declared seriously wounded or possibly dead with the advent of every medium or other device that might compete for people's time and attention. This was the case with the bicycle, the automobile, the motion picture, radio, and finally television. Of them all only television has had a serious impact on the newspaper business.

Several factors are involved in this competition. A major one is the persistence of illiteracy, in spite of efforts to combat it, and with this the growing number of people who can read but do not because of the increasing demands of contemporary life. A majority of people in the United States get their news from television rather than newspapers because it is more convenient and far less demanding of either time or attention. This is less true in other countries, in which the amount of TELEVISION NEWS is considerably less and often is controlled by the state, so that viewers turn to the medium more for entertainment than for news.

Television has also proved to be a more potent shaper of opinions and ATTITUDES than newspapers, at least in the United States, and a more effective political weapon in nations with government-controlled media. The late-twentieth-century trend in capitalist countries toward MONOPOLY and consolidation has produced a steady decline in the number of daily newspapers, and of newspaper owners as well, even though advertising revenues continue to rise. Newspapers are increasingly part of media conglomerates, or even of multifaceted, multinational organizations of which they may constitute only a small part, leading, in the opinion of some media critics, to a general uniformity.

Despite this situation and the competition of other media, newspapers in the late twentieth century have continued to hold their own as essential conveyors of information not duplicated elsewhere and as the medium most effective in holding governments accountable to the governed.

See also NEWSMAGAZINE.

Bibliography. John Tebbel, *The Compact History of the American Newspaper*, new and rev. ed., New York, 1969; idem, *The Media in America*, New York, 1974; The Times Newspapers, *The (London) Times: Past, Present and Future: To Celebrate 200 Years of Publication*, London, 1985.

JOHN TEBBEL

NEWSPAPER: TRENDS

This entry consists of seven articles:
1. Trends in Africa
2. Trends in Asia
3. Trends in Europe
4. Trends in Latin America
5. Trends in the Middle East
6. Trends in North America
7. Trends in the Soviet Press

1. TRENDS IN AFRICA

The vast expanse of Africa, inhabited by more than 500 million people, produces the fewest newspapers of any continent. Of the world's eight thousand daily newspapers, fewer than one hundred fifty are published in the forty-five countries of Africa. African newspapers have always been few, scattered, and concentrated in a handful of cities near the coast.

Historically, the press of Africa is a product of colonialism. The European colonizers and settlers imported printing presses to serve their own interests (*see* COLONIZATION). The first newspapers were official publications—the *Cape Town Gazette* in 1800 and the *Royal Gazette and Sierra Leone Advertiser*

in 1801. In the years following, two parallel traditions of journalism evolved, each directly influenced by the European incursion. First were the European, or "settler," newspapers, printed for the convenience and use of Europeans with the Africans as an eavesdropping audience. Later came the African nationalist newspapers, which, despite many obstacles, were published by Africans for many decades before independence. These early African newspapers fanned the flames of nationalism and, later, independence movements throughout the continent.

History. African journalism began in British West Africa. The first European papers appeared there, and the first journals published by Africans for other Africans were in the British colonies of Sierra Leone, Gold Coast (later Ghana), and, later, Nigeria. The guiding purpose of these African-produced newspapers, some of them handwritten, was politics; they were part of a strategy for gaining power. An indigenous English-language press developed in British West Africa originally to publicize African grievances and to criticize British rule. Later the press became a political weapon in the struggle for nationalism, to help organize political parties, and, finally, to win political independence itself. The first known newspaper in Nigeria was the *Iwe Irohin* in 1859, handwritten by missionaries in the Yoruba language. In time Nigeria became the principal center of journalism in black Africa.

In North Africa, too, an indigenous nationalist press, usually in Arabic, grew alongside the French colonial press. However, during the colonial era (roughly 1885–1960) the most important and dominant newspapers in North Africa were European publications.

A major and lasting influence on West African journalism was the establishment in the late 1940s of the London Mirror newspapers run by the redoubtable Cecil King. The *Daily Times* and *Sunday Times* of Lagos (Nigeria), the *Gold Coast Daily Graphic* and *Sunday Mirror* of Accra (Gold Coast), and the *Sierra Leone Daily Mail* (Freetown) dominated their areas in circulation and influence. Moreover, their Fleet Street style of tabloid journalism provided a model that was long emulated.

Other British influences came from the Lonrho group, which at one time owned newspapers in Tanzania, Uganda, Kenya, and Zambia, and from the Thomson group of newspapers in West Africa. Although most of these privately owned European enterprises were in time taken over by the independent African governments, they had a lasting impact on African journalism.

As independence neared, African politics and newspapers became closely entwined. Leading journalists were in many cases leading nationalists or political leaders. Nnamdi Azikiwe (known as "Zik"), a major figure of West African journalism, and his National Council of Nigerian Citizens party (NCNC) controlled 10 newspapers in Nigeria by 1959. Zik's *West African Pilot* played a crucial role in galvanizing the movement for political independence. His longtime political rival, Obefemi Awolowo, and his Action Group party had 7 newspapers. Similarly, in the Gold Coast during the 1950s KWAME NKRUMAH and his Convention Peoples' Party had 7 newspapers serving their cause. A total of 227 newspapers appeared in British West Africa during the last years of the colonial period: 52 in Sierra Leone, 70 in the Gold Coast, 100 in Nigeria, and 5 in Gambia.

East Africa was long dominated by the more staid *East African Standard* (Nairobi, 1902). The *Standard* and its sister papers, the *Uganda Argus* (Kampala, 1955) and the *Tanganyika Standard* (Dar es Salaam, 1930), were owned, staffed by, and published for English-speaking Europeans. These papers spoke for settler interests, showing little concern for Africans or their political aspirations.

The first African-owned paper in East Africa was *Muiguithania* ("The Reconciler" in Kikuyu), published in 1928 and edited by Johnstone Kamau, a young man later to be known as JOMO KENYATTA, independent Kenya's first president. By the time of the Mau Mau Emergency in the 1940s, there were about forty African vernacular newspapers being published, mostly in Kikuyu, all of which were eventually suppressed as seditious by the British.

French colonial policy did little to encourage African newspapers, and until the mid-1930s newspapers and journals could be published only by French citizens in either French West Africa or French Central Africa, a vast expanse including fourteen nations. The only successful and lasting newspapers were published in Dakar, Senegal, for French traders and colonial officials. *Le reveil du sénégalais* was founded in 1885 and *Le petit sénégalais* in 1886, but these were published by French nationals for other French nationals. The first French-language paper owned and operated by Africans themselves was the *Éclaireur de la Côte d'Ivoire* (Abidjan, 1935).

During the 1930s the Charles de Breteuil newspaper chain was the only group of its kind in francophone Africa. *Paris-Dakar* was launched in 1935, and in 1938 *France-Afrique* (which became *Abidjan matin* in 1954) appeared in the Ivory Coast. Other papers were started in Conakry and Cameroun, but francophone Africa was, and is, notable for its lack of newspapers.

During the 1950s European domination of the economic and cultural life of the Federation of Rhodesia and Nyasaland (later to become Zambia, Zimbabwe, and Malawi) was reflected in its press. Most newspapers and periodicals, including those intended for Africans, were European enterprises. Argus South African Newspapers controlled the *Rhodesian Herald* and *Sunday Mail* (Salisbury), the *Chronicle* and *Sunday News* (Bulawayo), and the *Umtali Post* until Zimbabwe gained its independence in 1980 and, in effect, nationalized these papers.

In South Africa throughout much of the twentieth century the Argus group and other British newspaper publishers, notably the South African Associated Newspapers (SAAN) group, developed the most extensive English-language newspapers on the continent, with the financial support of mining interests and based on the traditions of British newspapers. *The Star, Rand Daily Mail, Cape Argus, Sunday Times, Cape Times*, and others dominated South African journalism. This commercial press was later challenged by the politically oriented Afrikaans-language newspapers that faithfully served the political goals of the National Party, which gained control of the South African government in 1948.

The black press of South Africa has had a long history, mostly quite separate from that of the white newspapers. Between 1836 and 1977 there were more than eight hundred publications written by or aimed at nonwhites. Some were small, ephemeral newsletters of only two to four pages; others were full magazines or newspapers with circulations up to one hundred seventy thousand. However, any newspapers or publications that supported the political interests and goals of black South Africans have been systematically suppressed in recent years. Two successful black-oriented dailies, *World* and *Post,* were closed down by the government in 1977 and 1981, respectively. As a result of the growing conflict and civil strife over apartheid and political dominance, freedom of the press for the opposition English press, as for the black press, has been steadily declining. Despite their numbers Africans do not own or control any newspapers in South Africa.

The press after independence. The decade of the 1960s was a critical time for the press of Africa. As political independence came to colony after colony, the need for more newspapers seemed apparent and the growth of newspapers was predicted. Instead, however, newspapers remained small and undercapitalized, circulations limited, and ADVERTISING sparse; trained journalists were hard to come by, and potential readership was sharply constrained by illiteracy and poverty (*see* LITERACY). Furthermore, significant changes in ownership occurred as African governments assumed control of both newspapers and electronic media.

This direct role of government was evident in other trends of the 1960s: a decline in the number of independent newspapers (both African- and European-owned), nationalization of RADIO and television services (*see* TELEVISION HISTORY), and widespread establishment of government NEWS AGENCIES to control the flow of news in and out of the new nations. *See* NEW INTERNATIONAL INFORMATION ORDER.

At this time the most significant trend in African journalism was the proliferation of government and/or party newspapers. In Nigeria the federal government established its own group, the *Morning Post* and *Sunday Post* in Lagos, and each of the three regional governments did the same.

By 1970 the new look of African journalism had become clear: government- or party-controlled newspapers had taken center stage. European-owned newspapers gradually faded away except in Kenya and South Africa. The few independent African-owned newspapers such as the *West African Pilot* and *Nigerian Tribune* of Nigeria and *The Pioneer* of Kumasi, Ghana, were barely hanging on, while many small, irregular publications disappeared along with political opposition. In independent black Africa, Kenya remained something of an exception; two foreign-owned dailies, *The Standard* and *The Daily Nation,* continued to flourish under the one-party government of Kenyatta.

But political conditions were simply not conducive to the growth of vigorous, independent newspapers. Under colonial rule the African press had been a lively political press nurtured by nationalism and the independence movements, but the new governments that followed did not want outspoken papers that challenged politicians and their policies. Africa's new leaders felt the press should support the government and its development goals (*see* DEVELOPMENT COMMUNICATION).

The new one-party or military governments showed little tolerance for dissent or criticism. In Ghana, for example, Nkrumah bought out the British-owned *Daily Graphic* and made it a government publication; he shut down *The Pioneer,* an independent African dissenting newspaper, jailed its editor, and launched his own official newspaper, the *Ghanaian Times.* Journalists in Ghana and elsewhere became deferential civil servants, doing the bidding of politicians. Newspapers not yet directly under government control were harassed in various ways in Zambia, Rhodesia, Nigeria, Sierra Leone, Kenya, Uganda, and other countries, and their editors were often forced out of their jobs and into exile. A respected Kenyan editor, Hilary Ng'weno, expressed the frustrations of many African journalists:

In respect of the all-pervading power of the government, nothing has really changed from the bad old days of colonialism. Only the actors have changed; the play remains the same. Instead of a colonial governor you have a President or a field marshal. . . . Newspapers were

taken over and those which were totally opposed to being incorporated into the government propaganda machinery were closed down.

In addition to political barriers, the growth of newspapers in Africa was stymied by economic and social constraints deeply embedded in African societies. Such widespread conditions as low literacy, poverty, linguistic fragmentation, endemic disease, and malnutrition as well as transportation and production difficulties exacerbated the problems of producing profitable publications. Lack of investment capital, the high cost of imported newsprint and printing equipment, and difficulties of distribution all contributed.

In short, the newspaper did not take hold in Africa as a firmly rooted *African* institution. It remains an exotic plant imported from Europe and continues to struggle in a foreign and hostile environment.

Bibliography. Rosalynde Ainslie, *The Press in Africa: Communications Past and Present,* New York, 1966; Frank Barton, *The Press of Africa,* New York and London, 1979; William A. Hachten, *Muffled Drums: The News Media in Africa,* Ames, Iowa, 1971; William A. Hachten and C. Anthony Giffard, *The Press and Apartheid: Repression and Propaganda in South Africa,* Madison, Wis., 1984; George T. Kurian, ed., *World Press Encyclopedia,* 2 vols., New York, 1982; Dennis L. Wilcox, *Mass Media in Black Africa: Philosophy and Control,* New York, 1975.

WILLIAM A. HACHTEN

2. TRENDS IN ASIA

The Asian press underwent considerable change in the years after World War II. In many instances ownership and control of newspapers switched from European and local business interests to a mixture of national government, political party, and private enterprise, all often supportive of the status quo. Western-style freedom of press was replaced by GOVERNMENT-MEDIA RELATIONS that put the press in the role of promoting government policies. Perennial economic problems of the press were sometimes solved by local ingenuity, but more often through dependency on outside interests such as multinational corporations. In other regards change was slow. Mass readership has not been common except in Japan, Hong Kong, and Singapore. Newspapers in some areas such as India and the Philippines have problems addressing the needs and sensitivities of multiethnic and multilingual readers. Other problems persist: newspaper content tends to exploit the sensational, ignore the rural masses, and depend on foreign NEWS AGENCIES or local government sources.

History. Although missionaries brought printing presses to parts of Asia in the sixteenth century, newspapers appeared much later, mainly in the late eighteenth and the nineteenth century. Previously, newsletters were occasionally published for royal courts; these included the *kawaraban* in Japan as early as 1610, the *Royal Court Report* in Korea during the sixteenth century, and Tomás Pinpin's *Succesos felices* in Manila in 1637 (*see* NEWSLETTER).

Regularly published newspapers were introduced by the colonists and were designed to keep them in touch with their home countries or to propagate European religious, trade, or government policies. Even in countries such as Japan and Thailand, which escaped COLONIZATION, the first newspapers were either imitations of European-oriented papers (*Batavia shimbun* in Japan) or were started by missionaries (Dan Beach Bradley's *Bangkok Recorder* in Thailand). By the turn of the twentieth century, newspapers supporting nationalist and independence movements emerged. Notably in the Philippines, *La solidaridad* and its editors and contributors provided impetus for a nationalist movement. Korea's first modern newspaper, *Tongnip sinmun* (The Independent), listed goals of excluding foreign dominance, protecting national sovereignty, eliminating class distinctions, and expanding civil rights, while later Ceylon's nationalist movement was sparked by D. R. Wijewardene and his *Ceylon Daily News*. Most Asian countries had some newspapers that were characterized by nationalist motivation and politics.

Growing side by side with politically motivated newspapers were those that sought commercial success. The trend toward big-business journalism was most pronounced in Japan; the newspapers *Osaka asahi* and *Osaka mainichi,* predecessors of two of the three contemporary giants, claimed circulations in the hundreds of thousands by the 1890s. In the early twentieth century, newspapers that were more commercially than politically oriented were started in China, Hong Kong, Singapore, Malaya, the Philippines, India, and Ceylon. The result in a few countries, notably the Philippines, India, Ceylon, and of course Japan, was a trend toward concentration of ownership, resulting in the formation of newspaper groups.

As Japan advanced its military imperialism in the 1930s and 1940s, its press and the press of countries it occupied experienced similar hardships. Most editors were interned or sought refuge; all publications, except for a few used specifically by the Japanese military, were disbanded; and remaining media were reorganized as part of the PROPAGANDA apparatus. For example, in Japan the number of newspapers dwindled from 1,200 in 1937 to about 50 five years later. In occupied Japan in the postwar period, journalists who had supported the wartime military government and also those who had espoused Com-

munist principles were purged, and newspapers were censored. At the same time, most Asian countries, including Japan, witnessed an abundance of new newspapers. For example, 56 new papers sprang up in Burma between 1945 and 1946; 126 new papers in Japan by 1946; and 75 dailies in Indonesia by 1949. The freedom that came with the defeat of Japan and subsequent independence movements was not always matched with responsibility. At times newspapers were unabashedly reckless.

Government-press relations. Of all changes encountered by the Asian newspapers since World War II, the most sweeping have been those dealing with press-government relations. Trends toward authoritarian leadership altered the ways governments interacted with the press. Besides promoting a "guidance" concept to be used in conjunction with national development aims, most governments enacted or altered press laws, suspended offending newspapers, arrested errant journalists, restructured newspapers to include more government ownership and management, and imposed economic sanctions.

The guidance principle, coupled with self-censorship, prevails throughout the region. A subtle type of control, guidance is offered to journalists by officials who claim the press must diminish its role as critic and support government policies and institutions in the early years of newly emergent nations. Often, as in Bangladesh, Malaysia, Singapore, the Philippines, Indonesia, Pakistan, and Taiwan, the press practices self-restraint, avoids investigative reporting, includes all government speeches and campaigns, ignores opposition elements, and relies to a great extent on government news releases. The guidance comes in the form of public speeches by officials on the desired role of the press and the redefinition of press freedom, and telephone calls from officials offering "advice" and questioning editors' decisions.

In China, the Democratic People's Republic of Korea, the Indochina states, Afghanistan, and Mongolia the role of the press is in accord with Marxist-Leninist concepts of total integration with government and, in some instances, in harmony with Maoist concepts of mass line, anti-intellectualism, and antiprofessionalism. In China, for example, the press has been totally subject to the interests of society as defined by the authorities and by the party's opinion formation process. Communist presses are organized intricately along structural and functional lines, and are owned and controlled by the state or party.

In nearly all of Asia, legislation affecting the press has been scrupulously analyzed and strengthened through amendments, especially in the 1970s. Most Southeast Asian and many East and South Asian nations require annual licensing of newspapers; others require prohibitively expensive security deposits, such as the forty-seven thousand dollars levied on South Vietnamese newspapers in the early 1970s. Security, public order, and LIBEL and sedition laws have been harshly applied to newspapers and journalists; in Malaysia and Singapore the Internal Security Act provides for up to two years' imprisonment, without formal arrest, of journalists suspected of breaking these rules. Malaysia's sedition regulations specify four sensitive issues that cannot be discussed critically; Singapore's libel laws are used by the prime minister and other officials to subdue newspapers; and most countries have instituted or updated legislation to scrutinize foreign publications and journalists.

Harassment and arrest of journalists and suspension of newspapers occur when officials believe their guidance has not been accepted or laws have been broken. Extreme examples occurred in the early 1970s as governments and media made the transition from old-style authoritarianism, with its overt methods, to guidance and developmental communications, perhaps more dangerous because of their relative subtlety. In the Philippines in 1972, nearly all newspapers were closed permanently, scores of journalists were arrested, and new structures and purposes were given to the dailies that were founded at that time. Between 1973 and 1975 officials of the Republic of Korea arrested journalists and forced the merger or closure of opposition newspapers, including for a short time the main daily, *Dong-a ilbo*. The country that must, especially in its final years, have set a record for number of confiscations and suspensions of newspapers was South Vietnam. In 1970 Saigon authorities confiscated newspapers 250 times; 718 times in 1971; and 907 times in 1972. One daily, *Tin sang*, was confiscated no less than 166 times in 1971. After an assassination attempt on President Lon Nol in March 1973, all Cambodian newspapers were closed; they were reopened in May 1974, after each deposited $3,875 as security. In numerous other countries—India, Sri Lanka, Pakistan, Taiwan, Thailand, and Indonesia, to name a few—states of emergency or martial law drastically curtailed newspapers for substantial periods.

Another form of control includes economic restraints that were applied to newspapers through government control of newsprint and official advertisements. In Bangladesh the state rents office space and printing presses to newspapers and controls import licenses and newsprint and equipment allocations, while Nepalese authorities promise financially to support newspapers that favor "healthy journalism."

The economics of newspapers. Most Asian governments have recognized that punitive actions directed against the press contributed to a negative international image; in response, many purchased

and created their own newspapers. In the Philippines during the presidency of Ferdinand Marcos, a number of dailies were owned by his relatives and friends. In Malaysia many dailies have been owned by members of the ruling coalition. But the country that has most systematically controlled newspapers through ownership is Singapore. There, in 1974, the press law was amended to create two classes of newspaper shares—ordinary and management. The latter, carrying more voting weight, can be owned only by those approved by the Ministry of Culture. Another restructuring, which took place from 1982 to 1984, was more sweeping, as it accomplished the demise of three long-standing newspapers and their replacement by a new company of three dailies, Singapore News and Publications Ltd. SNPL ultimately merged with the country's main newspaper, periodical, and book publishers, Straits Times Press and Times Publishing, to form the largest industrial group in Singapore. Various reasons were given for this merger; some critics believed it was meant to create an official mouthpiece, while the government said it was to establish a "world-class player in the high-technology information and communications industry." The latter point is important because it illustrated Singapore's choice to invest in urban-oriented international information markets, rather than to pursue a development policy that would be more rural in its focus (*see* AGENDA-SETTING).

Actually, Singapore, through Straits Times Press, epitomized the trend of some developing countries to become involved in transnational business. By 1980 the Straits Times Press had engulfed, in whole or in part, media and other properties in England, Tahiti, New Caledonia, Singapore, New Zealand, Australia, Thailand, Brunei, Malaysia, Hong Kong, and the United States. By extension, Straits Times Press was tied in with corporate giants such as Dow Jones in the United States and Hachette in France. In other Asian countries between the 1960s and 1980s, newspapers became big businesses. Concentration of ownership became widespread in the Philippines through groups such as Times Journal and Express, in Malaysia through politically connected groups such as New Straits Times, in India through chains owned by business houses, and in Sri Lanka. Japan's press, with a number of newspapers in the million-circulation bracket, is highly concentrated; papers such as *Asahi*, *Mainichi*, and *Yomiuri* have scores of editions throughout the country.

The means of producing Asian newspapers were developed more rapidly than were methods to expand their markets. In the 1970s governments mounted projects to expand local newsprint industries. Many large-city newspapers adopted modern printing equipment; others, especially in Japan, tied in with new media. In most countries press revenues increased, and some efforts at professionalization of newspaper employees took place, especially since the 1960s. But the transformation was less than complete. Economic changes often were isolated to certain countries, or even to capital cities in those countries, and the consumption of newspapers in many instances remained low as production costs drove the prices of newspapers out of the reach of the masses and as newspapers resisted changing their contents from an urban to a more rural orientation.

Another problem for the press of these countries concerns the sources of news. Although regional news agencies, similar to the recently created Asian News Network, have been in existence for decades, in the 1980s they continued to take a back seat to large international services such as Associated Press, United Press International, Reuters, and Agence France Presse. Nearly all countries have national news services, but their credibility is suspect because of close government ties. A number of these agencies disseminate their own brand of development-oriented journalism, which, although well intentioned when it was conceived in Asia in the 1960s, has come to be associated with government-supported journalism. Dependency on foreign news agencies, authoritarian control of the press, concentration of ownership, a deepening metropolitan orientation, and a lack of local economic resources to finance autonomous development all combined to place sharp limits on the informational value of the Asian press.

See also GOVERNMENT REGULATION; MONOPOLY; NEW INTERNATIONAL INFORMATION ORDER; NEWSPAPER: HISTORY.

Bibliography. Lawrence Beer, *Freedom of Expression in Japan: A Study in Comparative Law, Politics, and Society,* Tokyo, 1984; John A. Lent, ed., *The Asian Newspapers' Reluctant Revolution,* Ames, Iowa, 1971; idem, *Newspapers in Asia: Contemporary Trends and Problems,* Hong Kong, 1982; D. S. Mehta, *Mass Communication and Journalism in India,* Bombay, 1979; Sir Charles Moses and Crispin Maslog, *Mass Communication in Asia: A Brief History,* Singapore, 1978; Nihon Shimbun Kyokai, *The Japanese Press,* Tokyo, 1949–; Rosalinda Pineda-Ofreneo, *The Manipulated Press: A History of Philippine Journalism since 1945,* Manila, 1984; Wilbur Schramm and Erwin Atwood, *Circulation of News in the Third World: A Study of Asia,* Hong Kong, 1981.

JOHN A. LENT

3. TRENDS IN EUROPE

The press in European countries has a long history and reflects differences in national tradition, economic development, and political systems (*see* NEWSPAPER: HISTORY). Despite these differences, the press in all these countries has tended to move through similar stages of development, albeit at varying rates.

After the period in which newspapers were initially established, the press in many countries was supported increasingly by government or political parties. The politicized press was particularly characteristic of western European countries in the nineteenth century and continued to be important in other countries through the twentieth century. This stage was followed, particularly in western Europe, by an advertiser-supported or commercialized press.

Both the history and the current state of affairs of the European press can be approached from a variety of perspectives. Some researchers who prefer materialist explanations focus on the economic and political context of the press, while other scholars—especially in the Western capitalist countries—accept a more idealist causality and emphasize the autonomy of the press, stressing the influence of individual publishers, editors, and journalists.

Western Europe. The largest western European countries have the longest history of newspaper publishing in the world. Although some of the traditional characteristics of the press in these countries are still apparent, significant changes—particularly the commercialization of the press—have accelerated since World War II. The first newspapers in Great Britain, France, and Germany were founded at the beginning of the seventeenth century. They were followed in the nineteenth century by the politicized press, after which changes in economic conditions led to the development of the commercialized, advertiser-supported press.

The British press is characterized by the dominance of newspapers published in London and by recognized distinctions between popular and elite newspapers. Concentration of power in a few newspaper conglomerates is also characteristic of the modern British press. Newspapers controlled by political parties have never had much significance in Great Britain. However, editorial policies do tend to favor particular parties; the Conservative party has normally received sympathetic treatment from both popular press and elite newspapers like the London *Times,* while the Labour party has been supported primarily by the London *Daily Mirror.*

In the Federal Republic of Germany (FRG) regional papers have played a more important role than they have in Great Britain, but here too there is an increasing trend toward concentration of ownership. Recognized as elite newspapers are the *Frankfurter Allgemeine,* a liberal paper, and *Die Welt,* a conservative paper published in Hamburg. Another category is the sensational "boulevard paper" represented by *Bild-Zeitung,* which has been published in several cities. Political party papers have traditionally played a role, but they have not been a dominant element in the FRG.

The structure of the French press has differed from

both the British and the FRG models. National newspapers have been less centralized in the capital city than they have been in Britain but more so than in the FRG. While the concentration of ownership has increased, it has not approached the level of concentration characteristic of the other two countries. In recent decades the Parisian daily *Le monde* has been considered the most widely known liberal, elite newspaper. Two examples of the popular press include *Le figaro* and *France-soir*. Political party papers have some importance; the Communist *L'humanité* achieved a higher circulation than most other Communist papers in the West.

One notable Swiss newspaper deserves mention—the *Neue Zürcher Zeitung*, an elite paper most often classified as liberal. It has been successful, despite its somewhat old-fashioned TYPOGRAPHY and appearance.

Southern Europe. In many respects the development of the southern European countries—Italy, Spain, Portugal, and Greece—lagged behind that of the large western European countries. Consistent with this, their newspapers are more likely to be aligned with specific political parties and less dependent on advertisers.

In Italy *Corriere della sera*, published in Milan, is widely read, but some experts believe that the most influential Italian newspaper is *L'osservatore romano*, which is published by the Vatican and reflects the opinions of the Catholic church.

In the southern European countries that shifted from fascist to more democratic regimes in the mid-twentieth century—Spain, Greece, and Portugal—the problems of the press are distinctive. Since these political changes occurred, these governments have respected the freedom of the press in principle but in practice have interfered with the press in various ways, including economic pressure. Yet the role of the press as a forum for political debate increased, and in Spain the political role of the press became particularly lively. *El país* (Madrid), founded in 1976, developed into a large and highly influential newspaper.

Northern Europe. The northern European press has differed in important respects from the southern European press, as well as from the press in western Europe. A large proportion of the newspapers are aligned with political parties, which suggests an earlier stage in press development. However, the largest newspapers are either not politically affiliated or are only nominally affiliated. The press system in general is highly developed. As in southern Europe, the distinction between popular and elite newspapers is less clear than in western European countries.

In Sweden the two newspapers with the largest circulations are both evening papers from Stockholm—the liberal *Expressen* and the Social Democratic *Aftonbladet,* which is owned by the labor unions. Perhaps the most influential newspaper, however, is the liberal *Dagens nyheter,* which is not affiliated with a political party.

Finland's leading newspaper is the liberal *Helsingin sanomat,* not affiliated with a political party. Its counterpart in Norway is the somewhat more conservative Oslo *Aftenposten.*

Denmark's small size led to a greater concentration of press ownership than in other Scandinavian countries. For the most part, political party papers disappeared. Two Copenhagen publishing firms own four papers with the largest circulations: the so-called lunch papers, *B.T.* and *Extra bladet,* and the two morning papers, the conservative *Berlingske tidende* and the liberal *Politiken.*

Eastern Europe. In the socialist countries of eastern Europe, the newspapers are not private enterprises but are published by the state, the Communist party, trade unions, youth organizations, citizens' organizations, and other such groups. There are also newspapers that target different geographical and social—rather than ideological—groups, as in the West.

There are very real differences between the aims and methods of journalism in the West and the East. They include different criteria for what constitutes news and a different presentation of argument in editorials. The socialist press has made some important contributions to journalism, such as the reliance on worker and peasant correspondents and the use of letters from readers as a way to facilitate communication among authorities, citizens, and the press itself.

The leading newspaper in each of these countries is that of the Communist party. They include *Neues Deutschland* in the German Democratic Republic, *Trybuna ludu* in Poland, *Rude pravo* in Czechoslovakia, *Nepszabadsag* in Hungary, and *Pravda* in the USSR. The Soviet Union has other important newspapers, including *Izvestia,* published by the Soviets (councils) of the People's Deputies; *Trud,* published by the trade unions; *Komsomolskaya pravda,* published by the Young Communist League; and *Literaturnaya gazeta,* published by the Union of Soviet Writers.

Economics of the press. The European press cannot be understood without a closer look at the press economy. The fundamental differences between the Western capitalist and the Eastern socialist systems are important; however, there are real differences between individual newspapers and between newspaper groups within each system, and these should not be overlooked.

The commercialization of the press in the western European countries created a situation in which ADVERTISING revenues determined the economic viability of newspapers. However, costs rose, especially since World War II, even faster than the advertising revenues that determined each newspaper's success or failure. These costs were due primarily to investment in expensive new printing technologies and to the rise in the cost of labor in both the printing and editorial branches of the press. This situation led to an economic crisis for several major newspapers—usually elite papers—even those that had enjoyed large circulations. Well-known examples include several of the London newspapers that have had financial difficulties since the 1970s.

These conditions strengthened the trend toward concentration of ownership and decreased the overall number of newspapers in most European countries. In several western European countries governments responded to this situation by providing substantial subsidies for newspapers. From the point of view of the so-called social responsibility theory of the press, it is easy to defend state subsidies, the aim of which is to maintain a diverse press consisting of both large and small papers. However, there is much doubt about the independence of the newspapers that receive financial support from the state. Nevertheless, there is evidence that in countries with a tradition of press autonomy the newspapers that receive state subsidies continue to feel free to criticize the government.

Role of the press. The press has sometimes been referred to as the fourth estate, having its own independent social function. This notion is particularly characteristic of those Western capitalist countries that have traditionally valued press independence. However, it has been supplanted to a great extent by the view that the press is closely linked to and influenced by the structure and power relationships of a given society. This view is held to be true regardless of the particular economic and political system, and, therefore, it provides a common point of departure for interpreting the press in both capitalist and socialist countries.

The short-term impact of the press on news events is no longer particularly important; the press has been overshadowed in this area by television coverage of political events, election campaigns, world affairs, and so on. The issue of the long-term impact of the press is more complex. For some segments of the population television has superseded newspapers completely (*see* TELEVISION HISTORY; TELEVISION NEWS). However, in all European countries there is an active minority or elite for whom television coverage of domestic and world affairs is too superficial and limited. For this group the role of the press, especially the so-called serious newspapers, remains paramount. Furthermore, political decision makers also rely on serious political journalism for information and analysis of events. Thus in some cases the press influences both PUBLIC OPINION and the perspectives of leaders.

According to some theorists, however, the quality and economic viability of serious journalism is declining. More and more, such newspapers alter their format and content to compete with the popular press. If this trend continues, newspapers may become more secure financially, but the press will lose much of its social and political role in the creation of informed public opinion and policy.

See also CENSORSHIP; GOVERNMENT-MEDIA RELATIONS; GOVERNMENT REGULATION; NEWS AGENCIES; NEWSMAGAZINE.

Bibliography. G. Bohere, *Profession: Journalist,* Geneva, 1984; Pertti Hemánus and Tapio Varis, *Mass Media Yesterday and Today,* Prague, 1983; John C. Merrill, ed., *Global Journalism: A Survey of the World's Mass Media,* New York, 1983; John C. Merrill and Harold A. Fisher, *The World's Great Dailies,* New York, 1980; Kenneth E. Olson, *The History Makers,* Baton Rouge, La., 1966; Kauko Pietila, *Formation of the Newspaper: A Theory,* Tampere, Finland, 1980; Fredrick S. Siebert, Theodore Peterson, and Wilbur L. Schramm, *Four Theories of the Press,* Urbana, Ill., 1956, reprint Freeport, N.Y., 1973; Anthony Smith, *The Newspaper, An International History,* London, 1979; UNESCO, *World Communications: A 200-Country Survey of Press, Radio, Television, Film,* 5th ed., New York and Paris, 1975.

PERTTI HEMÁNUS

4. TRENDS IN LATIN AMERICA

The press in Latin America has always been closely linked to the social and political history and conflicts of the region. Most of the newspapers that constitute the elite press of Latin America have experienced confrontations with governments, including CENSORSHIP and direct attacks on their journalists and printworks. On the other hand, the elite press newspapers have in many cases effectively defended their own social policies, which have sometimes represented the private interests of the newspaper owners. As a result of the newspapers' participation in social and political conflicts, the roles of journalist and politician have often been difficult to separate. In many cases the roles of publisher and banker or entrepreneur are also intermixed. The Latin American press has always been at the center of the storm during this region's frequent rebellions and revolutions.

History. The history of the Latin American press began in the eighteenth century, when Spain still controlled its New World territories (*see* COLONIZATION). Early newspapers include *La gazeta de México,* founded in 1722, followed by publications of similar name in Guatemala (1729), Lima (1743), Havana (1764), and Bogotá and Quito (1785). At the beginning of the nineteenth century the first Argentine and Uruguayan newspapers appeared: *El telégrafo mercantil* (Buenos Aires, 1801) and *La estrella del sur* (Montevideo, 1807).

The struggles for national independence—sparked

by the Napoleonic invasion of Spain—led to the appearance of newspapers that were committed to the objectives of the independence movements. The emancipation leaders were eager to found newspapers in the liberated countries. For example, *La aurora de Chile* (1811) and other comparable newspapers provided forums for patriotic intellectuals and attempted to promote the idea of independence. Simón Bolívar, liberator of Colombia, Ecuador, Peru, Panama, Venezuela, and to a large extent Bolivia, was an enthusiastic newspaper founder. He is credited with having stated that "the press is the artillery of thought," and he apparently transported a small printer on muleback throughout his entire military campaign in order to make full use of the power of the press.

Bolívar's struggles to create a single Latin America (a United States of the South) failed amid a multitude of disputes and political ambitions. The new nations soon found themselves involved in civil wars and other conflicts. Nevertheless, by the second half of the nineteenth century the majority of the Latin American countries had been established and were relatively stable. In this context the press was able to flourish. *El mercurio* (1869), founded in Valparaíso, Chile, became the basis for a large company, which operated without interruption from the time of primitive printing technology to the era of electronic production. *El comercio* of Lima (1839), *La prensa* of Buenos Aires (1869), *O estado de São Paulo* (1876), and *El día* of Montevideo (1886) are similar examples of both permanence and great influence over national and continental opinion.

The twentieth century brought with it the introduction of technologies and journalistic methods from the United States. The majority of the newspapers that were important through the century appeared between 1900 and 1920. Family-owned newspapers grew to positions of significant power and influence; examples of family organizations include Mitre and Gainza Paz (Argentina), Edwards (Chile), Batlle y Ordóñez (Uruguay), Santos (Colombia), Miró Quesada and Beltrán (Peru), and Mezquita (Brazil). Newspapers that were founded in these years include *El mercurio* (Santiago, 1900), *El diario* (La Paz, 1904), *El comercio* (Quito, 1906), *La razón* (Buenos Aires, 1905), *El tiempo* (Bogotá, 1911), and *Excelsior* (Mexico City, 1917). These newspapers constituted the main source of information until the arrival of RADIO in the 1920s and, subsequently, television in the early 1950s (*see* TELEVISION HISTORY).

Twentieth-century issues. Despite the presence of electronic media in Latin America, the role of the newspaper in the formation of public opinion and the expression of political debate continued to be significant. The Latin American newspapers can be grouped into three large political categories. The first

category is made up of the large traditional newspapers. Politically conservative, these newspapers reflect the interests of the families who were involved in various forms of private enterprise such as agriculture and mining during the nineteenth century. The second group, which arose from the time of the world economic crisis of the 1930s and the effects of World War II, can be classified as politically moderate. They are sympathetic to the concept of the welfare state and to strategies of national industrial development. Finally, the left and popular press increased its presence with the development of mass media and with the growing sympathies toward leftist political groups that accompanied the struggle against nazism during World War II and the subsequent revolution in Cuba. *See* DEVELOPMENT COMMUNICATION.

Socioeconomic conditions affected support for the press in Latin American countries. The more wealthy—and more literate—countries could support more and larger newspapers. For example, in 1970 in Chile, which had a population of 10 million and a LITERACY rate of 90 percent, one popular newspaper alone attained a circulation of 450,000; the three main newspapers together had a circulation of 1,100,000. In contrast *Excelsior*, in Mexico City, with a population of 10 million, did not even have a circulation of 150,000.

An increasing presence in the finances and management of the main newspapers was ADVERTISING. By the early 1960s the percentage of space devoted to advertising in the major Latin American newspapers ranged from 40 percent in *El nacional* (Caracas) to 73 percent in *O estado de São Paulo*.

Since the mid-1970s, research on and analysis of the Latin American press has increased. Much of it has been critical and has focused on the difficulty of maintaining independence, given the dependence on advertising and the newspapers' interrelationships with other sectors of the economy. Another criticism concerned the sources for foreign news. Since World War II the major NEWS AGENCIES expanded to control 60 to 75 percent of the international news published in the region. This led to concern about the structure and imbalance in the world flow of information—a problem that was recognized increasingly in other developing areas. *See* COMPUTER: IMPACT—IMPACT ON THE WORLD ECONOMY; NEW INTERNATIONAL INFORMATION ORDER.

In addition, there have been trends among the press to reject censorship, other forms of government control, and any actions limiting the freedom of the press. The Interamerican Press Association's (IAPA) annual report has had considerable influence on these policies. In the 1950s some newspapers suffered from censorship. The right-wing dictatorship of General Rojas Pinillas of Colombia led to the suspension of

El tiempo and *El espectador* in 1955. And in Brazil during the 1960s (following the 1964 coup d'état) the National Security Doctrine came into force with a rigorous censorship policy and violent actions (kidnappings, tortures, and murders) against journalists. Similar developments later occurred in Uruguay, Chile, and Argentina. Different experiments with censorship appeared in the left-wing governments. For example, Cuba applied a rigorous policy in this respect, giving the press a new role in "political education" (*see* POLITICAL SOCIALIZATION). By the beginning of the 1980s an attempt at "critical journalism" arose in Cuba, but still within the socialist framework. Nicaragua was another country where the radicalization of politics led to a confrontation between the traditional newspaper *La prensa* and the revolutionary government.

By the mid-1980s a large part of the Latin American press was in the process of technological transformation. This came about at the same time as a wave of redemocratization occurred in various Latin American countries, such as Brazil, Argentina, Uruguay, and Peru. As a result new prospects for journalistic development were opened up. The concept of "independent journalism" reemerged as an essential prerequisite for democratic stability and participatory development.

See also GOVERNMENT-MEDIA RELATIONS; GOVERNMENT REGULATION; LATIN AMERICA, TWENTIETH CENTURY; NEWSPAPER: HISTORY.

Bibliography. Simón Bolívar, *Cartas*, Vol. 1, *Obras completas*, Caracas, 1933; CIESPAL, *Dos semanas en la prensa de América Latina*, Quito, 1967; Dag Hammarskjöld Foundation/ILET (Latin American Institute for Transnational Studies), *Towards a New Information and Communication Order*, Uppsala, Sweden, 1982; Robert N. Pierce, *Keeping the Flame: Media and Government in Latin America*, New York, 1979, reprint (*Libertad de expresión en América Latina*), Barcelona, 1982; Fernando Reyes Matta, ed., *La información en el nuevo orden internacional*, Mexico, D.F., 1977.

FERNANDO REYES MATTA

5. TRENDS IN THE MIDDLE EAST

The first modern Arabic press in the Middle East was introduced in Egypt by Napoléon during his military campaign of 1798–1801. Aside from publishing Napoléon's declarations and orders, the press was used to publish two French newspapers and the first Arabic newspaper, which the French occupiers called *al-Tanbih*. The latter was used to publish legal cases and administrative news.

After the departure of the French from Egypt, no printing of newspapers or other publications took place until Muḥammad ʿAli Pasha, who in 1805 was sent by the Ottomans to govern Egypt, decided in 1821 to have a press to meet the demands of government and to satisfy his wish to spread knowledge, especially of science. He therefore bought and upgraded the press that the French had left and established a publishing house that later printed books, government documents, and the second Arabic newspaper, *al-Waqaʾi el-Masriyah*, in 1828. The third Arabic newspaper, *al-Moubasher*, was established by French settlers in Algeria in 1847.

Shortly thereafter the Arabs themselves engaged in the business of publishing newspapers. The first Arab to publish an Arabic newspaper, *Mirʾat al-Ahwal*, was Rizek Allah Hassoun from Aleppo, Syria, in 1855. In 1870 there were about twenty-seven newspapers and magazines published by Arabs. A survey conducted by Philip Tarazi revealed that by 1929 the Arabs had published 3,023 newspapers and magazines, of which some had perished but others were still in existence.

From the beginning many Arabs viewed the press as an instrument of struggle against occupiers and outdated traditions. The press, therefore, tended to concentrate on inciting and awakening the populace through its content, paying little attention to style, appearance, and technical improvements. Not all Arab papers, however, were nationalist in orientation. Some were loyal to the occupiers—be they Ottoman, French, or British.

The end of World War I marked the end of relations between the Arab world and the Ottoman Empire. By the end of the war, however, the Arab world fell prey to other foreign designs, particularly those of the British and the French. Both powers imposed stringent controls on the Arab press through administrations authorized to shut down newspapers and to prosecute editors for criticizing the occupiers.

The post–World War II era, which witnessed the emergence of independent Arab states, was characterized by Arab governments that viewed the press as an enemy. These states did not encourage the development of the press and did not hesitate to punish newspapers and journalists for criticizing them. Consequently, much of the press in the Arab world expressed little criticism and was transformed into a mouthpiece for individual governments. The fate of many of these newspapers was tied to that of the government in power. The overthrow of a government often meant the demise of those newspapers that were associated with it.

This turnover, among other factors, is why most of the modern Arab press dates back only to the 1960s and 1970s. Another reason is that a number of Arab countries achieved independence only in the 1960s. Moreover, ownership of the Arab press during the first half of the twentieth century was primarily in the hands of individuals. This often meant that the death of the owner or his abandonment of a newspaper marked the demise of that newspaper.

Relationship between government and press. The nature and role of the Arab press are directly and indirectly affected by the type of government that controls the country. In absolute monarchies such as Oman, Jordan, and Saudi Arabia there is limited freedom of the press on political issues and relative freedom on social and economic issues. Constitutional monarchies or sheikhdoms such as Kuwait are the exception. Kuwait has been known all along to have a freer press than most other parts of the Arab world; still, the Kuwaiti press is restricted, with a number of issues and subjects banned from public discussion. In the case of monarchies and sheikhdoms ownership of the press is usually private. However, governments have been known to support newspapers, directly through financial assistance and indirectly through astronomical ADVERTISING subsidies or through purchasing large numbers of newspapers that are later distributed by the government free of charge.

Authoritarian governments such as those in Syria, Iraq, and Libya have no freedom of the press. Other than the governing party no political parties are allowed to exist. Often the press is directly owned by the government itself or by the sole political party that runs the government. Usually the circulation of the press in these countries is extremely limited, and the people quench their thirst for news and analysis by listening to foreign broadcasts such as the BBC or by reading whatever foreign press might occasionally be allowed into the country. An underground press exists in some of these countries, the significance of which increases in proportion to the degree of suppression of freedom. This press is usually published by banned organized groups such as the Communists, student unions, or religious movements. On the other hand, the imported foreign press is often a mutilated source; some of these governments take pains to clip the news items relating to that particular country or simply tear off entire sections of newspapers or magazines.

The semidemocratic republics such as Egypt (which has been the largest PUBLISHING center in the Middle East) and Tunisia allow relative political freedom for the opposition within the limits set by the government in power. Opposition parties are given a legal status and permitted to publish their own newspapers, although not without restrictions. These restrictions have taken various forms, including "gentlemen's agreements" about what could be printed, and in at least one case the government limited the amount of printing paper that could be used by the opposition newspaper. Ownership of the press in these countries is usually associated with political parties, unions, and religious groups. Despite all the restrictions imposed by the Arab governments on the press, a number of journalists have developed the art of conveying their messages and thoughts to the public indirectly either between the lines or through political cartoons.

Variations. Lebanon's relationship to the press has been more the exception than the rule among Arab countries. Until 1977, and even during the upheavals of the 1975–1976 civil war, no CENSORSHIP of the press existed in that country. About two dozen newspapers and magazines continued to appear regularly, reflecting every shade of political opinion. In January 1977 censorship was imposed on all publications, forcing some papers to close down, if only temporarily. The absence of a strong central government to enforce the laws of the land made censorship regulations ineffective. Given the difficulties of publishing and distributing a newspaper in the war-torn country, the Lebanese also resorted to the airwaves. By March 1986 there were about forty-one private RADIO stations in Lebanon, although only one of them was officially registered with the government.

The violence and political turmoil in Lebanon, a country with one of the largest pools of experienced journalists and editors in the Arab world, forced not only many journalists but also entire publications to relocate, particularly to London, Paris, and Cyprus. (Under Anwar as-Sadat, Egypt too witnessed the emigration of opposition journalists to Europe and Kuwait.) Following the 1982 Israeli invasion of Lebanon, the core of the Palestinian press published in that country was also forced to relocate to Europe. These relocations introduced a new dimension—the expatriate press. These Arabic publications, although free of the daily harassments of censorship, political turmoil, and violence, were still unable to enjoy completely the freedom provided by the host countries. First, to survive, these news weeklies, such as *al-Mostaqbal, al-Hawadeth,* and *al-Watan Arabi,* have been forced to rely on certain commercial advertisers that favored only restrained criticism of certain Arab countries. Second, the readership of these publications is primarily in the Arab world, which means that if the Arab countries did not like what they saw, they could bar the publication from entering their borders. On the other hand, the presence of these Arabic publications in Europe helped increase the readership, thereby expanding their scope of interest and coverage. Moreover, these publications benefited from the availability of advanced technology, which improved their technical production and style.

It is important to note that the Palestinian press under Israeli occupation, although completely censored, enjoys more freedom than some of the Arab countries' presses. The Israelis have little to risk and much to gain from a policy of allowing selected critical articles to appear in the Palestinian press.

From Israel's vantage point the Palestinian press is important in defusing tension among the politically active segment of the population. The absence of this outlet could lead to a much more dangerous alternative, such as an underground press or possibly violent action. The press also provides Israel with "evidence" that its occupation is "liberal." Ultimately, however, it is the Israeli censor who becomes editor in chief of the Palestinian press because he has the power, which he frequently exercises, to censor any article, news item, editorial, picture, or advertisement.

Obstacles to press development. In comparison to many parts of the world, particularly industrialized countries, the percentage of Arabs who buy and read newspapers is small. The higher illiteracy rate among Arabs, coupled with social and cultural traditions that do not emphasize reading (most Arabs prefer to listen to the radio or watch television for the news), contributes to this phenomenon. The most important factor, however, is the Arab people's lack of trust in the press. Arab newspapers suffer from a serious lack of credible writers, thinkers, and investigative reporters. Many of the Arab newspapers fill their pages with translations from other sources because of lack of necessary resources owing to financial difficulties and the emigration of journalists. The pivotal question of credibility of the Arab press centers around the fact that these newspapers and magazines lack the freedom to express their opinions and to publish news items of their own choosing and are often viewed as the mouthpieces of the governments in power. As long as these factors persist, the Arab press stands little chance of expanding its readership.

See also ISLAMIC WORLD, TWENTIETH CENTURY; RADIO, INTERNATIONAL; TELEVISION HISTORY—GLOBAL DEVELOPMENT.

Bibliography. Bishara A. Bahbah, "Perspectives in Conflict: The Role of the Palestinian Media in the West Bank, the Gaza Strip, and East Jerusalem—A Palestinian View," *Journal of Communication* 35 (1985): 16–21; Adeeb Marwa, *Al-Sahafa, Al-Arabia*, Beirut, 1961; *The Middle East and North Africa, 1981–82* (28th ed.), London, 1981; *The Middle East and North Africa, 1986* (32d ed.), London, 1985; Munir K. Nasser, *Press, Politics, and Power: Egypt's Heikal and Al-Ahram*, Ames, Iowa, 1979; William A. Rugh, *The Arab Press: News Media and Political Process in the Arab World*, Syracuse, N.Y., 1979.

BISHARA A. BAHBAH

6. TRENDS IN NORTH AMERICA

The newspaper has had an enduring and pivotal impact within the communications systems and political life of North America. In the decades following World War II the number and circulation of newspapers increased somewhat, in spite of the rise of television (*see* TELEVISION HISTORY). Yet fundamental shifts were modifying the newspaper industry.

Rise of newspaper chains. Concentration of ownership in groups or chains, already a prominent phenomenon before the war, rose sharply after the war. In the United States the percentage of newspapers owned by chains rose threefold between 1945 and 1980, so that some two-thirds of the approximately seventeen hundred U.S. dailies, representing more than three-quarters of the total daily circulation, had come under group ownership. The top five groups, in terms of circulation, were Gannett, Knight-Ridder, Newhouse, Tribune Company, and Dow Jones. In Canada the concentration of ownership was even more pronounced. By 1980 two groups, Southam and Thomson, controlled 45 percent of the nation's approximately 115 dailies. In the United States and Canada the number of independent press voices had shrunk to a fraction of its prewar total.

In all but a score of cities, the newspaper had become a local MONOPOLY. In a strictly commercial system offering few alternative revenue sources—such as those furnished in some European nations by political parties—the newspaper depended heavily on its major advertisers. In turn, the latter found few incentives to support more than a single journal in a given market. Newspapers that had been fixtures on the scene for a century collapsed in the face of competition for advertisers. Gone were the *New York Herald-Tribune*, the Washington, D.C., *Evening Star*, the *Newark Evening News*, the Philadelphia *Evening Bulletin*, the *Ottawa Journal*, the *Winnipeg Tribune*, and others. These journals seemed unlikely to be replaced, as the costs of entry into the major metropolitan newspaper market were now reckoned in the tens of millions of dollars. (During its first two and a half years of existence, Gannett's risky national daily, *USA Today*, launched in 1982, lost an estimated $150 million.)

Attrition proved greatest among afternoon papers, although they remained the numerical majority. In competition with late-afternoon television news and with the newer suburban journals catering to affluent readers, and faced with distribution bottlenecks impeding timely delivery across sprawling metropolitan areas, the so-called PMs closed their doors by the dozen in U.S. and Canadian cities. Of the twenty largest papers published in the United States in the 1980s only one—*Newsday* on Long Island—remained a true afternoon daily.

The role of advertisers. Although the newspapers that survived enjoyed large profits, their dependence on ADVERTISING continued to deepen. Principally carriers of local advertising, newspapers as a whole comprised the largest advertising medium (followed by television and direct mail), generally garnering over a quarter of all media advertising revenues both in Canada and in the United States. While advertisements were allotted only about two-thirds of total newspaper space, their sponsors were furnishing fully four-fifths of average newspaper revenue. Moreover, totally advertiser-supported shoppers or freesheets, which were sprinkled with editorial matter, were becoming the fastest-growing segment of the industry.

Changes in the structure of the newspaper work force reflected the need to market a newspaper to potential advertisers and, on behalf of these same sponsors, to monitor and measure circulation with growing precision. The white-collar work force expanded after 1960, and, accordingly, the proportion of female newspaper workers had doubled by the 1980s. Meanwhile, highly skilled unionized printers were made increasingly redundant by computerized composing and typesetting systems. Only twenty-three computer terminals were in use in U.S. newsrooms in 1970; there were forty-one thousand at the end of 1981. By that time only 17 percent of publishing costs were going into wages for production workers.

Newspaper content and format also became increasingly skewed by the purported interests of advertisers' "most-needed audiences." Special sections covering fashion, life-style, science, SPORTS, FOOD, and especially business were devised to meet the advertisers' concern for targeting particular groups of readers. Such sections permitted the strategic placement of advertisements that were related to the subject matter of the articles.

Paradoxically, the focus on specific audiences occurred while the news content within the national and international market was becoming increasingly standardized. Syndicated columns, COMICS, features, and news services have long been employed to provide a major proportion of editorial content while spreading its cost across the entire news market (*see* SYNDICATION). Licensed product spin-offs from syndicated comic strips comprised a growing profit source for some retail advertisers, representing a further relationship between advertisers and the press. A further extension of the trend toward content standardization was made possible by SATELLITE technology, with regional editions of the same newspaper sponsored by regional and national advertisers. The *Wall Street Journal* pioneered this technique with regional editions around the globe; it was followed, at least at the national level, by the *Toronto Globe and Mail,* the *New York Times,* and others.

New developments. The strength of the newspaper chains, benefiting from economies of scale in everything from the acquisition of newsprint to advertising sales and marketing, permitted an ongoing restructuring of the newspaper industry. As RADIO and television broadcasting, followed by CABLE TELEVISION, began to challenge the role of newspapers for supplying news and advertising, the latter responded by acquiring a financial stake in the new media. Cooperative rather than competitive strategies generally followed. However, while joint ventures were becoming increasingly common, it was clear that newspapers had to depend—as a matter of survival—on their unique existing assets: printing and distribution facilities, intimate knowledge of local advertisers and their needs, valuable information-gathering and information-processing resources and staff.

With stiffening competition to supply electronic information services by means of new technologies, newspapers catapulted into the information market along with a slew of unrelated companies: TELEPHONE and computer firms, banks and brokerage firms, direct mailers, retailers. It was noteworthy that the new information services and technologies were no longer the domain of one relatively discrete media sector. An example of the newspapers' entry into this market was their commitment to "front-end systems"—computerized editorial systems that permit direct links between the paper and outside electronic networks. Once information was stored in newspaper computers, it could easily be transformed into new information products for electronic distribution. Another example was the use of in-house electronic libraries—computerized descendants of the old clipping library or "morgue"—to market news and information services. As the chains used their numerous local units as a springboard to national and international electronic information markets—Knight-Ridder, for example, planned "a web of regional data bases" around some of its twenty-nine papers—a variant of the television industry's network-affiliate relationship seemed to be taking shape (*see* DATA BASE).

As a result of competitive market strategies, information offerings varied widely (*see* VIDEOTEX). They included profiles of major companies, legislative tracking services, ocean shipping tariff lists, commodity and crop forecasts, even data-base management services for other information providers. Up-to-the-minute information was becoming available across an expanding set of professional, scientific, technical, and industry areas. It is important to note, however, that these specialized offerings were intended largely for a new public, comprising not individual citizens but corporate and organizational information users, and were priced not at twenty-five cents (the average newspaper price) but ranged up to thousands of dollars. Apparently the divergence between elite and mass news, which had existed roughly since the commercialization of the press in the mid-nineteenth century, was being succeeded by new kinds of disparities in information services.

Just as entry into these new information markets was no longer confined to any single media sector, so new information technology was also being employed by nonmedia interests to wrest from the newspaper some of its traditional functions. The power of the editorial, for example, was no longer limited to newspapers, or even to the news media, when direct mail and computerized mailing lists made it possible for sponsored opinions and likely supporters to be matched with unprecedented precision. Newspaper "advertorials," pioneered by the Mobil Corporation but later in routine use by other companies, intruded systematically into the newspaper's once unchallenged domain. For example, computerized PUBLIC RELATIONS networks such as Business Wire or PR Newswire fed messages from their clients directly into newsroom computers, creating an extraordinary access to publicity for those organizations that could afford such services.

Limits on press freedom. The newspaper also encountered increasingly sweeping and sophisticated moves by government agencies and private corporations to define and shape news accounts. The U.S. presidential press relations staff, for instance, had grown by the 1980s to include hundreds, whereas a generation earlier it had included only two or three persons. The president—indeed the entire executive branch—was frequently able to influence decisively the character of press accounts or to float "trial balloons" to test public reaction before making a commitment to a particular public policy. Newsgathering structures and processes were inevitably influenced by such pressures in the relative attention given to specific events. A 1984 economic summit conference among Western leaders in London was attended by no fewer than three thousand reporters, whereas the U.S. invasion of Grenada in 1983 was kept entirely off-limits to the press, and as a result the latter accepted future restrictions on wartime military coverage.

The independence of the press also received some setbacks in the courts. Although frequently overturned on appeal, initial LIBEL awards by juries turned consistently and dramatically against the press.

Highly touted in the wake of the Watergate presidential scandal, vigorous investigative reporting proved to be the province of only a handful of intrepid journalists such as Seymour Hersh, Alexander Cockburn, and I. F. Stone. A press corps inclined to be white, male, well educated, and relatively well off only infrequently directed sustained, trenchant criticism at institutions administered by analogous groups. Nevertheless, the newspaper continued to play a critical role in setting the political agenda—both for other news media, which tended to rely on a few top papers in developing their own coverage, and for the population as a whole. In consequence, the newspaper's role as a source of news and information in North America continued to bulk large, even as it became less independent of government, business, and other influences.

See also AGENDA-SETTING; CENSORSHIP; COMPUTER: IMPACT; DIRECT RESPONSE MARKETING; NEWSPAPER: HISTORY; PRINT-AUDIENCE MEASUREMENT; TELEVISION NEWS.

Bibliography. Ben H. Bagdikian, *The Media Monopoly,* Boston, 1983; Benjamin M. Compaine, Christopher H. Sterling, Thomas Guback, and J. Kendrick Noble, Jr., *Who Owns the Media?* 2d ed., White Plains, N.Y., 1982; Alfred M. Lee, *The Daily Newspaper in America,* New York, 1937, reprint New York, 1973; Gaye Tuchman, *Making News,* New York, 1978.

DAN SCHILLER

7. TRENDS IN THE SOVIET PRESS

The Soviet press began with the Bolshevik newspaper *Iskra.* Founded abroad by Lenin in 1900 and smuggled into Russia, it contributed to the workers' struggle against czarism and helped to form the Bolshevik party. The legal newspaper *Pravda* was first published on May 5, 1912, and became a landmark in the development of the Bolshevik press and the Russian revolutionary movement. It played an important role in the victory of the October Revolution of 1917.

The Soviet press played an active part in the fight against the White Guards and foreign invaders during the civil war (1918–1920) and in the efforts to rehabilitate the economy in the postwar period. During the first five-year plans the press gave priority to the socialist reorganization of farming, and it continued to perform essential communication functions during World War II.

Illegal newspapers issued in the Nazi-occupied territories helped to organize the partisan movement. The newspapers brought out in the rear furthered the Soviet people's efforts to supply the army with weapons, munitions, and food. Special newspapers were distributed among soldiers at the front to encourage them and to increase the efficiency of the army as a whole. After the war Soviet newspapers, along with magazines, MOTION PICTURES, RADIO, and later television (*see* TELEVISION HISTORY), concentrated on the rehabilitation of the economy.

Scope of Soviet journalism. The Soviet media have played an important role in Soviet society. By the late 1980s they comprised some 13,500 periodicals, including 8,273 newspapers (with a circulation of

181 million copies) and 5,308 magazines. In addition to 13 national radio services there were 175 local radio stations as well as thousands of regional and local radio centers. During the 1960s and 1970s television became increasingly popular, and by the 1980s practically every Soviet family had a television set. From a total of 14 million television sets in 1965, the number had grown to more than 100 million by 1985. Programming came not only from the national service but also from 120 republican and local television studios. The circulation of newspapers had likewise risen sharply, from 98 million in 1965 to 181 million in 1985.

Soviet journalism is served by two NEWS AGENCIES—Tass (Telegraph Agency of the Soviet Union), run by the council of ministers, and APN (Novosti Press Agency), run by public organizations. Tass is the sponsor of fourteen news agencies serving individual republics, disseminating information in their languages. The Soviet media are multiethnic; newspapers are published in fifty-five languages, while radio transmits programs in seventy-one languages and television in forty-five.

The Soviet system of journalism. There is no private ownership of the Soviet media. Soviet newspapers are issued by the Communist party, soviets of people's deputies, the Young Communist League, trade unions, the writers' and journalists' associations, and other popular, research, and professional organizations. Newspapers, magazines, and radio and television programs are disseminated at national, republican, territorial, regional, and district levels, and even within work collectives.

Among national newspapers are *Pravda, Izvestia, Komsomolskaya pravda* (Communist Youth Pravda), *Trud* (Labor), *Krasnaya zvezda* (Red Star), *Selskaya zhizn* (Rural Life), *Economicheskaya gazeta* (Economics Newspaper), *Sovetskaya kultura* (Soviet Culture), and publications serving major industries, professions, literature, arts, and the sports world. Newspapers serving individual republics include *Sovetskaya Rossia* (Russian Federation), *Pravda Ukrainy* and *Radyanska Ukraina* (Ukraine), *Tsinya* and *Sovetskaya Latvia* (Latvia), and *Tiesa* and *Sovetskaya Litva* (Lithuania).

Territorial and regional newspapers are issued every day. There are city newspapers in big cities and rural newspapers in the country. Some major enterprises issue newspapers for their workers. All in all, there are 41 national, 160 republican, 426 territorial, district, and regional, 711 city, and 3,021 rural newspapers, in addition to 3,317 run by big enterprises. There are evening newspapers in cities with a population of more than 1 million; they number 29 (*Vechernyaya Moskva, Vecherny Leningrad,* etc.).

Economics of newspapers. Although newspapers are cheap (from two to five kopecks for dailies and twenty kopecks for weeklies), most of them earn a surplus owing to their large circulations. Rural and evening newspapers give much space to ADVERTISING (three-fourths of a page in rural four-page newspapers), which adds to their income. There are advertisements in many other newspapers and magazines, but their number in the national and republican press is insignificant.

The role of media is growing as the new policy of "openness" (*glasnost*) involves more and more people in the political process. The Soviet media inform the public of the latest events at home and abroad; criticize the shortcomings in the work of various state, industrial, and agricultural bodies in a bid to involve more people in the management of the state and of industrial and agricultural enterprises; and promote socialist democracy.

Restructuring (*perestroika*) of the country's economic, social, and cultural life and accelerated socioeconomic progress are widely covered in the media, whose circulation grows every year. In the late 1980s the circulation of *Pravda* reached 11 million, *Izvestia* 8 million, *Trud* 18.5 million, and *Komsomolskaya pravda* 17 million.

Bibliography. *Mass Media in the Soviet Union* (in English), Moscow, 1979; Ellen Mickiewicz, *Split Signals: Television and Politics in the Soviet Union,* New York, 1988; Angus Roxburgh, *Pravda: Inside the Soviet News Machine,* New York, 1987; M. V. Shkondin, *Struktura sovetskoi pressi* (The Structure of the Soviet Press), Moscow, 1987; *Sovetskaya pechat v tsifrakh i faktakh* (The Soviet Press: Facts and Statistics), Moscow, 1986.

YASSEN NIKOLAEVICH ZASSOURSKY

NEWSREEL

For more than half a century, beginning long before the commercial introduction of television, the newsreel served as the world's only source of motion picture PHOTOJOURNALISM. It was usually a nine- or ten-minute potpourri of more or less newsworthy footage. Eight or nine items were strung together, separated abruptly from one another by a title and backed up, with the coming of sound, by a noisy musical score and a high-speed, invisible narrator. The newsreels appeared serially—usually twice a week—under well-known trade names and were seen in thousands of motion picture theaters around the world. It was a journalistic enterprise operating in an entertainment context.

Newsreels were corporate productions, backed by the resources of substantial news-gathering and motion picture distribution facilities. Some were distinctly national in release, rarely seen outside their countries of origin. Others, like the U.S. newsreels, were distributed globally; with the aid of foreign-

Figure 1. *(Newsreel)* Louis Lumière, *Le débarquement du Congrès de Photographie,* 1895. National Film Archive, London.

language versions they were seen by more than 200 million people each week. For many, especially the illiterate, the newsreel was a principal source of news.

Origins. Long before there were newsreels, there were *newsfilms,* individual short subjects on newsworthy topics. Newsfilms were released into theaters only as frequently as the cinematic availability of newsworthy subject matter allowed. The origins of newsfilms were *actualities,* short scenes of everyday people and events, showing unmanipulated activity of more or less general interest—citizens walking in the park, a train pulling into a station, workers

leaving a factory. It is with these humble actualities that one begins not merely the history of the newsreel but the history of all MOTION PICTURES.

At first, motion picture audiences demanded little more of actualities than the movement of recognizable people and objects. Gradually, newsworthiness was introduced, and vaudeville and music hall marquees headlined their newsfilms. Some of the earliest known newsfilm coverage includes celebrated SPORTS events photographed by the U.S. inventor THOMAS ALVA EDISON and his associates in 1894 and by the Englishman Robert Paul in 1896; the opening of the Kiel Canal by Kaiser Wilhelm II, photographed by the Englishman Birt Acres in 1895; and the coronation of Czar Nicholas II in Moscow, photographed by the Frenchman Francis Doublier in 1896.

The extent and volume of newsfilm coverage expanded rapidly during the first decade of the century. Despite its crudity, the primitive motion picture newsfilm provided a predominantly photographic kind of news coverage long before most newspapers and magazines of the period began to do so (*see* MAGAZINE; NEWSPAPER: HISTORY). By 1900, within five years of the commercial introduction of the motion picture and five years before the motion picture theater became a permanent entertainment phenomenon, every type of subject matter that was to characterize both motion picture and television journalism in the century ahead had already been pho-

Figure 2. *(Newsreel)* Charles Urban and a group of Kinemacolor cameramen, probably in New Delhi for the 1911 Durbar marking the accession of George V. National Film Archive, London.

Figure 3. *(Newsreel)* Fox News aircraft, a company-owned plane used to transport footage from camera to laboratory. Raymond Fielding Collection/20th Century Fox Movietonews, Inc.

Figure 4. *(Newsreel)* Fox cameraman shooting footage in England in the 1930s, from the reinforced roof of a Ford V8. Raymond Fielding Collection/National Film Archive, London.

tographed and presented to theater audiences: catastrophes, international celebrities, pageantry and ceremony, sports, political and governmental affairs, war and military events, industry and technology, education, spectacle, and novelty. Newsreel content could nearly always be classified by means of these established categories.

Rise of the newsreel. In 1909 the French firm of Pathé Frères introduced the world's first newsreel, the *Pathé Journal,* a newspaper of the screen containing several news subjects, which was released regularly in serial fashion (*see* PATHÉ, CHARLES). It was followed shortly by another newsreel series, produced in France by the Gaumont Company. Around 1910 the Pathé organization introduced a similar newsreel in England, followed by several competing British newsreels. In August 1911 Pathé Frères launched the first indigenously produced newsreel in the United States, under the title *Pathé's Weekly.* Two weeks later the U.S. firm Vitagraph was competing with its own reel. More than two dozen different U.S. newsreels were introduced in the years that followed, but only six survived and prospered for any length of time. Five of these were associated with major motion picture studios, their titles changing occasionally over fifty years: *Universal News, Fox Movietone News, Hearst Metrotone* (*MGM News of the Day*), *Paramount News,* and *Warner-Pathé News.* A sixth, independently released newsreel titled *Kinograms* survived from the late 1910s to the late 1920s, but it finally expired with the coming of sound.

World War I brought European film industries to a halt and destroyed the vigorous competition that had existed before the war. In the economic and creative vacuum that followed, the U.S. newsreel spread throughout the world, establishing its dominance within a few short years. The major newsreel companies opened overseas branch offices in major cities, assigning hundreds of staff and free-lance cameramen to photograph the millions of feet of news footage that annually found its way back to company headquarters in New York. The Fox newsreel alone had cameramen in fifty-one countries, reporting to nine producing centers in major cities. The same company exhibited its semiweekly newsreel releases in forty-seven foreign countries and in more than a dozen languages, each version tailored to the requirements of the exhibition situation involved. At its peak the weekly worldwide audience for this

◁ **Figure 5.** *(Newsreel)* Re-creation of the sinking of Admiral Cervera's fleet at Santiago Bay, Cuba, in the Spanish-American War, 1898. The photograph shows the pool, canvas backdrop, and miniature mountains and battleships constructed by E. H. Amet. *International Photographer,* 1933. Raymond Fielding Collection/International Photographer.

single company's newsreel was reported to be more than 200 million people. Each major studio distributed its newsreel under a "block-booking" plan; that is, a theater acquired it in the package deal along with the company's features and short subjects.

Over the years newsreels became streamlined, sophisticated operations. In addition to the two fresh issues of the newsreel delivered to theaters each week, special footage was rushed into theaters whenever the magnitude of an event warranted it. Sometimes the speed with which this occurred, especially in countries served by rapid rail or air transport, rivaled or exceeded the speed of coverage and publication provided by newspapers of the day. Films of the inauguration of Warren G. Harding in Washington were screened in New York six hours after the event. On another occasion, film coverage of the opening of a spectacular Armistice Day parade in New York was screened in theaters throughout the metropolitan area while the parade was still in progress. Compared with today's instant-replay, SATELLITE-distributed, electronic journalism, such examples of the speed of newsreel operation may not seem very impressive, but to audiences of the day they were extraordinary.

Newsreel content. The newsreel's content was fairly predictable, reflecting either the producer's conception of the public's interests or an obvious need for certain types of information. Analysis by researcher Leo Handel of U.S. newsreel content from 1939 through 1948 showed that in the peacetime year 1948, 88 percent of a typical reel was devoted to foreign news, sports, government news, political news, and national defense, in that order. The same analysis showed that in the wartime year 1943, 82 percent of a typical reel was devoted to war in Europe, national defense, war in the Pacific, sports, and government news, in that order.

Although the newsreel was popular with audiences and firmly established commercially, it was frequently criticized during its history for triteness and superficiality. Like the later TELEVISION NEWS programs, newsreels relied almost entirely on moving images to report and interpret news events. As in television, if you did not have pictures, it was felt you did not have much of a story. But, unlike television journalists, the newsreel's narrator was invisible; there were no stand-up reporters or "talking head" anchors to read the news. The newsreel had less than ten minutes in which to tell its several stories, no matter how complicated any single one might be. Because of these factors, the newsreel's treatment of complicated social, political, economic, and cultural issues was frequently sketchy, oversimplified, and trivialized.

The newsreel suffered the additional burden of having to operate in an entertainment context in which it played no significant economic function in generating income for exhibitors, distributors, or

Figure 6. *(Newsreel)* A staged scene from the *March of Time*'s September 1935 issue on Ethiopia, featuring an impersonation of Haile Selassie, played here by a *March of Time* office boy. Raymond Fielding Collection/Time, Inc.

Figure 7. *(Newsreel)* A simulation of a banquet held by Dominican dictator Rafael Trujillo, from the *March of Time*'s July 1936 issue. Raymond Fielding Collection/Time, Inc.

producers. Exhibitors received newsreels along with cartoons, travelogues, sports reels, and other block-booked trivia as a package designed to support the feature films that drew audiences to the theaters and that generated the principal income on which the industry relied. Unlike the television news medium that followed it, the motion picture newsreel was never allowed to stand alone. For this reason, it was rarely taken very seriously, from either economic or journalistic standpoints. An exception occurred during World War II, when numerous newsreel theaters

Figure 8. *(Newsreel)* Total equipment used by the Pathé company to film the coronation of Queen Elizabeth II in 1953. Raymond Fielding Collection/National Film Archive, London.

opened in the United States and some foreign countries to show only newsreels and DOCUMENTARY films. These theaters and their fare enjoyed considerable popularity until the conclusion of the war diminished much of their informational appeal.

Far more serious criticism of newsreel coverage centered on the occasional staging and faking of news footage when shots of the authentic event were not available. Such journalistic sins were not limited to any one country's newsreel output, nor were they absent from the subsequent operations of the television news industry. However, they were far more frequent, and more widely condoned, in motion picture newsreel circles than they were later in the broadcasting industry.

The March of Time. A journalistically more sophisticated variation on the newsreel was introduced in 1935 by the U.S. publishing firm Time, Inc., under the title *The March of Time.* An editorially interpretive twenty-minute reel, *The March of Time* was seen monthly in ten thousand theaters by as many as 25 million people in the United States alone, and by millions more in four foreign-language versions. *The March of Time,* as developed by executive producer Louis de Rochemont, was a unique form of cinematic journalism, its investigative and confrontational character anticipating by many years the more aggressive forms of television journalism. Censored in some countries, banned outright in others, the series lasted for sixteen years, treating political, social, and racial issues that the more conventional newsreels habitually avoided. Its most controversial feature was the practice of staging or "re-creating" news events at which newsreel cameras had not been present, using both professional and amateur actors who either looked or sounded like the newsmakers they impersonated, and sometimes integrating this staged material with authentic newsreel footage. The technique anticipated by many years the appearance on television of so-called docudramas, which combine the traditions of theater and journalism. *See* FACT AND FICTION.

The March of Time survived for more than fifteen years, finally disappearing from theater screens in 1951. In the following years all the other U.S. newsreels likewise vanished. The last, *Universal News,* ceased operations in December 1967. Theatrical newsreels continued to be produced in other countries, but as soon as widespread television journalism services became available newsreels tended to disappear from theater screens.

Newsreel archives. The motion picture newsreel is one of the very few major communications media ever to have gone out of business and disappeared. However, much of the footage has survived. It is estimated that perhaps as much as half a billion feet of negative were photographed by U.S. newsreel cameramen alone. Fortunately, a good deal of that original material still exists in the holdings of widely scattered ARCHIVES throughout the world. Some of the largest of these collections have been donated to public archives: the Universal newsreel is at the U.S. National Archives, the Hearst Metrotone newsreel at the University of California at Los Angeles, and the Fox Movietone collection at the University of South Carolina. Other newsreel collections are administered by commercial stock-shot libraries. Their holdings provide valuable resources for historical research and for the continuing production of so-called compilation documentaries. Because of the varying circumstances under which such material was photographed, the reputation for staging and re-creation that lingers over newsreel history, and the highly selective and superficial nature of all predominantly visual news media, historians approach this material with caution. They have found that some of the most revealing, instructive, and emotionally powerful footage exists in the outtake files of the archives—millions of feet of film never incorporated into the finished reels because they did not serve the purposes of the moment but which, for historical purposes, provide rich insights into the values, character, and behavior of human beings during the first half of the twentieth century. *See* ARCHIVES, FILM.

Bibliography. Peter Baechlin and Maurice Muller-Strauss, *Newsreels across the World,* Paris, 1952; Raymond Fielding, *The American Newsreel, 1911–1967,* Norman, Okla., 1972; idem, *The March of Time, 1935–1951,* New York, 1978; Jay Leyda, *Films Beget Films,* New York, 1964.

RAYMOND FIELDING

NIEPCE, JOSEPH-NICÉPHORE (1765–1833)

French physicist and pioneer in PHOTOGRAPHY. Joseph-Nicéphore Niepce is credited with having made the first successful and permanent image taken by a camera. The son of a lawyer with royal connections, he had the education, family resources, and leisure time to devote himself to being a gentleman inventor. The new art of lithography (*see* GRAPHIC REPRODUCTION; PRINTING), which was introduced to France in 1814, drew Niepce's attention. He sought to record the image of nature directly on a plate that could then be printed like an engraving.

Although Niepce's only surviving camera pictures date from about 1827, it is certain that he had obtained a camera image as early as 1816. For these early images he used paper sensitized with silver chloride and obtained a negative. Failing to make a positive image and overlooking the advantage of a negative—namely, the ability to replicate an image any number of times—Niepce continued to experiment to find a direct positive process.

Figure 1. *(Niepce, Joseph-Nicéphore)* J.-N. Niepce, the first surviving camera image, 1827. Heliograph. Gernsheim Collection, Harry Ransom Humanities Research Center, The University of Texas at Austin.

By using a plate coated with bitumen of judea, an asphaltlike substance that hardens when exposed to light, and by washing away the unhardened portions with oil of lavender, Niepce succeeded in producing a positive image. His initial attempts involved making copies of engravings, and he first achieved success in July 1822 by oiling a print of an engraving, placing it on a sensitized pewter plate, and then exposing it to sunlight. The area of the plate beneath the lines of the print did not harden and was washed away, and the bare metal of the plate was then etched and used to make prints.

Niepce's first surviving camera image is a view from a window at his estate showing the towers of the house and the courtyard (Figure 1). The image is grainy and of high contrast, and the exposure time was eight hours—all of which made his process impractical.

Unable to perfect his process, he signed a ten-year contract with LOUIS DAGUERRE in 1829 to collaborate on their investigations. However, in 1833, before any progress had been made, Niepce died.

Niepce's process of photography, which he called heliography, never became practical and was forgotten for many years. His importance lies mainly in his development of the first photomechanical reproduction technique, in his claim to having made the first permanent camera image, and in the impetus he gave to Daguerre in the invention of the daguerreotype, the first practical and widely used photographic process, which was completely different from Niepce's.

Bibliography. Gisèle Freund, *Photography and Society,* Boston, 1980; Beaumont Newhall, *The History of Photography from 1839 to the Present* (1949), 5th rev. and enl. ed., New York, 1982; Naomi Rosenblum, *A World History of Photography,* New York, 1984.

STEPHEN PERLOFF

NINEVEH

Capital of the Assyrian Empire at its greatest extent and site of the first great LIBRARY of antiquity, assembled by Ashurbanipal during his reign (668–627 B.C.E.). The first major excavations there were undertaken by A. H. Layard in 1846–1849, but the nearly twenty-five thousand tablets and fragments that made up the contents of the library itself were recovered in subsequent excavations over the next eighty years and were taken to the British Museum.

Creation and organization of the library. Ashurbanipal (see Figure 1) boasted that he was both literate, which is quite possible, and learned, which is not very probable. An inscription from his library reads: "[I am one who] with a sharp eye learned the most important elements of the scribal craft, although among the kings who preceded me, none had learned this skill. The wisdom of the god Nabu, all the cuneiform signs that can be made, I wrote on tablets, checked and collated, and deposited in my palace for my reading and perusal" (*see* CUNEIFORM). Ashurbanipal assembled and/or had copied tablets from private and institutional libraries in both Assyria and Babylonia. In his own words again, "According to the text of clay tablets and wax writing boards, copies from Assyria, Sumer and Akkad [Babylonia], I wrote this tablet with the assembled scholars." There is a letter from the king to one of his agents in Babylonia asking for specific compositions belonging to certain scholars to be sent to him, along with "rare tablets known to you there, but not available in Assyria." Letters from his agents to the king report on new acquisitions for the royal library.

These new acquisitions might consist of donated or confiscated texts from individuals or institutions, or copies made especially for the royal library. Acquisition lists of both kinds are extant. Catalogs listing texts by category, or listing the incipits (opening words) of individual tablets of multitablet compositions, are also known, but the details of the library's organization remain unknown. Unfortunately, the bulk of the library was excavated long before archaeology was put on a scientific footing; specific locations were not recorded, and the original arrangement of the tablets went unnoticed.

Ashurbanipal's amassing of tablets and copies from all the major centers of Mesopotamia was not simply a manifestation of bibliomania. There was great concern to establish the best text, which lay behind the effort to collect and compare exemplars from different scholars in different locales. And, in fact, tablets from Nineveh generally are of a much higher standard than texts written elsewhere in the first millennium B.C.E.

Format and content. Texts in the library were inscribed on single-column tablets of fifty or fewer lines, on large multicolumn tablets of up to three hundred and more lines, and on hinged multileaved and single-leaf wax-covered writing boards. Although we can estimate from acquisition lists that the writing boards comprised about 15 percent of the library's holdings, none have survived because of their perishable nature, and, in fact, only one has survived from all of Mesopotamia. *See* WRITING MATERIALS.

The contents of the library are primarily technical

Figure 2. *(Nineveh)* The Babylonian version of the flood narrative from the Gilgamesh Epic in Akkadian cuneiform script (fragment). Middle of the second millennium B.C.E. Reproduced by courtesy of the Trustees of The British Museum.

rather than literary in the narrow sense. Texts such as the Gilgamesh Epic, Enuma Elish (Creation Epic), or Ludlul Bel Nemeqi (the Babylonian Job) made up no more than 5 percent of the total (see Figure 2). The majority consisted of technical literature, such as omens, incantations, and rituals; medical lore; and philological compendia, used both for teaching

Figure 1. *(Nineveh)* King Ashurbanipal (668–627 B.C.E) and his queen feasting in an arbor. Alabaster relief from the palace at Nineveh. Reproduced by courtesy of the Trustees of The British Museum.

and for advanced study by scholars. Letters and other contemporary records provide ample evidence that such technical literature was regularly sought out and consulted. Ashurbanipal's library was thus an eminently practical enterprise, not simply an academic exercise. But the high scholarly standards and comprehensive goal that guided its formation, and which reflect the personal values of Ashurbanipal himself, set it apart from earlier tablet collections and justify the application of the term *library*.

See also ARCHIVES; BOOK.

Bibliography. A. Leo Oppenheim, *Ancient Mesopotamia*, 2d rev. ed., Chicago, 1977; Simo Parpola, "Assyrian Library Records," *Journal of Near Eastern Studies* 42 (1983): 1–30; Mogens Weitenmeyer, "Archive and Library Technique in Ancient Mesopotamia," *Libri* 6 (1956): 217–238.

JERROLD S. COOPER

NKRUMAH, KWAME (1909–1972)

First president of Ghana (1960–1966). Kwame Nkrumah's rise to power is closely related to his role as one of the pioneer journalists of the African nationalist movement. Born in what was the Gold Coast, in a small village where his father was a goldsmith, he received schooling at a Catholic mission. He started a teaching career but in his mid-

Figure 1. *(Nkrumah, Kwame)* Prime Minister Kwame Nkrumah waving to the crowd. The occasion was the creation of the sovereign state of Ghana, ninth member of the British Commonwealth, March 6, 1957. UPI/Bettmann Newsphotos.

twenties went abroad to continue his education. During ten years in the United States, first at Lincoln University (Pa.) and later at the University of Pennsylvania, he immersed himself in political activity, met many black leaders, organized an African students' association, and established its newspaper, *African Interpreter*. During a subsequent stay in England he took part in anticolonial meetings and for a time edited a monthly journal, *The New African*, which British authorities barred from the Gold Coast. But Nkrumah was becoming widely known, and in 1947, returning to the Gold Coast, he was appointed secretary-general of the United Gold Coast Convention (UGCC). When in 1949 he split from the UGCC to form the Convention People's Party (CPP), his organizational and journalistic skills served him well. He established three newspapers, one of which he personally edited, to publicize CPP policies, campaign for self-rule, and criticize the policies of the colonial administration. Besides publications, he furthered the cause with speeches, songs, drums, and town criers. In 1950 the colonial authorities sought to halt his activities by charging him with sedition. He was sentenced to three years in prison, but the imprisonment enhanced his role as the dominant political figure of the period. In 1951 an election was held for a newly authorized legislative assembly, and Nkrumah won a victory that brought his release from prison. In 1957, when the Gold Coast won independence, Nkrumah was made prime minister; in 1960, when it became the Republic of Ghana, he became president.

As president, Nkrumah committed considerable technical and financial resources to developing and expanding communications facilities. RADIO broadcasting was expanded, relay stations were established throughout the country, and an external broadcasting service was inaugurated in 1961 (*see* RADIO, INTERNATIONAL). A television station was started in 1965 (*see* TELEVISION HISTORY). In 1957 Nkrumah established a national news agency (*see* NEWS AGENCIES) and in 1959 a journalism training institution (*see* COMMUNICATIONS, STUDY OF); both were the first in sub-Saharan Africa.

Under Nkrumah, newspapers in six Ghanaian languages were regularly printed and distributed nationally, supplemented by a mass LITERACY campaign (*see* NEWSPAPER: TRENDS—TRENDS IN AFRICA). State-owned and party newspapers were expanded, but Nkrumah was expressly opposed to the private press. Privately owned newspapers either had been acquired by the state or were suppressed by the time of Nkrumah's overthrow in early 1966. President Nkrumah also made wide use of extension workers, mobile vans, and traditional promotion media to mobilize support and disseminate information about government policies. He subjected all communications in-stitutions to strict state control, declaring a MONOPOLY policy to be essential for national development, unity, and the building of a socialist state in Ghana. After his overthrow Nkrumah spent his last six years in exile in Guinea.

See also AFRICA, TWENTIETH CENTURY; CENSORSHIP.

Bibliography. Henry L. Bretton, *The Rise and Fall of Kwame Nkrumah*, London, 1966; Basil Davidson, *Black Star: A View of the Life and Times of Kwame Nkrumah*, London, 1973; Kwame Nkrumah, *Ghana: The Autobiography of Kwame Nkrumah*, New York, 1957.

S. T. KWAME BOAFO

"NOISE." *See* INFORMATION THEORY; MODELS OF COMMUNICATION.

NONVERBAL COMMUNICATION

Taken literally, nonverbal communication would mean any sort of communication that is not accomplished through words. In established usage, however, the term has a much more limited application. Typically it is used to refer to communication between people who are in each other's presence, and it is accomplished through BODY MOVEMENT, GESTURE, FACIAL EXPRESSION and orientation, posture and spacing (*see* INTERPERSONAL DISTANCE), TOUCH and SMELL, and those aspects of spoken utterance, such as intonation, voice quality, rate of speaking, and the like, that can be considered apart from the actual verbal content of what is said. Studies of nonverbal communication (also sometimes referred to as nonverbal behavior) are usually concerned with the part these aspects of behavior play in establishing and maintaining interactions and interpersonal relationships and typically have dealt with those aspects of communication that individuals are said to be unaware of or do not normally report. The use of gesture to convey explicit messages that can be glossed directly or translated into words, as in SIGN LANGUAGE, for example, is not usually considered part of nonverbal communication (although some authors have done so). *See also* INTERACTION, FACE-TO-FACE; KINESICS; PROXEMICS.

The term *nonverbal communication* first came into use in the early 1950s. It appears to have been first used in print by Jurgen Ruesch, and it gained wide currency as a result of a book Ruesch published with Weldon Kees in 1956 called *Nonverbal Communication*. Ruesch, a psychiatrist of Italian birth and Swiss education, was interested in the processes of interaction in psychotherapy. He moved to Boston, Massachusetts, in about 1940 and became involved in discussions with WARREN WEAVER, NORBERT WIENER, and, later, GREGORY BATESON in which concepts developed in INFORMATION THEORY and CYBERNETICS were applied to human interaction. The notion of "quantity of information," which had been developed as part of the mathematical theory of information (first evolved in the course of an endeavor to measure the transmission efficiency of telephone lines), required a way of thinking about information without any reference to the nature of the message transmitted. This meant that the information value of something could be considered regardless of the sorts of messages involved and regardless of whether any deliberate attempt to transmit messages had been made. When applied to the study of communication in human interaction, it led to the realization that all aspects of behavior that are detectable by another could be treated in information theory terms. Hence not only are such actions as SPEECH and gesture to be considered as signals, but all other aspects of behavior are as well, whether or not they are intended or designed to transmit messages. It is not only what A *says* to B that sends messages to B, it is also what A *does*.

The formulation of the notion of nonverbal communication that arose from these considerations has had several consequences. First, it has led to the investigation, from a communicational point of view, of many aspects of behavior that had been overlooked. Not only did nonverbal communication provide a new perspective for the long tradition in psychology of studies of expression, especially facial expression, but it also meant that aspects of behavior such as gaze direction, posture, and interpersonal spacing came to be studied. As a consequence of this notion, researchers began to realize that the way in which persons adjust or alter their behavior when in one another's presence was to be understood neither in purely practical terms nor in terms of some notion of expression, when expression is thought of simply as the translation into external forms of inner states. Rather, persons in the presence of others guide their behavior in relation to one another in the light of any information the behavior of each provides. Thus actions of all sorts can be viewed in terms of their possible significance as messages in interaction. All aspects of behavior, it appears, can function communicationally.

However, the notion of nonverbal communication has also encouraged the view that communication by actions can be studied independently of communication by words. It has suggested that there is a great divide in human communication, with words on one side and all else on the other. Yet this sharp distinction that the concept of nonverbal communication has seemed to encourage, in the hands of some authors, cannot be sustained. For example, it is impossible to establish consistent criteria by which to distinguish words and what they convey from everything else. Furthermore, from a functional point of view, as developments in the study of discourse and CONVERSATION have made clear, verbal utterance plays as crucial a role in the establishment and maintenance of interactive relationships as nonverbal aspects of human action do. At the same time, as studies of gesture show, aspects of human action that are definitely not verbal may nevertheless serve in the place of words or may serve as an essential component of referential communication.

A further drawback of the concept of nonverbal communication is that it tends to encourage the notion that it is one *sort* of communication only. A number of authors have made statements claiming a general character for nonverbal communication— that it is analogic, whereas verbal communication is digital, for instance, or that it is developmentally or evolutionarily more primitive. A close study of the communicative functions of nonverbal aspects of human behavior shows, however, that such statements cannot be maintained. At best the term *nonverbal communication* can be no more than a shorthand expression for referring to a range of quite diverse phenomena. Although the development of the concept, vague though it has been, has greatly expanded our way of thinking about human communication, it is also clear that it lacks coherence and probably should be dropped.

See also BODY DECORATION; CLOTHING; EYES; FACE; SPATIAL ORGANIZATION.

Bibliography. Robert Hinde, ed., *Nonverbal Communication*, Cambridge, 1972; Mary Ritchie Key, *Nonverbal Communication: A Research Guide and Bibliography*, Metuchen, N.J., 1977; Mark L. Knapp, *Nonverbal Communication in Human Interaction*, 2d ed., New York, 1978; Jurgen Ruesch, *Semiotic Approaches to Human Relations*, The Hague, 1972; Jurgen Ruesch and Weldon Kees, *Nonverbal Communication: Notes on the Visual Perception of Human Relations*, Berkeley, Calif., 1956; Klaus Scherer and Paul Ekman, eds., *Handbook of Methods in Nonverbal Behavior Research*, Cambridge, 1982.

ADAM KENDON

NORTHCLIFFE, ALFRED (1865–1922)

British MAGAZINE and newspaper publisher. Alfred Northcliffe was Britain's leading press lord in the early twentieth century. Unlike his great rival, Lord Beaverbrook (*see* BEAVERBROOK, 1ST BARON), Northcliffe was primarily a journalist. Like JOSEPH PULITZER and WILLIAM RANDOLPH HEARST in the United States, Northcliffe was a master of sensational journalism who owed his success to an uncanny talent for understanding and exploiting mass tastes.

Born in Dublin as Alfred Charles William Harmsworth, Northcliffe had an indifferent grammar and private school education in London. At the age of seventeen he was already a reporter for a Coventry newspaper, but he then made a lengthy detour into the magazine business. First the editor of *Youth,* he cofounded *Answers to Correspondents*—soon called merely *Answers*—with his brother Harold in 1888. His talent for satisfying mass tastes and Harold's remarkable business ability, particularly in the AD-VERTISING department, propelled the brothers to extraordinary success.

After creating an entire stable of mass-appeal periodicals, Northcliffe organized them into the Amalgamated Press (later the Fleetway Press), then the world's biggest magazine publisher. This achievement made Northcliffe rich but left him unsatisfied; he looked toward newspapers as the true source of power. In 1894 he acquired the London *Evening News,* which was verging on bankruptcy, and made the respectable but moribund paper into a counterpart of his cheap magazines. New *Evening News* features such as a women's column and short FIC-TION gained Northcliffe a reputation as the greatest innovator in British journalism.

Northcliffe followed his initial newspaper success with another, the London *Daily Mail,* which he founded in 1896. The *Mail* was truly revolutionary, with its makeup in the Pulitzer style and news to match. It also exemplified Northcliffe's instructions to the staff: "Explain, simplify, clarify." In another pioneering effort Northcliffe in 1903 started the London *Daily Mirror,* the first newspaper designed for women. Failing to enchant its audience of "gentlewomen," the *Mirror* was converted into a mass-circulation tabloid. Buying another financially ailing paper, the *Weekly Dispatch,* Northcliffe renamed it the *Sunday Dispatch;* it eventually attained the highest Sunday circulation in Britain. Then, after rescuing the struggling but soon to be distinguished *Observer,* Northcliffe climbed to the peak of his profession by gaining control of the London *Times*—an incredible feat for a man of his class and background. Marked by elements of farce and melodrama, his negotiations for the *Times* proceeded secretly by code, and the acquisition was not known to the public for several months.

The British government recognized his achievements by making him a baronet, then a baron, and finally 1st Viscount Northcliffe. But as a person Northcliffe was considered eccentric, even bizarre. He used the political power that his papers gave him in contradictory ways, provoking numerous controversies (the *Mail* was once burned on the London Stock Exchange), and his death, as trade unionist Roy Jenkins has said, "was a relief to almost everybody." The *Times* passed into the Astor family and his other papers into different hands.

See also NEWSPAPER: HISTORY; NEWSPAPER: TRENDS—TRENDS IN EUROPE.

Bibliography. Henry H. Fyfe, *Northcliffe: An Intimate Biography,* New York, 1930, reprint 1969.

JOHN TEBBEL

NOVEL, THE. *See* FICTION; FICTION, PORTRAYAL OF CHARACTER IN.

NUMBER

The number symbols and numeration systems known to humanity have been developed over the course of many centuries by many different cultures. The details of the origins of the *names* for numbers as well as the *symbols* used to represent them are not available for some systems, whereas for others there are fairly complete descriptions. The variety of approaches, however, share a few principles that constitute crucial elements not only of such number systems but also of humanity's cultural heritage.

Principles. The first is *abstract symbolization,* a written form for numbers that is different from concrete representation (e.g., with lines) and that has general application: "5" rather than "five sheep" or "five days" (*see* SIGN SYSTEM; SYMBOLIC LOGIC). The second is the principle of a *multiplicative base.* The most widely used system has ten as its base, but many others have been devised. For example, the numeral 234 in a base-twelve system would denote the number 328 in base ten: $328 = (4 \times 1) + (3 \times 12) + (2 \times 12 \times 12)$. In a base-five system the numeral 234 would denote 69 in base ten: $69 = (4 \times 1) + (3 \times 5) + (2 \times 5 \times 5)$. The third principle is *positional notation,* which allows users to distinguish numerals containing the same digits—348 is very different from 843, 438, and 384. Finally, the fourth principle is a numeral as well: *zero,* also called a "position holder," which allows distinctions between 19, 109, 190, and 1009.

Though related to the principle of a multiplicative base, the principle of position is independent. In ancient Egyptian numerals, for example, there are symbols for units (a simple slash), tens, hundreds, thousands, and so on, but the order in which the symbols are written is not critical. Egyptian numerals are additive in the sense that as many unit symbols, ten symbols, hundred symbols, and so on as are required are merely listed. Almost all early systems, including those of the Greeks and Romans, were of this relatively primitive type, additive and nonpositional. The Roman system was essentially additive

Figure 1. *(Number)* The Mayan counting system: the first nineteen numerals. Redrawn after David Eugene Smith, *History of Mathematics,* vol. 2, New York: Dover Publications, Inc., 1958, p. 44.

despite the subtractive complication (e.g., IV instead of IIII and IX instead of VIIII) introduced later.

Measuring and counting. Quantities were undoubtedly compared long before symbols for numbers were devised. The prehistoric man or woman who counted the days of the month by touching in sequence various body parts, one more each day, was ignorant of any summation system. Likewise the shepherd who counted the flock by moving his or her fingers along the notches in a tally stick did not need any written numeration system to know when an animal was missing. Such methods of comparing quantities supplemented people's limited immediate perception of number, which did not (and still does not) extend much past four. I is easily distinguishable from II and this from III or IIII. After four our perceptions waver: IIIII and IIIIII must be counted, explaining why numerals of many early systems, especially those based on the idea of tallying, change character at five. *See* PERCEPTION—STILL AND MOVING PICTURES.

These methods of comparison evolved into various concrete ways of indicating numbers—pebbles of different sizes (bigger ones being worth a fixed number of smaller ones), knotted skeins or rope (such as the Incan quipus), the abacus and other variations of the counting board, and of course the fingers on a person's hands and the toes on a person's feet, the likely source for the base-ten system. Base-twenty systems are suggested by the French words for twenty, eighty, and ninety—*vingt, quatre-vingts,* and *quatre-vingt-dix*—and evident in the Mayan system, which included a sort of nonfunctional zero and positional notation and allowed them to create a very accurate CALENDAR.

Problems of notation. It is difficult to avoid reading into earlier systems ideas or simplifications that were not there for the practitioners. For example, the Mayan and Babylonian systems were not completely positional. The Mayas had a position for ones and a position for twenties (their base), but the next position—because of their concern for the calendar—was for 360s and not 400s (twenty times twenty), and the next one after that was for 7200s (twenty times three hundred and sixty). Combined with their very

restricted use of a zero their principles generated ambiguity and, it would seem, great awkwardness: a dot was the symbol for one, a horizontal line the symbol for five, and the direction of increasing value from top to bottom. Thus two lines with three dots over them ($\underline{\overset{\textstyle\cdots}{\overline{}}}$) might represent either the number thirteen (ten plus three equals thirteen ones) or the number seventy (ten ones plus three twenties) or one of several other numbers, depending on the context or merely on the vagaries of how the symbols were mentally grouped. Even a single dot was indetermi-

Figure 2. *(Number)* Venerable Bede, *De Temporum Ratione,* fourteenth century. Colored drawing on vellum showing how to count on one's fingers. Phot. Bibl. Nat., Paris.

Figure 3. *(Number)* Chinese tradesman counting on his *suan pan* ("reckoning board"), a hand-held abacus. The Bettmann Archive, Inc.

six, the number assigned to the divine name of Yahweh. The Greek words for "God," "holy," and "good" all have the same numerical equivalent of 284 in the Greek alphabet.

The invention of zero. The invention of a functional zero within a system of positional notation constitutes a major achievement for the people of South India and for humanity at large. The Arabs borrowed this notion of zero, created algebra, and communicated much of their knowledge to western Europe. *See* ISLAM, CLASSICAL AND MEDIEVAL ERAS; MATHEMATICS.

It is most likely due to the lack of a zero that the abacus, in most places based on powers of ten, did not lead sooner to these discoveries. Had there been a numeral for zero, numbers could have been directly read from the state of the abacus, a zero symbol indicating an empty column on the abacus. Like Franciscus Vieta's (1540–1603) use of a letter to represent an unknown quantity, or the idea of René Descartes (1596–1650) of identifying a point on a bidimensional plane with an ordered pair of num-

nate, representing 1, 20, 360, or 7200, analogous perhaps to a 1 representing 1, 10, 100, or 1000. *See* AMERICAS, PRE-COLUMBIAN.

Similar remarks apply to the Sumerian-Babylonian system, the oldest known positional numeration system, dating from 1900 to 1800 B.C.E. The CUNEIFORM system of wedges and crescents was often an ambiguous hybrid of systems having multiplicative bases sixty and ten, with additive elements within each order or position. *See* CLAY TOKENS; EAST ASIA, ANCIENT.

Many early numeration systems, besides being additive and nonpositional, had numerals that were simply hieroglyphs or letters in a written LANGUAGE. Although the connection between WRITING and numeration is unclear, the necessities of trade probably played a significant role in the development of both. The relationship between language and numbers has a different character in numerology, widely practiced by different cultures, in which letters are assigned numerical equivalents. For example, the Hebrew words for "love" and "one" each have the same numerical equivalent of thirteen, and their "sum" is thus twenty-

Figure 4. *(Number)* A Russian abacus. The Bettmann Archive, Inc.

bers, inventing a zero was a stunningly simple idea that was "merely" a matter of notation. The Hindu-Arabic number system, and not just the notion of zero, is thus one of the most important technical discoveries in the history of humanity.

Bibliography. Carl B. Boyer, *A History of Mathematics,* New York, 1968; Tobias Dantzig, *Number: The Language of Science* (1930), 4th ed., rev., New York, 1959; Georges Ifrah, *From One to Zero: A Universal History of Numbers* (Histoire universelle des chiffres), trans. by Lowell Blair, New York, 1985; Otto Neugebauer and A. Sachs, eds., *Mathematical Cuneiform Texts* (Mathematische Keil-schrifte-texte, 3 vols., Berlin, 1935–1937), New Haven, Conn., 1945; David E. Smith, *History of Mathematics,* 2 vols., Boston and New York, 1923–1925, reprint New York, 1958.

JOHN ALLEN PAULOS

(ōᵘ), the fifteenth letter of the alphabet in English and other modern languages, and the fourth vowel letter. O was the fourteenth letter in the ancient Roman alphabet, corresponding in form and value to the ancient Greek O, derived from the sixteenth letter of the Phœnician and ancient Semitic alphabet, O, ◇, ▽, (Hebrew ע), called ʿain, i.e. 'eye'.

OCHS, ADOLPH S. (1858–1935)

U.S. newspaper publisher and exponent of "clean, dignified, and trustworthy journalism." At the age of eleven Adolph Simon Ochs went to work as an office boy at the *Chronicle* in Knoxville, Tennessee. He never graduated from high school or attended college, but by the time he joined the *Chattanooga Dispatch* at the age of nineteen, he had experience in news gathering, writing, and printing.

In 1878, using $250 of borrowed money, Ochs bought controlling interest in the *Chattanooga Times,* becoming the publisher of a paper before reaching age twenty-one. He turned his paper into a model of responsible journalism, printing national and local news rather than the viewpoints of special interests. The paper prospered, and Ochs prospered with it; he made many influential friends across the nation and served as chairman of the Southern Associated Press.

In 1896 Ochs borrowed $75,000 and, with a group of investors, purchased the moribund *New York Times,* which was losing $1,000 a day. He took over as publisher of the *Times* in August of that year. It was a tremendous gamble, but Ochs applied to the New York paper the principles he had used in Chattanooga. He refused ADVERTISING that was fraudulent or improper and refrained from sensationalism, hewing carefully to the slogan he had devised: "All the News That's Fit to Print." In 1898, to boost circulation, he reduced the price of the *Times* from three cents to one, the price of the "yellow" dailies. Although many predicted failure, the tactic succeeded brilliantly; both circulation and advertising revenue increased, and the paper showed a profit for the first time in many years.

Ochs kept close control over the *Times* from the beginning but permitted his reporting and editorial staff great latitude, never imposing his own views on his editors or permitting editorial viewpoint to take precedence over the news. Under Ochs the *Times* gained a position of national news leadership and maintained a tradition of responsible reporting. Ochs also served as director of the Associated Press (*see* NEWS AGENCIES) from 1900 to 1935 and was instrumental in beginning publication of the *New York Times Index* (which has become a guide to the news of the day) and in founding the *Dictionary of American Biography.*

See also NEWSPAPER: HISTORY.

Bibliography. Elmer Holmes Davis, *History of the New York Times, 1851–1921,* New York, 1921, reprint St. Claire, Mich., 1971; Harrison E. Salisbury, *Without Fear or Favor: The New York Times and Its Times,* New York, 1980; Gay Talese, *The Kingdom and the Power,* New York, 1969, reprint Garden City, N.Y., 1978.

ROBERT BALAY

OPERA

Opera unites DRAMA, POETRY, and SPECTACLE in musical PERFORMANCE. As a GENRE of communication, forms of drama in which actors sing some or all of their parts have occurred in many cultures. But from the seventeenth century in Italy opera developed as a large-scale form of public entertainment primarily in the Western world.

From the start the cultural status of opera derived from its support by royal and noble patrons, but the

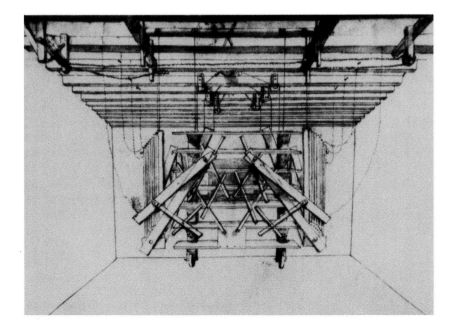

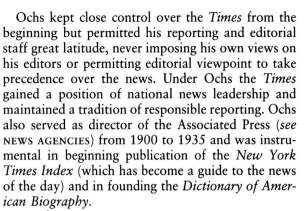

Figure 1. *(Opera)* Germanico sul Reno, descending cloud machinery. Spectacular stage effects, from the deus ex machina to machinery that allowed the heavens to open, were featured in performances at Venice's first public opera house, which opened in 1637. From Simon Towneley Worsthorne, *Venetian Opera in the Seventeenth Century,* London: Oxford University Press, 1954, plate 10.

Figure 2. *(Opera)* A curtain designed by Eugene Berman for *La serva padrona* (an opera buffa), by Giambattista Pergolesi. Jean-Jacques Rousseau used *La serva padrona*'s "naturalness" in music and plot to oppose traditional French opera during the "War of the Buffoons," a controversy that led to the inclusion in French opera of ordinary people as characters and more popular musical forms. From *Theatre Arts,* March 1963, p. 10. Courtesy of the Free Library of Philadelphia.

Figure 3. *(Opera)* Title page to *Le mariage de Figaro,* by Beaumarchais. Paris, 1784. Wolfgang Amadeus Mozart and his librettist Lorenzo da Ponte turned this play into a 1786 comic opera of love and manners to comment on the class constraints of servant and master, man and woman, by having them share ensemble singing and comic and serious roles. The Bettmann Archive, Inc.

reasons for its longevity and influence reside in its emotive and evocative musicality. Its capabilities for uniting and arousing a mass public were recognized, and in many countries the state supported an opera that glorified princely power. But as opera grew from being an Italian export of humanist values and lyrical melodies into a nineteenth-century expression of nationalist sympathies and romantic sensibilities, its revolutionary potential was equally exploited by its new patrons, the middle-class audience. Even though the twentieth century has seen its role as mass entertainment usurped by electronic forms, in scope, size, and spectacle opera remains a vital form of performance that has made its own accommodations to the new electronic media.

The relationship of words and music. The relationship between musical and nonmusical elements, particularly the words and dramatic structure, has been a central tension in the history of opera. Music was thought to enhance the emotional content of the word and to intensify its drama, and the nature of this relationship is the main focus of most theoretical writing. The best-known "reforms" of opera too

have called for the primacy of the word as its organizing feature.

As originally conceived by the Florentine Camerata during the 1590s, opera represented a humanist attempt to reclaim the expressiveness of the word as it was then believed to have been sung in the performance of Greek TRAGEDY. The realization of this literary doctrine in the performance of Jacopo Peri's *Euridice* in 1600 marks the conventional starting point of opera, not coincidentally because it is also the first published opera with verse play, or libretto, and figured bass.

However, even though many writers have seen the drama located in the content or MEANING of the words and the progression of the plot, composers have tended to override dramatic unities with musical ones, with themes and tonal relationships providing the ground, from figured bass to full orchestra. Composers' sensitivity to the poetic possibilities of the word did not necessarily make their musical settings work dramatically, as witnessed by the operatic failures of the most prominent nineteenth-century lieder composers, Franz Schubert, Robert Schumann, and

Figure 4. *(Opera)* Giuseppe Verdi, *I Lombardi.* Frontispiece from a piano score. In 1843, when Verdi staged this opera at La Scala, Italian patriots of the *Risorgimento* took up the battle cry of his Crusaders—"Today the Holy Land will be ours!" From Lorenzo Arruga, *La Scala,* Milan: Electa Editrice, 1975, plate 115. By courtesy of Electa Editrice, Milan.

Hugo Wolf. Whatever the import of the word in an opera's conception, many of the words are lost in its performance because of the technicalities of singing. In fact, even though the poetic union of that language and the melody forms part of its expressive quality, many enjoy opera without even understanding the language being sung. And if one sees opera as expressing affect, then the exact words—at least as information—are subservient to the suggestive harmonies, melodies, and rhythms. Overall, the organizing feature of an opera as a whole and what communicates in performance is the music.

Opera as a social institution. Opera has always been a transnational entertainment industry and in its first two hundred years was a major Italian export. Italian poets and composers took up residence in the courts of Vienna and Paris and the smaller German cities and principalities. With the establishment of public theaters came the professionalization of impresarios to manage the theaters, arrange for court entertainments, book opera touring groups, and handle the engagements for leading singers. Italians took the lead in this PROFESSION through the beginning of the nineteenth century, with Gioacchino Rossini as the "Napoléon of music" and Domenico Barbaja managing theaters in Vienna and throughout Italy.

Italian opera demanded Italian singers, and their ability, availability, and reliability in drawing audiences were key elements to an opera's financial success. The star-making machinery in Italy was constrained for its first centuries by church prohibition against female singing, but an underground industry developed to provide castrati (male singers who had been castrated at a young age to preserve their high voices) for the female roles. The castrati

were the first STARS, and they cultivated the benefits of celebrity through both financial and personal license. Their reputations crossed national boundaries faster than they could and helped them achieve international status.

Several communications factors encouraged the DIFFUSION of this Italian export. TOURISM, especially to Venice and other Italian cities, spread the reputation of and desire for Italian opera to such far-flung places as London and Saint Petersburg, and Italian touring companies followed the trade routes throughout Europe. Music PRINTING benefited opera, as it did other large-scale forms, particularly because the export of movable type had helped to standardize the various regional musical notation systems (*see* MUSIC THEORIES—NOTATIONS AND LITERACY). Although many operas composed before 1900 were not actually printed, Italy's role as a major center of music printing established Italian as the language of notation used to the present.

The Italian export was desirable because it represented the ideal expression of the reflected glory of princes in the age of Louis XIV. After Italian opera had been taken up by Cardinal Mazarin, Louis XIV's regent, it was natural for it to come of age in the life that was lived as a pageant. The noble rulers of up-and-coming cities and principalities found opera something they could buy, if not imitate, in the celebration of divine right. The excesses and waste of Italian baroque opera may have been the result at least as much of its use in competition among the nobility as of the form itself, for ART imitated life.

Printed pamphlets in the eighteenth century recorded the first resistance to baroque opera. This period also saw the rise of musical magazines, which

Figure 5. *(Opera)* Richard Wagner, *Der Ring des Nibelungen.* Drawing showing how Siegfried's slaying of the dragon was staged at the Paris Opera in 1902. Stagecraft was an essential component to Wagner's *Gesamtkunstwerk* ("total art work"), and he placed the audience in darkness and the orchestra in a pit to focus attention on the stage. From Charles Osborne, *The World Theatre of Wagner,* Oxford: Phaidon, 1982, p. 123. © Bildarchiv Preussischer Kulturbesitz, Berlin (West).

Figure 7. *(Opera)* Enrico Caruso recording for the Victor Company: a self-caricature. Singing into a megaphone to capture the sound was the method of acoustic recording used before microphones were introduced in the mid-1920s. From Roland Gelatt, *The Fabulous Phonograph 1877–1977,* New York: MacMillan, 1977, p. 144.

Figure 6. *(Opera)* Giuseppe Palanti, poster for *Parsifal,* by Richard Wagner. From Mario Monteverdi, *La Scala: Four Hundred Years of Stage Design from the Museo Teatrale alla Scala, Milan,* Washington, D.C.: International Exhibitions Foundation, 1971, p. 82.

carried criticism of musical compositions and performers. By the beginning of the nineteenth century music journalism gained an increasing role in the selection of stars, composers, and opera fashions. Many opera composers, from Hector Berlioz to Richard Wagner, made extra money writing for music publications.

The development of SOUND RECORDING in the late nineteenth century utilized opera in a new way. The

technical compatibilities between opera singing and the first recording techniques along with the social prestige of opera singing made opera arias a staple of the phonograph and Enrico Caruso its major star. Particularly in the United States, recorded sound provided opera in just the right four-minute segments to attract a new public and encourage support of its live performance. As RADIO broadcasting became available in the 1920s the home became a place in which opera melodies mingled with more popular tunes, and MOTION PICTURES of the 1930s drew upon opera stars in bringing sound to the screen. Television too used opera to lend prestige to its role as mass entertainment, and videocassettes of operas are today rented along with other filmed entertainment.

Meanwhile opera continued to provoke criticism. As a temple of music it did not please all the social critics, and some of the best invective of twentieth-century music criticism was leveled against opera by such figures as George Bernard Shaw and THEODOR ADORNO. Opera also fit into the growing specialty of professional musical study. Conservatories and universities invested in opera as a serious subject and turned out singers and composers for the opera industry.

Live opera continues to depend on the financial support of both its audiences and private individuals and is still a leading subject for daily music journalism. The twentieth century has found it socially allied with other high-culture institutions, and its electronic availability perhaps generates more support from these institutions than appeal for a mass audience, except for occasional superstars. Electronic media in particular, while contributing to the solidification of the opera repertoire of the past, have also revived an interest in its live performance, and opera continues to be both an extravagant and a vital form of musical and theatrical communication.

See also MUSIC HISTORY; MUSIC PERFORMANCE; MUSIC THEATER; SONG; THEATER.

Bibliography. Edward J. Dent, *Opera,* Harmondsworth, Eng., 1940, reprint Baltimore, Md., 1965; Max Graf, *Composer and Critic: Two Hundred Years of Musical Criticism,* New York, 1946; Donald J. Grout, *A Short History of Opera,* 2d. ed., New York, 1965; Paul Henry Lang, *The Experience of Opera* (orig. title: *Critic at the Opera,* 1971), New York, 1973; "Opera," *The New Grove Dictionary of Music and Musicians,* Vol. 13, London and New York, 1980 ed.; Henry Raynor, *Music and Society since 1815,* London, 1976; idem, *A Social History of Music: From the Middle Ages to Beethoven,* London, 1972; Hamish F. G. Swanson, *In Defense of Opera,* London, 1978.

MARSHA SIEFERT

OPINION LEADER

A concept used to designate influential individuals who do not hold formal positions of power or status. Although attention has been paid to the role of leaders in small or well-defined group settings (as in the work of KURT LEWIN), informal leadership in other contexts had been largely ignored as a research topic until the work of PAUL F. LAZARSFELD.

Lazarsfeld and his colleagues directed two large-scale studies of voting behavior in the 1940s that found less evidence of a direct "one-step flow" of influence through the mass media than expected. Instead many respondents attributed changes in their voting decisions to the influence of face-to-face communication (*see* INTERACTION, FACE-TO-FACE; INTERPERSONAL COMMUNICATION). The researchers labeled "opinion leaders" those persons who were regularly consulted for their views by people around them.

These informal opinion leaders resembled their followers in most respects: social status, age, education, and so on. Unlike them, however, opinion leaders paid closer attention to the mass media. In a later work Elihu Katz and Lazarsfeld stated that opinion leadership was specialized by topic, so that leaders influenced opinions only in those areas in which they were perceived to have some expertise or experience.

Lazarsfeld and his group hypothesized that ideas and information were transmitted by a "two-step flow" process, first *from* the mass media to opinion leaders and second *through* opinion leaders to the larger audience. However, the widespread DIFFUSION of television during the 1950s has altered the media environment significantly (*see* TELEVISION HISTORY). Research since then has transformed the notion of opinion leadership. Direct media influence has been suggested to be most important during the early "awareness" stages of opinion formation, and the multiplicity of media sources allows audiences access not necessarily mediated by opinion leaders. Thus research on the AGENDA-SETTING power of the mass media suggests the media's ability to direct public concern toward those issues to which the media give prominent attention or confer status. In the United States far fewer people engage in news conversation in an average day or week than watch a television newscast (*see* TELEVISION NEWS) or read a newspaper, and news media topics comprise only a small proportion of discussion topics that people describe as important on a typical day.

Electoral research also suggests that rather than a "trickle-down" process of information flow from leaders to followers, most interpersonal communication consists of "information sharing" among opinion leaders; these leaders may rarely talk to or influence followers. The main arena in which the original two-step flow model seems appropriate for voting behavior may be the nuclear FAMILY.

Nonetheless, research on information flow does confirm that the Lazarsfeld group's conclusions about the power of interpersonal sources, when activated, were well founded. Thus people who engage in interpersonal conversation about news topics are better informed than those who do not, other factors being equal. And word of mouth is still considered a powerful form of ADVERTISING, even though the role of opinion leaders in the influence flow process still needs more systematic study.

See also COMMUNICATIONS RESEARCH: ORIGINS AND DEVELOPMENT; ELECTION; MASS COMMUNICATIONS RESEARCH; MASS MEDIA EFFECTS; POLITICAL COMMUNICATION; PROPAGANDA.

Bibliography. Elihu Katz and Paul F. Lazarsfeld, *Personal Influence,* Glencoe, Ill., 1955; Paul F. Lazarsfeld, Bernard Berelson, and Hazel Gaudet, *The People's Choice* (1944), 3d ed., New York, 1968; John P. Robinson and Mark R. Levy, *The Main Source,* Beverly Hills, Calif., 1986; Everett M. Rogers, *Diffusion of Innovations* (1962), 3d ed., New York, 1983.

JOHN P. ROBINSON AND DENNIS K. DAVIS

OPINION MEASUREMENT

As a method of assessing PUBLIC OPINION, surveys have become a major form of enterprise in many countries, of interest to scholars and to those in government, industry, and not-for-profit associations as well as to the general public. Their rise has been largely a post–World War II development, spurred by the computer and other new technologies (*see* COMPUTER: IMPACT). The opinion survey has achieved this standing despite continuing disputes over the meaning of such concepts as "opinion" and "public opinion" and over appropriate ways of measuring them.

Wide dissemination of findings via newspapers, magazines, and television has tended to make opinion surveys a prominent feature of mass communication. Surveys of representative samples have created a new channel of communication between the general public and those in government, who do not rely simply on mass media reports of findings but often conduct or sponsor special surveys to guide administration and policy (see POLITICAL COMMUNICATION). Other methods of assessing public opinion are also used (e.g., CONTENT ANALYSIS), but the survey has become a constant and highly visible accompaniment to decision making.

Issues

Surveys depend on the willingness of individuals to express their opinions by answering questions posed by the surveyors. The validity of opinion measurements depends heavily on procedures that encourage respondents to answer candidly and not in a thoughtless or frivolous fashion. Some critics cast doubt on the ability of any survey procedure, no matter how carefully designed, to achieve valid results, arguing that all measurement procedures are reactive—that is, they create an awareness of being tested that produces artificial responses. While certain procedures may well create invalid responses, being surveyed seems to have become an ordinary experience for most respondents, not an extraordinary testing situation. Often the problem is to get respondents to act more attentively; one school of thought argues that the fact of being measured and the reasons for it should be emphasized more strongly to respondents.

The willingness to talk at all, and to express candid opinions, might seem far more dependent on political conditions in the society than on the procedures of the survey. The fear of being branded or punished for one's opinions, the belief that government is utterly indifferent to the people's wishes, the idea that only some are entitled to express political opinions—these might be so pervasive in certain places and periods as to make public opinion surveys unworkable or worthless. However, since World War II the method has found acceptance in many diverse countries. With well-planned procedures adapted to the local circumstances, the publics of a great many countries welcome the opportunity to express their views. The physical and social conditions in some countries may make nationwide surveys difficult. Some regions may be inaccessible; the population may be fragmented into linguistic enclaves, and a majority may be unable to read a printed questionnaire in any language; respondents may be hostile to interviewers of another ethnicity—indeed even to those of another clan or faction within the same ethnic group. Nevertheless, determined and resourceful researchers have managed to conduct useful surveys, although the stringent conditions have curtailed their extent and regularity.

Stages in the Conduct of Surveys

A survey measuring the opinions of a public on some issue or measuring other characteristics of a population (e.g., use of television) is a large, complex, and expensive inquiry. The public may be heterogeneous and spread over thousands of miles. Ideally, all types must be represented in the sample, whose members then must be located and agree to be interviewed. The samples used to achieve sufficient precision in the findings rarely are smaller than a thousand people, and for greater precision and other reasons often much larger. Reliable, comprehensive measurement and depth of understanding usually require multiple measurements on each individual. The voluminous raw data must be treated statistically and analyzed carefully to yield responsible conclusions on public opinion. This complex method may be divided into several major stages: design, collection of data, analysis of data, and report of findings. Each stage has many steps. The various technical principles and procedures must be adapted to the circumstances of each study, and are sometimes compromised by difficult conditions.

Designing the survey. The first step is to choose a basic research design suited to the problem and the resources available. Changes in public opinion following natural events or some planned intervention (e.g., a mass media campaign) are best studied by expensive "trend" designs in which equivalent samples of the public are surveyed by comparable procedures at two or more points in time, or by even more expensive "panel" designs in which the same sample is measured successively by comparable procedures. A single survey conducted in one brief interval of time may serve simply to describe public opinion at that point or also, with some modifications in the basic design and the instruments, to explain the patterns of opinion. It may also serve as a "quasi-panel" requiring retrospective questions on change.

Next, the public or population to be surveyed must be clearly defined, ideally in such fashion that everyone whose opinions should be counted is included within its boundaries and thus given a chance to be sampled and measured, and others are excluded. A useful term conveying the principle is *target population.* In theory this second step should govern later decisions, the method of sampling, data collection, and instruments being those best suited to achieve a representative sample and valid measurement of the target population. In practice those procedures often are predetermined for various practical reasons. The target population is then redefined and restricted to those who *can* be sampled and measured in ways already selected.

In most opinion surveys in the United States prior to 1970 the target population was defined as adults twenty-one years old or older; it was then changed to those eighteen years old or older as young adults became eligible to vote. Implicitly, the public was modeled on the electorate, those who had the right to vote their opinions. For surveys on national policy, that definition is reasonable, although teenagers might quarrel with it and want their opinions communicated to government. However, some might argue that the boundaries occasionally are drawn too broadly in surveys on particular issues. For example, on legislation on health hazards inside industrial plants, perhaps those working in industry are the exclusive public with a stake in the matter. Why dilute survey results by counting the opinions of those for whom the issues have few or no consequences? To be sure, defining the public too broadly is remediable. Groups with little or no interest at stake can always be distinguished in the analysis and presentation of findings or subtracted from the final count, although failures to make such crucial distinctions do occur. The more common problem is a too restrictive definition of the public, irremediable since those excluded from the start can never be given any weight in the results.

U.S. surveys redefine the public as adults living within the United States, since there is no feasible way to sample and measure the opinions of U.S. citizens living all over the world. Similarly, most surveys redefine the public as adults living in private households because it is difficult to gain access to and collect data from those residing in institutions— nursing homes, college dormitories, and military barracks as well as mental hospitals and prisons. These exclusions eliminate only a small fraction of the total public and do not seriously hamper the generalizability of findings. However, two other common redefinitions of the public should be noted. Since the 1970s, many surveys in the United States are conducted completely by telephone interviewing, mainly because face-to-face interviewing has become too costly; thus the public is redefined as those living in telephone households. In the affluent United States by 1980, 96 percent of households had telephone service. However, in less affluent times or countries, such surveys would exclude most people with modest incomes as well as the poor and the homeless. In addition, only an English-language version of the questionnaire is constructed and used by interviewers in most U.S. surveys. It would be too costly and

would present serious problems of comparability to have instruments and interviewers appropriate for all U.S. foreign-language groups. Perforce, those who cannot communicate in English are excluded. In summary, the public opinion reported in many U.S. surveys in the 1980s is the opinion of noninstitutionalized, English-speaking adults living within the continental United States in telephone households, a fact usually clearly stated but neglected by uncritical readers.

After the public has been clearly defined, a sample is designed and drawn from it, ideally by procedures known as *probability sampling*, which ensures that the set of individuals designated to be measured is representative of that much larger public. If the entire sample were measured—an unlikely achievement— the results would be the same as what would be found by measuring the total public in the same way, within a determinable margin of uncertainty at a stated probability. That *sampling error* is described in reports by words such as "ninety-five chances in a hundred, the results are within a margin of plus or minus 4 percent." Samples of the type and size used currently have small sampling errors, but this is only one component of the total error that may occur. Other errors arise from the inability to complete the measurements on all the designated individuals because they refuse to participate or are not home despite repeated calls, from flaws in the measuring instruments or how they were used during the collection of data, and from the ways the raw data are processed and analyzed.

Finally, long experience and careful experiments have produced sound general principles for formulating discrete questions and designing the total questionnaire and other instruments of measurement. The characteristics of the particular public to be surveyed (their literacy, education, limits of patience, time, etc.) may require modifying standard principles, and a predetermined method for collecting the data is also a limiting factor. The present technology of telephone interviewing, for example, makes questions with pictorial materials and interviewer ratings of visual characteristics impossible. Foresight is important, and no competent surveyor waits for hindsight to learn from mistakes in design after it is too late to correct them. Hence pretests, or trials of the provisional instruments on members of the public not drawn into the sample, often lead to necessary revisions.

Both the form and the content or coverage of the instruments are essential to adequate measurement of public opinion. A questionnaire is more than a series of standardized questions in a prescribed sequence, although that is its most crucial feature. The introduction, by stating a sponsor and purpose and such safeguards as confidentiality of the information provided, serves to encourage participation, candor, and thoughtful response and to satisfy ethical canons of informed consent. Instructions are essential to clarify ambiguities and specify the conditions to be followed: "Tell me the first words that come to your mind," "Just give me your opinion," "There are no right and wrong answers." A questionnaire is not confined to questions. When administered by interviewers, it generally includes their ratings of the respondent's interest, honesty, and so on; their reports of the circumstances (e.g., others present at the time); and even their character sketch of the respondent. And a questionnaire often is not confined to a single series of questions. Several forms varying the wording or sequence of questions may be administered to equivalent subsamples to determine the effects of the instruments on the opinions elicited.

The heart of the instrument, however, contains batteries of questions on each major variable or topic, the basic principle being that reliable and comprehensive measurement requires multiple questions for each topic. The types of questions composed by ingenious investigators show almost endless variety, but two major types are usually used in combination: "closed" questions forcing respondents to answer in terms of a limited set of fixed alternatives (e.g., "Do you favor or oppose ———?"); and "open" questions permitting them to describe or explain an opinion at length in their own words (e.g., "How do you feel about ———?").

In terms of content, sophisticated surveys do not limit the questions to opinion or ATTITUDES on the particular central topic of the survey. A wide range of variables is ordinarily included to deepen understanding and explain specific opinions. Opinions on other matters might be elicited to see whether the opinion is part of a broader position or IDEOLOGY— for example, on foreign policy. The cognitive realm, knowledge and belief, would be explored to see whether the opinion is informed or based on ignorance or misperception of the situation. An opinion question measuring support of a general policy might be followed by questions on the application of the policy to concrete cases to determine the breadth or depth of the support and the meaning implied by the general public. Questions measuring various hypothesized determinants of the particular opinion might be included—for example, questions on exposure to information and influence from mass or interpersonal communication. Wise investigators often ask a set of questions on voting and political involvement to differentiate the opinions of active versus apathetic members of the public, and questions to distinguish those with interests at stake. Invariably, a set of questions, sometimes wide-ranging, on the respondent's personal characteristics—age, education, occupation, religion, and so on—is asked to distinguish

the opinions of various segments of the larger public and to suggest possible explanations for the findings. And sometimes questions seemingly unrelated to the topic are asked for the sole purpose of evaluating errors of measurement. For example, the telephone number often is obtained to call back and check whether the interviewer had conducted or faked the interview. A question about "knowing" a fictitious event or "reading" a nonexistent book might be asked to see whether the respondent is confused or posing as informed. A set of such questions might be asked to estimate the magnitude of various kinds of response errors that have been identified. In these and other ways, instruments elaborate in form and content are designed to ensure accurate and comprehensive measurement.

Collection of data. Three survey methods, dramatically different in benefits and costs, are available for collecting data: personal interviewing, telephone interviewing, and self-administered mail questionnaires used to measure dispersed publics. Mail questionnaires are the cheapest method, permit reflection but allow influence from others to intrude, preclude control over the situation of measurement, eliminate the illiterate, and normally produce the lowest response rate. Personal interviewing, the most expensive method, gives interviewers maximum opportunity to make observations, but it permits their personalities to influence respondents. Telephone interviewing (sometimes assisted by computer terminals to display the questionnaire for the interviewer and for instantaneous tabulations of answers) eliminates the poor and the hard-of-hearing, the use of pictorial questions, and ratings of observable characteristics. Other distinctive properties not mentioned here may make a method appropriate to a given problem and a special public. Surveys sometimes combine different methods—for example, telephone or letter to make appointments and encourage cooperation, and personal interview thereafter.

All methods require follow-ups to pursue those initially not available or uncooperative and to reduce the potential error from nonresponse. The reasons for refusals should always be recorded to aid in estimating the error from that loss. All interviewing methods require careful training and supervision of the staff to reduce error, increase quality, and ensure proper use of the prescribed standardized instruments. The operative questionnaire is not what is printed but what is actually asked.

Analysis of data. Before analysis can begin, raw data must be refined and processed. Free answers to open questions must be classified or coded into categories. Tabulation and quantitative analysis of the voluminous data require conversion into machine-usable form for computer processing. A prelude to or early step in analysis is the construction of *indexes,* composite measures or scores based on combining questions or indicators to provide more reliable and comprehensive description of major variables.

Descriptive analysis of public opinion involves relatively few steps. The distribution of answers on single questions and of scores on composite indexes for the total sample are estimates of the opinions of the general public (as it was redefined). The separate distributions for subgroups within the total sample are the estimated opinions of various segments of the public, such as the classes, regional blocs, racial groups, and attentive and uninterested groups that compose it. These breakdowns, depending on the background questions asked, can be myriad and based on combined characteristics. For example, working women can be distinguished from nonworking women. These estimates, of course, are subject to all the sources of error noted earlier, and the magnitude of errors of sampling, nonresponse, measurement, and so on should be noted to qualify the findings or used to make corrected or adjusted estimates. This quantitative analysis should be supplemented by qualitative analysis, the use of individual answers, interviewers' reports, and so on to illustrate and enrich the abstract statistical findings. Explanatory analysis of survey data goes many steps beyond this point and is too complex to be treated here.

The report. The end point of the institution of public opinion measurement is the communication of findings to scientific audiences, mass audiences, and political elites. Therefore, a responsible report, appropriate for the particular audience and medium and containing the information on procedures specified by the standards of the associations for public opinion research, is the final stage and the fulfillment of the research.

See also POLL.

Bibliography. Richard W. Boyd and Herbert H. Hyman, "Survey Research," in *Handbook of Political Science,* Vol. 7, Reading, Mass., 1975; W. Edwards Deming, "Sample Surveys: The Field," in *International Encyclopedia of the Social Sciences,* Vol. 13, New York, 1968 ed.; Frederick W. Frey, Peter Stephenson, and Katherine Archer Smith, eds., *Survey Research on Comparative Social Change: A Bibliography,* Cambridge, Mass., 1969; Robert M. Groves and Robert L. Kahn, *Surveys by Telephone: A National Comparison with Personal Interviews,* New York, 1979; Stanley L. Payne, *The Art of Asking Questions,* Princeton, N.J., 1951; Morris Rosenberg, *The Logic of Survey Analysis,* New York, 1968; Howard Schuman and Stanley Presser, *Questions and Answers in Attitude Surveys: Experiments on Question Form, Wording, and Context,* New York, 1981; Judith M. Tanur, "Methods for Large-Scale Surveys and Experiments," in *Sociological Methodology, 1983–84,* San Francisco, 1983.

HERBERT H. HYMAN

ORAL CULTURE

A CULTURE without WRITING. Many of the standard comparisons between oral and literate cultures are flawed because the role of writing is misrepresented. Writing does not supplant oral communication; it is merely another channel of communication, substituting for the oral only in certain contexts but at the same time developing new ones. It is the same with the new electronic media; they are only substitutes for oral and written communication in certain contexts and are always dependent on them, just as writing is dependent on the oral use of LANGUAGE, which remains the primary means of human communication. *See also* LITERACY.

Issues in the Analysis of Oral, Literate, and Mixed Cultures

It is very important to distinguish between societies (or cultures) with and without writing and also between the written and oral traditions in societies with writing. Oral communication in societies with writing is not the same as it is in those without it. In the latter the oral tradition has to bear all the burden of cultural transmission. In literate societies, however, the oral tradition is vested with only part of the total body of literary activity, of standardized verbal forms. The café songs from Novi Pazar collected by Milman Parry and Albert Lord in the 1930s in Yugoslavia and the "fairy" stories of the European countryside collected by the Grimm brothers in nineteenth-century Germany formed part of popular culture, which was supplemented by printed romances and other works that were linked to the literacy-based manifestations of high culture that emanated from the towns (*see* ROMANCE, THE). And while these oral aspects of popular culture may be related formally to the oral productions of nonliterate societies, both their role and their content have clearly undergone important changes. From the standpoint of the total society, their role is now subordinate to those of written origin, although they are differently valued by different social groups and at different points in the life cycle. For example, religious practices and beliefs in literate cultures are based largely on scriptures and mediated by literate priests, so what is left in the oral tradition tends to be "magic" rather than "RELIGION," the peripheral rather than the core. In other words, the content of the oral tradition tends to be marginalized.

In addition to distinguishing between oral and literate cultures and between the role of oral and literate traditions in societies with writing, we must also distinguish among literate, nonliterate, and illiterate individuals. In some literate complex societies there are subgroups whose members communicate only in SPEECH. Comparisons between these subcultures and oral cultures in the fuller sense have to be made with great caution. A nonliterate is not the same as an illiterate, though they may have various attributes in common.

The notion of an oral tradition is very loose. In a nonliterate society the oral tradition consists of everything handed down (and ipso facto created) through the oral channel—in other words, virtually the whole of culture itself. In a society with writing both the literate and oral traditions are necessarily partial. Moreover, elements of the oral tradition, like folktales, inevitably get written down, whereas elements of the written tradition are often communicated orally, like the Indian Vedas. The fact that a sonnet is learned orally in school does not make it an oral production. From the standpoint of composition, even literate works are composed at least partially in the head—orally—before being written down. In other words, the interface continues to be of great significance. Bible stories, for example, become part of what is communicated orally between parent and child, even in societies or groups lacking a literate tradition but in contact with ones that have such a tradition.

The word *tradition*—a handing over, in the wide sense of intergenerational communication, indirect as well as direct—implies some notion of quasi-continuity, albeit if only over a single generation. The word is used in a more limited way to cover the literary tradition or its oral counterpart consisting of the FOLKTALE, legend, SONG, RIDDLE, and PROVERB—what are sometimes called *standardized oral forms* to avoid some of the possibly distorting ambiguities of using the term *literature* (i.e., to do with letters). No hard-and-fast line can be drawn between the verbal art forms of societies with and without writing, but certain genres such as the novel (or in music the symphony) are clearly products of the former alone. *See* GENRE.

Not only do the genres differ, but some of them change characteristics depending on whether they are oral or written. A written work necessarily has a fixed text, but an oral composition may be added to or subtracted from at any time and by different people. The notion of unity, so often mentioned in LITERARY CRITICISM, is much less useful in examining an oral product. What one hears on a particular occasion is less likely to be the product of a single human mind at a single point in time than is a literary work. The notion of the individual signature at the bottom of the canvas is out of place when the mural has been touched and retouched by numerous hands in the course of its preparation. *See also* AUTHORSHIP.

There is a danger here of falling into earlier errors of romantically inclined nineteenth-century scholars who contrasted the communal composition of ballads with the individual creation of lyric POETRY. The contrast is false, like other applications of this dichotomy; in this case it confuses composition, PERFORMANCE, and transmission. In oral societies each performance of a long poem such as the Bagre of the LoDagaa of northern Ghana reshapes the work and provides a new model for future versions, because performance is transmission. The process of composition, in the sense of the original act of creation, is impossible to reconstruct for lack of evidence or lack of relevance. On the other hand, it is in principle feasible to see how an individual has constructed his or her own performances, which tend to resemble one another more closely than versions by different performers. Individuals contribute, some being more creative than others, but their signatures rarely remain for long because of the very nature of oral transmission over time.

A further version of this fallacy recognizes the extent of variation but sees it as variation on an ideal or underlying version. For example, influenced by structuralist approaches, Robert Kellogg suggests that whereas written literature establishes communication between the minds of author and reader, the constant behind oral artistic activity is "an ideal performance, an aspect of tradition shared by performer and audience alike." He gives as an example of an oral work the Mwindo Epic of Zaire, which exists as an unperformed and very long and detailed ideal. This and similar contentions represent a misapplication of the idea of a deep structure and share the same difficulties as those that view oral literature as emerging from the spirit of the folk by common authorship. While it is clear that in oral societies individuals play a different role with regard to verbal performances, we must not introduce the idea of unanalyzable processes or mechanisms to account for the differences. *See* STRUCTURALISM.

Characteristics of Oral Cultures

What are the characteristics of an oral culture, as distinct from an oral subculture, or from an oral tradition in a society with writing? First, from the standpoint of communication, all interaction effectively takes place in face-to-face situations, a fact that gives a special importance to the individual who communicates information (*see* INTERACTION, FACE-TO-FACE). It is true that in literate societies the schoolteacher also holds a unique position as a transmitter of information, at least for children. But the "authority" behind the teacher lies ultimately in the BOOK, and intelligent, inquiring students soon learn to consult the LIBRARY directly. The teacher then becomes significant for the explanations of, commentaries on, and additions to the knowledge stored on the written page. In oral cultures all is stored in the heads of the adults, so the one who has seen most and lived longest remains a major source of knowledge. The elders have to be respected for this reason alone; they are irreplaceable storehouses of information about the past, that is, about the culture and traditions of the community. Such is true only in a limited sense of societies with writing.

Second, the fact that virtually the only store of information lies in human memories means that it is always susceptible to selective forgetting and remembering. There are, of course, techniques for preserving special kinds of information. But, unless deliberately directed, memory bends to other interests, tending to set aside what does not fit. This feature of oral storage and transmission contributes to the relatively homogeneous character of such cultures, in which uncomfortable dissonances tend to be forgotten while memory works with those experiences that link well with others.

As a result, many individual inventions or personal doubts tend to be either set aside or incorporated into the culture as if they had always been there. For example, innovations are a constant feature of religious activity, partly because of its creative complexity, partly because its solutions to practical problems of health and disease, of life and death, are always inadequate. The god who failed is replaced by a new creation or one imported from outside. Some of these creations are tried and rejected, others live on, producing a changing constellation that normally offers the appearance, to itself and to others, of a fixed tradition.

To the participants the tradition may be regarded as "the same," just as the versions of the Bagre are regarded by many as "the same." To interpret such statements as indications that each performance, each RITUAL, is a deviation from a disembodied ideal or that a hidden continuity lies at the level of deep structure has little justification in practice or theory. Variations occur, some of them leading to significant change; otherwise how would one account for the extraordinary variety of oral cultures in relatively small areas, such as Papua New Guinea? Some changes may be disregarded deliberately and some unintentionally; the determination of verbal sameness is often difficult. Since the long Bagre recitation of the LoDagaa has been written down, literate members of this society are able to perceive that the written version differs from current versions. This first written version has been invested with the authority of the ancestors, who recited it, giving rise to the notion of an orthodox version from which others have strayed. But it might equally be argued that in an oral culture the "genuine" version is the one produced by one's contemporaries—not the oldest but the youngest—because then the influence of present interests rather than past concerns will be reflected.

In the same way that change tends to get swallowed up by the nature of oral memory and the mode of oral transmission, so too do doubt and skepticism. Members of oral cultures do doubt from time to time the validity of their gods, their rituals, their premises. But only when these are written down does a real tradition of criticism emerge, a tradition that builds on itself. The generation of incredulity—disbelief—is partly a matter of placing alternative versions side by side, of recording systematically the outcomes of predictions, of perceiving in visual form the ambiguities of oracles. In oral cultures the slate tends to be wiped clean at every generation, maintaining the appearance of homogeneity of belief, of total attachment to cultural values.

Education, Social Relations, and Other Social Institutions

Part of the process of transmission between generations is what we call EDUCATION, referring to the deliberate act of TEACHING the young. In literate cultures the process is fairly formal and usually takes place in separate organizations: schools, colleges, and universities. In oral cultures, learning is inevitably a more contextualized process, taking place "on the job" rather than in a special setting. In formal schooling verbal accounts of acts and beliefs are little used compared with their written equivalents; reliance on the written word, in any case, permits a more abstract, more generalized, more analytical approach. Oral learning entails a greater amount of showing, of participation. Hence the world of childhood is less segregated from that of adults. Children sit or play when discussions and performances are taking place, absorbing at least the general atmosphere of these activities and occasionally, if they listen attentively, some of their content as well. Much more learning takes place publicly, since verbal communication depends on the voice, on face-to-face interaction. Whereas in literate cultures an individual can go off alone with a book, in oral cultures another partner is needed as narrator or instructor. Partly for this reason, the act of being alone, communicating to oneself, is sometimes regarded with some suspicion in oral cultures, possibly as a prelude to some malicious action such as witchcraft or sorcery. Solitary activities such as eating alone may take on a negative value; in this sense an individual's right to privacy is not necessarily prized because the interactive nature of human life is more immediately apparent to everyone.

In other words, what ÉMILE DURKHEIM saw as the mechanical solidarity of simpler societies is not only a matter of the division of labor. Social relations and values have to be upheld more obviously in face-to-face situations; there is no possible recourse to a text as an external source of guidance. It is the same with the very meaning of words. Semantic properties are validated in interaction; past meanings cannot be revived by historical etymology; that which is not carried in memory has disappeared for good. The restriction of linguistic communication to the oral channel accounts for some of those features that are commonly regarded as characteristic of the "primitive mentality." The greater concreteness and relative lack of abstraction must be linked to the dominance of the context of the interactive situation. Inhibitions are placed on the elaboration of general rules, which are more often implicit than explicit. In the terminology developed by sociologists MAX WEBER and Talcott Parsons, such societies tend to be particularistic rather than universalistic.

Social institutions are much affected by a limitation to the oral channel. Religions tend to have a more local focus, to be more clearly intertwined with everyday life. Legal transactions are less governed by general laws, by formal procedures. Precedent will rarely play a distinct part in lawmaking because recent judgments constitute the practice of the law itself. There are no written formulations that have outlived their usefulness to provide an embarrassing relic for the judge to modify and the legislature to undo by formal resolution. The homeostatic tendencies of memory usually consign to oblivion what is no longer wanted. Being limited to oral communication in the political field obviously restricts the buildup of bureaucratic government. While it does not prevent the rise of states, the relationship between the center and the periphery is likely to remain a weak link in the chain of messages. Both internal communication and central accounting can operate by adding mnemonic devices to oral storage, but the more complex the organization of the state and the economy, the greater the pressure toward a graphic representation of speech.

See also HUMOR; INSULT; MUSIC, FOLK AND TRADITIONAL; ORAL POETRY; SPEAKING, ETHNOGRAPHY OF.

Bibliography. Ruth H. Finnegan, *Oral Literature in Africa,* Oxford, 1970; Jack Goody, *The Myth of the Bagre,* Oxford, 1972; Jack Goody and S. W. D. K. Gandah, eds., *Une récitation du Bagré,* Paris, 1980; Robert Kellogg, "Oral Literature," *New Literary History* 5 (1973): 55–66; Albert Lord, *The Singer of Tales,* Cambridge, Mass., 1960, reprint 1981.

JACK GOODY

ORAL HISTORY

Essentially an account of firsthand experience, recalled retrospectively and communicated to an interviewer for historical purposes. Most practitioners would also argue that the interview should be recorded on a system of reproducible sound, thus preserving the spoken word as the original historical source. Oral history is a methodology, not a historical subfield such as political, economic, or social history. In its modern form it dates from the late 1940s, when tape recorders facilitated the collection and preservation of oral communications, but it had a number of precursors.

Forerunners

At least since the time of the ancient Greeks, historians have asked participants in past events to communicate their memories as part of the historical record. Although these accounts exist only as documents, many historians accept them as early oral history because they had the clear historical purpose of collecting information that did not exist outside the living memories of participants in the events. An interest in FOLKLORE was part of nineteenth-century romantic nationalism; numerous folk song and folklore groups were formed in Europe and North America. The purpose of these groups was to document and study the traditional and mainly rural societies that had been, or were being, replaced by industrial and urban societies. An interest in music and spoken lore prompted the recording of informants' recollections (*see also* MUSIC, FOLK AND TRADITIONAL). Similar retrospective evidence can also be found in the publications of early journalistic, sociological, and government inquiries into social and industrial conditions.

Most of these early reports were in the form of written transcripts, but by the end of the nineteenth century actual sound recording became possible and practical. The cylinder phonograph, which recorded sound on wax cylinders, was marketed widely and was used by anthropologists, folklorists, and ethnomusicologists to record recollections and songs that previously had to be laboriously transcribed on paper (*see also* SOUND RECORDING—HISTORY).

All these precursors of modern oral history had two things in common: informants related personal experiences, and informants were usually ordinary people, particularly working class, ethnic minorities, and underprivileged. This gave oral history a prime locus in those classes and groups in society that, although part of a literate society and even literate themselves, did not leave much documentary evidence of their own creation. If documented at all, they appear through the eyes of their middle-class and upper-class contemporaries. Relative economic, social, and political power affects the access particular groups have to the production and the preservation of documentary sources of all types. The oral communication of remembered experience can be used to shed new light on events that were distorted by contemporary social prejudice or by political CEN-SORSHIP. Giving a voice to the voiceless was a strong impulse in the development of oral history.

Modern Oral History

Given its precursors, it is rather ironic that modern oral history started in 1948 at Columbia University with historian Allan Nevins (1890–1971) recording "significant" Americans. This concern with prominent figures was outside the tradition of the American Folklore Society, the Chicago School of sociologists, and the Federal Writers' Project, which, as with early European work, was most interested in the experience of ordinary people. Nevins wanted to use oral history to supplement a dearth of personal documentation. Prominent people in the twentieth century wrote fewer diaries, letters, and so forth than their nineteenth-century counterparts (*see* DIARY; LETTER). Initially the oral communication was seen merely as a way to produce a document. Although modern American oral history started as a study of elites, it soon returned to its roots and spread in the 1960s as a record of nonelite groups. And although elite groups are still researched, the study of nonelites is now central to oral history throughout the world.

In its present form oral history allows historians to collect data that will illuminate particular subjects or groups about which too little information has survived from other sources. It is an ideal method for studying the recent past of unorganized workers, domestic life, ATTITUDES and IDEOLOGY at the grass roots, the experience of childhood, or indeed any historical dimension of the recent past that can be explored through lived experience. In Europe, for example, it is now virtually the only method of fully exploring the many underground struggles against fascism, because these were by definition clandestine and documented only by their opponents. The method is particularly strong in areas in which life is routine and fixed. Those most skeptical of oral history have been historians and biographers of elites. It has been argued that important figures can be too intent on concealing their mistakes and misjudgments and may be too experienced in avoiding the truth to be good subjects for interview methodology of any description. Nevertheless, even here the advantage of the voice for capturing atmosphere and the quality of relationships, particularly personal ones, is generally acknowledged.

Methodological Issues

Part of the methodological strength of oral history is that the source of the information is known. Also, any relationships between different aspects of experience—for example, between religion and politics, or social and industrial attitudes—are known and certain because it is the unified experience of one individual. The large numbers of cases necessary to establish such relationships by statistical induction are not required. But accounts do remain individual, and there must be some concern with the degree to which informants' lives are typical of their time and social location if generalizations are to be made on the basis of oral evidence. Although a BIOGRAPHY or life history can illuminate the wider history of the time, it is possible for it to stand alone as a study of an individual's development and psychology. History, however, is about social processes, so oral history must be concerned with using individual experiences as one type of evidence in establishing a wider account. As with all historical evidence, it is most illuminating when integrated with other sources. Nevertheless, the most popular disseminators of oral history have been authors (for example, Studs Terkel in the United States) who publish interview extracts with very little comment and little attempt to synthesize the various experiences into a historical account. This approach can be part of a radical/democratic impulse to allow ordinary people to speak with their own voices and not to have their experiences interpreted by another. But the result can be quite conservative: history is presented as a series of self-directing, individual lives without examination of the economic and social processes that shaped them. Individual experience can provide only a partial account of historical change; a great deal of power is exercised beyond the individual at the level of groups and institutions.

The value of retrospective oral evidence is entirely dependent on the accuracy of memory. Psychologists appear to know very little about how the process of remembering the past works or how accurately individuals can recall the previous events of their lives. Most oral historians operate on the commonsense notion that people do remember their pasts with greater or lesser accuracy in different contexts; practical experience has demonstrated to them that useful knowledge can be collected by retrospective interviewing. They are acutely aware of the problems of omission, suppression, and selectivity that may favor a recall of memories of pleasant rather than unpleasant aspects of life. Similar biases can be introduced by life-cycle factors. In basing, for example, descriptions of family history on accounts of the childhoods of elderly informants, one must be aware that it is a child's-eye view of the period. Many children are unaware of the domestic worries, conflicts, and stresses that must have been experienced by adults of the period. Careful interviewing and informed practice can, however, go a long way toward counteracting these potential pitfalls.

Many oral historians feel that oral history interviews have to be recorded and those records preserved as the original source. Some feel that type-scripts made from the recording contain all the historical information in the recording, but this is disputable. If the recording is erased, there is no proof that the transcription is a full one. A more fundamental objection is that typescripts, however accurate, are not oral. Oral communication is different in kind from written sources; it is richer in communicative power, containing as it does inflections, hesitations, expressions, and nuances that are not easily reproduced in written form. Both the oral and the aural qualities of the historical source may be thought of as part of its distinguishing feature. To accept this final point would, of course, rule out as full oral history any sources predating the mechanical reproduction of sound from wax cylinders—a rigorous position not all oral historians would share.

Oral History and Oral Tradition

It would be artificial to draw too firm a line between oral history and oral tradition, but there are differences. Many nonliterate societies have special remembrancers and storytellers who are the living repositories of all that is known or mythologized of their history. This material presents different problems of authenticity. In going beyond living memory and relying on information that has been transmitted orally from generation to generation and is not part of the direct, lived experience of the communicator, collectors of oral traditions work with data of a different quality from that of direct experience. Such information requires a different methodology for its evaluation and authentication.

See also AUTOBIOGRAPHY; ORAL CULTURE; PERFORMANCE.

Bibliography. Daniel Bertaux, ed., *Biography and Society: The Life History Approach in the Social Sciences,* Beverly Hills, Calif., 1981; David Henige, *Oral Historiography,* London and New York, 1982; *International Journal of Oral History,* Westport, Conn., 1980–; Trevor Lummis, *Occupation and Society,* Cambridge and New York, 1985; Ulric Neisser, ed., *Memory Observed: Remembering in Natural Contexts,* San Francisco, 1982; *Oral History,* The Journal of the Oral History Society, Colchester, Eng., 1972– (now includes *Life Stories/Récits de vie,* Colchester, Eng., and Paris, 1985–); Studs Terkel, *Hard Times,* New York, 1970; Paul Thompson, *The Voice of the Past,* Oxford and New York, 1978.

TREVOR LUMMIS

ORAL POETRY

Poems that are unwritten either because the cultures in which they occur are partially or wholly nonliterate (like the traditional native cultures of Africa, Australia, Oceania, and America) or because oral forms are cherished despite a population's overall LITERACY. The exact scope of the term is disputed, but it usually also includes POETRY originally composed and performed orally that has reached us through written transmission, like some of the early epics. Some scholars also include poetry transmitted or performed by nonwritten media, such as broadcast performances or modern pop lyrics.

Oral poetry takes many forms. Oral epics are widely found, particularly in Eurasia, from historic cases like the early Babylonian, Greek, and Indian epics to the later Finnish Kalevala and contemporary or near contemporary Asian examples like Kirghiz or Mongol narrative poetry or the modern Indian Pabuji epic. Ballads—shorter or more lyrical narratives—are particularly associated with Euro-American tradition but are found in arguably comparable form in various areas of the world. Panegyric odes are highly developed in Africa and Oceania, while short lyrics seem to be common everywhere, usually as words set to music, among them love lyrics, dancing and drinking songs, topical verse, war songs, laments, and lullabies (*see also* MUSIC, FOLK AND TRADITIONAL; SONG). Some forms do not fit easily into established Western genres: the great Australian Aboriginal song cycles; Polynesian mythological chants; verse set in prose NARRATIVE; dialogue verse; and short forms like spells, curses (*see* INSULT), street cries, or counting-out rhymes.

For a long time oral poetry was considered inferior, partly because of the Western emphasis on WRITING, partly through the various stereotypes that linked orality with "primitive" stages of development or, alternatively, glamorized it by romantic associations with nature or the "folk." Its study has also suffered by being split among a number of disciplines, each with its own preoccupations and interests. By the 1970s and 1980s it had partly emerged as a subject in its own right, relying on both historical analysis and contemporary field study. Oral poetry is a traditional form of literary expression widely distributed through the world and is now recognized as one important form of human communication.

Composition and Transmission

The genesis and distribution of oral poems have often seemed puzzling because of Western preconceptions about writing as the natural way to formulate and transmit literary compositions. However, much is now known about the processes by which poems are orally composed and communicated.

One process is prior composition followed by transmission through memorization. This was once the favored explanation for all oral poetry, supported by such varied examples as nursery rhymes, English ballads surviving in the Appalachian Mountains, or the Indian Vedic literature, all known (or claimed) to have come down over centuries. Changes in the text over time were explained by faulty memory. This view was also bolstered by a cluster of ideas that postulated communal or folk composition of oral items followed by long transmission through undifferentiated and uncreative "oral tradition." This generalized model has been queried recently for several reasons: reactions against earlier evolutionist and romanticist assumptions, evidence that memorized transmission is not as well established or widespread as once appeared, and, above all, the discovery of another oral process known as oral-formulaic composition.

The oral-formulaic process depends on creation by the performer during the act of PERFORMANCE. Results from the classic research carried out on Yugoslav traditional narrative poetry in the 1930s showed that oral versions even of "the same" narrative differed extensively because poets varied and, in a sense, improvised their performances according to their own interests and skills and the demands of a particular occasion. What was transmitted was not memorized texts at all but a stock of formulas at every level (from part-lines and sequences right up to major incidents, themes, and narrative patterns) on which poets drew for their own creative performances. This was a truly oral mode of composition-in-performance in which, unlike written texts, there was no concept of a correct version. Each performance was unique and authentic in its own right.

The elucidation of this oral-formulaic process had an immense effect on studies of comparable—or arguably comparable—oral forms throughout the world. Similar approaches have been applied to, for example, Chinese lyric poetry, Xhosa panegyrics, English ballads, Sumatran narrative songs, and blues and chanted sermons in the American South. Oral-formulaic composition has also been detected in historic texts, from ancient Greek and Indian epics to the early English Beowulf, Old Testament poetry, Hittite epics, and a range of medieval European poetry. By the 1960s and 1970s this form of composition was accepted as the typical process underlying traditional narrative oral poems, or even behind all oral poetry.

More recently some scholars have argued that, though the oral-formulaic process is indeed common (particularly in lengthy narrative verse), it cannot be assumed to be the only compositional process. Examples of long-considered composition followed by memorized performance have been found in, for example, Africa, Oceania, and native America. Such prior oral composition by reflective individuals working on their own, or in some cases in twos or threes, and separated from the occasion of actual performance contrasts with the composition-in-performance

of the oral-formulaic mode. In other cases composition and transmission and/or performance are split between different agents, or collective performance (as in choral singing) imposes a degree of textual fixity on the joint performers. Such examples have not necessarily displaced the oral-formulaic mode as one important form but have led to further questions about the variety of ways in which composition, transmission, and performance are related in the oral poetic traditions of differing cultures and genres.

Formal Features

Oral poems are not typographically distinguished from PROSE as in written literature, nor is the distinction always made clear in local languages. Many formal features characterize oral poetic forms and signify the artistic (rather than, as once supposed, merely "natural") properties of oral poetry.

First among these are prosodic systems. These are not always based on strict meter, though metrical patternings based on stress or quantity occur in some oral poems (chiefly in the European tradition); in some Asian poetry metrical patternings are based on syllable counting. Other prosodic features may perform much the same function as meter, among them alliteration, assonance, or end assonance (rhyme)—a controversial feature possibly more characteristic of European traditions but also found in, for example, Malay quatrains, medieval Chinese ballads, or Fijian heroic poems. Tone rhyme is a less usual feature but arguably occurs in tonal languages such as Chinese, Burmese, or Yoruba in which tonal patterning may be one of the formal poetic devices particularly effective in oral performance.

Parallelism is another important structural device, a type of repetition with variation in meaning or structure. This is a familiar form in biblical poetry ("Praise him with the sound of the trumpet/praise him with the psaltery and harp" in Psalm 150, for example); in Toda and Navajo poetry or the elaborate South African panegyrics, parallelism is one of the most significant prosodic features. Many subvarieties of parallelism have been distinguished, as well as variations such as chiasmus (cross-parallelism), deliberate change in word order in one of a series of parallel lines, and linking or chain parallelism. In other cases again, parallelism marks larger units such as verses or—a common form—question-and-answer sections in parallel format. The device is so widespread in oral poems that some consider it a characteristic feature of oral poetry.

The language of oral poetry is often distinguished from everyday speech, sometimes to such an extent that poets go through special training to acquire it, as with some Polynesian poetry or West African divination verse. Figurative language is also common, although its form and incidence vary among genres as well as cultures. It is popular in epic and panegyric; in southern Bantu poems, for instance, the hero is figured as a lion, leopard, storm, whirlwind. Metaphorical expression may underlie the whole structure of a poem, as with many of the overtly "nature" poems in the Polynesian tradition or the "miniature" Somali or Malay lyrics—highly condensed imagery that would surprise those who assume that oral poems must be simple. The complexity is also often heightened by music that sometimes forms one essential element of the poem as well as one of the local criteria for genre differentiation.

These formal features, along with local poetic canons and terminologies, are often taken as indicators of whether a particular case should be classified as poetry. That this is still problematic comes out in well-documented claims that some American Indian narratives are poetry and not, as once assumed, prose and controversies about African epics that turn partly on whether certain forms are prose or poetry (*see also* ETHNOPOETICS).

Whether there is a specifically oral style is another controversy. Some argue that the stress on parallelism, formulas, and perhaps repetition constitutes a defining quality of oral formulation, sometimes linking this with the composer's need to create without writing and the audience's need to understand even without having a text to study. Views about "primitive mentality" or the supposed resistance to change in oral culture are also sometimes drawn on here. Others argue against the existence of any one oral style, pointing to the variation in oral poetry among genres, cultures, and local expectations of audience reactions as well as the interaction and overlap between oral and written forms.

Modes and Contexts of Presentation

Oral poems are more than just texts, for they rely essentially on performance for their realization. The main modes of delivery are the singing, intoning, and spoken voice of one or more performers, sometimes supplemented by instrumental accompaniment. There are also specialized forms such as African drum poetry, in which words are communicated through percussion or wind instruments. It must be stressed here that performance forms an essential rather than (as in the Western written model) a merely contingent part of the oral poem itself.

The audience for oral poems is an essential element as well. There are occasional instances of solitary poetic delivery, but most oral presentations have audiences, who sometimes themselves take an active part in the performance. Thus some oral poems are performed jointly by a participatory group, particu-

larly in work and dance songs and some political and religious poems. Sometimes two groups alternate, taking turns as audience and performer, as with the interchange between relatives of the bride and those of the groom at weddings. In other cases performer and audience roles are completely separate, with the audience only influencing indirectly by its presence and behavior, as with 1930s Yugoslav heroic songs or nineteenth-century Kirghiz recitals. Between these two extremes are many variants in the roles of performer and audience: the exchange between leader and chorus typical of African lyrics; alternating performances by two individuals in Eskimo poetic duels or Polynesian song competitions; the differentiation between primary and secondary audiences when a poem is overtly directed to one party but known to be overheard by others; and a whole range of other variants, not least among them (if we take the widest sense of oral poetry) the distant yet in a sense personal relation between radio or television performer and audience.

The same variety applies to contexts for performance. Contrary to some assumptions, oral poetry is not always equally accessible to all members of a society or necessarily delivered in public. Cultural conventions determine both to whom particular poetic genres should be delivered and by whom. Some is court poetry composed and delivered mainly for the elite, some for specific groups like West African hunting or military societies' songs, some for just men or just women (as performers or audience or both) or particular age groups.

There are also conventions about the appropriate occasions for oral poetry. These vary according to local cultural conventions, but common ones include social occasions when people are relaxing and free of work (perhaps the most common settings for lengthy and specialized verse); work contexts in which poetry (often with music) accompanies such tasks as hoeing, paddling, grinding, or rocking a baby; religious rituals; and the celebration of recognized ceremonial points such as harvest, enthronement, initiation, marriage, or death.

Functions

Given the variety of contexts for oral poems, generalizations about their functions can be misleading. It used to be assumed that the function of oral literature was to uphold the status quo, socialize children into ancestral morals and wisdom, and generally inhibit change. This is sometimes one element, not least in the praise poetry for the powerful, but there are also poems that express rebellion, put pressure on authority, or encourage change. Political and protest songs are common, and even panegyrics sometimes subtly admonish as well as praise. Oral poetry can also play religious, ceremonial, artistic, and recreational roles for both individuals and wider groups. Indeed, the range of purposes for which it can be used is, like communication itself, almost infinite: to express hostility or love, intensify or resolve disputes, delight, scandalize, distance, worship, heal, innovate, conserve, add solemnity to public occasions, or clothe imagination in beautiful words. Much often depends on the actual occasion and the intentions of audience or performer. A poem can be used in one context to convey one message, in another (or in another listener's ears) for something quite different—a facet well exploited in political poetry. Nor is the element of individual expression by the poet lacking, as is revealed in the many intense love and mourning poems and the lengthy and carefully wrought personal poetry among, for example, the Eskimo, Somali, or Gilbertese.

Future Study

There are many continuing controversies and lines of possible development in the study of oral poetry. Some analysts concentrate on the oral-formulaic approach, stress the insights of ethnopoetics, or explore such approaches as linguistic or structuralist analysis, each with its own implications about the definition as well as the interpretation of oral poetry. Others disagree about the relative attention to be paid to performance as against text or whether to differentiate traditional or folk from other forms or the feasibility of taking a wide definition of oral in order to include both the many cases of overlap with written forms and the modern and arguably oral forms distributed and performed through electronic media. These and similar arguments will no doubt continue, but it can at least be concluded that the older generalizing assumptions about the "artless," "communal," or "primitive" nature of oral poetry can now be rejected, and oral poetry can be treated seriously as one of the long-established and still continuing forms of literary expression and communication.

See also ETHNOMUSICOLOGY; ORAL CULTURE; SPEECH PLAY.

Bibliography. Ruth Finnegan, Oral Poetry: Its Nature, Significance and Social Context, Cambridge, 1977; idem, ed., A World Treasury of Oral Poetry, Bloomington, Ind., 1978; A. T. Hatto, ed., Traditions of Heroic and Epic Poetry, London, 1980; Dell Hymes, "In Vain I Tried to Tell You": Essays in Native American Ethnopoetics, Philadelphia, 1981; Albert Lord, The Singer of Tales, 1960, reprint Cambridge, Mass., 1981; Felix J. Oinas, ed., Heroic Epic and Saga: An Introduction to the World's Great Folk Epics, Bloomington, Ind., 1978; Isidore Okpewho, The Epic in Africa: Towards a Poetics of the Oral Performance, New York, 1979; Jeff Opland, Xhosa Oral Poetry: Aspects of a Black South African Tradition, Cambridge, 1983; Jerome Rothenberg, ed., Technicians of the Sacred: A Range of Poetries from Africa, America, Asia and Oceania, New York, 1968; Dennis Tedlock, Finding the Center: Narrative Poetry of the Zuni Indians, New York, 1972, reprint Lincoln, Neb., 1978; Willard R. Trask, ed., The Unwritten Song: Poetry of the Primitive and Traditional Peoples of the World, 2 vols., New York, 1966.

RUTH FINNEGAN

ORATORY

The art of using SPEECH effectively in addressing an audience within political, legal, ceremonial, or religious settings. In the Western tradition of Greek and Roman RHETORIC, oratory is strongly associated with PUBLIC SPEAKING in political and legal settings, and it is defined as the art of getting the audience to take a particular perspective and eventually to accept the speaker's position or resolution on a particular issue (see HELLENIC WORLD; ROMAN EMPIRE). In the anthropological and linguistic literature, oratory also refers to the skillful PERFORMANCE of particular speech genres within ceremonial or magico-religious settings, such as curing sessions, initiation rites, weddings, and funerals. In these contexts the orator's task may include one or more from a variety of functions that range from interpretation of the occasion to creation of a context in which psychological, social, or even physical change can be said to occur. See also HOMILETICS; RELIGION; SPEAKING, ETHNOGRAPHY OF.

Characteristics and Contexts

The LANGUAGE of oratory is usually distinct from other ways of speaking in the same speech community. Oratorical speech tends to make more concentrated use of PROVERB, METAPHOR, parallelism, and repetition than is typically found in most everyday talk. It is, however, difficult if not impossible to predict in any speech community which specific linguistic features will characterize oratorical speech vis-à-vis other verbal genres (see GENRE). Although it is usually possible to distinguish between the language of oratory and that of CONVERSATION, other distinctions are problematic without an understanding of the relationship between oratory and other areas of verbal art, such as POETRY, verbal dueling, singing, and THEATER, within the same community (see INSULT; SONG). In fact, in some cases this very distinction may be questionable, given the interdependence of some of these genres in many communities around the world. Furthermore, despite the expectations of participants in a given social event regarding what constitutes oratorical language, individual performers often achieve fame by successfully mixing features from more than one genre (e.g., archaic formulas and jokes). Such controlled violations of the audience's expectations can help establish a particular atmosphere that the performer can then exploit for needed theatrical effects. *See also* DRAMA—PERFORMANCE.

The nature of the social activity in which oratory is used also affects both the actual form and content of oratorical speeches and their interpretation by the participants in the event. It is quite common, in fact, for a reflexive relationship to develop between oratory and the social event in which it is performed: the event is defined by the language used, whereas the language is said to be interpreted in light of the larger ongoing activity.

The Work of Orators

Like any other form of communication in any community, oratory is always tied to a tradition that both gives it MEANING and offers a background against which new values and new forms of expression can be tried. The most well-known and respected orators tend to be those individuals who establish a relationship with their audiences by addressing current concerns while at the same time displaying an impressive knowledge of the tradition (e.g., historical facts, myths, proverbs, metaphorical expressions).

For any orator the ability to communicate with an audience is not measured by linguistic skills alone. Knowledge of the appropriate linguistic repertoire and its organization in coherent units of talk must be accompanied by knowledge of effective paralinguistic features (e.g., voice quality, volume, tempo, pauses, and prolonged silence). Furthermore, culturally and situationally appropriate nonlinguistic behaviors, such as body posture, GESTURE, eye gaze, and FACIAL EXPRESSION, must accompany a speaker's verbal performance (*see* BODY MOVEMENT; EYES; FACE). The importance of such nonverbal expertise in a public speaker has long been recognized in the Western tradition of rhetoric, as documented by the special term, *actio,* given by the Romans to the nonlinguistic behavior that was supposed to accompany any public address. The introduction of modern mass media such as film or television can highlight certain aspects of nonlinguistic behavior (for example, facial expression) that could not be detected easily in a public performance in front of a large crowd. *See also* NONVERBAL COMMUNICATION.

Nature of Oratorical Speech

A tradition of oratory has been found in many different types of socioeconomic systems. Oratory has been documented among both so-called hierarchical and egalitarian societies. Societies vary, however, in terms of how they see the relationship between oratory and power.

Oratory and power. In many communities, such as the ancient Greeks, the Maori of New Zealand, and the Kuna of San Blas (Panama), oratorical ability is considered the entry point into politics, and the skills necessary for publicly addressing an audience are defined as directly linked to the exercise of power. In societies such as Bali and Samoa, however, powerful figures delegate others to speak for them in public, thus retaining the privilege of saving face or in some cases contradicting their spokespersons. Where this complementary model is adopted, such as in Tikopian political meetings (*fono*), the relationship between the chief and his spokesman is a complex one, in which the spokesman may take public blame and lose face on behalf of the chief but will then expect political and economic support from the chief on other occasions. *See also* POLITICAL COMMUNICATION.

The definition of oratory as the art of making any political or judicial decision acceptable to a given audience has been criticized by those social and cultural anthropologists who question the very ability of talk to affect social processes. In particular, the typically formalized and formulaic nature of oratorical speech has been cited as a means of so restricting an individual's choices that it is very difficult to do anything other than reaffirm or celebrate the existing social order. This perspective goes hand in hand with a deterministic view of the relationship between sociocultural context and talk, with the former always affecting the latter but not the reverse.

Oratory as action. Detailed studies of language use in a variety of cultural settings have instead stressed the dialogical, if not dialectical, relationship between speech and its social context. These studies have confirmed that in particular social settings people have to work out conflicts and to achieve an understanding of their own polity through speech. This view originated from an appreciation of words as deeds and not just labels for an already taken-for-granted reality. Many anthropologists, linguists, and folklorists are convinced that the action-producing force of oratorical speeches is also quite common to other uses of language. In particular, participants in conversation routinely employ a range of techniques to ensure preferred interpretations of what they are saying and to establish common ground and alignments with their addressees. It is thus quite common for speakers in all kinds of situations to try to get their audiences to see the world through their eyes, to get others to follow or at least to approve of their conduct. There may be little uniqueness, then, in the orator's use of language to win a case or to be elected, to celebrate the past and to make it relevant to the present, to play with words and to teach, to create the very context in which a distant or unlikely reality becomes the here and now (see SPEECH PLAY). All of these functions and contexts are in fact part of the inherent multifunctionality of speaking. Why in only some cases these activities would be glossed as oratory by either the participants or the observers is what future research must explain in reconsidering oratory as a universal category.

See also FORENSICS; ORAL CULTURE; PERSUASION.

Bibliography. Roger D. Abrahams, *The Man-of-Words in the West Indies*, Baltimore, Md., 1983; Richard Bauman, *Let Your Words Be Few: Symbolism of Speaking and Silence among Seventeenth-Century Quakers*, Cambridge, 1983; Maurice Bloch, *Political Language and Oratory in Traditional Society*, London and New York, 1975; Donald L. Brenneis and Fred R. Myers, eds., *Dangerous Words: Language and Politics in the Pacific*, New York, 1984; Alessandro Duranti, *The Samoan Fono: A Sociolinguistic Study*, Canberra, Australia, 1981; Laurence Goldman, *Talk Never Dies: The Language of Huli Disputes*, London, 1983; Gary H. Gossen, *Chamulas in the World of the Sun: Time and Space in a Maya Oral Tradition*, Cambridge, Mass., 1974, reprint Prospect Heights, Ill., 1984; Robert Paine, ed., *Politically Speaking: Cross-cultural Studies of Rhetoric*, Philadelphia, 1981; Joel Sherzer, *Kuna Ways of Speaking: An Ethnographic Perspective*, Austin, Tex., 1983.

ALESSANDRO DURANTI

ORGANIZATIONAL COMMUNICATION

The domain of human communication study and practice concerned with relations between communication phenomena and the functioning of those collectivities known as organizations. The field began to take shape in the late 1940s.

Approaches

Historically, specialists in the field have debated whether communication is a central component of the process of organizing or merely one of a number of variables affecting the ways in which an organization functions. Some theorists have proposed that *communicating* and *organizing* are virtually synonymous terms.

Indeed, as early as 1938 it was the businessman-turned-theorist Chester I. Barnard who declared in his classic treatise *The Functions of the Executive:* "In an exhaustive theory of organization, communication would occupy a central place. . . ." A more definitive statement appeared in 1951 when Alex Bavelas and Dermot Barrett, social scientists at the Massachusetts Institute of Technology, argued that communication, rather than being a "secondary or derived aspect of organization," should be regarded as "the essence of organized activity" and the most basic process to be studied if one is to understand organizational phenomena. This view was supported by such other communication scholars as Lee Thayer in the 1960s, Leonard Hawes in the 1970s, and Phillip K. Tompkins in the 1980s. Most behavioral scientists, however, have perceived communication as an independent, dependent, or intervening variable alongside other variables, such as organizational structure, technology, leadership style, working conditions, motivation, and the like. Communication specialists during the 1950s and 1960s tended to follow this trend as they examined the relationships between communication behaviors and such variables as job satisfaction, employee morale, group decision making, absenteeism, attitudes toward supervisors, and various indicators of productivity.

The view that puts communication at the center of organizational dynamics is still being challenged. However, the general premises underlying this position have become sufficiently influential that researchers are inclined to qualify carefully their use of the conventional constructs of organization theory: upward-downward-lateral, internal versus external, formal versus informal, tall versus flat, span of control, group decision making, performance appraisal, management by objectives, supervisory leadership, and so on.

Issues

Although in theory it would be fruitful to apply the concepts of organizational communication to the study of such entities as the family or the bowling club, virtually all systematic research in the field has been focused on formally designated and formally structured collectivities: business firms, government agencies, the army, voluntary associations, labor unions, religious organizations, academic institutions, and so on. This means that such aggregates as concert audiences, street-corner crowds, mobs, bus passengers, and spectators at athletic contests are customarily perceived as lying outside the purview of organizational communication. However, even though formal organizations have almost always provided the context of research, a major concern has been the innumerable ways in which informal (i.e., unofficial) groups and subunits within the larger, formal entity originate, function, and exercise influence on the formal organization. Indeed, the formal/informal dichotomy has been a persistent research theme. It can be applied not only to groups and channels but also to media (e.g., formal written reports versus conversations on the golf course), message formats (e.g., typed letters on official letterhead versus handwritten notes on scratch paper), and messages themselves (e.g., official pronouncements versus rumors).

In addition to the formal/informal distinction, there is also the troublesome internal versus external dichotomy. Traditionally the academic study of organizational communication has focused on the so-called internal phenomena, those communication events and behaviors thought to take place within the boundaries of an organization. This posture typically has resulted in the exclusion from study of such subjects as PUBLIC RELATIONS, ADVERTISING, and public affairs on the grounds that they belong under external communication. In the 1980s scholars were being urged to avoid such rigid compartmentalization and to recognize the artificiality of the external/internal dichotomy. Unfortunately most textbook definitions of organizational communication have continued to reflect the concentration on so-called internal phenomena, and research studies have continued to be framed within this traditional context.

Criterial Attributes of Organizations Used in Research

Organization theorists have found it difficult to define any universal set of attributes characterizing all organizations. However, it has been possible to identify a limited number of characteristics found in almost all *complex* organizations. One way to define a large, complex organization is to describe it as being of such size that it is no longer possible for all members to communicate, at any desired time and face to face, with all the other members. Within this framework scholars have perceived the following attributes as inherent in complex (especially large) organizations and have defined their research problems accordingly.

Interdependence. Whether an organization is defined in terms of human beings or of activities, the members or "units" are related in such a manner that no single component is a completely free agent. According to the general systems paradigm (dominant in the field during the 1960s and thereafter), any change in one part of the organization will produce changes in other parts. Reciprocity and circularity of causal chains must therefore be expected when examining so-called causes and effects of communication in an organizational context. For example, investigators have considered whether being informed leads to higher productivity in employees, whether more productive employees are ones who seek out more information, or whether a self-accelerating positive (response-enhancing) feedback loop is being enacted.

Differentiation of tasks and functions; division of labor. Under this heading fall such phenomena as specialization (of jobs, skills, knowledge, etc.), departmentalization (based on purpose, technology, location, etc.), and line versus staff distinctions. The classic account of specialization is Scottish economist Adam Smith's description of a pin factory in *Wealth of Nations* (1776). Functional differentiation is one of the basic forces behind the creation of various groups within the organization, some official (formal) and many more unofficial (informal): work groups, task forces, interest groups, committees, coalitions, cliques, leagues, and so on. Communication researchers have investigated such topics as semantic barriers, intergroup rivalries, and group dynamics as corollaries of the differentiation principle.

Goal orientation or purposiveness. No organization is a random aggregate of persons and activities. Although any organization exhibits a multiplicity of goals—including frequent conflicts between officially espoused objectives and goals being pursued by various subunits—and although goals are commonly stated in vague or ambiguous terms, all organized activity is in some sense purposive. The formulation, statement, and dissemination of goals represent important research problems in organizational communication.

Control mechanisms: hierarchy of status and authority. No coordination of effort can be accomplished without some sort of centralization; this means a minimum of two hierarchical levels. Many organizations are tall, pyramidal structures featuring layer upon layer of supervisors and managers; others are described as flat. Tall structures imply short spans of control; flat structures imply broad spans of control (span of control is, of course, a communication construct). The fact of hierarchy is not nullified by various power-sharing or delegation schemes, such as matrix structures, temporary task groups, labor-management teams, and the like. Even when work groups select their own supervisors on a rotating basis, such supervisors—while they occupy the position—still exercise hierarchical authority.

If one were to designate a single area in this field as the most intensively researched, it would almost surely be superior-subordinate (or management-employee) communication—the so-called vertical dimension. This orientation has accounted especially for a substantial corpus of research dealing with a wide range of topics subsumable under the rubric *communication climate*. A review of the climate literature shows the research findings largely clustered under five major dimensions, each hypothesized as contributing to organizational effectiveness: (1) a "supportive" style of supervisory/managerial leadership; (2) the use of participative decision making; (3) high levels of trust, confidence, and credibility (applicable in a reciprocal sense in both vertical and horizontal channels); (4) openness and candor, with particular focus on "upward" and "downward" communication; and (5) emphasis on high performance goals.

Control mechanisms: plans, policies, regulations, rules, premises, and role prescriptions. Whereas hierarchical controls are associated with persons exercising directive powers, these other forms of control gain their force by being incorporated into the basic structure of the organizational culture. Every member of an organization has at least one position or role, and much of his or her behavior (especially communication) is governed by the expectations and prescriptions attached to these roles. In other words, organizational members are ipso facto agents of the organization, and their communication behavior can reflect this fact.

Categories of Organizational Theory

Just as researchers have used different definitions of organization, so they have also used different theories of the organization to guide their work. To some extent the model chosen influences the categories of topics that are studied and the research techniques that are used.

The received model. The five criterial attributes described above represent basic premises of what may be called the received model of organizational functioning. It is grounded in the assumption that an organization is essentially a control system designed to increase the predictability of results. Subsumed under this model are two variants. The first is characterized by a focal concern for *control, productivity,* and *efficiency,* and the second by a focal concern for *human relations, human resources,* and *participation* (but all in a control frame of reference).

Investigators associated with the first variant typically study such phenomena as "information adequacy" (who receives what information, from what sources, at what times, with what effects); fidelity and distortion in message transmission; mass media (e.g., employee magazines); downward, upward, and horizontal channels; and communication skills. Those associated with the second variant have dealt with such topics as supervisory/managerial styles of communication (especially supportive versus nonsupportive); job satisfaction, "communication satisfaction," and morale; conflict resolution, including management-union BARGAINING; trust and confidence; and openness, including two-way feedback, reciprocity, self-disclosure, and candor.

Network analysis. Another research tradition in organizational communication incorporates some elements from both variants of the received model but also adds an important frame of reference: general systems theory (including its close relatives, INFORMATION THEORY and CYBERNETICS). This tra-

dition is identified with the study of *communication networks.* Concepts typically encountered in NETWORK ANALYSIS include unofficial versus official (i.e., organization chart) channels; patterns of centralization versus decentralization (centrality and peripherality); one-way versus reciprocated channels; network roles, such as liaisons, isolates, and bridges; and the creation of cliques. Network specialists stress the study of relationships rather than psychological variables; their vocabulary features terms like *input, throughput, output,* and *feedback loops.*

Political framework. This approach represents a radical departure from both variants of the received model and from network analysis. It posits the organization as a *political* entity—politics taken in the fundamental sense of the manipulation of power. Theorists adopting this view take a special interest, for example, in groups striving to gain power; hence they are concerned with coalitions and power tactics, including especially intergroup negotiation.

Interpretive or cultural paradigm. This approach, which emerged during the early 1980s, draws heavily on anthropological concepts and methods. Its central concerns are with symbolism, LANGUAGE, socially constructed reality, and shared meanings. Hence investigators commonly deal with such phenomena as RITUAL, METAPHOR, stories, myths, and ideologies.

The study of organizational communication has continued to be marked by contrasts. Many texts used in the field are written by managers, staff specialists, corporate editors, and others, who often focus on solutions to practical problems, such as how to conduct an interview or how to motivate subordinates. At the other extreme are academicians emphasizing theory and research. Their studies typically utilize constructs derived from organization theory and the social sciences, combined with concepts commonly regarded as components of communication theory. The 1970s and 1980s have also seen the rise of critics who argue that traditional concepts of organization theory have seriously crippled attempts to understand communication in organizations. Especially since the early 1970s the volume of research has grown dramatically. But it is clear that the field is far from finding consensus around a central, defined body of knowledge.

See also GROUP COMMUNICATION.

Bibliography. Carroll C. Arnold and John Waite Bowers, eds., *Handbook of Rhetorical and Communication Theory,* Boston, 1984; Samuel B. Bacharach and Edward J. Lawler, *Power and Politics in Organizations,* San Francisco, 1980; Chester I. Barnard, *The Functions of the Executive,* Cambridge, Mass., 1938; Marvin D. Dunnette, ed., *Handbook of Industrial and Organizational Psychology,* Chicago, 1976; Howard H. Greenbaum, Raymond L. Falcione, and Susan Hellweg, eds., *Organizational Communication: Ab-*

stracts, Analysis, and Overview, Vol. 9, Beverly Hills, Calif., 1984; Louis R. Pondy, Peter J. Frost, Gareth Morgan, and Thomas C. Dandridge, eds., *Organizational Symbolism,* Greenwich, Conn., 1983; Linda L. Putnam and Michael E. Pacanowsky, eds., *Communication and Organizations: An Interpretive Approach,* Beverly Hills, Calif., 1983; W. Charles Redding, *Communication within the Organization,* New York and West Lafayette, Ind., 1972; Everett M. Rogers and D. Lawrence Kincaid, *Communication Networks,* New York and London, 1981; Edgar H. Schein, *Organizational Culture and Leadership,* San Francisco, 1985; Lee Thayer, *Communication and Communication Systems,* Homewood, Ill., 1968.

W. CHARLES REDDING

OSGOOD, CHARLES (1916–)

U.S. psychologist whose writings—especially *The Measurement of Meaning* (1957) and *The Cross-Cultural Universals of Affective Meaning* (1975)—brought new insight into the meaning of MEANING and shed light on both the nature and the mechanism of human LANGUAGE behavior. Born in Somerville, Massachusetts, Charles Egerton Osgood received an A.B. from Dartmouth College in 1939, a Ph.D. from Yale University in 1945, and a D.Sc. from Dartmouth in 1962. He served as director of both the Institute of Communications Research and the Center for Advanced Study at the University of Illinois. He is widely known as a distinguished psycholinguist, cross-cultural psychologist, and critic of nuclear diplomacy by the superpowers. His reputation reflects the three interests that developed during his undergraduate days at Dartmouth and have continued throughout his life, with roughly equal emphasis: (1) psycholinguistic research and theory, (2) cross-cultural research on affective meaning and attribution of feelings, and (3) psychosocial dynamics and the prospects for humanity.

Osgood is most often associated with his work on the measurement of meaning and the SEMANTIC DIFFERENTIAL method. He assumed that meanings of words are mediated internal reactions to objects of judgment that can vary consistently in a limited but still unknown number of dimensions. Building on these assumptions, he developed a psychological theory of meaning that he named "affective meaning" and constructed a psychological measuring instrument termed "semantic differential" with which affective meanings can be quantitatively measured and analyzed. A typical semantic differential consists of both a set of concepts to be judged and a set of bipolar seven-point scales on which meanings of the concepts are rated. Each scale is defined by two qualifiers having opposite lexical meaning, such as good and bad, large and small, fast and slow. Subjects rate each concept on a set of bipolar scales, and

the generated "cube" of data is submitted to a statistical analysis, for which the logical-mathematical tool is factor analysis. Using the factor-analytic method, Osgood discovered that three dimensions, or factors, keep appearing, with a number of scales almost always loading high on the same factor, "clinging" to one another. This proved true despite differences in sex, age, culture, and language of subjects. Osgood named the three most salient factors *evaluation,* represented by such scales as good-bad and beautiful-ugly; *potency,* represented by such scales as strong-weak and large-small; and *activity,* represented by such scales as fast-slow and active-passive.

Osgood called this multidimensional structure of meanings a "semantic space" and showed that meanings of concepts can be allocated in such a semantic space along the evaluation, potency, and activity dimensions. In extensive cross-cultural field research in more than twenty countries Osgood and his colleagues were able to demonstrate the cross-cultural universality of such semantic spaces, or the generality of "affective meaning systems," according to which people judge various concepts. In general, Osgood's work on affective meaning systems profoundly altered the traditional, mentalistic views of meaning. Although his particular conceptualization of meaning is still subject to challenge, his continued cross-cultural work has provided evidence that meanings can be viewed as an important psychological process playing a central role in human language behavior and, most important, that the "structure" of meaning systems is universal to all humans (*see* LÉVI-STRAUSS, CLAUDE).

Osgood is also widely known as a pioneering psycholinguist. His contributions in this area, both theoretical and empirical, are often associated with his modeling of an intrapersonal communication process. In order to elucidate the complexity of human language behavior, Osgood developed a multistage model of human information processing, following CLAUDE SHANNON's contribution to INFORMATION THEORY. Osgood posited four basic stages in this model, each stage corresponding to a particular type of information processing in humans: *sensory recoding* (perceiving), *decoding* (interpreting), *encoding* (intending to act), and *motor recoding* (responding). According to Osgood's model, meanings of signs (*see* SIGN) are considered to be a psychological phenomenon that mediates decoding (input) and encoding (output). Meanings of a particular sign are thus taken at once as an internal response at the destination of information to the brain and as an internal, mediated stimulus at the source of information from the brain. Any overt response to the given sign is elicited by the internally mediated stimulus. This shorthand model of human information processing has proved useful for describing a decision-making process in groups as well as in individuals. For example, U.S. political scientist Robert North derived a model for internation foreign policy decision making from Osgood's psycholinguistic model.

Osgood's devotion to the study of human communications, coupled with his deep personal concern for humanity in the nuclear age, led him to develop a psychopolitical theory to provide a way for both the United States and the Soviet Union to step down their nuclear arms escalation. In *An Alternative to War or Surrender* (1962) he named this psychopolitical theory GRIT (graduated reciprocation in tension-reduction). Although the GRIT theory was originally intended to avoid a major nuclear war between the two superpowers, its applicability has proved so universal that it has been borrowed by scholars in other disciplines as well—by political scientists dealing with the dynamics of domestic as well as international conflict and the strategy for its resolution and by sociologists and psychologists coping with the pathology of and cures for serious disputes in family, racial, labor, and other interpersonal and intergroup relations.

YASUMASA TANAKA

OZU, YASUJIRŌ (1903–1963)

Japanese film director. Yasujirō Ozu was the creator of fifty-four films (of which thirty-two remain extant) devoted almost entirely to the GENRE the Japanese call home drama. Considered in Japan "too Japanese" for export, his films were for a long time little known to audiences elsewhere. But the minuteness and subtlety with which he examined the conflicts of the home eventually won him worldwide attention and honors. The ordinary home drama wanted only a little smile, a few tears, and a warm feeling on leaving the theater. Ozu desentimentalized the genre, stirring deep emotion, real smiles, real tears. The problems of the Ozu home drama are always pertinent and important: the tensions created by the old and the new, loving clashes between the generations. Ozu's pictures were always about the FAMILY (or the Japanese family surrogates, the SCHOOL and the office), but they show this family in dissolution. Ozu is the poet of social transition.

At a time (roughly the two decades following World War II) when the Japanese audience wished itself to be shown as it was rather than as it wished to be, the films of Ozu were very popular. He reflected his audience's dilemma, faced with both new and old, and suggested (in a manner exasperating to some, inspiring to others) that one could have sympathy with both. This postwar audience did not know it was viewing high art—Ozu being an artist whose art hides art—but viewers recognized their own lives. Once a new affluence arrived and the old ways vanished, a new generation found Ozu old-fashioned. Yet succeeding generations find in these films a wonderful lost world and discover a precision of observation, an economy of means, that has made Ozu something of a cult figure for contemporary filmgoers in Japan and elsewhere.

Just as Ozu limited what he showed, so he limited how he showed it (*see* FILM EDITING). The celebrated Ozu style (invariable camera placement; almost invariable camera immobility; the straight cut as the only cinematic punctuation; a typical and invariable method of construction in which, for example, sequences are separated by "placing" shots; a very controlled use of film space) is based on limitation. What is shown is what is necessary.

This extreme economy is the frame, as it were, that sets off the Ozu character, who emerges all the more human because of his or her "geometrical" setting. Given Ozu's genius for characterization, the father in *Banshun* (Late Spring, 1949), the daughter-in-law in *Tokyo monogatari* (Tokyo Story, 1953), and the mother in *Hitori musuko* (The Only Son, 1936) remain unforgettable. These people are not controlled by plot; rather, they seem controlled by life. Ozu disliked plot and said that to "use" people in this way was to "misuse" them.

Within the extraordinary economies of the Ozu film (each filmed in the same way, all with similar stories and similar titles, often using the same actors) one finds a freedom rare in cinema. As in other forms of art, it is the restriction that in part creates this flowering.

See also MOTION PICTURES—SOUND FILM.

Bibliography. Donald Richie, *Ozu*, Berkeley, Calif., and London, 1974.

DONALD RICHIE

P (pī), the sixteenth letter of the alphabet in English and other modern languages, was the fifteenth in the ancient Roman alphabet, corresponding in position and value to the Greek *pi*, π, Π, earlier Γ, Γ, originally written from right to left ⊓, and identical with the Phœnician and general Semitic *pi*, forms of which were ⌐, ⊓. During its whole known history the letter has represented the same consonantal sound. . . .

PALEY, WILLIAM (1901–)

U.S. broadcasting executive. William Paley, the son of a wealthy cigar manufacturer, purchased a small and shaky RADIO chain in 1928 and transformed it, through more than a half-century of explosive growth and complex technological change, into a major communications empire. When he bought it the chain was less than two years old, had had several names and owners, and had consistently lost money. One of the short-term owners, the Columbia Phonograph Record Company, had given it the name "Columbia." Paley took it over at a moment when it could not meet its forty-thousand-dollar bill from AT&T for cable connections. Always a shrewd, imaginative negotiator, Paley persuaded Paramount to become a 49 percent owner of the Columbia Broadcasting System (CBS) and to help him challenge the MONOPOLY position of the National Broadcasting Company (NBC), which had been founded in 1926. A few years later, when Paramount was in trouble and CBS was not, Paley bought back the Paramount interest. During the 1930s he persuaded stations throughout the country to become affiliates of the network, in part by offering them free programs in exchange for rights to broadcast CBS's commercially sponsored shows at specified hours. The affiliates gained programs too expensive to be produced locally, and CBS could promise advertisers a national audience during peak hours.

Though NBC remained dominant in audience ratings (see RATING SYSTEMS: RADIO AND TELEVISION) until the late 1940s, when Paley lured away some of its most popular entertainers, including Jack Benny and "Amos 'n' Andy," CBS garnered wide praise for its offerings in music, radio drama (e.g., Norman Corwin, ORSON WELLES), and especially the news. CBS's Edward R. Murrow, a widely respected journalist, vivified the European war for U.S. audiences in the 1940s and helped expose the excesses of Senator Joseph McCarthy in the 1950s.

Yet CBS was not without its controversies. McCarthyism influenced talent selection there as at other networks; QUIZ SHOW scandals eroded public faith; Murrow lost favor with his bosses and found himself interviewing celebrities. CBS nevertheless held public favor with enormously successful shows ranging from "I Love Lucy" in the 1950s to "All in the Family" in the 1970s.

As CBS consolidated its successful expansion into television and a variety of other profitable ventures, Paley continued to delegate significant authority without relinquishing control over the entire operation. In the 1970s the holdings included a major recording subsidiary, publishing ventures, a toymaker, and several companies that manufactured musical instruments. In 1978 CBS registered sales of more than $3 billion, a tribute in part to the business skills and political instincts of its presiding officer. Paley remained an offstage force even after he reluctantly retired. His career spanned more than fifty years of media history, an era commemorated in the Museum of Broadcasting, an institution he helped found and finance.

See also SPONSOR; TELEVISION HISTORY; TELEVISION NEWS.

D. L. LEMAHIEU

PALIMPSEST

Parchment manuscript from which the writing has been removed so that the surface can be reused. The term is from the Greek for "scrape again." Parchment, among the most durable of WRITING MATERIALS, could stand up under repeated scrapings and was costly enough to encourage the practice. It apparently began in the first century C.E. and continued through the MIDDLE AGES. In the process writings no longer considered important were obliterated— or partly so—to make way for other writings. It has been of interest to historians that removals were seldom perfect; traces of earlier writings could often be discerned and could sometimes be made legible by chemical or optical means. In some cases historians found the unsuccessfully obliterated material more interesting than the superimposed writing. The removals also gave some insight into historical shifts in interests and values.

The term *palimpsest* has been taken over in the art field for a canvas or panel on which a painting has been painted over another painting. Again tech-

Figure 1. *(Palimpsest)* An example of a palimpsest. M. 786, f.4v. The Pierpont Morgan Library, New York.

nical procedures, such as X rays, can often make the underlying material visible. These techniques hold special interest and financial importance when, for example, a work ascribed to the seventeenth-century Dutch artist Frans Hals is found to have underneath it a portrait of Queen Victoria. *See* FORGERY, ART.

WILBUR SCHRAMM

PAMPHLET

A nonserial publication, written for a general audience and not originally intended for permanent preservation. The pamphlet has rarely been studied as a medium of communication in its own right, partly because of the difficulty of distinguishing it from other genres of printed material such as books and broadsides (*see* BOOK). The lack of a precise definition is reflected in the numerous synonyms used interchangeably to describe such publications: brochure, tract, libel, booklet, and so on. Many definitions have limited the term to unbound works of a certain length, generally not more than one hundred pages, while others stress the essentially ephemeral nature of the pamphlet rather than its size. The term is most commonly applied to polemical publications, intended to persuade readers and rouse them to action, but it is sometimes also used for informational works meant to be disposed of after use, such as the leaflets given out by organizations like the U.S. Department of Agriculture. The difficulties in defining what is meant by a pamphlet make it equally difficult to measure the number that have been printed over the centuries, or even in distinct periods such as the French Revolution.

The term *pamphlet* was used as early as 1344 to refer to short manuscript works, but with the invention of PRINTING it became restricted to published texts. Wars and political controversies inspired early pamphlets. The Protestant Reformation was the first great social upheaval in which pamphlets played a central role; within a few years of MARTIN LUTHER's denunciation of indulgences thousands of titles had appeared. The pamphlet remained the leading medium for religious and political controversies throughout the next three centuries. Events such as the Thirty Years' War, the English Revolution, the wars of Louis XIV, and the American Revolution all occasioned floods of pamphlet literature, and the French Revolution inspired what was probably the greatest outpouring of all.

With that REVOLUTION and its destruction of traditional CENSORSHIP systems, however, the pamphlet found itself outstripped by a rival medium, the periodical. Newspapers and magazines, which could create a continuing bond with their readers and which offered publishers a much better chance of recovering their expenses, came to overshadow pam-

phlets in the Western world during the nineteenth century (*see* MAGAZINE; NEWSPAPER: HISTORY). Even so, the number of pamphlet publications remained substantial. In an analysis published in 1796 the French revolutionary politician Pierre-Louis Roederer explained the pamphlet's decline by noting that its impact was explosive but generally short-lived, in contrast to the more continuous and predictable impact of the periodical and the slow, unpredictable, but sometimes very durable effect of books. This punctual impact became one of the pamphlet's handicaps. Increasingly, success in political controversies depended on being able to keep one's troops together over a long period of time, and the periodical served this purpose much more effectively. As formal constitutional safeguards permitted wider uses of the periodical in most Western countries, the polemical pamphlet declined in significance. The distinction between pamphlets and other media became blurred, too, as it became more common for pamphlets to be nothing more than a collection of reprinted newspaper or magazine articles.

Even as the polemical pamphlet gradually sank from sight, the informational pamphlet continued to appear in large numbers. Some, such as the short tracts published by the Methodists and other religious movements, were produced by private groups; others were put out by government ministries and agencies. In the twentieth century commercial enterprises issued many publications that can be considered informational pamphlets. In addition to publicizing ideas, advice, or products to the general public, pamphlets in the modern world often serve to maintain internal communication within large organizations. Thus the pamphlet versions of the works of KARL MARX, V. I. Lenin, and Mao Zedong distributed to members of radical groups during the 1960s functioned to maintain ideological consensus within the group rather than to spread the gospel to outsiders.

Although pamphlets have often been interpreted as direct expressions of PUBLIC OPINION, in fact they have normally been the products of professional writers and probably served more to mold and manipulate opinion than to represent it. Pamphlet authors have included many of the great writers of the past five centuries, such as Luther, JOHN MILTON, Jonathan Swift, Voltaire, and Marx, as well as agitators who produced pamphlets almost exclusively, such as Thomas Paine and the Abbé Sieyès. Not all pamphlet texts originated as written works; many were transcriptions of sermons or political speeches. Many pamphlets are anonymous or pseudonymous, and in any event, even when written by celebrated authors, pamphlets often reflected the views of organized parties or interest groups more than those of the individuals who put the words on paper; they were rarely the direct result of a heartfelt individual impulse for expression. A few pamphlets, such as Swift's *A Modest Proposal,* have achieved the status of literature in their own right, but the vast majority have been forgotten once the controversy that inspired them ended.

In every age the essence of the pamphlet was to be easily readable, so that its message could be communicated to as wide an audience as possible. Pamphlet language was normally clear and simple, eschewing obscure words and complex ideas, although pamphlets have always been influenced by the literary style of their day (*see* STYLE, LITERARY). Thus seventeenth-century German pamphlets against Louis XIV imitated the baroque literary style of the period, while Paine employed a simpler, more direct language characteristic of the American world of his day. Pamphlet language was often freer than that employed in other media. The rhetorical violence of Luther's Reformation pamphlets is well known, and the scandalous *libelles* that helped undermine the French monarchy in the eighteenth century used obscenity to discredit high-ranking political figures like Marie-Antoinette. Some pamphlets of the premodern era employed woodcuts or engravings to illustrate their message, but more typically they lacked illustrations and such common features of books as tables

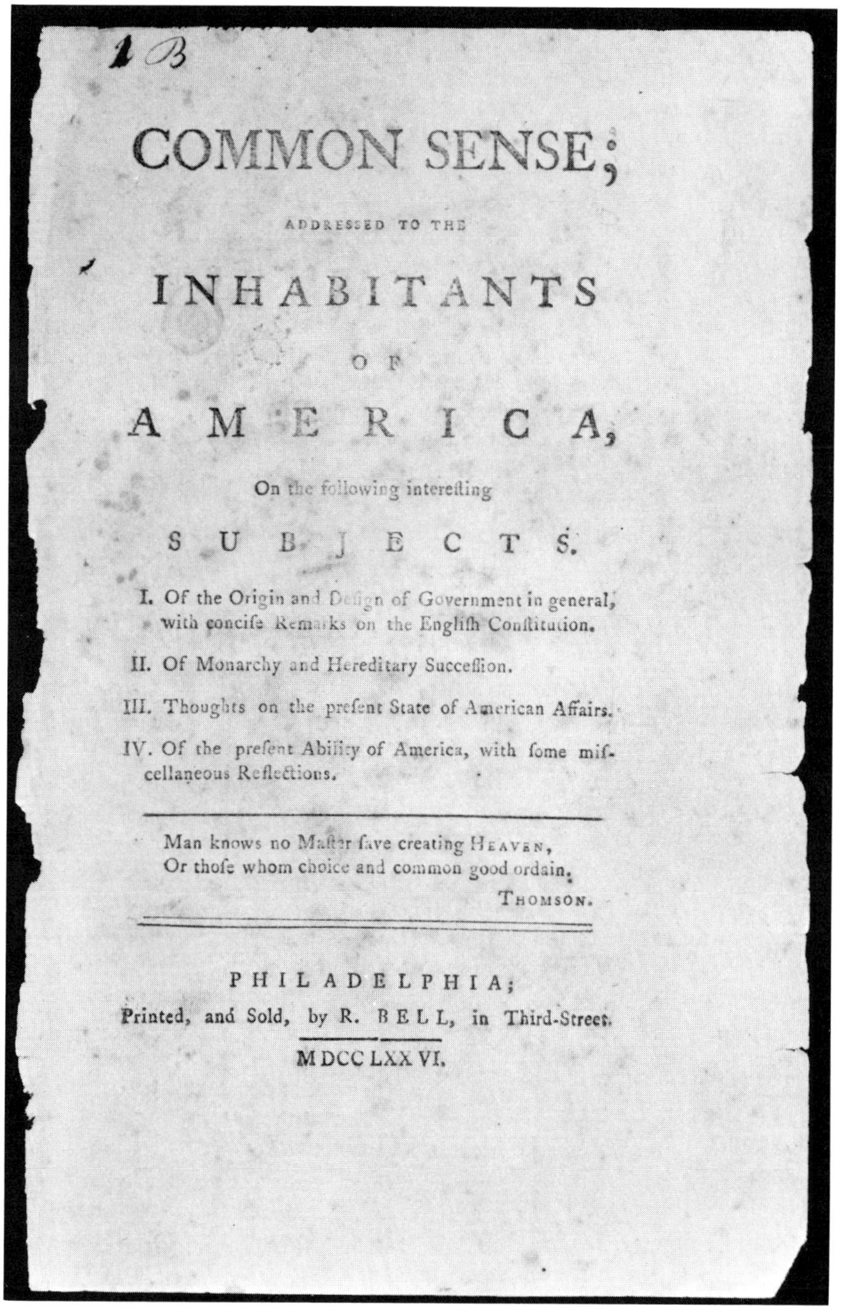

COMMON SENSE;

ADDRESSED TO THE

INHABITANTS

OF

AMERICA,

On the following intereſting

SUBJECTS.

I. Of the Origin and Deſign of Government in general, with conciſe Remarks on the Engliſh Conſtitution.

II. Of Monarchy and Hereditary Succeſſion.

III. Thoughts on the preſent State of American Affairs.

IV. Of the preſent Ability of America, with ſome miſcellaneous Reflections.

Man knows no Maſter ſave creating HEAVEN,
Or thoſe whom choice and common good ordain.
THOMSON.

PHILADELPHIA;
Printed, and Sold, by R. BELL, in Third-Street.
MDCCLXXVI.

Figure 1. *(Pamphlet)* Thomas Paine, title page of *Common Sense,* 1776. American Philosophical Society Library, Philadelphia.

of contents and indexes. Modern informational pamphlets, benefiting from more sophisticated printing technology, are more likely to have such features.

Production of pamphlets has never required special printing technology; any publisher capable of putting out books, magazines, or ordinary job printing has been capable of printing pamphlets. In view of their direct connection with current events, polemical pamphlets were ordinarily printed in haste, with little concern for typographical exactitude or style. Up to 1800, when mechanically powered presses began to replace the wooden handpress, print runs of pamphlets rarely exceeded two or three thousand copies, but a successful pamphlet would be reprinted in multiple editions, often in cities far removed from its place of origin. Pamphlets might be distributed by booksellers or by itinerant vendors or colporteurs who specialized in the dissemination of these easily transportable works. The authors and publishers of polemical pamphlets were normally more concerned with getting their message across than with making a commercial profit. Pamphlets, often subsidized by interested parties, were frequently given away, or, if they were sold, the distributor rather than the publisher often kept the money.

Pamphlets, as George Orwell noted in an essay on the subject, were uniquely suited to the conditions of Europe in the early modern period, when systems of censorship restricted writers' freedom without really abolishing it as in modern totalitarian systems. Easy to produce, pamphlets were hard to control, whereas periodical publications were compelled to offer readers some clue about the publisher's location so that they could subscribe for future numbers and were therefore easier for government officials to supervise. Despite formal censorship restrictions, pamphlets actually circulated fairly freely in most of the Western world in the centuries before 1800; indeed, many ostensibly clandestine publications actually had tacit permission to circulate or were even produced with government assistance.

Historians have credited specific pamphlets or waves of pamphlet literature with considerable impact on a number of movements, primarily in the early modern period. Luther and other Protestant pamphleteers presented their theological ideas in clear, simple language in their short works, making them accessible to a broad audience, and Paine's *Common Sense* decisively changed the nature of the debate about the goals of the American Revolution. But recent historical research has underlined the fact that pamphlets do not act in a vacuum; their success depends on appealing to favorable predispositions in their audience and on reinforcement through direct social contacts.

Although pamphlets are by their nature ephemeral literature, intended to be discarded when the context in which they were written has changed or when the information they purvey is no longer relevant to the individual reader, they have attracted collectors from early times, as the massive holdings of major research libraries, some of them assembled as early as the seventeenth century, demonstrate. Pamphlet literature has posed major challenges of cataloging and preservation for librarians, who have been virtually the only group to study and write about the GENRE systematically. Catalogs of major pamphlet collections, such as Knuttel's guide to the Dutch pamphlets in the Royal Library of The Hague or the Martin and Walter index to the Bibliothèque Nationale's French revolutionary pamphlet holdings, have been both triumphs of bibliographic industry and invaluable research tools for historians. Librarians have been acutely aware of the difficulty of staying abreast of current pamphlet literature, however. In contrast to books and periodicals, the vast flood of informational pamphlets that continue to appear in modern societies is almost impossible to trace; they constitute a virtually unnoticed and unstudied medium of communication.

Although often ignored in communications studies since World War II—the term does not even appear in the indexes of most U.S. mass communications textbooks—the pamphlet genre has proved adaptable enough to remain in existence from JOHANNES GUTENBERG's day to the present. While their present-day impact is difficult to measure, pamphlets remain a significant presence on the communications scene.

See also ARCHIVES; COPYRIGHT; GOVERNMENT REGULATION; LIBRARY; LITERACY; NEWSLETTER; PROPAGANDA; PUBLISHING.

Bibliography. Bernard Bailyn, *Ideological Origins of the American Revolution*, Cambridge, Mass., 1967; Lester Condit, *A Pamphlet about Pamphlets*, Chicago, 1939; Erich Everth, *Die Oeffentlichkeit in der Aussenpolitik*, Jena, 1931; Christian Jouhaud, *Les Mazarinades*, Paris, 1985; H. J. Kohler, ed., *Flugschriften als Massenmedium der Reformationszeit*, Stuttgart, 1981; George Orwell and Reginald Reynolds, eds., *British Pamphleteers*, 2 vols., London, 1948, 1951; Pierre-Louis Roederer, "Essai analytique sur les divers moyens établis pour la communication des pensées entre les hommes en société" (1796), *Oeuvres* 7 (1859): 84–87.

JEREMY D. POPKIN

PAPER. *See* BOOK; PRINTING; WRITING MATERIALS.

PARK, ROBERT (1864–1944)

U.S. sociologist. Born in Pennsylvania, Robert Ezra Park grew up in Red Wing, Minnesota, where his family moved after he was born. He went to the University of Minnesota for a year, then to the University of Michigan, where he was taught by JOHN DEWEY. Park, along with Dewey, became interested in a proposal for a new kind of newspaper, to be called "Thought News," which would report fluctuations in popular opinions as other newspapers reported changes in the stock market. The plan was abandoned, but Park remained interested in PUBLIC OPINION throughout his career.

After graduating from the University of Michigan, Park spent eleven years as a newspaper reporter for dailies in Minneapolis, Detroit, Denver, New York, and Chicago. This experience provided a solid basis for his later theoretical work on the mass media.

In 1898 he left journalism to enter Harvard University as a graduate student. There he studied psychology with Hugo Münsterberg and philosophy with WILLIAM JAMES and Josiah Royce. After receiving an M.A. in 1899, he moved to Germany and became a Ph.D. candidate at the University of Heidelberg. He studied sociology with GEORG SIMMEL, under whose supervision he wrote his dissertation, "Masse und Publikum" (Mass and Public), which picked up his old interest in public opinion. He received his doctorate in 1904 and returned to the United States.

After serving for a year as assistant in philosophy at Harvard, Park became secretary of the Congo Reform Association, which was greatly concerned with reported Belgian cruelty to blacks in the Congo. Making use of his newspaper experience, he wrote a series of articles on this subject for *Everybody's Magazine*. These articles and his job with the reform association brought him into contact with U.S. educator Booker T. Washington, at whose suggestion Park examined the condition of U.S. blacks in the South. Park, who entered into a kind of secretarial relationship with Washington and collaborated with him on *The Man Farthest Down*, continued to study minority problems for the rest of his life.

In 1914 he became a professor of sociology at the University of Chicago. Park was probably best known in academia for his *Introduction to the Science of Sociology*, written with Ernest W. Burgess and published in 1921, which was for years the leading college text in sociology. Like others of his writings, it included case studies and field observations, general and theoretical formulations, and suggestions for empirical study.

Park's works dealt with a wide range of subjects, including race relations, public morale and PROPAGANDA, cities, and human ecology, but his writings on the nature of news are of particular interest to the field of communications. News, as Park described it, has affinities with history but ultimately is not history. News deals primarily with discrete events in isolation, whereas history seeks to illuminate causal connections, to detail the succession of happenings that precede and follow a particular event, to put an event into context.

An event is considered newsworthy, according to Park, if when published "it will either startle, amuse, or otherwise excite the reader so that it will be remembered and repeated." Indeed, people typically react to news first by repeating it. This can lead to discussion and, because interpretations of events may vary, to disagreement. At this point the focus of the debate shifts from the news event itself to the issues it raises. From the "clash of opinions and sentiments" evoked by this debate, a consensus, or collective opinion, emerges. This, Park says, is public opinion. Thus "it is upon the interpretation of events, i.e., news, that public opinion rests." The circulation of news, Park continues, by orienting a society toward a considered end, is what makes political action possible. Sometimes, however, public debate on public issues leads merely to a superficial consensus that belies deep-rooted disagreement; other times overt dissension surfaces. In such cases conflict generally results.

Park believed that news plays a further important role in democratic societies. At certain times situations give rise to social unrest. As tension increases, the focus of public attention narrows, public discussion ceases, and public demand for some kind of action grows. Under these circumstances the influence of dominant community leaders is great, and dictators often are able to seize and hold power—provided they can maintain public tension. However, if news is freely circulated, public attention is dispersed, tension abates, and individuals are encouraged "to act on their own initiative." It is for this reason, Park declares, that dictatorships require some form of CENSORSHIP.

Park maintained that news has become more rather than less important with advances in science and methods of communication; changes in the modern world are so rapid and so dramatic that news is indispensable for understanding. As Park wrote, "Ours, it seems, is an age of news, and one of the most important events in American civilization has been the rise of the reporter."

Bibliography. Robert E. Park, *The Collected Papers of Robert Ezra Park*, ed. by Everett C. Hughes et al., Glencoe, Ill., 1950–1955.

WILBUR SCHRAMM

PATHÉ, CHARLES (1863–1957)

French motion picture executive. It is hard to overestimate Charles Pathé's role in the early evolution of MOTION PICTURES. The first great film industrialist, he built an empire encompassing every aspect of the business, from the manufacture of film stock and equipment to photoplay production, distribution, and exhibition. Known for his blunt yet complicated personality, Pathé supported experimental work and pioneered the NEWSREEL (*Pathé Journal, Pathé Weekly*), color processing, and other innovations.

Born in Chevry-Cossigny, France, Pathé began his career before the turn of the century by exhibiting phonographs in French fairground booths. This led to experimentation with other technological novelties, and by 1896 Pathé began marketing his own variation of LOUIS AND AUGUSTE LUMIÈRE's cinematograph. That same year Pathé, with brothers Émile, Jacques, and Théophile, created the Pathé Frères company to manufacture cameras and projectors as well as to make short films. Within a few years the company built large studios in Vincennes and Montreuil. Led by Pathé, French filmmakers soon dominated the pre–World War I film market. In 1901–1902 the company's profits totaled 421,000 francs; by 1907–1908 they had increased to more than 8.5 million. This rush of profits encouraged expansion, and by 1907 Pathé Frères had worldwide distribution facilities and chains of theaters in many countries, including Australia, Brazil, and Japan. In addition, Pathé studios in England, Germany, Italy, Russia, Spain, and the United States were grinding out films with the familiar Pathé crowing rooster symbol.

Pathé participated in the 1909 International Film Congress, which met in Paris in an unsuccessful attempt to establish patent control similar to that exercised by the Motion Picture Patents Company (of which Pathé Frères was a member) in the United States. That year Pathé sold more films in the United States than all U.S. companies combined and began leading the way toward the rental system. By 1914 the number of Pathé employees in France alone exceeded five thousand.

World War I proved disastrous for the French film industry. After August 1914 production and distribution were severely restricted because of CENSORSHIP and because the nitrate used in making celluloid was needed for armaments. Pathé also became a victim of the massive entry of Wall Street into the U.S. motion picture field, fostering a monopolistic HOLLYWOOD industry. To stave off bankruptcy, Pathé Frères disposed of many of its assets; parts of the manufacturing operation were sold to Eastman Kodak. In 1920, on the advice of his financiers, Charles Pathé reorganized the remaining Pathé-Cinéma holdings into two companies: Pathé-Cinéma, which limited itself to film-stock manufacture, processing, and sale of amateur camera equipment (see PHOTOGRAPHY, AMATEUR); and Pathé-Consortium, which was formed by Pathé and allied investors to concentrate on distribution and exhibition. But Charles Pathé was no longer in control, and in 1921 he was ousted from the company in a policy dispute. By the mid-1920s he was a declining force, although he continued to produce through a company known as Société d'Éditions Cinématographiques, which served as a personal vehicle for speculative film ventures, often

in support of promising young directors. He also served as a board member for a company called Société Générale des Films, which underwrote completion of the first part of Abel Gance's epic masterpiece *Napoléon* (1927). By the end of the decade Pathé was ready to retire from active involvement in the industry and settled in Monaco, where he resided quietly for another quarter of a century.

Bibliography. Richard Abel, *French Cinema: The First Wave, 1915–1929*, Princeton, N.J., 1984; Charles Pathé, *De Pathé Frères à Pathé Cinéma* (orig. published as part of Pathé's memoirs, 1940), Lyons, 1970; Georges Sadoul, "Napoleon of the Cinema," *Sight and Sound* 27 (1958): 183.

RICHARD ALAN NELSON

PEIRCE, CHARLES S. (1839–1914)

U.S. philosopher whose comprehensive theory of signs has been influential in developing a logical and formal basis for the analysis of communication and has been important in such fields as communications, LINGUISTICS, SEMIOTICS, and ANIMAL COMMUNICATION. Born in Cambridge, Massachusetts, Charles Sanders Peirce was the second son of Harvard mathematician Benjamin Peirce. He received a B.A. from Harvard University in 1859, and in 1862 he entered the Lawrence Scientific School, where he studied under Louis Agassiz, Jeffries Wyman, and Asa Gray. In 1863 he graduated summa cum laude with a B.S. in chemistry. Peirce worked as an astronomer at the Harvard Observatory and also for thirty years as a physicist for the U.S. Coast and Geodetic Survey. He had a difficult personality and held only one stable academic position—a part-time lectureship in logic at Johns Hopkins University from 1879 until 1884. In 1887 Peirce inherited some money with which he acquired an estate in Milford, Pennsylvania, where he lived in isolation and economic deprivation until his death.

Peirce's philosophical work was wide ranging and touched on many subjects, but the thread most relevant to the field of communications was his attempt to work out a theory of signs and to provide a program of inquiry into the problem of MEANING. After spending several years studying the works of German philosopher Immanuel Kant, particularly *The Critique of Pure Reason*, Peirce became interested in developing a system to reformulate Kant's a priori categories that in his philosophical system were considered true (of all possible experience) in order to let the human mind synthesize the sense data received from experience and thus to acquire knowledge. The reformulation of Kant by Peirce followed the study of the logical structure of argument. From Peirce's point of view the heart of the matter was to find the relationship between subjects and predicates in a single statement and premises and conclusions in a syllogism. Peirce called these relations a "sign relation." According to Peirce,

A sign, or *representamen,* is something which stands to somebody for something in some respect or capacity. It addresses somebody, that is it creates in the mind of that person an equivalent sign, or perhaps a more developed sign. That sign which it creates I call the *interpretant* of the first sign. The sign stands for something, its *object.* It stands for that object, not in all respects, but in reference to a sort of idea, which I have sometimes called the *ground* of the representamen.

These three elements—the ground, the object, and the interpretant—were central in Peirce's reformulation of Kant because they constituted an irreducible relationship of signification, and thus they designate the chief a priori modes that give us knowledge of the world. *See* SIGN; SIGN SYSTEM.

As noted, Kant's a priori categories help us to synthesize sense data and to understand the world. These data simply are; they do not refer to experience. In order to refer to something the human mind has to recognize it as something. This operation already involves, according to Peirce, a conceptualization, an interpretation in a very fundamental way. Thus raw data, impressions, or intuitions are not a part of this system. Humans are not able to know without the intervening conceptualization processes called cognitions (*see* COGNITION). Therefore, we can never reach the state of knowing on first impression or intuition of whatever phenomenon we are interested in; we can only know phenomena through a series of cognitions that relate to them. Every cognition is preceded by a priori cognition of the same object determined by a priori cognition, and so on ad infinitum. Peirce concluded that our series of cognitions or interpretations of sense data forms a series without beginning or end. The sign relation described above is fundamental to any conceptualization or cognition. Thus the series of cognitions is paralleled by a sign series. From these propositions Peirce concluded that thinking or knowing the world is a process involving an endless series of signs. Having eliminated intuitions, he could argue that the entire manifestation of consciousness is a sign series.

Peirce is also known as the intellectual father of pragmatism, the philosophical movement originating in the United States that was widely diffused by WILLIAM JAMES, who, along with JOHN DEWEY, recognized his debt to Peirce. Peirce's pragmatic concern was with meaning, which differed from James's interest in truth. In his pragmatic theory of meaning Peirce made two contributions. The first is a principle of scientific definition. Scientific theories or proofs are to be considered in terms of their observable consequences under laboratory or explicitly stated test conditions. Second, Peirce stressed the importance of taking into account the ends to which science is directed. This utilitarian aspect of science, according to Peirce, cannot be separated from the first methodological and ontological aspect. In sum, Peirce thought that the meaning of an idea corresponds to the ways we act on it or the habits involved in it and to the ways we operate with experiences as consequences of such an idea.

Peirce's theory of meaning posed several problems, one of which derived from the fact that according to this theory nothing was possible that was not actual or would not become actual. Nevertheless, Peirce's work was very influential on some thinkers of twentieth-century doctrines such as operationism, positivism, and philosophy of LANGUAGE and fields of inquiry such as communication, in which the problem of meaning is of central concern.

Bibliography. Bruce Kuklick, *The Rise of American Philosophy: Cambridge, Mass., 1860–1930,* New Haven, Conn., 1977; John A. Passmore, *A Hundred Years of Philosophy,* New York, 1980; Charles S. Peirce, *Collected Papers of Charles Sanders Peirce,* Vols. 1–6 ed. by Charles Hartshorne and Paul Weiss, Vols. 7–8 ed. by Arthur W. Burks, Cambridge, Mass., 1931–1960.

ABRAHAM NOSNIK

PERCEPTION

This topic is discussed in three sections:
1. Music
2. Speech
3. Still and Moving Pictures

1. MUSIC

Music is a form of communication involving composers, performers, and listeners. Perception of music occurs by means of physiological structures that make it possible to identify individual and combined pitches, durations, volumes, and timbres.

Physiological basis. Musical sounds are conveyed to the brain through the mechanism of the ear and the pathways between the ear and the brain. The conversion of SOUND waves into neural activity occurs in the cochlea (part of the inner ear), specifically in hair cells that are attached to a membrane. Sound waves cause the membrane to vibrate, and the vibrations result in electrical impulses in nerve fibers that end on the hair cells. Information concerning the pitch of a sound is conveyed by the placement of the nerve fibers that are activated and the periodicity of the activation. Their placement is also important in conveying sound quality, or timbre.

The mechanism of the ear provides only a preliminary analysis of the acoustic signal; most of the processing underlying the perception of music occurs in the brain. Its temporal lobes play a prominent role in such processing. Damage to these lobes, particularly to the anterior temporal region, may impair musical processing such as the ability to recognize melodies or rhythms or to identify the sounds characteristic of different MUSICAL INSTRUMENTS.

Musical illusions. Perceived musical sounds are composed of a number of attributes, such as pitch, loudness, location, and timbre. These various attributes are analyzed by separate brain systems, and the final perception results from a combination of information from these different systems. When more than one sound is presented at a time, the information may combine incorrectly so that musical illusions result. For example, if two melodic patterns are presented, one to each ear, and these patterns are in overlapping pitch ranges, listeners will typically reorganize the sounds so that a melody corresponding to the higher tones is heard in one ear, and a melody corresponding to the lower tones is heard in the other. Most right-handers hear the higher tones in the right ear and the lower tones in the left, regardless of where they did originate. Left-handers do not, however, display the same tendency. Analogous illusions occur under certain circumstances when sounds are presented through spatially separated loudspeakers and even in live performances in concert halls. They show not only that musical patterns may be profoundly misperceived but also that there are striking variations among individuals in the ways in which they are misperceived.

Grouping of musical sounds. In listening to music we do not simply process each sound as it arrives; rather, we form groupings out of combinations of sounds. The principles underlying such perceptual organization are analogous to those in vision and were formulated by the Gestaltists early in this century: (1) In accordance with the principle of proximity, we tend to group together sounds that are close in pitch or time and to separate out those that are further away. (2) We tend to follow pitch changes that move consistently in one direction, following the principle of good continuation. (3) Sounds that are produced by the same type of instrument tend to be grouped together, in accordance with the principle of similarity. (4) Sounds whose volumes change in correlation with each other are perceived as grouped together, following the principle of common fate.

Perception of pitch structures. The abstraction of musical patterns involves both the detection of low-level features and their combination into higher-level configurations. One prominent feature based on pitch is pitch class: tones that are separated exactly by octaves (whose fundamental frequencies stand in a ratio of 2:1) are perceived as equivalent in certain respects. Another feature is the interval: when the fundamental frequencies of two pairs of tones stand in the same ratio, the intervals formed by these tone pairs are perceived as identical. This is why a melodic or harmonic pattern retains its perceptual identity when it is transposed in pitch, provided that the intervals formed by the tones in the pattern are unaltered.

At higher levels abstractions are formed out of larger numbers of pitches. Virtually all traditional music is tonal; that is, one particular tone assumes prominence, with other pitch materials organized around it. In Western tonal music this central tone is termed the tonic, or keynote. Traditional musical styles also employ musical patterns and formulas that have statistical properties, which become internalized and can be recognized when we hear an unfamiliar piece composed in a familiar style. *See* MUSIC, FOLK AND TRADITIONAL; MUSIC HISTORY; MUSIC THEORIES.

Much twentieth-century Western art music provides an exception to the use of tonality as an organizing principle. Here attempts are made to organize tonal materials along different lines. Notably, the theory of twelve-tone composition, put forward by the composer Arnold Schoenberg, is based on the concept of a musical shape that retains its perceptual identity when presented backward or when its pitch relationships are inverted. Schoenberg likened a succession of tones that has been transformed in this fashion to a visually perceived object that retains its identity when viewed from a different position or through a mirror.

Perception of rhythm. Temporal patterns are organized by the listener in terms of successive divisions of time into approximately equal units. Patterns that can be divided in this way can be accurately perceived, and patterns that cannot be divided into equal time spans are perceived only poorly. Furthermore, a rhythmic pattern retains its perceptual identity when it is transposed to a different tempo, provided that the ratios of the time spans between successive sounds are preserved. This generalization holds, however, only for a certain range of tempi. At very fast rates the component sounds of the pattern fuse to produce timbres instead, and at slow rates temporal relationships are not perceived accurately.

Bibliography. Diana Deutsch, ed., *The Psychology of Music*, New York, 1982; Leonard B. Meyer, *Emotion and Meaning in Music*, Chicago, 1956; John R. Pierce, *The Science of Musical Sound*, New York, 1983.

DIANA DEUTSCH

2. SPEECH

The perception of SPEECH involves complicated processes whereby an acoustic signal generated by a speaker is decoded by a listener to determine the speaker's intended MEANING. The obvious ease of speech communication among native speakers of the same LANGUAGE belies the inherent complexity of speech perception as well as its intelligent nature. It is only as one tries to analyze the process of speech perception and to simulate it that one begins to appreciate speech perception as a skilled, intelligent process. As will be shown, analysis of this process involves LINGUISTICS, psychology, acoustics, and hearing science.

The Structure of Speech

Speech can be conceived of as being made up of segments called speech sounds, commonly referred to as consonants and vowels. These segments are the phonetic elements or phonemes of a language. Phonemes are linguistic units that have their bases in speech as it is perceived or spoken. All of the syllables and words of a language are composed of a relatively small number of phonemes. In the case of English, textbooks in phonetics may list as few as twenty-five consonants and twelve vowels for a total of thirty-seven elements. However, phonemes may be realized in slightly different ways depending on the surrounding context. Such contextually determined variants are called allophones. If these finer phonetic distinctions are included, the number of distinguishable speech sounds or allophones of English may reach fifty or sixty.

The phonemes and allophones of a spoken language can be characterized by a small set of distinctive features numbering about sixteen. These features have been inferred from analyses of the movements of the organs of speech, such as the tongue, lips, and jaw; from analyses of the perceptual attributes of the phonetic elements; and from linguistic analysis of the rules governing the sound sequences of a language. Thus, sounds are very often described as bundles of these features, and some theories of phonetic recognition make use of these features.

Linguistic theory includes the notion that phonemes are combined into larger morphological units called morphemes. A morpheme is defined as a minimal sequence of sounds that has its own meaning or grammatical function. Words are then made up of one or more morphemes. Thus, the word *talked* is made up of the verb morpheme *talk* and the past-tense morpheme *ed*. Morphemes are stored in the lexicon, and the rules of the morphological component of the GRAMMAR operate on morphemes to form words. The proper order of words and relationships among words in a sentence for a certain language are then controlled by the rules of the syntactic component. These rules generate what is called a syntactic tree, which reflects the functional groupings of the words in a sentence, such as subject noun phrase–verb phrase or verb–object noun phrase.

The acoustic waveform of speech carries relevant information—syntactic, morphological, and phonological—about the speaker's intended meaning. On hearing an utterance, the listener must extract this information from the waveform. Theories of speech perception must provide an account of how and in what steps this information is recovered by the listener.

Some researchers believe that the process of production of an utterance in any language can be modeled as a step-by-step procedure. In general, once the message is conceived, a syntactic tree is generated by the syntactic component with the appropriate structure. The morphological component combines the relevant morphemes (which are made up of phonemes) into words and inserts them under the proper nodes of the syntactic tree. The syntactic tree may or may not undergo any transformations. Next, the rules of the phonological component apply, converting any unacceptable sequences of sounds into acceptable ones, as well as determining the form of the positional variants of the phonemes (allophones). Thus, the word sequence *did you,* beginning a question, will be converted to and pronounced *didja*. Finally, the so-called phonetic implementation rules convert the sound sequences into sequences of commands to the relevant articulators (larynx, tongue, jaw, velum, lips, etc.). Speech is finally produced by forcing air through the vocal tract, and the acoustic wave radiates from the lips on its way to a hearer's ears.

A theory of speech perception must then explain how a listener extracts the phonemes from the acoustic waveform; how the listener groups the phonemes into morphemes and words; how the listener determines the syntactic structure of the utterance; and, finally, how the listener determines the speaker's intended meaning. Although researchers have examined all the stages of this process, the greatest amount of research on speech perception has concentrated on the lower end, that is, on the extraction of phonemes from the speech signal.

Acoustics

The acoustic signal generated by a speaker is made up of minute, rapid variations in the atmospheric pressure that are propagated through the air as an acoustic wave from a speaker to a listener. The frequency of the variations in atmospheric pressure that are of interest for speech perception range from about sixty to six thousand hertz. Spectral analysis or spectral estimation techniques allow the complicated acoustic waveform to be converted to a spectral representation. In a spectral representation the sound is represented by the distribution of intensities across the frequency range from sixty to six thousand hertz. The intensities of the components are usually given on a logarithmic scale expressed in sound pressure level. Because the acoustic signal generated by the speaker is changing constantly, the spectral estimation must be based on a relatively brief segment of the speech waveform and must be refreshed at frequent intervals so that changes in the spectral representation of speech can be tracked or followed. It is generally held that each spectrum should be based on a sample of .020 second to .040 second in duration and should be refreshed about every .001 second. These values seem to allow the input waveform to be analyzed with adequate temporal and spectral resolution, and it is generally believed that the listener's auditory system performs such spectral analyses.

Speakers generate two major classes of sounds. One class—called glottal-source sounds—is generated at the vocal folds or glottis. Usually these are voiced sounds wherein the vocal folds open and close in a periodic manner. Examples are sounds like the *ee* in *beat* or the *l* in *lip*. Whispered or aperiodic glottal-source sounds are generated by creating turbulence as air flows through a slit between the edges of the vocal folds. Burst-friction sounds are generated by forcing air through narrow constrictions in the vocal tract at supraglottal locations. These constrictions can be formed by bringing the tongue into contact with the more rigid parts of the vocal tract, such as the roof of the mouth, as in the sound *sh*. Burst sounds can be generated by stopping the airflow, building up pressure, and then suddenly releasing the air. For example, in making the sound of *t* the tip of the tongue is placed against the upper gum ridge to block the flow of air. When the block is removed, the sudden rush of air through the resulting narrow opening produces a burst-friction sound. During the time that the airflow is blocked, no sound is emitted. These periods of silence occur during the vocal tract closures associated with the stop consonants *p*, *t*, and *k* and may last from about .060 second to .120 second.

The Process of Phonetic Perception

The listener uses information from the sequence of glottal-source spectra, burst-friction spectra, and silences to decode the speaker's intent. Most theorists believe the listener transforms the acoustic wave through a series of stages to reach a stage wherein the speech is represented by a series of phonetic elements such as phonemes or allophones. Each such element represents a category; thus, these abstract representations are category codes. A major issue in speech perception is to determine how the acoustic patterns of speech trigger or induce the perception of a sequence of category codes that correspond to the allophones of a language. A great deal is known about this process even though certain aspects of it are not yet clarified.

For example, the perception of vowel sounds is highly dependent on the spectral patterns of the acoustic signal. Moving from the low-frequency end to the high-frequency end of the spectrum, a series of peaks in amplitude or spectral prominences are usually found. These are restricted regions with high concentrations of energy. Measurements of natural speech and perceptual experiments with synthetic speech have demonstrated that vowel quality is largely related to the positions of the first three spectral peaks. For a male speaker, the vowel *ee* in *beat* usually has peaks near 270, 2,300, and 3,000 hertz. In contrast, the vowel *aa* in *father* for the male speaker would have prominences near 730, 1,100, and 2,400 hertz.

The prominences in the spectra are related to the resonant frequencies of the speaker's vocal tract. These resonances and associated spectral prominences are frequently referred to as formants, are numbered from low to high as F1, F2, and F3, and are often used to succinctly describe the spectral pattern.

Almost all glottal-source spectra can be described in terms of formant patterns—F patterns—which can be quantified by listings of the values of F1, F2, and F3. Burst-friction sounds have been more resistant to such description. Generally they do not have much energy in the low-frequency range usually associated with the F1 of glottal-source sounds. Also, in the higher-frequency region, the presence of multiple peaks and valleys, some of which are small, makes the assignment of formant values difficult. Nonetheless, sustained friction sounds such as those of the consonant *s* in *sip* or *sh* in *ship* have distinct spectral shapes. The shapes to be associated with the friction sounds of *h*, *f*, and *th* are not yet well defined, perhaps because of articulatory variability augmented by the conditioning effects of neighboring sounds. The voiced fricative sounds such as *z* and *v* consist of a simultaneous combination of glottal-source spectra and burst-friction spectra. The voiced and voiceless stop consonants, that is, *b*, *d*, *g*, and *p*, *t*, *k*, have their acoustic bases in sequences of burst-friction sounds, glottal-source sounds, and silences. For example, for the *t* in *stop*, the *t* percept is generated by the following sequence. Initially, there is the burst-friction sound associated with s, followed by a silence associated with the tip of the tongue meeting the upper gum ridge, blocking the flow of air from the vocal tract. When the block is released, a brief burst of noise is generated, after which the vocal folds begin periodic vibration, and there is a transition to the following vowel. It is this whole sequence, then, that is responsible for inducing the perception of t.

Another class of consonants consists of the nasals such as m and n, and these are special cases of glottal-source sounds wherein the passageways to the nose are opened. This alters the F pattern in the region of the first formant, F1, usually by adding a nasal resonance and by weakening and broadening the first resonance of the oral part of the vocal tract. More detailed descriptions of the acoustic correlates of the perceived phonetic elements can be found in material cited in the bibliography below.

A complete account of the process of phonetic perception will include the solutions to several unresolved problems. One is that of *segmentation*. Consider the case of a simple sentence. As the speaker utters a sentence, a sequence of spectra is generated. If a spectrum is to be calculated every 0.001 second and if the sentence lasts 1.8 seconds, the sequence will contain 1,800 spectra. If the sentence contains fifteen allophones, which of the 1,800 spectra are associated with each of the fifteen allophones and which are simply parts of transitions and not associated with any of the allophones? At the present time, we have preliminary notions about the solution of this problem. For example, vowels are often associated with stationary or slowly changing glottal-source spectra, but the exact criteria for the segmentation of vowels are not known. Some consonants are similarly associated with either stationary or slowly changing glottal-source spectra or burst-friction spectra, and others, such as the stops—p, t, k, b, d, g— seem to be associated with very rapid spectral changes. Just as in the case of vowels, the exact criteria for the segmentation of consonants have not been established.

Another unresolved problem involves very large variations in the acoustic expression of an allophone related to its phonetic environment. Thus, the vowel oo, as in *boot*, may have a very different spectrum in the word *dude* as opposed to that found in the word *loop*. These are called coarticulation effects, and methods for describing the unifying characteristics of each allophone in the face of such variations are being sought.

Two other major problems are those of speaker normalization and rate normalization. The problem of speaker normalization is that the spectra generated by CHILDREN are higher in frequency than those generated by adult females, which, in turn, are higher

than those generated by adult males. Thus, the human perceiver must normalize these differences related to age and GENDER in order to recognize the linguistic content of the signal. Even though several models of such normalization are reasonably successful, consensus about which of these models best matches human performance has not been reached. It has also been argued that the acoustic expressions of the allophones vary with speaking rate. If that is so, the listener must normalize the interpretation of spectral changes in terms of the speaking rate of the current speaker. The details of the mechanisms of this hypothesized rate normalization are not known.

Characteristics of Speech Perception

Research on speech perception has elucidated several of its interesting characteristics. One of these is the *speech mode*. When a listener attends to a stimulus in the speech MODE, that stimulus is likely to induce the perception of phonetic codes even when the stimulus is not very speechlike. Similarly, when the listener attends to a stimulus in an auditory mode, as opposed to a speech mode, the stimulus may be heard as buzzes, noises, tones, and/or glides rather than as syllables or words.

Another characteristic is that of *categorical perception*. A large variety of acoustic expressions of an allophone induce the same categorical response from a listener, and thus many seemingly different spectral sequences may all induce perception of the same phonetic element. Furthermore, under certain circumstances, listeners do not perceive differences among members of the same category, although they clearly perceive objectively similar differences between members of different categories. The concepts of *speech mode* and *categorical perception*, along with other considerations, suggest that the decoding of the acoustic waveform into a string of phonetic elements may be done by a special perceptual system that is uniquely structured, with speech-specific mechanisms, for this perceptual task.

Another set of interesting characteristics of speech is revealed by studies of infant speech perception and of cross-language differences. It has been shown that infants of two to four months of age can discriminate intercategory pairs of speech sounds relatively independent of language. Soon thereafter, at six to eight months of age, infants categorize disparate members of that class into a single class. By adulthood, of course, listeners exhibit categorical perception of the allophones of their own language but are often unable to distinguish categorical differences in other languages. Taken together these findings suggest that as a spoken language is acquired and phonetic categories are learned, the listener becomes capable of distinguishing only those categorical differences in other languages that are either isomorphic with or otherwise do not conflict with those of the listener's native language. *See also* LANGUAGE ACQUISITION.

Other Factors in Speech Perception

The process of speech perception extends well beyond the issues discussed above. The listener not only uses information from the acoustic wave to decode the speaker's intention but also uses a variety of other sources of information. Specific information regarding the phonetic content of the message can be obtained from viewing the speaker's FACE and movements of the jaw and lips. Deaf persons, for example, can become skilled lip-readers and can achieve useful, although not perfect, levels of speech perception.

It it also well known that listeners use gestures and other elements in the situational context to determine the speaker's intended message. Additionally, very general knowledge of language and SEMANTICS often plays a crucial role in speech perception. *See also* BODY MOVEMENT; FACIAL EXPRESSION; GESTURE; KINESICS.

Theories of Speech Perception

Theories of speech perception seem to share a common four-stage structure; they differ in the exact nature of the processes occurring in the last three stages. All theories seem to agree that there is a stage 1, wherein the listener's auditory system performs a short-term spectral analysis on the incoming speech waveform. This analysis extracts the amplitudes of the lower harmonics of periodic signals and obtains smooth spectral envelopes of higher unresolved harmonics or of aperiodic signals. In this first stage the voice pitch of the periodic components and the shapes of the relevant spectra and their loudnesses are determined. Thus stage 1 converts the input waveform into auditory or sensory parameters. In stage 2 these sensory parameters are converted into perceptually relevant parameters. In some cases these parameters are lists of features, either auditory or linguistic. In motor theories the perceptually relevant parameters are thought to be abstract descriptions of the motor commands required to produce spectra that would match those determined by stage 1 processing. In still other theories the perceptual parameters are expressed in terms of abstract spectral patterns. In stage 3 the perceptual parameters of stage 2 are converted to linguistic terms. That is, based on the perceptual parameters and their changes over time, a sequence of allophones or phonemes is generated. Thus in stages 1–3 the acoustic waveform is converted into a phonetic-linguistic description. A distinction is often made between theories that posit a common acoustic pattern or class of patterns as the basis of phonetic perception and those that posit disjoint sets of acoustic patterns that are only uniformly related to phonetic perception through the intermediary of motor commands. The former are called acoustic invariance theories, and the latter are called motor theories or special-mechanism theories.

Unfortunately, a phonetic description does not map simply onto a lexical description or word because the phonetic expression of a word is highly dependent on context, rate of speaking, and dialect. Therefore, once the listener has gained a phonetic description of the speaker's utterance, the additional processing of stage 4 must be used to recover the intended lexical items.

Part of the problem of lexical access is that of grouping the phonetic string into meaningful morphological units such as syllables, morphemes, words, and syntactic groups. The process of lexical access appears to be affected not only by the phonetic content of the utterance but also by a number of other factors such as the frequency of occurrence of a word in the language, syntactic category information, and semantic relatedness. In this process the prosodic characteristics of speech play an important role. The prosody of speech is given by patterns of stressed and unstressed syllables, by the insertions of pauses of varying duration, and by the patterns of change in the voice pitch or intonation.

The next step in the process of speech perception involves a syntactic parsing of the utterance. An initial analysis scans the input from left to right and divides the words into phrasal groups based on their syntactic-category membership. Further processing takes as input these phrases and builds a coherent syntactic structure for the entire utterance. In the last stage of processing the meaning of the utterance is finally extracted on the basis of the syntactic structure, the words, and their meaning.

A complete theory of speech perception not only must describe the manner in which the acoustic waveform is converted by a listener into a string of phonetic elements (the focus of most research, as mentioned above) but also must deal with the way in which the listener uses prosody, rules of PHONOLOGY, visual input, knowledge of the situation, and general and linguistic knowledge to arrive at the speaker's meaning through several stages of processing. The transformation of the acoustic wave to a phonetic description is often isolated as a problem in acoustic phonetics, whereas the later stages of the process are thought to be in the linguistic-cognitive domain. *See also* COGNITION; LANGUAGE VARIETIES.

Implications

Speech perception involves high-resolution spectral analyses by the listener's auditory system and the conversion of the resulting spectral sequences to a string of phonetic elements known as allophones or speech sounds. In turn, the string of speech sounds must be grouped into a sequence of words that is used along with other information to determine the speaker's intended meaning.

The study of human speech perception and the search for a detailed description of the acoustic-phonetic CODE is an extremely exciting enterprise. The discovery of the detailed nature of this code may well rank as a major advance in the understanding of human perceptual and linguistic abilities. In speech perception the interplay of sensory, perceptual, linguistic, and cognitive functions is exquisitely coordinated in an everyday activity common to all human cultures. A more detailed understanding of each of the steps in the process will enhance our abilities to improve electronic voice communications, to provide easy voice communication with machines, to ease the process of second-language acquisition, and to assist those with hearing or language impairments.

See also SIGN LANGUAGE; SPEECH AND LANGUAGE DISORDERS.

Bibliography. Adrian Akmajian, Richard A. Demers, and Robert M. Harnish, *Linguistics: An Introduction to Language and Communication*, 2d ed., Cambridge, Mass., 1984; Peter D. Eimas and Joanne L. Miller, eds., *Perspectives on the Study of Speech*, Hillsdale, N.J., 1981; Norman J. Lass, Leija V. McReynolds, Jerry L. Northern, and David E. Yoder, eds., *Speech, Language, and Hearing*, Vol. 1, Philadelphia, 1982; James D. Miller, "Auditory Processing of the Acoustic Patterns of Speech," *Archives of Otolaryngology* 110 (1984): 154–159; J. M. Pickett, *The Sounds of Speech Communication*, Baltimore, Md., 1980; David B. Pisoni, "Speech Perception," in *Handbook of Learning and Communicative Processes*, ed. by W. K. Estes, Hillsdale, N.J., 1976; Eileen C. Schwab and Howard C. Nusbaum, eds., *Speech Perception*, Vol. 1, *Pattern Recognition by Humans and Machines*, Orlando, Fla., 1986.

JAMES D. MILLER AND MARIOS FOURAKIS

3. STILL AND MOVING PICTURES

Although both still and moving pictures are flat, they must either somehow resemble the three-dimensional scenes they represent or stand for them as words stand for things by arbitrary convention. As a limiting case, pictures may resemble their objects by providing the eye with the same pattern of light, or optic array (Figure 1). A stationary viewer, looking from the proper viewpoint with only one eye at such a surrogate (one that is made with perfect optical fidelity), cannot distinguish picture from scene. Although this conception underlies most technical discussion about pictures, almost no still or moving picture is even intended to meet these conditions. Pictures are neither arbitrary conventions nor optical surrogates.

Still Pictures

In the late 1400s, Leonardo da Vinci taught that by examining tracings made as in Figure 1, artists could learn what are now called pictorial *depth cues*, including linear perspective (Figure 2*ai*), textural perspective (2*aii*), interposition (2*aiii*; Figure 3*c*[1–3]), modeling through shading (Figure 3*a*), and aerial perspective (Figure 3*c*4). To traditional perceptual theorists and to philosophers concerned with how we come to know the world (notably George Berkeley in the early 1700s), depth cues underlie our perceptions of the real world as well as of pictures. However, if the eye moves while viewing a real scene (Figure 2*aiv*), near objects move more in the field of view than far ones (Figure 2*c*); but because all parts of a picture lie at the same distance, they move together (Figure 2*b*), revealing the picture as a flat dappled object.

This difference between picture and scene can be minimized (by increased viewing distance, shallower represented depth, etc.), but in most cases no real attempt is made to fool the eye. Most pictures are deliberately distorted or altered so that they do not provide the same light as the scenes they represent; indeed, pictures routinely use outlines to represent objects' edges and the modeling of form, although outlines exist neither in the scenes they represent nor in the light those scenes provide.

Because pictures and objects are so different, some theorists, including philosophers Nelson Goodman and Marx Wartofsky, argue that we learn a language of pictures from specific experience with them. In this view, and given the appropriate CULTURE, any picture can then arbitrarily represent anything. Although it is true that certain aspects of picture perception require pictorial learning, in that some viewers without Western schooling may not comprehend perspective in highly schematic sketches, we now know that pictures cannot in general be conventions acquired through experience with them. Julian Hochberg and Virginia L. Brooks reported in 1962 that a child of nineteen months, with no training whatsoever in pairing pictures with their objects or with the names of those objects (and who had almost no exposure of any kind to pictures), nevertheless was able, on first contact, to recognize objects not only in photographs and shaded drawings, but in line drawings as well.

Pictorial distortions. Distortions and departures from fidelity made with representational intent often serve nonarbitrary perceptual principles. In general, brightnesses in any scene must be rearranged in the interests of pictorial representation. Chiaroscuro, the arrangement of light and dark in a picture (Figure 3*a*), extends the apparent range of pigments by placing dark areas next to the region that is to look most bright (e.g., the face and the candle flame). This exploits the fact of simultaneous contrast, which is what causes the same gray ribbon to look lighter against the dark background in Figure 3*b*2. Such contrast-induced differences between two regions are not as manifest without a contour, so that the effects of the dark and light surrounds on the gray ribbon are not noticeable at 3*b*1, and the artist can maintain apparent unity of surface by avoiding contours where these would reveal contrast.

Familiar objects and people are usually drawn as though from straight ahead, that is, each from its own separate viewpoint perpendicular to the canvas (Figure 3*c*). This violates the conditions of Figure 1, in which the picture is so made as to provide the eye with the same pattern of light that it would receive, at a single viewpoint, from the scene itself. By showing each object from straight ahead, the picture is made internally inconsistent. This is done in part to remedy the fact that we normally view paintings from various positions away from the central station point (Figure 3*c*), so that then whichever object we may stand in front of is appropriately drawn, and the inconsistencies thus produced are not salient.

Gestalt theories. Even in a completely accurate surrogate, three-dimensional objects can look flat, figure and ground can reverse so that the spaces between objects assume visible shapes, and familiar shapes can become invisible. To Gestalt theorists in the 1930s such as Max Wertheimer and Kurt Koffka, "laws of organization" determine whether and how we perceive an object. Figure 4*a*, in which a familiar number is concealed in 4*a*i but not in 4*a*ii or 4*a*iii, demonstrates the *law of good continuation*: we perceive the alternative organization that best preserves smoothly continuing contours. The number is hidden in 4*a*i because to see it we must break the unfamiliar but smoothly continuing shape. Figure 4*b* looks flat because good continuation must be broken to perceive 4*b*i and 4*b*ii as dihedrals at different distances, but Figure 4*c* looks three-dimensional because the dihedrals would have to be broken at 4*c*i, 4*c*ii, and so on for the pattern to look like a set of closed polyhedrons.

As with depth cues, one may ask whether Gestalt "laws" are pictorial conventions. Learning and convention can certainly affect how organization occurs. Figure 5 is completed differently if taken as two words (CAT and DOG) than if taken as a pair of simple geometric shapes. Because they generally group together those parts that in fact belong to the same object, these principles are not arbitrary; rather, as Egon Brunswik argued in the 1940s, they may reflect the probable structure of the world. For example, it is very unlikely that edges of different objects lying at different distances from the viewer will so line up in the field of view as to form a single smoothly continuing contour. In general, only from one out of

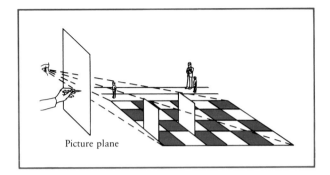

Figure 1.

all the myriad places from which the viewer could look at a pair of objects would their edges be aligned. For this reason the parts of a smoothly continuing contour probably comprise a single object. If learned at all, a law like good continuation is probably learned from experience with the world and not from pictorial convention.

The minimum principle. The *minimum principle*, proposed by Koffka in 1935, is that we perceive the simplest structure that fits the stimulus pattern. Various attempts have been made to measure simplicity objectively. Given an objective rule, a computer could *in principle* assess any picture before displaying it and display only those views for which the desired appearance is in fact the simplest alternative, for example, 4*c* rather than 4*b*.

The famous "impossible figures" discovered in 1958 by British father and son Lionel and Roger Penrose, and popularized in the graphic art of Maurice Escher, refute the minimum principle. Figure 6*a* looks three-dimensional although that is not a simple possible solution. Pictorial constraints are more piecemeal and local: in Figure 6*b*, if one attends intersection 6*b*1, the cube is then perceived so that the vertical edge at 6*b*2 looks nearer than the horizontal; observe intersection 6*b*2, and the perspective soon reverses, against any overall simplicity principle.

Structure through motion. Motion parallax refers to the fact that relative motion between the observer and a scene laid out in three-dimensional space results in a change in the position of the objects in the visual field, and objects at different distances move at different velocities in the pattern of light reaching the eye. These phenomena provide the moving observer with a rich source of information about the structure of the world and comprise a cue for depth. Shadows of unfamiliar three-dimensional structures that lack depth cues, and are perceived as flat when stationary, appear three-dimensional when moving.

In the 1960s and 1970s proponents of direct per-

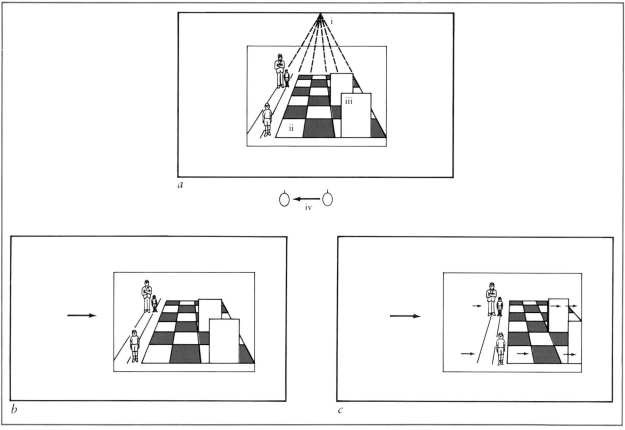

Figure 2.

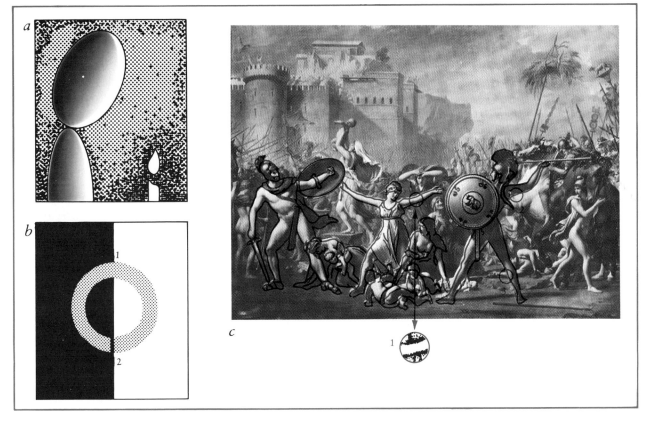

Figure 3c. *(Perception—Still and Moving Pictures)*   Drawing by the authors over a painting by Jacques-Louis David, *The Rape of the Sabines*, 1794–1799. Louvre, Paris. Alinari/Art Resource, New York.

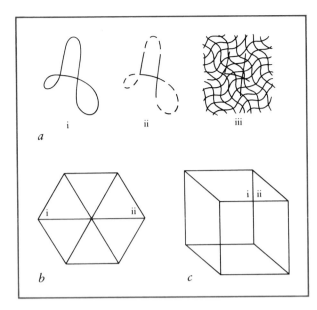

Figure 4.

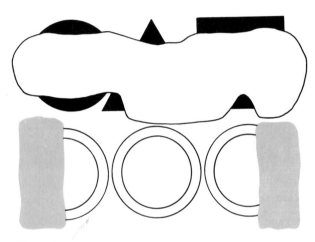

Figure 5.

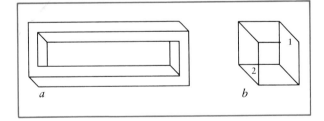

Figure 6.

ceptual theories, particularly James J. Gibson and Gunnar Johansson, proposed that the moving viewer's nervous system performs a reverse of the geometry represented in Figure 1. In this view our normal perceptions are of events, from which we extract the invariant object or layout that fits the changes in stimulation. Depth cues and Gestalt factors would then both be irrelevant.

As a more specific version of this approach, several psychologists and computer scientists in the late 1970s advanced versions of a *rigidity principle,* asserting that we perceive a rigid three-dimensional object or layout if one can be found that fits the moving pattern. Because most objects are rigid, when in motion we would normally perceive the world correctly if our nervous systems indeed followed this principle.

Even with rigid moving shapes in full view, however, in some cases we perceive instead quite different shapes undergoing nonrigid deformation. In 1949, Adelbert Ames showed that a trapezoid rotating continuously in one direction is perceived instead to oscillate, so that the larger end always appears nearer. Indeed, we now know a whole class of such illusions, in which the static depth cue of linear perspective seems to dominate the motion information and to contradict the rigidity principle. This goes against the theoretical assertions that were proposed to sidestep the complexities of cues and Gestalt laws. Moreover, moving pictures normally involve many practices that violate the rigidity principle with impunity.

The perception of motion and moving pictures. If an object moves relative to the direction of gaze, the object's image moves in the array of light reaching the retina at the back of the eye. Retinal movement that is too fast, too slow, or too brief is below threshold and not perceived. Much smaller and slower movements can be detected for *relative motion,* in which the distance between two seen objects changes, than for *absolute motion,* where the only change produced is the result of a single object moving in an otherwise empty field of view.

If a viewer's eye and the object are in lateral relative motion (Figure 9*a*), nearer objects move faster; as viewer and scene approach each other, there is an expansion pattern, with nearer objects expanding faster (Figure 9*b*). These motion patterns might provide information about spatial layout and are therefore important in direct theories of perception, but research does not show that we actually use such information reliably or with precision.

Moving Pictures: Why Do They Move?

Moving pictures do not, of course, actually move; they present still samples from the flow of motion at the rate of twenty-four and thirty per second for film and VIDEO, respectively. The perception of movement is usually, but incorrectly, explained as "persistence of vision." In fact, persistence results only in superposition (Figure 7*b*), although it does serve to mask the dark periods between still frames. In video, persistence of vision builds the whole picture from sweeps of a single moving dot of phosphorescence. *See* MOTION PHOTOGRAPHY.

Apparent movement from successive stills—stroboscopic movement—results from a complex range of sensory and cognitive processes only partially understood. (A closely related set of phenomena, in which apparent movement occurs between two stationary lights separated in time and space, has been studied with varied distances and times; these are summarized as Korte's laws.) We distinguish at least two processes:

1. Movement between nearby elements, regardless of the overall shapes of which they are a part. These movements are thought to rest on low-level motion-detecting mechanisms in the visual system that do not distinguish actual transitions from succession. With such small displacements as are normal in moving pictures (e.g., Figure 7a), movement is perceived correctly; with larger displacements (as in a too-rapid pan), spurious motion may occur between noncorresponding objects. In Figure 7c, 7c1 and 7c2 are successive frames providing a brief impression of movement (arrow *m*).

2. Movements perceived to account for change in views (e.g., Figure 7d). These movements bridge larger displacements and are more cognitive and inferential in nature. Because they are not immediately evident as sensory events, they require more time to grasp what has happened; it takes longer for the viewer to establish the new subjective viewpoint.

In viewing the world, these two components normally complement each other; on film, they agree only if certain precautions are taken.

Sources of movement in moving pictures. If the camera tracks a moving object with no background (Figure 8a), no motion is seen. Given a stationary background, which moves on the screen behind the stationary image of the moving object (Figure 8b), the larger or enclosing area appears stationary, and the object appears to move. (Indeed, in a moving visual environment in the real world, the stationary viewer perceives himself or herself to be moving.) The same effect, of course, can be achieved with a moving background and stationary object and camera (Figure 8c). How movement is perceptually partitioned (first systematically studied by Karl Duncker in 1929) has been the subject of intensive investigation by perception psychologists and computer scientists.

The camera has four primary component movements relative to the scene: (1) *track* (Figure 9a), in which the camera moves through the visual field parallel to the scene that is being recorded (a vertical tracking shot is called a crane shot); (2) *dolly* (Figure 9b), in which the camera moves toward or away from the subject matter; (3) *pan* (Figure 9c), in which

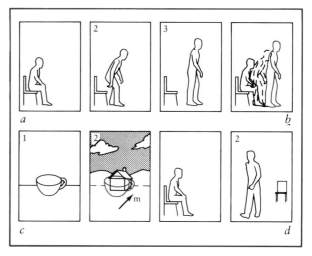

Figure 7.

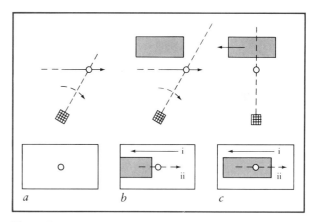

Figure 8.

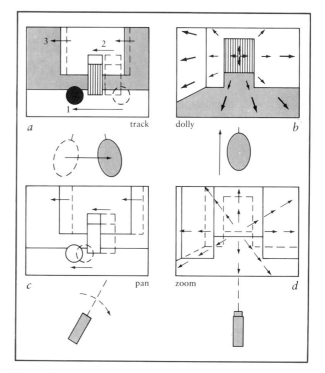

Figure 9.

the camera rotates in place to sweep the scene from side to side (a vertical pan is called a tilt); and (4) *zoom* (Figure 9*d*), in which the camera does not have to move but the focal length of the lens changes, enlarging or reducing the portion of the scene visible on the screen.

These motion picture techniques reveal three facts important in understanding visual perception:

1. Movement in telephoto or wide-angle shots must violate any rigidity principle. When the lens's focal length changes, the viewer's distance from the screen would have to change to maintain the relations of Figure 10*c*. If the viewing distance remains unchanged, the represented pirouetting dancer's arms must stretch and contract, in telephoto (close-up) and wide angle (long shot), respectively, if they are to fit the image on the screen as she turns. These are visualized as viewed from the top in Figures 10*b* and 10*d*. Such deformations are normally ignored. Given that no rigid objects in space will fit the swirl of moving patterns on the screen under these very common conditions, however, we cannot then say that we perceive people and things in moving pictures only by extracting the underlying rigid structures, in accordance with the rigidity principle.

2. Motion-produced stimulation is not fundamental to spatial perception. In pan and zoom, the lack of parallax conflicts with the static depth cues within the scene (Figures 9*c* and 9*d*). In Figure 9*c*, for example, the depth cue of interposition would show the tumbler to be nearer than the window, but the motions provided by the pan are equal, instead of being larger, for the nearer object (cf. Figure 9*a*). The fact that in moving pictures pan and zoom are routinely used in place of track and dolly (Figures 9*a* and 9*b*, respectively) shows that the parallactic information cannot be fundamental, as maintained by direct theorists, and that the pictorial depth cues are not merely conventions.

3. Represented space and events extend beyond the present stimulation. A major function of camera movement is to represent scenes far larger than the screen. This function is more economically filled by discontinuous changes or cuts. Cuts divide moving pictures into identifiable shots. The classic sequence (Figures 11*a–d*) from long shot, through medium shot, to a series of close-ups establishes the scene, indicates the players, and presents the action by changing distances or lenses.

Considered in terms of the light they present to the eye, moving pictures resemble the world even less than still pictures do. Much that is represented in the normal moving picture is never actually shown but is seen only in the mind of the viewer. In a limited

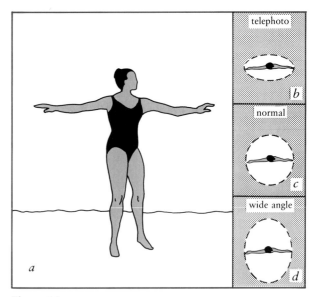

Figure 10.

Figure 11.

way, cuts between overlapping shots resemble the results of the eye movements that we usually make in glancing at the world, but in cuts, as opposed to normal vision, there is always the danger of spurious movement (see Figure 7*c*). With a cut from position 1 to 2 in Figure 12*b*, the camera "crosses the axis" and the man's contours in shot a (Figure 12*a*) turn into those of the woman in b, providing the viewer with a momentary (usually undesirable) disorientation. In Figure 12*c*, a group of dancers advancing leftward (arrow a) is perceived to jump backward (arrow b) because of the change in viewpoint. The care needed in cutting reminds us that the flow of images is not merely an identical surrogate for a sequence of glances.

Moreover, moving pictures routinely cut between shots that do not overlap at all (Figures 7*c*, 11*c*, and 11*d*), and these are surely not a general feature of

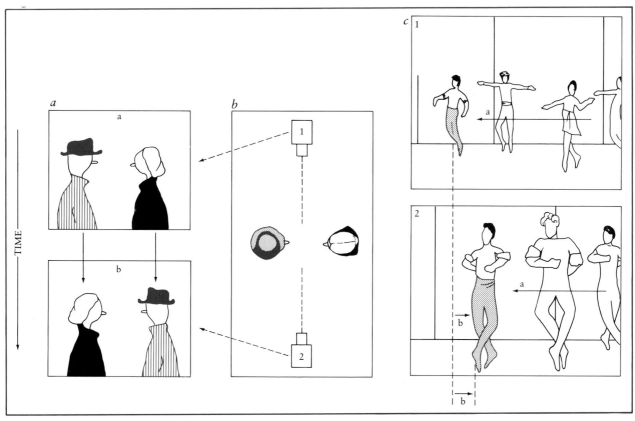

Figure 12.

normal vision. Nevertheless, cuts are ubiquitous and readily comprehended (if such pitfalls as those in Figures 7c are avoided).

What Then Are Pictures?

A picture—whether still or moving—need not look at all three-dimensional itself, nor need the entire shape be shown at any time in order to represent a three-dimensional object. How then is the picture like the object?

We must consider the processes by which we perceive the world itself before we can speculate about what they might share with picture perception.

- We do not see everything in detail at once. To see different things clearly, we need successive glances. No matter how flat the picture and how solid the scene, the two-dimensional relations within the optic array provide the medium within which eye movements are made. Picture and scene are very similar so far as this fundamental process of perceptual inquiry is concerned.
- Glances are *elective*. The viewer is not compelled to look at all parts of any picture (or of a real scene in the world) or to test its consistency, and perceptual tolerance of elisions (Figures 6 and 7d) may merely reflect this.

- Given that eye movements are made to answer visual questions, the viewer must keep some account of the questions and answers. That account constitutes a schema of the object or scene. The schemas that guide the viewer's perceptual inquiry in the world work with the picture as well.

The competent artist and filmmaker both aim at eliciting visual questions that make the subsequent visual answer comprehensible. Conventions guide this process. They provide expectations about what schemas are to be tested and about where information is to be found.

Conventions also provide MEANING for otherwise meaningless or unfamiliar patterns or events. Some arbitrary graphic symbols—such as electrical circuit diagrams, or film devices like the dissolve, signifying the passage of time or parallel action—are only meaningful with previous experience. Pictorial representations, both still and moving, are generally accessible and nonarbitrary when they draw on the characteristic processes by which we seek information about the three-dimensional world from the two-dimensional optic array.

See also GRAPHICS; MOTION PICTURES; REPRESENTATION, PICTORIAL AND PHOTOGRAPHIC; VISUAL IMAGE.

Bibliography. Rudolf Arnheim, *Art and Visual Perception: A Psychology of the Creative Eye*, rev. ed., Berkeley, Calif., 1974; James J. Gibson, *The Ecological Approach to Visual Perception*, Boston, 1979; Ernst H. Gombrich, *Art and Illusion: A Study in the Psychology of Pictorial Representation*, 4th ed., London, 1972; Ernst H. Gombrich, Julian Hochberg, and Max Black, *Art, Perception, and Reality*, Baltimore, Md., 1972; Julian Hochberg, *Perception*, 2d ed., Englewood Cliffs, N.J., 1978; idem, "Pictorial Functions and Perceptual Structures," in *The Perception of Pictures*, Vol. 2, ed. by Margaret Hagen, New York, 1980; idem, "The Representation of Space and Events in Video and Cinematic Displays," in *Handbook of Perception and Human Performance*, Vol. 1, ed. by Kenneth R. Boff, Lloyd Kaufman, and James P. Thomas, New York, 1986; Julian Hochberg and Virginia L. Brooks, "The Perception of Motion Pictures," in *Perceptual Ecology*, Vol. 10, *The Handbook of Perception*, ed. by Edward C. Carterette and Morton P. Friedman, New York, 1978; Calvin F. Nodine and Dennis F. Fisher, eds., *Perception and Pictorial Representation*, New York, 1979.

JULIAN HOCHBERG AND VIRGINIA L. BROOKS

PERFORMANCE

A mode of communicative behavior and a type of communicative event. While the term may be employed in an aesthetically neutral sense to designate the actual conduct of communication (as opposed to the potential for communicative action), performance usually suggests an aesthetically marked and heightened mode of communication, framed in a special way and put on display for an audience. The analysis of performance—indeed, the very conduct of performance—highlights the social, cultural, and aesthetic dimensions of the communicative process.

Conceptions of Performance

In one common usage performance is the actual execution of an action as opposed to capacities, models, or other factors that represent the potential for such action or an abstraction from it. In the performing arts this distinction can be seen in the contrast between composed guidelines or models for artistic presentations, such as playscripts or musical scores, and the presentational rendition of those works before an audience (*see* ACTING). A form of intersemiotic translation is involved here, a shift from the encoding of a message in one SIGN SYSTEM (CODE) to another. The transformation can go the other way as well, from performed action to transcribed text, as when a DANCE is transcribed into Labanotation or an orally performed FOLKTALE into written form. The approach to verbal art known as ETHNOPOETICS is centrally concerned with the problems of such transcription.

In this sector of performance studies, THEATER people, for example, have long been interested in the

Figure 1. *(Performance)* Yanagi Buncho, the celebrated actor Ichikawa Hakuyen or the Second Danjuro, represented in his main roles. The Bettmann Archive, Inc.

relationship between playscript and performance and the process of moving from the former to the latter. Folklorists, to take another example, contrast text-centered perspectives, which focus on disembodied, abstract FOLKLORE items, with performance-centered perspectives, which are concerned with the actual use of folklore forms.

The focus of debate on these issues centers upon how much and in what ways the script or score or folkloric tradition determines performance as against how much flexibility, interpretive choice, or creative opportunity rests with the performer. A corollary concern, in the fine arts especially, is how accurately a given version of a playscript or musical score represents the intentions of the playwright or composer. We do not, for example, have *Macbeth* written in Shakespeare's hand. Can we reconstruct what he intended, and, if so, how are we bound by that understanding in performance? As a general tendency, critics and scholars tend to vest authority in the musical or dramatic text and through it in the author of the artistic work, whereas performing artists tend to provide the strongest arguments for their own creative contribution to the artistic process. It is also clear that a neutral performance of a received and authoritative text is an idealist fiction; performance always manifests an emergent dimension, as no two performances are ever exactly the same. Beyond this, there is too much variation across the range of performing arts, cultures, and historical periods (and within each of these) to make a conclusive argument. Ultimately, the relative proportion and interplay of authority and creativity, the ready-made and the emergent, must be determined empirically, in the close study of performance itself.

A similar contrast between the potential for communicative action and the actual conduct of communication is found in linguistic usage in the opposition between competence and performance. This contrast was proposed by U.S. linguist Noam Chomsky and is central to the theory of generative grammar. In generative grammar competence is tacit grammatical knowledge, the formal structure of language as an abstract, idealized, cognitive system of rules for the production and comprehension of grammatically appropriate sentences. Performance, by contrast, is "natural speech," what the speaker actually does in using language. For Chomsky and other generative grammarians, competence is the primary concern of linguistic theory; a grammar is no more or less than a theory of competence for a given language. Performance tends to be seen as deviant, imperfect, encumbered by such "grammatically irrelevant" factors as distractions, memory restrictions, errors, shifts of attention and interest, and the like.

Other students of language, however, especially psychologists, sociolinguists, and linguistic anthropologists, are centrally concerned with performance.

For example, Dell Hymes, a U.S. anthropologist, argues that a socially constituted linguistics demands an alternative conception of competence and performance and their relative importance to linguistic theory. In this view, social function gives shape to linguistic form, language has social as well as referential MEANING, and the communicative function of language in the constitution of social life is fundamental to its essence. Hymes emphasizes "communicative competence," encompassing the whole range of knowledge and abilities that enable one to speak in socially appropriate and interpretable ways. It involves not only grammatical knowledge but also the knowledge and ability to greet, tell a story, pray, or promise. In this view, what transformational grammar would relegate to performance and thus exclude from the purview of linguistic theory assumes at least parity with grammar at the center of a theory of language. Performance here is an accomplishment.

In contrast to notions of performance as any doing of an act of communication are conceptions of performance as a specially marked mode of action, one that sets up or represents a special interpretive frame within which the act of communication is to be understood. In this sense of performance, the act of communication is put on display, objectified, lifted out to a degree from its contextual surroundings, and opened up to scrutiny by an audience. Performance thus calls forth special attention to and heightened awareness of the act of communication and gives license to the audience to regard it and the performer with special intensity. Performance makes one communicatively accountable; it assigns to an audience the responsibility of evaluating the relative skill and effectiveness of the performer's accomplishment.

To the extent that the skill and effectiveness of expression may become the focus of attention in any act of communication (some would argue that to some extent it is always so), the potential for performance is always present. In these terms, then, performance is a variable quality, relatively more or less salient among the multiple functions served by a communicative act. Accordingly, performance may be dominant in the hierarchy of functions or subordinate to other functions—informational, rhetorical, phatic, or any other. Thus, for example, a sea chantey sung on board ship primarily to coordinate a work task may be secondarily presented to and appreciated by the sailors for the skill of the chanteyman's performance; on the other hand, performance may become paramount if the same singer is featured onstage at a maritime folk FESTIVAL. The relative dominance of performance, then, will depend on the degree to which the performer assumes responsibility to an audience for a display of communicative skill and effectiveness as against other communicative

Figure 2. *(Performance)* Variations V (1965), by John Cage. Performed by Merce Cunningham and Dance Company at the Brooklyn Academy of Music. © 1967 by Peter Moore.

functions. It may range along a continuum from sustained, full performance, as when an operatic diva sings at La Scala, to a fleeting breakthrough into performance, as when a child employs a new and esoteric word in conversation with peers as a gesture of linguistic virtuosity. Situated somewhere between the two might be hedged performance, as when someone presents an off-color joke and claims it was picked up from someone else in case it is not well received by the audience, but tells it as well as possible in the hope that the skill and effectiveness of the presentation may be evaluated positively.

Integral to the conception of performance as a frame that puts on display the intrinsic qualities of the act of communication itself is the way in which this framing is accomplished, or in the Canadian sociologist ERVING GOFFMAN's term, how performance is keyed. Every act of communication includes a range of explicit or implicit framing messages that convey instructions on how to interpret the other messages being conveyed. This communication about communication was termed *metacommunication* by GREGORY BATESON. In empirical terms this means that each community will make use of a structured set of distinctive communicative means to key the performance frame so that communication within that frame will be understood as performance within

that community. These keys may include special formulas ("Once upon a time . . . ," "Did you hear the one about . . . ?"), stylizations of speech or movement (e.g., rhyme, parallelism, figurative language), appeals to tradition as the standard of reference for the performer's accountability ("The old people say . . ."), even disclaimers of performance ("Unaccustomed as I am . . ."). The culture-specific constellations of communicative means that key performance may be expected to vary from one culture to another, although areal and typological patterns and universal tendencies may exist.

Characteristics of Performance

Prominent among the cues that signal performance may be situational markers: elements of setting, such as a raised stage, a proscenium arch, or an altar; special paraphernalia, such as costumes or masks (*see* MASK); occasioning principles, such as seasonal festivals or holy days. All performance, like all communication, is situated, enacted, and rendered meaningful within socially defined situational contexts. The comparative study of performance, however, has tended to emphasize those events for which performance is a criterial attribute, what the U.S. anthropologist Milton Singer has called "cultural performances.'' Cultural performances tend to be the most prominent performance contexts within a community and to share a set of characteristic features.

First of all, such events tend to be *scheduled,* set up and prepared for in advance. In addition, they are *temporally bounded,* with a defined beginning and end; they are also *spatially bounded,* that is, enacted in a space that is symbolically marked off, temporarily or permanently, such as a theater, a festival ground, or a sacred grove. Within these boundaries of time and space, cultural performances are *programmed,* with a structured scenario or program of activity, as in the five acts of an Elizabethan DRAMA or the liturgical structure of an Iroquois condolence ceremony. These four features are in the service of an additional one, which is part of the essence of cultural performances, namely, that they are *coordinated public* occasions, open to view by an audience and to collective participation; they are occasions for people to come together. Moreover, involving as they do the most highly formalized and aesthetically elaborated performance forms and the most accomplished performers of the community, such performance events are *heightened* occasions, available for the enhancement of experience through the present enjoyment of the intrinsic qualities of the performative display.

Perhaps the principal attraction of cultural performances for the study of society lies in their nature as *reflexive* instruments of cultural expression. U.S.

Figure 3. *(Performance)* Bertolt Brecht, *Die Dreigroschenoper* (Threepenny Opera), Theater am Schiffbauerdamm, 1928. Deutsches Theatermuseum, Munich.

scholar Barbara Babcock has suggested that the term reflexive identifies two related capacities of performance, both rooted in the capacity of any system of signification to become an object to itself and to refer to itself, thus opening up to view the organizing and patterning principles by which the system is constituted.

First of all, performance is formally reflexive—signification about signification—insofar as it calls attention to and involves self-conscious manipulation of the formal features of the communicative system (physical movement in dance, language and tone in song, and so on), making one at least conscious of its devices. At its most encompassing, performance may be seen as broadly metacultural, a cultural means of objectifying and laying open to scrutiny culture itself, for culture is a system of systems of signification. Thus, Singer, in his efforts to understand the complex culture of India, concentrated his attention on such cultural forms as plays, concerts, lectures, ritual readings and recitations, rites, ceremonies, and festivals, because his "Indian friends thought of their culture as encapsulated in these discrete performances, which they could exhibit to visitors and to themselves."

Reflexive is a more potent term here than the still widely current *reflective*, which treats performances and other artistic forms as reflections, mirror images (though perhaps distorted ones, as in a fun house) of some primary cultural realities such as values, patterns of action, structures of social relations, and the like—an "art follows life" perspective. Recent performance studies in anthropology, as in the work of Roger Abrahams, Clifford Geertz, Richard Schechner, and Victor Turner, demonstrate that cultural performances may be primary modes of discourse in their own right, casting in sensuous images and performative action rather than in ordered sets of explicit, verbally articulated values or beliefs, people's understandings of ultimate realities and the implications of those realities for action. Geertz's analysis of the court rituals of what he calls "the theater state in nineteenth-century Bali" are especially revealing in this regard.

In addition to formal reflexivity, performance is reflexive in a social-psychological sense. Insofar as the display mode of performance constitutes the performing self (the actor onstage, the storyteller before the fire, the festival dancer in the village plaza) as an object for itself as well as for others, performance is an especially potent and heightened means of taking the role of the other and of looking back at oneself from that perspective, in the process that social philosopher and social psychologist GEORGE HERBERT MEAD and others like him have identified as constitutive of the self. Indeed, Mead himself cites the efficacy of drama in reporting situations through which one can enter into the attitudes and experiences of other persons. Such dimensions of consciousness of consciousness are not, of course, confined to cultural performances but may illuminate identity in any social context; a sense of being "on" or doing something "for the camera" in the course of ongoing social actions does constitute performance in the general sense developed here. However, when the attribution of a performance quality to social interaction carries with it a range of metaphorical meanings drawn more narrowly from theatrical performance in variations on the venerable "life as theater" trope, the analogy is best explored in terms of the conventions of theater or drama that are pressed into the service of the metaphor.

See also BODY MOVEMENT NOTATION; CANTOMETRICS; CHOREOMETRICS; MUSIC PERFORMANCE; ORAL CULTURE; ORAL POETRY.

Bibliography. Roger D. Abrahams, *The Man of Words in the West Indies*, Baltimore, Md., 1983; Barbara Babcock, ed., *Signs about Signs: The Semiotics of Self-Reference* (special issue), *Semiotica* 30, nos. 1–2, 1980; Richard Bauman, *Verbal Art as Performance*, Rowley, Mass., 1977, reprint Prospect Heights, Ill., 1984; Noam Chomsky, *Aspects of the Theory of Syntax*, Cambridge, Mass., 1965; Clifford Geertz, *Negara: The Theater State in Nineteenth-Century Bali*, Princeton, N.J., 1980; Erving Goffman, *Frame Analysis*, Cambridge, Mass., 1974; Richard Hornby, *Script into Performance*, Austin, Tex., 1977; Dell Hymes, *Foundations in Sociolinguistics*, Philadelphia, 1974; George Herbert Mead, *Mind, Self, and Society*, ed. by Charles W. Morris, Chicago, 1962; Richard Schechner, *Essays on Performance Theory*, New York, 1977; Milton Singer, *When a Great Tradition Modernizes*, New York, 1972; Victor Turner, *From Ritual to Theater*, New York, 1982.

RICHARD BAUMAN

PERSONAL SPACE. *See* INTERPERSONAL DISTANCE.

PERSUASION

The process whereby a person's cognitions, ATTITUDES, or behaviors toward an object are influenced by another person's communication about that object. The persuasion process has been subjected to intense theoretical analysis during several periods in Western history, but only during the past half-century has the theorizing been supplemented by concentrated empirical research.

Historical Background

Only in four scattered centuries has persuasion played so central a role in Western society that it became an art, a craft, and a science with a systematic body of theory. The first was the Hellenic century that can be dated from the 427 B.C.E. arrival of the Sophists in Athens to the death of Demosthenes in 322; AR-ISTOTLE's *Synagoge Technon*, which reviewed other Hellenic theories of persuasion, has been lost, but his own persuasion theory remains accessible through his *Rhetoric* and *Topics* (*see also* HELLENIC WORLD). A second persuasive age that left a lasting legacy of theory and techniques is the last century of the Roman Republic, dating from the Gracchi to the assassination of CICERO in 43 B.C.E. by the triumvirate who brought an end to the republic; Quintilian's *Institutio oratoria* provides a detailed summary of the persuasive techniques and theories of Roman orators (*see also* ROMAN EMPIRE). The reappearance of the *Institutio* in 1470 as one of Europe's earliest printed books began the third persuasive age, the RENAISSANCE century of eloquence that terminated with the murder of the French philosopher Petrus Ramus (Pierre de La Ramée), the period's foremost rhetorician, in the 1572 St. Bartholomew's Day Massacre. A fourth great age of persuasion is the present century of the mass media. *See also* RHETORIC.

Serious scientific study of persuasion began in the 1920s and grew quickly; currently well over a thousand empirical studies on how persuasive communications change attitudes and behaviors are published each year by basic and applied researchers in such fields as social psychology, marketing, and communication science. While the focus here is on persuasive communications from other people as a major determinant of the person's attitudes and behaviors, it should be recognized that attitudes and behaviors may be affected also by factors such as genetic endowment, transient physiological states, direct experience with the object, and participation in socializing institutions such as the childhood home, peer groups, schools, governmental structures, and social rituals.

An Input/Output Analysis of the Communication/Persuasion Process

The persuasion process can be analyzed on an input/output basis, the inputs being various components of the persuasive communications and the outputs being the successive steps that lead to the desired change in attitudes and actions. It is useful to group input communication variables into the five classes of source, message, channel, receiver, and target, each of which can be subdivided: source variables into credibility, attractiveness, and power cues; message variables into appeals, arguments, styles, organization, amount of material, and the like. These second-order input categories can be further subdivided, as when message style is analyzed into vividness, literalness, speed, HUMOR, and so forth. This hierarchy of input categories provides useful checklists for constructing and diagnosing persuasive communications. Their hierarchical structure allows the communication to be analyzed either by looking at the big picture or by focusing on specific aspects.

The output side of the persuasive process can be analyzed into a series of behavioral steps that leads to the intended change in attitudes or action. A dozen successive steps leading to persuasion are usefully distinguished, including exposure to the communication, attending to it, developing interest in it, comprehending its content, generating supportive cognitions, acquiring skills needed to comply, accepting the position advocated, storing this agreement in memory, retrieving the stored material when opportunity for acting arrives, decision making on the basis of the retrieved material, acting in accord with this decision, and consolidating the new position.

Constructing or evaluating a persuasive communication is facilitated by analyzing its potential for evoking each of the dozen steps; where some output step is found to be only weakly evoked, inputs can be added to the communication to elicit it. A number of errors common in constructing persuasive communications can be avoided by using such a checklist of steps. For example, a communication input such as humor or GRAPHICS may be added to evoke some output step such as interest in the message, but an examination of this output list suggests that the addition could impede other output steps, as when humor makes the message more enjoyable but distracts from comprehension of the arguments. With unimportant issues, the receiver may take a shortcut through these dozen steps, accepting or rejecting the message conclusion on the basis of incidental cues such as source credibility without paying attention to the arguments.

Source variables. The notion that the effectiveness of a given communication can be enhanced by attributing it to a favorably regarded source underlies efforts of advertisers and political campaigners to have their products or candidates endorsed by credible, attractive, and powerful persons and institutions. Credibility derives from the source's perceived expertise and trustworthiness. Expertise is attributed on the basis of the source's perceived general intelligence or specific acquaintance with the issue. The basis for the attribution of trustworthiness is the source's perceived general honesty and objectivity on the issue; for example, sources may be more trusted and elicit more agreement when they are perceived as arguing against their own best interests. Source attractiveness derives from the source's familiarity, similarity, or physical beauty. Source power derives from the source's control, or perceived control, over the target person's rewards and punishments, the source's desire for agreement, and ability to ascertain if the agreement has occurred; for example, source power is more effective in eliciting public compliance than private agreement.

While source credibility, attractiveness, and power typically enhance persuasiveness, these commonsense effects may be reversed in various circumstances. For example, revealing the source's persuasive intent may reduce credibility but enhance impact when the target person wants to ingratiate the source or when the source's interestedness is taken as a sign of expertise or when the revelation clarifies the point of the message. Likewise, the usual positive impact of source attractiveness can be reversed, for example, when the source's niceness is taken as an attempt at ingratiation or a willingness to tolerate noncompliance, when identification with the aggressor is involved, or when praise from a stranger is more convincing. And while source power generally enhances compliance, the reverse relationship obtains when a disadvantaged person dominates through weakness or a powerful source evokes reactance. Such reversals are reminders that persuasion theory should not only codify commonsense assumptions but also make explicit exceptional situations in which the usual relationships are reversed.

Message variables. The persuasive impact of a half-dozen illustrative classes of message variables will be considered: type of argument and appeal, style, inclusions and omissions, organization, amount of material, and extremity of position taken. As for type of argument, induction from a vivid example tends to be more persuasive than deduction from a general principle. The relative effectiveness of fear versus reassurance appeals can be studied by looking at messages urging people to get cancer examinations, either by stressing the dangers of waiting too long or by stressing the benefits of early detection. Fear appeals are more effective with people who feel invulnerable or are uninterested in the issue, but they may be counterproductive by motivating the person to cope with the anxiety rather than with the problem (for example, by repressing the whole topic rather than taking action on the danger). Reassuring appeals may thus be more effective in producing long-term behavioral results.

Figurative language and humor illustrate message style variables. Figures of speech, especially sustained metaphors, enhance persuasion by attracting attention, increasing perceived source competence, or providing aesthetic pleasure (*see* METAPHOR). Humor is used widely in commercial ADVERTISING and political ORATORY, but surprisingly little evidence for its persuasive effectiveness has been found. A considerable body of empirical research shows that humor decreases as often as it increases persuasive impact and seldom has the expected mediator or interaction effects. Faster speaking (up to one-and-one-half times the normal rate) enhances persuasion.

As for what is best included versus left out, persuasion is usually greater if the conclusion is presented explicitly in the message rather than left implicit for the audience to induce. It is more effective to deal explicitly and early with opposition arguments than to ignore them (unless there is near certainty that the audience will remain unaware of them). It is also more effective to include only very strong arguments and omit those of modest strength, because people tend to use a weighted-averaging model of cognitive algebra.

A "first the good news, then the bad" ordering of desirable and undesirable information in a message is more persuasive because starting with the bad news may cause the audience to tune out before the good news arrives. Whether there is a primacy advantage in creating the initial impression by presenting one's side first or a recency advantage in going last and leaving the freshest impression at decision time depends on spacing of the time gaps. Because of the negatively accelerated decay of memory and of proactive inhibition, the first side has the advantage when the two sides come in immediate succession and there is a delay before audience decision; but the second side has the advantage when there is an interval between first and second sides and the decision is made immediately after the second side.

Repetition has limited cost-effectiveness because persuasive impact increases only for the first three or four hearings and then levels off. When number and spacing of supportive arguments are considered, some evidence indicates that information-overload effects occur at high speeds of presentation, beyond which more information yields less impact. This negative return from increased information occurs only at unusually high rates of presentation, however.

A final type of message variable—extremity of the position urged—affects exposure, perception, and attitude change. The selective exposure postulate—that people seek out agreeable and avoid disagreeable information—is widely held by communication theorists, but empirical evidence shows that the desire to avoid discrepant information is often overridden by the advantages of becoming familiar with the opposition's position. Some evidence suggests that mildly discrepant material is perceptually distorted to appear more agreeing than it actually is, while highly discrepant material may be distorted slightly to appear more discrepant than it actually is. The more extreme the message position, the more change it produces in the audience, up to gigantic discrepancies where incredulity sets in, especially with suspect sources. For example, in simulated jury trials, the higher the award asked by the plaintiff's attorney (up to extravagantly high amounts), the more money the jury actually awards.

Channel variables. Channel variables include the sensory receptors by which the communication reaches the person (such as eye versus ear), the medium through which it is transmitted (such as print versus television), the contextual circumstances surrounding the transmission, and so forth. The television medium is thought to be particularly effective because of its vividness and the amount of time the average person spends watching it (over three hours per day in industrialized countries). Much research has focused on intended effects of television, such as advertising's impact on buying or the impact of political campaign materials on voting, and on such unintended effects as how the pervasive VIOLENCE in programs affects viewer aggression or how biased television representation of various demographic groups affects viewers' stereotypes. Some studies on each of these possible effects report statistically significant impacts but usually of small magnitude, and many studies find no significant effects at all. The smallness of the demonstrated effects of television may be due to methodological or conceptual deficiencies in the studies or to the impacts actually being less than commonly expected.

Examples of the source's NONVERBAL COMMUNICATION that are found to reduce persuasive impact include very high and low levels of eye contact, narrow pupil dilation, a closed and symmetrical posture, and self-grooming gestures. Examples of auditory nonverbal cues that tend to reduce persuasion by lowering perceived credibility, attractiveness, or power include high pitch, long latencies and other nonfluencies, hedges, and tag questions. It is dangerous to generalize about the persuasive effects of these nonverbal variables because of their nonmonotonic relationships and interactions with other variables.

Communication context variables affect persuasive impact. For example, hearing a persuasive communication in the presence of other people has been found to lessen impact even if the others are strangers. Also being in a benevolent mood when one hears a message often enhances its impact.

Receiver variables. Characteristics of the receivers (audience) that have been studied for their effects on persuadability include demographic characteristics, personality traits, and degree of active participation. There is a nonmonotonic relationship of age to susceptibility to social influence such that suggestibility reaches a maximum at about age nine, while conformity and persuadability peak a few years later. There is a marginal tendency for women to be more influenceable than men, while ethnic differences in susceptibility appear negligible. The relationship of many personality characteristics including self-esteem, anxiety, and depression to persuadability is that people at intermediate levels on such characteristics tend to be more influenceable than people very high or low on the variables. This inverted-U relationship of age and personality traits to persuadability suggests the operation of compensatory mediators. For

example, as age or self-esteem goes up, capacity for attention and comprehension increases, making the person more open to persuasion; but concomitantly skepticism and critical ability increase, reducing persuadability, these compensatory mediators accounting algebraically for why susceptibility is greatest at intermediate ages or self-esteem levels. Research on forced-compliance "dissonance" situations in which the person is induced to give a counterattitudinal speech indicates that internalized self-persuasion results to the extent that the speaker experiences the participation as voluntary and as having produced serious consequences.

Target variables. The extent to which induced attitudinal and behavioral changes decay as time passes after the communication depends on various factors. In the case of unimportant matters, very incidental aspects of the communication such as source attractiveness may induce the change, which is then likely to decay rapidly. Persuasion on more involving topics tends to be more persistent, because the recipient is motivated to assimilate the message arguments and generate further cognitive responses. There are even "sleeper effects" in which communications have delayed-action effects, their persuasive impact growing as time passes (*see* SLEEPER EFFECT).

A person can be made resistant to later persuasive communication by a variety of pretreatments. Prior anchoring of the belief to other beliefs, to the person's values, or to significant reference groups makes it more resistant to subsequent persuasive attacks. Preexposure to a weakened form of the attacking material also confers resistance to subsequent strong attacks, analogous to inoculation with a weak virus to stimulate disease resistance in a biologically overprotected person who might subsequently be exposed to the virus in strong form. Resistance can also be conferred by modeling, that is, having the person witness resisting behavior by other people. Training in critical ability and inducing resistant motivational states such as hostility have proven less successful in conferring resistance.

The selected communication variables reviewed here in relation to their persuasive impacts are representative of the wide range of variables that have been studied for their theoretical significance or practical importance. The field awaits general theories of persuasion that will integrate these many specific relationships that have been empirically observed.

See also POLITICAL COMMUNICATION; PROPAGANDA; PUBLIC RELATIONS.

Bibliography. Robert B. Cialdini, *Influence: The New Psychology of Modern Persuasion*, rev. ed., Glenview, Ill., and New York, 1985; Harold D. Lasswell, Daniel Lerner, and Hans Speier, eds., *Propaganda and Communication in World History*, 3 vols., Honolulu, Hawaii, 1979–1981; William J. McGuire, "Attitudes and Attitude Change," in

Handbook of Social Psychology, 3d ed., Vol. 2, ed. by Gardner Lindzey and Elliot Aronson, New York, 1985; Richard E. Petty and John T. Cacioppo, *Attitudes and Persuasion: Classic and Contemporary Approaches,* Dubuque, Iowa, 1981; D. W. Rajecki, *Attitudes: Themes and Advances,* Sunderland, Mass., 1982; Kathleen K. Reardon, *Persuasion: Theory and Context,* Beverly Hills, Calif., 1981; Mary J. Smith, *Persuasion and Human Action: A Review and Critique of Social Influence Theories,* Belmont, Calif., 1982.

WILLIAM J. MCGUIRE

PHALKE, DHUNDIRAJ GOVIND (1870–1944)

Better known as Dadasaheb Phalke, he was the "father of Indian cinema," maker of its first full-length fiction film in 1913. Dhundiraj Govind Phalke was born a Brahmin and raised to be a Sanskrit scholar. But he was attracted to the arts and trained first in drawing and later in PHOTOGRAPHY. In 1910 he saw *The Life of Christ* at the America-India theater in Bombay, and it changed his life; as the film rolled, Phalke visualized Indian gods and goddesses and their doings on the screen. It became his mission to make Indian films for Indian audiences.

Phalke saw his task as a part of the nationalist movement against British and other foreign influences. He journeyed to England, made friends with the editor of *Bioscope* magazine, and through him saw the "secret processes" of filmmaking at the Walton studios of Cecil Hepworth. He returned with the basic equipment he needed and made his first film, *Raja Harishchandra,* in 1913. The film was a huge success with both the press and the public. Phalke was hailed as a pioneer and went on to make three more films in quick succession, laying the foundation of a major GENRE of Indian cinema—the mythological film (*see* MYTHOLOGICAL FILM, ASIAN).

Phalke's wife, Saraswathi ("Kaki") Phalke, helped him immensely in realizing his dream of putting Indian images on the screen. When World War I's threat to supplies from abroad alienated his financiers, his wife cooked for his unit, pawned her jewelry to finance his business, and offered, at a time when prostitutes refused to act in films because it was beneath their dignity, to act as his heroine on condition that her name not be publicized and only her husband play the hero. His daughter Mandakini played the child-god Krishna in some of his films. His staff offered to work without salary. Even so, Phalke's independent production came to an end. The short films he had turned to during the scarcities of the war years could not sustain his business. In 1918 he joined the Hindustan Film Company, for which he made ninety-two full-length films. Although Phalke missed the creative independence of working in his own studio, his films continued to please large

Figure 1. (*Phalke, Dhundiraj Govind*)   Phalke at work. State Historical Society of Wisconsin, Erik Barnouw Collection.

audiences with their depiction of gods and goddesses. He portrayed miracles through the use of intricate SPECIAL EFFECTS, causing critics to compare him to Georges Méliès in France. In fact, after *Lanka Dahan,* Hepworth invited him to make films in England.

After the coming of sound Phalke made two talkie films, the last of them, *Gangavataran* (The Descent of the Ganges), in 1937. Although he made a hundred features and thirty documentaries (*see* DOCUMENTARY), only one reel of his first film, *Raja Harishchandra,* and some fragments of his documentaries have survived. He wrote articles advocating the recognition of cinema as an ART and an industry and promoting film appreciation, marking him as a visionary. In contemporary India Phalke is recognized as a pioneer, and the Indian government has instituted an award in his memory that is given annually for substantial contribution to the cinema. In his lifetime, however, except for the success of his very early films, Phalke generally went unrecognized.

See also MOTION PICTURES.

Bibliography. B. V. Dharap, "Dadasaheb Phalke: Father of Indian Cinema," in *Seventy Years of Indian Cinema, 1913–1983*, ed. by T. M. Ramachandran, Bombay and Springfield, Va., 1985; Narmada Shahane, *Studies in Film History: A Compilation of Research Papers Devoted to D. G. Phalke (1870–1944)*, Poona, India, 1970.

CHIDANANDA DAS GUPTA

PHONOGRAPH. *See* SOUND RECORDING.

PHONOLOGY

The branch of LINGUISTICS that studies the nature and behavior of SPEECH sounds. Many of the questions that occupy phonologists go back to prehistoric times: What is speech and how is it produced? How did articulate speech originate? What is the relationship between human speech and animal vocalization (*see* ANIMAL COMMUNICATION; ANIMAL SIGNALS; ANIMAL SONG)? How do given speech sounds come to be associated with given meanings (*see* MEANING)? How is pronunciation learned? Why does pronunciation vary with style of speaking, with speakers of different generations, and with those from different regions? The biblical tower of Babel story and the idea that speech was a gift from specific deities (e.g., Hermes for the Greeks, Sarasvatī for the Hindus) represent early attempts to answer such questions. For many of these topics, such as the origin of speech, there are still no adequate answers, but progress has been made on others. Perhaps the first significant accomplishment in phonology—and one that probably makes phonology the oldest of the behavioral sciences—was the system devised by the Hindu grammarian Pāṇini (ca. fourth century B.C.E.) for the description of speech sounds and how they vary when words are joined to form compounds or phrases. With some modifications, we use Pāṇini's descriptive system today. In the following abbreviated review of this system the phonetic symbols for speech sounds, which are those used in Webster's Collegiate Dictionary, are differentiated from traditional orthographic symbols by being enclosed between slashes.

Speech Sounds

Speech sounds may be characterized by their *manner* and *place* of articulation. Manners of articulation include, for example, *stops* (those sounds that completely block the air issuing from the lungs) and *fricatives* (those that let air pass through a narrow constriction and thus create audible high-frequency turbulence). Independent of other manners of articulation, sounds may also be *voiced* or *voiceless* depending on whether or not they are produced with accompanying vibration of the vocal cords. Places of articulation, where the speech sound's principal constriction is made, include, for example, the *labial* region and the *alveolar* region (the ridge on the palate behind the teeth). Using these and other classifications for manner and place, the articulations of the distinctive consonants of Midwest American English may be classified as in Table 1.

This system can be used—as Pāṇini did for Sanskrit—to describe in a consistent way the changes in pronunciation that words undergo when joined with other words. For example, when the word *don't* /dōnt/ becomes /dōnch/ in the phrase *don't you*, it may be characterized as a voiceless alveolar stop changing to a voiceless palatal affricate before a

Table 1. Consonants of Midwest American English

	Labial	Dental	Alveolar	Palatal	Velar	Glottal
Stops & Affricates						
voiced	b		d	j	g	
voiceless	p		t	ch	k	
Fricatives						
voiced	v	*th*	z	zh		
voiceless	f	th	s	sh		h
Nasals						
(voiced)	m		n		ŋ	
Resonants						
(voiced)			l r			
Glides						
(voiced)	w			y		

following palatal glide. This terminology permits the further generalization that (under certain circumstances) all alveolar stops are liable to become palatal fricatives or affricates when they appear before following palatal sounds; for example, /did/ changes to /dij/ in *did you,* /gas/ to /gash/ in *gas shortage,* and /wəz/ to /wəzh/ in *was she.* This is an example of a much more general process called *assimilation,* whereby the place or manner of articulation of a sound changes to be more like those of adjacent sounds. Thus the alveolar nasal at the end of /sən/ becomes the velar nasal /ŋ/ when it appears before a velar stop, as in *sun kissed.*

The Comparative Method

During the first half of the nineteenth century, in what is probably the greatest achievement of phonological science, a way was devised to answer at least partly the age-old question of how languages come to differ from one another. Danish scholar Rasmus Rask and Germans Franz Bopp, Jacob Grimm, and August Schleicher, among others, are credited with development and refinement of a technique— the *comparative method*—for the reconstruction of the history of languages: identifying the *sound changes* (changes in pronunciation) that gave rise to daughter languages from a parent tongue (*see* LANGUAGE). The comparative method utilizes practical knowledge about the usual construction of languages' sound systems and likely directions of sound change, a qualitative notion of probability (to recognize similarities in different languages that could not have arisen by chance), and the application of something not unlike the theory of optimization in MATHEMATICS (in the sense that it involves finding the shortest path between the posited parent language and the daughter languages—consistent with all other evidence, of course). After finding a set of cognate words in different languages, such as those in Table 2A in

Table 2. Selected Indo-European Voiceless Consonant Correspondences

	English	Latin	Greek	Reconstructed PIE initial consonant(s)
A.	father	pater	patēr	*p
	foot	pēs	poūs	*p
	fee	pecūs	pekō	*p
	spike	spīca	spilos	*sp
	sprout	sperma	spora	*sp
B.	thaw	tābēs	tēkein	*t
	three	trēs	treis	*t
	straw	sternere	sternon	*st

which borrowing of words can be ruled out, it is possible to deduce that the original forms for these words in the parent language—called Proto-Indo-European (abbreviated PIE)—started with the consonants or consonant sequences given in the rightmost column of Table 2A. The PIE *p (the asterisk marks the segment as hypothetical) remains as a voiceless labial stop /p/ in the daughter languages except in word-initial position in English (and other Germanic languages), in which a sound change has transformed it into a voiceless labial fricative. This conclusion is reinforced by the discovery of comparable sets of cognates such as those in Table 2B, which suggest that in the Germanic languages the change of a voiceless stop to a voiceless fricative also occurred at the dental place of articulation.

The same methods can be applied to words from a single language to deduce aspects of that language's history, in which case it is called *internal reconstruction,* but the time depth that can be penetrated in this way is often much shallower. It is possible, for example, to deduce common parent stems to such pairs of English words as *bake/batch, wake/watch,* and *book/beech,* in which the final velar stop /k/ would be original and the /ch/ the result of a sound change. Moreover, this finding would be a guide in reconstructing a parent form for *teach* that had a velar stop at the end. (In fact, *teach* is derived historically from the same source as *token.*) The phonological history reconstructed in this way has often been confirmed through subsequent discovery of ancient texts or inscriptions.

Structuralism

In the beginning of the twentieth century Swiss linguist FERDINAND DE SAUSSURE argued that a narrow focus on the purely superficial properties of speech sounds ran as much risk of missing the really important aspects of the communicative function of speech as a study of chess would if it focused only on the way the chess pieces were constructed. He also thought that more attention should be given to the present-day structure of a language, not only to its historical development. STRUCTURALISM, the approach to the study of speech sounds that implemented this program, was refined to a high level by a group of linguists in Prague. It sought to describe the underlying relationships that existed between the overt spoken elements of language. The function of /d/ in English, for example, is inherently different from that of /g/ in ways that could not be predicted by simply considering that the two differ in place of articulation. The /d/ contrasts with—is "crowded" by—its relatively numerous near neighbors, for example, /t, n, s, z, l, r/, whereas /g/ contrasts with fewer near neighbors, /k, ŋ/. This notion is not unlike the fundamental tenet of INFORMATION THEORY, that the measure of the information in a given signal is related to the number of possible different signals in the set from which it is drawn.

The Phoneme

A consideration of the function of speech sounds—whether or not they contrast with other sounds—led to the development of the concept of the *phoneme* (approximately 1890–1930). Regarded as the ultimate unit of speech, phonemes are the "chunks" that form words when strung together. For example, the stops at the beginning of the words *key* and *caught* are quite different: the former articulated in the midpalatal region, the latter almost at the rearmost margin of the palate. But they do not contrast functionally; substitution of one sound for the other would produce a strange English pronunciation but not different words. Therefore they are considered members—*allophones*—of the same phoneme, /k/. However, two sounds that are even more similar than these two allophones of /k/—/z/ and /zh/—do contrast, and the substitution of one for the other can create a different word, for example, *closure* /klōzhər/ versus *closer* /klōzər/ (i.e., something that closes). (As illustrated in this last example, phonemes should not be confused with the letters used to spell words, especially in English, which utilizes a very conservative orthography that reflects a centuries-old, not a current, pronunciation.)

Some who helped to develop and elaborate the phoneme theory, for example, Polish scholar Baudouin de Courtenay and EDWARD SAPIR in the United States, regarded it as essentially a psychological entity, the units used to store words and the chunks into which heard speech was divided and categorized. The attitude of most structuralists in the United States, however—following the lead of Leonard Bloomfield, who was influenced by the then-current behaviorist orientation in psychology—carefully avoided ascribing any mentalistic character to the phoneme or to any other phonological construct.

Generative Phonology

This antimentalist stance was challenged in the mid-1950s by Noam Chomsky and Morris Halle, both of the Massachusetts Institute of Technology, who encouraged phonologists to try to discover the psychological basis for native speakers' mastery of their language. This approach, called *generative phonology*, adapted the methods used to reconstruct language history to deduce the psychological structure underlying the surface forms of language. Competing grammars (the accounts of this structure) were evaluated on the basis of their overall generality and

simplicity. In principle, they asserted, there is, or should be, a parallelism between the way the linguist constructs a GRAMMAR of a language and the way the child learning its first language constructs its own mental grammar (*see* LANGUAGE ACQUISITION).

For example, given the related words *electric* and *electricity,* a common underlying stem /ēlektrik/ was posited for both, the stem-final /s/ in the latter word being derived by a *phonological rule* that changes /k/ to /s/ when it appears before a vowel like /i/. In some cases the posited underlying form may be quite abstract in the sense of being unlike any of the words derived from it. For example, /ōpak/ is said to be the form English speakers know—tacitly, not consciously—to be common to both *opaque* /ōpāk/ and *opacity* /ōpasitē/. It was argued that some principles governing phonological rules were so complex that they could not be learned and therefore must be innate, part of the human genetic endowment.

Other Approaches

In the wake of generative phonology (approximately since the mid-1970s) a vigorous and healthy debate over the content and methods of phonology has flourished. Most of the proposed alternative approaches accept the goals of generative phonology, that is, they seek the cognitive understructure that language is built on, but try to attain them with different means. Common to many of these schools is the assumption that what was perceived as the excessive power of the model of grammar used by generative phonology could be limited by finding more rigorous universal (cognitive) constraints on the form of grammars, for example, on the form and content of phonological rules, on the degree of abstractness of underlying forms, or on how rules may be sequenced. Some would rely more on experimental methods to restrain unbridled speculation. Others have argued that the bulk of sound patterns found in a language tell us more about its history and about the physics and physiology of speech than they do about the way language is represented in the mind of the native speaker.

Some of the social forces that determine a speaker's choice of style of pronunciation, such as the desire to show solidarity with the person spoken to, were explored in numerous field studies by U.S. linguist William Labov and his coworkers. These sociolinguistic studies not only clarified some of the ways speech is used to convey nonlinguistic information (social and attitudinal messages) but also speculated on how sound changes occur.

The data and generalizations accumulated by phonologists over the last two centuries have been applied in such diverse practical areas as language TEACHING, speech pathology, lexicography (dictionary making), speech synthesis, and automatic machine recognition of speech. *See also* LANGUAGE REFERENCE BOOK; PERCEPTION—SPEECH; SPEECH AND LANGUAGE DISORDERS.

Bibliography. Daniel A. Dinnsen, ed., *Current Approaches to Phonological Theory*, Bloomington, Ind., 1979; Eli Fischer-Jørgensen, *Trends in Phonological Theory*, Copenhagen, 1975; Erik C. Fudge, ed., *Phonology: Selected Readings*, Harmondsworth, Eng., 1973; D. L. Goyvaerts, ed., *Phonology in the 1980's*, Ghent, Belgium, 1981; Valerie Becker Makkai, ed., *Phonological Theory: Evolution and Current Practice*, New York, 1972; John J. Ohala and Jeri J. Jaeger, eds., *Experimental Phonology*, Orlando, Fla., 1986; R. H. Robins, *A Short History of Linguistics*, London, 1967, reprint (Indiana University Studies in the History and Theory of Linguistics) Bloomington, Ind., 1968; Alan H. Sommerstein, *Modern Phonology*, Baltimore, Md., and London, 1977.

JOHN J. OHALA

PHOTOGRAPHY

Invented as a practical picture-making medium in the third decade of the nineteenth century, photography is the most pervasive and influential means of depiction in modern culture. The basic elements of still photography—an optical system and a photosensitive receiving medium for the optical imagery—are also the foundations for other developments in mass communications technology. In addition to its most commonly considered pictorial uses, various nonillustrative applications of photography play a central role in modern communications technology. Nearly all contemporary books and printed materials are set by photographic typesetting equipment, composed by photocompositors, and printed by means of photographically produced plates (*see* ELECTRONIC PUBLISHING). The revolution in electronic data processing would have been impossible without the mass production of electronic circuitry, itself dependent on the development of highly sophisticated methods of photoengraving. The integrated circuits, which are basic to modern computers and electronic systems, are produced by the optical reduction of complicated circuitry that is photographically etched directly onto wafers of silicon (*see* MICROELECTRONICS). In sum, photography is not only an important means of depiction and illustration; it is also a critically important tool in the technology of information processing and transfer.

Theoretical Considerations

It is possible to make simple pictures by pressing translucent objects (leaves, engravings, swatches of lace, etc.) directly onto paper impregnated with suitable light-sensitive chemicals and permitting light to fall onto the object and pass through it to the photosensitive paper. The first experimental pictures made by photographic means were made in this manner (Figure 1). These pictures, usually called photograms, are photographic in origin but are somewhat like stenciled patterns. The object to be printed can be thought of as a kind of stencil, selectively transmitting light to portions of the photosensitive paper against which it is pressed, while blocking light from other portions of the paper. Photographs in the more general sense are made by means of an optical imaging system like a camera or an enlarger in conjunction with various kinds of light-sensitive materials.

Photography has been the subject of intense critical examination since the announcement of its invention in the late 1830s. W. H. F. Talbot called photography "the Pencil of Nature" and "a bit of natural magic," and LOUIS DAGUERRE referred to it as "the Mirror of Nature." Modern critics have viewed photographs as "stencils off the real" (Susan Sontag), "reality recorded" (Gail Buckland), "the scene itself, the literal reality" (ROLAND BARTHES), traces of the objects they represent (Rosalind Krauss), and essentially automatic productions (Stanley Cavell). Some, like Rudolf Arnheim, have claimed that photographs can only show the facts of the moment and are tied to what is termed visible reality; others, such as André Bazin, Edward Weston, and Beaumont Newhall, have insisted that photographs reveal a visible world beyond the reach of human vision.

Theoretical accounts of photography usually define it in opposition to all other graphic media.

Figure 1. *(Photography)* W. H. F. Talbot, photogram of flowers, 1839. The Metropolitan Museum of Art, New York, Harris Brisbane Dick Fund, 1936. (36.37)

Photographs are said to be mechanical in origin, and this, more than any other feature they may be thought to possess, is generally held to be definitive. It is often argued, for example, that a drawing, painting, or engraving originates in the mind of an artist, whereas a photograph necessarily originates in "reality." This mode of analysis is essentially ontological and places the burden of explanation for any particular photograph on the role played by the represented object in the sequence of events causing its depiction. Nearly all accounts of photography are causal in nature and emphasize the special relations said to hold between photographs and the objects they represent. Thus, according to philosopher Kendall Walton, "a photograph is always a photograph of something," whereas a drawing or painting need not be of anything at all. A further defining feature of photography is held to be its automatic character, which is fundamentally and crucially opposed to the manual genesis of other kinds of pictures.

Causal or ontological accounts of photography explain only a small part of what photographs are, and are so riddled with equivocal terminology and misleading emphases that they have proved incapable of providing comprehensive explanations of photography as a medium of depiction. Considered superficially, it seems as if a photograph of, say, the Taj Mahal necessarily depicts that structure because radiation of various kinds is mechanically reflected from it and ultimately, by means of the camera, onto the surface of a photosensitive film. Described in these terms, the photograph is understood to be a passive and necessarily accurate record of the Taj Mahal. On the causal view a photograph of a building is also a picture of it because the building was present before the camera at the time of exposure. But the presence of the building in front of the camera is only a necessary and not a sufficient condition of its photographic depiction. If the camera is not properly focused on the building, if the film receives too little or too much exposure, or if it is improperly developed, the resulting photograph may fail to represent anything standing in front of the camera at the time of exposure even though light reflected from the building initiated changes in the film.

According to theorists such as Walton, Sontag, Krauss, and Arnheim, if light reflected from the Taj Mahal enters a camera and exposes a piece of film, the resulting print from the film is necessarily a photograph of the Taj Mahal whether or not it happens also to be a picture of the building. That is, the print is equally a photograph of the Taj Mahal if it depicts the building, if it is blank, or if it is a dense, featureless black. This view does not correspond to our ordinary understanding, but, worse, it is incapable of explaining how it is that any photograph might also be a picture. A sunburn, after all, is caused by the action of the sun on human skin, which for these purposes may be considered a photosensitive medium. But a sunburn is not a photograph of the sun in the accepted meaning of that expression. Causal theories of photography cannot distinguish between light-induced changes in various media (including skin) and light-induced changes resulting in pictures of objects. The challenge to theorists of photography is to explain how light can be used to make pictures.

As a means of picture making, photography cannot be understood outside the context of the history of pictorial practice in the West. Most theorists of photography have attempted to explain it solely in mechanical, causal terms, but a comprehensive explanation of photography involves an appreciation of the subtle relations between ideas generally conceived of as artistic and matters thought to be scientific or technological in character (see ART; VISUAL IMAGE).

Art Practice and the Invention of the Camera

The inventors of photography characterized their inventions as mechanical processes by means of which the images on the ground glass of a camera obscura ("dark room") could be captured on sheets of paper without the aid of an artist. They saw photographs as the products of science and industry and not of the fine arts, a view found in many modern descriptions and analyses of photography.

The camera obscura evolved in Italy in the sixteenth century and was used by a number of picture makers in laying down lines for perspective views and assisting in the difficult task of representing foreshortened objects—problems that other artists and illustrators had mastered without such means (see REPRESENTATION, PICTORIAL AND PHOTOGRAPHIC). The earliest camera was nothing more than a completely shuttered room with a single, small aperture drilled in the door or a window shutter. When light is permitted to pass through a sufficiently small aperture into a darkened room, a dim, inverted, and laterally reversed image of illuminated objects outside will appear on a screen placed in the room, opposite the aperture. This phenomenon was known to the ancient Greeks and was studied in detail by the Arab and Latin students of *perspectiva,* the influential medieval theory of vision that flourished in the West from the tenth through the sixteenth century. Although the phenomenon was widely reported and studied, it was not until the art theory of the Italian RENAISSANCE had transformed the practice of painting in the West that pinhole images were thought of as a potential aid for picture makers.

According to theorist Erwin Panofsky, the tendency to emphasize spatial arrangement of objects and figures in Italian painting, together with an emphasis on foreshortened figures, reappeared in the West with the work of the late-thirteenth-century painter Giotto di Bondone. In Panofsky's view the period starting with Giotto and culminating two hundred years later with Leonardo da Vinci was one in which concerns about spatial organization and foreshortening brought about a confluence of artistic practice with scientific theory. This can be seen most vividly in Leon Battista Alberti's text on art theory and practice, *De Pictura,* written in Florence in 1434.

Alberti provides an analysis of vision in terms of what he calls visible things, concluding that a painter can paint what is seen because that is in fact nothing more than a series of conjoined planar surfaces. In other words, the elements of vision and the elements of painting are identical. Alberti's text provides the first written account of the theoretical basis for the use of linear perspective in painting together with the first codified rules for the construction of paintings in perspective. The formal values emphasized by Alberti include sharply outlined figures and objects, their rational (i.e., mathematically sanctioned) arrangement within a geometrically composed pictorial space, and the coherent use of light and shadow in the depicted space (Figure 2). Although these values were expanded and modified over the next two hundred years, his prescriptions for painting form the foundation of what might best be termed pictorial naturalism.

By the mid-sixteenth century most Western artists and illustrators had mastered the use of various techniques of perspective projection as well as the rules of foreshortening and the coherent treatment of light and shadow in painting, and their practice transformed the pictorial habits and expectations of their audience (*see* PERCEPTION—STILL AND MOVING PICTURES). Some of these techniques are reducible to rules and were discussed in great detail by authors of Renaissance texts on the practice of drawing and painting, but their appropriate application is nonetheless dependent on lengthy and difficult training. In 1558 Giambattista della Porta, in his encyclopedic *Magia Naturalis* (Natural Magic), mentioned the use of a camera for pictorial purposes, available to amateurs as a shortcut for the production of formally acceptable pictures. The manufacture of cameras meeting the requirements of artists and illustrators awaited advances in the design and production of appropriate lenses, and although improved cameras were used in the seventeenth and eighteenth centuries by amateur sketchers and some professional picture makers as well (Figure 3), it was not until the third decade of the nineteenth century that cameras were capable of meeting existing standards of depiction.

It is an important and often overlooked fact that camera and lens makers had to learn the specific needs of artists and illustrators before they could go about designing and producing instruments that would satisfy those needs. Cameras were designed to incorporate the pictorial requirements demanded by their users and cannot be thought of as machines for the production of natural imagery any more than a Jacquard loom can be thought of as a machine for the production of natural designs or pictures.

As improved cameras became available in the mid-eighteenth century the imagery they produced came to be thought of in popular terms as scientific or natural pictures. Camera images were easily likened

Figure 2. *(Photography)* Piero della Francesca, *The Flagellation of Christ,* ca. 1444–1451. Galleria Nazionale delle Marche, Urbino. Alinari/Art Resource, New York.

Figure 3. *(Photography)*   Athanasius Kircher, large portable camera obscura, 1646. Gernsheim Collection, Harry Ransom Humanities Research Center, The University of Texas at Austin.

to the images projected onto the retina of the eye, and this helped to create the impression of cameras as mechanical eyes. This reinforced the Albertian notion that vision itself was essentially pictorial in character. It was forgotten that cameras were designed to produce the kind of imagery routinely crafted by artists and illustrators. This kind of camera came to be conceived of as a mechanical picture-making machine that produced the natural images.

The myth of the camera's natural pictures, together with the discovery of previously unknown chemical elements and compounds in the late eighteenth and early nineteenth centuries, gave rise to the hope that a purely natural means of fixing these images might be found. In his introduction to *The Pencil of Nature* (1844–1845), the first book about photography to be illustrated with photographic prints, Talbot reminisces about the circumstances leading him to the invention of photography. After describing his frustration with his inability to draw freehand, or even to trace the images produced by his camera, he says:

And this led me to reflect on the inimitable beauty of the pictures of nature's painting which the glass lens of the Camera throws upon the paper in its focus—fairy pictures, creations of a moment, and destined as rapidly to fade away. . . . It was during these thoughts that the idea occurred to me . . . how charming it would be if it were possible to cause these natural images to imprint themselves durably, and remain fixed upon the paper!

Thus, from the very outset of the experiments leading to the invention of photography, the entire enterprise appeared to be essentially scientific and mechanical. The inventors of photography failed to understand that the camera was the product of a long-established depictive practice and that it had been designed to accord with the prevailing norms of representation. They viewed photography as an independent and scientific corroboration of existing pictorial practice when in fact the system of photography incorporates many key formal features of that practice.

Although the inventors of photography characterized their goal as fixing the camera's image, it is important to bear in mind that cameras do not produce a single, uniform imagery. For example, cameras using pinhole apertures produce images in strict conformity with the rules of linear perspective projection, whereas, strictly speaking, cameras with lenses do not. Moreover, some cameras (e.g., panoramic cameras made with lenses that rotate about an axis during exposure) produce imagery having an infinite number of principal vanishing points, whereas fixed-lens cameras produce pictures with a single principal point. Even with simple cameras intended for amateur use, the correspondence between what might be seen on a ground glass and what appears in a finished photograph is always a matter of degree.

The most obvious discrepancy between camera

image and photograph is seen clearly in black-and-white photography. Here not only is the range of colors represented by tones of black, gray, and white, but also the tonal responses will vary with different kinds of film. Panchromatic-, orthochromatic-, isochromatic-, infrared-, ultraviolet-, and X-ray-sensitive films provide very different tonal responses to the same camera image. Indeed, scientists value infrared, ultraviolet, and X-ray films because they can be used to produce photographs of structures that may not or cannot be seen in the image on a camera's ground glass. High-speed photography can be used to represent actions that occur in, say, a hundred-thousandth of a second and cannot be seen on the ground glass of a camera, whereas photographs resulting from exposures running many seconds, minutes, or even hours often show blurs and swirls that were never present on the ground glass. The characteristics of images produced by means of a lens depend on the lens focus as well as on the aperture setting used for any particular exposure. Under such circumstances the notion of a single kind of camera imagery is little more than fanciful. Properly understood, images are the result of the photographic process and are not its evanescent raw material.

Technical History

The earliest recorded attempt to produce photographs was made by Englishmen Thomas Wedgewood and Humphry Davy in the late 1790s. By pressing objects like leaves and lace in close contact with pieces of leather impregnated with a strong solution of silver nitrate and exposing these to the sun, they were modestly successful in making photograms, but these images turned dark with further exposure to light.

In 1824 two French brothers, Claude and JOSEPH-NICÉPHORE NIEPCE, produced the first successful photographs made with the camera. Using materials employed in lithography, they coated lithographic stones with a lacquer made of bitumen of judea and oil of lavender and exposed these in a homemade camera to the action of light for more than eight hours. They discovered that the image formed in the lacquer could be measurably enhanced by subjecting the exposed plate to the action of various chemicals, a process now known as development. The Niepces, who named the process heliography, hoped to treat the developed stones with the same chemicals used in lithography, ink them, and pull paper prints in the customary fashion, but the photographic image proved too fragile to withstand the necessary chemical treatment. Although heliography established the possibility of photography as a pictorial medium, the length of exposure time and the extreme difficulty of its operation made the process unworkable by all but the most dedicated experimenters (Figure 4).

In 1829 Joseph Niepce entered into a partnership agreement with Parisian painter-entrepreneur Daguerre for the perfection and commercial exploitation of heliography. Unlike Niepce, Daguerre was unschooled in scientific matters, but through luck and sheer obstinacy he managed to invent a practical photographic process, entirely distinct from heliography, that produced highly detailed and exquisitely modeled pictures. This new process, daguerreotypy, was sold to the French government in 1839 and was released to the world without patent (Figure 5).

The daguerreotype process required the buffing of a silver-coated copper plate until it reached a high polish, at which point it was exposed to iodine vapor, exposed in the camera, and developed by the fumes of heated mercury. The process produced one-of-a-

Figure 4. *(Photography)* Anonymous, table prepared for a meal, ca. 1829. Photograph on glass (original destroyed, reproduction from a photoengraving). Courtesy of the Société Française de Photographie, Paris.

Figure 5. *(Photography)* Louis Daguerre, still life, 1837–1839. Daguerreotype. Courtesy of the Musée National des Techniques, Paris.

kind pictures—it was not a print process—and although this was seen as a distinct fault, the ease and low cost of its operation made daguerreotyping an immediate success. The first daguerreotypes required many minutes of exposure in bright sun, but in less than four years new chemicals were employed along with the iodine, and exposure times were reduced to a matter of a few seconds in a daylit studio. These advances paved the way for studio portraiture, creating the conditions for commercial photography and for the development of a photographic supply industry.

The first negative/positive system of photography was invented by Talbot in England in the same year as the daguerreotype. Talbot's process, called photogenic drawing, involved coating writing paper with various compounds that deposited silver halides (e.g., silver iodide, silver chloride, and silver bromide) directly in the fiber of the paper. After exposing the sensitized paper to the action of light, Talbot washed the images in solutions that stabilized or "fixed" them. These pictures were tonally reversed (light tones appeared as dark deposits of silver, and dark tones appeared as blank areas), and Talbot discovered that by printing these negatives onto another sheet of paper he could reestablish the correct arrangement of lights and darks.

The photogenic drawing process was difficult to work, and in-camera exposures ran as long as two or three hours in bright sunlight. These problems led Talbot to experiment with more sophisticated chemistry, and in 1841 he patented an entirely new paper negative process called calotype that allowed for very rapid exposures (one or two seconds in bright sunlight) and for the relatively simple and rapid production of many prints from an individual negative (Figure 6). The process provided the technical foun-

Figure 6. *(Photography)* W. H. F. Talbot, *Chess Players*, 1842. Calotype. Gernsheim Collection, Harry Ransom Humanities Research Center, The University of Texas at Austin.

dation for modern photographic practice, but Talbot's patent restrictions, by limiting commercial use, worked against its widespread adoption. In addition the fibrous structure of the paper negative worked against the resolution of fine detail in finished prints, and many photographers found the soft, impressionistic quality of the prints objectionable.

In 1851 Frederick Scott Archer, an English amateur photographer, invented a variation of Talbot's process that permitted the production of highly detailed negatives on glass. The process, which came to be called wet plate because the sensitized coating had to be exposed and processed while wet, could be used to produce large numbers of highly detailed prints with ease and at a small cost. Within less than a decade the wet-plate process became the standard of the photographic trade and paved the way for large-scale commercial photography and for photographic publishing companies that annually sold millions of prints to an audience interested in photographs of current events, travel views, and pictures of celebrated aristocrats, politicians, artists, performers, and military men (Figure 7).

The mass production of photographic prints by publishing houses accounted for a large percentage of total photographic income until the 1890s, when inexpensive, type-compatible photomechanical reproduction techniques first became available. The inexpensive reproduction of prints in newspapers and books enormously extended the range of photog-

Figure 7. *(Photography)*   Timothy H. O'Sullivan, *Canyon de Chelly, Arizona, 1873.* International Museum of Photography at George Eastman House.

raphy as a means of communication in Western societies. *See* GRAPHIC REPRODUCTION; PHOTO-JOURNALISM.

The development of the technology of photography after the wet-plate period was spurred by the need for more sensitive and predictable photographic materials. Until the late 1870s photographers had to produce their own photographically sensitive plates and printing papers. During the early and mid-1870s photographic experimenters invented procedures for producing silver emulsions based on the use of gelatin. These emulsions revolutionized the practice of photography because coated plates and papers could be produced and stored for weeks or months before use and could therefore be manufactured by photographic suppliers. Moreover, they were hundreds of times more sensitive to light than previous photographic materials.

The new gelatin emulsions were responsible for the rapid growth of companies such as Eastman Kodak in the United States (*see* EASTMAN, GEORGE), Lumière in France (*see* LUMIÈRE, LOUIS AND AUGUSTE), and Ilford in Great Britain. These companies established sophisticated research-and-development laboratories that rapidly replaced amateur experimentation as the source of technological innovation in photography. The laboratories brought about a complete standardization of photographic materials and equipment. Eastman Kodak was particularly aggressive in photographic research and in the development of new markets for its products. The greatly increased speed of photographic printing papers allowed easy and inexpensive negative enlargement by means of electric light and encouraged the production of much smaller cameras whose negatives were designed to be enlarged. Beginning in the 1880s Eastman's production of clear plastic films coated with gelatin emulsions, together with the introduction of the Kodak camera, revolutionized the practice of photography throughout the world. The Kodak created an entirely new type of amateur photographer—the occasional snapshooter whose ability to make photographs is not dependent on any knowledge of the technical details of the medium. *See* PHOTOGRAPHY, AMATEUR.

Twentieth-century advances in the technology of photography have been aimed increasingly at the needs of the large amateur market. Advances in photochemistry, including the introduction of simplified color photography, have generally been elaborations of the silver gelatin processes invented in the nineteenth century coupled with major discoveries in the chemistry of dyestuffs. The incorporation of electronic components (e.g., computer-driven exposure meters) into the design of relatively inexpensive cameras has placed sophisticated equipment in the hands of many amateur photographers and, ac-

cordingly, has served to blur the distinction between amateurs and professionals.

Bibliography. Rudolf Arnheim, "On the Nature of Photography," *Critical Inquiry* 1 (1974): 149–161; Stanley Cavell, *The World Viewed: Reflections on the Ontology of Film*, enl. ed., Cambridge, Mass., 1979; Helmut Gernsheim, *The Origins of Photography*, rev. 3d ed., New York and London, 1982; Helmut Gernsheim and Alison Gernsheim, *The History of Photography, 1685–1914*, 2d ed., New York, 1969; Ernst H. Gombrich, *Art and Illusion: A Study in the Psychology of Pictorial Representation*, 4th ed., London, 1972; Nelson Goodman, *Languages of Art*, 2d ed., Indianapolis, Ind., 1976; Beaumont Newhall, *The History of Photography from 1839 to the Present* (1949), 5th rev. and enl. ed., New York, 1982; Joel Snyder, "Picturing Vision," *Critical Inquiry* 6 (1980): 499–526; Joel Snyder and Neil Walsh Allen, "Photography, Vision, and Representation," *Critical Inquiry* 2 (1975): 143–169; Susan Sontag, *On Photography*, New York, 1977.

JOEL SNYDER

PHOTOGRAPHY, AMATEUR

The emergence of mass-produced camera technology and associated supplies has profoundly affected the maintenance and transmission of information, social values, and cultural ideals. Cameras were initially characterized as tools of accurate reproduction (*see* GRAPHIC REPRODUCTION) and documentation, and later as tools of entertainment and artistic creation (*see* ART), but photographic activities have played an important role in the everyday lives of ordinary people as well. Business interests, technological developments, and social forces combined to promote popular participation in a relatively new MODE of pictorial communication—snapshots as a vernacular form of PHOTOGRAPHY. In this context GEORGE EASTMAN and EDWIN LAND did more than invent, manufacture, and market inexpensive cameras for popular use. They provided a process of photographic representation that had significant implications for interpersonal relations, for cultural continuity, and for the emergence of the home mode of pictorial communication. *See* REPRESENTATION, PICTORIAL AND PHOTOGRAPHIC.

Development

Although historians date the invention of still photography to 1839, it was not until the early 1890s that untrained nonprofessional photographers could purchase equipment and supplies marketed for mass consumption. The major thrust of development occurred between 1871 and 1888 and was largely the responsibility of Eastman and his colleagues George Seldon, Henry A. Strong, William H. Walker, and

Figure 1. *(Photography, Amateur)* Snapshot made with a Kodak, ca. 1890. International Museum of Photography at George Eastman House.

later Frank Brownell, among others. Major technological problems had to be solved because the photographic process was simply too complicated and cumbersome for use as a popular LEISURE activity. But by the late 1870s daguerreotypes, which put a positive image on metal, were being replaced by a wet-collodion process that put a negative photosensitive solution on glass plates. The plates were then printed on photosensitized pieces of paper to produce a positive image. However, the plates lost their photosensitivity as the collodion solution dried. A more permanent dry gelatin emulsion was invented to allow photographers to prepare many plates ahead of time, expose them as needed, and return later to a darkroom for processing and printing.

Increased competition, rising costs, and reduced profit margins led to the replacement of dry plates with a roll-film system. Here a continuous roll of paper-backed, emulsion-coated material passes between two rollers held inside a camera. Problems of film flexibility, fragility, tension, and initial cost, coupled with needs for camera redesign and photographic paper-coating machines, were addressed and solutions were proposed by 1884. But processing and printing the film were deemed too complicated even by professional photographers and certainly inappropriate for amateurs. Eastman then laid the foundation for what became known as the Kodak system, initiating a factory service for developing and printing film for professionals and amateurs alike.

Between late 1887 and early 1888 Eastman redesigned a camera for mass production and public consumption. The first Kodak box camera was marketed later that year, accompanied by the slogan "You press the button—we do the rest." The original Kodak box camera, which measured 3¼ by 3¾ by 6½ inches, with a fixed-focus lens of 57-mm focal length and an aperture of f/9, was loaded with a 100-exposure roll of film. After exposing the film the photographer sent the camera and its contents to the factory, where the film was removed, processed, printed, and returned to the customer, together with the camera and a fresh roll of unexposed film. After several modifications and improvements the Kodak system was accepted, and by 1895 an eager public had endorsed it; demands for both cameras and supplies soon outran their production. One estimate stated that by 1898 1.5 million roll-film cameras were in use throughout the world. By the turn of the century a foundation had been created for a mass market for amateur photography, one that continues to grow worldwide.

A new range of daylight-loading cameras was introduced in 1891, followed in 1895 by the Bullet models and Pocket Kodaks, which were Eastman's first daylight-loading cartridge cameras. Eastman sought to maintain his leadership by marketing the Brownie camera in 1902, taking another step toward putting photographic capabilities in the hands of persons of every income level. The first Kodak camera sold for twenty-five dollars, but the new Brownie models cost only one dollar. According to one account more than one hundred thousand Brownie cameras were sold within one year, and variations on the original model were sold until the late 1950s.

Eastman was not alone in his desire to develop a market for amateur photography. Competition was provided by European entries such as Lizar's Challenge (1898), Thornton-Packard's Automan (1901), and Busch's Cycam (1899) and the Tribees (1900), as well as a line of Houghton's Ensign cameras, among others. In addition, film manufacturers such as Agfa and Lumière introduced simple cameras for the mass market, as did leading professional camera makers like Voigtländer and Zeiss-Ikon.

Each successive line featured improvements in shutter speed and quality of lens and aperture; most lenses were fixed-focus ones set at f/16 for 1/25th of a second, a setting that seemed to satisfy most photographic situations chosen by the amateur photographer. By the end of World War II specific technical innovations originally developed in the 1930s, such as automatic exposure, miniaturization, color processing, and flash photography, had been improved and prepared for the mass market.

Land's invention of instant photography provided amateurs with a second system for simplifying the process, thereby increasing the leisure and social aspects of photography. The key to Eastman's success had been the separation of camera use from developing and printing (sometimes enlarging and copying) pictures, processes that could be performed with guaranteed success by specialists. Land changed this pattern of image production by creating a one-step system that eliminated the delay between taking and seeing the image.

On February 21, 1947, Land demonstrated his Polaroid instant camera, claiming the arrival of "a new medium." His first line of cameras weighed four pounds and sold for less than one hundred dollars. According to one report approximately half a million Model 95 Polaroids were sold between 1947 and 1952, and about two hundred million Polaroid pictures were taken. Like Eastman, Land sought to bring photographic activity within the reach of everyone, and he later marketed an inexpensive line of models for between fifteen and twenty dollars. Paradoxically, the competition between the two corporate giants increased the overall size of the market and escalated the general public's production of personal photographs.

Implications

Clear evidence for the increased use and enormous popularity of amateur photography is reflected in marketing reports produced for the photographic industry. Although worldwide figures are not available, according to the Wolfman Report published annually in the United States, 93.2 percent of U.S. families owned some type of camera as of 1983, and 79 percent of U.S. households were actually taking pictures as of 1981. A total of 11.75 billion still photographs were taken by U.S. amateur photographers in 1983, with no slackening of pace in sight.

The Wolfman Report uses the term *amateur pho-*

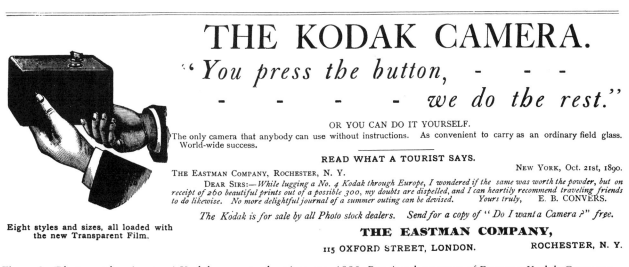

Figure 2. (*Photography, Amateur*) Kodak camera advertisement, 1890. Reprinted courtesy of Eastman Kodak Company. © Eastman Kodak Company.

Figure 3. *(Photography, Amateur)* "f/16 at 1/500th." Cartoon by Mort Gerberg, reprinted from the *New York Times*, December 4, 1977.

"f/16 at 1/500th."

Mort Gerberg

tographer to mean someone who is not a practicing professional or does not earn income primarily from some form of photographic specialization. Yet this broad classification subsumes many different kinds of photographic practice and behavior. As early as 1892 Eastman recognized two broadly conceived categories of nonprofessionals: the "true amateur," who wished to participate in all phases of the process (developing, printing, toning), experimented with camera equipment, and worked on creating special effects; and those who merely wanted to possess private pictures or memorandums of their everyday lives, family members, favorite objects, and special travels. Eastman estimated that the true amateurs were outnumbered by about ten to one, a ratio that has continued to increase dramatically. True amateurs also tend to be distinguished by their participation in local photo clubs or national photographic societies. As early as the 1890s journals such as *The Amateur Photographer* and *The American Amateur Photographer* were published by photographic societies in England and the United States, respectively. But these organizations were not dedicated to the interests of the majority of amateurs—people who were less interested in photography as an art form and more concerned that their "snapshots came out." These photographers found more relevance in such how-to publications as *The Kodak News* and *The Kodak Recorder*, both of which appeared in England, and *The Kodak Magazine*, published in the United States between 1900 and 1930.

The majority of mass-marketed, inexpensive cameras have been used primarily to produce *snapshots,*

a term borrowed in 1860 from the sport of hunting to refer to photographs made in a hurried manner, without deliberation. However, snapshot photography and amateur photography should not be understood as synonymous. The amateur photographer's ability to make snapshots is important to recognizing and appreciating a relationship between cultural significance and pictorial communication. *See* VISUAL IMAGE.

Amateur photography has reinforced the truism that members of contemporary society are the most "imaged" people in history. The frequency of photographic activity is not evenly distributed across all societies, but few people will be deprived of the privilege or dilemma of being photographed or taking photographs during the course of a lifetime. Travelers, missionaries, and anthropologists have contributed statements about indigenous values placed on personal photographs by people from relatively undeveloped or geographically remote regions of the world. People do not have to own cameras in order to have pictures of themselves. Native itinerant photographers, explorers, tourists, and even social scientists have contributed to this irreversible trend (*see* EXPLORATION; PHOTOJOURNALISM; TOURISM). Studies have documented how snapshots and private photograph collections are ranked among the most valued personal possessions. Social, psychological, and symbolic studies are also beginning to explain the immense popularity and ubiquity of amateur photographic forms as a medium of pictorial communication.

By allowing ordinary people to create pictorial

renditions of their own lives, amateur photography has altered the ways people can keep track of themselves and their pasts. Snapshot albums have been added to versions of personal life previously relegated to diaries (see DIARY), notebooks, and scrapbooks. Amateur photography has dramatically supplanted the ways ordinary people can share pictorial information across barriers of time and space. Collections of snapshots help people to retain pictorial representations of their lives and present future generations with visual evidence of their predecessors' existence.

The availability of inexpensive photography equipment has brought the potential for photographic communication to virtually everyone. It has enhanced the quality and quantity of detailed information that can easily pass between individuals, small groups of people, and generations. Ordinary people, untrained in photographic skills, can intentionally create and organize views of themselves, for themselves, and for sharing with others. A technological support system continues to develop to guarantee the renewed and continued growth of both an industry and a mode of pictorial communication. Amateur photography has fostered and enhanced the INTERPERSONAL COMMUNICATION of pictorial information on a mass scale.

Bibliography. Richard Chalfen, *Snapshot Versions of Life*, Bowling Green, Ohio, 1987; Brian Coe and Paul Gates, *The Snapshot Photograph: The Rise of Popular Photography*, London, 1977; Reese V. Jenkins, *Images and Enterprise: Technology and the American Photographic Industry, 1839–1925*, Baltimore, Md., 1975; Beaumont Newhall, *The History of Photography, from 1839 to the Present* (1949), 5th rev. and enl. ed., New York, 1982; Mark Olshaker, *The Instant Image: Edwin Land and the Polaroid Experience*, New York, 1978; Robert Taft, *Photography and the American Scene: A Social History, 1839–1889*, New York, 1938, reprint 1964.

RICHARD M. CHALFEN

PHOTOJOURNALISM

Photographs of current events published in newspapers and magazines are an influential aspect of news (see MAGAZINE; NEWSPAPER: HISTORY). PHOTOGRAPHY has been used as a news medium since the 1840s, but photojournalism requires techniques of GRAPHIC REPRODUCTION that were not developed until the late nineteenth century. Photojournalism is a complex international phenomenon shaping and shaped by individual careers, organizations, the technologies of making and publishing photographs, and the events recorded and distributed as news.

History. The first news photographs are considered to be the daguerreotypes of the aftermath of a fire that destroyed much of Hamburg, Germany, in 1842. The event was reported in the first issue of the *Illustrated London News* using a print from the British Museum of the city's skyline embellished with flames. The earliest illustrated newsmagazines (see NEWSMAGAZINE), including *L'illustration* (Paris) and *Die illustrierte Zeitung* (Leipzig), were limited to engravings and block prints of important public ceremonies and events; there was as yet no way to print a photo block alongside type.

This pattern was followed throughout the early illustrated press. Englishman Roger Fenton's photographs of the Crimean War appeared in the *Illustrated London News* and *Il fotografo* (Milan) in 1854–1855 as wood engravings. In the United States

Figure 1. *(Photojournalism)* Illustration from the cover of the first edition of the *Illustrated London News*, May 14, 1842. The Illustrated London News Picture Library.

View of the Conflagration of the City of Hamburg

A SCENE IN SHANTYTOWN, NEW YORK.
REPRODUCTION DIRECT FROM NATURE.

Figure 2. *(Photojournalism)* Stephen H. Horgan, *Shantytown* (taken by H. J. Newton), as published in the New York *Daily Graphic*, 1880. International Museum of Photography at George Eastman House.

Mathew B. Brady's team of photographers, which included Timothy O'Sullivan and Alexander Gardner, produced seven thousand wet-plate negatives of the U.S. Civil War, some of which were copied as engravings for *Harper's Weekly* and *Frank Leslie's Illustrated Newspaper*. Jacob Riis, a Dane who became a reporter for the *New York Tribune*, covered the harsh living conditions of immigrants in the city's ghettos in the late nineteenth century. His photographic documentation of the tenements was not published in the newspaper but appeared instead in Riis's book *How the Other Half Lives* (1890). Yet news photography drew on journalistic conventions for its agenda as topics were selected and defined as newsworthy: accidents and disasters, political and military conflicts, the living and working conditions of the poor, and public figures and ceremonies.

Since the 1850s inventors had experimented with ways of breaking the continuous tones of the photograph into a pattern of dots that could be transferred directly to a printing plate. U.S. photographer Stephen H. Horgan was the first to publish a halftone, as the screened photographic print was called, in a newspaper. Taken by H. J. Newton, the photograph, *Shantytown*, of a squatters' camp in uptown New York, appeared in the New York *Daily Graphic* in 1880. Munich printer Georg Meisenbach published a halftone in the *Leipziger Illustrierte* in 1883. Despite these successes newspapers resisted the costly reorganization of production and hiring of outside printers to screen photographs. Their investment in engravers also satisfied standards of visual ART and supplied more lively images than the slow photographic technology was capable of at the time. The first British picture newspaper, the *Daily Graphic*, used photographs primarily as models for woodcuts.

Publisher JOSEPH PULITZER's New York *World* was a leader in illustrated journalism by 1885, but the London *Daily Mirror* was the first newspaper illustrated exclusively with photographs.

Competition for exclusive coverage of the Spanish-American War led to excesses of "yellow journalism" in the 1890s. With Pulitzer's *World* and WILLIAM RANDOLPH HEARST's *New York Journal* in the lead, newspapers' lavish use of pictures, including faked and inaccurately labeled photographs, contributed to the war fever and increased circulation. This link with the yellow press also influenced more conservative publications to avoid photojournalism.

Such caution was especially pronounced in illustrated magazines, in which photographs were considered artistically inferior to the work of sketch artists and engravers. Prestigious U.S. periodicals, including *Harper's, Century,* and *Scribner's,* relied on a blend of commentary, FICTION, POETRY, and line art to appeal to upper-class readers. In the 1890s European and U.S. magazines began the shift to rotogravure. This adaptation of photogravure to rotary cylinder presses allowed rapid printing of large editions and the setting of type and halftones on the same page. Simultaneously, journalistic content gained importance as magazines began publishing serious commentary on national and international events. The Spanish-American War also stimulated competition in this segment of the press, and photojournalism became a component. *Collier's,* a leading magazine, carried reports from Cuba by British staff photographer Jimmy Hare and reporter Frederick Palmer throughout 1898–1899, supplemented by war photographs from others.

Typical of turn-of-the-century U.S. magazines, *Collier's* continued to publish news photographs after

RUTH SNYDER'S DEATH PICTURED!—This is perhaps the most remarkable exclusive picture in the history of crimi-
nology. It shows the actual scene in the Sing Sing death house as the lethal current surged through Ruth Snyder's body at
11:06 last night. Her helmeted head is stiffened in death, her face masked and an electrode strapped to her bare right leg.
The autopsy table on which her body was removed is beside her. Judd Gray, mumbling a prayer, followed her down the
narrow corridor at 11:11. "Father, forgive them, for they don't know what they are doing?" were Ruth's last words. The
picture is the first Sing Sing execution picture and the first of a woman's electrocution.

Figure 3. *(Photojournalism)* Tom Howard, *Execution of Ruth Snyder.* From the *Illustrated Daily News* (New York), vol. 9, no. 173, January 13, 1928. Newspaper Collection, The New York Public Library. Astor, Lenox and Tilden Foundations.

the war. Cropped to a variety of shapes, bearing the engraver's mark, and often with elaborate borders, the photographs appeared three to four weeks after an event. Thus magazines adhered to their conventions of artistic presentation while creating new patterns for photography as a news medium. By combining photographs and text and introducing credit lines and staff positions for photographers, magazines helped to establish photojournalism as a career.

By 1900 halftones were common in U.S. newspapers, and many dailies published weekly illustrated rotogravure supplements. The *New York Times* began its Sunday supplement after ADOLPH S. OCHS became publisher in 1896; it was soon followed by the *New York Tribune* and the *Chicago Tribune*. World War I produced a flood of news photographs that entered newspapers largely through supplements, such as the *New York Times' Midweek Pic-*

torial. Staff photographers covered routine events for their newspapers and occasionally produced a "scoop," such as William Warnecke's for the *New York World-Telegram* of the 1910 assassination attempt against Mayor William J. Gaynor. In 1919 New York's *Illustrated Daily News* became the first U.S. newspaper illustrated exclusively with photographs, following the tabloid format of the London *Mirror*. Competition was keen as other New York tabloids followed, including Hearst's *Daily Mirror* and Bernarr Macfadden's *Daily Graphic*, characterized by a sensationalistic coverage of crime and scandal. In 1928, when the *Illustrated Daily News* published a front-page photograph of convicted murderer Ruth Snyder's execution, its circulation was the highest of any U.S. daily newspaper.

International growth. Distribution of news photographs by agencies began in the 1890s, when several agencies in London and New York began

Figure 4. *(Photojournalism)* Martin Munkacsi, cover of the *Berliner illustrirte Zeitung*, September 29, 1929. Courtesy of Karin E. Becker.

supplying newspapers and magazines. However, the speed of distribution was limited by available methods of transportation until 1907, when the French weekly *L'illustration* installed a wire service with the *Mirror* in London, using a system invented by Arthur Korn in Munich. In 1924 American Telephone and Telegraph succeeded in linking Cleveland, Chicago, and New York for wire transmission of photographs from the national political conventions, and the Associated Press (AP) hired Bell Laboratories to develop its network. In 1935 AP's Wirephoto Service was established, serving approximately 40 of the agency's 1,340 member newspapers. Throughout the 1940s NEWS AGENCIES were a main source of photographs for newspapers without their own engraving shops. United Press International (UPI) became a major competitor in the 1950s as a result of its purchases of Hearst's International News Service (INS) and the ACME Photo Agency. That decade also saw radiophoto transmission increase international distribution as UPI established service to Latin America, Europe, and Asia. Intense competition in photographic technology continued between AP and UPI.

Relying primarily on staff photographers in their local bureaus, the two remained the largest news agencies transmitting photographs internationally. The greatest demand was for single, clear, graphic pictures of "spot" news events that included crime, accidents, and disasters. Regular coverage of public figures and ceremonies, including SPORTS subjects, was also important.

A decade after World War I Germany led a new style of photoreportage in popular magazines. Innovative editors, including Kurt Korff at the *Berliner illustrirte Zeitung* and Stefan Lorant at the *Münchner illustrierte Presse,* broke with earlier conventions of publishing single photographs or simple sequences and combined text and photographs in dynamically designed series or essays. The invention of the Ermanox and 35-mm Leica cameras with faster lenses enabled photojournalists to capture human movement for the first time without flash attachments. Stiff formal portraits quickly gave way to candid pictures of public figures and daily life by photographers such as Erich Salomon, Wolfgang Weber, Martin Munkacsi, Felix H. Man, and Alfred Eisenstaedt. Salomon's informal photographs of diplomatic meetings and Man's photo essay of Italian dictator Benito Mussolini at work remain classics of the style. In 1928 French editor Lucien Vogel created *Vu* (Paris) following a similar pattern. Photojournalists and editors were among those who began leaving Germany in 1933 to escape Nazi oppression. Lorant, for example, became founding editor of the *Picture Post,* the major British picture magazine, where he continued to publish photo essays by Man and others.

Issues and developments. The era of mass-circulation picture magazines in the United States dates from the first issue of *Life,* published by HENRY LUCE's Time, Inc., in 1936, and followed shortly by the Cowles magazine *Look. Life*'s staff included Margaret Bourke-White and Eisenstaedt. Adapting techniques and themes from German predecessors, the magazine established the photo essay as the most prestigious form of photojournalism. Stringers supplemented its growing staff of writers, editors, art directors, and photographers. Some *Life* photographers, including W. Eugene Smith, objected to lack of control over how their work was published, a problem intrinsic to the magazine's editorial structure. Specialization became more common at *Life,* as in the field as a whole. Munkacsi, for example, turned to fashion photography; Fritz Goro specialized in science. During World War II *Life* had a staff of sixty-seven hundred in nearly 360 offices worldwide and continued to dominate the national magazine ADVERTISING market. By the late 1960s television advertising and rising postal rates had eroded the profits of general-circulation magazines. With subscription sales and circulation at a near peak *Life* stopped weekly publication in 1972. When it resumed as a monthly in 1978, *Life* had no staff photographers, finding it more economical to hire free-lancers. As the number of specialty magazines continued to expand, free-lancing gained appeal as a career option for photojournalists.

Increasingly photojournalists work through agencies that sell their work to clients and are organized in various ways. Some hire photographers, then purchase their work outright; others pay photographers a commission on work sold. Dephot was a German agency producing important magazine work between the two world wars. Black Star, founded in New York in 1935, was a major source of photographs for *Life* magazine's early years. Magnum, led by Robert Capa, was organized as a cooperative of thirty photographers in Paris in 1936. By the early 1970s Magnum, Gamma, Sygma, and Contact were

among the top agencies specializing in international photojournalism, each with more than a million color and black-and-white photographs in its files.

Debates over appropriate ethical conduct and access to and treatment of sources persist within photojournalism. Spot news coverage frequently involves photographing people in distress, raising questions about photojournalism's role in recording human tragedy and its potential for invading PRIVACY. The view that news photographers focus on scandal and strife hangs over their work, fueled by the paparazzi practice of chasing celebrities for exclusive photographs. In contrast the history of photojournalistic access to U.S. courts is a case in which the self-monitoring of behavior, adoption of unobtrusive equipment, and research and lobbying by professional organizations gradually overcame the courts' expectation that camera coverage would necessarily be invasive and disruptive. In *Chandler* v. *Florida*

Figure 5. *(Photojournalism)* Margaret Bourke-White, *Dam Being Erected at Fort Peck, Montana.* First cover of *Life,* November 23, 1936. Margaret Bourke-White, Life Magazine © 1936 Time Inc.

Life comes with a tug.

A mother's face tightens white against her cheekbones, her face rushes red as she makes the final effort to deliver the child.

In the psychoprophylaxis method of delivery, such as the Lamaze childbirth method once reserved for the hardy few, the man stands next to his wife, letting her squeeze his hand, reminding her to push down. It is an alternative to the usual anesthetized, and isolated delivery room procedure.

Topeka hospitals report a growing number of Northeast Kansas parents are using the new method. In it the mothers are trained in the latter two months of pregnancy to develop conditioned responses through muscle relaxation and breathing exercises to intercept the pain stimuli and thus reduce pain. They learn what to expect at each phase of delivery and how to apply the breathing and relaxation techniques effectively.

Stormont-Vail and St. Francis hospitals report the method is growing in popularity with from two to six mothers, including some hospital personnel, each week choosing it.

"I was excited beyond belief. I kind of forgot what to do. It was a true high. I needed him to tell me what to do," she said.

"I couldn't do much being there but she needed me," he said.

"It was the most important thing to me, having him there."

Both believed the reserved waiting room where he could sit in a plastic molded chair surrounded by Redbook magazines and smouldering ashtrays was not the place to be at the moment of childbirth.

It's his baby too.

While Lynda Coburn was in labor at St. Francis Hospital, her husband Jerry was right there with her, ready to give both moral and physical support whenever needed.

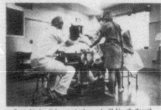

Dressed in hospital garments, Jerry sat with his wife throughout the delivery.

The Moment of Life
An Experience Shared

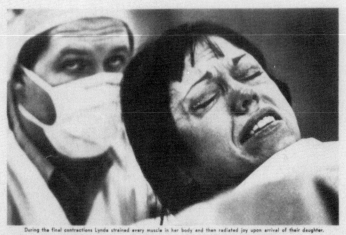

During the final contractions Lynda strained every muscle in her body and then radiated joy upon arrival of their daughter.

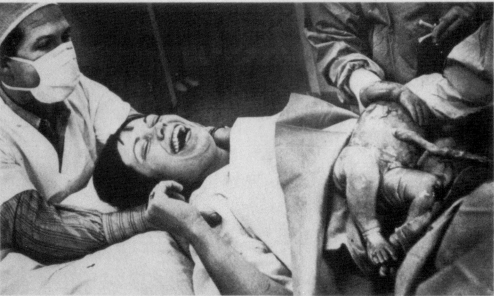

"One minute your stomach is so big and then in a second you have this hot, little, heavy, wet, body on top of you, alive . . . it's overwhelming."

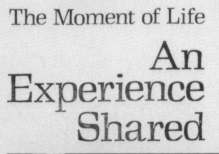

Jacki Lynn Coburn was born to Mr. and Mrs. Jerry Joe Coburn in St. Francis hospital at 11:45 a.m. on Thursday the 27th day of January, 1972.

photos by BRIAN LANKER

It was all over. Jerry walked from the now empty delivery room where moments earlier he had helped to deliver his daughter. "I didn't think it would move me that much, but I was very surprised and excited inside."

Figure 7. *(Photojournalism)*
President Richard Nixon and news
photographers, Washington, D.C.,
1973. Motordrive attachments capable of taking four frames per second and zoom lenses were standard
tools of photojournalism by the
1970s. UPI/Bettmann Newsphotos.

Figure 8. *(Photojournalism)* Susan Meiselas, Monimbo woman carrying her dead husband home to be buried in their backyard. From *Nicaragua: June 1978–July 1979.* © Susan Meiselas/Magnum Photos, Inc., New York.

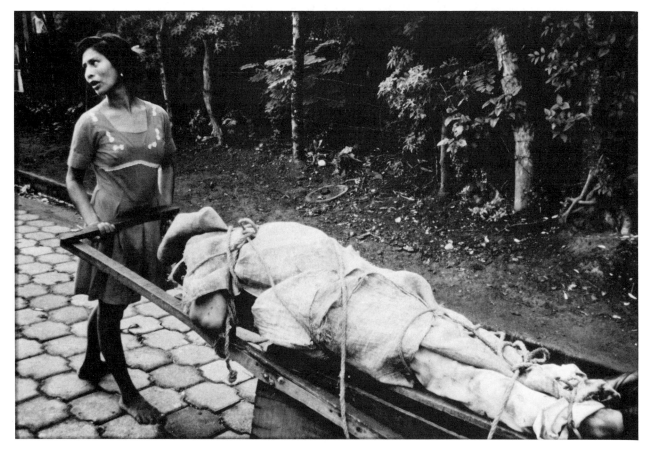

(1981) the U.S. Supreme Court held that states may allow camera coverage of trial proceedings, and most states moved to allow some form of access.

See also ETHICS, MEDIA; TELEVISION NEWS; VISUAL IMAGE.

Bibliography. Gisèle Freund, *Photography and Society*, Boston, 1980; Tim N. Gidal, *Modern Photojournalism: Origin and Evolution, 1910–1933*, New York, 1973; Rune Hassner, *Bilder för miljoner* (Pictures for the Millions), Stockholm, 1977; Wilson Hicks, *Words and Pictures: An Introduction to Photojournalism*, New York, 1952, reprint 1973; Sheryle Leekley and John Leekley, *Moments: The Pulitzer Prize Photographs*, New York, 1978; Arthur Rothstein, *Photojournalism: Pictures for Magazines and Newspapers*, 4th ed., Stoneham, Mass., 1983; Time-Life Books, Inc., *Photojournalism*, rev. ed., New York, 1983.

KARIN E. BECKER

PIAGET, JEAN (1896–1980)

Swiss psychologist, best known for his theory of child development. Born in Neuchâtel, Jean Piaget obtained a doctorate in biology in 1918. His philosophical interest in biological adaptation and the history of science led him to study precursors of adult logical thinking in the actions and explanations of CHILDREN. This developmental research was to occupy his whole life. From 1925 on, Piaget was a professor of psychology at the University of Geneva, and in 1951 he founded an interdisciplinary institute of genetic epistemology. His research, an empirically based reformulation of Immanuel Kant's epistemology, was published in more than one hundred books. Rejecting both sides of the nature/nurture issue, Piaget proposed a constructivist theory of knowledge development. Widely recognized as a theory of stages, Piaget's work is controversial and easily misunderstood. It has potential application within and beyond psychology to all disciplines dealing with human knowledge. Piaget's theory deals with concepts relevant to communication from a developmental basis.

For Piaget human knowledge at all levels is not something that exists objectively as a fact but something psychological that occurs within and between individuals, beginning with infants in their everyday actions. Sensorimotor knowledge is an integral component within the actions. It is conceptualized as the coordination, or the structure, of the action, through which infants relate to objects of action (an interesting event, another person or thing). The action as I/other relation is primary: there is not yet, strictly speaking, a separate I or a separate other. Action/object separation is clearly experienced for the first time around age two with the construction of what Piaget calls the "permanent object." There is a developmental-stage transition from sensorimotor ob-

jects of *action* to action-separated objects of *knowledge*. Children, who in the first two years have advanced in the sensorimotor logic of actions, have to reconstruct a logic appropriate to object knowledge. This second developmental series, beginning after age two as "preoperations," is completed at a first stage around ages six to ten in the form of what Piaget calls "concrete operations," followed in adolescence by "formal operations," the logic of adults. With the attainment of object knowledge (as distinguished from action knowledge), information as potential communication, apart from the intended action, becomes available. It is the difference between recognizing a traveled route and using a map. This difference involves symbolic information.

For Piaget the ability to construct symbols is a logical consequence of object formation. In symbolic play children make present (i.e., re-present) an absent event by assimilating past accommodations (e.g., gestures of attention to an airplane) to their present object knowledge (e.g., of airplanes). In turn, the internalization of symbolic gestures leads to the formation of internal representation—mental images, fantasy, imagination, dreams. In sum, for Piaget symbols are external or internal actions (gestures) that refer to the object knowledge of the symbol user.

PLAY and fantasy differ from a third symbol type that directly intends interpersonal relations and communication. Piaget recognized this difference by limiting the adjective "symbolic" to the first two and referring to the third type as "semiotic"; however, his theory of symbol formation pertains to all three types. Societal LANGUAGE is the most prominent semiotic system, but other conventional systems (e.g., MATHEMATICS, maps, traffic signs) are here included (*see* SEMIOTICS; SIGN; SIGN SYSTEM; SIGNAGE). Language has an "objective," factual existence and seems to be learned through imitation of an outside model. Nonetheless, in Piaget's theory its acquisition has two prerequisites: object knowledge and the general ability to form symbols. This sequence explains why language is acquired at a certain age—but not earlier—and within a relatively short period. The MEANING of words is found in object knowledge. Consider the sentence "This is not a bird; it's an airplane." Comprehension of this sentence requires mental reference to a contrast of subordinate classes that as such has to do not with language but with object knowledge and understanding. In short, for Piaget (as for U.S. linguist Noam Chomsky) LANGUAGE ACQUISITION is not just the taking in of (accommodation to) objective information. It primarily requires assimilation of that information to knowledge structures, which implies subjective construction. This construction is observable in childish speech errors, such as "goed" and "unsick"; but the most telling evidence is the situation of profoundly deaf children born into hearing families. Even without any special educational efforts many young deaf children, deprived of an outside model, spontaneously begin to use manual and visual gestures in a manner strictly analogous to verbal language. In other words, as they communicate within their family they literally invent or coconstruct a new language.

This last example illustrates forcefully that on the question of the language-thinking relation clear distinctions are in order regarding logical thinking, symbols, communication, and societal language. Without the first three, there can be neither language nor personal development. With these three as a basis, natural language is assimilated as the children are exposed to it. Thus in Piaget's theory language cannot be considered the source or the determining instrument of human logic, symbols, or communication; it is the other way around. This position is frequently misunderstood, as if development for Piaget were private and solitary, untouched by language or society. But for Piaget human knowledge, by itself, is a social relation (as indicated above), and communication through action is already implied in sensorimotor development. With object formation around age two, symbolic communication becomes possible, and positive social relations remain the necessary occasions to motivate children away from their original egocentric position to a mature, socialized perspective. Piaget's operations (beginning around age six) in fact provide the minimum logical constraints through which children's thinking becomes socialized and open to free and responsible cooperation. In short, logical thinking is for Piaget an implicit form of interpersonal relating, and the potential contribution of societal language is precisely to bring this implicit communicative power to fruition.

See also COGNITION; EDUCATION; LOCKE, JOHN; VYGOTSKY, LEV.

Bibliography. Hans G. Furth, *Knowledge as Desire: An Essay on Freud and Piaget*, New York, 1987; Howard E. Gruber and J. Jacques Vonèche, eds., *The Essential Piaget*, New York, 1977; Jean Piaget, *Play, Dreams and Imitation in Childhood* (La formation du symbole chez l'enfant), trans. by C. Gattegno and F. M. Hodgson, New York and London, 1962.

HANS G. FURTH

PLATO (ca. 428–348/347 B.C.E.)

Greek philosopher. As one of the seminal thinkers of the Western intellectual tradition, Plato made fundamental contributions to concepts of human communication, both in his own development of dialectic and in his important theoretical statements on EDUCATION, POETRY, RHETORIC, and WRITING. In his *Republic* he offers one of the first UTOPIAS. Plato also contributed through his own literary example; his philosophical fame tends to obscure the fact that he was the greatest PROSE writer of classical antiquity.

Born in the glorious days of Periclean Athens, Plato witnessed the downfall of Athens in the Peloponnesian War and the trial and death of his friend and mentor, Socrates (399 B.C.E.). His aristocratic background prepared him for a political career, but he finally gave up hope of political reform in Athens and turned to philosophy and political theory instead. His three longest works (*Gorgias, Republic,* and *Laws*) deal with the themes of moral, social, and legal reform. He twice accepted invitations to serve as adviser to Dionysius II, tyrant of Syracuse, but his efforts to influence public affairs in Sicily came to naught. He returned to Athens, where his philosophical school in the Academy gathered a distinguished group of mathematicians, astronomers, and philosophers—among them the young ARISTOTLE, who spent twenty years at the Academy. Plato's school remained a center of philosophical study for centuries.

All of Plato's written work is in dialogue form except for the *Apology* (a courtroom speech in defense of Socrates) and a few letters whose authenticity is contested. Other followers of Socrates also composed Socratic dialogues, but Plato transformed the GENRE into a literary instrument of unique power and versatility. At least three of these dialogues (*Protagoras, Symposium,* and *Phaedo*) are among the masterpieces of world literature. The earlier dialogues depict Socrates discussing questions of ethics and education and exposing inconsistencies in his interlocutors' reasoning. Scholars disagree on the historical reliability of these works. Some regard them as a faithful portrait of Socrates; others believe that, although the personal character traits of Socrates may be reliably portrayed, the philosophical thought of the dialogues was, from the beginning, developed by Plato in his own way. That is certainly true for the great "middle" dialogues (*Symposium, Phaedo, Republic,* and *Phaedrus*), in which Plato's metaphysical doctrine of Forms or Ideas is expounded. A third group of later dialogues, beginning with the *Parmenides,* is quite different. The doctrine of Forms is subjected to criticism (in *Parmenides* and *Sophist*), the dramatic form becomes more mechanical, and the figure of Socrates fades into the background. Among the late dialogues the most influential has been the *Timaeus,* which presents a grandiose cosmology in the form of a creation myth; it incorporates much of the earlier tradition of Greek natural philosophy and much contemporary astronomy, MATHEMATICS, and biology, all reinterpreted within the framework of the creation of the world by a demiurge or craftsman god, who looks to the Platonic Forms as his model for producing order in the world of nature.

As a writer Plato is a master of characterization, including brilliant imitations of different rhetorical styles. His own style is extraordinarily versatile, ranging from informal CONVERSATION to the solemn diction of myth (*see* STYLE, LITERARY); the tone varies from light COMEDY to intense DRAMA and (in the death scene of the *Phaedo*) outright TRAGEDY. The most highly developed literary form of their day, Plato's dialogues took the place occupied by the great Attic tragedians of the preceding age.

Plato presents his literary work to rival the poets on the one hand and the rhetoricians on the other. His chief competitor in Athens was Isocrates with his school of ORATORY. Plato deals with oratory at length in the *Gorgias* and *Phaedrus*. In the *Gorgias* he attacks professional rhetoric as a spurious imitation of moral and political philosophy. In the *Phaedrus* he presents an alternative vision of ideal rhetoric as the instrument of philosophy: the language of PERSUASION to be put in the service of truth. But the same dialogue expresses grave doubts about the capacity of any written words to communicate important ideas with accuracy; the BOOK is like a statue, which seems to be alive but cannot answer questions. Dialectic, the power to clarify thought by question and answer, is the only method for philosophy, but it requires a living exchange between teacher and pupil. As a second best to the spoken word, Plato chose to write dialogues.

As a political thinker Plato was opposed to what he considered the degenerate democracy of Athens, but he regarded the arbitrary rule of a tyrant as even worse. In the *Republic* he offers the rule of philosopher-kings as a salvation for humankind, with abolition of the FAMILY and of private property for the ruling class. In the *Laws*, written in his old age after the bitter experience of Syracuse, he settles instead for the rule of law in a moderate blend of democracy and aristocracy, with an enlightened reform of the law courts and a careful system of checks and balances among the magistrates. He was certainly no liberal in the modern sense, but the portrayal of him as a protofascist (by Austrian-British philosopher Karl Popper and others) is much overdrawn. The ideal state of his *Republic* is a unique blend of authoritarian government with revolutionary modern ideas, such as free public education (including mathematical science) and equal participation of women in public life.

As a metaphysician Plato presents the vision of a realm of unchanging, supersensible Being constituted by Forms, in contrast to the changing physical world of sensible Becoming. The world of nature derives its structure and reality by participation in the realm of Forms. According to the myth of recollection, every human soul has had some prenatal contact with the Forms, and conceptual thought for the embodied soul thus consists in "recollecting" the Forms. The study of mathematics is essential for training the soul to turn away from the empirical pseudoreality of the world of change and become able to grasp the intelligible Being of the eternal Forms.

The influence of Plato's thought has remained great throughout Western intellectual history. In the form of Neoplatonism it dominated late antiquity and provided Augustine and other Christian theologians with their metaphysical framework. The creation story of the *Timaeus* was assimilated to that of Genesis, and the Forms became Ideas in the mind of God. The theory of recollection was reformulated in the seventeenth century as the doctrine of innate ideas, a doctrine reflected in our own time in U.S. linguist Noam Chomsky's theory of innate linguistic structure.

Bibliography. Paul Friedländer, *Plato* (in German), trans. by Hans Meyerhoff, 3 vols., New York, 1958–1969; W. K. C. Guthrie, *A History of Greek Philosophy*, Vols. 4 and 5, Cambridge, 1975, 1978; A. E. Taylor, *Plato: The Man and His Work* (1926), 7th ed., London, 1960, reprint 1966.

CHARLES H. KAHN

PLAY

Behavior with a genetic basis that is voluntary and pleasurable and that results in an altered state of consciousness while leaving one in control of one's actions. Play can be realized only in contrast to nonplay behaviors. The experience of the play state may be sufficient motivation for engaging in play behavior.

This definition implies that one ought to distinguish between the experience of play (as a state of being) and play behaviors as they may be observed in play events. Anthropologists Victor Turner and Helen Schwartzman also have noted that the major difficulty in defining and studying play is distinguishing the act from the experience. For example, urban Zulu males engaged in a soccer match or Dani CHILDREN playing flip-the-stick may be said to be participants in play events. However, while an observer may assume they are experiencing play, it is unlikely that this assumption can be verified.

Mihaly Csikszentmihalyi has stated that play is a state of subjective experience because its existence is contingent on there being an awareness of alternatives: "[W]e play when we know we are playing. . . . If we could not conceive of acting by a set of rules that are different from those to which we have learned to adapt, we could not play." He also has developed the concept of *flow*, which is related to playfulness. While flow is a process of involvement in a given reality and playfulness refers to one's attitude toward the reality in which one is involved, these two processes tend to evoke each other. Csikszentmihalyi is clear, however, that neither flow nor playfulness should be confused with play forms or play behavior.

Inherent in virtually all of the literature on play and communication is the assumption that both phenomena are social. Even the play of a child alone is often interpreted as play with a fictionalized character or a make-believe playmate.

Whether considering the play of a single child chasing butterflies or that of scores of Choctaw Indians involved in a stickball contest, one needs to be mindful of the seemingly simultaneous use—either actual or potential—of the sensory organs of the player. A variety of stimuli may be received and treated as parts of a single integrated message by an actor in a play event. That is, TOUCH, SMELL, vision, hearing, even taste, may be used along with myriad internal psychophysiological cues in formulating a play message. Such a message may be to oneself or to one or more others. However, the content of any play message—the symbols defining play and appropriate play behavior—is not only species specific but also culture specific.

Communication and Theories about Play

The work of GREGORY BATESON, summarized in *Steps to an Ecology of Mind* (1972), stimulated interest in the analysis of play and communication. Bateson's understanding of metacommunication, or the frame that tells individuals that behavior is not to be interpreted in its usual denotative sense, has had a significant impact on the study of play during past decades.

According to Bateson, while human communication operates at many contrasting levels of abstraction, there must be one level, implicit or explicit, that defines the subject; he called this the metalinguistic. The level of abstraction that defines the relationship between the communicators Bateson labeled the metacommunicative level. With regard to play this means that one individual must communicate, "This is play." For playful communication to ensue, another must respond, "OK, I'll play too."

The message "This is play" is not a single, static signal, however. In play events all behaviors are transformed in some way (e.g., exaggerated or repeated) and are marked continuously as play. As Schwartzman pointed out, "the message 'This is play' always acts as both a context and a text," and "the messages *are not delivered sequentially but simultaneously.*" Schwartzman further stated that because

"play actions are never quite what they seem to be (e.g., 'This nip is not a bite'), metacommunicative messages must be contained in *every* action that is play. There can be no single signal."

A metacommunicative message serves as a frame or context, providing information on how another message should be interpreted. Such a frame defining a metacommunicative message may precede or follow the textual message. For example, a humorous frame can be established by beginning, "Have you heard the one about . . . ?"

Often overlooked is the fact that players engage in and disengage from play. This engagement process is an intrapersonal one since no one can be forced to play. One may be coerced into capitulation, but the metacommunicative response "OK, I'll play" is first and foremost an intrapersonal one.

U.S. anthropologist Anthony F. C. Wallace's work on communication and RITUAL seems to be relevant to the perspective on play presented here. Wallace concluded that social ritual was allo-communicative, while solitary ritual was auto-communicative, and that auto-communication occurs when individuals send messages to their own psychophysiological systems.

Applying Wallace's conclusions to play, it follows that an individual sends signals to his or her internal psychophysiological system, which produces particular responses necessary for the specific play behavior. However, once initiated these systems may respond with signals of their own. Not only does the player's intended message result in the desired behavior of running toward another in an effort to tag that person, but also the player's body produces messages that may result in laughter, euphoria, and a distorted sense of time (such that the player forgets to come home for supper at the parentally designated hour). These messages from the internal systems may be understood as an important part of the context of play—a context that is continuously open to new signals and changes in the character of the context.

Play, then, presents two messages. The first is the metacommunicative message or statement of intent: "This is play." The second is a statement of contextual reality. These two are integrally related and must be understood as a continuous experientially defined frame until superseded by a new and different metacommunicative message.

The contextual reality of play is not limited to the social texts that are communicated. There are also the messages to one's own psychophysiological systems. Moreover, once the individual's psychophysiological systems have received a play message, these systems respond, and such responses become part of the contextual reality that affects ongoing communications.

This view of play is congruent with those that

emphasize play as a biologically structured adaptive process. Steve Tipps has suggested that there are neurological bases for play's adaptive function. He has argued that play has a positive emotional quality that enhances experiential exploration and neural alertness to the environment, which results in neurological growth and provides structures for more complex play behaviors. The physical symbolic exploration associated with play leads to pattern making that enables individuals to manipulate abstract ideas and to behave creatively.

Charles Laughlin and John McManus also have argued that play is to be understood within a biological matrix. They have defined play as a subprocess of the empirical modification cycle, or EMC. The EMC is a biogenetic feedback and feedforward arrangement that allows the organism to develop an internal model (or cognized environment) of the external world (or operational environment). The cognized environment is not a pictorial representation of the operational environment but an adaptive mechanism. The cognized environment is so structured that it directs the production of behavior that proves adaptive for the organism within the operational environment.

Play, in the model proposed by Laughlin and McManus, is a subprocess of the EMC by means of which an organism intentionally "complexifies" its operational environment for the purpose of optimizing development of its cognized environment (or internal model of the external world). This is accomplished either by increasing the sensory information about the external world as previously modeled or by increasing the spatiotemporal range of the external world.

For Laughlin and McManus social play is not a fundamentally different process from other play, but it has a different object. Social play functions to establish or modify channels of neurophysiological transport necessary for optimal interorganismic coordination within and between social groups. What is important, then, is that during social play, organisms are measuring one another's rhythms.

Conclusions

The following points summarize the foregoing discussion on the play/communication relationship.

1. A player may be understood as both a transmitter and a receiver of messages.
2. Play may involve the simultaneous use of multiple sensory channels for transmission and reception. However, a number of different cues may make up the message "This is play."
3. Codes for play may be shared by many (but not necessarily all) members of a culture. Such codes, however, are usually culture specific.

4. Signs or symbols can have meaning as communicative cues only as members of sets, not as isolates. However, as U.S. anthropologist Ray Birdwhistell has noted, even context- or event-specific cues are subject to modification cues that signal the reliability of the cue by transmitting information about the context, the sender (i.e., the signature), and the intended receiver (i.e., the address).
5. Play is a continuous process from the point of engagement until the player disengages. In this sense a play occurrence can be regarded as the outcome of a binary mechanism since one is either at play or not at play. The triggering of a play state, however, may involve a complex of cues.

Whether play is defined as activity, experience, or biological process, the researcher is presented with certain conceptual and methodological problems. The activity approach ignores the obvious: play is intrinsic to the player and is not a set of easily classified, observable behavior patterns. However, those who would approach play as an affective state or a biologically structured process present empirical researchers with a significant dilemma. If no specific behavior can be equated with play, how can one determine when play is taking place? Perhaps by exploring the communication inherent in play, both the auto- and the allo-communicative aspects, some of the theoretical and methodological barriers to understanding play will be overcome.

See also ETHOLOGY; SPORTS.

Bibliography. Gregory Bateson, *Steps to an Ecology of Mind*, New York, 1972; Mihaly Csikszentmihalyi, "Some Paradoxes in the Definition of Play," in *Play as Context*, ed. by Alice Taylor Cheska, West Point, N.Y., 1981; Charles D. Laughlin, Jr., and John McManus, "The Biopsychological Determinants of Play and Games," in *Social Approaches to Sport*, ed. by Robert M. Pankin, East Brunswick, N.J., 1982; Edward Norbeck, "The Anthropological Study of Human Play," *Rice University Studies* 60, no. 3 (1974): 1–8; Jurgen Ruesch and Gregory Bateson, *Communication: The Social Matrix of Psychiatry*, New York, 1951; Helen B. Schwartzman, *Transformations: The Anthropology of Children's Play*, New York, 1978; Steve Tipps, "Play and the Brain: Relationships and Reciprocity," *Journal of Research and Development in Education* 14, no. 3 (1981): 19–29.

ANDREW W. MIRACLE

PLEBISCITE

A time-honored method of ascertaining the popular will. It conforms to an ancient Roman tradition of frequent and direct consultation on significant questions with as many citizens as possible. The earliest plebiscites were by voice vote in assemblies, but the more recent ones have all been by secret ballot among eligible voters. Although political scientists today generally favor representative over plebiscitarian forms of democracy as better adapted to the requirements of modern complex society, the plebiscite still has its uses.

Derived from the Latin, *plebiscite* means quite literally the submission of any kind of question to a popular vote. It is in this respect the equivalent of a referendum, but the term has, over the years, acquired a more restricted meaning. One designates as plebiscites only voting on matters of sovereignty or basic constitutional reform. Moreover, where the results of a referendum can be either legally binding or advisory, the outcome of a plebiscite is usually accepted as the expression of a sovereign popular will against which there is no recourse.

Uses in Europe. The plebiscite in this modern dress dates from the French Revolution, when the concept of self-determination first emerged and made the nation the focus of loyalty. On the premise that a change of sovereignty should take place only with the consent of the people concerned, the 1790–1791 Constituent Assembly held a plebiscite in the papal territory of Avignon and the Comtat-Venaissin and, later, in Savoy and Nice. Even though the voting took place under French military occupation, historians generally agree that these plebiscites were a genuine effort to ascertain popular preferences. They are less confident about subsequent plebiscites by which Napoléon gained the ratification of a new constitution and conferred upon himself first the title of life consul and later that of emperor. Some fifty years later his nephew had himself crowned by the same means.

Notwithstanding these early abuses, the idea behind the plebiscite gained ground with the advance of democracy and the resurgence of nationalism in the mid-nineteenth century as the appropriate way to implement these principles. In 1848 the leaders of the Italian Risorgimento were able to demonstrate with the results of referendums among the people of Lombardy, Venetia, Parma, Piacenza, Modena, and Reggio the existence of a strong desire for union with Sardinia into a single nation. Other plebiscites were held to settle the territorial reorganization of the Danubian principalities; the first, in 1856, was followed by a second ten years later and led to the establishment of Romania as a national state.

In considering the use of the plebiscite as an instrument to legitimize changes in territorial sovereignty, one has to concede that, at least until World War I theoretical discussion ran far ahead of practice, with favorable views voiced mostly by French and Italian writers; the main opposition came from Germans, while Americans seemed pretty well divided.

Those in favor argued that political units coincident with nationality would promote internal democracy, be conducive to tolerance, and ultimately find expression in greater international cooperation. Opponents believed that disregard of strategic considerations could allow the preference of a small population to play havoc with the balance-of-power system, which they saw as the cornerstone of international stability. That these views were to some extent reflections of national interest was demonstrated when Prussia, with its unilateral annexation of northern Schleswig in 1866, overrode the call for a plebiscite as it did again a few years later when it annexed Alsace-Lorraine. The two acts struck a shattering blow at the principle. The only bright spot in the picture until the end of World War I was Sweden, which was persuaded to grant Norway its independence as the result of a 1905 plebiscite to which it had reluctantly consented.

Types. Plebiscites can be informal and unilateral or formal and by agreement among the parties with an interest in the outcome. The earliest modern plebiscites were clearly of the informal variety, called by the victorious French in the obvious expectation that the people would want to affiliate with the nation whose armies promised liberty, equality, and fraternity. Over time plebiscites have more often been held under provision established in bilateral and multilateral treaties, as illustrated in the territorial changes effected through the Treaty of Versailles (1919), which incorporated the principle that people sharing a common language had a claim to common nationhood. When the negotiators attempted to redraw boundaries so as to maximize self-determination, they found that sometimes there was no obvious line of demarcation in national sentiment. For these situations a plebiscite proved a useful corrective. U.S. President Woodrow Wilson, to cite one example, had believed that all of the previously German province of Upper Silesia should rightfully be ceded to Poland, yet when 60 percent of the inhabitants voted to remain German the province was partitioned along lines duplicating as closely as possible the actual ethnic frontiers.

The success of this kind of plebiscite is highly contingent on close supervision by an impartial authority to ensure that citizens are free to express their preference. But the problems do not end there. A plebiscite, even when the balloting is conducted fairly, tends to inflame national passions. Nor do the ballots always record permanent national preferences rather than momentary fears, prejudices, and economic interests as perceived in the specific circumstances. Studies of Japanese Americans who opted for repatriation in 1942, and of Québecois during more recent balloting on whether they wanted to remain part of Canada, have shown that expression of "national loyalty" or the apparent desire for "independence" can be affected by the administrative context in which the question is framed and by specific political and economic grievances.

Uses in the Third World. Although there has been continuing reliance on plebiscites to resolve issues relating to territoriality—such as those between Italy and Yugoslavia over Trieste and between Germany and France over the Saarland—the arena since World War II has shifted to the Third World, where the claims of former colonies for full sovereignty were as yet unmet (as in Algeria). The change in venue brought other changes. Whereas plebiscites in Europe had been over territories fervidly disputed by neighboring states, so that international authorities had merely to concern themselves with the impartial administration of the vote, most plebiscites in the Third World involved political entities with no common history other than previous colonial rule. Their supervision introduced new complexities. One was how to define the alternatives for a population in the absence of fully developed ways for articulating its interests; another was the delineation of the appropriate voting area where the only clear boundaries were those defined by a colonial administration. Efforts by the supervisory bodies of the United Nations to define these issues for these populations have led to charges of partial disenfranchisement.

This is in contrast to most of the West, where constitutional government has long been in place. Here the questions (or propositions) that people vote on are usually defined within the framework of an already existing consensus. Since they are, quite legitimately, called referendums, the term *plebiscite* in its original meaning has fallen into partial disuse. However, the fundamental issue of the plebiscite as a valid measure of the public will is the same as for the referendum. With all its shortcomings, one is hard put to argue for a better and more effective institutional means of direct consultation with the public at large.

See also ELECTION; POLITICAL COMMUNICATION—HISTORY.

Bibliography. István Bibó, *The Paralysis of International Institutions and the Remedies,* New York, 1976; Friedrich Otto Hertz, *Nationality in History and Politics,* London, 1944, reprint 1966; Michla Pomerance, *Self-Determination in Law and Practice: The New Doctrine in the United Nations,* The Hague, 1982; A. Rigo Sureda, *The Evolution of the Right to Self-Determination: A Study of United Nations Practice,* Leiden, 1973; Oji Umozurike, *Self-Determination in International Law,* Hamden, Conn., 1972; Sarah Wambaugh, ed., *Plebiscites since the World War,* 2 vols., Washington, D.C., 1933; idem, *The Saar Plebiscite,* Cambridge, Mass., 1940.

GLADYS ENGEL LANG

POETICS

The study of literature in its characteristic, specific properties. Poetics consists of a theoretical and an analytical branch. Theoretical poetics inquires into general, universal properties of literature and literary categories—genres (*see* GENRE), structures, historical formations. Analytical poetics studies the specific properties of particular literary works, of individual writers' oeuvres, of literary styles (*see* STYLE, LITERARY), and so on.

Poetics and criticism. Poetics has often been confused with, or subsumed under, LITERARY CRITICISM. However, a sharp contrast between the activity of the critic and that of the poetician can be postulated in theory and observed in history. Criticism is an axiological, value-assigning activity that integrates and reintegrates literary works into the historically changing hierarchy of a cultural system. Poetics is a cognitive activity that gathers knowledge about literature and integrates it into the store of knowledge acquired by the human and social sciences and into the macrotheoretical frameworks established by AESTHETICS, SEMIOTICS, communication theory (*see* COMMUNICATION, PHILOSOPHIES OF), and so on. The discourse of criticism is based on evaluative judgments, the discourse of poetics on descriptive (observational and theoretical) statements.

The confusion between criticism and poetics has been heightened by the standard practices of literary study, in which the most popular and most frequently discussed documents, beginning with ARISTOTLE's *Poetics,* are "mixed" texts blending evaluation and description (*see* LITERARY CANON). To discriminate between the critical and cognitive aspects of such texts does not decrease their intellectual value; rather, it means that not only criticism but also poetics can claim for its pantheon such classics of literary thought as those by Aristotle, Johann Wolfgang von Goethe, or Samuel Taylor Coleridge. Modern poetics, however, owes its establishment and development to hundreds of scholars whose work has been undeservedly neglected by the literary establishment. Contemporary literary thought is dominated by the contribution of scholars who have dealt with literature as poeticians rather than as critics: FERDINAND DE SAUSSURE, Boris Ejkhenbaum, ROMAN JAKOBSON, Vladimir Propp, Jan Mukařovský, William K. Wimsatt, Jurij Lotman, ROLAND BARTHES, Paul Ricoeur. The expansion of poetics into a comprehensive theory of literature, postulated implicitly by Aristotle and explicitly by Boris Tomashevski, has become a reality.

Foundations of poetics. The cognitive activity of poetics is based on two fundamental assumptions: that literature is the art of LANGUAGE produced in a creative act of poiesis and that its study is governed by the general requirements of scientific inquiry. On the first assumption is built the ontology of poetics, on the second its epistemology. These ontological and epistemological assumptions are bound together by logical necessity. A science of literature is possible only if literature is recognized as a specific artistic activity. If it is seen, on the contrary, as a branch of IDEOLOGY or morals, as a representation of individual or social consciousness, or as a set of historical or cultural documents, then there is no justification for developing an autonomous discipline of literary scholarship; literature would be properly studied within the framework of philosophy, ethics, psychology, sociology, political science, history, and anthropology.

Epistemologically the systematic study of literature requires historical continuity. Although the topical agenda of poetics is largely determined by cultural context, its epistemology does not follow patterns of cultural change. Rather, the history of poetics consists of a progressive expansion of its conceptual systems and methods of inquiry and a continual examination of the principles whereby its theories are formed, confirmed, or refuted. Being scientific, poetics can monitor and adopt advances in related sciences, as well as follow the continual probing into the foundations of scientific inquiry by philosophers of science.

From its inception poetics has been characterized by a structural, systemic tendency and occupied with developing mereological (parts and wholes) models in order to describe literary phenomena as complex and highly organized wholes made up of elements, constituents, or parts. The first such model of poetic structure, Aristotle's model of the TRAGEDY, is a logical one set out in accordance with the general postulates of his philosophy of science. By identifying six necessary and sufficient constituents of tragedy, Aristotle demonstrated the validity of the first principle of literary mereology: literary structures are decomposable into parts but cannot be reduced to the sum of those parts. His model is a representation of a generic structure (of a literary genre). It initiated an abstract poetics, a theory of universal structures that treats particular literary works only as examples.

In the second stage of its development, in romantic poetics, the scope of the mereological model was substantially expanded (see ROMANTICISM). It was now to represent not only a restricted repertoire of literary universals but also, and perhaps more important, the rich and inexhaustible variety of particular structures manifest in individual works. This expansion, typified by Wilhelm von Humboldt's 1799 study of Goethe's poem *Hermann und Dorothea*, was facilitated by the adoption by poetics of the organic model cultivated in natural science. Goethe's morphology of living nature and especially his con-

cept of metamorphosis provided poetics with the long-sought theoretical link between a universal Ur-structure and the structural variability of its particular manifestations. The fascination of this organic model for the study of poetic structures survived long after its nineteenth-century dominion over theoretical thinking crumbled. Modern narratology—a special branch of poetics concerned with the study of NARRATIVE structures—is founded on the work of Wilhelm Dibelius and Propp, both of whom were inspired by the organic model in general and by Goethe's morphology in particular.

In the meantime Saussure outlined a semiotic mereology of signifying systems totally free of the organic METAPHOR (see SIGN SYSTEM). When the representatives of Russian formalism in the 1920s and of the Linguistic Circle of Prague in the 1930s, following Saussure's inspiration, perceived literature as a system of signification, the history of the semiotic version of the mereological model began. Russian formalism laid the foundations of modern structural poetics. In pioneering studies of verse structures and narrative forms, the "algebra" of the mereological model was designed. Proceeding from this foundation the scholars of the Prague school (Mukařovský, Jakobson, Felix Vodička, and many others) advanced structural poetics by a meticulous examination of poetic structures on all levels (phonic, grammatical, semantic, thematic) and in all genres (lyric POETRY, prose narrative, DRAMA). In Russian formalism and Prague STRUCTURALISM the potentials of a semiotic theory of literature were developed far beyond the mereology of "immanent" structures. Prague school poetics, formulated within the broader framework of semiotic aesthetics and ART theory, is the first systematic exposition of a semiotic theory of literary communication in all of its basic stages: production, reception, and transduction, or intertextual transmission (see INTERTEXTUALITY).

At the same time as the foundations of modern structural poetics were being laid in the Slavic countries, a radical reformulation of the principles and goals of literary criticism—pointing in a similar direction—was taking place in England and the United States. Several prominent poet-critics, from T. S. Eliot to John Crowe Ransom, challenged the traditions of Anglo-American criticism by perceiving poetry as a special kind of aesthetic experience and COGNITION rather than as an ideological tool or an expression of the poet's personality. At the same time I. A. RICHARDS, although postulating a sharp distinction between literature and science (based on an opposition between "emotive" and "referential" uses of language), endeavored to transform literary criticism into a science of literature. Stimulated by these initiatives, U.S. critics of the 1930s and 1940s (usually lumped together under the label New Criticism) accomplished a dramatic conversion of criticism into literary theory. The representatives of the older generation (including, along with Ransom, Allen Tate, Cleanth Brooks, and R. P. Blackmur in particular) were hindered by a conservative "humanist" ideology, but the younger generation (Wimsatt, Monroe C. Beardsley, Northrop Frye, and others) proceeded confidently to establish a modern theory of literature in North America. This process was aided by an infusion of the results of interwar European poetics into the U.S. context, brought about by the immensely popular *Theory of Literature* (1948), by René Wellek and Austin Warren. The New Critics are especially close to the research project of structural poetics in emphasizing the autotelic and specific character of poetic utterance. They may lack a systematic model of poetic structure, but their particular concepts, such as irony, paradox, ambiguity, and texture, represent a significant enrichment of the mereology of poetics.

In French structuralism of the 1960s and 1970s the heritage of prewar central European structuralism was not cultivated, but a direct link to Russian formalism, especially to its abstract poetics, was established. Focusing primarily on universal structures, the French structuralists advanced theoretical poetics by developing formalized mereological models. By integrating modern LINGUISTICS (Émile Benveniste), structural anthropology (CLAUDE LÉVI-STRAUSS), social semiotics (A. J. Greimas), and poetics (Barthes, Julia Kristeva, Gérard Genette, Tzvetan Todorov, Claude Brémond), French structuralism became a powerful intellectual movement with worldwide influence.

The scope of theoretical poetics in the Moscow-Tartu school (flourishing in the 1960s and early 1970s) was as broad as that of the Prague school. The scholars of this group absorbed not only the abstract poetics of Russian formalism but also the postformalist project of a cultural semiotics (MIKHAIL BAKHTIN). The inspiration derived from generative linguistics, INFORMATION THEORY, and mathematical statistics made possible a high-level formalization of the mereological model of poetics. The main contribution of the Moscow-Tartu scholars (Lotman, V. V. Ivanov, A. N. Toporov, and others) consists in integrating literature into the system of systems of CULTURE. In the grand project of a semiotics of culture, theoretical poetics provided stimuli for theories of creative semiosis and of signifying practices in other arts, the mass media, RELIGION, philosophy, political ideology, and so on.

Literature and language. Because poetics conceives of literature as the "art of the word," it has to study systematically the relationship between literature and language. The concept of poetic language has thus become a crucial and controversial issue. The definition of poetic language requires a framework in which the oppositions between the language of literature and other uses of language can be identified. Aristotle differentiated firmly between the language of poetry and the language of ORATORY, a differentiation on which his division of poetics from RHETORIC rests. In subsequent centuries poetics and rhetoric jointly devised a detailed categorization of tropes and figures of speech, the rudimentary conceptual system for the study of poetic language (*see* SYMBOLISM). The romantics made a sharp distinction between poetic and prosaic language, although the interpretation of both poles of this opposition was a matter of controversy. In the romantic conception poetic language is characterized primarily by formal distinguishing features. A semantic theory of poetic language was proposed in 1892 by the German philosopher of language Gottlob Frege. According to Frege, sentences of ordinary language (including the language of science) have truth-values, that is, are either true or false; sentences of poetic language, however, are exempt from truth-valuation, being neither true nor false. Frege's SEMANTICS is compatible with an influential contemporary semantics derived from Saussure, according to which poetic language is freed from referentiality and able therefore to focus on radical manipulations of the sound (*significant*) and MEANING *(signifié)* nexuses. The Russian formalists put the problem of poetic language at the core of modern poetics, characterizing it, in contrast to practical language, by a lack of communicational utility. This contrast was superseded when the Prague school replaced formal and semantic distinctions with a functional differentiation. In Mukařovský's system (outlined in 1938) an aesthetic function of language appears in contrast to other, communicative functions of language (referential, emotive, and appellative). Jakobson's influential model, proposed in 1960 under the influence of communication theory, defines a "poetic function" in contrast to five communicative functions: referential, emotive, conative, phatic, and metalingual.

Literature and "reality." Poetics has often been criticized for treating literary works exclusively in terms of their "immanent" properties and textual devices. In fact, its efforts to reveal the specific features of verbal art have necessarily been accompanied by a simultaneous probing of the relationship between literature and the world ("reality"). One of the most enduring formulations of this relationship, the theory of mimesis, entered the history of Western thought primarily through Aristotle's *Poetics* (although the first formulation of the idea that art imitates existing things can be attributed to Socrates). Associating mimesis with the productive activity of poiesis, Aristotle counterbalanced PLATO's radical conception of art works as imitations twice removed from essential reality. During the RENAISSANCE the idea of mimesis reentered Western aesthetics and poetics in the Aristotelian version, which allowed emphasis on the participation in the mimetic process of the poet's individuality and of the poet's particular perception of reality.

In neoclassicism the idea of mimesis was transformed into a norm requiring poetry to correspond to "nature" (*see* CLASSICISM). In the eighteenth century, however, the idea of mimesis was seriously questioned and an alternative theory ultimately formulated, inspired by German philosopher Gottfried Wilhelm Leibniz's doctrine of possible worlds. The Swiss poeticians J. J. Breitinger and J. J. Bodmer and the German aesthetician A. G. Baumgarten assigned to poetry the power of creating imaginary (fictional) worlds as possible alternatives to the actual world. In nineteenth-century REALISM and naturalism the idea of mimesis reemerged in a different formulation, that of literature as an inquiry into human nature and the nature of society, parallel and analogous to scientific analysis. In contrast, the poetics of modernism and the AVANT-GARDE have perceived literature as a purely verbal structure and so deemphasized its relationship to reality. More recently a new version of possible-worlds poetics has emerged whereby literature is perceived as the construction of fictional worlds whose relationship to reality is a variable one, ranging from similitude to absolute contrast. By thus asserting the potential infinity of the poetic universe, poetics reaffirms its alliance with the anticonventional, totally open practice of contemporary poiesis.

Bibliography. M. H. Abrams, *The Mirror and the Lamp: Romantic Theory and the Critical Tradition*, New York, 1953; Sture Allén, ed., *Possible Worlds in Arts and Sciences* (Proceedings of Nobel Symposium 65), Stockholm, 1987; Jan M. Broekman, *Strukturalismus: Moskau-Prag-Paris*, Munich, 1971; Lubomir Doležel, *Occidental Poetics: Chapters from a Research Tradition*, forthcoming; Victor Erlich, *Russian Formalism: History and Doctrine*, 3d ed., The Hague, 1969, reprint New Haven, Conn., 1981; D. W. Fokkema and Elrud Kunne-Ibsch, *Theories of Literature in the Twentieth Century*, London, 1977; Tzvetan Todorov, *Introduction to Poetics* (Poétique), trans. by Richard Howard, Minneapolis, Minn., 1984; Boris Tomashevski, *Teoriía literatury: Poetika*, 4th ed., Moscow, 1928.

LUBOMIR DOLEŽEL

POETRY

Poetry and definitions of poetry are cultural products; both vary according to prevailing social structures and habits of mind. Perhaps the only definition of poetry that covers all the phenomena usually understood by the term is that it is an ART form characterized by a distinctive structuring of LANGUAGE. Such a definition leaves imprecise two difficult questions: the nature of art and the nature of poetic as contrasted with other kinds of language. Thus the term *poetry* can refer either to a small class of texts that are indefinable in purely formal terms and are held to embody special human values, or to all texts that exhibit certain formal properties, in which case the distinction between "poetry" and "verse" tends to disappear. These two aspects of poetry—its function as an art form and its distinctiveness as a MODE of linguistic organization—can be emphasized and related to each other in different ways.

Origins and Functions

The origins of poetry cannot be separated from those of music; rhythmically patterned language, joined with rhythmic and melodic SOUND, vocal or instrumental, is associated in preliterate societies with activities such as the marking of important events in family and political life, the memorializing of a community's history and religious traditions, the public assertion of authority, preparation for military activity, communal work, prayer, and RITUAL (*see* MUSIC, FOLK AND TRADITIONAL; RELIGION). These verbal artifacts (*see* ARTIFACT) are like poetry in the modern sense in being distinguished from quotidian uses of language by a higher degree of formal organization, by the capacity to undergo repetition without loss of efficacy, and by unusual emotional effects; but they are more utilitarian in their social function than would be allowed for in many modern accounts of poetry.

The Western tradition of written poetry (and literature) began in Greece with the Iliad and the Odyssey of Homer, probably composed out of traditional oral materials in the eighth century B.C.E. and perhaps at first transmitted orally (*see* ORAL POETRY). Although they are vast and entertaining narratives, these epic poems were also regarded as sources of moral and religious authority throughout antiquity, and the other early Greek epic poet, Hesiod, was explicitly didactic. Lyric poetry, in the most general sense, first emerged clearly in the seventh century, dealing with personal feeling rather than NARRATIVE or instruction; it was closely associated with music and was related to the more public utterances of hymns and encomia. Greek DRAMA grew out of the choral lyric and reached its height in the fifth century B.C.E. Other prominent genres, not clearly separable from one another, included satire, short narratives such as the fable and the epyllion (minor epic), and the pastoral; the brief epigram was also popular (*see* GENRE).

Thus Greek poetry, in its diversity of forms and

functions, laid the foundations for the Western poetic tradition, which continued in classical and medieval Latin CULTURE and duly passed to the modern European languages. The fifteenth and sixteenth centuries in particular saw a growth of vernacular literatures as part of the nationalistic trend of RENAISSANCE culture and politics, but the influence of classical forms increased in this period, to remain strong (though constantly reinterpreted) through the following two centuries (*see* CLASSICISM). Toward the end of the eighteenth century the shift of emphasis from the formal and rhetorical to the emotional and expressive became pronounced, and ROMANTICISM, though still indebted to the writings of antiquity, gave rise to assumptions about the nature of poetry that were to remain influential throughout the nineteenth and twentieth centuries despite the challenges of modernism and postmodernism (*see* AVANT-GARDE).

Poetry can be traced further back in other cultural traditions: to Sumerian CUNEIFORM writings and EGYPTIAN HIEROGLYPHS of the third millennium B.C.E. and to Hittite, Babylonian, Indian, and Hebrew texts of the second millennium B.C.E. (and if we could decipher the early Minoan language known as Linear A we might include Cretan writing). Chinese and Persian poetry go back at least to the first millennium B.C.E. (*see* EAST ASIA, ANCIENT; SOUTH ASIA, ANCIENT). This early poetry shows the same close relationship between music and verse as its European counterpart, and a similar range of religious and political functions.

Poetry as Effective Art

Changes in poetry throughout history have been accompanied by changes in its INTERPRETATION and evaluation. As a form of language that makes a particularly strong and lasting impression on the hearer or reader, poetry serves a number of ends related to the more general understanding of art of the time. It can be seen, for instance, as primarily concerned with the evocation of emotion. PLATO, indeed, banished poets from his ideal republic partly because of this power of verse (and its accompanying music); ARISTOTLE, in reply, pointed to the healthy psychic effects of aroused and discharged emotion. The treatise *On the Sublime,* attributed to Longinus in the first century C.E., continues to find readers in whom its emphasis on the emotional effect of poetry strikes an immediate chord, and many modern accounts of poetry stress this aspect with varying degrees of psychological sophistication. Whatever the specific emotions aroused, poetry must always produce pleasure, and this capacity has often been proposed as a defining characteristic. Poetry is thus set in opposition to other kinds of language, which are

seen as concerned largely with the communication of MEANING, with PERSUASION, or with rational argument. Hence the repeatability of a poem: if its raison d'être is a highly particular and fundamentally emotional experience, the reader cannot carry away some extractable nugget or summary and discard the poem.

Such an account of poetry aligns it closely with the nonverbal arts to the extent that they are regarded as affective rather than cognitive, and like many accounts of poetry it leaves PROSE literature in an uncertain region somewhere between indubitably poetic and indubitably nonpoetic uses of language. Poetry is taken to be the purest form of literature, and lyric as the purest form of poetry, because they are the least contaminated by the rational and instrumental modes of ordinary language. This view springs from an aesthetic tradition in which the example of romantic poetry and Immanuel Kant's theory of the "disinterestedness" of the response to beauty—its freedom from any motive or purpose beyond itself—have played an important part (*see* AESTHETICS).

It is sometimes argued that the emotion experienced by the reader is or should be identical to that experienced by the poet; the poem is in this view a vehicle of affective communication. The appeal of this simple theory is evident, but the history of poetic creation and poetic response shows it to be far from universally applicable. Its popularity springs no doubt from the quality of the response evoked by some poetry—a vivid sense of the feelings of another individual. If the poem is in dramatic form, however, those feelings may belong to an invented character and may have little to do with the emotions of the writer. Any poem, however autobiographical, will allow a reading that distinguishes between the persona it creates and the poet who created it. *See* AUTHORSHIP; READING THEORY.

Another inheritance from romantic literature and Kantian aesthetics is the centrality of the concept of imagination to many discussions of poetry. The poem is seen as the most imaginative, or freely and fully creative, use of language, and this is related to its emotional power and its distance from the rational and the practical. The term resists definition but reflects a quality of poetic language that has been felt by many writers and readers. Some would emphasize poetry's mimetic power, seeing it as the most accurate means of imitating the internal and external worlds of human experience, and others would regard the ambiguity of poetic language as a defining feature.

A complementary and sometimes contradictory emphasis frequently has been given to the special moral or social value of poetry, and many poems have been written out of a desire to teach or improve as well as to express or communicate. The particular emotional and imaginative forcefulness of poetry becomes the servant of a larger aim. We could include here the overtly presented moral and religious values of the early epics, the religious purpose of much medieval verse (*see* MIDDLE AGES), the Renaissance view of poetry as the vivid depiction of virtue and vice, the romantic insistence on poetry's power to enhance imaginative sensitivity, and the political function of poetry written in revolutionary situations.

These interrelated views of poetry—all of them significant in the history of poetry itself—imply that the term has an evaluative dimension; a text that bears formal similarities to poetry or is presented as poetry but that does not have the aesthetic, emotional, or moral effects demanded of poetry cannot be a poem. One result of this is that the category of poetry is highly unstable, varying from period to period, place to place, and individual to individual. Some stability is provided by the social and economic systems in which poetry is produced and evaluated—notably the PUBLISHING and mass media industries and various educational institutions—as well as by the relatively limited sector of the population for whom it is of any importance (*see* TASTE CULTURES). Thus many verbal artifacts that appear to have the intrinsic properties characteristic of poetry, such as pop and rock songs, sporting chants, and jokes and conversational routines, are judged to fall outside its domain (*see* ETHNOPOETICS).

Poetry as Organized Language

A different approach, which emphasizes not the effects of poetry as a mode of art but its relation to other kinds of language, has been of equal importance in the history of poetry. This approach grows out of the tradition of RHETORIC initiated in antiquity and central to the writing and reception of poetry until the romantic period, a tradition that laid great emphasis on the formal features of language and was buttressed by an emphasis on such matters as prosody and stanza form. Although with romanticism the mechanics of form began to be regarded with some suspicion as a possible hindrance to creativity, these questions could not fail to be of importance to anyone engaged in the writing of poetry, until the rise of free verse in the twentieth century made it possible—although still not very usual—for a poet to write without a strong consciousness of the formal choices involved.

Most attempts to determine the difference between poetic and other uses of language emphasize one or both of two kinds of deviance: an unusual degree of patterning, and a departure from accepted linguistic rules. Patterning of rhythm is most characteristic of

poetry. How this is achieved depends on the exact nature of SPEECH in a particular language. Pitch, duration, volume, and timbre or voice quality all coexist in speech but with interrelations that vary widely from language to language. In poetry these elements are organized in a more regular way than is usually the case. A poetic tradition makes certain basic forms or meters familiar to readers, enabling them to associate a given poem with a whole group of poems and to respond to small variations from the norm.

For example, in English the most salient features of speech rhythm are the succession of syllables and the different degrees of stress on them. The predominant tradition in the history of English literary meters is that of accentual-syllabic verse, in which both the placing of stressed syllables and the number of syllables is controlled. Another tradition, older and more characteristic of popular verse, controls only the main stressed syllables. Sequences of stressed and unstressed syllables are grouped into units, with two main types predominating: four beat and five beat. The four-beat sequence is almost universal in popular verse and SONG and is used in much literary verse as well; it is manifested in a variety of line lengths and stanza forms (all versions of a fundamental four-beat structure) and is usually associated with rhyme. Five-beat verse is largely limited to the literary tradition and has been used for some of the major poetry in English, including William Shakespeare's plays and JOHN MILTON's epics. It is employed much more strictly than four-beat verse, almost invariably in a duple accentual-syllabic meter (alternating stressed and unstressed syllables, with certain allowable variations) and in a ten-syllable line; it can be rhymed or unrhymed. The underlying metrical patterns of English verse are clearly related to those of other languages; in particular the four-beat structure is widespread across cultures.

Other elements also may be patterned: vowels and consonants, to produce different kinds of rhyme (including alliteration and assonance) or more complex patterns such as those of Celtic prosody; numbers of syllables or words (as in Japanese and Chinese poetry, respectively); individual words (as in the villanelle and the sestina); or syntactic structures (to produce a metrics of parallelism, such as that of most ancient Near Eastern poetry). Poems may be visually patterned, and all written poetry has a visual dimension; some forms of "concrete" poetry exist primarily as graphic structures. Patterning of any of these elements can be regular, as in rhyming or alliterative verse, or unsystematic. The minimal degree of patterning is division into lines. Even if no other verbal organization is present, sentences divided up on the page are read—in the twentieth century, at least—as a poem, with the enhanced attention that this implies.

When line division is not used, doubt arises about CLASSIFICATION; hence the category of the prose poem, which became firmly established in the nineteenth century after the example of French poet Charles Baudelaire, although there are a number of less self-conscious precedents.

The breaking up of continuous prose into segments could also be regarded as a minimal instance of the other kind of deviation that characterizes poetry— the infringement of rules. Here what is ignored is the rule of layout, which specifies that lines should reach the right-hand margin except at the end of a paragraph (and possibly the associated rule governing the insertion of pauses in delivery, although practice in the reading of verse varies widely). Other types of infringement include various kinds of figurative language (see METAPHOR), ellipses, changes in parts of speech and other syntactic irregularities, unusual collocations (e.g., of adjective and noun), and shifts in register, as well as the employment in some periods of a distinctive vocabulary and style that are not found outside poetry (poetic diction).

These devices of patterning and deviation are often seen as the instruments whereby the special effects of poetry are achieved by increasing the richness and specificity of the language and by focusing the reader's attention on the meanings of the words; but they are as often seen as focusing attention on the language and form of the poem itself. This apparent contradiction runs through many descriptions of poetry and also typifies the paradoxes of the creative process. Whereas successful prose could be described as that in which the language becomes transparent in order to present the content as vividly as possible, successful poetry seems to heighten awareness of the medium and the subject matter at the same time. By the same token the poet tends to be more conscious than the prose writer of the medium that is being shaped into meaningful sequences.

The way in which poetic language draws attention to itself was a particular concern of the Russian formalists in the second and third decades of the twentieth century. They valued this phenomenon as a revitalization of both language and the world it represents. But the project of distinguishing between poetry and prose in formal terms is rendered difficult if not impossible by the fact that apart from regular patterning most of the features adduced as defining characteristics of poetry can also be found in nonpoetic language; the distinction therefore tends to collapse back into a mechanical distinction between verse and prose. Out of this work grew a theory of linguistic functions, most influentially propounded by ROMAN JAKOBSON. The poetic function is one of several, and although it is dominant in poetry it exists in a subordinate role in other uses of language. It is defined as the focusing of attention on the linguistic

text itself, but there remains some uncertainty regarding whether this is brought about by the distinctive characteristics of poetic language or by the habits of readers confronting something already defined as poetry. See POETICS.

The adequacy of this or any characterization of poetry is not open to wholly objective scrutiny, given the embeddedness of literature within the cultural forms that also govern the way we describe it. The term *poetry* and the range of phenomena to which it refers remain elusive and shifting, although the activity of exploiting the multiple resources of language to produce pleasure and profit, to move and to improve, remains a feature of all human cultures.

Bibliography. Derek Attridge, *The Rhythms of English Poetry,* London and New York, 1982; Ruth Finnegan, *Oral Poetry: Its Nature, Significance, and Social Context,* Cambridge, 1977; Paul L. Garvin, ed. and trans., *A Prague School Reader on Esthetics, Literary Structure, and Style,* Washington, D.C., 1964; Geoffrey N. Leech, *A Linguistic Guide to English Poetry,* London, 1969; Winifred Nowottny, *The Language Poets Use,* London, 1962; Alex Preminger, ed., *Princeton Encyclopedia of Poetry and Poetics,* enl. ed., Princeton, N.J., 1974; Thomas A. Sebeok, ed., *Style in Language* (Conference on Style, Indiana University, 1958), Cambridge, Mass., 1960; W. K. Wimsatt, Jr., ed., *Versification: Major Language Types,* New York, 1972.

DEREK ATTRIDGE

POLITICAL COMMUNICATION

This topic is discussed in three sections:
1. **History**
2. **Impact of New Media**
3. **Broadcast Debates**

1. HISTORY

Any transmission of messages that has or is intended to have an effect on the distribution or use of power in society can be considered political communication. The term is generally applied to messages concerning power in nation-states but can also refer to communication in a church, SCHOOL, FAMILY, or any other setting in which power is at stake. Indeed, with the expansion of state power all over the globe in the past century, private life has been increasingly politicized, subject more and more to state policy. Defining the limits of the political has grown correspondingly more difficult.

We may picture the world divided into spheres of the governors and the governed. Sometimes the governors communicate among themselves (elite communication), sometimes they address the governed (hegemonic communication), sometimes the governed address the governors (petitionary communication), and sometimes the governed communicate among themselves (associational communication). This schema is overly simple, but it facilitates defining the field of discussion and clarifying historic trends.

Early Modern Europe

With the invention of the printing press and the spread of print shops throughout Europe in the late fifteenth and sixteenth centuries, a technical possibility emerged for expanding political communication that was not exclusively elite communication (*see* PRINTING—HISTORY OF PRINTING). But printed news and political opinion remained largely within the realm of elite communication until the mid-1700s—later in many countries. Church and state supervision of printers and CENSORSHIP of printing tried to keep pace with the spread of the new technology.

Only when representative government became institutionalized did political communication move from predominantly elite communication to the hegemonic and petitionary forms of communication that link governors and governed. Representative government developed in England and in the American colonies in the 1600s, but even there it took another century to establish the principle that the voting public had a right to know what the legislature was doing.

In 1726 James Franklin (Benjamin's older brother) became the first person on either side of the Atlantic to record in the public press the votes of individual lawmakers on a bill before the legislature. This became standard practice only in the 1770s in England; the English press did not gain full rights to listen to parliamentary debates until after 1800. The tradition of SECRECY and privilege was persistent. The U.S. Senate acted completely in secret for its first four years. While the eighteenth-century press was by no means muzzled in the English-speaking world, most newspaper political writing and pamphleteering did not report information about what politics was so much as express (often very freely) opinions about what it should be (*see* NEWSPAPER: HISTORY).

The PAMPHLET and the broadside developed as important forms of communication in eighteenth-century Europe and in colonial America. Perhaps the most famous pamphlet of that time was Thomas Paine's *Common Sense*. It went through twenty-five editions and gained thousands of readers in 1776 alone. It helped pioneer a new style of political writing. Earlier pamphleteers in America were lawyers, merchants, planters, or ministers, who typically wrote to others of their peer group in a florid style full of classical references. Paine's style of writing was as republican as his politics: "As it is my design to make those that can scarcely read understand, I shall therefore avoid every literary ornament and put

it in language as plain as the alphabet." Paine was original in this rejection of the elite political language of the past. The move away from elite communication as the exclusive domain for political messages was under way.

The pamphlet, like the newspaper, had roots in the seventeenth century but was still a break from more traditional means of expressing or shaping PUBLIC OPINION. In the eighteenth century, in the American colonies, without written constitutions or school texts on government (or many schools), people learned about politics by participating—usually in a subordinate and deferential role—in rituals of authority. People learned about government by attending courthouse sessions or public executions. Voting itself was as much an act of hegemonic communication as of petitionary communication. In the state of Virginia, for instance, it was typically an act of deference since there was no secret ballot. The sheriff would ask the voter whom he favored in the presence of the candidates. The fortunate candidate would then thank the voter. Candidates "treated" voters to rum, not so much to buy votes as to express the paternalism of the gentry toward the lower orders. Politics was not so much a separate sphere of activity as it was just one more expression of the etiquette of a deferential society in which inequality was taken for granted.

In contrast, New England's political culture made more room for petitionary political expression. Town meetings voiced objection to the Stamp Act of 1765 (a British law requiring publications in its American colonies to bear a tax stamp) by written instructions to their representatives in the colonial assembly. The instructions were typically printed in newspapers, spreading the ideas of resistance (see Figure 1). Political writing in the colonies was directed to the legislature, not to the public, until at least the 1720s. Political expression in print was at first elite communication. But by the 1750s pamphlets and newspapers were directed to voters and might be printed in several thousand copies and read aloud at the polls. Elites were not happy with this inclusion of a larger (although still narrow by modern standards) public, but parties out of office sought to broaden their political base by such means to unseat incumbents. This intraelite rivalry led even social conservatives to appeal to a wider public. Colonial elites did not want to democratize society, but their hesitation in encouraging mob violence directed at British imperial officers lessened over the years.

The riot may have been the archetypal form of petitionary communication in the eighteenth century. In England and France so-called food riots were generally an assertion of the local community's right to consume available food at a fair price. These often tumultuous but only occasionally violent gatherings

Thursday, *October* 31, 1765.

THE
PENNSYLVANIA JOURNAL;
AND
WEEKLY ADVERTISER.

NUMB. 1195.

EXPIRING: In Hopes of a Resurrection to LIFE again.

I AM sorry to be obliged to acquaint my Readers, that as The STAMP-ACT, is fear'd to be obligatory upon us after the *First of November* ensuing, (the *fatal To-morrow*) the Publisher of this Paper unable to bear the Burthen, has thought it expedient to STOP a while, in order to deliberate, whether any Methods can be found to elude the Chains forged for us, and escape the insupportable Slavery; which it is hoped, from the just Representations now made against that Act, may be effected. Mean while, I must earnestly Request every Individual of my Subscribers, many of whom have been long behind Hand, that they would immediately Discharge their respective Arrears, that I may be able, not only to support myself during the Interval, but be better prepared to proceed again with this Paper, whenever an opening for that Purpose appears, which I hope will be soon.
WILLIAM BRADFORD.

Remember, O my friends! the Laws, the Rights,
The generous plan of power deliver'd down,
From age to age, by your renown'd fore-fathers,
(So dearly bought, the price of so much blood)
O let it never perish in your hands!
But piously transmit it to your children.
Do thou, great Liberty, inspire our souls,
And make our lives in thy possession happy,
Or our deaths glorious in thy just defence.
ADDISON'S Cato.

LIBERTY is one of the greatest Blessings, which human beings can possibly enjoy. When we are deprived of this earthly happiness, we are fettered with the Chains of inimical servitude. Nations, who are born for the mutual support of each other, should preserve a steady attachment to the welfare and happiness of that nation with whom they are united, that their mutual alliance of friendship might be sincere and permanent. When this union is separated by the illegal encroachments on that Liberty, which is the Soul of Commerce, and the support of Life, it degenerates into implacable Enmity, which in time grows inveterate, and finally recoils upon those who have been the means of its unhappy dissolution. The *Liberty of the Press* has very justly been esteemed one of the main Pillars of the Liberty of the People. While this is maintained, the first Steps to Oppression are detected, and the Attention of the People reasonably awakened. When this is suppressed, the suspicion of the People, and their Ruin may admit of so sudden a transition, as renders the Success of the first impracticable, and the Mischiefs attending the latter unavoidable. So dangerous a thing to lawless Power, that the farthest approaches to it are resolutely opposed, or vigorously punished. So essential is this to Freedom, Property, and Happiness, that the most plausible Attempts to curtail it, even in the smallest Degree, have always been most strenuously opposed by the virtuous, free, and unbiassed Patriot. It is the Privilege of Britons to speak Truth with impunity, and even to fear no Danger from specious Error whether in Religion or Politicks. The want of attending to this has produced needless Enquiries, and inexcusable Censures of what is true in Fact or too much taken for Speculation.—But how unhappy is it to a Patriot from this last Relief in a dangerous and sick. To pine and die while under a Physician allowed to explore the Cause, or prescribe the Cure of our manifold Disorders! The loss of Reason, and absence of Pain in some Distempers, is a fatal symptom of the desperate Circumstances of the Patient.

And in all political Disorders the more contented we are under them, so much the worse are they, and so much the worse are we for them. It is a very happy Circumstance attending public Virtue and public Spirit, that the more it is vilified, the more illustrious it always appears. No Falshood formed against it can prosper, for it at once detects and confutes the darkest and most inveterate Calumny. But although public Virtue cannot be affected by the Indulgence of the most unlimited Freedom of speaking or writing, yet Oppression and Tyranny as it derives all its Influence from its Secrecy, may be extremely benefited by the Reverse. For this reason, in Countries subjected to the insatiable Demands of Power and Avarice, the first Attempts to inspire People with a just Sense of their Condition, are commonly nipt in the Bud. It is of the last Importance to the Views of designing Men to shut up the most successful and universal Channel of Information from the People, when they are forming such Schemes as need only to be known in order to be Opposed. Besides the Deprivation of our whole Liberty may be justified on the same Principles as the Deprivation of any individual Part, such as the Liberty of the Press undoubtedly is.

How amiable is the Enjoyment of Liberty! But how detestable are the Bonds of Servitude! 'Tis therefore sincerely to be hoped, that that old *New-England* Spirit so exemplarily free in former Times, will never condescend in Submission to new and unwarrantable Restrictions.

A Day, an Hour of virtuous Liberty,
Is worth a whole Eternity in Bondage.

May we all as loyal Subjects, and free born Britons exert our utmost to preserve the Rights and Liberties of our Country, in a Manner that shall add Honour to our Endeavours, that future Posterity may reap the Benefit, and bless the Hands which were the Instruments of procuring it.

That Glory then, the brightest Crown of Praise,
Which every Lover of his Country's Wealth,
And every Patron of Mankind deserves;
Will gracefully adorn such Patriot's Deed,
And leave behind an Honour that will last
With Praise immortal to the End of Time.

Thursday last arrived here the ship Philadelphia Packet, Capt. Budden, from London, by whom we have the following advices.

R O M E, *July* 24.
THE harvest in this country hath not proved so good as we hoped. This event hath engaged the congregation established for inspecting into the supplies of provisions for this capital, to seek all possible means to prevent a fresh scarcity.

St. James's, August 17. The king has been pleased to appoint the most honourable the Marquis of Rocking-ham to be lord lieutenant of the west-ridings of the county of York, and of the city of York, and county of the same city; and also Custos Rotulorum of the north and west-ridings in the said county of York and of the city of York, and county of the same city; and Ainsty, otherwise Aynstry, of York.

The king has been pleased to appoint the right hon. William Earl of Dartmouth, Soam Jenyns, Edward Eliot, John York, George Rice, John Roberts, Jeremiah Dyson, and William Fitzherbett, Esqrs; to be commissioners of trade, and for inspecting and improving his majesty's plantations in America, and elsewhere.

The king has been pleased to grant unto the right hon. Richard Viscount How, the office of treasurer of his Majesty's navy.

St. James's, August 27. By the last letters from Col. Desmaretz, his majesty's commissary at Dunkirk, we are assured, that orders were given by the French ministry, for immediately setting about the demolition of the jettees, which are the support of the harbour of Dunkirk.

Warsaw, August 1. The tribunal of Great Poland, held at Posnania, has granted permission to the Lutherans at Lobsens, to open their church, which has been shut near twenty years, to provide a minister, and to perform divine service in public.

Corunna, July 17. The detachment of one hundred men drafted for Louisiana, are on the march for Ferrol, where they are to embark on board the Unicorn frigate with a governor, two capuchin friars, a commissionary at war, and some civil officers.

Cadiz, July 23. Letters brought by the last post from Gibraltar say, the report before spread, that the Algerines have killed their Dey, and declared war against all the European powers except England and France, proves not true.

L O N D O N.
August 17. On Thursday at the king's arms tavern in Cornhill, an elegant entertainment was given by the committee of North-American merchants to Richard Glover, and Charles Garth, Esqrs; when those gentlemen received the thanks of that body, for their endeavours to prevent the soldiery from being billeted upon the private houses of their fellow-subjects in America.
Part of a letter from an officer in the East-India service, dated from the Arietur camp, January 8, 1765.
"In my last I acquainted you that we did at last reduce Madure. The army has since conquered the Arietur county for the Nabob, of 100,000l. revenue a year. We are now under orders to attack another chief, or polygar contiguous to this country; both chiefs have mutually maintained an independency of the Nabob till now; nearly on account of the impenetrable woods they are possessed of. You certainly have heard before of the memorable battle Major Munro gained at Bengal over Suja Dowla, one of the most formidable powers of India. The consequence of this battle gives the company the command of trade in the greatest part of the Mogul's dominions; and, without exaggeration, the East-India company at present may be brought in comparison with Alexander the Great, whose command, from the river Indus to the river Ganges, was not so much respected as their's."

It is said the new m----y, taking into consideration the present deplorable situation of the Canadians, have determined to take up all the Canada bills at par, with interest to the present time; and afterwards to demand, in the most spirited terms, immediate and full payment of France, under pain of all the consequences that can result from a refusal.

The new lords of trade and plantations will hold a board on Monday next, for the first time, at the Cock-pit Whitehall.

We hear the rent rolls of the several proprietary estates in America, obtained by former grants under the crown are ordered to be made out; as also an estimate of the annual produce of their land tax, in order to introduce a more equitable form of levying his majesty's revenues in that part of the world.

They write from Gibraltar, that English officers and seamen are engaging both there and at Minorca by foreign agents, to serve on board his Sardinian majesty's ships of war in the Mediterranean.

August 20. The right honourable the Earl Cornwallis, lieutenant colonel to the 11 regiment of Foot, is appointed one of his majesty's aids de camp, with the rank of colonel of foot in the army.

We are informed, that a gentleman lately very popular in this country, is soon to reside at Lousanne, in Switzerland, where he intends publishing his friend Mr. Churchill's poems, with explanatory notes; and we are likewise informed, that he has an intention of publishing, at the same place, a history of England wrote by himself.

By a vessel arrived at Guernsey from Belleisle there is advice, that the French are erecting several batteries at Sandy Bay, on the south east of the island, and in the great road where the descent was made in the late war by the seamen and troops under Admiral Keppel and General Hodgson.

Aug. 21 We hear lord Viscount Spencer is shortly to be created an earl.

All thoughts of any further changes are said to be entirely laid aside.

It is reported, that a person of high rank, on being lately offered a great employment, refused accepting ... of the STAMP, ... that ... could not consistently with the love he bore to the British nation, which would ever be the object of his care and attention.

Monday some dispatches said to be of importance, were received here from Holland, but the subject has not yet transpired.

Private letters from Paris mention, that the true reason ... of the said STAMP

◁ **Figure 1.** *(Political Communication—History)* The "Tombstone Edition" of *The Pennsylvania Journal and Weekly Advertiser,* October 31, 1765. This satire appeared the day before the Stamp Act was to be enforced. The Historical Society of Pennsylvania, Philadelphia.

threatened hoarders and profiteers and led to searches of storehouses and private homes for hoarded grain and seizure of food shipments. In London riots were often directed toward Parliament and in this respect were the most directly political. In the American colonies riots also became expressly political as local issues became assimilated to the single theme of opposition to British rule. The eighteenth-century mobs were a kind of halfway house of political consciousness: in part concerned only with local economic issues, in part developing a sense of political rights, in part a tool of the gentry that organized or incited the riots, in part an emerging separation from the traditions of deference. The eighteenth-century riot typically resisted the encroachment of state power; it was a reactionary form of collective violence and died out by the mid-nineteenth century in England, France, and the United States, to be replaced by more organized violence based on social or political associations and directed toward a broad political program. *See* DEMONSTRATION.

Political communication also took place through the calendar of the year's activities. In Boston, March 5 was celebrated in the 1770s as the anniversary of the Boston Massacre. Public orations were an important part of the commemoration, and they served, in Sam Adams's view, "to preserve in the Minds of the People a lively Sense of the Danger of standing Armies." The mobilization of opinion through holidays and celebrations greatly accelerated with the French Revolution. Jacobin revolutionary leaders established republicanism as a pseudoreligion. Jacobin clubs throughout France employed revolutionary catechisms, prayers, hymns, communal feasts, civic altars, and Trees of Liberty (a symbol borrowed from the American Revolution) to encourage republican sentiment. Indeed, the French Revolution provided the first self-conscious, directed, and total effort at political indoctrination in history. Where earlier rulers had sought compliance or loyalty, the French leaders wanted commitment. They believed with other Enlightenment thinkers that human beings could be fundamentally changed and that "men could be led to practise social virtues if moral lessons were constantly associated with pleasant sensations." Hence music, festivals, spectacles, and dramas were all drawn into the service of political education (*see* POLITICAL SOCIALIZATION). With the French Revolution the interest of the state in hegemonic political communication began to encompass control over the private

life and passions of individuals, not just their public behavior (see Figure 2).

Political Parties and Newspapers

The nineteenth century saw two significant developments in political communication in western Europe and North America. First, the political party emerged as the central institution of opinion formation and articulation. Second, the newspaper grew substantially as an avenue of political communication.

The political party is, as Benjamin Disraeli put it, "organized opinion." It is even more important than this suggests. French political scientist Maurice Duverger wrote that "parties create public opinion as much as they express it; they form it rather than distort it; there is dialogue rather than echo." Like political communication generally, parties began as intraelite institutions and only later became a link between rulers and citizens. The modern political party, the mass-based party, developed in the United States and western Europe in the nineteenth century. In England a Parliamentary party moved toward a mass party system as the Reform Bills of 1832, 1867, and 1884 broadened the electorate. In the United States the mass party developed in the Jacksonian period, from 1828 to 1840. Other European party

Figure 2. *(Political Communication—History)* *Feast in Honor of the Supreme Being,* June 8, 1794. "The true priest of the Supreme Being is Nature, her Temple the Universe, her Religion Truth, her services the joy of a great People assembled to tighten the bonds of Fraternity, and Swear the death of Tyrants." Bibliothèque Nationale, Paris. Giraudon/Art Resource, New York.

systems emerged in the middle to late nineteenth century.

The rise of the party in England was connected with the extension of the franchise to the working class. This is a vital story in itself, for the vote is the primary expression of petitionary communication in democratic societies. The growth of the franchise concerns not only who is eligible to vote but how voting is conducted. The working class in some countries had the franchise before they were able to exercise it freely. Not until 1872 in Great Britain, the 1890s in the United States, 1901 in Denmark, 1918 in Prussia, and the 1930s in Hungary was a secret ballot a protection within the electoral process.

Many of the developments in political communication in the nineteenth century accompanied working-class (and later feminist) agitation for the vote. In Great Britain this included popular lecture series, workingmen's educational institutes, indoor and outdoor mass political meetings, union organizing, demonstrations that spurred the Chartist and other reform movements, and a tradition of banners that accompanied the demonstrations and outdoor meetings. In the United States similar kinds of activities developed with the emergence of the mass-based political party. In ELECTION campaigns from at least 1840 on, banners, torches (for nighttime parades), campaign buttons, handkerchiefs, and other paraphernalia became part of popular political culture. The election, from the mid-nineteenth century on, has been the chief institution of dramatized IDEOLOGY and legitimating political RITUAL.

The idea that party opposition to the governing party is legitimate developed and became institutionalized in the nineteenth century. In the United States the Federalists and Republicans did not at first see themselves as alternatives in a two-party system; each side hoped to eliminate the other. Eighteenth-century political thinkers took party loyalty to be an insidious substitute for loyalty to the public good. Edmund Burke, in 1770, was probably the first to state effectively the case for party competition as a legitimate structure within representative government. But it was the United States that first developed the legitimacy of party opposition early in the nineteenth century, and also the United States that first incorporated a large electorate and the machinery of mass-based political parties. In Great Britain the idea of an organized opposition had roots in the seventeenth and eighteenth centuries but did not develop into a genuinely organized and led opposition until the late nineteenth century.

As parties became the main institutional locus of political expression, newspapers became the major medium. The French Revolution stimulated a POLITICIZATION of the news media in Europe. In Scotland the editorial voice of the newspaper (the leading article, or leader) acquired importance for the first time in the early nineteenth century. The eighteenth-century Scottish newspaper had been an advertising medium without political influence. The Edinburgh *Review* certainly exaggerated when it claimed in 1860 that journalists were no longer hack writers but were "men of fixed opinions, consummate knowledge, and deliberate purpose," but it recognized that the press had become an established political institution.

At the same time, the French Revolution led to a reaction and increased censorship of the press in many parts of Europe. In Great Britain a key distinction emerged between the "respectable press" and the "pauper press." Radical journalists in the early 1800s ran papers of much greater circulation than even the leading newspaper of the age, the *Times* of London. But while political expression in the latter was tolerated, the readership being "safe," government's fears of the working class led to efforts to limit the reach of the radical journals. A newspaper tax and an advertisement tax, which the bourgeois papers were wealthy enough to pay, could not be paid by the working-class press. Hence these "unstamped" papers were denied access to the mails, and a paper like William Cobbett's famous *Political Register* had to be sold and distributed by its own readers (Figure 3).

The British stamp tax was ended in 1836 and the advertisement duty in 1853, opening the way to a newspaper press of vastly increased circulation and influence. The social and economic basis of the new popular press was an improvement in the production and distribution of newspapers, connected with improved technology in printing and paper making and the growth of the railroads in the mid-nineteenth century. (In France and England, bookstalls at the railroad stations were a major marketplace for reading matter.) The success of newspapers was as much a result as a cause of political communication: the drive for a wider franchise and the gaining of the franchise gave more people a stake in political life and reason to want to inform themselves about it.

In France a daily newspaper press at prices that a growing middle-class readership could afford was inaugurated in the 1830s. Stimulated by the freedom of expression that the French Revolution unleashed, hundreds of papers sprang up (and expired) in France in the first decades of the nineteenth century. The press became closely allied with politics. In 1830 and again in 1848 journalists played central roles in overthrowing governments, and freedom of the press was a burning issue. A close accommodation between government and the press developed after 1848. During much of the nineteenth century the French press deposited "caution money" with the government as an advance against fines. The size of this deposit and

Figure 3. *(Political Communication—History)   A Free Born Englishman!* Satirical cartoon published after the passing of the Six Acts, which raised taxes on all newspapers and established penalties for seditious libel, 1819. Reproduced by courtesy of the Trustees of The British Museum.

the nature of the fines limited the growth of the press and led to a press more venal than that in England or the United States. In the late nineteenth century the French commercial press was notoriously corrupt. The Russian government paid millions of francs to the French press from 1889 to 1905 to help raise loans in France; respected journalists took bribes to write favorably about Russia. As for the French government, it operated on a similar system of secret funds, subsidies, and bribes to attract favorable press publicity.

In the United States an active party press in the early 1800s gave way to a self-consciously "independent" commercial press, the "penny press," that arose in New York, Philadelphia, Boston, and Baltimore in the 1830s. These papers were distinctive in that they were cheap, were sold on the street by newsboys rather than solely by subscription, attended to local news (early U.S. newspapers had copied most of their news items from London papers), and paid greater attention to areas on the border between public and private life—the social life of elites and the police and court reports. While the penny papers were not all affiliated with political parties and were the first papers to seek commercial success without government printing contracts (a major source of income for the earlier press), they remained engaged in the political field of battle. Indeed, nineteenth-century newspapers frequently grew up (and died) with specific parties and movements. The press was an instrument of political and cultural association and was often more an institution of associational than of elite or hegemonic communication. *See* BENNETT, JAMES GORDON; DAY, BENJAMIN H.; GREELEY, HORACE; HEARST, WILLIAM RANDOLPH; PULITZER, JOSEPH.

In countries without the institutions of democracy political communication was very different. In Russia, as late as 1703, all foreign and domestic news was regarded as a state secret. Only at the end of the eighteenth century did literature emerge from patrimonial subservience as an independent field. Catherine II (r. 1762–1796) encouraged a new level of free expression. In the nineteenth century several institutions among the privileged developed as centers of critical discussion: the salon, the universities, and the periodicals. From the 1860s on, a student movement became a constant feature of Russian life. With the reforms of Alexander II (r. 1855–1881) freeing the serfs and establishing limited local self-government, opportunities for political expression grew. While censorship, including the requirement of a prepublication government stamp, existed throughout the nineteenth century, it was not strictly enforced. A secret police provided a strong system of social control, but the severity of the repressive apparatus generated its opposite number in the dramatic terrorist activities of the czar's opposition. Further, dissidents used the privileged place of literature as a political field of expression. One of the most influential political documents in history was Nikolai Chernyshevsky's novel *What Is to Be Done?* (1863). This utopian novel describes a revolutionary "new people" who dedicate themselves to liberation through selfless struggle. It was the Bible of Russian radicals and deeply influenced V. I. Lenin himself, who wrote a revolutionary pamphlet with the same title (1902).

Twentieth-Century Developments

The mass-based party and the newspaper were the great inventions of nineteenth-century political communication. The twentieth century's contributions have been the Leninist party and the rise of what might be called the PUBLIC RELATIONS state.

USSR and China. Lenin created the new-model political party, not as part of a multiparty system within constitutional government but as a revolutionary army and instrument of mobilization. Today, about one adult person in ten in the Soviet Union is a Communist party member, recruited through youth organizations and obligated to study political doctrine, attend meetings, and often serve as a leader of youth groups and an administrator of party institutions.

The Bolshevik Revolution (1917) and the first years of Soviet rule established, besides the party, another major institution of political communication, "agitprop"—organized agitation (promoting a few, simple ideas to masses of people) and PROPAGANDA (promoting many and complex ideas to a literate elite) on behalf of building the new Soviet citizen. Agitational events directed by the state have included the massive annual FESTIVAL on May Day and on the anniversary of the October Revolution, the erection of heroic statues, and the development of a cult surrounding the person of Lenin (even before his death). During World War I a newsprint shortage limited the value of this conventional source of propaganda, and the Bolsheviks substituted with "agit-trains" and "agit-ships." The "Lenin Train" was covered with frescoes depicting workers and soldiers; it carried books, leaflets, posters, films, and trained agitators themselves to the front.

Agitators operate extensively in the Soviet Union. There is a vast system of mass oral media. More

than 15 million lectures are given annually (figures for the 1970s). Because of the vastness of the system it is difficult to monitor and operates to a large extent outside the critique and control of party officials, although most lecturers are party members. Related models have been adopted in other Communist states. In Cuba two mass organizations, the Committees for the Defense of the Revolution and the Central Organization of Cuban Trade Unions, organize people for mass demonstrations. In China, Mao Zedong's "mass line" policy developed in the 1940s advocated that the party

take the ideas of the masses (scattered and unsystematic ideas) and concentrate them . . . then go to the masses and propagate and explain these ideas until the masses embrace them as their own, hold fast to them and translate them into action, and test the correctness of these ideas in such action. Then once again take them to the masses. . . .

This policy grew out of the efforts of the Communist army to organize the masses in the 1940s and continued as an instrument of hegemonic communication in China after 1949.

The People's Republic of China, like the Soviet Union, relies heavily in its campaigns of mass indoctrination on INTERPERSONAL COMMUNICATION rather than on the mass media for its key efforts at hegemonic communication (see Figure 4). This is not to say that newspapers, RADIO, and television play no role in it. In the Soviet Union there are thousands of

Figure 4. *(Political Communication—History)* A mass calisthenics display at the opening ceremony of the Third Sports Meet of the Chinese People's Liberation Army, May 11, 1975, Beijing. UPI/Bettmann Newsphotos.

newspapers that serve not only to report government views on political and economic affairs but also to act as a forum for complaint and criticism. Soviet papers publish hundreds of thousands of letters to the editor. These letters often complain of bureaucratic mismanagement, and many of the letters lead to government remedies. The letters columns are a form of quality control of party and government officials and also serve as a means of legitimating the political system as a whole while criticizing some of its machinery. In China, as in the Soviet Union, the electronic media have developed more slowly, but they are also becoming important media for hegemonic communication.

Electronic media and public relations. The image of all-powerful electronic media in political communication comes not from the Communist countries but from the development of propaganda and public relations in the West during and after World War I (1914–1918). The fear that governments could manipulate the masses at will was greatly stimulated by Adolf Hitler's spellbinding abilities as an orator, not only in front of large crowds but as transmitted around the world by radio broadcast. Hitler was very interested in how the media could be used to solidify his leadership (*see* GOEBBELS, JOSEPH). The actual Nazi media policy involved much more than skillful exhortation, however; during the 1930s a combination of concentrated social pressure, economic strangulation, arbitrary use of police power, and physical terror eliminated opposition parties, the opposition press, and public expression of dissident opinion.

Radio and television broadcasting (*see* TELEVISION HISTORY) emerged in the twentieth century around the world as government-controlled or government-regulated media of communication. Government control of broadcasting ranges widely: from the U.S. system, where broadcasting is primarily in private commercial hands, to the British "arm's-length" system of a government-appointed broadcasting authority that operates with a high degree of autonomy, to more tightly state-directed systems like the French, to systems where broadcasting is explicitly conceived as an instrument of government policy making, like the Soviet (*see* GOVERNMENT REGULATION).

Perhaps the most striking and original use of the electronic media for political communication to date was the Ayatollah Khomeini's use of TELEPHONE and tape recorder in engineering the Iranian revolution of 1979. In Paris, in exile, Khomeini had better communication (by telephone) to his followers in Iran than he did when in Iran. And his voice (distributed by audiocassette) reached more people than he could have reached face to face from within the country.

In liberal societies in the twentieth century elections have remained the central institution for both

Figure 5. *(Political Communication—History)* Austrian electoral campaign billboard, 1980. Photograph by Lee Ann Draud.

hegemonic and petitionary communication, but the character of elections has changed. The authority of the political party has declined notably in the United States and, to a lesser degree, in European countries. Candidacy for office is now less dependent on grooming by party service and more reliant on candidates' abilities to gather around them organizations personally loyal to them and to reach directly to the voters through the mass media. Campaigning has increasingly been run not by party loyalists but by professionals in public opinion, public relations, and ADVERTISING (Figure 5). The vast reach of the media, especially television, has provided a more direct link between national candidates and the public, much less mediated by party leaders. In the United States this gives the president and presidential candidates at least the illusion that an election is a personal PLEBISCITE. Democratic reforms have led to a vast increase in the importance of primary elections, and the United States has moved closer to plebiscitary democracy (Figure 6).

Apart from electoral communication, the field on which hegemonic and petitionary communication meet, a major change in twentieth-century political communication has been the institutionalization of the hegemonic function as part of standard government operations. Propaganda or public relations has become a major governmental function. Government agencies in the United States began hiring press relations specialists in the 1920s, and this has been a key government function ever since. From World War II on, foreign policy has become a more impor-

Figure 6. *(Political Communication—History)* The 1980 Republican Convention, Detroit, Michigan. UPI/Bettmann Newsphotos.

tant aspect of U.S. government functions, national security has become a more central concern, and secrecy has been more often invoked as a barrier between government and the press. While the U.S. government remains more open in its information policies than France, Britain, or most other liberal democracies, the government is nonetheless increasingly self-conscious about using the mass media as a forum for PERSUASION. Whether one calls it news management or public relations or image building, it is a sophisticated derivative of the propaganda that became part of the property of governments, both autocratic and democratic, from World War I on.

In many parts of the world, of course, governments have come to use a much wider array of tools of information control than would be accepted as legitimate in North America or western Europe. In some of the more liberal nations of Latin America, for instance, direct press censorship is rare, but many other measures effectively limit political debate. In Mexico, Argentina, and Brazil suspension of publication of offending newspapers has been widely prac-

ticed. In Mexico the state controls newsprint and has withheld it from dissident publications, and the state has used its control of the banks to exert economic leverage on the press. The Latin American press, like an earlier U.S. or European press, is generally much more effective at publishing dissenting opinion than at publishing potentially embarrassing news (*see* NEWSPAPER: TRENDS—TRENDS IN LATIN AMERICA). This, of course, is true not only of Latin America. In France there is a tolerance of government secrecy and a relatively modest demand for information about government compared to the Anglo-American tradition. France's liberal legal framework for political expression is not realized in actual political information because of toleration of a rather secretive administrative bureaucracy.

Overview

Political communication as discussed here is a much smaller realm than politics as such. This is true in two respects. First, where people do not have the civil rights of political participation, access to political voice, or enough education and wealth to feel a sense of efficacy in the political sphere, the opportunity for political expression is absent or reduced. Second, where key decisions are removed from public view, where the key decision to be made is less "How shall I stand on a public issue?" than "What issue will be treated publicly?"—questions, in short, of AGENDA-SETTING—the vast majority of people with little or no access to the agenda-setting corridors of power are left out of politics. Even in representative democracies with relative freedom of association and freedom of speech and the press, most political communication concerning the actions of nation-states remains elite communication.

See also DIPLOMACY.

For further information about political communication in different parts of the world before the seventeenth century, *see* EAST ASIA, ANCIENT; HELLENIC WORLD; ISLAM, CLASSICAL AND MEDIEVAL ERAS; MIDDLE AGES; ROMAN EMPIRE.

For further information about political communication in regions of the world during the twentieth century, *see* AFRICA, TWENTIETH CENTURY; ASIA, TWENTIETH CENTURY; AUSTRALASIA, TWENTIETH CENTURY; ISLAMIC WORLD, TWENTIETH CENTURY; LATIN AMERICA, TWENTIETH CENTURY.

Bibliography. Karl Deutsch, *The Nerves of Government*, New York, 1963; Eric Foner, *Tom Paine and Revolutionary America*, New York, 1976; James A. Leith, *Media and Revolution*, Toronto, 1968; George Rude, *Ideology and Popular Protest*, New York, 1980; Michael Schudson, *Discovering the News: A Social History of American Newspapers*, New York, 1978; Anthony Smith, *The News-*

paper: An International History, London, 1979; Charles Tilly, "Collective Action in England and America, 1765–1775," in *Tradition, Conflict, and Modernization: Perspectives on the American Revolution*, ed. by Richard Maxwell Brown and Don E. Fehrenbacher, New York, 1977; Raymond Williams, *The Long Revolution*, London, 1961, reprint New York, 1975; idem, "The Press and Popular Culture: An Historical Perspective," in *Newspaper History from the Seventeenth Century to the Present Day*, ed. by George Boyce, James Curran, and Pauline Wingate, Beverly Hills, Calif., 1978.

MICHAEL SCHUDSON

2. IMPACT OF NEW MEDIA

The new media of any age can contribute to change or stability in political institutions and processes. Historians have linked the rise of print media to such developments as the expanse of empires and have tied the rise of electronic media to major changes in political campaigning. Since the 1970s scholars have grappled with the implications of newer media taking shape through advances in the computer and telecommunications, accelerated by developments in MICROELECTRONICS, microwave RADIO relays, satellites (*see* SATELLITE), and FIBER OPTICS. In doing so, they have addressed classic political questions: Who controls these media? Whose interests are served by changing technologies? How might the new media be organized to enhance democratic institutions and processes?

Media Control

Control is a central issue because communications technology is likely to serve the interests of those who control its use. At least four competing perspectives have emerged from discussions of control. The first is a democratic marketplace view, which sees technology ultimately controlled by public (consumer) needs and preferences, operating through normal marketplace processes within the context of democratic institutions. This perspective is characteristic of the scholars most optimistic about the impact of the new media.

A second, more technocratic perspective is characteristic of critics of the media. These have argued that new media are driven more by military and industrial applications than by public communication needs, that public preferences are controlled through marketing techniques, and that the new media increase the likelihood that communications will be controlled by a technological elite, experts who are primarily responsive and accountable to the economic elite of a society.

A third perspective can be called a pluralist view of the new media. Pluralists argue that technology is shaped by the pulling and hauling of competing groups of elites. The new media are thus controlled by a pluralistic process of conflict and cooperation among a variety of actors with different resources and stakes in the political process. Pluralists view technocrats as among the influential actors but consider public officials, economic elites, and the public to be important actors as well.

A fourth perspective, reinforcement politics, views communication technologies as malleable resources that can be controlled by the dominant coalition of interests within an organization or society. Technologies enhance the power of already powerful groups and thereby reinforce the prevailing power structure of a political system rather than affecting any particular configuration of power.

Interests Served

Are the new technologies neutral, or are they inherently biased toward serving certain groups and interests and therefore potentially able to create power shifts? Again, four competing perspectives have emerged, variously viewing the technological changes as (1) neutral, (2) democratic, (3) elitist, and (4) dual in their political effects.

View 1: neutrality. A prevalent view is that the media are politically neutral, if not apolitical. Many in the television industry, for example, have argued that the nature of the content, not the technology, shapes the effects of a medium. In contrast, some prominent media scholars have maintained that media exert a bias in political communications that is independent of their content. Comparing oral and written traditions, HAROLD INNIS argued that the political organization of societies is dominated by a written tradition because written communications, particularly in printed forms, can be more permanent, less constrained by distance, and more centrally controlled. Other scholars, following Innis, have pointed to attributes of radio and television, as well as newer technologies, that differentiate them from earlier media in their impact on political communication systems.

View 2: democratic bias. A dominant perspective within communications institutions sees in the new media an overall democratic impact. According to Edwin Parker, the newer media provide the public with more information packaged in more ways, less controlled in contents and timing, with more processing capacity and improved feedback. Harlan Cleveland has echoed this thesis, claiming not only that the new electronic media can spread information far and wide but that they will inevitably do so and thus accelerate the erosion of hierarchies and power monopolies while promoting the development of more open, less secret, and more participative decision making. Ithiel de Sola Pool, referring especially to the development of INTERACTIVE MEDIA, has labeled them "technologies of freedom," leading to more varied choice for the public. Others have offered images of the new media breaking down communication barriers between nations and classes, as in MARSHALL MCLUHAN's "global village."

View 3: elitist bias. A third line of speculation argues that the media exert a nondemocratic, elitist bias in political communication by creating bottlenecks, with powerful entities in a gatekeeper role in communication systems. Many have suggested that the complexity of high technology further distances elites from a public that is increasingly uninvolved and uninformed about the decisions of large public and private institutions in society. They have pointed to the expense and complexity of high technology as factors that exacerbate knowledge gaps among individuals and organizations, which in turn accentuate economic and political inequalities. Kenneth Laudon has noted that the interactivity of such new media as two-way cable systems masks the degree to which they simply erect more efficient vertical communication networks between elites and masses rather than create horizontal networks among the public and groups. He argues that they are more likely to facilitate manipulation of the public than to foster greater democratic participation.

View 4: conflicting influences. A fourth view is that the implications of communication technologies are inherently countervailing if not often contradictory. Pool developed such a dual effects theme in discussing the social implications of the TELEPHONE, but examples can be found in discussions of a variety of new media. The telephone, Pool and others found, can erode as well as provide PRIVACY; it can reinforce as well as circumvent an organizational hierarchy, and it can facilitate centralization and decentralization simultaneously.

Given these four competing views on whose interests the new media serve, most students of political communication recognize that the implications of media derive only in part from their various technical features. They are more or less malleable technologies, whose functions are also shaped by the extent to which they are used for different purposes within particular institutional arenas. From this perspective the bias of the new media is an outcome of a political process that determines who will control the media in specific settings.

Political Uses of Media

Empirical research in the 1980s focused on how different actors and groups shape the purposes for which the new media are employed. Wide speculation as well as empirical research addressed such questions, with an ample amount of both utopian and dystopian conclusions. The entry of new media into four institutional settings has been the focus of both empirical and speculative inquiries: (1) political campaigns, (2) governmental communications, (3) the public communication arena, and (4) international communications.

Political campaigns. Campaign communications concerns the diverse media used in political campaigns and elections (*see* ELECTION). Particularly in the United States, new technology has increased the sophistication and use of direct mail in campaigns by permitting a greater volume of more personalized and targeted correspondence. Computer-assisted telephone dialing and interviewing systems, interactive cable and VIDEOTEX applications, and other developments in opinion polling have increased the speed and sophistication of the candidate POLL in ways that can dramatically enhance a campaign's effectiveness in marketing its candidate or cause. Computing also extends the potential for matching data in different mailing lists, PUBLIC OPINION polls, voter registration records, housing data, censuses, and other data bases to compile more detailed data banks about the individuals who compose the voting public (*see* DATA BASE). Techniques of profiling can be used in conjunction with these data banks to predict the likely supporters of a candidate or cause so that mailings and other contacts can be more precisely targeted (*see* CONSUMER RESEARCH). Video conferencing has permitted candidates to develop their own closed-circuit television campaigns, independent of the broadcast networks. Together the new media offer channels of communication between candidates and voters that can do more than complement the mass media. They can provide a different set of messages from those conveyed over the mass media, yielding different agendas and different effects on public opinion and voting behavior (*see* AGENDA-SETTING).

New technologies have been used extensively in campaign planning and administration. Desktop computers have brought budgeting, accounting, and payroll applications along with specially designed campaign management software within the reach of even modestly financed campaign organizations. Electronic mail and conferencing systems have also been used in managing communications among campaign personnel and coordinating the work of geographically dispersed speech writers, media consultants, and field staff.

This increasing centrality of computing and telecommunications raises several issues. These new media bring new skills and actors into the political fray, bolstering the role of new kinds of campaign consultants. Their rise may undercut the value of other consultants but also diminish the role of unskilled volunteers, whose jobs can be increasingly taken over by the media specialists.

The application of the new media to campaigns and elections may have dual effects, both centralizing and decentralizing. On the one hand, the electronic media permit candidates to bypass the traditional mediating institutions of parties and interest groups, as well as journalists, and reach their audience directly via mailings and teleconferences. In this respect the media might weaken parties, facilitate the development of more single-issue interest groups, and lessen the influence of media gatekeepers, thereby decentralizing control over campaigns. On the other hand, greater reliance on electronic communications media may lessen the role of distance and travel on interest group formation and decision making. Such an outcome could erode local political organizations and enhance regional and national organizations. Furthermore, by permitting groups to appeal to a national audience, the new media might centralize control of the campaign in national organizations, parties, and interest groups that can marshal the economies of scale, resources, and specialists necessary to conduct a high-technology campaign.

The utilization of newer media may also have redistributive effects, altering the relative influence of different socioeconomic groups in society. Differential access to electronic media by various socioeconomic groups could translate into disparities in access to other political resources. More affluent members of the public have greater access to computing resources such as electronic bulletin boards, word processing, high-speed printers, and campaign management software. Thus the new media may increase inequities rather than level the influence of groups.

Governmental communications. Here the focus is on the values of computing and telecommunications for more effective and responsible government. Modern reformers and futurists have often viewed new communication technology as a path to more democratic participation in government and greater governmental responsiveness to public opinion. They have seen its potential as "citizen technology." Yet this same technology can be used for manipulating public opinion. Whether the media will ultimately erode or enhance democratic institutions and processes are questions that have received increasing attention since the 1970s. Three issues have dominated such inquiries: whether the technologies can be used to (1) further communication between citizens and government, (2) facilitate responsible decision making, and (3) improve the functioning of bureaucracies.

The first issue, revolving around the use of the media as a citizen technology, raises perhaps the most dramatic and controversial questions. Proponents of the idea argue that the new media eliminate the major physical barriers to more direct democratic participation in government. They see interactive communication systems such as cable and videotex providing means for the public to be better informed and more frequently polled on public issues. Those who doubt such democratic results see a greater risk of unrestrained majorities and of an apathetic and uninformed public. They point out that since the 1950s government applications of computing and telecommunications have seldom involved the public in ways that even remotely approach utopian images of citizen technology. For the most part computing has been used to automate administrative functions and the routine processing of large-volume record-keeping and record-searching operations. The information applications adopted by governments at various levels, such as cablecasts of local council meetings or of national legislative proceedings or government reports in VIDEO format, have generally used one-way channels.

With developments in teleconferencing, videotex, and personal computing, old images of citizen technology have been resurrected. Like the telephone, these technologies could facilitate horizontal communication among citizens and thereby enhance the development of groups within a pluralist society. However, the new media have rarely been effectively applied to such purposes.

Studies relating to the second issue, the role of the new media in decision making, have likewise led to mixed conclusions. The computer revolution generated images of large computer and TELECOMMUNICATIONS NETWORKS serving as an information utility to provide both the public and decision makers with essential information at all levels of government, so that decisions could be based more solidly on the merits of each case. Empirical studies have tempered these expectations, finding computer-based information systems used more often to legitimate decisions made on other grounds. Nevertheless, the existence of numerous decision-support systems does often play a positive, albeit political, role in the policy process.

As for the third issue, the impact of the media on the functioning of bureaucracies, findings have likewise been ambiguous. The new media are often used with the intention of affecting power relationships. However, the routine use of computing and telecommunications by public agencies might also have indirect and often unintended political implications. Relations between citizens and institutions may have been altered by the migration of more information from the individual into the automated files of private and public organizations. The consequence of this drift could be an alteration of the relative power of individuals in relation to institutions, both public and private.

Relationships between public and private institutions, as well as among governmental institutions, may also be affected by the application of the new media in public bureaucracies. The most common hypothesis is that the accumulation of power in national agencies and bureaucracies will be reinforced by their relatively greater utilization of computing and telecommunication resources when compared to their local counterparts. Research has supported the generalization that national governments have adopted communication technologies earlier and more extensively than local governments (see COMPUTER: HISTORY). However, power shifts are not always straightforward. For example, national computing resources such as those created by law enforcement systems have sometimes tended to reinforce the effectiveness of state and local agencies, since local enforcement agencies can obtain access to much of the same data and information resources that are available to national agencies.

Relations among the executive, judicial, and legislative branches of government may also be affected by changing technology. The rise of television has often been cited as one factor contributing to the increasing influence of chief executives (see TELEVISION HISTORY). The greater use of new communications technologies within executive agencies and bureaucracies may have enhanced their decisional effectiveness relative to other branches of government. But the technological advances of large federal agencies may also have outstripped the ability of the executive to monitor and lead the bureaucracy.

Public communications arena. Public communications concerns the array of communications facilities available to government, business, and the public. Since the 1960s developments in computing and telecommunications (such as interactive cable communication systems) have made it possible to think of changing the basic infrastructure of public communications. In the United States during the late 1960s the electronics industry and a high-level presidential commission saw social and political opportunities in a nationwide broadband communications network to provide an "electronic highway" into every home and business to carry all kinds of information and services. Similar initiatives were proposed in Japan and western Europe at about the same time. The potential for integrating broadcast, cable, data, and telephone communications networks generated both utopian and dystopian visions of a "wired nation." Ralph Lee Smith, Peter Goldmark, and others in the 1970s presented positive visions of a wired nation in which private cable operators could build this electronic highway much as the telephone network was constructed. A more integrated network held the promise of providing more channels of communication, a greater diversity of programming, a more equitable distribution of services, and an opportunity for new constituencies to become involved in broadcasting. Instead of television being an elite medium of communication between the few and the many, it could become a more democratic medium of social exchange and public services as well as entertainment.

In the United States visions of the wired society faded with the growing recognition of the limitations of interactive cable, the economic problems of the cable industry, and the rise of a host of newer media that competed with CABLE TELEVISION services. In the 1980s competition among media generated a new vision of an emerging marketplace of electronic networks and services. It was hoped that marketplace competition among telephone, cable, newspaper, television, videotex, and videocassette media would create a pluralistic array of communication channels and services leading to more democratic patterns of public communications.

Critics of these utopian visions have argued that the wiring of communities, along with an increasing array of new media, have actually lessened the diversity of communications, increased concentration within the media industry and the cost of communication services, driven out commercially unprofitable services, threatened personal privacy, and widened the gap between the information poor and rich in societies.

International communications. International communications concerns the array of facilities available for communications across national boundaries. Advancements in video recording systems, fiber optics, microwave relays, and satellite communications have expanded the multiplicity, capacity, and reach of worldwide telecommunications networks. The development of these systems has lessened technological limitations on international communications and correspondingly focused attention on economic, cultural, and political factors that promote and impede communications across national borders. As with domestic public communications, issues of who controls and whose interests are served loom large in discussions of this arena. See INTERNATIONAL ORGANIZATIONS.

Some students of the new media have argued that technological change has fundamentally undercut the ability of nations to control the international flow of communications. The videocassette recorder, for example, limits a nation's ability to control the importation of foreign programming through traditional means. Likewise, prospects for the widespread use of direct broadcast satellites have raised questions of whether nations will continue to be able to control the character of broadcast offerings. Others have argued that the new media can be shaped in ways that will permit nations more control over international flows of communications. One aim of the French national cable plan, for example, was to provide a communications infrastructure that would facilitate public efforts to provide a balance of programming, ensuring access to an ample array of French as well as other foreign and more commercial programming. Likewise, even if direct broadcast satellites became economically feasible, the use of satellite broadcasting could be effectively blocked by nations through a variety of technical measures.

However, the thesis that the new media will reinforce the economic, cultural, and political interest of those actors and nations that already control international communications has been widely accepted. International communication networks are complex and costly, two features that have buttressed the dominant role of the most economically and technologically advanced nations in creating and distributing news and television programming (see NEWS AGENCIES). The new media of computing and telecommunications are also high-technology products that may allow greater choice to consumers, as a videocassette recorder or personal computer does, but they do not allow control over the production or distribution of the technological infrastructure and its basic content. The interests served by advancements in international communication systems were perhaps the most controversial issue in the politics of communications during the 1980s, given their economic, cultural, and political implications.

Economically, if one acknowledges the trend of most advanced industrial societies toward increasingly information-based economies, then international communication infrastructures represent nothing less than new trade routes. Nations concerned with balancing international trade, and such organizations as multinational corporations requiring extensive and efficient communication systems, are naturally affected by the availability of international networks and services. Large developed nations, which have been the major exporters of communication products and services, have tended to support the development of international communication systems, whereas small developing nations, which are among the major importers of these products and services, have been more ambivalent in their support.

Culturally, many nations have raised concerns over the maintenance of their traditions and values in the face of mass media institutions that threaten to homogenize the public around commercial rather than public service broadcasting and foreign rather than domestic programming (see MASS MEDIA EFFECTS). This issue has surrounded radio and television broadcasting for decades. However, the newer media of cable, satellites, and video recording systems raise this issue anew because they challenge existing institutional mechanisms for ensuring national controls. For example, culturally defined standards for the handling of personal information are threatened by the ease with which personal data files could be processed in so-called data havens, that is, other nations or territories with less restrictive data protection and privacy regulations (see GOVERNMENT REGULATION).

In the area of governance the new media raise such critical issues as national sovereignty. With regard to computer communications, for instance, Canadians have been among those who have voiced concerns over the amount of information vital to the Canadian economy that is processed on computers in the United States. To some this places Canada in a dependent situation, leading to a national campaign for independence from U.S. computers as a means for ensuring Canada's political sovereignty. See COMPUTER: IMPACT.

Future Focus

Changes in the technology of communications have raised new issues for students of political communications and have broadened traditional definitions of both the media and political communications. The new media have been portrayed as facilitators of democracy by some and as instruments of repression by others. The same technologies have been depicted as potentially able to inform or enslave a society, to create a more open or closed society, and to decentralize or centralize political control. Speculation rather than empirical research has dominated such inquiries. Clearly, a variety of research strategies will be needed to assess such speculations and to clarify the worldwide political implications of the rise of new communications technologies.

See also COMMUNICATIONS, STUDY OF; MINORITIES IN THE MEDIA; POLITICAL COMMUNICATION—HISTORY; PRESSURE GROUP; TELECOMMUNICATIONS POLICY.

Bibliography. Gerald Benjamin, ed., *The Communications Revolution in Politics*, New York, 1982; James N. Danzinger, William H. Dutton, Rob Kling, and Kenneth L. Kraemer, *Computers and Politics: High Technology in American Local Governments*, New York, 1982; William H. Dutton, Jay Blumler, and Kenneth L. Kraemer, eds., *Wired Cities: Shaping the Future of Communications*, White Plains, N.Y., 1986; Starr Roxanne Hiltz and Murray Turoff, *The Network Nation: Human Communication via Computer*, Reading, Mass., 1978; Harold A. Innis, *Empire and Communications* (1950), rev. by Mary Q. Innis, foreword by Marshall McLuhan, Toronto, 1972; Erwin G. Krasow, Lawrence D. Longley, and Herbert A. Terry, *The Politics of Broadcast Regulation*, 3d ed., New York, 1982; Kenneth C. Laudon, *Communications Technology and Democratic Participation*, New York, 1977; Theodore J. Lowi, "The Political Impact of Information Technology," in *The Microelectronics Revolution*, ed. by Tom Forester, Oxford, 1980; Robert Meadow, ed., *New Communication*

Technologies in Politics, Washington, D.C., 1985; Vincent Mosco, *Pushbutton Fantasies: Critical Perspectives on Videotex and Information Technology,* Norwood, N.J., 1982; Edwin B. Parker, "Democracy and Information Processing," in *The Information Utility and Social Choice,* ed. by Harold Sackman and Norman Nie, Montvale, N.J., 1970; Ithiel de Sola Pool, *Technologies of Freedom: On Free Speech in an Electronic Age,* Cambridge, Mass., 1983; Herbert I. Schiller, *Who Knows: Information in the Age of the Fortune 500,* Norwood, N.J., 1981.

WILLIAM H. DUTTON

3. BROADCAST DEBATES

On-the-air debates between opposing candidates for high office, using debate procedures that have evolved since ancient times (*see* FORENSICS), have been an intermittent feature of U.S. television since 1960, when Richard M. Nixon and John F. Kennedy met in four confrontations publicized as the Great Debates. Planned for television, the debates were also carried by many RADIO stations. They were later thought to have helped Senator Kennedy—Democratic candidate for the U.S. presidency, less well known than his Republican rival, Vice-President Nixon—to win the presidency. Debates were regularly proposed in subsequent elections for offices at various levels, national and regional, but these required extensive negotiations that were not always successful in reaching agreement. Better-known candidates always risked more but could not afford to seem fearful of the challenge. Negotiations centered on debate procedures, choice of moderator and intermediaries to pose questions, limits on the range of topics, scheduling, locations, and ground rules of all sorts. In some instances judicial or legislative approval was required.

Such debates, on radio or television or both, have been tried elsewhere to a very limited extent (in France, for example, in 1981 and 1985) but have remained essentially a U.S. phenomenon for reasons closely related to its commercial broadcasting system. Early in the system's evolution, U.S. stations and networks began classifying political speeches as ADVERTISING and charging candidates (or parties) commercial rates for access to home audiences. Most European countries ban such sales. In most European democracies free time is proportionally allocated to opposing parties according to criteria such as the number of members in the legislature, votes in a previous election, or party membership statistics. The U.S. practice, because of its financial requirements, is seen as undemocratic—a criticism also voiced in the United States. Another objection to the existing system has come from U.S. broadcasters themselves. A political broadcast, especially in prime time, has

generally meant cancellation of a sponsored entertainment program and inevitably the loss of a portion of the audience to a competing program. To put on a debate was therefore a commercial hazard regardless of the outcome. The proposed solution was that the Great Debates be carried free of charge by all commercial networks. Although this would not end the sale of time for political appeals, broadcasters at least hoped to minimize it and to shunt it as much as possible toward spots instead of longer periods. Thus the U.S. system of political broadcasting has remained essentially a time-sale system, supplemented by free debates when agreement could be reached. *See also* TELEVISION HISTORY.

Research

Although televised political debates have taken many forms, explicit rules of procedure have always been a feature. In the Kennedy-Nixon debates each contestant was allowed an introductory statement that was not challenged. Rather than debate each other directly, contestants replied to questions put to them by journalists. The questions were not known to the candidates in advance but were within certain areas previously agreed on (e.g., foreign affairs, the economy). A moderator assigned speaking turns and kept track of time allotted for each response. Debates have most often followed this pattern, with minor variations, and have been broadcast in prime time.

Debates constitute a distinct form of political communication. Through them the electorate is given an opportunity to assess the candidates' competence and compare their stands on issues. Debates tend to be among the few occasions during a campaign when implications of policy statements can be explored in some detail. Furthermore, the debates represent severe tests of the candidates because the initiative is with the questioners and also because evasive or inconsistent replies—the politician's staple diet—are readily seized upon.

The impact on the electorate of the 1960 presidential debates, and to a lesser extent of subsequent debates, has been the subject of numerous studies, some of which assessed both initial impact and its erosion over time by interviewing the same people on several occasions. It soon became apparent, however, that debates cannot be meaningfully studied as isolated events but require an approach capable of accounting for multiple sources of influence and their interactions. Factors like party loyalty, habitual voting patterns, candidates' appearance and style, the press and broadcast media's coverage and commentary, as well as political discussions at home and at work all come into play during an election campaign.

The context surrounding the debates is also relevant. Debates have become media events that take place with a great deal of advance publicity. They are treated by the electronic and print media as a great sporting contest. Commentaries before and after the debates tend to concentrate on who might win or who has won. Given the power of media to focus audience attention, such commentaries affect the public's perceptions of the debates. U.S. political scientist Thomas E. Patterson demonstrated this by using two matched samples: one interviewed immediately after the 1976 debate between Jimmy Carter and Gerald Ford (before subsequent commentaries were available) and the other interviewed twelve hours later. Patterson found that the majority of the first sample considered Ford the winner, but the majority of the second sample named Carter, echoing the choice of media commentators.

Even people who express little interest in politics attend to debates. Studies have shown that after a debate the politically uninterested were as well informed about candidates' positions on issues and their differences as people who said they took an interest in politics. Furthermore, people's descriptions of the candidates became more varied and less stereotyped after a debate and the subsequent commentaries, particularly with regard to the newcomers (e.g., Kennedy in 1960, Carter in 1976). All studies have reported some gain in knowledge and interest, but the degree has varied depending on the timing of the debates. Interest and knowledge gains were small when the presidential debates were held at a time when people's views had already crystallized and greater if they took place before an early primary (as was the case in the 1980 debates between George Bush and Ronald Reagan).

The influence that debates have over people's votes has generally been small. On the average only 3 percent of the voters admit being affected, a figure similar to that obtained in Britain when the electorate was asked about the influence of party political broadcasts on voting decisions. But in the future the influence of televised debates may increase because party loyalty is a declining influence in a number of countries, the percentage of undecided voters is on the increase, and more voters make up their minds late in a campaign. Given these trends—and the media's prominent role in election campaigns—televised debates may well play an increasing role among the diverse sources of influence on the voter's decision.

See also AGENDA-SETTING; POLITICIZATION.

Bibliography. Hilde T. Himmelweit, Patrick Humphrey, and Marianne Jaeger, *How Voters Decide*, London, 1985; Donald R. Kinder and David O. Sears, "Public Opinion and Political Action," in *Handbook of Social Psychology*, Vol. 2, 3d ed., ed. by Gardner Lindzey and Elliot Aronson, New York, 1985; Sidney Kraus, ed., *The Great Debates*, Bloomington, Ind., 1962, reprint 1974; Thomas E. Patterson, *The Mass Media Election*, New York, 1980.

HILDE T. HIMMELWEIT

POLITICAL SOCIALIZATION

The process by which people acquire political orientations and patterns of behavior as they mature cognitively and affectively over the course of their lives. The study of political socialization has been developed as a factual inquiry into the content, causes, and consequences of such learning, involving a variety of social scientists including political scientists, psychologists, sociologists, educational researchers, and communication researchers.

When U.S. sociologist HERBERT H. HYMAN published *Political Socialization* (1959) few empirical studies existed that explored what people learn about politics and government or how they come to learn about such matters. But since that time an impressive volume of work has appeared exploring topics like childhood and adolescent patterns of political learning; differences among younger and older cohorts of individuals due to different generational experiences; how and what people learn about their own political systems and those of other nations; and differences in patterns of political learning based on socioeconomic status, gender, ethnic background, religious preference, and so on.

A great deal has been learned about how people adapt to the complex and shifting political environment in which they find themselves, a process that includes increased understanding of politics and government as well as the formation of emotional commitments that help in finding one's way through a wide variety of political objects and stimuli.

A recurrent theme in much of this research is that most people begin to acquire an extensive repertoire of political orientations and behaviors as early as the preschool years. Well before the time of formal schooling, people in complex societies begin to incorporate at least rudimentary images and practices of authority, national identity, and habits of learning that facilitate the gathering and internalization of more abstract, differentiated modes of relating themselves to politics and government.

Most political scientists approach these questions with a strong sense of the need to understand the political socialization phenomenon from the standpoint of its bearing on how people conduct themselves politically at later stages. Such political relevance involves both the political choices and the actions taken as individuals; as members of politically active groups, strata, or geographical regions; and as members of the wider political system. Therefore, such scholars focus especially on those aspects of preadult political learning that seem to have direct consequences for adult political behavior—and thus effects on the structures, relationships, and processes of the political system in general.

However, political socialization involves much more than the individual and collective adaptation of people to the political world that surrounds them. Political socialization is also an important dimension of more general processes of social communication. People may to some extent learn about politics and government through personal observation and reflection, but for the most part they are forced to view and understand the political realm indirectly, through various modes of personal and impersonal POLITICAL COMMUNICATION. In technologically advanced societies political messages are carried out through a great variety of means: television, RADIO, newspaper, and NEWSMAGAZINE coverage of political happenings (see ELECTION). But movies, books, handbills, signs, intrafamily or peer-group discussion, videocassettes, computers, loudspeakers, SCHOOL curricular material, patriotic rituals and observances (see POLITICAL SYMBOLS), graffiti, popular songs, poetry, and CHILDREN's literature may also yield examples of politically relevant content. It is not difficult to find many examples of the ways people communicate with one another about politics, thus helping to make sense of what would otherwise be a remote, confusing, and somewhat intractable set of entities. Much of this INTERPERSONAL COMMUNICATION about politics is carried on in a low-key, unofficial, indirect, sporadic, informal, and unselfconscious fashion. But the political system is an unavoidable feature of life, and even those least disposed to becoming politicized find exposure to some forms of political communication inevitable (see POLITICIZATION).

In the United States in the late 1950s empirical research by pioneers like Fred Greenstein, David Easton, and Gabriel Almond focused primarily on what is learned and how and when it is learned. Their work was particularly concerned with developing a better conceptual and observational handle on what people learned about politics from early childhood into adulthood. There was less attention to the sources of such learning or to the conditions that shaped those influences in the socialization process. During the 1960s more research analyzed the role of the contributing agencies of political socialization, especially FAMILY, school, and peer group. This work has shown that the presumed effects of such obvious interpersonal political sources were by no means as potent as it was supposed; in the United States only specific areas of content (e.g., political party identification) or specific categories of individ-uals (e.g., black adolescents) were notably affected. Work in other countries has generally confirmed the limitations of interpersonal sources of political learning—whether family, school, or peers—even though there are several specific effects of each that may be found under certain conditions.

Media Influences in Political Socialization

Investigation of the complex relationships between mass media communication and political learning has become increasingly salient. What most people know or feel about the complex social aggregates and patterns of action identified as political events, processes, or systems is in a direct sense very limited. People can no longer rely—as they might have done in simpler, smaller, less differentiated political systems—on direct experience and observation for developing political thoughts and emotions. The mediated communications of greatest currency in a society are the ones with the highest political learning potential. Television, given its high levels of aggregate political communication exposure, seems under most circumstances to be the most significant of such influences.

Empirical studies have consistently reported that there are two basic types of media influence: (1) on political information and (2) on political values. These are relatively independent of each other. Available evidence suggests that political cognition—understanding, knowledge, beliefs, perceptions, and definitions of political reality—is pervasively affected. Television and the print media have the most important and sustained effects, particularly on what people grasp about the main structures, events, personnel, and principles of politics and government (see AGENDA-SETTING).

More difficult to establish but nonetheless evident in a variety of circumstances are PERSUASION effects. The influence of the mass media on political preferences, identifications, images, emotions, commitments, motivations, and values—either positively or negatively—is demonstrably present. But such effects are not as consistent across different intervening conditions as they are in the area of political knowledge. Intentionally persuasive communication through the media affects only certain groups of readers, listeners, and viewers.

The content of media-stimulated political knowledge from preadolescence through young adulthood takes many forms, although only a few of these have been well studied. They include such matters as learning one's own national symbols and other political community identifications and the equivalents for foreign peoples; the identity and functions of chief political actors, particularly those in positions of authority; the major institutions of politics and government; politically relevant identifications such as political party affiliation or social class membership; major political events and activities, such as wars and elections; issues and problems of public policy; the connections among various sectors of society and the government; features of the legal system, including police and the courts; and general value and belief systems.

Even those who are very young but who have exposure to these matters through the media are likely to begin forming relevant orientations to politics that begin to shape patterns of future political behavior. At first such content may come mostly via the entertainment uses that children make of television. With early adolescence, the patterns of media exposure and attention, and thus of influence, are likely to shift. As people approach adulthood, public affairs programming on television is more attended to, and print media become increasingly important sources of political information. During later adolescence and early adulthood this pattern is extended, so that higher proportions of hard news provided by the print media are utilized to form political images and bases of knowledge. However, some of the earlier media-use patterns persist, even for individuals whose motivations lead them to the highest levels of political information seeking.

Patterns of media consumption at different age levels are more difficult to associate with affective or persuasive effects. Yet it is possible to find evidence suggesting that there are both direct and indirect effects traceable to exposure to particular media or to specific media content in preadult life. For example, CONTENT ANALYSIS studies of television programming have shown that portrayals of political leaders and of politics in general might be related to people's level of trust in the political system, its efficacy, and its fairness.

There are also a number of suspected indirect media effects on political orientations (e.g., in antisocial behavior such as approval or use of VIOLENCE) as a possible consequence of heavy viewing of crime and police shows on television. The implicit approval of the use of aggressive means to resolve disputes (e.g., by police authorities) may lead some viewers to a greater propensity to focus heavily on the use of military force to address international disputes or to condone a lack of official observance of the rights of criminally accused persons or of those who dissent politically. Equally, media reinforcement of GENDER or racial stereotypes may well slow progress in eradicating patterns of discrimination in society. Thus what are often taken to be relatively innocuous entertainment presentations of violence or social stereotypes may indeed have important, if not yet fully unraveled, political consequences (*see* CULTURAL INDICATORS; MINORITIES IN THE MEDIA).

Some Unanswered Questions

Most of the work on political socialization thus far has strongly suggested that media influences, especially when supported by interpersonal influences, can be very powerful teachers about politics. But we still do not know the extent to which the mass media depend on interpersonal support and reinterpretation for their effects, nor do we understand well the interactions among socialization institutions such as the family, the school, and the mass media.

Despite these and other unanswered questions, the influence of the mass media on processes of political socialization appears to be already substantial and growing, especially in industrialized nations that rely extensively on the more technologically advanced and persuasively used media. Such effects are likely to be important not only for how the young are brought up to think about political matters but also for the continuing process of resocialization of adults as they seek to cope with an increasingly complex political environment.

Bibliography. Steven H. Chaffee, ed., *Political Communication: Issues and Strategies for Research*, Beverly Hills, Calif., 1975; Jack Dennis, ed., *Socialization to Politics*, New York, 1973; David Easton and Jack Dennis, *Children in the Political System*, New York, 1969, reprint Chicago, 1980; Sidney Kraus and Dennis Davis, *The Effects of Mass Communication on Political Behavior*, University Park, Pa., 1976; Dan D. Nimmo and Keith R. Sanders, eds., *Handbook of Political Communication*, Beverly Hills, Calif., 1981; Stanley A. Renshon, ed., *Handbook of Political Socialization*, New York, 1977.

JACK DENNIS

POLITICAL SYMBOLS

Any word, image, object, act, or event that evokes loyalty, encourages obedience, asserts or justifies a claim, or promises salvation in this world or in any other, functions, whether by design or not, as a political symbol. On the most general level these symbols give concrete and often visible expression to something intangible. Strongest in their appeal to the eye are emblems such as the flag, the badge, the seal, the totem, or other insignia, and even modes of dress that a group adopts or inherits and through which its members signify their status as well as their belongingness. But even simple visual symbols can stand for something more complex. Thus the scepter is the visible sign of royal authority, the cross of Christianity and its associated beliefs, the hammer and sickle of communism as a political movement, the swastika of the racist IDEOLOGY of the short-lived German Third Reich, the spinning wheel of MOHANDAS GANDHI's campaign for resistance to British rule.

Figure 1. *(Political Symbols)* Some flags of member states in front of the United Nations, New York. United Nations photo 150,480/Yutaka Nagata.

Important as these kinds of iconic representations may be, the overwhelming number of political symbols consist of words that are found in texts. LANGUAGE influences the nature of politics as much as it does ordinary discourse. Through symbols, brute force is converted into legitimate authority, and many political acts consist largely of words: a proclamation, the issuance of an order, or the change in the wording of some law.

Myths. As a first step in any analysis of this symbolic environment, the political master symbols with a consistent bearing on social structure and the exercise of power must be distinguished from the more ephemeral and polemical RHETORIC that marks a particular conflict. The social constructions that incorporate the fundamental assumptions regarding the pattern of authority within a society form what HAROLD D. LASSWELL designated the political myth.

One of the main constituents of the myth is a doctrine of beliefs about liberty, or manifest destiny, or some set of ethical principles to provide the rational underpinnings of constituted authority. These doctrinal assumptions find expression mostly in sacred pronouncements and philosophical tracts, but they also find their way into the more popular media. They still must be enunciated and made to apply to everyday life through the political formula embodied in the basic laws and regulations by which a society is governed. But no rule is secure unless bolstered by the appropriate sentiments. Hence attention needs to be paid not only to what people believe but also to the things they admire, such as the heroes represented in statues, monuments, and history books as well as the shrines at which the past is worshiped and events are commemorated with all the pageantry and ceremony—like the singing of anthems, the salute to the flag, and the required pledge of allegiance—through which the identifications and sentiments appropriate to the achievement of political goals are kept alive and reinforced.

It should be clear that political symbols are not a special type of sign with distinctive characteristics. Rather, what makes them political is the way they are used in the political process to establish, consolidate, or alter power relationships. It is through their common allegiance to symbols—of creed, class, guild, generation, dynasty, nationality, and so forth—that collectivities are internally unified and self-consciously differentiate themselves from others. A place name that is purely descriptive for a geographer may constitute a meaningful identity once it becomes the focal point for the crystallization of sentiment.

Symbolic acts can be used not only to maintain but also to challenge the existing order. A demand formulated strictly in terms of self-interest will have less political clout than the same demand made in the name of a larger social entity, such as a class, all the oppressed, or even all of humanity, while recourse to an accepted principle invests it with some legitimacy. The more inclusive the group and the more widely accepted the principle, the greater the potential appeal.

Importance of language. The bearing of language on potential political effectiveness underlines the extent to which political conflict is in fact a battle over words and gives rise to questions about their relation to "real" interests (*see* LANGUAGE IDEOLOGY). Conflict over issues that are largely symbolic, in which the concerns are less material than moral, is hardly an epiphenomenon. It takes an idea of justice to convert a condition like the lack of power or wealth into a sense of deprivation, to formulate it as the violation of some right, which is then related to some meaningful identity. But people will argue about whether or not a right applies; therefore, the moral force behind any claim depends on the support it has from PUBLIC OPINION, although public opinion can also be manipulated by those in power or by skillful propagandists who play on people's fears (*see* PROPAGANDA).

The use of these and other propagandistic devices to influence public opinion is a fact of political life. Subject to analysis is the extent to which symbolic appeals facilitate rational judgments or whether they

Figure 2. *(Political Symbols)* The hammer and sickle on Communist party election posters, Rome, 1976. UPI/Bettmann Newsphotos.

are mere slogans, accepted not because of what they overtly state but because of their latent meanings. The themes used by some agitators deliberately play on the impulsivity of their following. They mobilize by providing a conventionally acceptable political rationale for displays of hostility and aggression against villains and members of accursed groups with assumedly great power to do evil. Despite the evident psychopathological strains in some kinds of politics, not all radicalism is essentially irrational and without social roots (*see* TERRORISM).

Sometimes symbolic crusades against infidels and supposedly dissolute members of society often mask a very real threat. In the United States the insistence of whites in the South after the Civil War (1861–1865) that blacks be kept segregated was intended to reduce economic competition and defend a preferred life-style, which whites saw undermined in numerous other ways. Similar arguments, more vehement in their racism, are offered by the white South African minority in support of that country's apartheid system, in which race remains the dominant symbol of identification for both the advocates of change and those who continue to block the progress of the black majority toward full political, social, and economic equality.

Developments following the overthrow of Moḥammad Reza Shah Pahlavi of Iran in 1979 illustrate how religious symbols can be used to consolidate power. The shah had been the chief proponent of his country's rapid modernization program against substantial popular opposition, and he was eventually replaced by Ayatollah Ruholla Khomeini, who, by appealing to traditional Islam, managed to install a new regime based on the capability of the mullahs to rally people to his cause (*see* DEVELOPMENT COMMUNICATION; ISLAMIC WORLD, TWENTIETH CENTURY). Social strata and entire societies threatened with dislocation by the march of modernity have also sought to preserve their old ways of life by abandoning this-worldly pursuits in order to seek moral regeneration through collective adherence to some aesthetic ideal, cultivation of personal piety, or indulgence in some kind of purging of the soul.

Revolutionary movements differ in their preference for symbols associated with science, technology, and progress in social organization over traditions and versions of the past (*see* POLITICAL COMMUNICATION—HISTORY; REVOLUTION). The key symbols, whether of a movement or of a society, are important clues about how meanings are organized. One can, for example, trace changes in the associations with a term like *democracy* from the rule of the mob, a negative image, to the idea of representative government and, subsequently, to personal freedom. One can likewise gain an understanding about how a society views itself, its past achievements, its future, and its relation to other societies and make further comparisons across polities. There is a language of democracy as well as a language of tyranny, a language of a newly liberated nation and a language of an old empire. They undoubtedly differ in both vocabulary and style. The confidence one can have in inferences from the symbolic output about a society depends on the adequacy and validity of propositions about the symbol producers and those to whom they appeal. Hence the analysis of symbols must be conducted in conjunction with an analysis of the situational context in which they are used.

Bibliography. Hugh Dalziel Duncan, *Communication and Social Order*, New York, 1962; Murray Edelman, *Politics as Symbolic Action*, Chicago, 1971; Jacques Ellul, *Propaganda: The Formation of Men's Attitudes* (in French), trans. by Konrad Kellen and Jean Lerner, New York, 1965; Joseph R. Gusfield, *Symbolic Crusade: Status Politics and the American Temperance Movement*, Urbana, Ill., 1963; Harold D. Lasswell and Abraham Kaplan, *Power and Society*, New Haven, Conn., 1950.

KURT LANG AND GLADYS ENGEL LANG

POLITICIZATION

The process by which an institution, person, event, or activity not considered political acquires political MEANING and relevance. Instead of being dealt with privately or in some other nonpolitical forum, the subject becomes an issue of political concern. Politicized issues may be featured in ELECTION campaigns, provide a source of disagreement among candidates, inspire differences among political parties, or be seen as falling under governmental responsibility and even as requiring government action. See POLITICAL COMMUNICATION.

Politicization is most common in societies in which government tends to intervene in the economy, social life, and services; is involved in EDUCATION and cultural activities; and often tries to enforce certain standards of morality. At the same time, because of urbanization, increases in the relative size of the politically conscious upper and middle classes, and the development of an elaborate and extensive mass media system, people are—or have the opportunity to be—politically informed, aware, efficacious, and active. As a result, both the size of the political realm and the level of political conflict expand.

Role of the mass media. The mass media are central to the politicization process. Depending on what they report, how often and in what way they portray it, and the perspectives they provide, they can variously create, have no effects on, hinder, or even prevent politicization (see MASS MEDIA EFFECTS).

Much depends on the determinants of news. Relevant here are the backgrounds, values, and socialization of journalists; their definitions of news; their reliance on public officials as sources; and the ways they present news. Editing material, presenting it in brief segments on TELEVISION NEWS programs or in limited spaces in newspapers, encapsulating it for RADIO in a narrow frame of reference—all these requirements for presenting news have the effect of altering it or, at best, transmitting only a fragment of what has occurred.

The influence of the media can be seen, for example, when some economic issues are politicized but not others. During the 1980s U.S. media gave considerable publicity to claims and evidence that an abundance of imports from Asia was increasing U.S. unemployment and to concomitant calls for import quotas, tariffs on certain kinds of foreign goods, and subsidies for severely affected domestic industries. In contrast, and in part because of lack of media coverage, foreign investment *in* the United States was of little concern. In developing countries, however, foreign investment *from* the United States and other industrialized nations was a highly politicized matter (*see* DEVELOPMENT COMMUNICATION—ALTERNATIVE SYSTEMS).

Causes of Politicization

Although five of the most significant causes of politicization overlap, each is intimately linked to its coverage and presentation by the mass media. These overlapping causes are (1) social trends, (2) particular events, (3) activities of interest groups, (4) politicians' RHETORIC, and (5) governmental decisions.

Social trends. Social trends can bring to the fore ATTITUDES and behavior that raise concerns not currently thought of as politically relevant. But much depends on whether and how the media report these trends. Reporting is facilitated if the trends are palpable and can be personalized. For example, as the twentieth century progressed, people in the United States became increasingly aware of the forcibly imposed limits on the freedom and equality of blacks, especially those living in the South. Demands were made on government to respond, and the issue entered political discourse. Federal, state, and local governments eventually passed civil rights laws and created regulatory agencies designed to rectify, at least to some extent, the abuses. But it was the media that, by personalizing this trend and highlighting the moral dimensions of the conflict, brought the struggle for blacks' rights strongly to public attention, thus exacerbating the pressure on government to respond. Indeed, David J. Garrow argues that the Reverend Martin Luther King, Jr., and his associates devised a strategy to attract widespread and sympathetic media coverage of their cause by provoking attacks from violence-prone white southern officials (*see* MINORITIES IN THE MEDIA).

Particular events. Particular events can inspire politicization, especially if they fulfill such news values as VIOLENCE, conflict, and destruction and if they can be taken to symbolize outstanding inequities (*see* POLITICAL SYMBOLS). When, on March 25, 1911, the Triangle Shirtwaist Company went up in flames in New York City, killing 146 workers, extensive press coverage and editorials sparked a nationwide crusade for safer working conditions. In New York, a newly created Factory Investigating Commission sent inspectors into the tenements, factories, and workshops. Appalled by their reports, the commission sponsored numerous laws requiring safer working conditions, fire escapes and multiple staircases, and shorter working hours for women and children. Similar alarms and appeals for governmental response were sounded during the 1980s following the massive international news coverage of the release of deadly chemicals from a Union Carbide plant in Bhopal, India. Television images and detailed accounts of the disaster in the Indian and world press provoked vigorous debate in the Indian Parliament for new environmental and occupational health laws.

Even more alarming (and thus politicizing) was the nuclear plant accident at Chernobyl in the Soviet Union in 1986, when radiation was released into the atmosphere and spread across much of the world. Western media in particular led with the story for several days, even though their extensive coverage was often more speculative than factual—a problem caused in part by the Soviet government's determination to control the flow of information. The disaster reignited antinuclear passions, especially in western Europe. Demonstrations in France, the Federal Republic of Germany, and other countries often resulted in confrontations with the police (*see* DEMONSTRATION).

Interest groups. Interest group leaders often encourage social trends and try to capitalize on particular events to instill their objectives in the political world and bring them to the attention of policymakers and the public (*see also* OPINION LEADER). The mass media can be indispensable aids. As an example, consider the success of the self-described public interest group Common Cause in using the *New York Times* during the 1970s as a conduit, even a publicity agent, for the organization's views. Common Cause received favorable coverage because it possessed legitimacy and credibility, reinforced by the number and social standing of its members. Its expressed purposes were widely viewed as desirable by journalists. Meanwhile, at Common Cause media-conscious staff were involved in creating events of interest to the media, giving them visibility, bringing

them to reporters' attention, emphasizing the events' newsworthy details, and organizing them into stories for the press. In part because of this favorable coverage from one of the most influential newspapers in the United States, Common Cause's objectives—public financing of presidential election campaigns, LOBBYING disclosure laws, conflict of interest laws, and financing disclosure laws—became items on the agenda of political debate in the United States and were enacted. *See* PRESSURE GROUP.

Politicians' rhetoric. Politicians, especially prominent public officials, possess the power to politicize because they are a major source of news for the media. Heads of state are conspicuously blessed in this regard because virtually anything they say is news. They are prone to politicize an issue particularly if they believe they can benefit from the results. Election campaigns offer expanded opportunities for politicization because candidates, particularly those seeking the presidency from major parties, can supplement (even replace) news coverage with campaign advertisements on television, in newspapers, and elsewhere. They often bring to the fore issues of public irritation, concern, discontent, or fear that previously lacked a pronounced political dimension. Chile offers a significant example. The issue of foreign investment became highly politicized in the 1964 presidential election between leading candidates Eduardo Frei and Salvador Allende. It was widely believed that many of Chile's economic and social problems were caused by uncontrolled foreign interests, especially U.S.-owned copper mines. Hence, many politicians, intellectuals, and activists felt that foreign investment should be used more for the benefit of the domestic economy than to maximize the profits of foreign corporations. The candidates' rhetoric in the election highlighted this concern. Frei, of the moderate Christian Democratic party, proposed the "Chileanization" of the copper industry through state purchase of majority ownership in the mines. The Marxist-oriented Allende proposed the more radical road of nationalization. Allende lost to Frei in 1964, but in 1970, as the candidate of the Popular Unity coalition—whose major policy thrust was nationalization—he won the presidency. The Chilean Congress, under Allende's guidance, nationalized the copper industry.

Governmental decisions. These can also have politicizing effects. When, in its 1973 decision of *Roe v. Wade*, the U.S. Supreme Court in effect legalized abortion, it politicized a subject that until then had been primarily personal and private. Henceforward, intense pressure would be brought on the legislative and executive branches of government for action by both those favoring and those opposing abortion. The mass media can be instrumental in such politicization. Many Supreme Court rulings receive little if any media coverage, while others are widely reported. Given the media's fascination with some topics and disinterest in others, the amount and depth of coverage is not necessarily consonant with a case's significance.

Entertainment

There is more to media content than news coverage and campaign commercials. In commercial mass media systems there are also regular advertisements (*see* COMMERCIALS) and a wide variety of programming in radio (e.g., music, talk) and television (e.g., movies, SPORTS, soap operas, game shows, situation comedies, and so on; *see* QUIZ SHOW; SOAP OPERA). At first view media entertainment would appear to lack any politicizing potential; however, it is often saturated with political meaning. It identifies what topics are important and even how to think about them (*see* AGENDA-SETTING). Much of the material contains underlying values that in turn encourage politicization. Programming may propound the desirability of economic growth and the facilitating role of government. It may stress the centrality of fairness and distributive justice in society and thus the government's responsibility to ensure them. Conversely, individualism—people's personal responsibility for their fate—may be the value upheld and goverment considered unnecessary or irrelevant; this perspective discourages politicization. On the one hand, shows can highlight specific problems faced by women and minorities, portray general social and economic problems, and suggest that government action is called for. On the other hand, entertainment programs can ignore issues or, even if they raise them, indicate that *personal* (e.g., love, ambition, individualism, luck), not *political,* solutions are appropriate. *See* CULTURAL INDICATORS.

Differences among Systems

While some media content includes deliberate attempts at politicization, usually by public officials or political activists, much of it is devoid of conscious intent, and any politicization effects are inadvertent or accidental. One reason is that in predominantly democratic societies the media possess considerable autonomy and independence. In contrast, the media in autocratic societies are usually controlled by and operate at the behest of the people running the state (*see* GOVERNMENT-MEDIA RELATIONS).

In autocratic states many decisions affecting the media system are apt to be made by those holding party or government positions, while the public is usually denied a significant say. Diverse political parties rarely exist, vigorous opposition to the ruling elite is curtailed, and criticism of the authorities is discouraged. State control of the media is consequently often used to depoliticize, to remove or prevent subjects from entering the restricted political arena (*see* CENSORSHIP; GOVERNMENT REGULATION). But there are exceptions. The media in autocratic states sometimes contribute to widespread politicization promoted directly by those in power, as was the case in China during the Cultural Revolution (1966–1969). During that period many kinds of personal behavior normally regarded as private were treated by rulers and media alike as having political meaning and implications (*see* ASIA, TWENTIETH CENTURY). At other times—for example, during a conflict among members of the ruling elite or the emergence of previously dormant opposition—the media in an autocratic state may obtain a much greater degree of freedom. Although this freedom may be brief, it often lasts long enough to release a torrent of information and ideas politicizing repressed or suppressed subjects that were previously confined to unofficial or underground press and publications.

When states move away from autocracy, the media's freedom usually increases concomitantly. Brazil in the 1970s is a notable example. As the military leaders jockeyed for power and political parties emerged, newspapers in particular became sources of information, centers of debate about public policies, and raisers of issues. Thus newspapers were central to the resurgence of political processes and the movement of topics and issues from private to public life.

Politicization is sometimes viewed as unnecessarily endowing private lives and problems with political elements, making them grist for ill-considered governmental intervention. But there is another, positive side: politicization as awakening.

See also POLITICAL SOCIALIZATION.

Bibliography. David J. Garrow, *Protest at Selma: Martin Luther King, Jr., and the Voting Rights Act of 1965,* New Haven, Conn., 1978; Claus Mueller, *The Politics of Communication,* New York, 1973; David L. Paletz, *Political Communication Research: Approaches, Studies, Assessments,* Norwood, N.J., 1986; David L. Paletz and Robert M. Entman, *Media Power Politics,* New York, 1981.

DAVID L. PALETZ

POLL

Polling is a special application of the sample survey method to the study of political behavior. (Other applications of this method—for example, for social science, marketing, and public policy research—are excluded from this definition of polling.) By surveying representative samples of the public, polls seek to measure and analyze the state of PUBLIC OPINION and how it responds to events and public debate surrounding those events. In each poll questions are asked of a representative cross-section of the public concerning such matters as understanding and knowledge of public issues, preferences regarding how those issues should be handled, evaluation of the nation's political leadership, and the public's hopes, aspirations, fears, and concerns. The aggregate survey results are reported as public opinion concerning the topics covered at the time the survey was conducted.

Polls contrast sharply with other sources of information about public opinion, such as grass-roots soundings by local political leaders, meetings with community and organization leaders, and CONTENT ANALYSIS of letters to news media or to elected representatives. Reliance on those other sources assumes that public opinion can best be determined by investigating its expression through formal channels of communication and by community and institutional leaders. In contrast, polls rely on quantitative methods intended to produce representative, objective measures of the opinion of all the people included in the universe from which the sample is drawn. Polls measure public opinion in terms of the total sampled population, all of whose opinions are treated as relevant and significant. Therefore, when polls measure public opinion they give substantial weight to the views of all sorts of people, regardless of how uninvolved or uninformed about specific issues. On the other hand, such informal opinion is often overlooked by methods that, by focusing on formal leaders, are prone to emphasize established interests.

Origins

Modern public opinion polling has its roots in pre-election straw polls conducted by newspapers and magazines. Initially straw polls attempted to do little more than measure voting preferences, playing a minor role in news coverage of ELECTION campaigns. They were essentially journalistic stunts conducted because of their presumed value for increasing circulation. Sampling methods were primitive, and those polled were asked only to mark their voting preferences on paper ballots and return them either by mail or by personally putting them into ballot boxes. Despite the crudity of these methods, the results of the straw polls were often better predictors of election outcomes than were the forecasts based on canvassing, personal observation, and judgment made by politicians, journalists, and other "experts." By the 1930s some straw polls were treated as trustworthy measures of voting intentions and not merely as a journalistic curiosity.

In 1936 the most prestigious U.S. straw poll was the one conducted by the *Literary Digest*. On the basis of 2 million mail ballots returned from a total of 10 million that had been mailed to telephone subscribers and automobile owners, the *Literary Digest* incorrectly forecast that the incumbent president, Franklin D. Roosevelt, would be defeated by the Republican challenger, Alfred M. Landon. This massive error demonstrated that sheer numbers were insufficient for accurate measures of voting intentions and set the stage for the emergence of polls based on small but carefully selected samples.

The growth of modern public opinion polling. In October 1935 GEORGE GALLUP founded the American Institute of Public Opinion (the Gallup Poll), a syndicated newspaper service based on frequent polls of representative national samples. The concept underlying this service is that the opinions of the general public on current issues are both newsworthy and politically significant. At virtually the same time, *Fortune* magazine engaged the services of ELMO ROPER to conduct periodic public opinion polls, which were published as the Fortune Poll. Shortly thereafter King Features contracted with Archibald Crossley to conduct public opinion polls that it syndicated to its newspaper clients. It is noteworthy that while all three of these polling ventures were sponsored by news media, Gallup, Roper, and Crossley themselves came from the world of ADVERTISING and marketing research. This alliance of news media and marketing research has continued to characterize much of public opinion polling.

Two important differences between straw polls and the methods used by Gallup, Roper, and Crossley were, first, the use of relatively small samples with preassigned quotas (i.e., specific numbers of women and men, people of different ages and income levels, etc.) and, second, the use of interviewers who collected the information in people's homes to avoid a self-selection bias in the sample. Gallup, Roper, and Crossley all correctly forecast a Roosevelt victory in 1936. The markedly superior performance of their polls to the *Literary Digest* poll established the credibility of their methods and marked the emergence of public opinion polling as a staple of political journalism.

Public opinion polling suffered a severe setback in 1948, when every poll incorrectly forecast that President Harry S. Truman's bid for reelection would be defeated by the Republican contender, Thomas E. Dewey. Illustrative of the severity of the credibility crisis that resulted is the fact that the Social Science Research Council funded an intensive study of the methodological sources of this error.

Acceptance of public opinion polls was partially restored during the 1950s, but it was not until the extremely close 1960 presidential election, when just about every poll forecast a victory for John F. Kennedy despite the narrowness of his lead over Richard

M. Nixon (50.1 percent), that their credibility was firmly reestablished. The following decade was characterized by considerable expansion in media-sponsored polling: television networks, newsmagazines, and individual newspapers began to conduct polls on a regular basis, (see NEWSMAGAZINE). By 1985 there were seven regularly conducted media-sponsored national polls in the United States, while state and local polls were being conducted by more than 150 newspapers and television and radio stations.

A major innovation introduced by the television networks in the late 1970s and early 1980s was to interview voters as they left their voting places. The results of these exit polls are used to develop early forecasts of voting returns and to analyze voting patterns.

Academic polling in the United States. Four academically based survey centers were established during the 1940s: HADLEY CANTRIL organized the Office of Public Opinion Research at Princeton (later dissolved); Harry Field, the National Opinion Research Center at Denver University (later moved to the University of Chicago); PAUL F. LAZARSFELD, the Bureau of Applied Social Research at Columbia University (later absorbed into the Center for the Social Sciences); and Rensis Likert, the Survey Research Center at the University of Michigan. These research centers increasingly directed their attention to studies of voting behavior, the measurement of social trends, and policy research rather than conducting public opinion polls as such. By the 1980s academic involvement in polling public opinion was most active at the state level, with some twenty-three academic survey research centers forming a Network of State Polls. Many of these centers regularly conduct public opinion polls.

International spread of polling. Interest in public opinion polling spread rapidly to Europe, with Gallup affiliates established in Great Britain in 1937 and in France in 1938. The outbreak of World War II halted growth temporarily, but there was a rapid expansion of polling throughout western Europe in the postwar years. In addition to the establishment of additional Gallup affiliates, International Research Associates was organized by Elmo Wilson with affiliates in most of western Europe. The following decades saw a further expansion to South America, Africa, and Asia. By 1985 Gallup International had affiliates in thirty-five countries, and International Research Associates in thirty. Independent polling organizations were formed in many of these countries to compete with the international networks.

Private polls. One of the most significant aspects of the rise of public opinion polls has been their use by political leaders and parties. In addition to the publicly reported polls sponsored by news media, public opinion polls are conducted for politicians and political parties for their private, confidential use. A pioneer user of private opinion polls was Roosevelt, who in 1941 relied on them to gauge how successful he was in generating public support for his policy of providing military aid to Great Britain. During the 1950s Claude Robinson of Opinion Research Corporation conducted polls for the Republicans, while Louis Harris's polls for Kennedy figured prominently in the 1960 presidential election campaign.

By the end of the 1970s private polls had replaced local party units as the primary source of information about grass-roots public opinion. As precinct-level party organizations atrophied and mass media of communication proliferated, politicians increasingly turned to privately sponsored polls to identify public ATTITUDES toward themselves and their opponents, the issues of greatest salience to the public, and the effectiveness of their election campaigns. A new politics came into being, based on the interactive use of polls and mass media of communication to measure and influence public opinion.

The use of polls by special-interest groups. As the credibility of polls as a source of public information became established, special-interest groups began to use them to further their policies and positions. This use of polls by special-interest groups has taken three forms: advocacy, PUBLIC RELATIONS, and communications planning.

Advocacy polls are conducted specifically to develop "proof" that the public endorses the position advocated by the sponsoring organization. Such polls have been used to support LOBBYING efforts by industry and labor groups and also by citizen action groups. They have covered a wide range of topics, including taxation, environmental protection, abortion, and military spending (see AGENDA-SETTING). On occasion, conflicting special-interest groups have sponsored their own polls, with contradictory results. In such circumstances the polls themselves have become matters of controversy.

Public relations polls are conducted in the expectation that the public release of their results will enhance the public standing of the sponsoring organization. For example, a special-interest group will sponsor a poll on some topic of current general interest—changing patterns of family life, fear of crime, the role of religion, the changing status of women in modern society—even though the topic has no apparent relation to the group's specific interests. The poll results are publicized as a public service in the expectation that the public's attitude toward the sponsoring group will be improved.

Special-interest groups also sponsor polls for their private use when planning public communications campaigns. This use is directly analogous to the use of polls by politicians. The poll results are used primarily as information about public opinion that can contribute to the development of effective public communications. Selected results are sometimes released as part of the campaign.

Issues in Polling

The history of public opinion polling is characterized by high expectations regarding its power as a source of information about public opinion, questions about the accuracy and meaningfulness of poll results, and concerns about the effects that polling has on the political process. The interaction among these issues has on occasion resulted in bitter controversy.

Preelection polls. An evaluation of polls methodology sponsored by the Social Science Research Council to analyze why polls failed to forecast Truman's reelection in 1948 identified the major limitations of preelection poll methodology then in use. These included the reliance on quota sampling instead of probability sampling, the lack of an adequate method for differentiating likely voters from nonvoters, the failure to conduct last-minute polls to detect late shifts in candidate strength, and the lack of a satisfactory method for allocating undecided voters.

Since 1948 methods used for preelection polls have undergone considerable change. Most polls now use sample designs that employ probability procedures at most stages of selection. Progress has been made in developing techniques for identifying likely voters and for treating undecided voters. Of particular importance, poll results are now reported as measurements of candidate strength as of the time the polls are taken rather than as predictions in the strict sense of the word.

As a result of these changes some polling organizations have achieved very accurate records in their preelection polls. This has created another problem in its turn. Experience with preelection polls that correctly pointed to the winner in very close elections—such as in the 1960 and 1968 U.S. presidential elections—created unrealistically high expectations of poll accuracy. As a result, preelection polls that are within expected sampling error of election results but have the wrong candidate ahead are often cited by the uninformed as evidence of the unreliability of polls.

Problems in accuracy persist, especially with respect to primary elections. Periodic failures to forecast elections correctly continue to occur, as happened in Australia in 1984 and in the United States in 1980. These failures indicate that room for improvement in preelection poll methodology remains. Nonetheless, news media and politicians continue to rely on polls as their main source of information about voting intentions.

Conflicting polls. On occasion polls conducted by different organizations report apparently conflicting results. For example, the measurements of public approval of the incumbent president by the Gallup and Harris polls differ occasionally from each other to a degree greater than would be expected because of random sampling error. Conflicts have also occurred regarding public opinion on such issues as abortion, disarmament, and nuclear freeze, and whether treaties such as SALT II and the return of the Panama Canal to Panama (1979) should be ratified.

Critics point to conflicts between polls as evidence that poll results cannot be relied on as valid measures of public opinion. Pollsters have answered these criticisms by noting that conflicting results are to be expected when interviewing dates differ and when question wording differs. When major events intervene between interviewing dates, and especially when public opinion is in flux, differences between polls are to be expected. With respect to question wording, a considerable body of evidence attests that apparently minor variations in wording can sometimes lead to significant differences in responses. It is often the case that purportedly conflicting results are based on questions that differ appreciably from one another. Another possible source of variation is the position of questions in an interview, since question order may also significantly affect how a question is answered.

More generally, conflicting polls underscore the dangers of simplistic interpretations of poll results, which assume that there is "a public opinion" that can be validly summarized in the answers to a single question. Public opinion is a dynamic, often inconsistent quality of the body politic that cannot be fully comprehended by any one or two questions.

Effects on the electoral process. The possibility that preelection polls have BANDWAGON EFFECTS (the assumed propensity of voters to vote for a candidate primarily because they believe he or she will win) is a perennial issue. The probability of a candidate's winning is an important consideration to politicians when deciding whom to support. Consequently, preelection polls are an important influence on the nominating process within political parties and on the decisions of major financial contributors. However, there is no empirical evidence that bandwagon effects occur to any appreciable degree among rank-and-file voters.

In addition to influencing who is nominated, polls play a central role in the planning and evaluation of political campaigns. Some feel this has contributed to democratic government in that polls sensitize politicians to the public's concerns and desires and, therefore, make them more responsive to their constituencies. Others disagree, noting that the result has been to induce politicians to abdicate their leadership function and to follow the polls in their efforts to get elected.

Polls make it possible for politicians to reach out directly to the public, bypassing traditional institutional channels of communication. To some this represents a democratization of politics, weakening the ability of power elites to control the political process. An opposing view is that this bypassing has brought about the disintegration of organized political activity, leading to declining voter turnout and enhancing the ability of well-financed aspirants to political office (with little prior political experience) to manipulate the political process and achieve high office. *See* POLITICAL COMMUNICATION—HISTORY.

Regulating Polls

Concern over the possible undesirable effects of polls on the electoral process has created pressure to regulate polls. In Western-style democracies those advocating regulation have focused their attention on assumed bandwagon effects among the general electorate, although those effects have never been clearly demonstrated. Thus, in the Federal Republic of Germany, preelection poll results cannot be published during the final days preceding an election. Efforts to enact comparable legislation in the United States have been unsuccessful, primarily because restricting publication has been viewed as a form of CENSORSHIP. Some states in the western United States have tried to circumvent this objection with respect to exit polls by prohibiting interviewing within the immediate vicinity of the voting places.

Regulation has also been an issue in nations with authoritarian governments. In such nations the freedom to conduct polls without government interference is subject to infringement. In response to this possibility the World Association for Public Opinion Research has included in its professional code a provision asserting the freedom to poll independent of a government.

Public opinion polling has become a major commercial venture as well as a critical link between people and their governments. Its importance is widely recognized, and concern over the possible social and political consequences resulting from it is likely to continue into the twenty-first century.

Bibliography. Leo Bogart, *Silent Politics: Polls and the Awareness of Public Opinion*, New York, 1972; Jerome S. Bruner, *Mandate from the People*, New York, 1944; Albert H. Cantril, ed., *Polling on the Issues*, Cabin John, Md., 1980; Hadley Cantril, *Gauging Public Opinion*, Princeton, N.J., 1944, reprint Port Washington, N.Y., 1972; idem, *The Human Dimension*, New Brunswick, N.J., 1967; George Gallup and Saul F. Rae, *The Pulse of Democracy*, New York, 1940; Norman C. Meier and Harold W. Saunders, eds., *The Polls and Public Opinion*, New York, 1949; Harold Mendelsohn and Irving Crespi, *Polls, Television, and the New Politics*, Scranton, Pa., 1970; Frederick Mosteller, Herbert Hyman, Philip J. McCarthy, Eli S. Marks, and David B. Truman, *The Pre-election Polls of 1948*, New York, 1949; Claude E. Robinson, *Straw Votes*, New York, 1932, reprint 1979; John P. Robinson and Robert Meadow, *Polls Apart*, Cabin John, Md., 1982; Charles W. Roll, Jr., and Albert H. Cantril, *Polls: Their Use and Misuse in Politics*, New York, 1972.

IRVING CRESPI

POLO, MARCO (1254–1324)

Venetian known for his account of travels during twenty-five years (1271–1295) in eastern regions of Asia. The extraordinary observations Marco Polo related, particularly about the Chinese court of Mongol emperor Kublai Khan, were received by many Europeans as fantasy, but in the course of time much of what he wrote was confirmed. His observations became for generations the main source of European information and imaginings about eastern Asia. His account was read with special interest by cartographers and explorers and had an influence on Christopher Columbus, whose geographical calculations were guided to some extent by what Marco Polo had written, particularly in what he reported having heard about Cipangu (Japan).

Marco Polo's merchant family had traded throughout the Middle East for generations. About 1260, during a time of comparative tranquility in central Asia, his father (Niccolò) and uncle (Maffeo) extended the range of their travels eastward to the Mongol Empire with a journey of nine years. Marco was about fifteen when his father and uncle returned, and when they set out again in 1271 he went with them. They reached their destination, the court of Kublai Khan, about four years later. The Polos appear to have been employed in some official role during their stay at the court. Marco was sent on investigative and administrative missions to many parts of the Mongol Empire.

The Polos ended their eastern sojourn after some twenty years to accompany a Mongol princess and her retinue by sea to her wedding in Persia. They continued onward to Venice. Soon thereafter Marco was captured in a sea battle with the Genoese and taken to a Genoese prison, where he spent about a year before he was able to return to Venice to live out the rest of his life.

The book on which his fame rests was dictated to a fellow prisoner in Genoa named Rusticiano or Rustichello. The amanuensis, a writer of romantic tales, is thought to have added a few embellishments of his own. Where the work rests on Marco Polo's

Figure 1. (Polo, Marco) Marco Polo as portrayed in a German edition of his book, 1477. The surrounding caption reads: "The noble knight [sic] Marco Polo of Venice, the great traveler who describes for us the grand wonders of the world that he himself has seen, from the rising to the setting sun, of a sort not previously known." The Bettmann Archive, Inc.

direct observations (as opposed to what he related having heard) the account has proved remarkably accurate. On his deathbed, asked to recant his Asian stories, Polo responded that he had told only half of the marvels he had seen. *Il milione* (translated in English as *The Travels of Marco Polo*) remains an informative glimpse of an early bridge between East and West.

See also CARTOGRAPHY; EAST ASIA, ANCIENT; EXPLORATION; SILK ROAD.

Bibliography. Luigi Foscolo Benedetto, ed., *Il milione, prima edizione integrale*, Venice, 1928; Henry H. Hart, *Venetian Adventurer*, Stanford, Calif., 1942, reprint (*Marco Polo, Venetian Adventurer*) Norman, Okla., 1967; Leonardo Olschki, *Marco Polo's Asia* (L'Asia di Marco Polo), trans. by John A. Scott, Berkeley, Calif., 1960; Marco Polo, *The Travels of Marco Polo* (in Italian), trans. by Ronald Latham, Harmondsworth, Eng., 1958; Milton Rugoff, *Marco Polo's Adventures in China*, New York, 1964.

POPULAR CULTURE. *See* CULTURE; LITERATURE, POPULAR; MUSIC, POPULAR; TASTE CULTURES.

PORNOGRAPHY

A MODE of discourse, a way of thinking, talking about, and depicting sexual practices that is generally seen as differentiating sex from any spiritual or sentimental meaning on the one hand and from procreative functions on the other. Pornography defines erotic desire by isolating it from the contexts of medicine and scientific rationality as well as from aesthetic analysis; thus it slips through the categories of thought that we use to organize our knowledge and CULTURE. And yet it has become, at least in Western countries, part of the public agenda, a matter for commissions and government inquiries, confirming the observation once made by the French social historian MICHEL FOUCAULT that we are the only civilization in which officials are paid to listen to people talk about sex.

Despite the public attention given to pornography and the strong views held about it, there is little consensus on how to define, operationalize, or recognize it. Some persons refer to content (e.g., frontal nudity of female figures); others refer to style and presentation, an "auteur theory" that looks at camera angles or the painter's perspective on the nude; and still others define pornography by the responses it induces among its viewers (e.g., sexual arousal or voyeurism). The arbitrary nature of these definitions reflects the fact that *pornography* is a legal term and not one ordinarily used by art historians or literary critics. Yet there is a discernible pattern to the diverse texts that legal codes have labeled pornographic, a common structure that makes it possible to speak of pornography as a distinctive GENRE.

First, pornography violates societal norms because it presents forms of sexual behavior held unacceptable in themselves, or because it presents publicly acts that are judged acceptable only when they occur in private, or both. By transgressing the norms governing "appropriate" sexual behavior or appropriate depictions of sexuality, pornography is always controversial and is generally accused of profaning society in a way that is expected to evoke shame or disgust. In most societies this disgust is expressed through legal restraints and CENSORSHIP. Pornography may also be a parody of the social structure. Sixteenth-century pornography, for example, was often about clergy who disregarded their sacred vows of chastity, whereas much eighteenth-century pornography was about the court and the moral turpitude of the nobility. In the nineteenth century the central character of the anonymous sexual AUTOBIOGRAPHY *My Secret Life* was a gentleman who conducted his adventures with the spirit of an entrepreneur. Pornography's second layer of social satire adds a sense of political decadence to its deeper mockery of a system of values.

Second, the violation of sexual norms in pornography is presented as if it were a natural part of everyday life, fully permitted and widely practiced. It is this nonjudgmental attitude toward proscribed behavior that creates the shock and embarrassment we experience and may even contribute to the pleasure, for pornography that does not shock fails as ENTERTAINMENT (although it still may fulfill its function of sexual arousal).

Finally, the characters in pornography are nearly always one-dimensional figures with no past, no inner life, no emotion, no sense of self-discipline or constraint. Male or female, they have no identity or capacity to resist any sort of external stimuli. Their relationships exist only for purposes of sexual gratification and are terminated should any other sentiment intrude. These unreal characters reside in a world in which the ordinary consequences of behavior are canceled. They do not fear pregnancy, and there is no risk of sexually transmitted disease. Means and ends follow a pleasure principle rather than the logic of society or biology.

Within the broad category of pornography is a subset of sadomasochistic texts based on the theme of bondage. Bondage, or a master-slave relationship, is seen as created through and subsequently demonstrated by administering or receiving pain. VIOLENCE may be the mediating factor between pain as a physical sensation and bondage as a social relationship. What is often overlooked, as some contemporary feminist theorists have noted, is the key aspect of sadomasochism as playing with power and power roles, the acting out or manipulation of relationships in sexual form that remain hidden, implicit, and usually unchallengeable in other contexts.

Sadomasochism touches a sensitive social nerve by linking pleasure and pain, yet its presumed effects on behavior and ATTITUDES are the cause of most controversy. Many feminists, for example, are concerned with the functions of sadomasochistic pornography in which women and children are portrayed as desiring or freely consenting in violent acts of male sadism (*see* FEMINIST THEORIES OF COMMUNICATION).

It is frequently alleged that the volume of pornography has increased in recent decades and that contemporary pornography is qualitatively different—both more realistic and more violent—from older forms. Although such claims are difficult to investigate, certainly pornography is more readily available than ever before as the result of new media and distribution technologies such as VIDEO and CABLE TELEVISION. The use of PHOTOGRAPHY and CINEMATOGRAPHY has also raised concern over the po-

tential exploitation of real-life participants in pornography. As long as the production of pornography is not a legitimate form of enterprise, there is no system of accountability and no way of protecting the interests of the work force. Many law-enforcement officials believe there is a business connection between the production and sale of pornography and organized crime, but there is little evidence to show this and no way to prevent it.

Social scientists have attempted to account for pornography as a phenomenon and to explain its attraction. Although their theories differ, they represent a larger liberal point of view that itself reflects the rapid changes characterizing sexual norms and attitudes in all Western industrialized societies since World War I. In general the theories support a more permissive and less restrictive approach to sexual attitudes and practices, a greater appreciation of the normality and therapeutic values of sexual fantasy, and a distrust of the motives behind conservative forces.

The oldest and best known is the psychoanalytic theory, which understands pornography as a form of wish-fulfillment fantasy, the consequence of necessary sexual sublimation (*see* PSYCHOANALYSIS). As with dreams and other forms of fantasy, pornography is here viewed as being essentially harmless, perhaps even contributing to mental health by lowering psychological tension and restoring psychic equilibrium through catharsis. Pornography is thus seen as both a diagnostic of civilization and a safety valve.

An unhealthy aspect of pornography, in this view, is the motivation of the censor or of those who crusade for decency and the restoration of traditional morality. What underlies such obsessional behavior, Freudians suggested, is a pathological denial of the powerful attraction felt for illicit sex and guilt at having these indecent, improper feelings. By publicly condemning evil, the censors display to themselves and others what they know privately to be untrue—the purity of their own thought.

A second, more sociological theory locates sexual frustration, particularly that of men, in the constraints imposed by monogamous marriage. The view suggests that as long as this institution is held to be socially desirable and productive, men will be forced to find gratification for their residual sexual energies outside marriage through prostitution. According to this theory prostitution is the price to be paid for the nuclear monogamous family. Pornography is seen as the functional equivalent of prostitution, and as an activity that, like prostitution, should be recognized and brought out from the shadows of illegal behavior.

If either of these theories—psychoanalytic or sociological—were valid, one would expect pornography to have declined significantly with the advent of certain social changes. The first theory, for example, predicts that as we become less inhibited about our sexual activity and better informed about sexuality there will be less need for pornography. The second predicts that as marriage systems become more flexible, as the reality of both premarital and extramarital sex is recognized, and as divorce is more easily available, the need for pornography will decrease. Yet modern Western society has undergone these changes without an accompanying decline in the production of pornography.

A third, more reasonable hypothesis is based on humanistic psychology and proceeds from the assumption that sexual behavior is primarily learned and can be performed either in an instrumental and technically proficient way or in a creative and expressive way. Pornography is seen as falling into the second category by creating a mood and contributing to an atmosphere that may help people to experiment with sex.

Pornography in this view is a minor and enhancing part of a life-style. According to a major U.S. study, men and women of all backgrounds and socioeconomic levels used pornography. No evidence from user behavior or personality profiles indicated that those who enjoyed pornography were abnormal in any way. Furthermore, more literate and culturally sophisticated audiences demanded a better quality of pornography, something less vulgar than the usual tabloid or adult film.

In the 1960s criticism of the theories about pornography was part of a larger critique of earlier liberalism. Conservative thinkers took the permissive morality that trivialized pornography as symptomatic of a breakdown in civilization in which all values had become relative and all ethics pragmatic. Pornography was merely the tip of this iceberg and could not be redeemed by claims of artistic merit or the tastes of cultural elites.

To leftists pornography was similarly regarded as an expression of a sick society, the malaise of a bourgeois capitalism that dehumanized all relationships and converted sexuality into a commodity. The radical power of eros to humanize relationships was, according to this view, co-opted by the system and had become part of a counterrevolution. Casual recreational sex was a pseudoliberation representing freedom from the legacy of Victorian attitudes but effecting no corresponding transformation in interpersonal relations or the power structure. Whether pornography was used as a stimulant or as a form of entertainment, it was an expression of modern alienation and its consumption a form of conformity.

One prominent feminist position, too, starts from a critical analysis of the social structure as exploitative, alienating, and coercive. But the distinctive feature of the social structure for women is its patriarchal character—that is, a system of male privilege, authority, and power that keeps women dependent on men in the home, segmented in the labor force, and marginal in political life (*see* SEXISM). This pattern of sexual inequality could not exist without a symbolic system to legitimate it. All forms of culture—literature, RELIGION, science, social theory, ADVERTISING, and popular culture—reinforce the system; pornography is merely the extreme, the most misogynist form of a pervasive androcentric culture. From this perspective, sadomasochistic pornography that depicts women as freely cooperating in their own humiliation and physical pain is a self-serving male myth. Men who sincerely claim that they do not approve of pornography and abhor any form of sadomasochistic fantasy reap its benefits anyway, for pornography's long-term consequences are the intimidation of women and the strengthening of male control.

Feminist criticism of pornography falls into three categories, each centered on one aspect of the issue: the values pornography is seen to embody, pornography as a social problem, and pornography as POLITICIZATION. In the first view, pornography is said to degrade women apart from any consequences it may have; it is frequently compared with "hate" literature, although the two are thematically different. Hate literature has a strong paranoid appeal, whereas pornography appeals to male narcissism, but both treat a class of persons as objects.

The social-problem view is less concerned with values or the intrinsic nature of pornography and more with its possible extrinsic effects on male audiences. These hypothesized effects include rape and other overt forms of sexual aggression, the justification of violence against women or the belief that it was invited, and desensitization with respect to acts of sexual cruelty. Thus feminist critics have maintained that there are specific behavioral outcomes, attitudinal changes, and moral deteriorations that may result from even minimal exposure to any form of pornography, although the consequences are most obvious in the case of sadomasochistic pornography.

The third perspective examines the impact of pornography on women, how it might shape women's understanding of their own sexuality (e.g., making the clitoris the site of sexual pleasure as if it were a penis) and contribute to their passivity and depoliticization. Pornography and popular romances (*see* ROMANCE, THE) are viewed as simply different sides of the same coin. Both devalue women in a way that leads to material disadvantage.

Implicit in both critical theory and this strain of feminism is a rejection of an earlier view of pornography as having no deleterious social effects and as best left unregulated. In the new frameworks, particularly that of feminism, pornography constitutes a violation of human rights. Recent empirical research has challenged the older, benign view and has been used by both conservatives and liberals attempting to mandate censorship. This research, which is mainly experimental and based on psychological behavioral theory, shows that the catharsis process, the vicarious discharge of aggressions or antisocial impulses, is not consistently demonstrated. On the contrary, according to the studies, people tend to be incited by certain material and may imitate what they see, especially if they see it often. Communication scholars generally resist any simplistic model of media causation (*see* MODELS OF COMMUNICATION), particularly one based largely on generalizations from a few experimental studies, but tend to regard persistently repeated patterns of communication as potentially strong influences (*see* CULTIVATION ANALYSIS).

Feminists themselves are divided on the subject of censorship and regulation. Many believe it is possible to seek the elimination of violence against women and to achieve structural equality while still supporting freedom of expression. Some are skeptical of legalistic solutions to political and social problems. Moreover, they argue, censorship and other forms of regulation have their own unanticipated consequences—"a chilling effect"—on the political culture. They recall that Margaret Sanger and many of the early advocates of family planning were prosecuted under existing antiobscenity laws. Other feminists are convinced that priority must be given to structural equality as measured by equal pay, day care, control of reproductive functions, the Equal Rights Amendment, and other indicators; when these are achieved, any undesirable social effects of pornography will be defused. And still others view censorship as obstructing research and the kind of open dialogue on sexuality from a feminist perspective that is essential for reconstructing our knowledge of sexuality. In short, there are many objections to censorship that fully recognize the misogynist values in pornography.

The current research agenda on pornography appears to offer a choice between the classic psychoanalytic theory of catharsis and behavioral modification. Many investigators are dissatisfied with both and seek a different paradigm for understanding the effects of pornography on individuals as well as on the quality of life. Some scholars have begun to study pornography as a text, an iconic system that can be understood as revealing fundamental messages about the nature of erotic pleasure and desire. There is a question, too, of whether pornography is a code term for something else, a concrete example of a universal archetype of the profane arising out of the imperatives of social organization. Thus all human societies have a dual culture, the sacred and the profane

existing in a reciprocal relationship. Sexuality may be the most enduring form of this dialectical tension, but it is not the only one.

Pornography symbolizes the profane through sexual scenarios. It insults and subverts the established code of sexual morality without repudiating it or offering a radical alternative. The psychological discomfort pornography engenders stems from the juxtaposition of tabooed behavior and a value-free attitude toward it. Sociologically, pornography reflects the ever-shifting boundaries of sexual norms; politically, it tests the state's concern in maintaining those boundaries. Yet pornography may have less to do with sex and the social psychology of prurience than with a dilemma of the modern mind, becoming a way of measuring the cultural and intellectual tolerance of a society and the emotional maturity of the individual faced with ambiguity.

Bibliography. Harry M. Clor, *Obscenity and Public Morality*, Chicago, 1969; Kate Ellis, Nan Hunter, Beth Jaker, Barbara O'Dair, and Abby Tallmer, eds., *Caught Looking: Feminism, Pornography, and Censorship*, New York, 1986; Michel Foucault, *The History of Sexuality* (in French), trans. by Robert Hurley, New York, 1978; A. Nicholas Groth, with H. Jean Birnbaum, *Men Who Rape: The Psychology of the Offender*, New York, 1979; H. Montgomery Hyde, *A History of Pornography*, London, 1964; Walter Kendrick, *The Secret Museum: Pornography in Modern Culture*, New York, 1987; Laura Lederer, ed., *Take Back the Night: Women on Pornography*, New York, 1980; Steven Marcus, *The Other Victorians*, New York, 1966; Ann Snitow, Christine Stansell, and Sharon Thompson, eds., *Powers of Desire: The Politics of Sexuality*, New York, 1983; Carole S. Vance, ed., *Pleasure and Danger: Exploring Female Sexuality*, Boston, 1984; Robert Paul Wolff, Barrington Moore, Jr., and Herbert Marcuse, *A Critique of Pure Tolerance*, Boston, 1969.

THELMA MCCORMACK

PORTRAITURE

Although it is not possible to define the term *portrait* to everyone's satisfaction, it may be described as a recognizable likeness of an individual. The GENRE is not universal but is associated with the West in particular, first in classical antiquity and again from the RENAISSANCE to the present. Even in Western CULTURE the genre has been far from constant: the kinds of people portrayed, the social functions of the portrait, its visual conventions, and the messages conveyed by this "silent language" have all been subject to continuous change.

A world survey. There is an obvious danger of circularity and ethnocentrism in defining the portrait in Western terms and then discovering that it is essentially a Western genre. However, some repre-

clear who is being portrayed (rulers and their households) and where the images were displayed (in tombs). The Chinese portraits of emperors and officials, often life-size, seem to have been intended for public viewing (Figure 1), while the miniatures of Mogul rulers, like those of the shahs of Iran and the Ottoman sultans, were a private form of ART—indeed, a secret one, since the Islamic tradition was hostile to images of living beings. In Japan, monks and poets as well as political leaders were not infrequently portrayed. In all these cultures images of women are rare; among the best known of the exceptions are the Egyptian queen Nefertiti (fourteenth century B.C.E.; Figure 2) and the court beauties and courtesans portrayed in Japanese picture scrolls and prints (if these are recognizable likenesses of individuals—an uncertainty). Despite these examples, it would appear from a comparative point of view that a strong concern with portraiture is one of the many peculiarities of Western culture.

The Western tradition: functions. The Western concern with portraiture cannot be explained without placing it in context and surveying the social functions of the portrait, whether religious, political, or private. The religious (including the magical) function seems to be both the oldest and the most widespread, deriving from the cult of skulls in prehistoric

Figure 1. *(Portraiture)* Unidentified artist, *The Emperor K'ang Hsi* (1662–1722), Chinese, nineteenth century. Colors on silk. The Bettmann Archive, Inc.

sentations of heads or whole figures that seem to modern Western eyes to be individualized have survived from a variety of regions and periods. Well-known examples include the funerary statues of ancient Egyptian pharaohs, the Mochica "portrait jars" (Peru, ca. 500–800 C.E.), the brass heads of Ife (Nigeria, fifteenth century C.E.), and the paintings of Chinese mandarins, Japanese shoguns, and Mogul emperors.

For lack of evidence, little can be said about the Peruvian and West African examples. We do not know what kinds of individuals were portrayed (assuming that these heads were indeed individual likenesses), and the functions of these objects are also uncertain. In the case of ancient Egypt it is at least

Figure 2. *(Portraiture)* Queen Nefertiti, Egyptian, ca. 1360 B.C.E. Painted limestone. Ägyptisches Museum, West Berlin. The Bettmann Archive, Inc.

times. Here the portrait is seen as a means of survival after death. In Egypt, in the first centuries after Christ, portraits of the deceased were painted on their coffins. In ancient Rome portraits modeled in wax or carved in marble (Figure 3) were carried at funerals and were associated with the cult of the ancestors (like photographs among some Chinese today). In the later MIDDLE AGES, death masks were employed in funeral ceremonies (*see* MASK), while the faithful sometimes offered wax images of themselves to saints or had themselves represented in the religious paintings they commissioned (Figure 4). In early modern times there was a vogue for "memorial portraits," painted shortly after the death of the "sitter." Portraits might also be commissioned by the living to remind themselves of the process of aging

Figure 4. *(Portraiture)* Tomb effigy of Edward III, 1386. Gilt bronze. Westminster Abbey, London. By courtesy of the Dean and Chapter of Westminster.

Figure 3. *(Portraiture)* Patrician carrying busts of his ancestors, Roman republican period, ca. 50 B.C.E–15 C.E. Marble. Palazzo Barberini, Rome. Alinari/Art Resource, New York.

and the inevitability of death. *See also* ART, FUNERARY.

The political function of the portrait—PROPAGANDA, the pictorial eulogy of rulers—also goes back a long way. In ancient Greece and Rome, as in the ancient Near East, portraits of rulers—Alexander the Great, Augustus—were displayed in public places. The "state portraits" of the Holy Roman Emperor Charles V, Louis XIV of France, and others served similar functions. The multiplication of portraits of Queen Elizabeth I of England and Maurice of Nassau both revealed and encouraged the popularity of their respective dynasties. In our own day the huge photographs of political leaders displayed in public places carry on the tradition, their colossal scale reminiscent of Assyria or the late ROMAN EMPIRE. Related to the ruler portrait is the official portrait, glorifying the office rather than its holder and sometimes displayed, as in eighteenth-century Venice, as part of the ritual of inauguration. Dutch group portraits of the seventeenth century are among the best-known examples of this type, which still persists in the portraits of company heads or the presidents of universities. These pictorial eulogies are balanced by pictorial criticisms, from the defamatory paintings of the later Middle Ages to the cartoons that have been part of

Western political life since the seventeenth century.

Besides these public functions, portraits have a variety of private uses. The sixteenth-century Italian bishop Paolo Giovio had a gallery in his house at Como filled with the portraits of famous men, and his example was widely imitated. The surviving busts of ancient Greek and Roman poets and philosophers were presumably destined for similar settings. From the Renaissance on, it became customary for artists to paint their own portraits and for collectors to buy portraits by artists they admired even if the sitter was unknown to them. In the early modern period, the houses of the nobility (and, following their lead, the bourgeoisie) were filled with portraits of family members—a private form of propaganda, a secularized version of ancestor worship, a status symbol. Double portraits commemorated weddings, while miniatures were exchanged between lovers and friends. PHOTOGRAPHY has allowed these practices to spread down the social scale, and photograph albums have replaced the albums of portraits owned by Renaissance princes and Mogul emperors. Over the long term, the gradual democratization of the portrait has been accompanied by the diversification of its functions.

The Western tradition: conventions. Despite the apparent timelessness and photographic realism of many Western portraits, the genre needs to be interpreted as a system of signs, a CODE of conventions that has gradually been elaborated and transformed. Images of individuals, for example, were not always expected to be recognizable likenesses. Contracts for late-medieval English tomb SCULPTURE reveal that what was required was "a man in armor" or "a lady"—in other words, a record of social status rather than individual personality. This tradition may explain why so many sixteenth-century portraits now look alike (though it may be the case that we are unable to see significant variations of detail).

Artists have long been expected to proceed with tact as well as—or rather than—accuracy. The Renaissance painter Piero della Francesca represented the Duke of Urbino in profile to hide the fact that the duke was blind in one eye (Figure 5). The ancient Greek painter Apelles was said to have used the same expedient. Although Oliver Cromwell is supposed to

Figure 5. *(Portraiture)* Portrait of Federico di Montefeltro from *The Urbino Diptych*, by Piero della Francesca, 1465. Uffizi, Florence. Alinari/Art Resource, New York.

have told Peter Lely to paint "pimples, warts and everything as you see me," flattery has persisted into the age of the photograph.

In the system of signs known as the portrait there are two main elements: posture and properties. Like the body itself, representations of the body speak a silent language (*see* KINESICS). There is a repertoire of hand gestures (*see* GESTURE) that has been considered appropriate in various periods for different social types, including the imperious gestures of rulers: the hand on the heart, protesting sincerity; the hand on the hip, signifying self-confidence; and the hand supporting the head of a philosophical or mel-

ancholy sitter. The Napoleonic gesture of the hand tucked into the waistcoat, apparently neutral before his time, has since come to symbolize power—an example of the importance of association in the ascription of meaning. Even the position of the sitter's legs may communicate a message. The eighteenth-century English painter Thomas Gainsborough liked to portray men with crossed legs, a pose of aristocratic nonchalance, but when he represented Mrs. Thicknesse in this posture he offended the proprieties of the time (Figure 6). The frozen rigidity of many sixteenth-century portraits should probably be read as an expression of aristocratic hauteur. As for

Figure 6. *(Portraiture)* Thomas Gainsborough, *Portrait of Mrs. Philip Thicknesse,* 1760. Oil on canvas. Cincinnati Art Museum. Bequest of Mary M. Emery.

Figure 7. *(Portraiture)* Édouard Manet, *Portrait of Stéphane Mallarmé*, 1876. Oil. Louvre, Paris. Giraudon/Art Resource, New York.

contemporary male portraits that show the sitter slumped in a chair or standing (more exactly, slouching) with hands in pockets, these should be interpreted as cases of formalized informality, additions to the repertoire of posture rather than a rejection of it (Figures 7 and 8). Today it is not slouching but posing that offends the proprieties.

In a similar manner, messages about sitters, more especially about their social status and roles, have long been conveyed by representations of CLOTHING and a whole arsenal of accessories. Rulers who never took part in battles were careful to have their portraits painted in armor. Eighteenth-century ladies were often represented in costumes with "the general air of the antique," because modern clothes, according to the doyen of British portrait painters, Sir Joshua Reynolds, would "destroy all dignity." The properties surrounding sitters have long been contrived to support what sociologists ROBERT PARK and ERVING GOFFMAN have called social "front." Among the most important of these symbols of power and status and indicators of taste are the classical column (often combined with the velvet curtain); the throne-like chair; the classical bust; and dogs, horses, and servants, which can all be managed so as to give the sitter an air of dominance. Statesmen have their official papers, scholars their books, gentlemen of leisure their hunting gear, and eighteenth-century ladies of fashion their teacups, fans, and oriental screens. For the past century or so, the cigar, pipe, or cigarette has contributed to the visual rhetoric of relaxation and informality (the sitter's customary cigar was omitted from Graham Sutherland's portrait

Figure 8. *(Portraiture)* Alice Neel, *Portrait of Henry Geldzahler*, 1967. Oil on canvas. The Metropolitan Museum of Art, New York. Anonymous Gift, 1981. (1981. 407)

of Winston Churchill precisely because the portrait was an official one).

Clear enough in essential outline, the property system, like the posture system, is blurred by individual variation and by change over time. In a sixteenth-century portrait of a lady, a dog was probably intended to signify fidelity (that of the sitter to her "master," not that of the dog to the sitter); in a nineteenth-century portrait it may imply only that she loves animals. The CLOCK, once an intimation of mortality like the hourglass, was transformed into a status symbol, or even, in the case of Jacques-Louis David's *Napoléon* (1812), into a piece of propaganda ("at night I work for the welfare of my subjects"). Meanings cannot be read mechanically from gestures or accessories; the observer needs to bear in mind the fact that each portrait represents a transaction between two individuals: the sitter and the artist. In the long history of such transactions, the balance of power has gradually shifted in the artist's favor. Photographs now satisfy the demand for both realism and flattery, while painted portraits (apart from those of royalty, still tenaciously traditional) have come to communicate what the artist wants.

Two basic tendencies are discernible in twentieth-century portraiture: the decorative and the expressionist. Both can be found in milder form before the late nineteenth century, but they have since become much stronger. The decorative tendency subordinates the sitter to the general design, as in the case of the

Figure 9. *(Portraiture)* Gustav Klimt, *Portrait of Emilie Flöge,* 1902. Oil on canvas. Historisches Museum der Stadt Wien, Vienna.

Figure 10. *(Portraiture)* Francis Bacon, *Portrait of Isabel Rawsthorne,* 1966. Oil. The Tate Gallery, London. ▷

Austrian art nouveau painter Gustav Klimt (Figure 9) or of the U.S. painter James Whistler, who underlined the point by giving his portraits titles such as *Arrangement in Grey and Black* (1872). There is little room here for the portrayal of character. In the case of the expressionist tendency, the artist is much concerned with character—so much so, in fact, as to produce caricatures, which sacrifice outward appearance to inner truth (see CARICATURE). An outstanding example of this trend is the work of the Austrian painter Oskar Kokoschka, and it has been carried to an extreme by the Irishman Francis Bacon (Figure 10). Sitters are now often shocked by their portraits, as Churchill was by Sutherland's—or at best ambivalent.

Bibliography. James D. Breckenridge, *Likeness,* Evanston, Ill., 1968; Marianna Jenkins, *The State Portrait: Its Origin and Evolution,* New York, 1947; John Pope-Hennessy, *The Portrait in the Renaissance,* New York, 1966; "Portrait," *Encyclopedia of World Art,* Vol. 11, New York, 1966; David R. Smith, *Masks of Wedlock: Seventeenth-Century Dutch Marriage Portraiture,* Ann Arbor, Mich., 1982; Roy Strong, *The English Icon,* London, 1969; Malcolm Warner, *Portrait Painting,* Oxford, 1979.

PETER BURKE

POSTAL SERVICE

In praise of the Persian couriers the Greek historian Herodotus (484?–425? B.C.E.) wrote the famous motto:

Neither snow, nor rain, nor gloom of night stays these couriers from the swift completion of their appointed rounds.

Despite its renown, the Persian postal system was neither the earliest nor the largest in the ancient world. References survive to the exchange of messengers and verbal messages between rulers, or between rulers and their people, even before the age of WRITING (see ORAL CULTURE). The custom of sending oral news by courier continued even after writing was invented, but the advent of writing made it possible for messengers to ride or run their routes carrying CLAY TOKENS, notes, and letters written on bamboo (in China) or papyrus (in Egypt), and prompted the regularization and scheduling of such services. See EAST ASIA, ANCIENT; EGYPTIAN HIEROGLYPHS; HELLENIC WORLD; LETTER.

Early History

Message services operated in China at least by the time of the Chou dynasty (ca. 1027–256 B.C.E.) and probably earlier. Private mail, however, was not admitted to the Chinese system until 1402 C.E. Before that time the messengers carried only official messages. CONFUCIUS paid perhaps unintentional tribute to the efficiency of the system when he wrote, "The influence of the righteous travels faster than a royal edict by post-station service." When MARCO POLO returned to Venice from his trip to China he was able to tell Europeans just how elaborate the Chinese postal system had become by the time of the Yuan dynasty (1260–1368), founded by the Mongol Genghis Khan: five routes with sixteen hundred post stations were staffed by seventy thousand men and forty thousand horses. Postal couriers were reported to cover as much as 250 miles a day over favorable terrain.

The Assyrians in Asia Minor, the Egyptians in North Africa, and the Greeks in Europe all had messenger systems, but none of them was as developed as the Persian. The Persian monarchs, particularly Darius I (r. 521–486 B.C.E.), quickly grasped the principle that control of government and control of communication are inseparable. The system they built ranged from the Persian Gulf to Asia Minor and had strings of stations at fourteen-mile intervals stocked with horses to bear royal messengers from post to post. The Persians even had "secret mail," achieved by shaving the heads of messengers and writing messages on their scalps. When the hair grew enough to conceal the writing, the couriers (who were usually slaves) were sent on their routes. At the destination, their heads were reshaved to reveal the message.

The Bible contains several references to messenger and post systems in ancient times. In the Book of Job the prophet complains, "My days are swifter than a post; they flee away." The Book of Esther makes reference to the variety of animals used to carry messengers through deserts and mountains when it speaks of "posts that rode upon mules and camels."

The Roman postal system. The Roman emperor Augustus (r. 27 B.C.E.–14 C.E.) is credited with establishing the *cursus publicus,* an official postal system like those of China and Persia, used to bind together the growing empire and contribute to solving the political and commercial problems that grew along with it (see ROMAN EMPIRE). This system was not only designed to transmit messages by couriers but was also intended to provide accommodations in the posts for officials on special missions or individuals granted special permit to use it. Five main trunk lines originated in Rome, with end points in Carthage, Asia, Macedonia, Spain, and northern Europe (Germany, Britain, and Gaul). Couriers rode horses or guided chariots pulled by two or four horses over paved roads that helped the system achieve a degree of speed and efficiency not to be matched in Europe until after the MIDDLE AGES.

Figure 1. *(Postal Service)* A post rider bearing the news of the Peace of Münster, 1648, which ended the Thirty Years War. The Bettmann Archive, Inc.

FIG. 58 [Page 259

ENLARGING MICROSCOPICAL DESPATCHES DURING THE SIEGE OF PARIS.

Figure 2. *(Postal Service)* Clerks enlarging and copying microscopic pigeon-post messages during the Siege of Paris, 1870–1877. Gernsheim Collection, Harry Ransom Humanities Research Center, The University of Texas at Austin.

The decline of the Roman Empire meant the dismantling of the *cursus publicus*. The eastern parts of the road system were absorbed by Muslim states, which under the rule of Caliph Muʿāwiyah had created their own postal system. The Arabic system had its center in Baghdad, from where six main roads originated (*see* ISLAM, CLASSICAL AND MEDIEVAL ERAS). In Europe only small parts of the system were kept in operation by smaller kingdoms, and it was only when Charlemagne created the Holy Roman Empire in 800 that a serious attempt was made to re-create the equivalent of the *cursus publicus*—without much success.

Middle Ages. During the Middle Ages monasteries and universities created their own messenger services, for whatever official systems existed either were not open to the public or did not have the range these two institutions required (*see* UNIVERSITY). Monasteries needed to maintain contact with one another throughout Europe and with the headquarters of their religious orders. As universities began to attract students from afar, the need for a means to maintain contact with their families evolved into an elaborate (and eventually quite profitable) system of messengers. The university and monastery systems, along with other commercial systems emerging in medieval Europe, provided the most efficient means of exchanging letters or correspondence of all types to parties other than governments, which began to feel threatened by the possibility of widespread conspiracy if opponents that were "safe" when apart were brought together by the posts. The efforts to bring postal systems under official control thus date from those early days, though the beneficiaries were not very willing to give them up and often received large amounts of money as compensation for their troubles.

In other parts of the world elaborate systems were also in operation. In Peru the Incas had a corps of foot messengers who delivered verbal messages as well as messages encoded in *quipus*, cords of different lengths that purveyed meaning in themselves and also in the knots tied in them. The Mayas, centered in what is now southeastern Mexico and Guatemala, also maintained a large system of roads and messengers (*see* AMERICAS, PRE-COLUMBIAN). The countries of Europe, of course, knew nothing about postal developments in the Americas until European explorers found their way across the Atlantic (*see* EXPLORATION). At the other end of the world Indian rulers had established messenger systems perhaps as early as the first century C.E. By the sixteenth century the Mogul emperor Akbar (r. 1556–1605) had runners said to cover as much as eighty or ninety miles a day.

Europe after the Middle Ages

At the beginning of the fourteenth century extensive private postal services started to appear in Europe. In Switzerland several cantons (provinces) established their own postal systems. In Austria the Paar

Figure 3. *(Postal Service)* A commemorative postcard carried by the first airplane mail, Allahabad, India, 1911, bearing the signature of the pilot, H. Pequet. The Bettmann Archive, Inc.

FIRST "AERIAL POST," ALLAHABAD, FEBRUARY 18, 1911.

family built up a national post service. However, the most widely successful of these private enterprises was established by the Taxis (originally Tassis) family, which came from northern Italy and settled in Germany. Roger de Tour et Tassis (as the name is found before it was germanized into Thurn and Taxis) organized an extensive postal system for Holy Roman Emperor Frederick III (r. 1440–1493), who granted the family special favors. In turn, the Thurn and Taxis family developed a system that was a model of efficiency and speed, operating on regular and reliable schedules. Prompt delivery was a goal. The lead riders wore a small yellow post horn embroidered on the front and back of their jackets, which evolved over time as an accepted symbol of national postal services and the hobby of philately. The Taxis postal system lasted through political and commercial difficulties for more than five hundred years, but the French Revolution and the increasing tendency of governments to seize the lucrative postal systems were mortal blows to it. The family's remaining commercial assets were purchased by Prussia in 1867.

Modern Transportation

The introduction of modern systems of transportation was an important step toward significant improvements in postal systems. From the time animals were first used for postal transport until about 1830, the best that could be expected of a postal system was approximately fifteen hundred miles in seven days. The most efficient stagecoach services in Europe and the United States reached a speed of approximately nine miles an hour. With continentwide and intercontinental demand for faster service, a transportation breakthrough was imperative.

Railroads. The railroads made it possible for the first time to carry mail faster than could be done on horseback or in a stagecoach. Better roads meant that stagecoaches could often deliver mail the next morning in cities as far as 120 miles from London; but railroads could provide the same level of service as far as 400 miles away. This was due not only to the speed of the trains but also to the development of "railway post offices," special coaches in which mail was sorted for distribution along the route. The railway thus became the heart of a complex system of sorting and distribution of mail. Furthermore, the extension of railways across continents immensely speeded up delivery of the mail. In the United States, Omaha was linked to San Francisco in 1869. In Russia, the Trans-Siberian Railway Service was in full operation by 1904. The transcontinental railroads and their related postal services were credited with opening up the American West, while the Trans-Siberian rails reduced by at least one-half the time it took to carry letters between Europe and eastern Siberia and northern China.

Shipping. By water the steam engine also speeded up postal delivery. The steamship made intercontinental mail service much swifter and more dependable. Long shipping routes were considerably shortened with the digging of important canals like the Suez (1869) and the Panama (1914). Mail service between Europe and East Asia no longer had to be routed around the Cape of Good Hope, and steamships going from the Pacific Ocean to Europe no longer had to go around Cape Horn. Shipping also contributed to the efficiency of the post by using the great canal and river systems, which made it possible to deliver to and from points not always served by mail trains.

Other systems. Throughout history several other types of services were tried in efforts to bypass or resolve specific problems. For example, pigeons have been used for message delivery in many places and times. When NEWS AGENCIES began to appear in the nineteenth century, they occasionally used pigeons to transmit news items. During the Napoleonic wars the Montgolfier brothers in France carried mail in their invention, the balloon, which was also used to carry letters out of Paris during the Prussian siege in 1870. Another experiment was rocket mail, but the results were dubious. One of the most promising variations on these pre-airmail experiments was mail service by German zeppelin. By 1932 these dirigibles had made 590 regularly scheduled flights to points around the world (including 172 transatlantic crossings). The system came to a tragic end with the crash of the zeppelin *Hindenburg* at Lakehurst, New Jersey, in May of 1937.

The automobile and the airplane. The first real difference in postal transportation since the railroads came with the automobile and the airplane. As the railways had taken over the responsibility of carrying the mail long distances, so the automobile took over the short ones—between collection points to central post offices, between post offices and mail trains, between nearby towns, rural mail delivery, and so on. But the real change in long-distance delivery came with airmail.

Until the end of World War II airmail was a special event. The first contract flight carried mail between New York and Washington, D.C., in 1918, while the first international service delivered mail between London and Paris in 1919. For a time airmail was limited to short distances and at higher rates than other mail. It was clear, however, that airmail could make its greatest contribution over long routes. The first transcontinental flight in the United States took place in 1920. By 1923 mail planes were flying on a

Figure 4. *(Postal Service)* A view of the general mail facility, Washington, D.C., 1986, showing two of the three optical character readers that sort thirty thousand to forty thousand letters per hour. Courtesy of the United States Postal Service.

twenty-four-hour schedule in most Western countries, and by the late 1920s the vast distances between Europe and Asia were covered by airmail routes. Transoceanic airmail started in the 1930s.

Modern transportation and postal systems were reciprocally influenced. The need to carry mail provided an incentive to extend and speed up transportation, and the income earned by carrying mail furnished a subsidy to each new transportation system during the years when support was most needed. Thus it may be argued that the postal system helped support the courier routes, the stagecoaches, the building of good roads, the use of inland and ocean waterways for transportation, the railroads, and, to a certain extent, the introduction of the automobile and the airplane.

Modern System Organization

A basic postal system includes the collection, sorting, and delivery of mail. Before systems were opened to public use collection was less of a problem, since the governments that owned and operated the system or the private concerns that maintained their own delivery systems also provided the messages to be carried. When mail service was opened to the public many new problems arose.

Post offices were very scarce at first, which made it difficult to send and receive mail. Service within cities was not available until after 1653, when the *petite poste* ("local post") was created in Paris; many other cities soon followed the example. Collection boxes at street corners and home delivery did not come about until the nineteenth century, after several failed attempts (children, for example, would stuff

the first mailboxes in Paris with unsavory contents). These and other developments made apparent certain organizational problems, like the need for reliable timetables for collection and distribution as well as for prompt local delivery. In London a civilian named William Dockwra set up a private "penny post," in which letters could be prepaid, stamped with time of posting, and delivered almost hourly within the city. This scheme was so successful that it was closed down in 1685, after only five years, because it infringed on the government MONOPOLY. But the public missed it, and the system was later reinstituted under government control.

Also in England, but in the nineteenth century, postal reform became the main preoccupation of Rowland Hill, who in 1837 published a pamphlet, *Post Office Reform: Its Importance and Practicability*, that perhaps did more than anything else to reform the postal system. He demonstrated that the cost of transporting the mail was an insignificant part of the total cost. Most of the expense came from the time it took postal clerks to figure out the charges, based on distance, to keep the accounts, and to make reports. Furthermore, it was expensive to collect part of the charge from the recipients of letters, as was then common. Hill suggested establishing a uniform postal fee—based on weight—to be paid only by the sender, who would affix an adhesive stamp that could be bought in advance. Much of the cost and delay involved in handling mail would thus be eliminated. The first STAMPS, depicting Queen Victoria, were sold in England in 1840, and the new methods for handling the post were soon adopted throughout the world.

Improvements in efficiency meant that the postal

system could be used for other services, such as rural delivery of mail (beginning in France in 1829), parcel post (to carry packages at fixed rates for weight and distance), money orders, distributing benefits from government, and collecting some taxes. In many countries post offices also became telegraph offices, with these services linked in one administration.

COLONIZATION during the nineteenth century fostered the introduction of European-style postal systems in many parts of the world. The need for fast and safe mail delivery between nations resulted in an international postal conference meeting in Bern, Switzerland, in 1874. An international treaty for cooperation in handling mail was drafted, approved, and signed by twenty out of twenty-one countries attending (France signed almost one year later). The General (later called Universal) Postal Union set forth rules and procedures for exchanging mail and other postal services between countries, and its membership increased rapidly (see INTERNATIONAL ORGANIZATIONS).

Contemporary Developments

During the twentieth century further advances in transportation and TELECOMMUNICATIONS NETWORKS have resulted in faster and more efficient mail services. The widespread availability of computers (see COMPUTER: IMPACT), coupled with SATELLITE and other telecommunications systems, has made possible electronic message services sent through complex computer-based networks. This virtually instantaneous form of communication is likely to increase in importance over time.

Specialized delivery services represent another area of competition to postal systems. Emulating private courier systems of several hundred years ago, companies have appeared in several countries that, for substantial fees, will deliver letters or packages overnight or in considerably less time than through regular post. Whether the government-owned and -operated postal systems will continue to grow and provide efficient services will depend in large measure on how well they stand up to these and other future challenges.

Bibliography. Alvin F. Harlow, *Old Post Bags: The Story of the Sending of a Letter in Ancient and Modern Times,* New York and London, 1928; Max Piendl, *Thurn und Taxis 1517–1867: Zur Geschichte des fürstlichen Hauses und der Thurn und taxisschen Post,* Frankfurt am Main, 1967; Zaven M. Seron, *From the Winged Heels of Mercury,* Redwood City, Calif., 1984; Lauren Zilliacus, *Mail for the World: From the Courier to the Universal Postal Union,* New York, 1953.

MAX R. KENWORTHY

POSTER

A technological extension of the historical use of walls or other public space to convey messages. As a concise combination of word and image intended for easy and instant comprehension, the poster was the result of the invention of lithography (see GRAPHIC REPRODUCTION), a PRINTING process making possible the distribution of multiple identical copies. It is usually studied more with respect to its functions as PROPAGANDA and ADVERTISING than as a VISUAL IMAGE; yet besides translating the visual ART movements of the twentieth century into a consumer medium, the poster's impact and methods have sometimes influenced the form and direction of art.

The one figure most responsible for the development of the poster was French artist Jules Chéret, who in the 1860s began to produce color lithographic posters from his own press in Paris. Through his use of the traditions of the European MURAL, as in the work of Italian painter Giovanni Battista Tiepolo, Chéret was able to combine the GENRE of the circus advertisement with that of the decorative fresco. His works enlivened the new ARCHITECTURE of Paris and gained recognition for posters as the "gallery of the street." Chéret's style also influenced many artists, most notably Henri de Toulouse-Lautrec.

Table 1. Art Nouveau Schools

Art Nouveau (United States)	Art Nouveau (Great Britain)
Will Bradley	Aubrey Beardsley
Maxfield Parrish	The Beggarstaff Brothers
Edward Penfield	(James Pryde and
	William Nicholson)
Jugendstil (Germany)	Dudley Hardy
	John Hassall
Peter Behrens	*Secession* (Austria)
Julius Engelhard	
Thomas Theodor Heine	Gustav Klimt
Walter Schnackenberg	Julius Klinger
Franz von Stuck	Koloman Moser
Olaf Gulbransson	*Stile liberty* (Italy)
Le style moderne (France)	Marcello Dudovich
	Adolpho Hohenstein
Eugène Grasset	Giovanni Mataloni
Henri Meunier	Leopoldo Metlicovitz
Leonetto Cappiello	*Modernista* (Spain)
Henri Ibels	
Adolphe Willette	Alexandre de Riquer
Alphonse Mucha	Miguel Utrillo
Jean de Paléologue	

Figure 1. *(Poster)* Jules Chéret, *Les Girard*, 1879. Lithograph, 22⅝ by 17 in. Collection, The Museum of Modern Art, New York. Acquired by exchange.

the Bauhaus to the vocabulary of pictorial language. In the Soviet Union constructivism found expression in the work of Gustav Klutsis, El Lissitzky, Aleksandr Rodchenko, and the brothers Vladimir and Georgij Stenberg, among others. In Germany the ideas of the Bauhaus were translated into poster designs by artists such as Oskar Schlemmer and Joost Schmidt. Edward McKnight Kauffer in England and Cassandre (Adolphe-Jean-Marie Mouron) in France took the new elegance of the formal styles into the popular field of poster design in the 1920s and 1930s. Throughout the twentieth century major painters

Figure 2. *(Poster)* Joost Schmidt, *Staatliches Bauhaus Ausstellung*, 1923. Lithograph, 26¼ by 18⅝ in. Collection, The Museum of Modern Art, New York. Gift of Walter Gropius.

Toulouse-Lautrec gave a greater emphasis to the element of CARICATURE and also reduced his designs to flat patterns, often satirical in nature.

Both Chéret and Toulouse-Lautrec can be identified with art nouveau, a movement in art and DESIGN deriving much of its style from Japanese art and depicting in ornamental and decorative terms new social developments, new technology, and new expressions of the spirit. The worldwide influence of art nouveau was such that the poster, as perhaps its principal representative, was within twenty-five years of its introduction established as an international art form (see Table 1).

Posters reflected the addition of twentieth-century developments such as cubism, constructivism, and

Figure 3. *(Poster)* Cassandre [Adolphe-Jean-Marie Mouron], *Étoile du nord*, 1927. Giraudon/Art Resource, New York.

such as Pablo Picasso, Henri Matisse, Oskar Kokoschka, Marc Chagall, and Joan Miró acknowledged the importance of the medium by contributing posters to their own exhibitions or creating original and influential designs.

An important development that paralleled the stylistic influence of art movements was the consolidation of the role of the professional graphic designer. Posters representing the spirit of the corporate product became a significant part of advertising display in the 1950s, spurred by the coordination of design in such firms as Olivetti in Italy, which set the pattern for industrial designers around the world. A classic example of complete design coordination is the London Underground rail system, which in the 1930s was approached as a single design exercise that included the commissioning and display of posters as an intrinsic part of the scheme, thus continuing and indeed extending the notion of the public art gallery.

The rise of professional design consultants, agencies, and groups of studios and companies, along with the establishment of graphic design as a course of study, influenced the form of the poster itself, which was often the work of an industrial designer (or group of designers) involved in overall design policy rather than the creation of an independent artist. In the latter half of the twentieth century the field of commercial advertising through posters was dominated increasingly by large Western advertising agencies such as the Push-Pin Studios in the United States or the Belier Agency in France.

Technical considerations also affected poster form and style. Developments in color PHOTOGRAPHY made possible the production of clear, high-quality images and contributed to the movement toward poster REALISM in the United States in the 1920s and 1930s (a movement also given commercial impetus by the effective photographic display of advertised products in distinct and accurate detail). The use of photography in posters must also take into account John Heartfield's influential photomontages of the 1930s, as well as the sophisticated work of the Atelier Yva in 1920s Berlin or of El Lissitzky in Moscow. Much AVANT-GARDE work in fact linked photography with other design elements such as TYPOGRAPHY to produce new and startling juxtapositions. In later decades similar effects were achieved by the creative photography of artists like Herbert Matter in Switzerland, George Tscherny in the United States, and Gan Hosoya in Japan.

Figure 4. *(Poster)* Poster for *Zemlya*, 1930, directed by Aleksandr Dovzhenko. National Film Archive, London.

In the 1960s psychedelic designs provided an alternative to the established tradition of simple, formal design exemplified in the "new objectivity" movement centered in Switzerland in the 1950s. Just as the new objectivity had its origins in earlier artistic developments such as the Bauhaus, psychedelic design can be traced to the exhibition of German *Jugendstil* posters in Berkeley, California, in 1965. Once again poster design was renewed from its own past, just as the ideas of earlier artists like Josef Witzel were reinterpreted in the work of, among others, Victor Moscoso in the United States and Michael English in Britain.

The poster as a tool of POLITICAL COMMUNICATION has an extensive history in the twentieth century. World War I saw the widespread use of the recruitment poster, and many countries used the form effectively to arouse patriotic fervor and to urge specific citizen actions. In the Soviet Union the poster was a principal means of proclaiming the ideals of the socialist state, at first through the revolutionary posters of Rodchenko and Klutsis and later through the work of artists such as Oleg Savostiuk and Nikolai Babin. Soviet posters are traditionally heroic in subject and in most cases naturalistic in style. The gigantic images in Red Square have their counterparts in the political murals of the People's Republic of China and even, to some extent, in the billboards of the West. Chinese poster art is frequently notable for its mix of traditional imagery and contemporary POLITICAL SYMBOLS and icons (*see* ICONOGRAPHY). Individual artists who have made original contributions to the ideological poster include Jan Lenica in Poland and Raúl Martinez in Cuba. An appropriate example of the poster's immediacy and vitality during politically turbulent times may be found in its own place of birth. In May 1968 the streets of Paris carried the revolutionary posters of the Atelier Populaire, a militant collective of students, artists, and workers. The art produced by this cooperative enterprise was at once crude and powerful, thus renewing the elements that characterize the poster of impact.

Historically, the poster has drawn upon various styles and traditions in art and the mass media. Effective imagery continues to borrow from such diverse areas as film ANIMATION, COMICS, PHOTOJOURNALISM, and cinematic techniques (*see* CINEMATOGRAPHY), including EXPRESSIONISM, surrealism, and AVANT-GARDE FILM, to convey its message most directly and simply.

See also GRAPHICS; REPRESENTATION, PICTORIAL AND PHOTOGRAPHIC.

Bibliography. Dawn Ades, *The 20th Century Poster: Design of the Avant-Garde,* ed. by Mildred Friedman, New York, 1984; John Barnicoat, *A Concise History of Posters: 1870–1970,* New York and London, 1972; Maurice Bau-

Figure 5. *(Poster)* Tadanori Yokoo, *The City and Design Isamu Kurita,* 1966. Silk screen, 41 by 29½ in. Collection, The Museum of Modern Art, New York. Gift of the designer.

wens, ed., *Les affiches étrangères illustrées,* Paris, 1897; Ernest Maindron, *Les affiches illustrées, 1886–1895,* Paris, 1896; Josef Mueller-Brockmann, *Geschichte des Plakates,* Zurich, 1971; Alain Weill, *The Poster: A Worldwide Survey and History,* Boston and Paris, 1984.

JOHN BARNICOAT

PRAGMATICS. *See* MEANING; SEMANTICS.

PRAYER. *See* RELIGION.

PREACHING. *See* HOMILETICS; PUBLIC SPEAKING.

PRESSURE GROUP

Until the 1960s the prevailing model of pressure-group activity in developed democracies focused on relations between organizations representing the diverse interests of a pluralistic society and the agencies of government, in which news media publicity played little part. Direct and regular access to decision processes was the favored goal, and prime avenues of influence included formal and informal contacts with legislators and officials (*see* LOBBYING), membership on advisory committees, establishment of a right to be consulted over policy developments, a role in providing expert information and testimony in policy inquiries, representation in party platforms and machinery, and the occasional offering of financial contributions and other favors. This model featured a strong party system (into which group demands were channeled and within which interest-group coalitions were formed) and a spirit of compromise and moderation to allow for the adoption of broadly acceptable interim solutions to policy problems. The intrusion of media-based communication into such a system could have been disruptive to the process of coalition building. Press publicity was mainly a way for newly formed and less established groups to gain notice.

Since the 1960s, however, because of the combined impact of several political, social, and communication transformations, a more "media-centric" model of pressure-group activity has come to the fore. Without displacing the more traditional patterns, this new model has often supplemented, bypassed, and penetrated them. According to this model, media attention is a vital source of potential influence and power, creating perceptions of public support that policymakers must heed. Groups must therefore give much higher priority to the publicity field, recognizing that it is a competitive arena in which many rivals are also seeking footholds and that it is dominated by the standards of journalism to which their own media materials must conform. This in turn generates pressure to develop self-conscious news-management strategies, influences the kinds of appeals and demands that will be ventilated, can provoke conflict inside groups over what is thought necessary to break into the news as distinct from what would be more true to an organization's purposes, and may redistribute overall power and status differentials among groups in society.

Media strategies. Many pressure-group needs may be served by effective press and publicity organization. One is the need to sustain relations with members, demonstrating the group's effectiveness, perhaps even informing members about activities (especially if the group's own internal communication channels are weak and underused). A second is to stake the group's claims with policymakers as the legitimate representative of its clients and holder of significant support in the citizenry at large or among relevant attentive publics. A third is to mobilize demands for action that policymakers might otherwise ignore. A fourth is to keep the group's priorities and definitions of key issues in the forefront. A fifth is to bring an issue into the open with different criteria from those that would apply if it were insulated from publicity. A sixth is to counter the occasional bouts of bad news that most groups can expect to experience. A seventh is to benefit from the "looking glass" function of media, striving to ensure a closer conformity of media portrayals to the group's own image of its purposes, values, and identity.

Publicity Problems and Techniques

The publicity organization and techniques of pressure groups may be regarded as responses to five basic problems that they face in trying to optimize coverage:

1. A threefold uncertainty over whether their activities and statements will appear in the news, how they will be framed there, and whether they will have the intended influence on PUBLIC OPINION generally, on activists and members, and on policymakers. Planning and professionalization of the publicity function are devices to overcome such uncertainties.
2. Keen competition for attention in major media newsholes. There are many groups and typically only limited space left over after the activities of leading politicians have been covered. Alertness is required to "cash in" on stories already in the news, tying the group's cause to a prominent controversy, current crisis, or publicized scandal.
3. Sustaining a tolerably continuous presence amid the highly episodic flow of political stories. Relations with editors, producers, and specialist correspondents are cultivated to gain recognition as accredited witnesses in the established "news net."
4. Complications of tailoring publicity to the needs of different news outlets, varying by medium (television, radio, newspapers, magazines), scope (national, regional, local), level (quality, tabloid), and editorial leaning. To cope with these and other diversifying factors, specialists with insider knowledge are needed.
5. Journalistic norms of objectivity and neutrality, distancing reporters from groups' causes and priorities. Consequently stories must be imbued with *news* values, not *organizational* values; they must stress events rather than processes, action rather than meaning, and controversy rather than consensus.

At the most general level three broad approaches to the mass media—not mutually exclusive—may be distinguished. Groups may go in for (1) marketing and ADVERTISING, (2) complaints and criticism, and (3) news management. Advertising campaigns bypass journalists' selection mechanisms and give an organization full control of the message, but such campaigns can usually be afforded only by wealthier bodies and may start with several credibility counts against them. Complaints about unfair coverage, stereotyping, and negative portrayals of groups may reach the professional consciences of editors, journalists, and producers, but for full effectiveness they require sanctions in the background. These might include the likelihood of disruption, unwanted controversy, withdrawal of patronage, and boycotts of advertisers, as well as the imposition of more directly political penalties. In the United States numerous advocacy groups used such tactics in the 1960s and 1970s to wrest from the networks rights to be consulted over program ideas and scripts, and secured identifiable changes in prime-time programming as a result. Most groups, however, need strategies for coping with—if not managing—the news, because this reaches virtually all citizens on a daily basis.

News-management techniques tend to draw on several elements. One is the alert opportunism that is quick to recognize hooks in news originating elsewhere onto which material favorable to a group's ideas and policies can be pegged. Another common feature may be labeled "adaptation," including the creation of media events attractive to reporters; the casting of verbal material into language that is terse, crisp, and arresting; releasing statements in the name of an already prominent leader or personality; and issuing controversial challenges that other leaders and officials must answer. In effect, groups may also offer journalists what Oscar Gandy has called "information subsidies," comprising all those devices that groups can adopt to reduce the costs to reporters of obtaining newsworthy material. These include press releases that tell the story as journalists would write it, arranging events and conferences at times optimal for news organizations' deadlines and routines, and providing a digest of new information that cannot be obtained elsewhere without effort. Such measures not only make a reporter's job easier and less costly; they also stand a chance of converting him or her into a vehicle of group PROPAGANDA.

Nevertheless, groups that cater to journalistic needs in such ways may pay a price for the publicity they gain. A "spurious amplification" may set in (e.g., inflammatory rhetoric and extravagant demands to make stories more arresting), distorting what the group stands for. Personalization may convert a group's policy concerns into the drama of a leader's individual fight for justice. The need to fashion media events may upstage a group's more long-term goals, trivialize its objectives, and open it to ridicule. Organizations are often under pressure to suppress or mask their normal processes of internal debate; outbreaks of conflict within the group can be exploited for negative news stories. There is also a "here today, gone tomorrow" quality about publicity successes. Even if symbolic and token concessions have been extracted from legislators and officials, the bulk of effective policy may remain intact after the publicity peak has receded.

Pressure Groups and Democracy

Models of pressure-group activity highlight severe difficulties in attaining democratic accountability through communication in modern conditions. The earlier approach was only thinly democratic and favored established interests through its emphasis on inter-elite accommodation. Although the media-centric model appears to give greater weight to mass preferences, their grounding in informed choice cannot be guaranteed. The outcomes of complex processes of mutual adaptation among pressure groups, politicians, and the institutions of journalism may be faddish (sporadically responsive to short-term opinion shifts) and simplistic (responsive to demands encapsulable in slogans and one-liners). Such dangers are to some extent countered, however, by the employment of specialist correspondents equipped to deal with issues in depth in their spheres, by the centrality of quality newspapers in national press systems, and by the survival among leading journalists of analytical and interpretive notions concerning their role in POLITICAL COMMUNICATION.

More insidious perhaps is a threatened subjection of public communication to Machiavellian perspectives of realpolitik. Not fully articulated yet, such perspectives presume, first, that group actors should not leave opinion formation to chance; second, that they are involved in a competitive struggle not only with their political opponents but also with the press itself, in a battle over what version of political reality will be communicated to the public; and third, that sentimental notions such as a free marketplace of ideas, the social responsibility of the press, and the role of the informed citizen in decision making should be discarded as illusions. Should such perspectives gain further ground, the democratic legitimacy of the public opinion process might seem increasingly hollow.

See also AGENDA-SETTING; POLITICIZATION.

Bibliography. Jay G. Blumler, "Election Communication and the Democratic Political System," in *Political Communication Research: Approaches, Studies, Assessments,* ed. by David L. Paletz, Norwood, N.J., 1987; idem, "Political Communication: Democratic Theory and Broadcast Practice," in *Public Opinion and Social Change,* ed. by Horst Baier, Hans Mathias Kepplinger, and Kurt Reumann, Opladen, FRG, 1981; Roger W. Cobb and Charles D. Elder, "Communication and Public Policy," in *Handbook of Political Communication,* ed. by Dan D. Nimmo and Keith R. Sanders, Beverly Hills, Calif., 1981; Oscar H. Gandy, Jr., *Beyond Agenda Setting: Information Subsidies and Public Policy,* Norwood, N.J., 1982; Todd Gitlin, *The Whole World Is Watching: Mass Media in the Making and Unmaking of the New Left,* Berkeley, Calif., 1980; Martin Harrison, *TV News: Whose Bias?* Hermitage, Berkshire, Eng., 1985; Gladys Engel Lang and Kurt Lang, *The Battle for Public Opinion: The President, the Press, and the Polls during Watergate,* New York, 1983; David L. Paletz and Robert M. Entman, *Media Power Politics,* New York, 1981; Gaye Tuchman, "The Newspaper as a Social Movement's Resource," in *Hearth and Home: Images of Women in the Mass Media,* ed. by Gaye Tuchman, Arlene Kaplan Daniels, and James Benet, New York, 1978.

JAY G. BLUMLER

PRINT-AUDIENCE MEASUREMENT

Until the mid-1930s, magazines and newspapers described the delivery of their editorial and ADVERTISING content by the number of copies sold. At the time, the major competitor to print media in the United States was commercial RADIO. To quantify delivery, radio developed the concept of *audience*, the total number of people tuned in to a given program. Print media—particularly magazines—responded with a similar concept, also labeled audience.

World War II delayed further development of methods and concepts. After the war, research on the conceptual development of print-audience measurement was resumed, particularly in the United States and western Europe. The data from such studies have come to be a major element in selling advertising space and evaluating media schedules.

Definitions

Although advertisers desire measures of exposure of readers to their advertising, most of the work in this field has aimed to develop measures of exposure to the average issue of a publication. The definition of *exposure* has been the number of persons exposed to one or more pages. Operationally, two methods have been dominant: (1) a recognition method in which respondents in a survey are asked if they recognize a particular issue or not, and (2) a recall method in which respondents are asked whether they have seen any issue of a particular publication for the first time in the last publication period (i.e., within the preceding week for weekly publications or within the preceding month for monthly publications). Respondents are commonly selected through standard sampling methodologies. If the surveys are perfectly administered and if respondents have perfect memory, the recognition and recall methods should provide the same or nearly the same results, namely, audience estimates that vary only because of sampling error.

Recognition Methods

These methods are used regularly in North America, seldom elsewhere. In the United States and Canada hundreds of magazines have been studied by these methods. The usual procedure is the "through-the-book" or "editorial interest" technique. In an interview that may also seek the demographic characteristics of the respondent and information about his or her recent purchasing behavior, the respondent is first shown logotypes of MAGAZINE titles and then asked which have been read, looked into, or held in one's hand over a relatively long period such as the preceding year. The purpose of this "screen" or "filter" is to reduce the number of titles about which the respondent is asked more detailed questions. Next, for each title not eliminated in the first phase, the respondent is given a copy of the magazine and asked to page through it. These copies are "aged": for weekly magazines, issues about six weeks old are used; for monthlies, copies that are two or three months old. It is believed that such aging provides a time period in which most of the readership will have accumulated, but not so old that respondents will have forgotten their prior experiences. In most cases the issues are not complete; they have been "stripped" of advertising and of regular features that might be confused from one issue to another.

Respondents are told to indicate which editorial items look interesting. After going through the entire issue, respondents are asked whether this is the first time they have seen the particular issue. Those indicating they have seen it before are labeled readers of that particular issue. Because such interviewing goes on over all or most of the year, the total number of readers is designated the Average Issue Audience.

Usually a second interview is administered, either during the same session as the first one or several weeks later. The format of the interview is much the same, except that different issues are shown to the respondents. As a result, each individual can be said to be a reader of 0 of the 2 issues, 1 of the 2 issues, or 2 of the 2 issues. These data, when aggregated across individuals, are used to extrapolate the behavior of a subpopulation to more than two issues in order to develop measures such as *reach* (the total number of persons exposed to one or more issues out of n) or *average frequency* (the average number of exposures among the persons reached).

Recall Methods

Recall methods are used internationally. They are used in more surveys than recognition methods, and with more variations. As in the recognition methods, they usually begin with a screening phase, which reduces the number of titles about which further questions are asked. Next, if the publication is a weekly, the respondent is usually asked, "Have you read or looked at any issue of this publication within the last seven days?" Alternatively, the respondent may be asked when the last reading occurred. In some cases the question focuses on whether any issue of the publication has been seen for the first time during the seven-day interval.

Another set of data, collected either before or after the readership question, relates to frequency of reading. Respondents are asked to estimate their usual frequency of reading or their most recent frequency of reading, using a scale that is either numerical or verbal, such as "How many of the last twelve issues have you seen?" or "Do you see every issue, most of the issues, or . . . ?" These data are often used to assign readership probabilities to individuals. For all the persons claiming to see six of every twelve issues, one can compute the "readership" from the recall question.

A variant of the recall method is the "read yesterday" technique, a forebear of the more common recall techniques. Here one asks respondents to recall what magazines they have read or looked into the day before. The rationale for this method is that it reduces the time period over which the respondent must recall behavior. When weighted properly (i.e., multiplied by seven for weeklies and thirty for monthly publications), such data can provide estimates of the Average Issue Audience. However, the technique does not provide data for reach and frequency extrapolations without additional questions being added. Also, to conform completely to the conceptual model, a question should be asked about issues read for the first time the day before.

Characteristics of the Methods

In the United States, where both general methods have been used, it has been found that they provide very different results for the titles studied. A controlled experiment by the U.S. Advertising Research Foundation showed that weekly magazines were estimated to have audiences 25 percent larger by the recall method, and monthly magazines almost 100 percent larger. Further, there were insufficient regularities to enable the results of one method to be calibrated to the other.

Several studies have been done with both methods in which respondents were surreptitiously seen reading magazines in public places and were then questioned at an appropriate later time. Generally, the results showed that 50 percent of the observed reading was not recaptured by these techniques. Studies of subscribers showed, in spite of their having received a magazine by mail, a failure to recapture almost 10 percent of the readers. These are considered estimates of *underclaiming*.

Several studies of overclaiming have also been published. In one, copies of a number of women's monthly magazines not yet distributed were used as stimuli for the recognition technique. After discounting for claimed regular readership, it was found that from 2 to 5 percent of nonreaders claimed readership. This could lead to a very large absolute number because it must be applied to the vast majority of persons who are not, in truth, readers of a particular title. Another study used the recall method with nonexistent or foreign titles. In this study also a significant percentage of the respondents claimed readership of these titles, and more than 50 percent

of those included in the Average Issue Audience claimed readership of half or more of the recent issues of these nonexistent titles.

Such findings clearly throw doubt on the validity of widely used measurement techniques. Assessing validity is difficult, requiring an independent, objective measure of readership behavior. In the increasingly competitive media environment, with its sharp struggles for advertising support, the search for reliable measures of reading behavior is certain to continue.

See also CONSUMER RESEARCH; NEWSPAPER: HISTORY; RATING SYSTEMS: RADIO AND TELEVISION.

Bibliography. Harry Henry, ed., *Readership Research, Theory and Practice: Proceedings of the First International Symposium (New Orleans, 1981),* London, 1982; idem, ed., *Readership Research: Proceedings of the Second International Symposium (Montreal, 1983),* Amsterdam, 1984.

ROBERT J. SCHREIBER

PRINTING

This entry consists of the following articles:
1. History of Printing
2. Cultural Impact of Printing

1. HISTORY OF PRINTING

Printing is a blanket word that embraces three different but related concepts. (1) It is usually taken to mean the multiplication of documents consisting of words, pictures, or other signs by means of some controlling surface, image, or set of codes. And the assumption is that all the resulting copies are identical or very similar to one another. (2) It is also taken to mean the transfer of ink or some other substance by impressing one surface against another. Such an action relates to (1) above but does not necessarily lead to multiplication. (3) An essential stage in some but not all printing is the assembly of prefabricated or predetermined characters (letters, numbers, and other signs) that relate to a particular language or set of languages.

Many printed items involve multiplication, impression, and the assembly of prefabricated characters. However, none of the three is essential to printing.

The Invention of Printing

It is confusion over what is meant by the word *printing* that leads us into difficulties when trying to answer the question When was printing invented? If we take printing to mean either the multiplication of more or less identical images or the transfer of ink by impressing one surface against another, the pro-

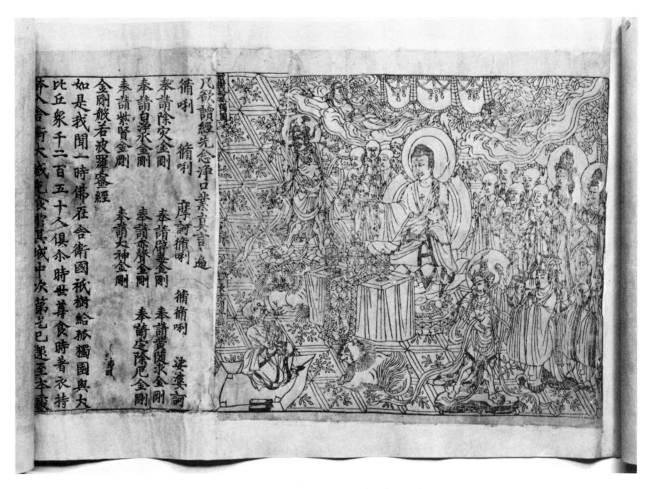

Figure 1. *(Printing—History of Printing)* The "Diamond Sutra" (Chin-kang-ching), 868 C.E. By permission of the British Library.

cess is well over a thousand years old. Textiles were printed in Europe as early as the sixth century C.E., and religious documents in Japan and Korea by the eighth century. These items were printed from wood blocks, which had their nonprinting parts cut away so that they were lower than the parts that printed. Large numbers of documents, mainly Buddhist texts, were printed by such means in East Asia before the close of the ninth century (see Figure 1). The earliest datable printed text is held to be the *Dharani Sutra*, which was printed in Korea between 704 and 751. *See* EAST ASIA, ANCIENT.

In the West the technique of printing wood blocks on paper probably dates from the late fourteenth century, although the first such items it is possible to date come from the early fifteenth century (see Figure 2). In both the East and the West the multiplication of large numbers of documents depended on the availability of a cheap substrate; it was no accident

Figure 2. *(Printing—History of Printing)* Biblia Pauperum, fifteenth century. Colored woodcut. Marburg/Art Resource, New York. ▷

that printing was developed after the invention of paper and, in the case of printing in the West, after paper began to be manufactured in Europe. *See* WRITING MATERIALS.

If we take printing to mean the assembly of prefabricated or predetermined characters rather than the multiplication of copies, we come up with different dates for its invention. Again, printing has to be considered an invention that belongs to East Asia. The Chinese were responsible for the assembly of prefabricated characters made of clay as early as the mid-eleventh century, and of wood from the beginning of the fourteenth century. Metal types, made by sand casting, were produced in Korea in the early thirteenth century and were in wide use there in the first half of the fifteenth century.

How is it, then, that we commonly refer to printing as an invention of the mid-fifteenth century in Europe? The answer lies not just in Western parochialism and not just in the fact that the invention of movable type in the East came up against difficulties posed by languages with thousands of different characters. It lies partly in the methods used for the production of the prefabricated characters.

The person who is now generally credited with the invention of printing with prefabricated characters, usually called printing from movable type, is JOHANNES GUTENBERG, who was active first in Strasbourg and then in Mainz between about 1436 and 1460. Gutenberg was a goldsmith by trade, and his main contribution was to discover a way of casting letters from adjustable molds. Though we do not know precisely what his mold was like, it allowed the dimensions of the types to be controlled so that they could be fitted together physically. It also accommodated letterforms of varying widths and ensured that all letters aligned perfectly with one another visually.

Gutenberg's method of manufacturing type allowed him to imitate with remarkable success the letters and combinations of letters used by scribes (*see* WRITING). It is supposed that he initiated the techniques used by later manufacturers of type, called typefounders. These techniques involved the following stages. A letter was cut in relief and in reverse on the end of a steel shaft, called a punch. The end of the punch was struck into soft copper, thereby producing an indented letter the right way around. This piece of copper was tidied up, in which form it is known as a matrix, and was placed in an adjustable mold. Molten metal, composed mainly of lead, was then poured into the mold with a ladle, and within seconds a single piece of type was produced, with its character standing in relief and in reverse. Such pieces of type were subsequently brought together and prepared so that they aligned and fitted together perfectly. Once they were properly finished, they could be kept in a way that allowed them to be brought together to form lines of words.

We credit Gutenberg with the invention of printing, rather than anonymous artisans in East Asia or their rival European claimants such as Coster of Haarlem (who was for a long while regarded as a serious contender), because Gutenberg devised a convenient and accurate way of replica casting that allowed him to bring together letters to form an infinite number of different messages. His invention proved good enough to compete with the work of the scribe in terms of appearance, and yet allowed for the editing and correction of texts.

Gutenberg's invention ousted writing only because it was competitive economically. The apparatus and materials needed for type manufacture were expensive, and both typecasting and composition were slow. These initial costs could be justified only if numerous copies were printed from the type. The discovery of a way of multiplying documents was therefore central to Gutenberg's invention, and the manufacture of a press must, therefore, be seen as a second and important part of it. Presses were not new: they had been used in the Rhineland for winemaking since Roman times and had been used in more recent years by papermakers too. We know nothing about the first printing presses, but in order to adapt the paper press to taking copies of documents Gutenberg must have made substantial changes to it. He also needed to develop an ink that took to his metal types more easily than the ink used by woodcutters, and it is supposed that he took advantage of the improvements made by painters in the use of oil as a medium for binding pigments.

Gutenberg's invention was a synthesis of many elements, none of which was absolutely new. Though he failed to make the most of it commercially, he set standards that ensured its exploitation by others and established the value of the use of interchangeable characters in the composition of text. The production for which he is best known is the forty-two-line Bible (ca. 1452–1456), known as the Gutenberg Bible, one of the greatest achievements in printing and a landmark in the history of BOOK production (see Figure 3).

The Origination of the Image

The word *origination* is used here to describe the stage at which the marks that appear in a printed item are determined. It is intended to cover, on the one hand, words and pictures and, on the other, physical materials and electronically coded data. In addition, it has to include methods that involve the production of the printing surface, as well as others that do not.

The origination of verbal messages in printing is

Figure 3. *(Printing—History of Printing)* Bible, Latin Vulgate. The Gutenberg Bible, Mainz, 1455(?), f.161v– 162r. Rare Book Division, The New York Public Library. Astor, Lenox and Tilden Foundations.

known as typesetting, composition, or character assembly and involves the use of prefabricated or predetermined characters with standard spacing between them. Both the composition of characters into words and lines and their subsequent organization into larger groupings belong to the origination stage.

All type continued to be set by hand—in much the same way as it must have been set by Gutenberg— until the middle of the nineteenth century. And it was not until the end of the century that typesetting machines were widely adopted (Linotype, 1886; Monotype, 1897). These machines used a keyboard, which was an essential ingredient in streamlining the process of composition. Linotype and Monotype machines have largely been replaced by different kinds of composition systems, the most important of which is photocomposition, which had its roots in the late nineteenth century but was not adopted seriously until after World War II. With the growth of offset lithography, particularly from the 1970s, photocomposition quickly supplanted metal typesetting. The first generation of photocomposition machines made use of photographic negatives of characters, through which light passed to form images on paper or film. Later photocomposition machines stored the shapes of the characters as binary electronic codes. The

characters were given a material form by defining thousands of minute dots with a laser beam. All methods of photocomposition involve the exposure of characters on photosensitized paper or film, which can then be used to produce a printing surface.

The typewriter, which was first successfully marketed by E. Remington & Sons in 1874, can also be considered a means of composition. It appears to have been first used in connection with printing from the mid-1930s in the United States and the 1940s in Great Britain. With the introduction of electric typewriters, and particularly the IBM 72 Selectric composer in the mid-1960s, it was rapidly taken up as an alternative to metal composition and photocomposition.

In the early 1980s laser printing began to challenge photocomposition. As in most advanced photocomposition systems, laser-printed characters are defined digitally by electronic codes, but they are made visible by xerography. The process of laser printing involves the deposit of very fine black powder on paper in response to electrical charges determined by digital codes. The major conceptual difference between photocomposition and laser printing is that the first involves the origination of a controlling image, which is then used to produce a printing

Figure 4. *(Printing—History of Printing)* Albrecht Dürer, *Saint Augustin*, 1514. Engraving. Musée
Condé, Chantilly. Giraudon/Art Resource, New York.

surface from which copies can be multiplied, whereas the second was designed to produce a series of separately generated documents and therefore combined origination, production of the printing surface, and multiplication. However, the images of the most advanced photocomposition machines have resolutions of over two thousand lines to the inch, whereas existing laser printers have resolutions of only three hundred to four hundred lines to the inch.

A disadvantage of all composition systems is that the user is limited to the particular characters available on the system. This ranges from eighty-eight on a standard typewriter to many thousands on the most flexible photocomposition systems. The only composition method that copes with all known characters in all languages is handwriting; for this as well as other reasons, handwriting has been used for the origination of the texts of some printed documents.

The origination of printed pictures was closely linked with the production of printing surfaces until the development of PHOTOGRAPHY. Consequently, printed images have reflected the limitations and possibilities of the various methods of production. One limitation printed pictures had in common for many centuries was that they were usually printed in monochrome—although many were hand-colored afterward. Isolated examples of color printing can be found from many periods, but commercial color printing in Europe can be said to have begun in earnest in the second half of the 1830s. The earliest printed pictures were simple outline images, which were intended to be colored by hand; but by the end of the fifteenth century, and principally through the contributions of Albrecht Dürer, methods of making marks were developed that allowed images to be printed in monochrome that did not require hand coloring. These methods involved cross-hatching and the use of swelling and tapering lines, and they became an essential part of the printmakers' repertoire for representing tone, form, and texture for almost four centuries (see Figure 4).

With the successful application of photography to printing processes in the second half of the nineteenth century, the artist was freed from the restrictions of print production methods. Consequently, any image an artist makes today can be reproduced tolerably well, whatever form it takes. The path to this achievement was opened up by the development of the halftone screen and three- and four-color process printing at the end of the nineteenth century (see Figure 5). Such methods have been supplemented by electronic techniques of scanning and digitally storing images, which allow them to be modified in innumerable ways without manual intervention.

The 1980s witnessed a converging of the techniques used for character assembly and picture origination. Electronic methods reduce all marks, however

Figure 5. *(Printing—History of Printing)* Jakob Husnik, screenprint, 1873. Gernsheim Collection, Harry Ransom Humanities Research Center, The University of Texas at Austin.

they are made, to a series of minute dots. The advantage of this technique was that, almost for the first time since the days of woodcut books, words and pictures could be originated and produced by exactly the same means. The bringing together of words and pictures in common technologies led to the use of the term *marking engine* to describe the means of originating marks, whatever their form.

The Printing Surface

Until the end of the eighteenth century there were two essentially different kinds of printing surfaces, relief and intaglio. In relief printing, ink was deposited on those parts of the printing surface that were higher than others. In intaglio printing, ink was forced into the hollows of a plate by inking its whole surface; the surface was then wiped clean, leaving the ink in the hollows.

Printing from type, woodcut, and wood engraving (a refined version of woodcut developed in the eighteenth century) all belong to the relief category. Copper engraving (often called line engraving), etching, aquatint, and mezzotint all belong to the intaglio category (see Figure 6). Copper engravings were made with a sharp tool, known as a burin, which cut grooves of varying depths into the surface of the

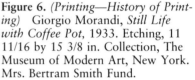

Figure 6. *(Printing—History of Printing)* Giorgio Morandi, *Still Life with Coffee Pot,* 1933. Etching, 11 11/16 by 15 3/8 in. Collection, The Museum of Modern Art, New York. Mrs. Bertram Smith Fund.

copper. Etching involved coating a copper plate with an acid-resistant ground, removing this ground where the image was to appear, and etching the exposed metal with acid. Both methods were developed in the fifteenth century. Mezzotint and aquatint were the tonal versions of copper engraving and etching and were developed in the seventeenth and eighteenth centuries, respectively.

This simple dual division of printing into relief and intaglio was shattered in the closing years of the eighteenth century when Aloys Senefelder, a Bavarian, invented lithography (see Figure 7). Lithography differs from the other processes discussed in that it does not depend on physical differences between printing and nonprinting areas, but on chemical (strictly speaking, electrical) differences. The process rests on the antipathy of grease and water and the attraction of these two substances to their like and to a common porous ground. The porous ground that was initially found most appropriate was limestone, hence the use of the word *lithography.* From the middle of the nineteenth century plates of aluminum and zinc were used increasingly instead of stone. In most branches of lithography the printing area is, to all intents and purposes, on the same level as the nonprinting area. For this reason lithography is regarded as the first example of the third main category of printing processes known as planographic.

The invention of lithography did more than introduce a new printing process. It was so versatile that it could imitate most of the existing processes tolerably well. What is more, it had as one of its major branches the technique of transfer lithography; henceforth pictures and writing done on a specially prepared paper could be transferred to stone, and so too could prints produced by most of the other printing processes. This removed one of the greatest drawbacks of printing, and particularly of the printing of pictures. Hitherto, all printed images had to be made in reverse, so that they appeared the right way around when printed. The transfer process allowed an image to be drawn and written the right way around, since it was reversed when transferred to the stone.

The ways in which printing surfaces could be made increased dramatically in the mid-nineteenth century, and one contemporary writer listed as many as 156 different ways of producing prints. In order to give longer runs in intaglio printing, steel came into use about 1820, and steel facing of copper plates about 1840. Wood engraving was refined and became the bread-and-butter method for producing pictures that needed to be printed with type, although copies usually were made by stereotyping (taking casts in lead) so that the original could be preserved and more than one press used at a time.

The greatest change in the manufacture of printing surfaces came with the application of the photographic process, which in the negative/positive version developed by William Henry Fox Talbot in 1839, can also be regarded as a kind of printing because it allowed for the multiplication of identical copies of an image (see Figure 8). Photography was applied to all the major printing processes before the close of the nineteenth century and began to be

Figure 7. *(Printing—History of Printing)* Henri de Toulouse-Lautrec, *L'estampe originale*, 1893. Color lithograph: folio cover jacket. 17¾ by 23¾ in. The Metropolitan Museum of Art, New York, Rogers Fund, 1922. (22.82.1)

Figure 8. *(Printing—History of Printing)* William Henry Fox Talbot, *The Open Door*, 1843. Salt print from a paper negative. 5 7/16 by 7 3/8 in. Arnold H. Crane Collection, Chicago.

applied to lithography as early as 1850. The most important commercial application of photography to printing came with the manufacture of relief blocks, both line and halftone, by means of a combination of photography and chemical etching. Such blocks could be printed along with type and had effectively replaced wood engraving by the end of the nineteenth century.

In the twentieth century the most significant developments have been the commercial growth of screen printing, a stencil process that had its origins in the nineteenth century, and the extraordinary impact of xerography since World War II. Xerography was invented in the United States by Chester Carlson in 1938. It involves transferring a very fine black powder from an electrically charged surface to paper

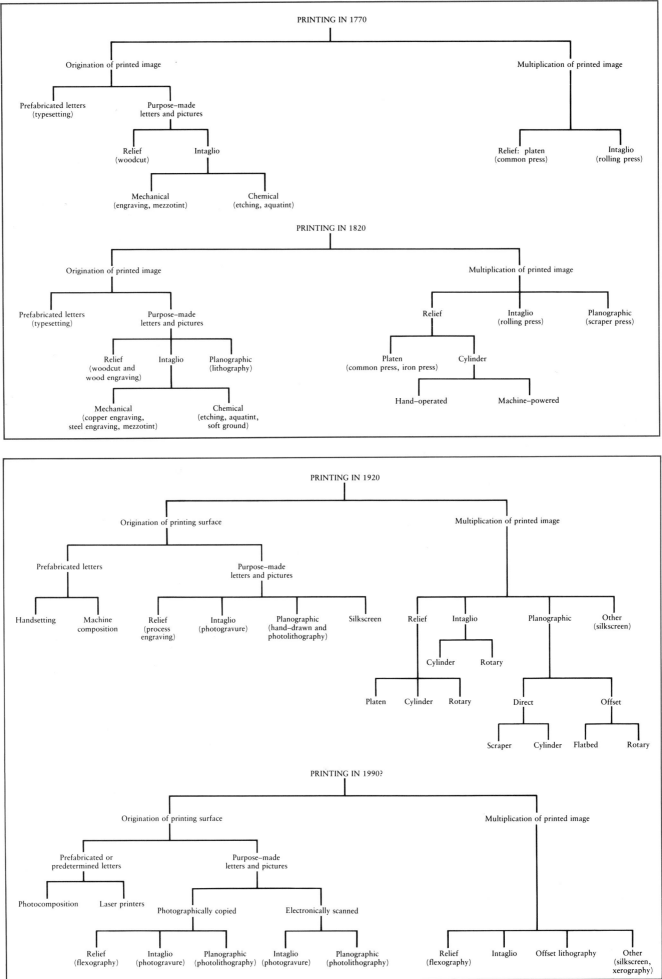

and was used initially for office copying. It has developed rapidly in quality, and some machines enlarge and reduce and can produce images in color. Like photography and screen printing, xerography differs fundamentally from the traditional printing processes discussed above in that it does not depend on the pressure of one surface against another. Other printing methods have been developed, such as ink-jet printing, that likewise do not depend on pressure. They are described by the generic term *nonimpact printing*.

The Multiplication of Copies

Though the multiplication of copies is not an essential feature of what we call printing, the economic, social, and intellectual consequences of printing derive from its ability to produce identical copies of a document in large numbers. The ways in which printing can multiply copies may be considered in three categories: printing without presses, printing with the handpress, and printing with machines.

It seems likely that the earliest woodcuts were printed by pressing the block against the material on which it was to be printed or by placing it with the inked surface face up, laying the material on top, and rubbing the back of it all over. The invention of the printing press in the middle of the fifteenth century effectively did away with these methods, although the second of them continues to be used for proofing purposes in some crafts.

The oldest surviving printing presses probably date from no earlier than the seventeenth century. What we know about the earliest presses derives mainly from woodcut illustrations of the late fifteenth century. Such presses, known as common presses, were made of wood and were used mainly for printing pages from metal type (see Figure 9). The type was placed on the bed of the press and inked up with leather-covered inking balls. The paper to be printed was held in place with a tympan and frisket and was brought down above the type. The bed of the press was then positioned beneath a flat surface (the platen), which applied pressure to the type and paper by means of a worm screw and lever.

Common presses continued to be used into the middle of the nineteenth century, although by this time most had been replaced by iron presses. The first successful iron press was invented by Earl Stanhope and was in use in Great Britain by the first years of the nineteenth century. It was modeled on the common press in most respects, but allowed for larger areas to be printed with less effort with the help of a system of compound levers. It was followed

◁ **Table 1.** Charts Showing the Development of Printing Techniques

Figure 9. (*Printing—History of Printing*) An English printing office, 1619. The motto says, "In serving others, we are worn away." The Bettmann Archive/BBC Hulton.

by many other kinds of iron presses, the most popular being the Columbian (1817) and Albion (ca. 1822).

Such platen presses, which applied pressure across a broad area by forcing one flat surface against another, were appropriate for relief printing but not for intaglio or planographic printing. These other methods required greater pressure, and the simplest way of achieving this was to reduce the area over which pressure was applied. Intaglio printing solved the problem by laying the inked-up copper plate and paper on a plank and forcing them between two cylinders. The pressure was applied successively along a line and had to be great enough to force the ink out of the sunken lines onto the paper. Such presses are known as rolling presses; the first of them were made of wood, but from around 1830 they began to be made of iron.

The first successful lithographic presses also applied pressure successively, but by means of a wooden scraper. This was less rigid than a cylinder and was therefore less likely to break stones. Numerous kinds of scraper presses were manufactured in the first half of the nineteenth century. The ones that achieved greatest success were those that placed the lithographic stone on a bed, which was then pulled under pressure beneath a scraper. Most lithographic presses of this kind incorporated a tympan to protect the paper from the friction of the scraper and therefore owe something to both the platen press and the rolling press.

All the nineteenth-century handpresses discussed above continue to be used for craft purposes. They even continued to be used industrially for proofing purposes into the twentieth century, although long before this they had been replaced by powered machines when large runs were needed.

Steam power was first used in printing in 1810 when the German engineer Friedrich Koenig applied it to a platen press. However, Koenig's claim to fame as the inventor of the powered printing machine rests on his cylinder machine, which was first used to print *The Times* (London) on November 29, 1814. This machine had a moving bed on which the printing surface traveled successively under inking rollers and an impression cylinder, and this principle of working has formed the basis of a wide range of cylinder presses manufactured since. Successful powered machines were not developed for lithographic printing until shortly after the middle of the nineteenth century, and not for intaglio printing until almost the end of the century.

In the complicated history of powered machines two significant developments need to be highlighted: the rotary printing press and offset printing. In rotary presses the printing surface is cylindrical, and so too is the surface that applies the pressure. This means that it is possible to feed a continuous sheet of paper between the two cylinders, thereby doing away with the slow business of feeding individual sheets by hand. The rotary principle was first applied to calico printing in the late eighteenth century. The first successful rotary machine for printing on paper relied on hand feeding and was used for printing parts of *The Times* (London) in 1848. But in the 1860s William Bullock in the United States and John Walter in Great Britain both manufactured reel-fed rotary machines. Presses of this kind printed something in the order of ten thousand copies an hour, compared with about two hundred sheets an hour (printed on one side of the sheet) on the handpresses of the early nineteenth century, and around one thousand sheets an hour on the first powered cylinder machines (see Figure 10).

The second major development, offset printing, was first explored commercially in connection with lithography. In offset printing an image is transferred from the printing surface to an intermediary (usually a rubber cylinder) and from there to the material that has to receive it. It was developed as a solution to the problem of printing on the insensitive surface of metal and was first practiced by the firm of Barclay and Fry in London in 1875. By about 1880 it was being used successfully for the printing of biscuit tins. Tin printers of this period used flat lithographic

Figure 10. *(Printing—History of Printing)*   The Hoe ten-feeder horizontal rotary printing machine. From a catalog of the firm R. Hoe and Co., 1867. Smithsonian Institution, Washington, D.C. Photo No. 73-5136.

stones; however, the real significance of the offset principle of printing was not felt until it was adapted to rotary printing and used for printing on paper. This was first proposed in the United States in 1903 by Ira W. Rubel, who seems to have stumbled on the offset idea quite independently as a result of accidentally offsetting a print from a rubber impression cylinder. Rubel developed his idea commercially, and within a few years offset presses were being manufactured in the United States and Great Britain. Though a latecomer in the history of printing, offset lithography accounts for the majority of the world's printing.

Apart from xerography, the twentieth century did not witness fundamental changes in the ways in which documents were multiplied. Improvements were made in such areas as the printing of two, four, or more colors at one pass through the press, in methods of drying, and in the computer control of inking, drying, and pressure.

Electronic Publishing

All advanced printing of the last quarter of the twentieth century involved computing at the composition stage, and most computers need a printer or other marking engine to produce marks on paper (*see* COMPUTER: IMPACT). But printing and computing began to converge in a more coherent way in an area called ELECTRONIC PUBLISHING. The term, which is not used very precisely, describes the electronic capture, storage, handling, and dissemination of information from credited sources, such as publishers, and also the much less formal electronic communication between individuals and groups of people. It is used when a large part of the communication is electronic, whether the material is presented on-screen, on paper, or in both forms. Only such communication on paper would normally be called printing, but it is becoming increasingly difficult to consider printing separately from other means of presenting information to users. In its fully developed form, electronic publishing may include the electronic capture, storage, handling, transmission, production, and dissemination of information, and even the involvement of the user in selecting what information is presented. But the activity would still be called electronic publishing even if some of these stages were omitted—for example, when the production is done by printing (photocomposition and offset lithography).

The origination of verbal messages, called data capture by computer scientists, is being done increasingly on microcomputers equipped with word-processing software or on dedicated word processors. Such devices have simple keyboards and are widely available and easy to use; this means that authors can do their own typing. However, this approach to text origination means that codes have to be inserted, either on the microcomputer or at a later stage, if the material is ever to look like traditional printing. These codes are necessary to tell the typesetting system how to format the material and where to use such typographic variants as italic and boldface types. An alternative approach, if the material has already been cleanly typed or printed, involves the use of an optical character recognition (OCR) machine. Such "reading" machines began to be developed shortly after World War II, but they have not been taken up for text composition as quickly as was predicted. Speech input devices of a fairly rudimentary kind have also been developed, and it is possible that improved versions will provide yet another means of capturing straightforward data. Pictorial images used in electronic publishing are scanned and coded electronically so that they can be stored and, if necessary, manipulated in many ways. Since both pictorial and verbal images are reduced to binary codes, they can be brought together and handled in precisely the same way. This facility allows for the visual arrangement of pictures and words on computer-controlled page-makeup terminals.

The real advantages of electronic publishing lie not so much at the data-capture stage, but in what can be done with the data afterward. The storage and handling of data really belong to computer science; they are referred to here because, like Gutenberg's method of manufacturing type in relation to printing, they lie at the heart of electronic publishing. They will probably determine the degree of its economic success, and it seems likely that electronic publishing will succeed only if the data, once captured, can be used for a variety of purposes. For example, different selections of data might be made available for different readerships, or users may themselves choose the selection they want through an interactive terminal. Additionally, however, electronic publishing offers the advantage of storing vast quantities of data in a compact and relatively cheap form, such as the compact disc.

Developments in SATELLITE communications make it possible for information to be transmitted around the globe in coded form in a matter of seconds. Such data can be reconstructed as readable information where it is required. Techniques of this kind are regularly used for newspaper production, and similar "facsimile" methods of transmitting graphic messages are also available for office communication through public telephone networks. A transmission stage, which is foreign to traditional printing, is central to much electronic publishing; and some publishers provide users with a choice between reading information on-line to the computer and on a screen, or in a paper version. An equally important development is on-demand printing and publishing—that is, the production of a document when you want it and, possibly, in the form that suits you best.

Developments in electronic publishing in the last quarter of the twentieth century have led to changes in communication far greater than those that came about with Gutenberg's invention of movable type in the mid-fifteenth century. They have brought pictures and words together and have opened the way for the combination of audio and visual messages. We are too close to the beginnings of electronic publishing to see how it is likely to develop, but it is already clear that it has complicated the relatively simple interpretations of printing outlined above. The use of predetermined characters is as central to most electronic publishing as it was to Gutenberg's invention, but printing has become part of a larger communication system and just one of a number of means of making available messages stored as binary codes.

See also PUBLISHING; TYPOGRAPHY.

Bibliography. W. Turner Berry and H. Edmund Poole, *Annals of Printing: A Chronological Encyclopaedia from the Earliest Times to 1950*, London, 1966; Harry Carter, *A View of Early Typography up to about 1600*, Oxford, 1969; Geoffrey Ashall Glaister, *Glaister's Glossary of the Book*, 2d ed., Berkeley, Calif., and London, 1979; William M. Ivins, *Prints and Visual Communication*, London, 1953, reprint Cambridge, Mass., 1969; Lucien Alphonse Legros and John Cameron Grant, *Typographical Printing-Surfaces: The Technology and Mechanism of Their Production*, London and New York, 1916; Joseph Moxon, *Mechanick Exercises on the Whole Art of Printing, 1683–4*, ed. by Herbert Davis and Harry Carter, 2d ed., London, 1962, reprint New York, 1978; Victor Scholderer, *Johann Gutenberg: The Inventor of Printing*, London, 1963; John W. Seybold, *The World of Digital Typesetting*, Media, Pa., 1984; Hans W. Singer and William Strang, *Etching, Engraving, and Other Methods of Printing Pictures*, London, 1897; Michael Twyman, *Printing 1770–1970: An Illustrated History of Its Development and Uses in England*, London, 1970.

MICHAEL TWYMAN

2. CULTURAL IMPACT OF PRINTING

Printing made its strongest initial cultural impact on the literate elites who had always been dependent on scribes (see section 1, above). The spread of LITERACY and the development of mass markets for the printed word followed much later. It is, therefore, the shift from one kind of literate culture to another that constitutes the greatest cultural significance of the typographical revolution—certainly in its early years. Some of the most important components of this shift include (1) the increased dissemination of ideas and information, (2) increased opportunities for standardization, (3) the reorganization of contents and layout, (4) the potential for improved editions, and (5) preservation.

Increased dissemination. Patterns of BOOK consumption were significantly affected by increased production. While more copies of any given text were spread, different texts were also being brought together for the single reader to peruse. In some regions printers produced more scholarly texts than they could sell and flooded local markets. In all regions a given purchaser could buy more books at lower cost and bring them into the study or LIBRARY. In this way the printer, who duplicated a seemingly antiquated backlist, was still providing the scholar with a richer, more varied literary diet than had been provided by the scribe.

More abundantly stocked bookshelves obviously increased opportunities to consult and compare different texts. Some medieval coastal maps had long been more accurate than many ancient ones, but few eyes had seen either. Much as maps from different regions and epochs were brought into contact in the course of preparing editions of atlases, so too were technical texts brought together in certain physicians' and astronomers' libraries. Contradictions became more visible, divergent traditions more difficult to reconcile. Even while confidence in old theories was weakened, the enriched READING matter also encouraged the development of new intellectual combinations and permutations.

Cross-cultural interchange stimulated mental activities in contradictory ways. The first century of printing was marked above all by intellectual ferment and by a somewhat wide-angled, unfocused scholarship. Certain confusing cross-currents may be explained by noting that new links between disciplines were being forged before old ones had been severed. In the age of scribes, magical acts were not clearly distinguished from mechanical crafts; mathematical formulas were easily confused with cabalistic charms. When technology went to press, so too did a vast backlog of occult lore, and few readers could discriminate between the two. Hieroglyphs were set in type more than three centuries before their decipherment, and these sacred carved letters were imbued with significant MEANING by readers who could not read them. They were also used simply as ornamental motifs by architects and engravers. Given baroque decoration on the one hand and complicated interpretations by scholars, Rosicrucians, or Freemasons on the other, the duplication of Egyptian picture WRITING throughout the Age of Reason presents modern scholars with puzzles that can never be solved. By the end of the Enlightenment the still undeciphered hieroglyphs had come to stand for everything that was secret and everything that was known (*see*

EGYPTIAN HIEROGLYPHS). Thus one should not think only about new forms of enlightenment when considering the effects of printing on scholarship. New forms of mystification were encouraged as well.

In this light it seems necessary to qualify the assumption, expressed by the historian Myron Gilmore, that the first half-century of printing gave "a great impetus to wide dissemination of accurate knowledge of the Western sources of thought, both classical and Christian." The duplication of the Hermetic writings, the Sybilline prophecies, the hieroglyphs of "Horapollo," and many other seemingly authoritative, actually fraudulent esoteric writings, worked in the opposite direction, spreading inaccurate knowledge.

Primers, ABC books, catechisms, calendars, and devotional works were widely disseminated by early printers. Increased output of such materials, however, was not necessarily conducive either to the advancement of scholarship or to cross-cultural exchange. Catechisms, religious tracts, and Bibles filled some bookshelves to the exclusion of all other reading matter. The new wide-angled, unfocused scholarship went together with a new single-minded, narrowly focused piety. At the same time practical manuals also became more abundant, making it easier to lay plans for getting ahead in this world— possibly diverting attention from uncertain futures in the next one. It would be a mistake to press this last point too far, however. During the first centuries of printing the output of conflicting astronomical theories and tables offered very uncertain guidance. Devotional manuals and spiritual guidebooks provided clear-cut advice. Readers who were helped by access to road maps, phrase books, conversion tables, and other aids were also likely to place confidence in guides to the soul's journey after death. The fixing of precise dates for the Creation or for the Second Coming occupied the very same talents that developed new astronomical tables and MAP PROJECTION techniques.

As these comments suggest, during the first century of printing many dissimilar effects came relatively simultaneously. Both religiosity and secularism intensified. In addition to disseminating new works and ideas, printing increased the circulation of traditional materials—a fact often overlooked by modern scholars attempting to identify new trends in the era of early printing. Many medieval world-pictures were duplicated and distributed more rapidly during the first century of printing than they had been during the so-called MIDDLE AGES; they became more visible to poets and playwrights of the sixteenth century than they had been to minstrels and mummers of the thirteenth century. Furthermore, given the use of woodcuts and engravings to depict medieval cosmologies, these older world-pictures were not merely being preserved but were being rendered in new visual forms. In view of such considerations, how printing changed patterns of cultural DIFFUSION deserves much more study than it has yet received. Some scholars have emphasized the standardizing effects of printing. But individual access to diverse texts is a different matter from bringing many minds to bear on a single text; the former issue is apt to be neglected by too exclusive an emphasis on standardization.

Opportunities for standardization. Although it has to be considered in conjunction with many other issues, standardization certainly does deserve closer study. While the books produced by the early printing presses did not achieve the degree of standardization that became possible later, copies were sufficiently uniform for scholars in different regions to correspond with one another about the same citation and for the same emendations and errors to be spotted by many eyes.

The implications of standardization go beyond textual emendations and errors. They are also relevant to calendars, dictionaries, and other reference guides and especially to maps, charts, diagrams, and other visual aids. The capacity to produce uniform spatiotemporal images is often credited to the invention of writing without considering how difficult it is to produce many identical copies of such images by hand. The same point applies to systems of notation, whether musical or mathematical. Indeed, the standardization of mathematical tables, diagrams, and maps helps to explain why the exact sciences (such as astronomy) advanced so rapidly during the age of the handpress.

Standardization also entered into every operation associated with TYPOGRAPHY, from the replica casting of precisely measured pieces of type to the subliminal impact upon scattered readers of encounters with identical type styles, printers' devices, and title page ornamentation. Calligraphy itself was affected. Sixteenth-century specimen books stripped diverse scribal hands of personal idiosyncrasies. They did for handwriting what pattern books did for dressmaking, furniture, and architectural motifs or ground plans and what style books did for typography itself.

Reorganization of contents and layout. Concern with surface appearance necessarily governed the handwork of the scribe, who was fully preoccupied trying to shape and space uniform letters in a pleasing, symmetrical design. An altogether different procedure was required to give directions to compositors; every scribal text that came into the printer's hands had to be reviewed in a new way. Within a generation the results of this review were being aimed in a new direction—away from fidelity to scribal conventions and toward serving the convenience of the readers. The resulting innovations began to appear in the era of the incunabula; they made texts more lucid and intelligible. Competition between printers encouraged the relatively rapid adoption of any innovation that won favor with the purchasers. In short, providing built-in aids to the reader became for the first time both feasible and desirable.

The tasks faced by early printers led to the invention of new tools, production methods, and symbols. Scholars concerned with modernization or rationalization might profitably think more about the new kind of brainwork fostered by the silent scanning of maps, tables, charts, diagrams, dictionaries, and grammars. They also need to look more closely at the routines pursued by those who compiled and produced such reference guides. These routines were conducive to a new *esprit de système*. In the preface to his pioneering atlas, Abraham Ortelius likened his *Theatrum* to a "well furnished shoppe" that was so arranged that readers could easily find whatever instruments they might want to obtain.

The use of arabic numbers for pagination suggests how the most inconspicuous innovation could have weighty consequences—in this case, more accurate indexing, annotation, and cross-referencing. Most studies of printing have quite rightly singled out the increasing frequency of title pages as the most important of all the changes in format. How the title page contributed to the cataloging of books and the bibliographer's craft scarcely needs to be spelled out. More attention needs to be addressed to the contribution of this innovation to new conventions of placing and dating in general.

Improved editions. When turning out successive editions of a given reference work or set of maps, printers did not only compete with rivals and improve on their predecessors; they were also able to improve on their own performance. The sequence of editions turned out by a Bible printer (such as Robert Étienne) or an atlas maker (such as Ortelius) shows how the drift of scribal culture had been not merely arrested but actually reversed.

In making this point one is likely to run up against objections posed by scholars who have learned to be skeptical about the claims made on behalf of early printers. Prefaces that repeatedly boast of improvements are belied by actual evidence of uncritical copying. Some comparisons of scribal with printed versions show how an age-old process of corruption could be aggravated and accelerated after print. But in the very course of accelerating a process of corruption, which had gone on in a much slower and more irregular fashion under the aegis of scribes, the new medium made this process more visible to scholars and for the first time offered a way of overcoming it. In the hands of ignorant printers trying to make quick profits, texts tended to get garbled at an ever more rapid pace. But under the guidance of techni-

cally proficient masters, the new technology also provided a way of transcending the limits that scribal procedures had imposed upon earlier masters. Under proper supervision, fresh observations could at long last be duplicated without being blurred or blotted out over the course of time.

Some sixteenth-century editors and publishers simply duplicated old compendiums. But others created vast networks of correspondents and solicited criticism of each edition, sometimes publicly promising to mention the names of readers who sent in new information or who spotted errors. The requests of publishers often encouraged readers to launch their own research projects and field trips, which resulted in additional publications. Further interchanges set off new investigations, the accumulation of more data making necessary more refined CLASSIFICATION, and so on. The sequence of improved editions and ever-expanding reference works was a sequence without limits—unlike the great library collections of the age of scribes.

Insofar as the change from a sequence of corrupted copies to a sequence of improved editions encompassed all scholarly and scientific fields, it probably affected the intellectual community as a whole. It seems likely that the invention of printing contributed to an increasing acceptance of the idea of progress and a fading away of the earlier "decay-of-nature" theme. A series of new and augmented editions made the future seem to hold more promise of enlightenment than the past.

The new process of data collection initiated by printing helps to explain why systems of charting the planets, mapping the earth, synchronizing chronologies, codifying laws, and compiling bibliographies were all revolutionized before the end of the sixteenth century. In each instance Hellenistic achievements were first reduplicated and then, in a remarkably short time, surpassed. In each instance the new schemes, once published, remained available for correction, development, and refinement. Successive generations could build on the work left by sixteenth-century polymaths instead of trying to retrieve scattered fragments of it. The intellectual revolutions of early modern times owed much to the features that have already been outlined. But the great tomes, charts, and maps that are now seen as milestones might have proved insubstantial had not the preservative powers of print also been called into play.

Preservation. Of all the new features introduced by the powers of print, preservation is possibly the most important. To appreciate its importance, we need to recall the conditions that prevailed before texts could be set in type. No manuscript, however useful as a reference guide, could be preserved for long without undergoing corruption by copyists, and even this sort of preservation rested precariously on the shifting demands of local elites and a fluctuating incidence of trained scribal labor. Insofar as records were seen and used, they were vulnerable to wear and tear. Stored documents were vulnerable to moisture, vermin, theft, and fire. However they might be collected or guarded, their ultimate dispersal and loss was inevitable. Information that was transmitted by writing from one generation to the next had to be conveyed by drifting texts and vanishing manuscripts.

The incapacity of scribal culture to sustain a simultaneous advance on many fronts in different regions may be relevant to the problem of the RENAISSANCE. Italian humanist book hunters, patrons, and dealers tried to replenish a diminished supply of ancient texts that were being neglected by scribes serving medieval UNIVERSITY faculties. Their efforts have been heralded as bringing about a permanent recovery of ancient learning and letters. However, if one accepts the criteria of totality and permanence to distinguish prior revivals from the Renaissance, then probably the advent of the scholar-printer should be heralded instead. Once Greek type founts had been cut, not even the disruption of civil order in Italy, the conquest of Greek lands by Islam, or the translation into Latin of all major Greek texts were enough to cause the knowledge of Greek to wither again in the West. A cumulative process of textual purification and continuous recovery had been launched.

Typographical fixity also encouraged more explicit recognition of individual innovations and the staking of personal claims to specific discoveries and creations. Once the rights of an inventor could be legally fixed, profits from innovations could be achieved by open publicity, and individual initiative could be released from guild protection. It is no accident that printing was itself the first invention to become entangled in priority disputes. Rival national claims on behalf of the German JOHANNES GUTENBERG versus the Dutchman Laurens Coster and the Frenchman Nicolas Jenson set the pattern for many later arguments.

By 1500 laws were already being devised to accommodate the patenting of inventions and the assignment of literary properties. Competition over the right to publish a given text raised controversial issues involving MONOPOLY and piracy, and possessive individualism began to characterize the attitude of writers to their work (see COPYRIGHT). In the words of Michael B. Kline, the "terms of plagiarism and copyright did not exist for the minstrel. It was only after printing that they began to hold significance for the author."

The accumulation of fixed records also made it feasible for each new generation to begin where the prior one had left off. In the age of scribes distinction between the recovery of a lost art and the discovery of a new one had been blurred. When unprecedented innovations had occurred, there was no sure way of recognizing them as such, for no one could ascertain precisely what had been known—either to prior generations within a given region or to contemporary inhabitants of other lands. "Steady advance," as George Sarton says, "implies exact determination of every previous step." In his view, printing made this determination "incomparably easier." He may have understated the case. Progressive refinement of certain arts and skills could and did occur in the age of scribes, but no sophisticated technique could be securely established, permanently recorded, and stored for subsequent referrals.

During the early years of printing map publishers began to produce new and improved editions of atlases and star maps, which showed that modern navigators and stargazers knew more things about the heavens and earth than did ancient sages. New editions of ancient texts began to accumulate, uncovering more schools of ancient philosophy than had been dreamed of before. Scattered attacks against one authority, by those who favored another, provided ammunition for a wholesale assault on all received opinion. Incompatible portions of inherited traditions could be sloughed off, partly because the task of preservation had become less urgent. Copying, memorizing, and transmitting absorbed fewer energies since reference books were no longer blotted out or blurred with the passage of time.

The preservative powers of print thus help to explain the victory of the moderns over the ancients as well as the increasing popularity of ideas of progress during the age of the handpress. On the other hand, five hundred years of printing and the concomitant accumulation of fixed records have brought about problems of overload that were unimaginable in the age of scribes. Each new generation of artists and writers has had to meet the unprecedented challenges posed by an ever-growing record of the past.

See also ARCHIVES; AUTHORSHIP; CARTOGRAPHY; PAMPHLET; PUBLISHING; WRITING MATERIALS.

Bibliography. Richard Altick, *The English Common Reader: A Social History of the Mass Reading Public*, Chicago, 1957; Curt Buhler, *The Fifteenth Century Book: The Scribes, the Printers, the Decorators*, Philadelphia, 1960; Elizabeth L. Eisenstein, *The Printing Press as an Agent of Change: Communications and Cultural Transformations in Early Modern Europe*, 2 vols., Cambridge and New York, 1979; Lucien Febvre and Henri-Jean Martin, *The Coming of the Book* (L'apparition du livre), trans. by D. Gerard, London, 1976; Myron Gilmore, *The World of Humanism 1453–1517*, New York, 1952; Harvey J. Graff, ed., *Literacy and Social Development in the West: A Reader* (Cambridge Studies in Oral and Literate Culture, No. 3), Cambridge,

Mass., 1982; William M. Ivins, *Prints and Visual Communication*, London, 1953, reprint Cambridge, Mass., 1969; Michael B. Kline, *Rabelais and the Age of Printing* (Études Rabelaisiennes IV, Travaux d'humanisme et renaissance LX), Geneva, 1963; Martin Lowry, *The World of Aldus Manutius*, Ithaca, N.Y., 1979; Walter J. Ong, *Orality and Literacy: The Technologizing of the Word,* London and New York, 1982.

ELIZABETH L. EISENSTEIN

PRIVACY

Privacy as a social value and a legal right encompasses a variety of related claims to personal autonomy generally understood as "a right to be let alone." In the context of changing modes of communication between and about individuals, privacy also means the right to exercise control over information about oneself. These principles have a long history and have continued to evolve as new technologies pose increased threats to individual privacy.

Until the end of the nineteenth century the right of privacy was considered almost coextensive with private property and protection against trespass. The struggle in England over "general warrants" and the American colonists' battle against "writs of assistance" (used by the crown to enforce tax and tariff measures) led to a fundamental expression of this concept of privacy in the Fourth Amendment to the U.S. Constitution, which guarantees "the right of the people to be secure in their persons, houses, papers, and effects against unreasonable searches and seizures."

However, the communications revolution, with its increased threats to privacy, led to an expansion of the legal concept of privacy. The development of such mass media as newspapers, magazines, and television led to the development of a privacy right against intrusion into personal affairs and against unwanted publicity. New forms of communication such as the TELEPHONE led to laws protecting personal communications from unwarranted interception by government or individuals. And the advent of the computer and the computerized DATA BASE made it necessary to give individuals control over the collection, use, and dissemination of personal and public information held by government and business. New communications technologies continue to pose privacy issues that are yet to be resolved. *See* COMPUTER: HISTORY; MAGAZINE; NEWSPAPER: HISTORY; TELEVISION HISTORY.

The law of unwarranted intrusion. In the late nineteenth century, which witnessed the rapid rise of mass-circulation newspapers and magazines, two U.S. lawyers, Samuel D. Warren and Louis Brandeis (who later became a noted Supreme Court justice), pub-

lished an article in the *Harvard Law Review* in which they advocated that privacy law should protect the individual not only from unwarranted trespass as embodied in the Fourth Amendment but also from emotional distress caused by unwarranted intrusion into private affairs. Written in an era of yellow journalism, which relied on sensationalism and gossip to sell papers, the article suggested a new legal right that would later form the basis for even broader concepts of informational privacy.

As a result, laws in all Western countries recognize the right of private individuals to sue a newspaper or a television station for unwarranted invasion of privacy. Such rights generally extend to unauthorized use of one's name or likeness in ADVERTISING. They may also extend to fiction that is recognizably based on someone's private experience or to sensationalized journalistic "revelations" about individuals. In the United States such rights are severely limited by the First Amendment to the Constitution, which guarantees freedom of speech and of the press. The rights are especially limited in the case of "public persons," such as officeholders or others who have sought the limelight themselves. If information is at all newsworthy, broad latitude is granted to the press to publish it. In a number of countries some protection against unwarranted invasion of privacy is guaranteed by statutes that limit the information that public agencies or private entities such as banks and credit companies may make public. Other laws permit individuals to sue any person who invades their personal privacy.

Privacy in communications. The development of the telephone paved the way for another major expansion of the right of privacy. In *Olmstead* v. *United States* (1927) the U.S. Supreme Court had to decide whether government interception of a phone conversation by a wiretap was a search and seizure under the Fourth Amendment. The majority held that the interception was not a violation because nothing tangible was seized. Justice Brandeis, in a dissenting opinion, argued that the Fourth Amendment must be interpreted to protect "the right to be let alone—the most comprehensive of rights and the right most valued by civilized man," and that a wiretap was as intrusive if not more so than other searches and seizures. Four decades later, in 1967, the Court adopted the Brandeis view; it decided that citizens had a "reasonable expectation of privacy" in private telephone conversations and that the government must obtain a judicial warrant based on probable cause in order to intercept wire communications.

The standards regarding when and how the government could legally intercept private telephone conversations were established for the United States by the Safe Streets Act of 1968. The act prohibited the interception of aural communication—communication that can be overheard by the ear—unless the government first obtained a warrant and met standards aimed at minimizing intrusion. The legislators could not know at the time that the law would put electronic mail—which was still in the planning stage—in an uncertain position, for it is not aural communication. It travels over telephone lines and may substitute for a phone call, but it is technologically different, raising a new set of issues.

Computers and privacy. From the mid-1970s, the issue of protection of personal information revolved around the explosive growth of the computer and its ability to collect, search, compare, and merge private information about individuals. The "rise of the computer state," as one author has described it, came about during the period when individuals were increasingly required to supply personal information to banks, credit bureaus, hospitals, and businesses in order to participate in a modern transactional society. As a result, people's privacy can no longer be protected merely by laws or policies embodying "the right to be let alone." Instead citizens in modern societies need laws that give them control over what information may be collected, maintained, and disseminated by third-party record holders.

In a number of Western countries codes of "fair information practices" have been developed to set forth principles for protecting information in third-party records. These codes are based on the principles that only relevant and necessary data should be collected, that the subject should know what data are being collected, that information collected for one purpose should not be used for another purpose, and that people should have a right to see and challenge collected data about themselves.

Canada, the Federal Republic of Germany, and some other Western countries formed national privacy protection agencies or commissions to ensure that fair information practices were respected by their governments and private enterprises. In the United States, after the Watergate scandal in the early 1970s had revealed abuses of government records by government officials, who used personal information in them to conduct surveillance and political harassment, public pressure resulted in the adoption of the Privacy Act of 1974, which embodied a code of fair information practices but did not establish any privacy or data protection agency. Passed at a time when public support for privacy protection was high, the act was later weakened by the government in its concern to detect fraud and abuse in government benefit programs. The concern led to moves to link the computers of different government agencies, field agents, and central data bases. For example, federal employee payrolls were compared with student loan records to detect loan defaulters, immigration records were compared with welfare rolls to detect illegal aliens receiving benefits, and private bank records were compared with welfare rolls to detect concealed assets. Although many were sympathetic with the government's desire to improve efficiency and reduce fraud, there was concern that widespread computer linkage would create a national data base with detailed information collected on each citizen and that privacy would be even harder to protect when all the information was linked. Other fears were raised about the integrity of such computer networks—whether the information would be safe from computer hackers and other intruders or from employees who ignored privacy protection procedures in performing their jobs.

There were a variety of views about what should be done. Some felt that third-party records should be protected by statutes that would clearly restrict the use and accessibility of the records. One such statute was the Cable Telecommunications Act of 1984 (*see* CABLE TELEVISION). With the development of interactive cable television systems permitting subscribers to order products, vote in polls, conduct banking from home, and select among different subjects to watch, it became clear that operators of such systems had access to information that could reveal a great deal about each subscriber's habits, life-style, and even political beliefs. To protect this sensitive information, the act required cable companies to report to their subscribers what personal information about them is collected, used, and disseminated, and prohibited companies from releasing "personally identifiable information" without notice and consent. The government could not obtain such information without a court order, and subscribers could fight such government requests in court. Similar statutes in the United States protected bank and credit records. Other suggestions for improving the protection for third-party records included the creation of the National Data Protection Agency to oversee privacy protection in the United States.

In the 1980s such issues intensified as the amount of data flowing across international borders grew. A number of countries became concerned that inadequate protection for privacy in other countries would injure their citizens, and possible prohibitions on transnational computer links and information exchanges were debated. In response to these problems several European countries developed an international code of fair information practices. *See* INTERACTIVE MEDIA.

See also GOVERNMENT REGULATION; LIBEL; POLITICAL COMMUNICATION—IMPACT OF NEW MEDIA; SECRECY; TELECOMMUNICATIONS POLICY.

Bibliography. David Burnham, *The Rise of the Computer State*, New York, 1983; David Flaherty, ed., *Privacy and Data Protection: An International Bibliography*, White

Plains, N.Y., 1984; John Shattuck, *Rights of Privacy*, Skokie, Ill., 1977; Robert Ellis Smith, *Privacy: How to Protect What's Left of It*, Garden City, N.Y., 1979; United States Privacy Protection Study Commission, *Personal Privacy in an Information Society*, Washington, D.C., 1977; Alan Westin and Michael A. Baker, eds., *Databanks in a Free Society: Computers, Record-keeping, and Privacy*, New York, 1972.

JERRY J. BERMAN

PROFESSION

Professions are a special category of occupations. The attributes that make them special are not clearly defined, but in most societies medicine, dentistry, the law, the high clergy, ARCHITECTURE, and some specialties of engineering and accounting are considered professions. There is substantial agreement about the general dimensions of professional status. The cognitive dimension is always privileged. It centers on the body of knowledge and techniques that members of a recognized profession presumably apply in their work and on the training needed to acquire such knowledge and skills. Formal professional training is generally located at the postsecondary level of modern educational systems. Credentials conferred by them are not an indispensable or sufficient component of professional status, but they serve as a means to guarantee professional exclusiveness.

A second dimension stems from the professions' alleged service orientation and nonvenal or anticommercial ethics, which justify the privilege of self-regulation professions claim—a privilege that is usually granted to the established ones. There is no empirical evidence to confirm that the behavior of individual professionals is more ethical, on the whole, than that of people in less honored occupations; however, this is undeniably an important part of the IDEOLOGY of organized professions and an aspect of their PUBLIC RELATIONS stance. It seems to be supported by the available evidence that in advanced societies professionals of both sexes are more likely than other workers to report commitment to their work and to find intrinsic satisfaction in it. This leads into a third dimension of profession, the evaluative one. It underscores professional autonomy and prestige, endorsing the widespread notion that professionals not only command more social respect and cultural authority than other specialized workers but are also entitled to higher material rewards. Established professions rank high on scales of occupational prestige, and professional status is coveted. However, this status, like income, is highly variable—both within and across the same profession's boundaries—and it is never irreversibly achieved.

In advanced industrial societies more people than ever before in history have contacts with at least some professionals, mainly in the fields of health and EDUCATION. The modern idea of profession thus becomes part of the common lore, influenced and modulated by the mass media. Television SOAP OPERA and other forms of broadcast DRAMA, which are globally marketed commodities (*see* TELEVISION HISTORY), include among their dramatis personae a proportion of professional characters far in excess of their proportion in the world at large; they also reinforce vague notions of "professional-managerial" status or of "educated labor." But the boundaries of profession remain vague. They represent a phenomenon of social practice, without clear definition or internal homogeneity. Difficulties of definition are compounded if more than one profession, more than one historical period, more than one society are considered. To note that even the Anglo-American term *profession* has no exact counterpart in the French *profession libérale* or the German *freie Berufe* is tacitly to underscore that definitions cannot impose a sequence of compulsory steps toward professional status, inevitably modeled on the road followed by established professions. For instance, if a definitional or taxonomic approach to the new and burgeoning specialties is applied in a field such as broadcasting, there is as much risk of illustrating mere contingencies—which occupations were better able than others to organize their members into an association or which activities were easier to integrate into the existing university curricula—as there is of measuring the advance toward mature professionalism.

Nonetheless, if professionalization continues to play a role in the changing social division of labor, some parameters will have to be used to demarcate what can be considered, at least temporarily, professional. Features such as full-time involvement in a specialized area of the social division of labor, representative professional associations, formal training, examinations and credentials, state licenses, demands for market control, and the claim to speak with quasi-ultimate authority in a field that society deems important become yardsticks in the comparative study of different occupations that claim (or could claim) professional status. The recent revival of social science interest in the professions is distinguished by a deliberate emphasis on the theories of professionalization that always underlie the use of such yardsticks.

This revival is largely historically based, sensitive to the idiosyncratic and transient characteristics of the professional phenomenon in each society. It is quite compatible theoretically with the sociological approach of Everett C. Hughes, which considers even the most powerful profession as any other occupation, whose practices and striving for social power must be examined empirically without prejudging the outcomes. In both the historical and the inter-actionist perspective the attainment of professional status and privileges is conceived as a continuous and reversible negotiation: at the individual level, between the expert practitioner and his or her client or employer; at the collective level, between the spokespersons for professional groups, who often present their claims as a movement for reform, and the relevant audiences to which such claims are presented. Ultimately the most significant audience is the state, from which professional leaders hope to obtain collectively a preferential treatment in support of individual entitlements.

Professionals and the state. The two major models of professionalization are essentially distinguished by the role assumed by the relevant state authorities in each. In one model the state takes the initiative in providing institutional mechanisms and supports, as is done in most eastern European countries for THE-ATER and MOTION PICTURES. The class of experts thus defined becomes "the best" or the only legitimate one. Whereas the state-driven model draws attention to the particular dependence of all modern states on the service of experts and to policies that implicitly connect backwardness to educational deficiencies of the labor force, its historical origins can be traced to the building of centralized administrations and systems of schooling by the absolutist European monarchies and their successors.

The starkest illustration is perhaps France, where, even in the seventeenth century, there existed royal *écoles* and *académies* and, after the Revolution, an educational hierarchy, capped by the École Polytechnique, the related schools of applied engineering, and, for the production of a professoriat, the École Normale Supérieure. State-driven professionalization does not necessarily create as clear-cut a professional elite as the French *polytechniciens,* who drew as much prestige from their service to the state as from their topflight scientific education. However, when the state sustains a hierarchy of prestige, profound effects on the social ranking of all practitioners are felt; it has a decisive influence on professional authority and success. Thus throughout the nineteenth century French architects struggled to obtain for the École des Beaux-Arts as close an association with the state as that enjoyed by the engineers of the École des Ponts et Chaussées. Obviously the advantages they sought were not only the prestige of the relationship but also the instant MONOPOLY of lucrative state commissions and state employment.

A further and more important consequence is attached to state-driven professionalization. The officials involved in professionalization policies intend to sponsor the emergence of adequate competence, superior to what the civil society had been able to spawn without help. Having defined the require-ments and often financed the institutional supports of professional expertise, the state (or at least one sector or faction within the state) logically considers the discourse and practices of "its own" experts as truer, more significant, and more authoritative than those of competitors, heretofore defined as nonprofessional. When the state establishes a hierarchy of prestige it also contributes to creating hierarchies of people, facts, and ideas.

For French philosopher MICHEL FOUCAULT discourse, which perforce must be that of *some* experts, provides the reasons, the "regime of rationality," for specific systems of codified practices and prescriptions. Such are the programs that govern the organization of the prison, the clinic, the school, the factory. Discourse creates its own conditions, the codes of conduct that it justifies, and the domain wherein it becomes possible to produce intelligible truths and falsehoods. Discourse is a fundamental part of the "equipment of power," the power not merely to repress but to discipline, by determining both the needs and their satisfaction. If it is practically impossible in Foucault's work to distinguish the discourse of experts from the power of the state, indeed it must be because the basis of his reflection is the centralized French state, active in the production of those cadres who are going to be the authorized speakers for a superior rationality. Conceding a monopoly of reason, the state still reserves the power to reorganize the professional corps it has helped to create when this becomes politically necessary or, as in the example of French medicine, when institutionally entrenched clinical interests resisted for too long the scientific dominance of bacteriology. Too close an embrace obviously endangers the autonomy inherent in the monopolization of rational discourse. Beyond the limit we find German physicists under Adolf Hitler propounding "Aryan physics" or Trofim Lysenko reinventing genetics under Stalinist rule.

Professionals and the market. Even in the alternative market-driven model the modern state is still the ultimate guarantor of rationality. State-subsidized hierarchical systems of schooling serve to legitimate and standardize, by the very image of ordered ascension they project, the rationality of the discourses produced at the top. Free and compulsory education justifies not only the linkage between education and occupational rewards that is professionalization's goal but also the undisputable superiority of certain forms of knowledge, tacitly presented as accessible to all those with enough intelligence and motivation. What changes in the market-driven model is the initial locus of the drive toward professionalization. Particularly in the Anglo-American world, the professionalization movements of the late eighteenth and nineteenth centuries can be seen as the response of professional leaders to both the expansion of market opportunities and the decline of traditional warrants of professional probity. To induce and guarantee an investment in training, markets of professional services can be neither so narrow that they exclude the competent nor so broad that they admit all competitors. And it is on the basis of a protected market, wherein organized professions attempt to control the supply of producers, that social status can be attached to learned and specialized work.

In England the movements of professional reform merged politically with the ascension of the industrial bourgeoisie and the middle classes, challenging the narrow aristocratic monopolies that existed by royal charter and the social exclusiveness of aristocratic education. But the reconstruction of professional monopoly was delayed, in part because of the permanence of aristocratic models of status, open largely to the bourgeoisie by Victorian educational reforms. In larger part the delay was caused by a neglect of technical and scientific education, which Great Britain could afford for a time because of its protected position as the world's pioneering industrial power. The professional associations, central agents of the reform movement, retain to this day unparalleled control over training, qualification, and policy.

In the United States professional monopolies based on social rank and education were formally eliminated in the Jacksonian era, retaining their informal functions in the exclusive urban circles in which upper-class clienteles tended to choose professionals from among "their own." Here the enormous diversity of the population, the possibilities of geographic mobility over an immense territory governed by multiple and overlapping political units, directly linked the fate of professionalization to the establishment of a disparate, heterogeneous, uneven, but nonetheless nationally recognized educational system. The diversity and openness of the latter to this day account for the accessibility of professional status to new occupations.

The inevitable restrictions of access that surround esoteric knowledge are socially and morally justified by the modern, state-sanctioned systems of education because their hierarchy has confirmed the merit of the knowers. They do more than that: epistemologically, the superiority of all forms of expert knowledge depends on their connection to systems of schooling in which science is taught. In this institutional matrix the epistemological superiority of science, publicly (and falsely) demonstrated by its technical applications, extends ideologically to all bodies of knowledge credentialed by official schools. Through the system of schools the modern state actively affirms the superiority of science over all other forms of knowledge. For professions that have no other immediate form of showing technical mastery, the state provides not only legal privilege, not only power, but also an indirect connection with the only methodology of truth that is publicly recognized as legitimate in our society.

Bibliography. Alan D. Beyerchen, *Scientists under Hitler*, New Haven, Conn., 1977; Burton J. Bledstein, *The Culture of Professionalism*, New York, 1976; Michel Foucault, *Discipline and Punish: The Birth of the Prison* (Surveiller et punir), trans. by Alan Sheridan, New York, 1977; Eliot Freidson, *Professional Powers: A Study of the Institutionalization of Formal Knowledge*, Chicago, 1986; idem, *Profession of Medicine*, New York, 1970; Gerald L. Geison, ed., *Professions and the French State, 1700–1900*, Philadelphia, 1984; Thomas L. Haskell, ed., *The Authority of Experts*, Bloomington, Ind., 1984; Everett C. Hughes, *The Sociological Eye*, 2 vols., Chicago, 1971; Terence J. Johnson, *Professions and Power*, London, 1972; Magali Sarfatti Larson, *The Rise of Professionalism: A Sociological Analysis*, Berkeley, Calif., 1977.

MAGALI SARFATTI LARSON

PROPAGANDA

Communication, verbal or nonverbal, that attempts to influence the motives, beliefs, ATTITUDES, or actions of one or more persons. From the Latin "to propagate" or "to sow," the word appears in many languages with only minor variations in spelling and pronunciation.

History. Use of the term, and the concept behind it, became common after the Vatican established in 1633 the Congregatio de Propaganda Fide (Congregation for Propagating the Faith), devoted to missionary work. In more recent times the word has acquired pejorative connotations in most countries, with notable exceptions: Nazi Germany, with its Ministry of Enlightenment and Propaganda; and the Soviet Union and the People's Republic of China, with their official agitation and propaganda ("agitprop") services. Elsewhere at the present time, to call someone a propagandist is to discredit him or her as a source of communication.

Yet efforts to influence other persons include countless activities not regarded in this light, among them what is ordinarily called EDUCATION. The grade-school teacher, for example, is expected to influence pupils to become good citizens. To distinguish propaganda from such other, more accepted activities, popular definitions of propaganda generally make use of three subjective and seldom clear-cut criteria. First, the attempt to influence is described as *biased*. But this attribute raises difficulties. What is bias? Teachers consider the version of history they teach to be true and that taught in another country or by someone in a different tradition to be subject to distortion. Those who reject the propaganda desig-

RED CROSS OR IRON CROSS?

WOUNDED AND A PRISONER OUR SOLDIER CRIES FOR WATER.

THE GERMAN "SISTER" POURS IT ON THE GROUND BEFORE HIS EYES.

THERE IS NO WOMAN IN BRITAIN WHO WOULD DO IT.

THERE IS NO WOMAN IN BRITAIN WHO WILL FORGET IT.

Figure 1. *(Propaganda)* British poster from World War I: David Wilson, *Red Cross or Iron Cross?* Trustees of the Imperial War Museum, London.

nation adhere to a doctrine of truth acceptable to themselves or to others in a given society during a specific historical period.

Second, the attempt to influence is considered to be motivated by *personal gain.* This allows propaganda to include such prominent contemporary activities as ADVERTISING, PUBLIC RELATIONS, political campaigns, LOBBYING, even courtship. Any communicator, however, is likely to gain by the act of communicating, whether it be the salary paid, the boost to the ego, the admiration of peers, or the support rendered the IDEOLOGY or regime one admires. Thus the attribute of personal gain, like that of bias, has only limited usefulness.

Third, the attempt to influence is portrayed as *intentional.* The propagandist presumably desires a specific outcome: to boost sales, to improve the client's reputation, to win the ELECTION, to push the bill through a legislative body, to discredit and demoralize the enemy, possibly to marry the person courted. It is clear, however, that the motivations of many judgments and actions are not fully conscious and the consequences not fully intended. The innocent person who praises a toothpaste, a candidate, or a philosophical doctrine is unaware of the bias but for that reason may be more influential than the deliberate professional. The attribute of intention, like the other two, contributes little by way of clarification.

Use of the attributes of bias, personal gain, and intention to refine the definition of propaganda raises issues that go beyond definition problems. It raises questions concerning the epistemological, ethical, sociological, and psychological foundations of behavior in society. Since these issues cannot be universally delineated for all times and for all cultures, a clearcut definition of propaganda is neither possible nor desirable. And the word is so carelessly used—as a brand rather than a designation—that sociologists, social psychologists, political scientists, and others have grown to eschew the very word in their studies, calling instead on such respectable and more neutral labels as social change, PERSUASION, attitude change, or communication itself. Practitioners have likewise avoided the term; instead of propagandists they are public relations counsel, information specialists, or official spokespersons, who issue policy statements, news releases, reports, and white papers. But under whatever terminology, the growth of propaganda and propaganda organizations in the twentieth century has been exponential.

Twentieth century. Statistical evidence reflects, in all parts of the Western world, a vast increase in advertising, public relations, and lobbying activities, and also, everywhere on the planet, an increase in radio stations (and to a lesser degree in television stations) owned, sponsored, or clearly controlled by governments. In the 1980s, for example, there were more than four thousand shortwave radio stations seeking to reach foreign nationals; the Voice of America spoke in forty-two languages; the Soviet Union spoke in twenty-one languages to Europe, eleven to Africa, six to the Middle East, twenty to Southeast Asia, four to East Asia, three to Latin America, and one to North America (see RADIO, INTERNATIONAL). Attached to most embassies are so-called cultural attachés who transmit, via the mass media and through lectures and other forms of persuasion, their government's viewpoint to the people of the country where they are stationed and who facilitate contacts and exchanges toward the same end.

The phenomenal growth of propaganda organizations may be partly attributable to an increase in LITERACY almost everywhere, but it stems more particularly from the conflicts between and within almost all modern societies. Both hot and cold wars have been accompanied by attempts to fortify one's own countrymen and to weaken the enemy. Developing countries in Africa, Asia, and Latin America have been invaded or permeated by outside powers who have quarreled with one another and who have sought to impose their own values or way of life on the indigenous populations. Regimes with new or authoritarian philosophies seek to resocialize their older citizens and to socialize their younger ones (*see* POLITICAL SOCIALIZATION). As commercial companies in Western countries have become more numerous, more diverse, and larger, competition for the support of consumers and clients has grown keener. Multinational corporations, when they have failed to become monopolies, compete with one another in order to increase profits and the capital available for research and development.

These conflicts have produced, and in turn have been facilitated by, noteworthy advances in technology, engineering, and the social sciences. During World War I direct communication with enemy forces was essayed by agents and through leaflets (including safe-conduct passes to soldiers tempted to surrender) dropped erratically from kites, balloons, and planes or shot across battle lines by special cannon. In World War II radio played a significant role, and leaflets were more accurately and diffusely targeted from planes. Since the late 1940s television has disseminated nationalist propaganda, and fading short-wave programs have been supplemented by clearly audible radio communications available from satellites in space (*see* SATELLITE; TELECOMMUNICATIONS NETWORKS). Television viewers and radio listeners are offered almost instantaneous, simplified versions of events so that they feel informed without the opportunity to review or reflect upon what they have seen or heard (*see* TELEVISION NEWS). Transistor radios have enabled even seminomads to be reached. Plays in professional and amateur theaters and MOTION PICTURES have propaganda objectives as well as artistic merit.

Social science has contributed the PUBLIC OPINION survey to contemporary propaganda. Within determinable margins of error it is possible through interviews with or questionnaires directed to carefully selected samples to ascertain the predispositions, intentions, and actions of a population in almost every conceivable respect. With a high yet imperfect degree of accuracy one can know in advance who will win an election or for what reasons consumers accept or reject a product. Public officials or those aspiring to be elected thus obtain insight into opinion patterns and tailor their propaganda accordingly. The mass media, especially U.S. radio and television, are dependent on survey data to avoid being too far ahead or behind their target audiences. Systematic polls and CONSUMER RESEARCH consequently tend to replace virtually everywhere the less reliable methods of intuition, projection, or chatting with the boys and girls down the street (*see* OPINION MEASUREMENT; POLL).

Channels and techniques. Propaganda employs the same devices as any other form of communication to reach and affect an audience. Consequently, the researcher addresses the challenges within the oft-cited and appropriate question posed by political scientist HAROLD D. LASSWELL: "Who/ says what/ in what channel/ to whom/ with what effect?" A verbal communication, or a nonverbal one such as an action or a physical object, is planned on the basis of experience, prejudice, shrewd or reckless guessing, or formal or informal research. It may (or may not) be pretested on a (not necessarily) representative sample of the intended audience. Eventually, either once or continually, it is transmitted by a medium of communication; for propaganda a mass medium is preferred. Then the transmitted message, action, or object is or is not perceived by an audience. The perception, when or if it occurs, may or may not accurately reflect the communicator's standpoint, and it may or may not affect the intended perceivers. The effect, whatever it is, may or may not eventually influence or determine their actions. Whatever changes in motives, beliefs, attitudes, or actions occur in turn may or may not determine the predispositions and behavior of the audience in the future.

Experiments with captive audiences in schools, universities, and laboratories, as well as empirical observations of real-life and historical situations, aim to determine the effectiveness of various propaganda or communication techniques. Each investigation usually has some value in its own right but is limited by the choice of persons serving as subjects and by the social-psychological or situational variable or variables being examined. No magic formula for success has emerged; the consequences of propaganda campaigns, therefore, are often surprising.

As a result of their role within and outside their own societies, propagandists tend to place greater emphasis on some techniques than on others. Unlike many educators, they intentionally bias their communications in a manner that supports their viewpoint largely unequivocally. They may realize, nevertheless, that their audience is suspicious, and so they attempt to bolster their own credibility whenever their identity cannot be concealed or disguised. In World War II, for example, the British Broadcasting Corporation (BBC) struggled to appear impartial even among Germans and other enemies by reporting, consonant with military security, not only favorable but also unfavorable news concerning Britain and its allies. The Voice of America sought to adhere to the same self-proclaimed "strategy of truth" by broadcasting "bad" news "for the record" on unimportant programs or by downplaying it.

Sometimes propagandists are able to conceal their bias and intention by not completely revealing their own identity. The communicator appears to be a

Figure 2. *(Propaganda)* First anniversary of the founding of the People's Republic of China, October 1, 1950. Workers carry hundreds of portraits of Mao Zedong in the National Day Parade. The Bettmann Archive, Inc.

disinterested peer when in reality he or she is an intentional or paid rumormonger whose efforts would be discounted if his or her objective in spreading innocent-sounding tales were known; or unintentionally he or she may be performing the same function after being told the tale by someone else and believing it (*see* RUMOR). Propaganda deeds, moreover, may achieve successes not intended fully or at all by the original communicators. The pyramids of ancient Egypt may have been erected primarily for funereal purposes and to honor the illustrious dead; they then may have strengthened citizens' respect for the ruling elite. Throughout the centuries they have served as reminders of their origin and are major tourist attractions. During a war a bombing raid may be planned to disrupt an enemy's logistical line; a secondary consequence may be a lowering of civilian morale or, under some circumstances, a stiffening of morale.

Propagandists, pursuing their own goals, are likely to realize that they generally must overcome resistance if their messages are to be perceived and learned. The resistance results from the audience's indifference or hostility to them or their aims. They try, therefore, most deliberately to bring those messages to people's attention. They bribe or persuade the controllers of the media to transmit them. Advertisements or announcements become almost unavoidable when they are on billboards or posters, when they appear next to inviting reading matter in printed media, or when they are inserted at strategic points in television and radio programs. Endorsements are obtained from public or respected figures. The issues or problems at stake are simplified so that they can

be easily grasped via slogans, clichés, epithets, and fashionable terminology. Then the action required of propagandees is either obvious ("Buy the product") or is suggested unsubtly ("Vote for me") or subtly ("Surrender, resistance is futile"). *See* COMMERCIALS.

Over time, since persons may become bored or may change, the content of propaganda is suitably varied, so that the audience is made to seek new or modified goals. An audience is created or retained when its members are attracted by the compelling quality of an advertisement, when they turn on their television sets to be entertained or informed by a particular program, when they attend a meeting ostensibly out of curiosity or for social or conventional reasons, when they view a monument or visit a museum—and thus they learn what the propagandist would have them learn. They may have insight into the fact that they are being seduced, yet they tolerate or enjoy the seduction without being fully aware of its consequences.

When propaganda is successful, most of the audience or its critical members subscribe to the propagandist's viewpoint, dismiss alternatives as false or misleading, or behave as the communicator would have them behave. They tend to believe that there is no better product or person, no other political viewpoint that can possibly be as satisfactory, no country worth supporting other than one's own, or no other theology that can bring everlasting salvation.

Countering propaganda. A sure-fire method to combat propaganda has not been discovered other than a complete immersion in the propaganda of one's own side or society, with a resulting immunity to the hostile viewpoint of actual or potential opponents or enemies. Various devices, however, offer audiences partial protection. Newspapers in the United States sometimes add the label *advertisement* or its equivalent to paid printed matter that might not be immediately perceived as commercial propaganda. Similarly, television and radio stations may state that what will be or has been disseminated is a "paid political announcement." Candidates in a political campaign deliberately expose or refute their opponents and proclaim themselves to be oracles of truth. LIBEL and other laws as well as custom inhibit or prohibit the expression of some communications, including what is considered obscene, antisocial, in violation of national security, or leading too directly to "dangerous" consequences. Propagandists in democratic societies nevertheless enjoy considerable freedom of speech and assembly.

Shortly before World War II a U.S. Institute for Propaganda Analysis prepared and distributed materials for secondary schools and reports for the general public that sought to teach an analytic skill by explaining and applying to current propaganda seven catchy devices dubbed name calling, glittering generality, transfer, testimonial, plain folks, card stacking, and bandwagon. Speeches and publications by public officials and organizations could be dissected and labeled with these rhetorical modes. The same kind of skepticism is probably encouraged by a competent, scholarly CONTENT ANALYSIS of any communication or by a documented account of historical events; the techniques and trends of the past presumably presage the present and the future. Education, however defined, advocated, or practiced, can be supposed to include the objective of making students less vulnerable to "pernicious" or "immoral" propaganda. *See* BANDWAGON EFFECTS; RHETORIC.

Frontal attacks on what is arbitrarily or conventionally called propaganda are at best only a prelude to improving communication or liberating audiences from alleged machinations. The reactions of children, adolescents, and adults depend on the contents of what they perceive and on their own predispositions (*see* CHILDREN—MEDIA EFFECTS). It is insufficient merely to label a communication propaganda because it employs detectable rhetorical devices or because it is thought to originate from a biased source deliberately seeking personal gain. Knowledge of the devices and the use of propaganda as an epithet, however, alert audiences and analysts alike to the issues of truth and falsity or of goodness and badness that otherwise might be evaded.

See also POLITICAL COMMUNICATION—HISTORY; POLITICAL SYMBOLS.

Bibliography. Michael Balfour, *Propaganda in War, 1939–1945*, London and Boston, 1979; Leonard W. Doob, *Public Opinion and Propaganda*, New York, 1948; Jacques Ellul, *Propaganda: The Formation of Men's Attitudes*, trans. by Konrad Kellen and Jean Lerner, New York, 1965; Carl I. Hovland, Irving L. Janis, and Harold H. Kelley, *Communication and Persuasion*, New Haven, Conn., 1953; Paul Kecskemeti, "Propaganda," in *Handbook of Communication*, ed. by Ithiel de Sola Pool, Frederick W. Frey, et al., Chicago, 1973; Harold D. Lasswell, Daniel Lerner, and Hans Speier, eds., *Propaganda and Communication in World History*, 3 vols., Honolulu, Hawaii, 1979–1980; Daniel Lerner, ed., *Propaganda in War and Crisis*, New York, 1951, reprint 1972; Charles E. Osgood, William H. May, and Murray S. Miron, *Cross-Cultural Universals of Affective Meaning*, Urbana, Ill., 1975; Ernest Richert, *Agitation und Propaganda*, Berlin, 1958.

LEONARD W. DOOB

PROSE

The category of linguistic communication that is not in a metrical or rhymed arrangement. This definition has resulted in a diverse application of the term, from broadly characterizing all ordinary LANGUAGE to more narrowly specifying certain classes of nonverse writings by virtue of qualities such as explicitness, argumentation, fictionality, expositional stance, or eloquence. The broader application tends to devalue the discourse as unimaginative and commonplace (thus a proser is a tedious writer, part of a prosaic world), and the narrower one tends to heighten its value, as in such discriminating expressions as the German *Kunstprosa* ("art-prose"). The puzzling thing about prose is that the narrower application can really do without the term at all; each of these kinds of writings—exposition, philosophy, the novel, belles lettres, and so forth—is itself a GENRE or set of genres that can be aligned alongside POETRY, whereas the broader application seems not to know when to stop. Witness the astonishment and also pride of Jean-Baptiste Molière's *bourgeois gentilhomme*, in the 1670 play of the same name, when he learns that since "all that is not verse is prose" he must have been speaking prose all his life.

A consideration of the changing status of the term *prose* requires an investigation of its origins. This has been done for poetry, of course, and although findings are still in healthy contention, strong hypotheses have been put forward, such as that poetry comes from the repeated utterances that were part of RITUAL (*see* ORAL POETRY). Not so for prose. To go back to the earliest recorded utterances, at least in the West, is to find prose practically nowhere (unless again it is just another name for everything) and certainly not to find it then used as a category. Sayings, lists, oaths, and inscriptions are articulated in particular ways, sometimes with traces of rhythmic arrangement, that do not lend themselves to the term *prose.* Early utterance often bears clearly the marks of oral composition (*see* ORAL CULTURE), and, however loosely, such marks (e.g., repetition, formulas, figures of sound, parallelism, or epigrammatic style) suggest verse to us today. The more we see that transcribed oral utterances had these features, inspired to a great extent by the need to be remembered and to resonate, the less likely we are to see such utterances as "pure" prose. Further inquiry leads to the conclusion that although most definitions of prose—such as the one that begins this entry—do not limit it to WRITING, it is a term born of literate CULTURE (*see* LITERACY). This gives rise to many confusions, in which certain writings are characterized as prose just because they are not poetry, whereas they are more profitably dealt with if considered to be ORATORY, enumeration, dialogue, notation, or certain forms of NARRATIVE. (Some confusions are of course intentional, such as the prose poem.) In fact ethnographers see distortions resulting from the fact that transcriptions of unrhymed oral storytelling and histories (*see* ORAL HISTORY) are often categorized as prose as if they were to be read like nineteenth-century short stories.

Most strikingly, prose often comes into its own domain not as some outgrowth of natural language production such as SPEECH but generally at the point at which verse has to cede to nonverse much of its legacy in oral cultures. This explains the fact that although verse is usually considered to come after prose (and thereby to represent some kind of refined work on a raw, natural, and omnipresent prose flow), prose makes its appearance after verse in most Western cultures.

The ascension of prose is a slow process; prose is not "natural" in an oral society. Speech is articulated in all sorts of ways unaddressed by the poetry/prose distinction. Even the advent of writing does not bring forward prose in any specialized sense. Many ethnographers, such as Ron Scollon in speaking of the Athabaskan Indians, have observed that a tribe that has writing may still not have prose. Classicist Eric Havelock points out that in ancient Greece

while the last half of the fifth century begins to see the acceptance of prose as a viable means of publication, acceptance does not become complete until the fourth. This is three hundred years after the invention of the alphabet had rendered the monopoly exercised by poetry over the contrived word theoretically obsolete.

And Frank Byron Jevons, discussing in 1895 the earliest recorded Greek attempts to write prose, those of Pherecydes in 570 B.C.E., noted that

in everything but meter they are poetry, not prose; and whereas in poetry an author could compose artistic sentences of some complexity, in prose at this time he could only ejaculate short and simple expressions, in their baldness rather resembling a child's attempt at writing than a philosopher's.

In Greece verse and nonverse competed on the oratorical podium. The artful recitations of the poets were challenged by the Sophists Gorgias and Isocrates, who showed that true poetry (here, beauty) could be achieved in a richly styled and figured nonverse public speech. The need for a third alternative was felt by ARISTOTLE, who took to task both forms of grandiloquence when he said that the appropriate style for important issues argued at court was a "bare" though not dull one. Although this seems to be a debate about style (*see* STYLE, LITERARY) and not genre, it was actually a search for a means of communication closer to the Greek's evolving sense of fact or objectivity. But Aristotle could not give any principles of this bare, clear style, and the debate remained suspended between unrealistic extremes—the constraints of meter and sound versus total freedom from constraints, artful elaborateness versus dry and artless simplicity. *See* RHETORIC.

There was apparently no specific word for prose as such in Greek. The word Aristotle uses in opposition to verse, and that translators thus give us as *prose,* is *logos* ("thought," "reason," "discourse," or, especially in Athens, "speech," "oration") and sometimes *koine* ("common speech," the style of everyday talk). The prose histories of Herodotus and Thucydides relied for their material on the public speeches of the major historical figures. As Havelock has shown, the Greeks were brilliant in their ability to process ideas in a way uncharacteristic of oral culture and at the same time to discover or devise kinds of oral modes (*see* MODE) in which to do the processing, as in PLATO's dialogues. *See* HELLENIC WORLD.

Prose in Rome still looks like oratory, which shares its communicative framework with recited verse. There we see the appearance of the term's ancestor, *prorsus,* from the word meaning "straightforward," but the more general Latin expression (the one on CICERO's lips) is *oratio soluta,* "unfettered oration or speech." Translators also say *prose* when faced with certain uses of *sermo,* which, like *koine,* means "talk," "conversation," or "conversational style." The Romans pushed forward the interests of prose less in what they said about it than in what they did with writing. Writing, as Canadian scholar HAROLD INNIS has pointed out, is necessary to extend an empire's power through space. The extensive administrative use of writing was continued by the church, which in its particular forms of scriptural exegesis (*see* SCRIPTURE) initiated a good deal of writing *on* writing. *See* ROMAN EMPIRE.

The Bible made no distinction between poetry and prose, but hellenized Jews and early Christians took the Greco-Roman tradition and applied it retrospectively, finding as poetry those parts of the Bible that would be poetry in their world. St. Jerome went so far as to find Greek meters in the Psalms, a finding that neither he nor anyone else has been able to demonstrate. Was the rest of the Bible then (only) prose? (There is continuing criticism of the King James version of 1611 because it writes the Bible *as* prose.) The distinction was so compelling that a basic stylistic figure such as biblical parallelism was looked upon in the so-called poetic books as an indicator of meter, whereas in the nonpoetic books it was considered only a rhetorical figure. The distinction challenged those who believed that as divine inspiration the Bible could appropriately be neither poetry nor prose.

The church brought its increasingly self-contained Latin literate tradition into the MIDDLE AGES, where it stood beside a rich oral tradition that was in the vernacular and in verse only. Medieval France is one of the richest places to catch prose in the making; what writing there is in French is, up to 1200, in verse only. Vernacular writing was an attempt to record, and was thus modeled on, oral PERFORMANCE. Verse was so emphatically considered the authoritative medium in the vernacular for historical truth that any Latin prose translated into French was translated into French verse. Then, relatively abruptly, verse was considered to "lie," and the nonrhymed was seen as more truthful. More than an attack on rhyme or meter, this was a move away from any writing that by virtue of being in verse bespoke the oral system of transmission (e.g., jongleur, minnesinger, scop) that had become unreliable. The rejection is in favor of a more impersonal and unchanging document as evidence in the modern sense, a kind of evidence that, being finally "unspoken," lacks the accompanying interpretation that a speaker or remembrancer would naturally provide in an oral culture but whose consequent rawness is not troubling to readers now who are ready to take on the burden of such interpretation armed with a changing set of critical faculties, a new kind of literacy. Such changes become clear as we watch prose evolve and as French court writers begin to derhyme already existing verse epics. What gains acceptance here is the idea that prose is the kind of discourse that can convey matter with a minimum of formal changes enacted upon it, which makes it closer to some conception of fact, so that facts are seen somehow to come in prose.

Once prose reaches this status, verse gravitates in other, more specialized, directions (e.g., toward lyric), and prose comes to be regarded as the language of knowledge. The founders of the English Royal Society (1662) pick up the Aristotelian distinctions and attack rhetoric and eloquence as affectations and corruptions of any utterance that aims to put forth objective truth. Clearly this is a battle to be waged on the now-established territory of prose, not verse, and it is prose that the Royal Society explicitly seeks to improve. It is as if prose is to fulfill its destiny by becoming transparent. For founder Thomas Sprat the enemy here is unabashedly "the luxury and redundance of *speech*" and the ideal a "return back to the primitive purity, and shortness, when men deliver'd so many *things*, almost in an equal numbers of *words* . . . bringing all things as near the Mathematical plainness as they can." Such intentions signify a pursuit of a kind of communication with a new epistemological stance, a writing seen to stand on its own at a distance from aspects of its uttering context. Prose is becoming a particular way of putting things forward. There are obvious consequences of this in terms of scientific communication (for which the Royal Society was in fact founded) and logical discourse. Canadian education researcher David Olson, for example, finds in literacy "techniques of examining an assertion to determine all of its implications," leading to what he calls "essayist technique" and to one aspect of expository prose. There are less obvious but nonetheless powerful consequences in terms of representation and FICTION, such as the subjectivity, apparent illogic, and unique kinds of worldview offered by the quintessentially prose genre of the modern novel.

Bibliography. Wlad Godzich and Jeffrey Kittay, *The Emergence of Prose*, Minneapolis, Minn., 1987; Eric Havelock, *Prologue to Greek Literacy*, Cincinnati, Ohio, 1971; James L. Kugel, *The Idea of Biblical Poetry*, New Haven, Conn., 1981; David R. Olson, "From Utterance to Text: The Bias of Language in Speech and Writing," *Harvard Educational Review* 47 (1977): 257–281.

JEFFREY KITTAY

PROVERB

A verbal GENRE of folklore also widely employed in literary contexts. The proverb is seldom more than one sentence long, and it usually expresses one main idea. The message of the proverb is formulated in a way that implies a summary of the wisdom of collective experience. This effect is often enhanced by the insertion of introductory formulas at the beginning (such as "It is said . . ." or "The old people say . . ."), the specific wording of the formula following the poetic conventions of the culture and the kind of authority upheld by its norms. Poetic language, rhyme, rhythm and/or meter, alliteration, assonance, repetition, and other devices associated with oral forms may be used. Like all genres of verbal FOLKLORE, the proverb has multiple uses and is performed in recurring situations. The folkloristic research of proverbs is usually called paremiology.

Many proverbs have an international distribution, and the genre as a whole, as well as specific proverbs, have frequently been studied in distributional and comparative perspective. Distribution has in some

·GRANDIBVS EXIGVI SVNT PISCES PISCIBVS ESCA·
Siet sone dit hebt sik zeer langhe ghiweten dat die groote vissen de cleine

Figure 1. *(Proverb)* Pieter Bruegel the Elder, *Big Fish Eat Little Fish*. Engraving by van der Heyden, 1557. From H. Arthur Klein, ed., *Graphic Worlds of Peter Bruegel the Elder*, New York: Dover Publications, Inc., 1963, p. 139.

cases been explained as a result of cultural contact but is also ascribed to similarities of circumstance and experience.

The proverb is used by members of a cultural (ethnic, regional, professional, etc.) group to communicate an interpretation of a behavioral or interactional situation. The amount of proverb use and the skill with which proverbs are employed depend on an individual's competence in proverb lore, which usually is determined by such factors as memory, acquaintance with a proverb repertoire, and verbal-folkloristic creativity. Proverbs are usually applied in situations characterized by conflict, skepticism, or other kinds of oppositionally structured mental dispositions. Invoking the authority of a proverb in such contexts transfers the difficulty from a personal to a conceptual level, thereby restoring equilibrium to the specific occurrence that threatens the community's traditional values.

Use. Proverbs are used to emphasize and enhance the ritual aspects of any interactional behavior by engaging its formal and traditional characteristics. The application of a proverb imbues the specific situation with cultural meaning by linking it to a chain of situations, all of which may be interpreted by the same proverb. Proverbs may also be conceived of as a repertoire of available, optional verbal strategies to be invoked in certain situations. Since proverbs reflect tensions in feelings and logic, they may as a cultural repertoire exhibit a rather conflicting and paradoxical worldview or collective psychology: "Look before you leap," but "He who hesitates is lost"; also "Absence makes the heart grow fonder," but "Weeds grow on the untrodden path."

Proverbs have a variety of relations to other genres of folk literature and to other parallel systems in literature, mass communications, and everyday speech. In folk literature proverbs may be linked to various NARRATIVE forms, both as narrative springboards and as formal headings, or as a logical conclusion to which the narrative leads. They may also summarize a narrative, appear in close proximity to it, or become a point of reference to it by appearing separately. In both FICTION and nonfiction literature, proverbs may be invoked like quotations, a rhetorical genre to which they generally bear many similarities. The main difference is that the quotation is attributable to an identifiable individual source, whereas the proverb relies on a collective authority. In literature proverbs may also be used to stress a specific cultural coloring and identity and to create a more markedly folkloristic discourse.

An example of a genre of literature that utilized proverbs is the proverb play, developed in the eighteenth century in France by Louis Carmontelle (1717–1806). The title of the play is a proverb, and the action onstage illustrates the point of the proverb. An example of such a play is Alfred de Musset's *Il faut qu'une porte soit ouverte ou fermée* (A Door Must Be either Open or Shut, 1848).

Sources. There is sometimes a relatively direct connection between the oral and the written expression of proverbs. Written collections of popular short sayings may come to be quoted proverbially. Later, however, the connection between the spoken proverbs and their written source may be partially or totally forgotten. Thus the Old Testament books of Proverbs and Ecclesiastes, parabolic passages of the New Testament, and collections of wisdom lore of the humanistic period (notably Erasmus's *Adagia*) have become standard sources of proverb lore of Western culture.

Certain genres of certain cultures tend to dominate the proverb lore of those cultures and become sources for additional generation of proverbs, such as legal discourse in the Jewish Aramaic tradition of the Babylonian Talmud (ed. ca. 500–550), the *Schwank* anecdote genre in German (a short narrative ending in a punch line), and wisdom novellas in Arabic tradition or POETRY in Iranian tradition: "If you have one virtue and seventy defects, he who loves you will see nothing but that one virtue" (following a line of the thirteenth-century Shirazi poet Saʿdī). Some cultures have proverbial subgenres that are not proverbs per se because they do not consist of a complete sentence or express a complete idea. In Finnish, for example, proverbial comparisons are a dominant form among proverbial subgenres: "The words drop as matches from the tail of a black cat" (said about especially slow speech); or the so-called Wellerism (named after a Charles Dickens character, Sam Weller, who often used this form) or dialogue proverb in Swedish, Danish, Norwegian, and Anglo-Saxon traditions, such as the Swedish " 'You never get too much of God's word,' said the farmer as he hit his wife on the head with the Bible."

Collections. It is important to mention that these dominant genres are not the only ones found in the areas mentioned here. Any absolute comparison of genres and geographical locations would be quite impossible because interest, motivation, and strategies in eliciting and collecting proverbs have been of varying focus and intensity in different eras and different places. It is not unusual, therefore, to find a Wellerism in the Kurdish tradition: " 'The ears resemble those of a rabbit,' said the man who was compelled to eat donkey meat." Parallels can produce curious surprises. The Chinese equivalent of "penny wise, pound foolish" has been explained as "You go to bed to save the candle and you beget twins."

Proverbs as a folk literary genre began to be collected very early in history. Several ancient literatures show proverb compilations, notably the ancient Sumerian and the ancient Egyptian cultures. Well-known collections are the Egyptian Wisdom of Amenemope and the Neo-Babylonian Proverbs and Sayings of Aḥiqar (Aḥikar). In modern cultures proverbs survive and are regenerated in numerous ways. For example, there have, generally speaking, been no major changes in most of the traditional ways of communication with proverbs: in everyday speech, especially in situations in which the mode of speech is prescriptive; in educational situations; in religious or ideological preaching; and in political contexts. Research has shown that politicians use proverbs in commenting on subjects about which there is special tension or controversy, for example, U.S. President Jimmy Carter's application of "God gives the cold weather but he also gives the coat" in a speech on the occasion of the signing of the Camp David peace agreement between Israel and Egypt. In 1959 Nikita Khrushchev promoted U.S.-Soviet detente with "Two mountains never meet, but two people can." Proverbial texts may also be used to communicate moral and political messages in printed form to enormous masses of people, as did the Little Red Book of Mao Zedong, distributed widely in many languages. Proverbs have been quoted in judicial proceedings in cultural contexts as varied as a tribal court in Nigeria, the Jewish courts of Babylonia (quoted in the Talmud), and the courts of the Spanish Inquisition that questioned heretics in the sixteenth century.

Modern uses. Modern mass media have made innovative uses of proverbs. Unchanged, slightly changed, or heavily parodied proverb structures may be found in headlines of newspapers all over the world. Proverb application here serves functions similar to those in traditional face-to-face interaction, namely, to enhance the authority of what has been said or done, to heighten the aesthetic quality of the text, and to achieve rhetorical effectiveness. Proverb use is a way to catch the ears and eyes of readers and media audiences in general and therefore also can be a device in the commercial promotion of media products. The most developed commercialized use of proverbs, however, is their application in ADVERTISING. Jingles may consist of literal quotations of proverbs or slightly changed, easily identifiable proverbs, as well as traditional proverbs with a sophisticated twist. The use of proverbs in advertisements especially exploits the traditional association between proverbs and authority, thereby strengthening the validity of the communicated message. Many banks have made use of "A penny saved is a penny earned."

Modern urban culture has generated variations in proverb use that follow the changes in repertoire of the popular culture itself. In the past, chapbooks contained proverbs along with ballads, legends, and other folk literary material; the oral narrator, in the past as well as the present, inserts proverbs in the narrative performance. Pop music with catchy lyrics often includes genuine proverb texts or references of a more concealed character, in which case the traditional structure serves as a means to create something familiar and easily imprinted in the memory. In American black music, especially jazz, proverbs may become themes for variation and improvisation much as musical themes in the same sequence. *See* MUSIC, POPULAR.

Bibliography. Alan Dundes and Wolfgang Mieder, eds., *The Wisdom of Many: Essays on the Proverb,* New York, 1981; Galit Hasan-Rokem, *Proverbs in Israeli Folk Narratives,* Helsinki, 1982; Matti Kuusi, *Parömiologische Betrachtungen,* Folklore Fellows Communications no. 172, Helsinki, 1957; idem, *Towards an International Typesystem of Proverbs,* trans. by R. Goebel, Folklore Fellows Communications no. 211, Helsinki, 1972; Wolfgang Mieder, ed., *Ergebnisse der Sprichwörterforschung,* Bern and Frankfurt am Main, 1978; idem, *International Proverb Scholarship: An Annotated Bibliography,* New York, 1982; Grigorii L'vovich Permîakov, *From Proverb to Folktale: Notes on the General Theory of Clichée* (in Russian), Moscow, 1979; Lutz Röhrich and Wolfgang Mieder, *Sprichwort,* Stuttgart, 1977; Archer Taylor, *The Proverb, and An Index to the Proverb,* Hatboro, Pa., 1962.

GALIT HASAN-ROKEM

PROXEMICS

Term coined in 1963 by the U.S. anthropologist Edward T. Hall for his studies of the cultural patterning of mutual sensory involvement of people in face-to-face encounters. His particular emphasis was on how this patterning is related to physical and interpersonal space. The study of significant sound contrasts in a spoken language is known as phonemics, so Hall called the study of the significant contrasts in spatial organization in interaction within a given culture *proxemics.* Since the mid-1970s the term has come to denote all types of studies of human spatial behavior in social interactions. Such studies complement research in territoriality, crowding, and privacy and contribute to the body of data used by architects and environmental designers (*see* ARCHITECTURE; SPATIAL ORGANIZATION).

In the original conception of proxemics, physical settings (layouts of furniture, houses, streets, towns) together with the activities of people and their spatial perceptions form an intricate and dynamically balanced system in any given culture. The interactants' posture, orientation, eye contact, TOUCH, body heat, and SMELL, as well as style of speech and loudness of voice, vary according to their activity, relationship, feelings, and the type of spacing adopted for the duration of their encounter. *See also* BODY MOVEMENT; GESTURE.

According to Hall, members of Western societies regularly use four concentric *proxemic zones,* which he labeled, from smallest to largest, "intimate," "personal," "social-consultative," and "public" distances. Proxemic zones differ in terms of the quality and richness of the sensory input that those in them can obtain from one another through their EYES, ears, nostrils, and faculty of touch. At the intimate distance (e.g., mother-infant interaction) touching, heightened attention to body noises and smells, and the use of a narrowed field of vision play a crucial role. At the social-consultative (e.g., interview) or public (e.g., priest addressing a congregation) distances the information is gleaned through omnidirectional hearing and general 60- or 180-degree vision. There is a two-way relationship between the shifts in style of language used and the manner in which people orient their bodies, look at each other, and listen to each other. Thus, the head-on orientation, frequent and prolonged eye contact, and a semiformal manner of speech are both reasons for and consequences of the social-consultative distance.

The number of distinguishable proxemic zones, their size, and their relationship to behavior and layout of the setting are subject to people's perceptions and interpretations of space, and these, in turn, are structured by the culture in which the people have been reared. Members of different cultures could be thought to be living in different sensory worlds.

The study of proxemics involves intensive naturalistic observations, often using photographic, film, or VIDEO recordings, and also laboratory experiments, interviews, and analyses of literature, visual arts, and the language of a given community. Hall's work has been influenced by the views of linguists EDWARD SAPIR and BENJAMIN LEE WHORF on the interdependencies between culture and language. It has also been stimulated by research in KINESICS, paralanguage, INTERPERSONAL DISTANCE, and studies of spatial behavior in animals (*see* ANIMAL COMMUNICATION; ANIMAL SIGNALS).

See also INTERACTION, FACE-TO-FACE; NONVERBAL COMMUNICATION.

Bibliography. Edward T. Hall, *The Silent Language,* New York, 1959, reprint 1973; idem, *The Hidden Dimension,* New York, 1966; idem, *Handbook for Proxemic Research,* Washington, D.C., 1974.

T. MATTHEW CIOLEK

PSYCHOANALYSIS

In addressing the profound influences of psychoanalysis on ideas about human communication, the focus here will be on (1) major theoretical contributions of psychoanalysis to understanding communication, (2) clinical contributions of psychoanalysis to understanding obstacles to communication, and (3) implications of psychoanalysis for any theory of communication.

Psychoanalytic Theory

The contribution of psychoanalytic theory to the study of communication began with the first major work in psychoanalysis itself, SIGMUND FREUD's *The Interpretation of Dreams* (1900). The dream, which Freud described as "normal psychosis," serves as the model for communication in psychoanalytic theory. At the center of this theory is Freud's and his followers' accounts of the role of the unconscious in psychic life.

Freud's examination of dreams was meant to demonstrate how the mechanism of repression operates in relation to the unconscious. Simply stated, dreams communicate by a process of indirection unconscious wishes that otherwise remain unrecognized by the dreamer. It is the purpose of psychoanalytic interpretation to give a MEANING to dreams, in effect to reconcile two discrepant truths: what one dreams and what one's dreams mean.

Of course, the only MODE available to communicate what one dreams is some form of symbolic representation such as LANGUAGE or ART (*see* SYMBOLISM). For the typical patient, talk is itself the manner in which dream-work is made available for interpretation. Psychoanalysis raises talk—any talk—to a level of importance unprecedented in the history of interpretation. The purpose of psychoanalytic theory and therapy is to match the truth of an interpretation with the truth of the dream itself. In this way a patient is able to discern not simply what has been repressed but also the elaborate means that have been taken by the mind to conceal its meanings and intentions.

The dream makes of everyone, as Freud said, a natural poet and thus raises everyone at least hypo-thetically to the level of the most culturally esteemed of communicators. But the social esteem reserved for poets is, to this extent, parodied in the Freudian elevation of the natural talent of dreamers. Freud's discovery was that creativity had its predicates in the life of the unconscious. It is no coincidence that numerous artists and poets have been reluctant to undergo analysis, precisely because of its power to provide interpretations that would rationalize both motive and achievement.

In psychoanalytic theory the unconscious of each individual constantly communicates itself. In waking life these communications are symbolized in a broad range of behaviors: jokes (*see* HUMOR), SLIPS OF THE TONGUE, facial tics, compulsions—in short, in the extensive expressional life of human beings. By attempting to account theoretically for all actions and occurrences, psychoanalysis has claimed to show the organization of meaningfulness beneath the manifest surface of dreams and the random, seemingly insignificant aspects of waking life. Interpretation always threatens to become overinterpretation. Psychoanalytic theory has been criticized for its indeterminacy. But it is a retrospective rather than predictive science. What is communicated by way of analysis is thus imposed as interpretation rather than exposed as fact.

The method of free association, the recounting of dreams, and the interpretive questioning and offering of analytic constructions by the analyst are all intended to direct the patient to a limited range of unconscious predicates, including sex; death; and parental, sibling, and spousal relations. These predicates are themselves only representations of instinctual processes that are permitted entry into the mind through a series of distortions. The history of the psychoanalytic movement after Freud is in many respects a history of the relative weights attached to the influence of these predicates on psychic life.

The Clinical Setting

The clinical setting remains the locus for working out the aims of psychoanalytic technique. It is worth noting that the setting for psychoanalytic encounters calls for the patient to recline on a couch while the therapist is seated nearby. In other forms of therapy (e.g., psychotherapy, family therapy, group therapy) much greater emphasis is placed on face-to-face encounters (*see* INTERACTION, FACE-TO-FACE). From the standpoint of psychoanalysis the reclining patient, alone with his or her thoughts, is essential to the process of free association. The therapeutic setting is intended to encourage a form of communication that imitates the patient's dream state during sleep.

The emphasis that psychoanalytic treatment has placed on matters and relations pertaining to sexuality is so well known that a popular undermining of certain psychoanalytic insights has occurred. The patient's discovery of the Oedipus complex has therapeutic efficacy only to the extent that interpretations lead to resistances that in turn point the way back to a recognition of wishes (and, no doubt, events) that have been repressed. Freud was the first to admit that the analyst often fails to enable the patient to recollect what was repressed. But as long as the analyst can produce in the patient an "assured conviction" of the truth of a construction, the same therapeutic result will be achieved.

At stake in the production of assured convictions are the phenomena of transference and countertransference, two master terms in the vocabulary of communication in psychoanalysis. The concept of transference stipulates that through the patient's participation in analysis strong identifications with the analyst, both affectionate and hostile, develop. But the analyst is an "object" substituted for significant others in the patient's life. By clarifying in the course of analysis how these substitutions or displacements from the past operate, the analyst gives therapy. In this sense therapy is communication.

The significance of countertransference, both clinically and theoretically, has been a subject of considerable debate, and the function of language has figured prominently in this discussion. Psychoanalysts committed to a "drive model" explanation of neurosis view countertransference—those feelings and identifications that the analyst has for the patient—as fundamentally disruptive to the therapeutic aims of analysis. Countertransference points back to the analyst's unresolved neuroses and conflicts and thus interferes with the communication between analyst and patient.

On the other hand, a "relational" or "object relations" model incorporates the functions of transference and countertransference and treats them as essential components in the therapeutic process. This model concentrates on interpersonal and interactional dimensions in human development rather than on biological factors such as instincts, as is more characteristic of the drive model. In the drive model the obstacles to communication are viewed primarily as the result of imbalances in the psychic economy of the patient; an emphasis is placed on conflicts that arise from instinctual aggression and sexuality. In the relational model these obstacles are defined as conflicts that emerge from human relations themselves, including the relation between analyst and patient. The tension produced between competing explanatory models of human growth has been productive for the improvement of clinical psychoanalysis.

One example of a relational view of communication can be found in the work of British psychoanalyst Charles F. Rycroft, who has argued that the capacity for interpersonal relations depends on a person's ability not only to use objects to satisfy libidinal wishes but also to use language to maintain a continual separation of self from object, whether the object is present or not. SPEECH mediates between and connects the biological and the social. In psychoanalytic terms speech demonstrates that the id has been acted upon by external forces and in particular by the superego.

The debate among clinicians about the consequences of subscribing to one theoretical model or another is not likely to be resolved, in part because the relation between analyst and patient is neither separate from their biological existences nor grounded solely in their social and cultural milieus. At the same time, for therapeutic purposes theory is never divorced from the particular persons who participate in analysis and the circumstances in which the analysis takes place. HARRY STACK SULLIVAN once wrote that "communication is an exquisite triumph of trial and profit from shrewdly observed error." The authority of the analyst is established in the ability to communicate interpretive understandings of conditions that are both in and beyond the control of analyst and patient alike.

Implications

The contributions of psychoanalysis to theories of communication have been more preliminary than definitive. The writings of psychoanalyst Ernst Kris and psychologist David Rapaport, for example, contain provocative discussions of the importance of the psychoanalytic perspective for theories of mass communication.

Kris has noted that totalitarian and democratic forms of PROPAGANDA can be usefully distinguished in psychoanalytic terms. In the case of totalitarian propaganda the leader qua communicator is accepted as the audience's ego ideal. Identification in the superego alone produces a rigid CODE of emotional reaction in the audience and thus a submissive type of identification. This submissive reaction signifies a collective moment of regression in which intellectual and moral independence are renounced. On the other hand, democratic propaganda is said to produce two types of identification, one in the superego and the other in the ego. Kris linked ego identification in particular with what he described as the "birth of criticism," that is, a mode of identification in which members of an audience do not share the same reactions.

In following Kris's line of reasoning it is interesting to consider the implications for mass communications theory. A certain degree of "healthy" regression applies to all social orders, in which members may share in the multiplicity of assured convictions that rituals of all kinds offer (see RITUAL). Freud's criticism of RELIGION as an illusion was similar to Kris's warning about regressive identification toward the state. But the similarity ends insofar as religion attempts to particularize the contents of experience in ways that separate persons from one another while binding them together in like faiths. Mass communications and modern propaganda are vehicles for universalizing the contents of experience in ways that unite persons while binding them to no faith in particular. The democratic and totalitarian orders have thus mastered the therapeutic utility of communication, appealing to and defining expectations with the assured conviction that no communication is infallible, especially when it is no longer useful.

Rapaport proposed exploring the structures of consciousness in which communication takes place, referring to them as "channels of communication." He cautioned that the generalizations made about identification and projection in clinical psychotherapy should not be simply transposed to group and mass phenomena. The danger implied suggests the central dilemma and responsibility of any elite, including the psychoanalytic, that would claim to educate. Rapaport concluded: "How to *indicate* without dishonestly *concealing* and without prematurely and destructively *revealing* the secret of one's life one cherishes or dreads, is the great enigma of communication."

Of all contemporary social movements, feminism has posed by far the most fundamental challenges to the organizing principles of psychoanalysis (see FEMINIST THEORIES OF COMMUNICATION; GENDER; SEXISM). In many respects these challenges turn precisely on the nature of human communication, between men and women, parents and children, even nation-states and their citizenry. The power dynamics inherent in these relations present one of the clearest expressions of the endless balancing between the biological and the cultural and between elites and masses. It is the natural function of elites to define the guiding principles of any CULTURE. As this function is assumed negationally in the form of criticism of prevailing balances, the therapeutic mode comes to take the place of earlier modes of communication.

The psychoanalytic framework has always presupposed the dyadic relation of analyst and patient. Treatment is administered on a one-to-one basis. The assimilation of psychoanalytic insight into social-scientific generalization may be limited to the extent that each intends to serve different aims. The humanities have been far more favorable toward the proposition that there can be no genuine creativity without criticism, for criticism—whether poststructuralist, deconstructionist, or otherwise—reveals the precedence of interpretation over what is interpreted (see AUTHORSHIP; STRUCTURALISM).

The priority of interpretation over what is interpreted parallels the analyst's position vis-à-vis the patient. Both relations are indubitably relations of authority. Psychoanalysis has shown the complexity inherent in these relations. It has sought to improve them. In so doing it has also exposed itself to the same relentless criticism that it seeks to communicate as a healthy state of mind. Its optimism is founded on discontents that can no more be frozen and resected than they can be once and for all times identified. Communication in psychoanalysis connotes a process. This triumph of the therapeutic comes, it may be expected, with its own discontents.

See also JUNG, CARL.

Bibliography. Merton M. Gill, ed., *The Collected Papers of David Rapaport*, New York, 1967; Jay R. Greenberg and Stephen A. Mitchell, *Object Relations in Psychoanalytic Theory*, Cambridge, Mass., 1983; Paul H. Hoch and Joseph Zubin, eds., *Psychopathology of Communication*, New York, 1958; Ernst Kris, *Selected Papers of Ernst Kris*, New Haven, Conn., 1975; Robert Langs, *Interactions: The Realm of Transference and Countertransference*, New York, 1980; Louis Paul, ed., *Psychoanalytic Clinical Interpretation*, New York, 1963; Philip Rieff, *Freud: The Mind of the Moralist*, 3d ed., Chicago, 1979; Jürgen Ruesch, *Therapeutic Communication*, 2d ed., New York, 1973; Charles Rycroft, *Imagination and Reality*, New York and London, 1968.

JONATHAN B. IMBER

PUBLIC OPINION

Definitions of public opinion tend to fall into two categories, considering it either as a collection of individual opinions or a kind of social organization. The first school is represented by Albert Venn Dicey, a nineteenth-century legal scholar who described public opinion as "a general term for the beliefs held by a number of individual human beings." Those who define public opinion as what is found by attitude surveys follow a similar approach. *See* OPINION MEASUREMENT.

A different point of view was expressed by sociologist CHARLES HORTON COOLEY, who saw public opinion as "no mere aggregate of separate individual judgments, but an organization, a cooperative product of communication and reciprocal influence." Ferdinand Tönnies, a German sociologist, took a similar approach when he described public opinion as the unified opinion, or what passes for it, of a group of people, especially when it approves or disapproves. He notes that this is the sense in which the term is used in the German legal code of his time, which calls for appropriate punishment for anyone who "originates or disseminates information about another person that is designed to make this person appear contemptible or to lower his standing in public opinion. . . ."

Another division is between those who use public opinion mainly or exclusively with reference to politics and those who apply the term to a broader range of phenomena. A frequently quoted definition advanced by Hans Speier describes public opinion as "opinions on matters of concern to the nation freely and publicly expressed by men outside the government who claim a right that their opinions should influence or determine the actions, personnel, or structure of their government." Other social scientists see public opinion as also playing a role in economics, science, RELIGION, and many other domains. All usages at all times tend to assume that public opinion can exercise influence. Its power may be strong or weak, but the fact that it has the potential to exert force is one of the basic characteristics by which it is recognized.

History

Although the term *public opinion* was not generally used before the eighteenth century, earlier references to the phenomenon can be found. A letter from King Shamshi-Adad of Assyria (1815–1782 B.C.E.), for example, warns his viceroy against tampering with the land allotments of the inhabitants of the Euphrates region, since such action would surely provoke "loud public outcry."

Austrian historian Wilhelm Bauer concludes that public opinion was an active force in the politics of classical Greece and Rome and had to be taken into account by the government, whether a dictatorship or a democracy. Indeed, the art of PERSUASION became so highly developed in ancient Athens that ARISTOTLE's *Rhetoric* is still used as a text today. To illustrate the importance of public opinion to Roman politicians, Bauer quotes from a letter sent to CICERO by a friend when he was temporarily away from the capital: "If anything of greater importance of a political nature should occur, I will diligently describe to you its origin, the general opinion about it, and the prospects for future action that it opens up."

Bauer and other historians who examine public opinion in previous centuries often treat the channels of communication as indicators, from whose nature and extent the existence and characteristics of public opinion can be inferred. Thus, during the medieval period in western Europe, when information channels extending beyond the village market were few, expensive, and often dangerous, public opinion played a relatively minor role. Currents of opinion did, however, have some importance in those locations that were better served by communications and where literate people congregated: Rome, other religious centers, and royal and ducal courts. But for the great

majority of the population, questions posed by daily life were usually settled by religion, custom, and the local authorities. *See* MIDDLE AGES.

As communication channels revived, the role of public opinion grew. The Italian city-states, which flourished from about 1200 to 1600, provided forums for lively debate on issues of all kinds among interested and concerned people, many of whom could read and write. Dante Alighieri (1265–1321) is labeled by Bauer as the first modern publicist, a social critic who used his pen and talent in mobilizing public opinion to oppose the abuses of his time. Tightly built urban centers, providing almost ideal conditions for the communication of ideas, developed north of the Alps also. Antwerp's stock exchange, the first institution of its kind, was founded in 1460 and rapidly became a world-class center for news and RUMOR.

The printing press, an even greater aid to communication than the city, spread rapidly throughout Europe following JOHANNES GUTENBERG's first use of movable type in 1436 or 1437. It provided much of the fuel for the religious and national strife that enveloped Europe in the sixteenth and seventeenth centuries (*see* PRINTING). Regularly printed newspapers started to appear in several German principalities shortly after the year 1600. By the end of the century the major cities of Europe and some in other continents had newspapers, even though many were heavily censored or regulated. By the middle of the eighteenth century, when the French and American revolutions were brewing, substantial numbers of people in Europe and North America had become members of a group that political scientist Gabriel Almond has labeled the "attentive public." These were literate people, mostly well-to-do, who took a continuous interest in political, social, and cultural affairs of the day. Typically, they lived in cities and read newspapers, many of which had by this time gained sufficient freedom to print news about controversial subjects and, as historian Stephen Koss notes, were regarded by the authorities as "vehicles of turbulence."

When, at the end of the eighteenth century, the ancien régime in France was toppled and existing governments all over Europe were threatened, observers commonly blamed or praised public opinion for having played a major part in the upheaval. It became a subject that preoccupied politicians, political philosophers, and journalists. There was no doubt about its significance, although there was still some question about exactly what it was.

Formation of Public Opinion

For public opinion to form, three elements must be present: communication channels, issues, and publics. As historical surveys demonstrate, mass media are not necessary; more primitive channels are in some cases quite adequate, although a combination of mass media and interpersonal channels appears to be optimal. An *issue* may be defined as a question affecting a substantial number of people for which there is no generally accepted "right" answer, and which is therefore a likely subject for discussion. A *public* includes those people who give their attention to an issue; they must have at least some interest in it and must be able to learn something about it. Communication links issues with members of the public and may link members of the public with one another. The study of the formation of public opinion is essentially the study of the way these linkages are created.

A schematic description of the emergence of an organized body of opinion might identify the following stages. (1) An individual forms an attitude about an issue as a result of exposure to communications about it. If this attitude is then expressed in words, action, or gesture, it becomes an opinion. If it is never expressed, it does not become an opinion and plays no part in the public opinion process. Some individual ATTITUDES become part of public opinion on an issue only because they are expressed to a public opinion interviewer or in a voting booth. (2) Ordinarily, people voice their opinions about issues to members of one or more face-to-face groups to which they belong. If members of the FAMILY, neighborhood, or work group are in substantial agreement, a common opinion on the issue may develop. Opinions that meet strong opposition among a person's associates are likely to be changed, or the individual holding them may break with the group (*see* GROUP COMMUNICATION). (3) Through the mass media or interpersonal networks, people become aware of opinions among the larger public. If they find support for their own views, they tend to express these more often and more confidently; if they meet disapproval, they are more likely to remain silent. (4) When partisans become aware of others who share their opinions, a "we" feeling may come into existence. This body of opinion may grow by a snowball or spiral process until nearly everyone who is disposed to agree shares the "we" feeling.

In practice, public opinion on each issue follows a slightly different course. Not all stages can be identified in each case, and varying proportions of a public may be included in the body of opinion on an issue.

Whether person-to-person communications or the mass media are more important in the formation of an attitude on an issue depends on the individual's social environment and on the nature of the issue. People who have loose-knit networks of friends and acquaintances tend to rely more on the mass media for information about issues and for guidance in forming their own attitudes; those belonging to intimate social groupings are more likely to acquire information and attitudes via word of mouth. Usually, mass media (including books and magazines) and personal sources complement and reinforce each other. A person may learn about an issue from a RADIO broadcast, talk about it with friends, and then go to a newspaper for further information (*see* NEWSPAPER: TRENDS). The resulting attitude is likely to be influenced strongly by a person's preexisting attitudes and values and by his or her social and economic situation.

Group pressures. Once attitudes are formed, and expressed as opinions, they often are modified so as to harmonize with the opinions expressed by others with whom one associates. Even if the attitudes themselves do not change, it is customary for them to be formulated in a way that does not do violence to the group consensus, if there is one. And the more closely group members are linked by a network of INTERPERSONAL COMMUNICATION, the more likely it is that a consensus will exist. The result of CONVERSATION about a subject within a group is ordinarily the formation of a common opinion, to which most members conform at least outwardly. Nonconformists are likely to remain silent or, if they differ strongly, to leave the group.

Dramatic examples of the power of neighborhood groups to enforce conformity could be found in the United States before the Civil War, when antislavery advocates living in the slave states of the South left those states by the thousands and settled in Ohio or in the Kansas-Nebraska territory. They could no longer live in communities with which they differed on such a vital issue. More mundane examples of group pressure can be seen prior to almost any ELECTION, when family, neighborhood, and work groups all tend to influence the voting intentions of their members.

When an issue is given attention by the mass media, the result is usually to encourage wider discussion and to promote the aggregation of opinions on the issue into one or more larger bodies of public opinion. Political scientist Bernard C. Cohen observed in connection with foreign policy questions that the media are not especially successful in telling us what to think, but are stunningly successful in telling us what to think *about*. Scholars later gave the name AGENDA-SETTING to this ability of the press to direct public attention to certain subjects.

Social movements. The opinion mobilization process is furthered also by the mass media's ability to stimulate group formation and even social movements. Tom Burns, a student of public opinion in eighteenth-century England, notes that the radical press, including pamphlets, was of great importance in "articulating and promoting opposition and protests" and that newspapers "could themselves provide the occasion for regular, semiclandestine meetings, it being common practice for them to be read aloud in public houses and coffee houses throughout the country." Much the same process could be observed in the growth of the women's movement in the United States and other countries in the 1960s and 1970s.

Examination of the women's movement, or of any major social movement, shows the reciprocal relationship between social movements and public opinion. A movement may arise in response to popular sentiment on an issue, but then one of its principal objectives becomes to influence the public. The opinions of those concerned about air, water, and soil pollution stimulated several movements to protect the environment, and most of these movements then launched massive publicity campaigns.

Information media frequently make it possible for individuals who otherwise might feel that they are alone in holding their opinions or are members of a small minority to gain courage from the knowledge that others agree with them. Perception of others' opinions affects one's willingness to speak out. Some researchers have found that those who think the attitude they hold on an issue is gaining ground are more likely to express this attitude. A circular process develops: more people voice their opinion when they think it is gaining ground, and some who hear this opinion are emboldened to express themselves. At the same time, those who hold dissenting opinions are less and less likely to be heard from. Eventually, opinion on one side of the issue dominates the public channels of communication; opinion on the other side exists but is not heard. This phenomenon has been called by Elisabeth Noelle-Neumann "the spiral of silence."

The spiral process can lead to a variety of configurations of public opinion. Only rarely are all members of a public prevailed upon to accept a particular point of view; there are almost always some holdouts. Even in regard to questions of fashion in CLOTHING or SPEECH, nonconformists often flout the preferences of an overwhelming majority. Or there may be several contending bodies of opinion, each of which has "spiraled up" to a point where it has absorbed all, or nearly all, of those amenable to its point of view on the issue in question. This is often the state of public opinion prior to elections in those democratic countries in which two major parties enjoy almost equal support.

Social Effects of Public Opinion

There are two major categories of social effects of public opinion, usually labeled *social control* and *decision making*. The idea that public opinion can play a role in social control—namely, in causing individuals and groups to conform to social norms and standards of behavior prescribed by larger or superordinate societal units—is implicit in the way the term is frequently used. In a popular French novel from the late eighteenth century a young woman is warned against associating with a man of bad repute, since even if he should change his ways public opinion would remain against him. In *Henry IV* Shakespeare has the king urge his son to have more regard for opinion, and not be seen too often in bad company. Similar statements can be heard today.

Sociologists have noted the part played by public opinion in social control. Edward A. Ross, in the first volume of the *American Journal of Sociology* (1895), spoke of public opinion as "an instrument of discipline . . . the judgment the public pronounces on an act as to whether it is righteous or wicked, noble or ignoble." ROBERT PARK and Ernest W. Burgess, in their early and influential sociology text, *Introduction to the Science of Sociology* (1921), designate public opinion as the dominant form of social control in secondary groups and cities, where "fashion tends to take the place of custom." Tönnies went even further, attributing to public opinion much of the social control function that had in former times been exercised by religion.

To exercise such a function, the existence of public opinion must be known to the person or group whose behavior is to be controlled. GOSSIP cannot influence behavior if the victim never learns about it. The victim may go about his or her business, not comprehending the social snubs or economic discrimination he or she encounters. Politicians, corporations, and government agencies frequently subscribe to clipping services or commission private polls (*see* POLL) to learn about public reactions to their activities. If the "image" is bad, the offending behavior may be corrected, or, more commonly, a PUBLIC RELATIONS campaign may be undertaken. Those who, fearing public disapproval, attempt to keep secret their activities and sometimes their thoughts are implicitly paying tribute to the effectiveness of public opinion as a form of social control.

Related to social control is the decision-making function of public opinion in society. In social control a consensus forms and influences some behavior that deviates from a norm; in decision making, the consensus determines what the group as a whole should think or do.

The decision-making function of public opinion is most obvious when it is formalized in a constitution that calls for elections. Less obvious but more common is the case in which public opinion comes into play in problematic situations where no laws, customs, norms, or other rules apply, or where there is a dispute about their suitability.

Public discussion of an issue frequently leads to the establishment of norms of conduct or the passage of laws. Park saw some rules of behavior as "judgments of public opinion in regard to issues that have been settled and forgotten." Prior to the mid-twentieth century, for example, it was accepted that a male passenger in a public conveyance should offer his seat to a female passenger if she had none. This norm of conduct came under question as the women's rights movement gained momentum. There was a period of discussion; dominant opinion came to hold that it was not required for the male passenger to stand. This judgment came to be embodied in a new norm.

Whether a law or some other kind of rule is or is not an outgrowth of the public opinion process, it cannot survive without public support. The statement of eighteenth-century Scottish philosopher David Hume that it is on opinion only that government is founded is regarded by some scholars as being extreme, but that it includes a large measure of truth is rarely disputed. Social scientists have found that any law, unless it is accepted by a substantial majority, is likely to become a dead letter. Similarly, public acceptance of a solution to a crisis, worked out by politicians, is often the outcome of a consensus built through publicity and wide discussion. Such a consensus was created, for example, during the Watergate affair in the United States and was one of the reasons the potentially divisive issue did so little damage to the country.

Change and Manipulation of Public Opinion

Communication channels, issues, and publics are the principal elements involved in the change of public opinion, just as they are involved in its formation. Issues change not only because of new developments but also because old problems are settled. When discussion of a question leads to the establishment of a new norm, the enactment of a law, or the election of a particular candidate to office, public opinion on that issue tends to disappear.

On occasion one issue is pushed off center stage by another issue. Only a few subjects can be prominent in interpersonal channels of communication on any one day. Gossip places a premium on novelty and freshness; issues wear out and are replaced. The mass media are similarly limited. We sometimes say that a subject is "forced off the front page" by more sensational news.

Changes in public opinion may also occur because publics change. People become interested in different things. The bitter religious wars of seventeenth-century Europe were stilled not so much because accommodation between the Protestant and Catholic forces had been reached but because attitudes toward religion changed. As the advancement of science and the industrial revolution brought new ideas and concerns, especially to those with more EDUCATION,

religious questions that previously had been disputed with vigor came to be seen as less important. Smaller publics continued to debate these questions, but much of the public for the religious issue had been lost.

Those who seek to influence or manipulate public opinion frequently make practical application of what is known about its formation and change. If they have the power, they control and regulate the channels of communication, emphasize some issues while ignoring others, and do their best to mobilize publics that will favor their policies.

Those who have power can often keep issues under control. A government can release or withhold a controversial report. Those who have less power may not be able to create or eliminate issues in this manner, but they can emphasize certain subjects and ignore others. It is customary for political candidates, with the help of their campaign advisers, to select and emphasize certain issues, hoping to direct public attention to them. Advertisers do the same thing. They may not be able to improve a product, but they can stress some of its characteristics and gloss over others. One reason diplomats at international conferences fence so fiercely over the agenda is that whatever is talked about is likely to influence public opinion one way or the other (*see* DIPLOMACY).

Equally common, or perhaps more so, are efforts by opinion manipulators to build publics and mobilize bodies of opinion. Jean Stoetzel notes that one of the most elegant techniques of PROPAGANDA is to build on scattered, private opinions, and to crystallize these into public opinion: "Vague hopes can be utilized" and "diffuse discontent can be merged into a revolutionary current." Those who are leaning toward a particular party or candidate, or are already exercised about an issue, can often be mobilized by campaign propaganda and incorporated into a body of supporting opinion.

Nearly everyone is concerned with the manipulation of public opinion. Even those who take no interest in public affairs are likely to try to influence the opinion that other people have of them. And most of us, at one time or another, engage in propaganda designed to mold opinion regarding issues that affect our community, organizations to which we belong, or our country as a whole.

See also NEWSPAPER: HISTORY; OPINION LEADER; POLITICAL COMMUNICATION—HISTORY.

Bibliography. Wilhelm Bauer, *Die öffentliche Meinung in der Weltgeschichte* (Public Opinion in World History), Potsdam, 1929; Bernard Berelson, Paul F. Lazarsfeld, and William McPhee, *Voting: A Study of Opinion Formation in a Presidential Campaign*, Chicago, 1954; Tom Burns, "The Organization of Public Opinion," in *Mass Communication and Society*, ed. by James Curran, Michael Gurevitch, and Janet Woolacott, London, 1977; Charles

Horton Cooley, *Social Organization: A Study of the Larger Mind,* New York, 1909, reprint New York, 1962; Albert Venn Dicey, *Lectures on the Relation between Law and Public Opinion in England during the Nineteenth Century,* London, 1905, reprint New York, 1978; C. Wendell King, *Social Movements in the United States,* New York, 1956; Gladys Engel Lang and Kurt Lang, *The Battle for Public Opinion: The President, the Press, and the Polls during Watergate,* New York, 1983; Harold D. Lasswell, Daniel Lerner, and Hans Speier, *Propaganda and Communication in World History,* 3 vols., Honolulu, Hawaii, 1979–1980; Dan D. Nimmo, *The Political Persuaders: The Techniques of Modern Election Campaigns,* Englewood Cliffs, N.J., 1970; Jean Stoetzel, *Esquisse d'une théorie des opinions* (Outline of a Theory of Opinions), Paris, 1943; Ferdinand Tönnies, *Kritik der öffentlichen Meinung* (Critique of Public Opinion), Berlin, 1922; David Weaver, "Media Agenda-Setting and Public Opinion: Is There a Link?" in *Communication Yearbook 8,* ed. by Robert N. Bostrom and Bruce H. Westley, Beverly Hills, Calif., 1984.

W. PHILLIPS DAVISON

PUBLIC RELATIONS

Information activities and policies by which corporations and other organizations seek to create ATTITUDES favorable to themselves and their work and to counter adverse attitudes. Public relations may be administered by an in-house department or by special public relations agencies or counselors engaged for the purpose. The term *public relations* is used at some corporations to cover all kinds of informational activities addressed to the public, including advertising; in more typical usage, it excludes advertising. This article discusses nonadvertising aspects. The two fields have developed separately, although in recent years a number of large advertising agencies have taken over the ownership of major public relations agencies. For the range of information services generally included in advertising, *see* ADVERTISING.

Genesis

In the early years of the twentieth century, public relations emerged as a distinct occupational pursuit in the United States to provide counsel and policy guidance to large business corporations. Often the managements of these companies found themselves the target of government, press, and public criticism for their allegedly insensitive or unethical business practices. Their leaders turned to early public relations counselors to help create greater public understanding and support for their operations.

Several of these pioneer counselors played significant roles in shaping the early practice of public relations. For example, Ivy Lee, a former newspaperman, served the Rockefeller family for many years,

and the prestige of that support gave an important endorsement to this field. Two senior executives of the American Telephone and Telegraph Company, Theodore N. Vail and Arthur W. Page, provided role models that influenced other large companies in structuring their public relations operations. Finally, in Edward L. Bernays, who described public relations as "the engineering of consent," the profession found a particularly articulate spokesman, able to exercise considerable influence on both corporate and academic audiences. After the era of these pioneers, the number of public relations practitioners increased considerably, but the profession did not produce leaders of comparable stature and importance.

Up to the post–World War II period, clients for these services were largely business corporations and their trade associations. Since then, however, other groups—including local and national governments and a host of not-for-profit institutions such as schools, hospitals, health care agencies, religious groups, and political parties—have made extensive use of public relations techniques, although different terminology may be used.

The Field

A past president of the Public Relations Society of America once suggested, half in jest, that the practice of public relations could be defined as "what public relations people do"; the suggestion has merit and some obvious limitations. The field encompasses many different activities depending on the needs and financial resources of the client and the particular climate of opinion that obtains when the client organization defines its problems. On a policy-making level, public relations professionals are expected to counsel top management with respect to the early identification of significant social, economic, and political issues that might adversely affect their operations. This emphasis on issue management contrasts with earlier concerns of public relations workers, who concentrated on the identification of particular hostile or uninformed audiences considered to be prime targets for a public relations information program. The issue-management approach, on the other hand, recognizes that people of diverse social, economic, and ideological backgrounds may find themselves on common ground with respect to their attitudes on controversial public issues.

Apart from counseling management, public relations professionals carry out a wide range of more routine tasks designed to ensure a continuous flow of information to key publics. These activities usually include the preparation of speeches and background briefing papers for major executives and a wide range of periodic reports to employees, customers, community groups, shareholders, and others interested in the current and future plans and activities of the organization in question. In addition, public relations staff personnel are expected to cultivate ongoing and friendly relations with representatives of the media, with their employers' professional and trade associations, and with relevant government regulatory agencies and policy-making bodies.

Organizations that can afford to staff large public relations departments will often employ personnel with special communications skills. Some devote their talents to creating special exhibits for trade shows or for meetings of important OPINION LEADER groups. There is a long-term tradition for programs designed to reach students and teachers, with the intention of helping to shape the thinking of tomorrow's leaders. Booklets and speaker programs frequently are part of the effort to reach educators and other molders of community opinion such as religious leaders. In recent years growing attention has been given to recruiting public relations personnel with expertise in dealing with the concerns of consumer groups, environmental protection organizations, and diverse elements in the population with a special interest in affirmative action programs.

Among innumerable devices and approaches available to public relations practitioners, a favorite Bernays plan was to organize citizen committees dedicated to a public purpose, which would somehow dovetail with the purposes of a client. During a 1930s flu epidemic Bernays stirred up concern about unsanitary glassware in soda fountains and restaurants as channels of infection, and persuaded various health officials to serve on a Committee for the Study and Promotion of the Sanitary Dispensing of Foods and Drinks. Its pronouncements were prominently reported in the press and on radio. Its participants were largely unaware that the committee was designed to set the stage for a promotion campaign on behalf of Dixie paper cups, a Bernays client. In such situations it seemed best for the role of the public relations adviser to remain out of the limelight. Bernays once discovered during a lunch with Lee that both were public relations advisers to American Tobacco Company. Both had held these positions for some time, each totally unaware of the other's similar involvement. Bernays writes in his memoirs: "I never asked Ivy Lee what he did for American Tobacco. The result of his work wasn't noticeable to me, nor was my work noticeable to him. When my advice called for action, it was usually the company that carried it out." This penchant for behind-the-scenes counsel makes it difficult to chronicle fully or accurately the achievements of public relations.

Training and Professionalism

There are no legal constraints anywhere in the world to prevent anyone from claiming to be a public relations expert. From time to time some public relations leaders have advocated licensing for their field, but most appear vehement in opposing such intrusion of government into their profession. Professional societies serving the public relations field exist in many countries of the world at both local and national levels. Their preoccupation with defining and enhancing ethical practices reflects their concern with the ambivalent image of the field within the intellectual community and the mass media, which perceive public relations as a manipulative and self-serving occupation available to a client for hire. Film, television drama, the press, and politicians reinforce this stereotype when they dismiss actions or statements by public figures as simply "public relations gestures." Related to this problem is the growing trend on the part of many organizations to use other names to describe the public relations function: public affairs, media relations, public information, and external relations, to name a few. This practice may reflect a hostility and suspicion encountered by public relations personnel within the organizations they serve. In contrast to a traditional-line department that can point to hard data to demonstrate its contributions to the growth and well-being of the organization, a public relations department almost never generates comparable data. Perhaps for this reason, public relations executives are rarely moved into top operating management positions of large organizations. More often, the public relations department is used to provide on-the-job sensitivity training to a high-potential executive who might benefit from a limited assignment to a department dealing with the "people problems" of business.

Despite its critics inside and outside the profession, public relations shows every indication of being a growth field in many countries. Clearly, many companies and institutions feel the need for this expertise in trying to reach audiences that are already saturated with an endless barrage of sophisticated messages from other sources. With the future characterized as an information society, many executives look to public relations for help in charting a reasonable course of action and policy in dealing with that future.

Bibliography. Robert O. Carlson, "Public Relations," *International Encyclopedia of Social Sciences*, Vol. 13, 1968 ed.; Scott M. Cutlip and Allen H. Center, *Effective Public Relations*, 6th ed., Englewood Cliffs, N.J., 1985; Philip Lesly, ed., *Lesly's Public Relations Handbook*, 3d ed., Englewood Cliffs, N.J., 1983.

ROBERT OSKAR CARLSON

PUBLIC SPEAKING

The role of public speaking can be traced as far back as the third century B.C.E. in Egypt and China. It has had different roles in different societies. Western scholars have argued that only a political democracy will produce public speaking of high quality in both content and artistry. With the death of the Roman Republic "a hush fell upon eloquence," Tacitus said. The Western tradition has its roots in Greek thought, Roman law, and eighteenth-century rationalism. But public speaking has been important in societies without this tradition.

China. China especially appears to have had a richly developed tradition of public speaking. Perhaps public speaking developed more fully in China because of the role of the sovereign. Chinese rulers ruled "by the mandate of heaven," and when there was widespread disapproval of the ruler it was assumed that the mandate had been revoked and revolution became a duty. Therefore rulers had to convince the people that their decisions were correct and consider disagreements with their views.

Three kinds of speeches were identified in ancient China. The first was charges to armies before a battle; the second was instructions, which the ruler gave to ministers or ministers gave to the ruler; the third was announcements, the persuasive statements the king gave to the court or the people.

This third form can be illustrated by three speeches given by Pwan-Kang of the Yin Dynasty, who reigned from 1401 to 1374 B.C.E. and who moved the capital from the north to the south bank of the Yellow River for protection from floods and marauding tribes. To stem the restlessness of people forced to leave homes and the burial grounds of their ancestors, he gave three speeches. The first was to his court and the others to the general population. Each speech was adapted to the particular audience and offered a mixture of authority assertion, ancient sources of wisdom, and conciliation. These speeches make clear that even a ruler of that era had to be persuasive. They also reflect the Chinese value of harmony with the ancient past. Chinese speeches used examples and analogies from the ancient authorities (including the *Book of History*, which is mostly a collection of speeches dating from the twenty-third century B.C.E.). Further, the speeches were depersonalized in established and ritualistic ways: the speaker's purpose was to clarify community meaning rather than to argue for a change. Even modern Chinese communicators have tended to reconcile Marxism with the traditional public speaking assumptions of ancient China. *See also* EAST ASIA, ANCIENT.

Figure 1. *(Public Speaking)* Speaker in Hyde Park, London, 1933. The Bettmann Archive/BBC Hulton.

India. Principles of public speaking in India can be traced to the rhetorical traditions of Hinduism, as embedded in its ancient literature. The role of the speaker was to reveal hidden truths that were part of the basic nature of the universe, not to argue for a particular position or to try to refute counterpositions offered by others.

The idea of universal truths was questioned later by those who argued over who knew the real truth. In the century of the birth of Buddha, debating seems to have become a prominent feature of Indian intellectual life (*see* FORENSICS). Heads of families met in community halls to debate both legislative and judicial matters. Brahmins; priests of Jainism, Hinduism, and Buddhism; and wandering skeptics debated before large audiences. The rigid caste system limited participation to the Brahmins, who were originally created "from the mouth of Pursha," the creator of the world. Only they could memorize the sacred texts or even listen to them.

Buddha (ca. 563–ca. 483 B.C.E.), whose first recorded speech was the "Sermon in the Deer Park," seems to have been a compelling speaker. He felt that effective oral presentation was crucial for the spread of doctrine and stressed to his disciples the arts of delivery. He used parables, questions, and humor that would be relevant to his immediate listeners.

Native Americans. European explorers to the New World commented on the oratorical skill of the natives they encountered—among them Malinche, a Tarascan woman who spoke several American Indian languages and who served as a diplomat for Cortés. Another was the San Juan Indian Pope, who led the Pueblo rebellion of the 1680s in what is now the southwestern United States, proclaiming that the Great Father had told him the foreign invaders must be driven out.

For many tribes of North American Indians, the council fire meeting was the setting for much of the ORATORY. A tribe's best orator was not necessarily a warrior or chief, but one who knew tribal history and traditions and was also a persuasive speaker. The content of an orator's speech was drawn from tribal experience, in consultation with other wise men of the tribe. Like speakers in some oriental societies, they did not so much argue as explain, using analogies to nature's ways. The use of METAPHOR was common, and brevity was admired.

The last half of the eighteenth century is considered the golden age of American Indian oratory. Joseph Brant (Mohawk), Tarhe (Wyandot), Little Turtle (Miami), Logan (Cayuga), Red Jacket and Cornplanter (Senecas), and Farmer's Brother were among the most accomplished public speakers. In the nineteenth century Sitting Bull, Red Cloud, and Spotted Tail (Sioux), Chief Joseph (Nez Percé), and Little Crow III were outstanding. Even today public speaking based on tribal history and nature is important to Native American life.

Ancient Greece. The distinguishing feature of the Western tradition of oratory (as opposed to the non-Western) was speeches that argued policy (*see* RHETORIC). The fourth century B.C.E., the golden age of Athens, produced great speakers like Lycurgus, Demosthenes, Hyperides, Aeschines, and Dinarchus, who all excelled in the debating of policy. Demosthenes' speeches against Philip of Macedon are models of Greek deliberative oratory. He was a master of both style and argument, and his delivery was called "thunder and lightning."

One of the most celebrated speakers of his day was Pericles, whose speech honoring warriors killed in the Peloponnesian War (431 B.C.E.) is recounted by Thucydides. It has served as a standard for commemorative orations, never equaled except perhaps by Abraham Lincoln's "Gettysburg Address." *See also* HELLENIC WORLD.

Ancient Rome. The period of Roman democracy produced many outstanding orators, but the greatest legal and deliberative speaker was Marcus Tullius CICERO (106–43 B.C.E.), who, in addition, was the author of several influential books on oratory. He was so impressive as a speaker that the Roman rhetorician Quintilian said, "Cicero is the name, not of a man, but of eloquence." He is best known for his combination of analytical argumentative skill and strong audience motivations. *See also* ROMAN EMPIRE.

The preaching tradition. When the Roman democracy ended, the significance and quality of deliberative and forensic speaking declined. But a new kind of public speaking—preaching—was to emerge from the Christianization of Europe. The two most important preachers in the New Testament were prime actors in that drama: Jesus and Paul.

A later period of great preaching came in the fourth and early fifth centuries, with Augustine, Tertullian, and Chrysostom. Although they considered the writings of ARISTOTLE and Cicero pagan documents, they drew heavily on classical rhetorical theory.

In the scholastic period from the eleventh to the fourteenth century such speakers as Peter the Hermit and Urban II were noted for their persuasive oratory on behalf of the Crusades (*see* CRUSADES, THE). The next two centuries are memorable for the preachers of the Reformation: Huldrych Zwingli, John Calvin, Hugh Latimer, and MARTIN LUTHER. Richard Baxter, who preached in the seventeenth century, is perhaps the most important name in English Puritanism. Puritan preaching is characterized by close attention to text and avoidance of excessive emotion. Perhaps the most significant Catholic orator of that time was Jacques-Bénigne Bossuet.

Methodist George Whitefield, who was influential

in both England and the United States, and Puritan Jonathan Edwards (United States) were dominant preachers of the eighteenth century. The circuit-riding preachers of the nineteenth century drew on the techniques of Edwards, ushering in a tradition of text-bound, free-will evangelism that can be traced through Charles Finney, Dwight L. Moody, Billy Sunday, Aimee Semple McPherson, and others to the radio and television evangelists of another day.

William Ellery Channing made the early nineteenth-century case for Unitarianism. Liberal Protestantism represented by the social gospel found its most important exponents in George Herron in the nineteenth century and Harry Emerson Fosdick in the twentieth. Bishop Fulton J. Sheen became the most important Catholic orator of the twentieth century through his humorous and stylistically elegant television sermons, which were viewed by millions. *See also* HOMILETICS; RELIGION; RELIGIOUS BROADCASTING.

England. The Glorious Revolution of 1688 inaugurated the British parliamentary tradition of debate, which has produced outstanding orators on a host of important issues such as taxation, empire, slavery, reform, and war. The late eighteenth century has been called the golden age of British political oratory. Its great speakers included William Pitt the elder and William Pitt the younger, Charles James Fox, Richard Sheridan, William Wilberforce, and Edmund Burke. Burke is of special note because his orations advocating conciliation with the American colonies served as student models of organization and argument for more than a century.

Thomas B. Macaulay, Benjamin Disraeli, and William Gladstone were the great parliamentary speakers of the nineteenth century. Probably the most widely heralded speaker of the twentieth century was Winston Churchill. As prime minister, rallying the British against Nazi Germany, he became famous for such phrases as "blood, sweat and tears." In the words of Edward R. Murrow, he "mobilized the English language and sent it into battle." His oratory was marked by an elegance of metaphor and rhythm. Nazi Germany, too, was spellbound by oratory, as Adolf Hitler used Germany's shame over the loss of World War I, the devastation of the Great Depression, and German racial myth to weave powerful appeals that combined scapegoating with master-race theories.

The United States. The most revered leaders of the young republic—George Washington, Thomas Jefferson, and Benjamin Franklin—are recognized for significant individual speeches such as Jefferson's "First Inaugural," which has been a model for subsequent presidents. However, the most famous orators of the revolution were people like James Otis, Samuel Adams, and Patrick Henry, who, despite the questionable authenticity of his "Give me liberty or give me death,"

was an acknowledged oratorical leader both of the revolution and of the debates over the Constitution.

What has been called the golden age of American oratory, the first half of the nineteenth century, was characterized by classical allusion and complex but balanced sentences. The most important speakers of the day were Daniel Webster, Henry Clay, and John C. Calhoun. Their debates on the slavery question, revolving around constitutional rather than moral grounds, culminated in the Compromise of 1850. Daniel Webster's fame as an orator rests not only on his role in Senate debates but also on his arguments before the U.S. Supreme Court and on ceremonial orations such as his "Bunker Hill Monument Address."

The early nineteenth century was also the period when professional lecturing first became organized and featured speakers like Ralph Waldo Emerson and Wendell Phillips. In 1826 Josiah Holbrook suggested community "lyceums" for the presentation of educational lectures. Professional lecturing was further developed by later movements such as Chautauqua. More moralistic in its tone, it featured such popular speeches as William Jennings Bryan's "Prince of Peace" and Russell Conwell's "Acres of Diamonds." Chautauqua lasted into the middle of the twentieth century.

Various nineteenth-century reform movements in the United States produced a host of celebrated public speakers. Many spoke for women's rights, including Lucretia Mott, Lucy Stone, Ernestine Rose, Elizabeth Cady Stanton, and especially Susan B. Anthony. These women exhibited a variety of styles, some quiet and reasoning, others condemnatory and abusive. Some argued that women were superior in conventional morality and would improve the conduct of political life; others argued for a radicalization of contemporary values by advocating such causes as free love. In the last half of the twentieth century the women's movement has dealt with a variety of issues, most notably the proposed Equal Rights Amendment.

The slavery issue and the Civil War produced notable speeches by William Lloyd Garrison, Wendell Phillips, and black orator Frederick Douglass. Unique among public speakers of the period was Lincoln, whose attempts to save the Union included careful reasoning, modest but precise style, and complex, even mystical thought. His "Cooper Union Address," the "Gettysburg Address," and his two inaugural addresses are considered masterpieces.

The role of black orators increased during the following century. They included Booker T. Washington, president of Tuskegee Institute, who stressed the need for education and meanwhile asked blacks to be patient, in contrast to the more militant W. E. B. Du Bois, who called for full social and economic equality and organized the movement that became the National Association for the Advancement of Colored People. Meanwhile, Marcus Garvey led a Back to Africa movement, arguing that any attempt to assimilate with whites was futile. In later decades this nonassimilation position was held by powerful speakers of the Nation of Islam, most notably Malcolm X, who used mordant humor to ridicule white separatist policies.

Probably the most influential speaker of the civil rights movement in the 1960s was Martin Luther King, Jr., who won broad support among both blacks and whites. His speaking reflected his origins in the black church. It was characterized by value-intensive language, repetition, metaphor, and alliteration with minimal argumentation. His speech "I Have a Dream" is regarded as a modern classic.

With late-nineteenth-century industrialization came serious social problems and the amassing of huge fortunes. Socialism became a serious political force under the leadership of the carefully reasoned public addresses of Eugene V. Debs and, in the twentieth century, Norman A. Thomas. Existing industrial conditions were defended by Andrew Carnegie and other social Darwinists like William Graham Sumner. The Populist-Progressive movements countered, led by some of the most effective public speakers in U.S. history. William Jennings Bryan used Christian analogy and spoke the value language of the Midwest; his best-known speech is "The Cross of Gold." Albert Jeremiah Beveridge used elaborate appeals to patriotism, destiny, and racial superiority to spearhead the wave of enthusiasm for imperialism.

Perhaps the most effective speaker of the period was President Theodore Roosevelt, who, in speeches like "The Man with the Muckrake," was able to speak for the capitalist system and reform at the same time. The scholarly and puritanical Woodrow Wilson was a careful but moralistic speaker for reform. After World War I he campaigned widely for a greater U.S. role in international affairs via membership in the League of Nations, but he was defeated in the Senate by such orators as Henry Cabot Lodge.

In the following decades, with the rise of the broadcast media, new oratorical practices were added. The transition was epitomized by Franklin D. Roosevelt, who, in the midst of the Great Depression, began his term of office by telling a nationwide radio audience, "The only thing we have to fear is fear itself." His subsequent "fireside chats," delivered from a private room and heard by millions in their private homes, brought a new atmosphere of intimacy to a public function and has been used by every president and many other politicians since that time. The assembled crowd and the podium began to lose their central role. The age would still have orators, like Gamal Abdel Nasser of Egypt, Fidel Castro of Cuba, and many others, but even they were heard by most

of their people via broadcasts. With the ascendancy of television, national leaders throughout the world increasingly addressed their people in a conversational mode by means of the tube and microphone. Traditional oratory still flourished, but a new tradition of conversational public speaking was in the making.

Bibliography. William N. Brigance (Vols. 1 and 2) and Marie K. Hochmuth [Nichols] (Vol. 3), *A History and Criticism of American Public Address*, New York, 1943, 1955; Edwin C. Dargan, *A History of Preaching*, 2 vols., New York, 1905, 1912, reprint 1968; John F. Dobson, *The Greek Orators*, London, 1919; James L. Golden and Richard D. Rieke, *The Rhetoric of Black America*, Columbus, Ohio, 1971; Chauncey A. Goodrich, *Select British Eloquence*, New York, 1853; Richard C. Jebb, *The Attic Orators from Antiphon to Isaeas*, 2 vols., London, 1876, reprint New York, 1962; Louis T. Jones, *Aboriginal American Oratory*, Los Angeles, 1965; James H. McBath and Walter R. Fisher, eds., *British Public Addresses: 1828–1960*, Boston, 1971; Robert T. Oliver, *Communication and Culture in Ancient India and China*, Syracuse, N.Y., 1971; idem, *History of Public Speaking in America*, Boston, 1965.

MALCOLM O. SILLARS

PUBLISHING

This topic is discussed in two sections:
1. History of Publishing
2. Publishing Industry

1. HISTORY OF PUBLISHING

Broadly defined as the selection, reproduction, and circulation of written materials, publishing preceded the advent of PRINTING technology. However, as a discrete and specialized activity, it appeared only with the invention of printing and the beginnings of trade in the printed BOOK.

The introduction of movable type in Europe in fifteenth-century Germany and its spread to other countries made possible the publication of a wider range of works—among them scriptures, broadsides, pamphlets, maps, music, ballads, almanacs, newspapers, dictionaries, books, encyclopedias, periodicals, and "ephemera," including catalogs and posters. Each product, whether concerned with information or with recreation, has had its own history within a developing pattern of communications, shaped not only by technology but by economic, social, and political forces, of which the rise of LITERACY has been the most important. *See* CARTOGRAPHY; ENCYCLOPEDIA; NEWSPAPER: HISTORY; PAMPHLET; SCRIPTURE.

Figure 1. *(Publishing—History of Publishing)* Printers' marks. *(a)* Aldus Manutius, Italy, early sixteenth century, *(b)* Espasa-Calpe, S.A., Mexico, twentieth century, *(c)* Thames and Hudson, London, twentieth century.

The different units concerned with the preparation and distribution of printed publications have their own histories as well. They continue to represent a wide range in type and scale of operations and draw on traditional craft skills as well as on modern technology. Although there are now large integrated publishing concerns, some multinational, which publish different kinds of products (books, magazines, newspapers) and which through ELECTRONIC PUBLISHING have themselves become part of bigger media complexes, smaller specialized units continue to operate alongside them. In addition, there are traditional concerns, notably university presses, with a far longer continuous history than most other institutions in the field of communications.

While by its nature the whole activity of publishing involves an approach to the public or to specialized publics, some of the most interesting aspects of the history of publishing can be discovered only in still largely unexplored publishers' archives. The fact that more cataloging of archives is being carried out and that the whole subject of the history of the publishing industry (see section 2, below) is now being explored with increasing sophistication is in part a by-product of communications changes in the late twentieth century. The changing world of the book is being reexamined in the light of the history of film and television. Strictly bibliographical studies are now supplemented both by biographical and literary studies concerned with particular authors and by more general economic and sociological studies. The political dimension also is receiving more attention.

In the organizational history of the printed book, specialization in production preceded specialization in distribution, and it was not until the early nine-teenth century that the distinctive role of the publisher was defined. Usually, according to the more recent definition, publishers were neither printers nor bookbinders. Nor were they general wholesale or retail booksellers. Their function was to arrange the production of books bearing their own imprints (usually at their own expense, though not necessarily of their own selection) and the subsequent distribution. Between the sixteenth and nineteenth centuries economic risks had passed from the printer to the bookseller and eventually from the bookseller to the publisher. There had also been a shift from control by authority to COPYRIGHT in the joint interests of publisher and author, although it was not until the nineteenth century that a system of payment to authors in the form of royalties on sales was established.

In most countries the chronology of change was not determined solely by market forces. The entrepreneurial role of the publisher took time to establish itself, and both patronage and control played a significant role in the handling of what was often considered to be a dangerous new mode of communication, whether old or new titles were being published. The authority of state, church, and university was enforced, although attempts were made to escape the CENSORSHIP of these institutions by means of guild organization and later through underground publishing.

Early history. In China, where printing from wooden blocks had been invented between the sixth and ninth centuries and from movable type during the eleventh century, the profit motive counted for little, and there was strong official initiative in determining what was printed and published. For this reason, the effects of

Neapolis

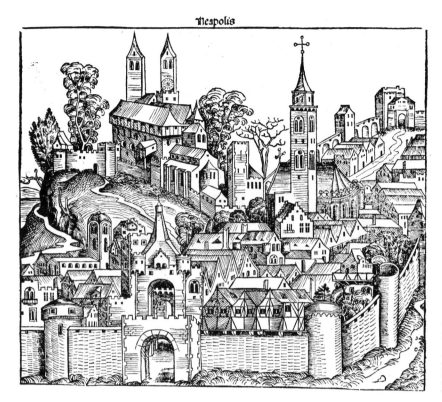

Figure 2. *(Publishing—History of Publishing)* "Neapolis"; a detail from Hartman Schedel's *Liber chronicarum* ("The Nuremberg Chronicle"), published by Anton Koberger, 1493. Rare Books and Manuscripts Division, The New York Public Library. Astor, Lenox and Tilden Foundations.

printing on the scope and scale of publishing were severely restricted. In Europe, by contrast, the spread of printing encouraged commerce, sharpened religious and political controversy, favored the development of national languages, and played a key part in the scientific revolution of the seventeenth century. Yet there were controls there also. The Vatican decreed in 1543 that no book might be printed or sold without permission from the church, and the first list of banned books, the *Index*, was drawn up in 1559; while in Protestant England, where the Tudors feared subversive as well as heretical books, the chartered Stationers Company, founded in 1403, was given control of a licensing system that lasted almost continuously until 1694, when prepublication censorship was abolished. France instituted an even tighter system of control in 1618, the Chambre des Syndicats, which included two royal nominees. Control had interesting by-products, however. In England it influenced both the growth of copyright and the development of libraries; in 1610 the Stationers Company undertook to give Thomas Bodley's eight-year-old library in Oxford a copy of every book printed in England, a privilege later extended to a number of other libraries by act of Parliament. *See* LIBRARY.

Before the rise of printing, books had been distributed in Europe by stationers, controlled by the universities. As a result, book copying, including the copying of secular texts, had become a sizable activity in a number of cities. With the invention of printing there was a huge increase in the number of titles and sales and a significant change in book format. Before 1500 there were at least thirty-five thousand book titles in western Europe, and 20 million copies had been printed, two-thirds of them in German cities, among which Frankfurt and Cologne were preeminent. Many of them made their way to readers in other countries. So, too, did printing and publishing techniques. The trade was innovative and competitive, and one entrepreneur, Johann Rynmann of Augsburg, who died in 1522, published nearly two hundred books without printing any of them.

From the start, publishers of printed books, like their readers, were concerned with the books' appearance, design, and TYPOGRAPHY as well as with their content. Early printer-publishers, operating within the increasingly diverse cultures, included Anton Koberger of Nuremberg, whose books crossed many frontiers; the Estienne (Stephanus) family in France, who were to publish books—and dictionaries—without a break for five generations; Christophe Plantin, first of Paris and then of Antwerp; and later in the sixteenth century another Dutch publisher, Louis Elzevir, who like Plantin founded a flourishing family business. In Italy, where German printers had established themselves in the 1460s, book format was radically changed in 1501 when Aldus Manutius

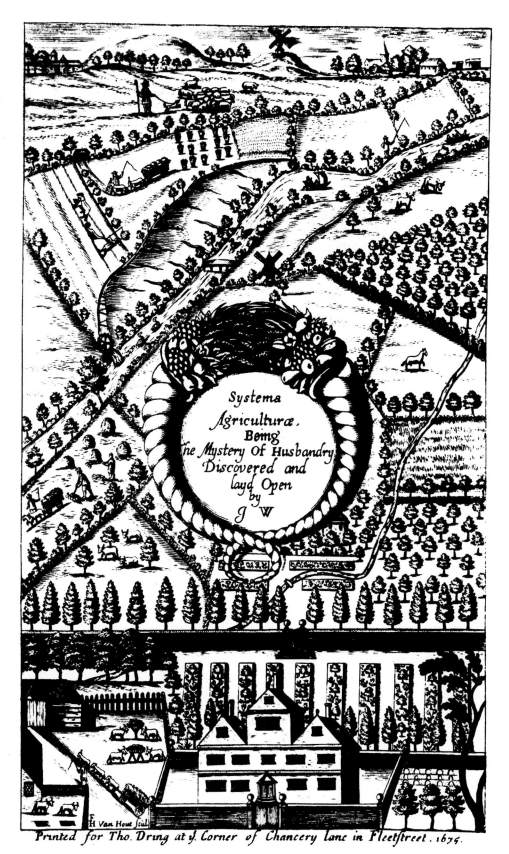

Printed for Tho. Dring at y. Corner of Chancery lane in Fleetstreet. 1675.

Figure 3. *(Publishing—History of Publishing)* Title page from a book on agriculture, 1675. Engraved by Frederik van Hove. From Alexander Nesbitt, ed., *200 Decorative Title-Pages,* New York: Dover Publications Inc., 1964, plate 109.

designed books in manageable sizes, replacing huge, awkward codexes. The first book printed in the New World was produced in Mexico in 1538 and concerned Christian doctrine. Its printer, Juan Pablos, had been sent over by a printer-publisher of Seville, Juan Cromberger. Further north Stephen Daye and his sons produced their first book, a book of psalms, in Massachusetts in 1640.

Eighteenth century. In the eighteenth century, an age when the reading public, including a coffeehouse public and a circulating-library public, grew in size and sophistication, the novel developed as a literary form in a culture that from the beginning of the century had attached interest and prestige to belles lettres. There were financial consequences. Enterprising booksellers benefited from rising demand, and some of the publishing businesses founded then survived into the twentieth century, among them the Weidmann Company in Leipzig and the Longmans Company in England. One of the eighteenth-century Weidmann partners, Philipp Erasmus Reich, is said to have invented the net price agreement in the book trade and to have pioneered the idea of a booksellers' association. In England, where there were far-reaching commercial developments, the first copyright act in the world was passed in 1709. It was an attempt to limit both privilege and piracy in an effort to reconcile the interests of printers, publishers (depending financially on their MONOPOLY of their most profitable books), authors (increasingly conscious of their standing in society), and the public. It was the first in a long series of such enactments.

Before the royalty system of rewarding authors, one way of financing the publication of a book was to divide expenses among a number of booksellers who were styled partners; the system had first been introduced in fifteenth-century England. Another was to appeal to the public for subscriptions, a device also said to have been devised in the fifteenth century by the English printer WILLIAM CAXTON. The *Encyclopaedia Britannica* in 1768 was financed in this way. It was a characteristic product of its time, a compendium of knowledge to be set alongside the French *Encyclopédie* (*see* DIDEROT, DENIS), the circulation of which—and its influence in France and overseas—has been carefully plotted by Robert Darnton in a pioneering study of publishing as communication.

By the end of the eighteenth century a considerable measure of freedom to publish had been won in most countries. In England the licensing system was not revived after 1694, and while security of state was still treated as a paramount interest, the freedom of the press began to be decreed a bulwark of liberty. Even control in the name of security of state was difficult as the volume of published material increased; although in 1783 Lord Chief Justice Mans-

field observed in a case about seditious LIBEL that "the liberty of the press consists in printing without any previous license subject to consequences of the law," he added that "the licentiousness of the press is Pandora's box, the source of every evil." In the United States, where from the start there was no formal censorship, there were laws of libel, and Mansfield's complaint remained relevant in the twentieth century. In France, where until the Revolution a forceful publisher like Charles-Joseph Panckoucke had served the regime of censorship, the National Assembly of 1789 stated unequivocally that "the free communication of thought and opinion is one of the most precious rights of man: every citizen may therefore speak, write and print freely." Although freedom was short-lived, French publishing took on a new shape in the nineteenth century, when two great publishing firms—Hachette in 1826 and Larousse in 1851—were founded.

Nineteenth century. The biggest changes in the nineteenth century were technological, in the use of paper and illustrations as well as in printing and binding, and in commercial organization. Before the advent of electrical power there came the iron press and the age of steam. Coinciding with the development of mass literacy, made possible by public schooling, and the end of "taxes on knowledge," these changes raised output and lowered costs—dramatically in the case of paper. There were economic considerations independent of the new technology, however. For example, price regulation of books, foreshadowed in the eighteenth century, was established in Germany in 1887 under the auspices of a trade organization founded in 1825, and in Britain in 1901 under the auspices of a publishers' association founded in 1896. Copyright legislation, too, was extended after bitter experience of book piracy, particularly in the United States, where Harper, Scribner's, Dutton, and Little, Brown had entered the publishing business. The first international system of copyright was initiated by the Berne Convention of 1885. Some countries remain outside this agreement.

There have been variations in the speed of change in different countries, as there have been in the crucial relationships between publishers, authors, and readers as set out both in contracts and in advertisements. The development of the publishing pattern was part of a bigger communications pattern, including the coming of the railway and the telegraph, regular ocean transport, the daily newspaper, mass retailing, and the public library. There was a greater demand for both information and diversion. Some publishers tried to satisfy both; others specialized. "Railway literature" was designed for diversion. It included the novel as well as the MAGAZINE. Textbooks provided one major source of information,

Figure 4. *(Publishing—History of Publishing)* Twentieth-century paperbacks. *(Top left)* Gustave Flaubert, *L'éducation sentimentale,* Paris: Gallimard, 1965; *(top right)* Eugène Ionesco, *Rhinoceros,* New York, 1960, courtesy of Grove Press, a division of Wheatland Corp.; *(bottom left)* H. A. Murena, *El nombre secreto,* Caracas, © Monte Avila Editores C.A., 1969; *(bottom right)* Louisa May Alcott, *Little Women,* New York: Bantam Books, Inc., 1983.

but many other kinds of informational materials were published as well. A number of authors began to employ literary agents from the 1870s onward, and some of them organized themselves in bodies like the British Authors' Society (1884) and the Authors League of America (1912). Meanwhile, a publishers' scouting system developed in the United States to discover manuscripts that might not otherwise have been noticed.

Twentieth century. Twentieth-century book publishing continued to reflect economic, social, political, technological, and cultural change, uneven though these changes were in different parts of the world. There were alternating booms and slumps in total sales in countries with private publishing businesses; competition, often fierce, between firms; changes in management styles; and the establishment of publishing consortia. The book club was a major social innovation with economic and cultural implications. The expansion of education, including higher education, at times greatly extended the market for all kinds of books. A paperback revolution, beginning in the 1930s but spreading through many countries in the 1950s and 1960s, led to a chain of developments in printing, photography, and computerization. It has sometimes been suggested that in an electronic age the book is dead, but what has happened rather is that books changed their appearance—and in some cases their uses. The largest modern publishing houses developed individual departments dealing with editing (an increasingly specialized function), manufacturing, accounting, and marketing—often by highly sophisticated promotion methods—as the rhythms of publishing became noticeably more hectic during the second half of the century.

See also ADVERTISING; AUTHORSHIP; GOVERNMENT REGULATION.

Bibliography. Richard D. Altick, *The English Common Reader: A Social History of the Mass Reading Public,* Chicago, 1957; James Barnes, *Free Trade in Books: A Study of the London Book Trade since 1800,* Oxford, 1964; Cyprian Blagden, *The Stationers' Company: A History, 1403–1599,* Cambridge, Mass., 1960, reprint Stanford, Calif., 1970; George Boyce, James Curran, and Pauline Wingate, eds., *Newspaper History from the Seventeenth Century to the Present Day,* London, 1978; G. A. Cranfield, *The Press and Society: From Caxton to Northcliffe,* New York, 1978; Robert Darnton, *The Business of Enlightenment: A Publishing History of the Encyclopédie, 1775–1800,* Cambridge, Mass., 1979; Robert Escarpit, *Le littéraire et le social: Elements pour une sociologie de la littérature,* Paris, 1970; Lucien Febvre and Henri-Jean Martin, *L'apparition du livre* (The Coming of the Book), Paris, 1958; idem, *Livre et société dans la France du XVIIIe siècle,* 2 vols., Paris, 1965, 1970 (Vol.

1 ed. by G. Bolleme, J. Ehrard, F. Furet, and D. Roche); John Lough, *Writer and Public in France from the Middle Ages to the Present Day,* Oxford, 1978; Martin Lowry, *The World of Aldus Manutius,* Ithaca, N.Y., 1979; Henri-Jean Martin, *Livre, pouvoirs et société à Paris au XVIIe siècle,* 2 vols., Geneva, 1969; Robin Myers and Michael Harris, eds., *Development of the English Book Trade, 1700–1899,* Oxford, 1981; Lucy Maynard Salmon, *The Newspaper and the Historian,* New York, 1923, reprint 1976; Anthony Smith, *The Newspaper: An International History,* London, 1979; Susan R. Suleiman and Inge Crosman, *The Reader in the Text,* Princeton, N.J., 1980; Suzanne Tucoo-Chala, *Charles-Joseph Panckoucke et la Librairie Française, 1736–1798,* Paris, 1977.

ASA BRIGGS

2. PUBLISHING INDUSTRY

A network of organizations that interact regularly in the selection, production, and distribution of printed material. Particularly prominent are the newspaper (*see* NEWSPAPER: HISTORY), MAGAZINE, and BOOK publishing industries. Another important publishing sector in many countries is the direct mail industry (*see* DIRECT RESPONSE MARKETING). Also significant has been the development of ELECTRONIC PUBLISHING, in some ways an industry unto itself but with strong connections to the others.

The roots of publishing as an industrial activity predate even JOHANNES GUTENBERG's invention of the PRINTING press. Still, publishing remained almost a handicraft activity until about the nineteenth century; that is, one organization was often the publisher, printer, and seller of the reading matter, and that organization often comprised only a few people. Only in nineteenth-century Western society did the book publisher become distinct from the printer and the distributor. Moreover, each of these roles involved in getting material from the writer to a growing number of readers began to require the efforts of large and complex organizations. See section 1, above.

Structure

The structure of an industry typically refers to the pattern of interdependent behaviors—the roles—that characterize organizations making up the industry (*see* ORGANIZATIONAL COMMUNICATION). For example, a particular book publishing industry's structure might be found in the activities that printing firms, publishing firms, law firms, authors' guilds, wholesalers, retailers, libraries (*see* LIBRARY), and other entities carry out with one another.

The influences on the organizations that make up a publishing industry inevitably relate to the provision of resources to those organizations. People, supplies, permissions, information, services, money—these are the material and symbolic resources that organizations involved in publishing must continually obtain from their environment (the other organizations in the industry and the society at large) if they are to survive. But the need for scarce resources faces all industries in any society. Decisions must be made about the amount and nature of resources that ought to go to publishing as opposed to other sectors. The activities of the people who constitute the organizations must be directed toward ensuring that they have the resources they need to carry out their work. That involves trying to adapt to the demands of their environment as well as trying to shape the demands of the environment to fit their needs.

A broad spectrum of resource-related considerations influences the structure of a publishing industry and, along with it, the amount and nature of published materials available in a society. One obvious prerequisite for a publishing industry is authors whose work can be selected for publication (*see* AUTHORSHIP) and a READING public that can support them (*see* LITERACY). Another is a set of spoken and unspoken values within the society about the benefits and drawbacks of certain approaches to the public dissemination of knowledge. A third is paper and the machines on which the selected material can be prepared, produced, and reproduced. A fourth prerequisite is the presence of distribution networks that can allow the producers to disseminate material efficiently to appropriate markets.

Illiteracy as a barrier to publishing is relatively unimportant in the developed world though still very much a concern in developing countries (see Figure 1). But illiteracy is usually only part of a wide complex of difficulties that publishers meet in Africa, Australasia (Oceania), and much of Asia and Latin America. The result is a startling disparity between the publishing output of the world's nations (see Table 1). The situation of the book industry in Africa is indicative. Potential book publishers on that continent typically confront strong oral traditions (*see* ORAL CULTURE) that militate against literacy and the desire to read, hundreds of different languages and dialects that have no written counterparts (*see* AFRICA, PRECOLONIAL), scarcity of skilled book-industry personnel, and a shortage of well-equipped modern printing establishments. They also find that elite African writers and readers have become dependent on the European languages for EDUCATION, commerce, administration, and intellectual communication. These elites tend to import most of their books and even turn to large transnational book publishers when they want to write books. *See* AFRICA, TWENTIETH CENTURY; DEVELOPMENT COMMUNICATION.

The amount and extent of indigenous publishing

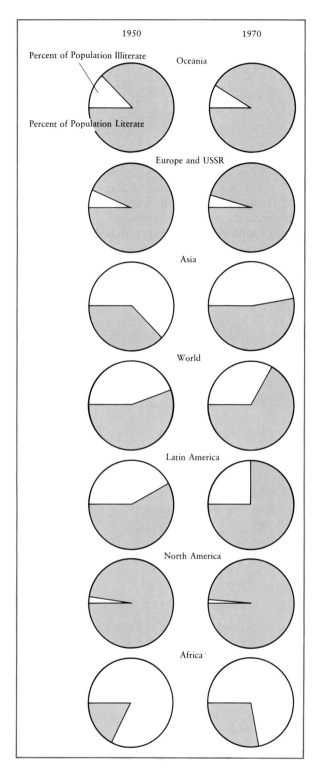

Figure 1. *(Publishing—Publishing Industry)* Changes in world illiteracy, 1950–1970. Redrawn after United Nations, *World Statistics in Brief*, 1978.

Table 1. Publishing around the World

Percentage Distribution of Population				
	1955	1965	1975	1982
Africa	10.8	12.2	13.1	10.9
North America	8.8	8.4	7.7	5.5
Latin America	9.0	9.8	10.6	8.3
Asia	41.1	42.2	44.2	58.3
Europe (incl. USSR)	29.5	26.7	23.7	16.5
Oceania	0.7	0.7	0.7	0.5

Percentage Distribution of Book Production				
	1955	1965	1975	1982
Africa	1.1	1.6	1.9	1.8
North America	5.2	13.6	16.2	15.3
Latin America	4.1	4.5	5.1	5.9
Asia	20.1	14.3	15.3	20.4
Europe (incl. USSR)	69.1	64.7	60.0	55.1
Oceania	0.4	1.2	1.6	1.5

Number and Circulation of Daily Newspapers (1982)			
	Number	Circulation (in millions)	Circulation (per 1,000 inhab.)
Africa	160	9	18
North America	1,830	68	269
Latin America	1,200	33	86
Asia	2,500	164	61
Europe (incl. USSR)	2,420	235	311
Oceania	110	6	264

Production and Consumption of Newsprint (1982, in metric tons)		
	Production	Consumption
Africa	0.3	0.3
North America	12.7	11.3
Latin America	0.5	1.7
Asia	4.3	5.4
Europe (incl. USSR)	7.2	7.4
Oceania	0.7	0.8

Production and Consumption of Other Printing and Writing Paper (1982, in metric tons)		
	Production	Consumption
Africa	0.3	0.6
North America	15.4	15.3
Latin America	1.8	1.9
Asia	8.2	8.4
Europe (incl. USSR)	16.1	14.6
Oceania	0.3	0.3

Source: Adapted from *Statistical Yearbook*, 1984 (Paris, UNESCO). For caveats and fullest interpretation of data, see source.

that takes place in developing countries with such problems can be modified somewhat by several factors: government policies on state educational publishing, the development of local library services and purchasing power, and government policies toward capitalist, state-run, and foreign publishing. When the state decides to enter book publishing, it nearly always assumes a MONOPOLY on primary textbooks (*see* TEXTBOOK), often for ideological reasons. When state publishing is not emphasized, schoolbook production often goes to transnational textbook companies. During the past several years government ministries of education in large developing countries have forced those companies to make their books conform to specific national guidelines. Still, the strong hold by the transnationals on textbooks and technical volumes has meant that indigenous firms have had to mine other domains—for example, popular and light local FICTION, advice books, and study guides.

Governments control key resources: permission to publish, protection from foreign competition, tax benefits that might improve cash flow, employment laws affecting the availability of personnel, and laws encouraging or discouraging monopolies or other trade restraints. Government laws that grant permission to publish can be said to operate on three levels: structural, technical, and content. *See* GOVERNMENT REGULATION.

The structural level involves rulings that dictate actual organizational processes and relationships in a publishing industry. An example was the 1945 decision by the U.S. Supreme Court striking down an Associated Press bylaw that permitted the wire service to grant exclusive service to a newspaper for a particular area. At a technical level rulings relate to standards of a mechanical, electronic, or otherwise scientific nature that organizations in a publishing industry must uphold. Postal edicts relating to weight, size, and construction represent technical regulations that affect the operations of book, newspaper, and magazine publishers as well as mail-order advertisers (*see* POSTAL SERVICE). The third level of regulation, the content level, involves specific messages and message policies. These may range from direct prohibitions on certain kinds of ideas to broader rulings on subjects such as COPYRIGHT, obscenity, PORNOGRAPHY, and deceptive ADVERTISING. Government regulations in these areas often spark societal controversies. *See* CENSORSHIP.

Government policies are among the factors that encourage or discourage certain niches in publishing. The concept of a niche refers to a distinct combination of resources that organizational leaders find capable of supporting their organization in specific goals and activities. So, for example, in Western capitalist countries some publishers find that they can make money turning out religious books; others turn a profit creating elementary and high school textbooks; others do it by emphasizing reference books. Each area is a different niche. Generally, when one publishing firm perceives a niche, attempts to exploit it, and thrives, other firms enter to compete in the niche until no additional organizations find entry profitable.

A publisher may exploit only one niche or may try to mine other market segments as well. In the United States and Europe the years since World War II have seen the growth of huge media conglomerates such as Bertlesmann (based in the Federal Republic of Germany), Rizzoli (based in Italy), Pearson and Thomson (based in England), and Gulf and Western, Time Inc., and CBS (based in the United States). These companies are involved in a wide variety of print and nonprint media.

Some critics charge that their activities have had an unhealthy influence on publishing. In the book industry, for example, the contention is that conglomerate takeovers of the major trade firms have led to unrealistically high profit expectations and, as a result, to the concentration by these firms on the most popular authors to the detriment of talented but lesser-known writers. Further, the critics contend that these activities are leading to a lack of diversity in mainstream publishing and to a subordination of print to other media. Publishing companies are said to judge book material as part of a larger project involving lucrative subsidiary rights—a theatrical film, a television movie, a magazine or newspaper series, a videocassette, and the like. Other observers argue that book publishing is highly diversified despite the growth of conglomerates and cross-media projects.

The specific way in which a publishing organization approaches its niche depends on three major factors: the firm's tradition, its executives' conceptions of their audience, and the needs of the major patron organizations with which they interact. Patron organizations make purchases of published materials before those products reach the public. As such, they provide publishing firms with the cash flow that is most directly responsible for their survival. In the case of U.S. newspapers and magazines, the major patrons are advertisers; they purchase space in the hope that readers will buy their products. In the book industry patrons vary widely depending on the kind of book. The trade book segment's patrons are general bookstores that purchase the publishers' titles with the aim of retailing them profitably. Elementary-school text companies, on the other hand, may look to school boards as their patrons, and college text companies may look to universities and UNIVERSITY bookstores.

Selection activities. The relationship between publisher and patron often greatly influences the material to be selected. Evidence suggests that it helps set the boundaries on the kinds of people who are the targets of the material, the frequency at which the publisher releases the material to the public, and the amount it costs to produce and release the material. In book publishing, for example, a trade publisher's interactions with bookstores will likely influence the number of titles it puts out each season (the length of its list) as well as the kinds of titles it puts out (the nature of its list). In the magazine, newspaper, and direct mail industries, as in other advertiser-driven industries, the producer-patron dealings have given rise to a market research industry (*see* CONSUMER RESEARCH) that feeds both parties data with which to negotiate their relationship.

Once the executives of a publishing organization have a conception of the mandates in their niche, they must search for material with which to find success in that area. Different kinds of publishing operations search in different ways depending on the executives' understanding of their marketplace. Book companies and many magazines typically contract with writers on a free-lance basis, often by using literary agents as efficient intermediaries. That allows the publishers the freedom to hire the best people of the moment without long-term commitment and payroll. Newspapers, on the other hand, tend to hire reporters on an extended basis, largely because the daily mandate to "cover the news" requires the presence of a predictable group of creators at all times.

Production activities. Editors guide writers and select manuscripts based on a conception of the published work and the technological process that will create it. Decisions about the look of the published product are guided by competitive considerations, aesthetic considerations, and costs. The process of preparing the product necessarily goes hand in hand with the selection process. For example, a children's book editor involved in producing a book jointly with a publishing firm in another country (an activity called international copublishing) might caution the illustrator that the drawings must be appropriate to both the U.S. version and its French translation. Similarly, a magazine editor, knowing how much space is left in an issue, might caution a free-lance writer not to exceed five hundred words in a proposed article.

Even if a manuscript is solicited, it may be rejected. And even if it is accepted, it will go through a gauntlet of editorial work before being printed. Innovations by major companies in linking word processing, storing, retrieving, and printing capabilities of computers to publishing situations have resulted in increasingly closer ties between the editorial and printing phases of the publishing process. In magazine and newspaper companies computer-run production systems have substantially increased the efficiency of editorial departments. Editors can call up and reshape articles at a moment's notice. They and their writers can also work closer to printing and distribution deadlines than ever before. And they can experiment with changes in the graphic designs of their periodicals much more easily than in the past. *See* COMPUTER: IMPACT—IMPACT ON THE WORK FORCE; GRAPHIC REPRODUCTION.

Distribution activities. A major publisher is primarily distinguished from a minor one by distribution clout—the ability to support the dissemination of a large number of printed copies to a large number of outlets quickly and efficiently. The specifics of distribution clout vary by industry and with the niche that a company has chosen within the industry. In the direct marketing industry, distribution concerns revolve mainly around postal and TELEPHONE rates. In the local daily newspaper industry, in which the newspaper firms themselves typically handle circulation, the mandate is to produce tens of thousands— even hundreds of thousands—of copies for efficient delivery to points throughout the target area. Doing that in a city on a daily basis requires a printing-to-delivery system that is hugely expensive. It makes starting a newspaper to compete with existing ones very difficult, if not prohibitive.

Several distribution approaches characterize different segments of the book and magazine industries. When it comes to getting books to stores and libraries, book publishers sell to the outlets directly at a discount and/or they work through large wholesalers, often called jobbers. Mass-market publishing has grown remarkably in the United States and Europe since World War II, largely on the strength of broad-based wholesaling. The approach is to format books in such a way that they can be carried not only in trade outlets but also in places that used to sell only magazines: newsstands, drugstores, discount chain stores, and supermarkets. The low price of these mass-market (mostly paperback) books has not been related primarily to the softcover, pocket-sized format that has characterized them, but rather to the huge numbers of copies printed for each title—numbers that were thought justified because of the wide access to outlets of the magazine jobbers that distribute them.

Bibliography. Phillip G. Altbach and Sheila McVey, eds., *Perspectives on Publishing*, Lexington, Mass., 1976; John P. Dessauer, *Book Publishing: What It Is, What It Does*, New York, 1974; S. I. A. Kotei, *The Book Today in Africa*, Paris, 1981; Alan M. Meckler, *Micropublishing*, Westport, Conn., 1982; E. Lloyd Sommerlad, *The Press in Developing Countries*, Sydney, 1966; Joseph Turow, *Getting Books to Children: An Exploration of Publisher-Market Relations*, Chicago, 1979; idem, *Media Industries: The Production of News and Entertainment*, New York, 1984;

Thomas Whiteside, *The Blockbuster Complex*, Middleton, Conn., 1981.

JOSEPH G. TUROW

PUBLISHING, ELECTRONIC. *See* ELECTRONIC PUBLISHING.

PULITZER, JOSEPH (1847–1911)

U.S. newspaper publisher. Joseph Pulitzer's great innovative paper, the New York *World*, carried JAMES GORDON BENNETT's formula of sex and politics to new heights. Pulitzer died just before his creation became one of the most respected newspapers in the United States. Like his newspaper, Pulitzer was a strange, complex personality, contradictory and eccentric.

Born in Makó, Hungary, he left home at seventeen and tried in vain to enlist in one of Europe's armies, but none would accept him. He was described then as "about six feet two and a half inches tall, ungainly in appearance, awkward in movement, lacking entirely in the art of human relations." In Hamburg Pulitzer found a recruiting agent for the U.S. Union Army who got a bounty of five hundred dollars for every man he could enlist as a substitute in the draft;

Figure 1. *(Pulitzer, Joseph)* Cartoon of Joseph Pulitzer, ridiculing his absenteeism from the U.S. Congress to concentrate on "The World." The Bettmann Archive, Inc.

he signed Pulitzer up at once. Jumping ship in Boston Harbor, Pulitzer enlisted in the First New York Cavalry but found army life intolerable. His most prominent characteristic was the incessant asking of questions, and he despised anyone who withheld information—journalistic qualities that led to numerous fights and eventual discharge.

After the Civil War Pulitzer migrated to Saint Louis, where he worked on the *Westliche Post*, the German-language daily, and became the city's leading reporter. Eventually elected to the Missouri House of Representatives, Pulitzer could have had a career in politics (he also served briefly in the U.S. Congress, 1885–1886), but instead he bought two newspapers and combined them into the *St. Louis Post-Dispatch*, still one of North America's best newspapers. Crusading was Pulitzer's journalistic stock-in-trade, and it made him rich enough to buy the New York *World* from financier Jay Gould in 1883. He launched it on a remarkable career with a ringing statement of journalistic idealism that is still quoted. Crusades for liberal causes resounded from the editorial page, but the news columns purveyed the kind of sex, scandal, and corruption that Bennett had exploited earlier. In short, the front page was for the laborer, the editorial page for the idealistic intellectual. The marked contrast did not entirely please either class. Yet Pulitzer felt compelled to carry sex and crime to even greater extremes when WILLIAM RANDOLPH HEARST came to New York in 1896 and began a direct rivalry with his *Journal*.

In this epic confrontation Pulitzer displayed extraordinary courage. Suffering for years from a steadily worsening neurological condition, he was half blind and so sensitive to noise that he could live only in a soundproof apartment. Eventually this sensitivity led him to spend most of his time on his luxurious yacht, editing the *World* from wherever he happened to be with incredible tenacity and intelligence. He fought Hearst ferociously at his own game, particularly in their historic battle for circulation during the Spanish-American War, but at a ruinous cost in both money and health. Hearst's genius for mass journalism was the greater, and Pulitzer's determination to lead that market proved to be a mistake. Nevertheless, he contributed to the development of the press by sending FICTION writer Stephen Crane (1871–1900) to cover the war in Cuba, introducing a kind of personalized, impressionistic reporting of men under fire that flowered in World War II with the work of Ernie Pyle (1900–1945) and others.

After the war Pulitzer withdrew from the dubious contest with Hearst, leaving the working-class audience to his rival and concentrating on making the *World* a great liberal, democratic organ. It spoke courageously and passionately for free speech, personal liberty, and constitutional government. It fought hard against privilege and what Pulitzer called "the money power."

Like Bennett before him and E. W. SCRIPPS after him, Pulitzer died on his yacht. He left behind a newspaper that became perhaps the best ever published in New York before it failed in 1930, losing its identity and becoming the *New York World-Telegram*, a Scripps-Howard paper. Pulitzer's other legacies are the two institutions founded initially by his will, the Pulitzer Prizes in U.S. journalism and literature and the Graduate School of Journalism at Columbia University, whose *World* Room, decorated with materials from his old paper, embraces his memory.

See also NEWSPAPER: HISTORY; NEWSPAPER: TRENDS—TRENDS IN NORTH AMERICA.

JOHN TEBBEL

PUPPETRY

The art of designing, constructing, and operating puppets and marionettes, usually in theatrical PERFORMANCE. A puppet (from Latin *pupa*, "doll") is an articulated figure controlled by external means. Most puppets represent human or animal forms, though they may also give movement to normally inanimate objects or abstract shapes. While puppets can be life-size or larger, most are considerably smaller than their operators.

Puppets are classified according to their means of control. Hand or glove puppets, of the familiar Punch-and-Judy type, are controlled directly by the puppeteer's hand inside a cloth sleeve that forms the figure's body. Rod puppets are controlled from below by slender rods. Shadow puppets are two-dimensional cutout figures, also controlled by rods, that are held against a backlit screen to project black-and-white or tinted shadows. Marionettes are controlled from above by strings. The name ("little Mary") is believed to have been derived from the practice of using puppets in medieval church plays, though this may be merely fanciful. Various combinations of control methods are also possible.

Early history. Puppetry seems to be at least as old as the THEATER itself and to have shared the DRAMA's early connections with magic and RELIGION. The Greek historian Herodotus (fifth century B.C.E.) records the ancient Egyptian practice of displaying moving figures of the gods in holy processions. Hopi Indians used large articulated figures of the sacred snake in their corn ceremonies. Much of the shadow-puppet art of East Asia has a firm basis in religion (*see* EAST ASIA, ANCIENT).

Like the drama, puppetry soon broke free of its religious associations to become a performing art in its own right. It has been suggested that the objects displayed to the prisoners in PLATO's famous Allegory of the Cave are glove puppets, already familiar from popular entertainment. And in the late classical period a puppeteer (*neurospastes,* "string-twister") is reported as performing in the theater of Dionysus in Athens. Medieval examples are numerous for various European countries, and a fresh infusion of vitality came from Italy in the sixteenth and seventeenth centuries. Eastern puppetry represents an even more ancient tradition, and in the Western world the art has continued with vigor to the present day.

Though the history of puppetry has been continuous, its reputation, particularly in the West, has been less consistent, varying widely according to period, social class, and country. At most times and places it enjoyed considerable popularity as a folk art or, as the English director Peter Brook has called it, "rough theatre." Various cultures have created their own puppet heroes or antiheroes, differing in their names and national characteristics but sharing an irreverent, even anarchic spirit that delighted in the flouting of taboos and the affronting of contemporary mores. Expressive of popular resentment against moral, legal, and political sanctions, these figures, being nonhuman, were comparatively safe from CENSORSHIP or reprisal and traditionally enjoyed a freedom to criticize far greater than that permitted to the human theater.

Eastern traditions and trends. It is in East Asia that the kinship of puppetry and serious drama is most clearly attested. This is particularly true in Japan, where from the seventeenth century on the two arts have been ranked side by side.

The Japanese puppet theater, Bunraku, has several distinctive features. Its figures, exquisitely crafted and standing some four feet high, are manipulated by a combination of hand, rod, and trigger control. Each puppet has three operators. The master controls the trunk, the right arm, and the head—particularly the eyebrows, which convey a wide range of expressions. The first assistant controls the left arm, and the second the feet. They work, after long apprenticeship, as a closely knit team. All are visible during the performance; though the assistants wear black, the masters often wear bright kimonos. All are, however, by convention invisible. (See Figures 1 and 2.)

Bunraku shares many of the characteristics of its human counterparts, the Buddhist-inspired No and the melodramatic Kabuki. Musical accompaniment underlies the words and movement. A chanter narrates the action and recites the speeches. Many scripts have been taken directly from the human theater, and vice versa: Chikamatsu Monzaemon, "the Japanese Shakespeare," wrote with equal facility for both forms. Costumes, properties, ACTING styles, and staging devices have been similarly interchanged, and the massive complex of the Japanese National Theater contains a smaller auditorium for the Bunraku players.

Other oriental countries have preferred the shadow show (hence the name *ombres chinoises* for such performances in Europe). The Chinese tradition, in particular, suggests an early religious connection between shadow puppets and the spirits of the dead. Here the figures are some twelve inches high and made from animal skin worked until translucent and delicately colored. In modern times plastic has been substituted. As in Japan there is a close affinity between the puppet and the human actor. Plots have commonly derived from the Peking OPERA, although the showmen permitted themselves considerable latitude in interpretation, and the puppet tradition was

Figure 1. *(Puppetry)* Bunraku; the puppet and three operators. From Barbara Adachi, *The Voices and Hands of Bunraku,* Tokyo, New York, and San Francisco: Kodansha International, 1978, p. 31.

oral rather than literary (*see* ORAL CULTURE; ORAL POETRY). Staging, too, followed the principles of the larger theaters, using one item of furniture to suggest a whole environment.

Java also cultivated a traditional shadow show, *Wayang kulit*, drawing on material from the two great Hindu epics, Ramayana and Mahabharata (see Figure 3). Another form cultivated there was *Wayang golek*, rod puppets, which in turn inspired *Wayang topeng*, human actors wearing masks and miming to the declamations of a chanter (*see* MASK; MIME). Clearly, those cultures that have cultivated masked and nonrealistic acting have been more sympathetic to the puppet theater than those in which the realistic style is paramount.

European traditions. The English-speaking world has provided a famous example in Mr. Punch. His origins are obscure. Suggestions include Pulcinella (see Figure 4), a favorite clown of the Italian commedia dell'arte, and—less probably—Pontius Pilate as portrayed in the religious drama of the MIDDLE AGES. Hook-nosed and humpbacked, Punch is a delightful villain. In the traditional scripts he defies every standard imposed by morality and society. He mocks, beats, and kills his wife, Judy, and murders their baby; he kills several other figures, including an interfering neighbor and the policeman sent to arrest him; and when finally caught he hangs the executioner in his own noose. In some versions Punch even escapes the ultimate punishment by killing the Devil himself.

Anthropologists and drama theorists have seen in Punch a direct descendant of the RITUAL combat of

Figure 2. *(Puppetry)* Bunraku; a puppet repairer. From Barbara Adachi, *Backstage at Bunraku*, New York and Tokyo: Weatherhill, 1985, Figure 39.

Figure 3. *(Puppetry)* Shadow puppets from Java: Petrok, Yudistira, Demi Srikandi, and Burisrawa. Reproduced by courtesy of the Trustees of the British Museum.

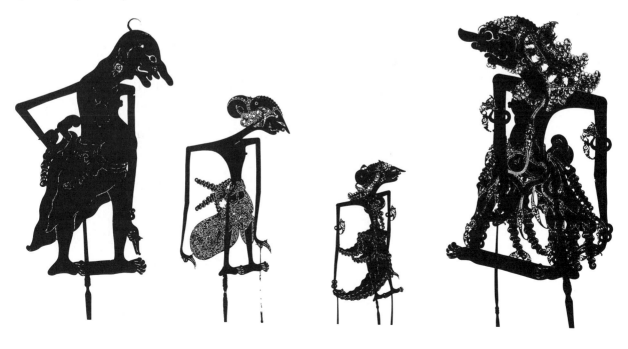

Figure 4. *(Puppetry)*   Pulcinella. The Bettmann Archive, Inc.

preindustrial society. As entertainment the Punch-and-Judy shows reached their apogee of popularity in the nineteenth and early twentieth centuries. Until the outbreak of World War II Punch booths could be seen on every English seaside beach. Their scripts, in the manner of the commedia dell'arte itself, were highly topical, introducing into the traditional plot characters and allusions of the day. (See Figure 5.)

France produced a similar figure in Guignol, who made his first appearance in Lyons around the end of the eighteenth century and was given local color as a representative of the people. A Lyonnaise silk-worker, he was shrewd and scornful of false pretenses, like Punch an unruly figure who, as puppet, could say and do things impermissible on the human stage. Also like Punch, his career was marked by mayhem—hence the term *Grand Guignol* for horror plays in the larger theaters.

Petrushka performed a similar function in Russia, as did Kasperl and Hanswurst in Germany. In the Mediterranean world the Greco-Turkish culture evolved Karagöz, a shadow puppet whose fantastic and often obscene adventures served as an outlet for opposition to the restrictions of Turkish officialdom (see Figure 6). Karagöz is a man of the people, poverty-stricken and always hungry. His plays are

Figure 5. *(Puppetry)*   A Punch-and-Judy show on Bournemouth Beach, 1954. The Bettmann Archive/BBC Hulton.

Figure 6. *(Puppetry)* Hadjivat, the jinn, and Karagöz. From Hellmut Ritter, *Karagös, Türkische Schatten-spiele.* Hannover: Orient-Buchhand-lung Heinz Lafaire, 1924, Figures 16, 17, and 18.

full of slapstick, and his favorite weapon is the watering can. These shows could once be viewed, on stretched sheets lit by oil lamps, throughout the Greek countryside. Only a few examples survive, in more sophisticated form, in major cities. Elsewhere, however, the liberty of expression has endured. Adolf Hitler's regime in Germany, which encouraged pup-

petry as a native folk art, found itself forced to tolerate the puppets' outspoken political satire. In Fascist Italy also the puppet theater took liberties that would have had human actors arrested.

These popular manifestations have often intertwined with, or inspired, more serious dramatic works. It has been argued on impressive scholarly authority

Figure 7. *(Puppetry)* Jim Henson, *The Great Muppet Caper,* 1981. The Museum of Modern Art/Film Stills Archive. Courtesy of Henson Associates Inc.

that the Karagöz show has affinities with the comedies written by Aristophanes for Athenian audiences in the fifth century B.C.E. Alternatively, it has been suggested that the shadow play derives from the Greek new comedy of the Alexandrian age. This form was carried to Asia Minor by Greek performers, was translated there into puppet form, and returned with the Turkish conquerors in the fifteenth century. In the Western world Johann Wolfgang von Goethe's massive two-part poetic drama *Faust* (1813, 1831) is said to have been inspired by a local puppet show. Alfred Jarry's bizarre and anarchic *Ubu roi* (1896), claimed as the earliest manifestation of the theater of the absurd, derived from the author's boyhood experiments with puppets, particularly the Lyonnaise Guignol. Igor Stravinsky's *Petrushka* (1911), created for the Diaghilev Ballet, raised the Russian folk figure to the level of high art. And one of George Bernard Shaw's last plays, *Shakes versus Shav,* was written for marionettes.

Trends in the West. In spite of the general denigration of puppetry in the West, theorists and practitioners have always been eager to proclaim its aesthetic virtues. Often they have been influenced by the East. Heinrich von Kleist (1777–1811) wrote an essay in praise of the form. George Sand (1804–1876) wrote for hand puppets. The symbolist playwright Maurice Maeterlinck (1862–1949) wrote for marionettes. Their common understanding was that for certain purposes puppets surpass human actors because they transcend the trivial and individual. Like the mask, they have the power to abstract, or convey the essence of an idea. Edward Gordon Craig (1872–1966) devised a theory of the human actor as *Übermarionette* totally susceptible to directorial control. In the U.S. production of Stravinsky's *Oedipus Rex* the characters were puppets of superhuman size controlled by operators within. A related example is provided by the Bread and Puppet Theater, which employs huge cartoonlike figures to illustrate political and social themes.

Despite these examples, serious uses of puppetry in the Western world have been comparatively few. England in the eighteenth century enjoyed a thriving tradition in which the puppet theater served as an adjunct to its live counterpart, taking successful London plays through the provinces in miniature form. By the late nineteenth century, however, puppetry was thought of largely in terms of children's entertainment. The same has been true in the United States, where puppeteers have aimed increasingly at juvenile audiences and have been more concerned with mechanical dexterity than the quality of the material presented. Professional companies have subordinated artistic values to commercial necessity. While

Waldo Lanchester's company, based for many years in Stratford-upon-Avon, England, included an early Italian opera in its repertoire, the traditional circus proved more successful on tour. The so-called puppet revival in the United States in the 1930s, linked to Remo Bufano and Paul McPharlin, was largely local in its impact and had no great effect on the state of the art. More recently Jim Henson's work, first with the Muppet figures for television and subsequently with his imaginative films, has enlarged the popular audience and suggested more sophisticated uses of the art in association with electronic media (see Figure 7).

Europe has developed a more durable artistic tradition. In Austria the Salzburg Marionette Theater offers exquisite productions of Mozart operas performed to Salzburg Festival recordings and uses the magic of the medium to illuminate, particularly, *The Magic Flute.* Germany has similar companies. In France, Yves Joly developed a school of nonfigurative puppetry, animating familiar household objects, like umbrellas, to illustrate sociological or satirical themes.

A distinctive form indigenous to Sicily has long combined literary qualities with strong popular appeal. The material, drawn from heroic verse sagas of the RENAISSANCE, deals with tales of chivalry and romance, crusades and battles, divided into installments that may run on for months. The figures, several feet high and extremely heavy in order to create a massive clanking effect, are supported from above by a thick metal rod passing through the top of the head. Stringing is minimal; the sword arm is the most mobile part of the body. Like the Greco-Turkish Karagöz, the heroic Sicilian marionettes could once be seen throughout the country and even accompanied emigrants to the Italian quarter of New York. Performances, though still traditional family affairs, have greatly decreased and are centered chiefly in Palermo.

The status of puppetry as a serious theatrical art is highly developed in the Soviet Union. Moscow has its State Puppet Theater, whose presiding genius, Serge Obraztsov, toured on several occasions in the West. It offers productions for children and for adults with equal acclaim.

See also COMEDY; FOLKLORE; MUSIC PERFORMANCE; MUSIC THEATER; TRAGEDY.

Bibliography. Olive Blackham, *Shadow Puppets,* London and New York, 1960; Donald Keene, *Bunraku: The Art of the Japanese Puppet Theater,* Tokyo, 1965; Charles Magnin, *Histoire des marionettes en Europe depuis l'antiquité jusqu'à nos jours,* 2d ed., Paris, 1862.

PETER D. ARNOTT

Q

(ki*ū*), the seventeenth letter of the modern and the sixteenth of the ancient Roman alphabet, was in the latter an adoption of the Ϙ (κόππα, *koppa*) of some of the early Greek alphabets. The Phœnician letter from which this was derived had the forms Ϙ, Φ, ϙ, and was used as the sign for the deeper or more guttural of the two *k*-sounds which exist in the Semitic tongues (Hebrew ק, Arabic ڧ).

R

(ā.ɪ), the eighteenth letter of the modern and seventeenth of the ancient Roman alphabet, is derived through early Greek Ꝛ, Ᵽ from the Phœnician ꟼ, representing the twentieth letter of the early Semitic alphabet. In general the character denotes an open voiced consonant in the formation of which the point of the tongue approaches the palate a little way behind the teeth. . . .

QUIZ SHOW

Quiz programs and game shows are among the most ubiquitous of broadcast genres, popular worldwide on both RADIO and television (*see* TELEVISION HISTORY). They range from simple spelling matches and school quizzes broadcast on small stations and based on traditional formats to network productions involving elaborate rituals and offering such enticing prizes as automobiles, stereos, and vacation trips to exotic places. While formats and stakes vary widely, the basic appeal of all such programs is the same: they are contests in which results hang in the balance. Contestants are in most cases ordinary people with whom those at home can identify. A rooting interest develops; quiz addicts are not mere viewers and listeners but avid participants.

Quiz and game shows differ from almost all other broadcast entertainments in that outcomes are not predetermined. Questions and instructions may be scripted, but the main events are not. As in sports, the tensions, risks, fumblings, uncertainties, successes, and failures are real. Those at home sense this and their reactions thus differ from reactions to fiction; no suspension of disbelief is required. The reality gives a special edge to the experience. A quiz viewer who has identified with a winning contestant may feel a sense of personal achievement and triumph not experienced by a drama watcher.

The anger that erupted in the United States during the late 1950s when it was revealed that contestants on some top-rated quizzes, notably "The $64,000 Question" and "21," had been given answers and had even rehearsed was a measure of the extent to which viewers had experienced the programs as reality. When what had been perceived as real turned out to be fiction, they felt duped and betrayed. Even President Dwight D. Eisenhower felt a need to comment on the event. It was, he said, a "terrible thing to do to the American people." The U.S. Congress reacted with legislation outlawing quiz fixing, and the networks developed new supervisory procedures.

The nature of a viewer's participation in quiz programs can be complex. Viewers may identify with specific contestants (their representatives in the action) and at the same time measure themselves against those contestants. There is no disgrace for the viewer in missing a question the contestant proves able to answer; it is a victory for "our side." On the other hand, there may be special satisfaction in knowing an answer the contestant missed. A viewer's sense of self, of personal achievements or failures in life, and awareness of the contestant's status, occupation, and educational level (such details are commonly brought out in preliminary interviews) may all color the viewer's experience and the self-measuring process. And in moments of success there is always the sense that,

Figure 1. *(Quiz Show)* Charles Van Doren, a contestant on "The $64,000 Question," who was later discovered to have been given answers in advance. The Bettmann Archive, Inc.

given the chance, the viewer might be the one on the screen. Quiz shows can also serve an even wider purpose. In the late 1950s, with the personal involvement of Prime Minister David Ben-Gurion, Israel Radio initiated a yearly Bible Quiz. The quiz became a major national event, its winners became famous overnight, and the program played an obvious role in rooting Israeli national identity in the biblical past. In the 1960s quiz programs were introduced into South Vietnam by Armed Forces Radio and Television.

With the perennial success of quizzes and games, producers have ceaselessly experimented with variations and new combinations of the essential elements. In the quest for high ratings, celebrities have sometimes been a part of the strategy, often teamed with ordinary contestants. Celebrities have also been enlisted as masters of ceremonies. In a quiz series hosted by Groucho Marx on U.S. radio and television, "You Bet Your Life," his anarchic preliminary interviews with contestants became high spots of the series. In several series, panels of the famous or not so famous have been faced with novel challenges. On "What's My Line" panel members were confronted with a person unknown to them and had the task of guess-

Figure 2. *(Quiz Show)* "Wheel of Fortune," with hostess Vanna White. Courtesy of Merv Griffin Enterprises.

Figure 3. *(Quiz Show)* "Blankety Blank," hosted by Terry Wogan. Copyright BBC (Enterprises) 1986.

ing, through a limited number of questions, his or her occupation. Each program presented several such challenges, the final one being to guess the identity of a masked mystery celebrity. This simple formula proved so involving that the series ran for many years in both the United States and Great Britain. Britain has launched many quiz successes of its own, such as "Brains Trust" and "Mastermind." Italy has been a devotee of elaborate game shows.

Television quiz and game programs, because of their spontaneous nature, have not proved suitable for translation via dubbing or subtitling. Such series have consequently not become export commodities along the lines represented by drama series. However, successful series have in some cases been reconstituted abroad under license from their originators. Programs known in the United States as "Password," "Match Game," "The Price Is Right," and "Sale of the Century" have appeared in diverse languages in various parts of the world, using the original formulas and procedures but with local participants. Such transplants have met with varying success, but in some cases they have proven more popular than the original series. For example, in the 1960s "Call My Bluff" had only a brief run in the United States but has been telecast for more than twenty years on the BBC in Great Britain.

After the quiz scandals of the 1950s, large prizes were for a time avoided in the United States, but after confidence returned the value of prizes began to mount again, apparently heightening the sense of drama for the home viewer and stimulating participant applications. The growing readiness of manufacturers to donate prize merchandise became a factor in the escalation. Series like "The Price Is Right" and "Wheel of Fortune" became not only popular sponsored programs but also effective merchandising instruments for the donors, whose products were presented as the epitome of the good life, the ultimate reward.

MARK GOODSON

RADIO

Medium transmitting SOUND via electromagnetic waves. Evolving during the first quarter of the twentieth century amid disputes over its proper use, it became during the second quarter of the century the most ubiquitous mass communication medium ever known. Its offerings ranged from ENTERTAINMENT to news, EDUCATION, ADVERTISING, and POLITICAL COMMUNICATION. During this period the technology of television was developed largely within the radio industry, and after midcentury television rapidly replaced radio as the dominant mass medium in many countries (see TELEVISION HISTORY). Yet radio, with a somewhat changed role, remained a worldwide presence and a powerful social influence.

Development

The existence of electromagnetic waves was theorized by Scottish physicist JAMES MAXWELL in 1867 and clearly demonstrated in 1888 by German physicist Heinrich Hertz. The nature of these "Hertzian waves," as they were known for a time, caused astonishment. That they could pierce night, fog, mountains, and walls suggested, in the words of British physicist Sir William Crookes, "the bewildering possibility of telegraph without wires, posts, cables or any of our present costly appliances." Many scientists began to labor to achieve this possibility, including Édouard Branly in France, Adolphus Slaby in Germany, and Aleksandr Popov in Russia. In 1895

in Italy GUGLIELMO MARCONI succeeded in sending messages over large distances using the code of dots and dashes developed by SAMUEL F. B. MORSE for TELEGRAPHY. When Italian authorities showed no interest in the achievement, Marconi took his little black box to England, where its value to the vast British empire was readily perceived. Substantial funds were raised to create the Marconi Company. When it held demonstrations for the British navy off the southern coast of England in 1897, major naval and military powers sent observers. The equipping of all kinds of ships with "wireless" for communication with one another as well as with shore points proceeded rapidly in the following years. Wireless telegraphy was precisely what navies needed to coordinate large maneuvers, and they considered it their special instrument, bringing to the seas the advantages that wired TELEPHONE systems had brought to land.

If navies were content with dots and dashes, others were not. Among them was the Canadian-born electrical engineer REGINALD FESSENDEN, who showed that continuous radio waves could be used as a carrier for voice and music. He set up his own company to refine the process and to market equipment and by Christmas Eve of 1906 was ready for a historic demonstration. In various parts of the Atlantic Ocean wireless operators, listening on earphones for dots and dashes, heard a short speech sent by Fessenden from Brant Rock, Massachusetts, followed by phonograph music. He also sang, read from the Bible, and closed with a Christmas greeting. A number of wireless operators on ships of the United Fruit Company, alerted in advance, heard the transmissions. This company was already finding wireless valuable for coordinating the activities of scattered banana plantations and directing ships to the most profitable markets, and it later established its own wireless manufacturing subsidiary. The Fessenden version of wireless acquired the name *radiotelephony*, or *radio*, although the term *wireless* persisted.

Radio stirred wide curiosity and excitement. Although in many countries the military considered it their domain, activity originated from numerous other sources. Particularly in the United States the air was soon filled with a confusion of code, chatter, and music from amateur experimenters ("hams"), researchers at universities and electrical companies, independent inventors, and army and navy transmissions—all interfering with one another to some extent. There was little agreement on the goals of the experimentation. The hams looked on it as an exciting hobby, the exploration of a new domain. The military looked on radio, as on Marconi's wireless, as a point-to-point communication device invaluable except for one drawback: people could eavesdrop. Still others, like Fessenden, considered this drawback to be radio's greatest asset. This view was espoused by U.S. inventor LEE DE FOREST, whose Audion vacuum tube, patented in 1907, brought radio transmission to a new level of clarity and became the basis for the electronics industry. De Forest felt there should be stations sending out continuous music, news, and other matter for the inspiration and delight of whoever might tune in. This was called *broadcasting*, originally an agricultural term meaning to scatter seed over a broad area rather than sowing in designated places. All this seemed visionary to most people—interesting, but hardly useful. There was, after all, no way to make it pay.

With the advent of World War I the broadcasting idea seemed evanescent. In the warring nations the airwaves suddenly became exclusively military terrain. When the United States entered the war in 1917 lone inventors like De Forest were ruled off the air, and thousands of ham operators, ordered to seal their equipment, were not even allowed to listen in. Major electrical companies such as General Electric, Westinghouse, Western Electric (a subsidiary of the American Telephone and Telegraph Company, AT&T), and American Marconi (a subsidiary of the Marconi Company of Britain) received huge government orders for electronic gear for ships, planes, tanks, and trenches. It was very secret. The public now heard no more about radio except through magazine FICTION describing its use in ESPIONAGE and dramatic wartime rescues. The broadcasting notion appeared to be dead. *See also* CRYPTOLOGY.

Postwar Resurgence

As the war ended, government contracts abruptly ceased, and electronic assembly lines lay idle. As countless hams unsealed their equipment and resumed their activities, Westinghouse and, later, other companies gave new thought to the broadcasting idea. If they were to establish stations offering schedules of music and other programming, would the public buy listening equipment of the sort the companies had manufactured for the military—compact and easy to operate? Might the revenue from such sales support broadcasting activity and earn a good profit as well? Approached in this way, broadcasting seemed not quite so visionary.

Station KDKA in Pittsburgh, launched by Westinghouse in time to broadcast returns for the 1920 U.S. presidential ELECTION, along with other stations launched immediately afterward in various cities by Westinghouse and others, put this idea to the test with great success. Crowds lined up at radio counters appearing in department stores. The U.S. Department of Commerce, seeking to avoid SPECTRUM chaos, began to issue broadcasting licenses and assign wavelengths. In many cities amateur installations emerged from attics and garages and became radio "stations."

On both sides of the Atlantic the age of broadcasting had begun, but it developed along two separate lines.

In the United States the radio boom was a free-for-all from the start. Four dominant companies—General Electric, Westinghouse, AT&T, and United Fruit—had taken over American Marconi and turned it into a new entity, the Radio Corporation of America (RCA). This takeover, buying out British interests, was instigated by the U.S. Navy, which wanted the industry in U.S. hands. Aside from this corporate group many other interests were plunging into broadcasting: newspapers, hotels, universities, department stores, and churches (*see* RELIGIOUS BROADCASTING). Broadcasting seemed at first an inexpensive prestige device. As costs mounted, however, a new entrant came on the scene: the SPONSOR. In 1922 the sale of blocks of time, to be used as a sponsor wished, became a feature of U.S. broadcasting, first over separate stations and then over hookups. This arrangement attracted increasing numbers of corporations and led to the formation of the National Broadcasting Company (NBC) in 1926 as an RCA subsidiary and the rise of the Columbia Broadcasting System (CBS) in 1928 under WILLIAM PALEY, a member of a cigar-manufacturing family that had already found radio an effective promotional tool. Many major manufacturers began purchasing nationwide hookups, embarking on ventures that would transform advertising and PUBLIC RELATIONS. Pondering what kinds of programming might best serve their merchandising needs or corporate images, sponsors arrived at a range of solutions, including the SOAP OPERA, the QUIZ SHOW, symphonic music, jazz, masterpieces of literature, astrological forecasts, military bands, SPORTS events, COMEDY, barbershop quartets, and crime DRAMA. Advertising agencies became the producers or supervisors of most sponsored network programs as well as of the COMMERCIALS within them. Commercials were discreet and formal at first but grew longer and more insistent. Merchandising offers proliferated. Startling contrasts characterized the schedule. Because time was money, the pace was fast and often frenetic.

Events in Europe took a different turn. Because of the close proximity of foreign borders, and because of the past identification of radio with military and espionage activity, most European governments considered it essential to take control of radio broadcasting (*see* GOVERNMENT REGULATION). They also saw its future role as resembling those of institutions such as the SCHOOL, LIBRARY, or MUSEUM, serving to enlighten the public and therefore meriting government support—perhaps funded in part through license fees levied on set owners. Such ideas prevailed in most European countries and in their colonies overseas (*see* COLONIZATION). There was as yet no powerful advertising force pressing for a different

Figure 1. *(Radio)* Broadcasting the presidential returns, KDKA, Pittsburgh, Pa., 1920. State Historical Society of Wisconsin, Erik Barnouw Collection/The New York Public Library.

system because the war had devastated much European business and industry.

In England, starting in 1922, radio was entrusted to the British Broadcasting Company (later, Corporation), or BBC. The corporation was financed through license fees collected by the government, but it was sheltered from government control and other pressures by a charter that gave it considerable independence. Under JOHN REITH, who headed the BBC for its first sixteen years, that independence was resolutely defended. Policies were based not on what listeners might say they wanted but on what the BBC decided they needed, because "few knew what they wanted, fewer what they needed." The BBC therefore spent little on PUBLIC OPINION surveys. The idea of catering to public tastes repelled Reith; it was a betrayal of the task of leadership, which called for unified control and a focus on public service.

Reith's BBC and European systems similarly organized as centralized services developed programming different in tone from most programming in the United States—or in Latin America, where radio tended to follow the U.S. pattern (*see* LATIN AMERICA, TWENTIETH CENTURY). The European tone was staid, judicious, more leisurely. Its content was informative and dedicated to cultural values.

Although their tones differed, there were parallels between U.S. and European broadcasting. The same genres took root in Europe and the United States and then elsewhere (*see* GENRE). Eventually the two traditions began to influence each other. Radio almost everywhere had developed a powerful hold. The 1929 stock-market crash and the worldwide depression of the 1930s had a shattering impact on THEATER, vaudeville, and, for a time, the motion picture industry

(*see* MOTION PICTURES). Artists displaced by these media gravitated into radio, which could send an increasingly richer assortment of offerings into homes.

Growth of the Medium

In the late 1920s there was a sudden interest in the use of shortwaves, partly as a result of experimentation by ham operators. When broadcasting was officially launched in the United States in 1920, using medium-wave channels, amateurs were assigned to a shortwave band, which at the time was considered a sort of banishment. But they soon discovered the extraordinary if sometimes erratic ability of shortwaves to span vast distances. This finding led in two directions. The colonial powers of Europe established shortwave radio stations to broadcast to their overseas possessions; in Asia, Japan did likewise. At the same time, shortwaves began to be used as a relay device to inject special international pickups into domestic broadcasting. Radio began to be a significant news medium. During the 1930s MOHANDAS GANDHI, Benito Mussolini, Adolf Hitler, Franklin D. Roosevelt, and many other leaders were heard internationally via shortwave relays. Growing political tensions speeded this development. Major broadcasting systems established foreign representatives in key locations. Edward R. Murrow went to Europe for CBS in a position that evolved into a major news role. As war came, Murrow was responsible for an innovation that became a news standard: the news roundup, with such colleagues as William L. Shirer and Eric Sevareid reporting from various European capitals.

While radio grew as a news medium it also grew

as a dramatic medium. SERIAL drama had proved an early addiction, but longer forms emulating stage drama were slower to evolve. Modern stage drama proved to be an unsatisfactory model. Only when radio writers began to think of radio as a freer NARRATIVE medium did it develop its own excitement. In radio the imagination was the stage, and nothing was impossible. The narrator, often an intrusion in the theater, was welcome in radio. The use of SOUND EFFECTS became a radio specialty, as in "Lights Out," a long-running Arch Oboler horror series, and "The Shadow," in which ORSON WELLES for a time played the central role. More surprising was the sudden interest of British poet laureate John Masefield and U.S. poet Archibald MacLeish, who both proclaimed radio an ideal medium for POETRY. MacLeish's verse play *The Fall of the City* (1937), inspired by the Nazi threat to Europe, was performed on both CBS and the BBC and each time created a sensation. In his preface to the play's published edition MacLeish asked poets if they were really satisfied with writing "thin little books to lie on the front parlor tables." Through radio the poet might address the many rather than the few.

Radio's audience continued to grow. One-third of all U.S. homes had radio in 1930, a proportion that by 1935 had increased to two-thirds. By 1938, when Welles and his Mercury Theatre company dramatized H. G. Wells's *The War of the Worlds,* radio was acknowledged to be a powerful social influence. Yet the panic that ensued when thousands of listeners reacted to the broadcast as if it were news of an actual Martian invasion prompted increased concern over the effects of radio and vividly demonstrated that the medium was a fertile area for social science research (*see* COMMUNICATIONS RESEARCH: ORIGINS AND DEVELOPMENT).

Feud. The evolution of radio witnessed a bitter struggle in the United States between two pioneers of the industry that was to have great repercussions. DAVID SARNOFF had been a telegrapher at American Marconi and an early advocate of broadcasting. He had risen to the top of RCA, which had become the dominant power of the industry to an extent that constantly raised MONOPOLY issues. EDWIN H. ARMSTRONG had started as a ham hobbyist and became a major inventor. In the 1920s Sarnoff suggested that Armstrong devise "a little black box to eliminate static." In March 1933 Armstrong invited Sarnoff to his basement laboratory at Columbia University to witness the result. What Sarnoff found was not a black box but a roomful of equipment that represented an entirely new radio system: frequency modulation (FM). Its startlingly alive, static-free quality was clearly a vast improvement over the existing system, which was based on amplitude modulation (AM). But Sarnoff's goal was the introduction of commercial television, and RCA's profits from radio were being poured into the achievement of that goal. Armstrong's FM, if introduced as a rival to AM, seemed certain to bring an upheaval in radio and to endanger the radio profits Sarnoff counted on for his television plans. Besides, FM required more space in the spectrum, space that Sarnoff wanted for television. Armstrong became aware during the following months that Sarnoff was attempting to block what Armstrong considered his major life achievement. The resulting battle was fought out over many years in patent offices, Federal Communications Commission (FCC) hearings, and courtrooms. In the end both television and FM, in their final form, were held back until the postwar era, when FM not only acquired separate channels but also became the sound element of television. But the bitter struggle precipitated both Armstrong's suicide and lawsuits that, decades later, were all won by the Armstrong estate.

U.S. regulation. Radio's early years brought demands for regulation from differing directions. The newspaper press viewed radio as a threat to its circulation and advertising revenues. Educators decried the influence of advertising and big business on radio programming. Throughout the 1920s, as the number of radio stations grew, technical problems became acute. The increasing interference among stations prompted some (in defiance of their Department of Commerce channel assignments) to shift their dial positions, thus escalating the chaos. As a climax to the confusion a court ruling declared that the Department of Commerce did not have the power to license stations. This finally caused Congress to pass the Radio Act of 1927, creating a five-member board, the Federal Radio Commission (FRC), to regulate the industry and set STANDARDS. At first the FRC was meant to be temporary and to be abolished when the problems were solved, but it was made permanent. After his inauguration President Roosevelt, in order to make more of his own appointments to the commission and to bring telephone and broadcasting under the same jurisdiction, sought a new regulatory act. The Communications Act of 1934, essentially a redrafting of the 1927 Radio Act with only minor changes, established the Federal Communications Commission, which has regulated U.S. broadcasting since then under the resilient rubric of serving "the public interest, convenience, and necessity."

Wartime radio. Radio expanded rapidly during and just after World War II—before television came to the forefront. Soon after the United States entered the war the U.S. War Department decided to organize a network to serve its troops. By 1944 it had some eight hundred outlets operating out of Quonset huts near overseas army camps, in trucks moving behind troops, or through sound systems in battleships or airfields. Each of these outlets received a weekly shipment of sixteen-inch disk recordings representing some thirty hours of programming, largely U.S. network programs from which the commercials had been deleted. Each outlet was authorized to add local programming of its own, and each received through shortwave relay supplementary programming such as coverage of baseball and football games and elections. There was also a special series entitled "Command Performance," based on requests from the field and featuring HOLLYWOOD talent. All this was seen as a powerful morale factor for U.S. troops, but each outlet also had an eavesdropping audience. Such broadcasting was a logical focus for espionage. At the same time, listeners in many countries were acquiring a taste for the U.S. radio comedy styles of such performers as Bob Hope, Bing Crosby, and Jack Benny, all heard frequently on the armed forces system.

Other warring nations put radio to intensive use. In some areas, such as Africa, transmission facilities were expanded in order to counter enemy broadcasts and to rally the population to wartime purposes. Radio personalities such as Axis Sally in Europe and Tokyo Rose in the Pacific attempted to influence Allied troops with a mixture of popular dance music and PROPAGANDA. And the assumed effectiveness of Nazi radio propaganda, under the aegis of JOSEPH GOEBBELS, was a major impetus in much of the MASS COMMUNICATIONS RESEARCH conducted in the United States in the 1930s and 1940s.

Near the end of the war radio acquired an important new SOUND RECORDING technology: magnetic recording. A primitive wire recorder was used by some of the Allied correspondents covering the 1944 Normandy landings. This device allowed reports to be recorded during the action, and the recordings could be censored if necessary (see CENSORSHIP) and then used for relay to home audiences. As Allied troops advanced into Germany they discovered that captured German radio stations had a much superior form of magnetic recorder—the tape recorder—which permitted rapid and precise editing. During the following years the tape recorder became a basic tool of radio journalism and brought an upsurge in radio DOCUMENTARY.

After Television

Listeners who had relied on broadcasting throughout World War II hardly imagined that they were experiencing the twilight of network radio. Yet within a few years television had seized the public fancy. In nations with commercial systems it also seized the fancy of sponsors, and many left radio for television. Program sponsorship by major corporations had given network radio, particularly in the United States, a

Figure 2. *(Radio)* "The Mosquito Network," Guadalcanal, 1944. Armed Forces Radio Service, World War II. State Historical Society of Wisconsin, Erik Barnouw Collection.

period of extraordinary prosperity; its departure brought a correspondingly rapid decline. By 1952 television, with far fewer stations, surpassed radio in revenues. Most new television stations were established by the owners of radio stations. Television took radio's management, programs, audience, advertising, and profits. As networks reduced their role in radio, radio's focus shifted to local programming. On many stations this meant recorded music and talk. Change was less precipitate in noncommercial systems, but even there a simplification began.

Radio had to change in order to survive, and in the decades after World War II it adapted by developing new genres and formats. In response to listener demographics and ratings (see RATING SYSTEMS: RADIO AND TELEVISION) stations were geared to particular groups, interests, and musical preferences. Some stations took advantage of radio's unique participatory capabilities and promoted talk shows in which listeners were encouraged to phone in and join on-air discussions. The disc jockey was an integral part of still another U.S. programming innovation: formula or "top-40" radio, in which a limited playlist of best-selling phonograph records was repeated around the clock. With help from radio the phonograph industry boomed, and new forms of popular music appeared and spread (see MUSIC, POPULAR).

The development in 1948 of the transistor, a much smaller replacement for the Audion vacuum tube, led to the miniaturization and true portability of radio receivers (*see* MICROELECTRONICS). Radio became something that could literally be taken through the day, serving as a backdrop or accompaniment to other activities (*see* LEISURE). Radio stations proliferated in the United States—from about one thousand in 1946 to nearly thirty-five hundred in the mid-1950s to some ten thousand in the 1980s. One result was the rapid growth of FM as opposed to AM stations. The crowding of the AM portion of the spectrum and the vulnerability of AM signals to electrical interference—particularly in urban areas—seemed by the 1980s to pose a threat to the future of AM. AM countered with such innovations as stereophonic sound, and its stations became increasingly specialized in attempts to target specific audiences.

International Developments

The postwar expansion of radio was widespread and was abetted by increasing broadcast commercialization in many parts of the industrialized world. The availability of relatively inexpensive radio technology gave it an advantage in developing regions as well. In large rural areas of Africa (*see* AFRICA, TWENTIETH CENTURY), Asia (*see* ASIA, TWENTIETH CENTURY), and Latin America radio served as a link with population centers and played a significant role in development projects (*see* DEVELOPMENT COMMUNICATION). SATELLITE technology brought radio to places television could not reach, and its voices were increasingly numerous and diverse. Stations ranged from government-operated to clandestine enterprises. International radio burgeoned during the postwar decades, stemming from political, commercial, and religious interests (*see* RADIO, INTERNATIONAL). Many nations authorized low-powered community stations, often serving and controlled by small groups: Eskimo settlements in northern Canada, students on university campuses, South American Indian villages in the Andes. In Australia, Aboriginal groups experimented with ethnic radio (*see* AUSTRALASIA, TWENTIETH CENTURY). Japan inaugurated a class of mini-FM stations not requiring licenses if broadcasting no farther than half a mile. Local and community programming and control in western Europe, particularly in Italy, the Netherlands, Britain, Denmark, Switzerland, and parts of the Federal Republic of Germany, developed in response to pressures for CITIZEN ACCESS.

Radio's scope has increased with its reach. Commercial broadcasting, for example, is only one use of the radio spectrum. Other types of radio service include marine, industrial, aviation, military, and citizens bands (*see* CITIZENS BAND RADIO). Radio wave technology has even contributed to advances in space exploration (*see* CETI). The future expansion of radio's role lies in two directions. The first, typified by radio's contributions to Third World development and its ability to give voice to the concerns of communities and nonmainstream groups as well as government and big business, centers on the participatory dimensions of radio applications. The second direction is that taken by radio and related technologies as they function in increasingly complex TELECOMMUNICATIONS NETWORKS. While new, competing technologies increase the capacity to communicate, they raise the issues—of control, access, and benefit—that have reverberated throughout radio's history and that today dictate the agenda of international TELECOMMUNICATIONS POLICY.

Bibliography. Erik Barnouw, *A History of Broadcasting in the United States*, Vol. 1, *A Tower in Babel*, Vol 2., *The Golden Web*, New York, 1966, 1968; Asa Briggs, *The History of Broadcasting in the United Kingdom*, Vol. 1, *The Birth of Broadcasting*, Vol. 2, *The Golden Age of Wireless*, London, 1961, 1965; Andrew Crissell, *Understanding Radio*, London and New York, 1987; Sydney W. Head, *World Broadcasting: A Statistical Analysis*, Philadelphia, 1975; Elizabeth Mahan, Sergio Mattos, and J. Straubhauer, *Broadcasting in Latin America*, Philadelphia, 1987; Sir Charles Moses and Crispin Maslog, *Mass Communication in Asia: A Brief History*, Singapore, 1978; UNESCO, *World Communications: A 200-Country Survey of Press, Radio, Television, and Film*, 5th ed., New York and Paris, 1975.

LAWRENCE LICHTY

RADIO, INTERNATIONAL

RADIO transmissions from one territorial entity to listeners in another, with the intention of influencing ATTITUDES, opinions, and beliefs in favor of the broadcasting nation or source—in other words, for PROPAGANDA purposes. More than a hundred organizations in various parts of the world engage in this activity, ranging from regional operations of one or two kilowatts, broadcasting in a few languages for an hour or two of airtime per day, to the giant complexes of the United States and the Soviet Union, with worldwide coverage, transmitter power in the tens of thousands of kilowatts, using shortwave and medium wave, and broadcasting in dozens of languages and for more than 250 hours of airtime per day.

History. The transmission of Morse-coded messages designed to influence opinion abroad dates back to World War I, but the earliest voice broadcasts of this sort took place in 1923, when a German station sought to enlist the sympathies of European listeners with accounts of the French occupation of the Rhineland. Those broadcasts lasted only a few days, as did broadcasts from the Soviet Union to Romania in 1926 in which the Soviets asserted the justice of their territorial claim to Bessarabia.

The first continuing experimental international radio station was established in the Netherlands in 1927. It was to provide Dutch citizens living outside the country, especially in the Dutch East Indies (Indonesia), with a link to the homeland. Great Britain began experimental overseas transmissions in the same year and for somewhat the same purpose, as did Germany in 1929, France in 1931, and several other European countries and Japan during the 1930s. The Soviet Union inaugurated a continuing international service in 1929, at first as a means of explaining the benefits of communism but increasingly with both veiled and direct attacks on capitalism. It was the world's first continuing international radio station to specialize in propaganda for external consumption.

These stations were all shortwave operations, which can cover huge distances—sometimes erratically. Most international radio since that time has been in the shortwave bands, although some countries have supplemented this with medium-wave broadcasts, especially when aimed at nearby populations; these transmissions have sometimes intruded on domestic radio, which uses mainly medium waves. Shortwave transmissions have made some use of relay stations to strengthen communication over large distances, especially in recent decades.

In the early 1930s Fascist governments in Germany and Italy began to make intensive use of international radio to present their own policies and to attack those of their opponents. The Soviet Union then concentrated more of its broadcasts on anti-Fascist themes, but other European countries did not seek to combat hostile broadcasts until the late 1930s, and even then their replies were more defensive than offensive. As tensions increased, the USSR, Germany, and Italy restricted listener access to foreign broadcasts by interfering with incoming signals (jamming), confiscating sets capable of receiving broadcasts from abroad and making available cheap sets that could not receive them, and/or making it illegal to listen to such broadcasts and especially to pass on to others what one had heard.

When World War II broke out many of the nations in western and central Europe had international stations. Some were taken over by the Nazis in their conquests, but a few of the exile governments established stations in their colonies (e.g., in the Belgian Congo and the French Congo) and found outlets over Britain's British Broadcasting Corporation (BBC) and the U.S. Voice of America (VOA). The BBC began international broadcasting in foreign languages only in 1938, and the VOA came into exis-

tence in 1942, but both expanded foreign-language services very rapidly, both to benefit the exiles and to present the Allied point of view to listeners in Europe, the Americas, and the Pacific. Several U.S. and British allies, notably Canada and Australia, also began to broadcast internationally as part of the war effort.

Alongside those official activities arose the clandestine stations. A few such stations had operated during the Spanish civil war. Usually carrying colorful names (e.g., the Nazi "Station Debunk") that disclosed nothing of the station's actual origins, source of financial support, or location, the stations often pretended to represent "true" PUBLIC OPINION within the target country and even occasionally portrayed themselves as the operations of patriots broadcasting from a secret location within the country itself. Such stations were labeled "black" operations, in contrast to "gray" stations (no identification of location but no outright DECEPTION) and "white" stations (full and true identification of source). Most clandestine stations used informal and even vulgar language and indulged in harsher attacks on the enemy than did their official counterparts. Most were on the air for a matter of weeks or months, because often they were used as tactical weapons in a particular theater of military operations. In the closing months of World War II in Europe, Nazi Germany placed six or seven clandestine stations in operation, some directed to Soviet soldiers, others to British or U.S. forces, all intended to sow dissension among the Allies.

World War II saw the rise to prominence of "personality" broadcasters such as Lord Haw-Haw, Tokyo Rose, and Colonel Britton. The speakers playing those fictional roles generally used forceful, informal delivery and spoke to listeners in a personal, intimate manner in marked contrast to the formality of most earlier international broadcasters. Many had their devoted fans, although sometimes for the wrong reasons. For example, U.S. servicemen claimed to listen to Tokyo Rose in part because they found her brand of propaganda obvious to the point of being amusing. Wartime broadcasts often featured propaganda campaigns in which set themes (e.g., "Your leaders are misleading you" or "Your allies are unreliable") were highlighted on a daily basis and in various program formats. Both personality and thematic broadcasting have remained common elements in international radio. Among the international broadcasting personalities prominent in the 1970s and 1980s were such figures as Radio Moscow's Joe Adamov, the BBC's Anatole Goldberg, and VOA's Willis Conover.

After World War II some governments debated whether to disband international stations on the grounds that they might not be necessary in peacetime. Several stations were reduced in size and the

VOA was nearly dissolved, but the coming of the cold war gave international radio a new lease on life. The Soviet Union assisted the development of international stations in eastern Europe, the United States encouraged the resumption of international broadcasts by the Federal Republic of Germany and Japan, and clandestine stations, now associated with pro- and anti-Communist causes, began to reappear. In the early 1950s the United States established Radio Free Europe, Radio Liberation (later Radio Liberty), and Radio Free Asia, all ostensibly public-supported (but in reality CIA-funded) stations designed to help "roll back communism." Most Communist nations countered those broadcasts with jamming, which many of the Western stations countered in turn by broadcasting on more frequencies or by "cuddling," broadcasting so close to a domestic station of the target nation that any jamming would also affect the domestic station.

During this period two further types of international service were developing rapidly. International religious stations had existed since the early 1930s but had been small and few in number (see RELIGIOUS BROADCASTING). In the late 1940s to mid-1950s such stations proliferated, especially in Africa and Asia. Generally backed by U.S. Protestant churches or groups, the stations sought to convert "heathens," Muslims, and even Roman Catholics. They were joined in the 1960s and 1970s by Islamic international stations based in Egypt, Libya, and Saudi Arabia, but those stations were uninterested in gaining converts; they existed to sustain the faithful. International commercial stations began to operate in the 1930s in Europe, southern Africa, and the United States. Most of them went off the air during the war, but a few came back after the war and were soon joined by others in North Africa, the Middle East, Asia, and later the Caribbean. Dominated by the target country's popular music, brief newscasts, and commercial messages, such stations sound much like typical U.S. commercial radio.

Third World nations, too, began to develop international services in the 1950s. Several of them, notably Egypt's Radio Cairo and Voice of the Arabs and Ghana's Radio Ghana, carried strongly anticolonial broadcasts and frequently hyperbolic praise for their national leaders. Possession of an international radio station became something of a token of modernity, and even some of the poorest nations, such as Bangladesh, acquired stations whether or not there was money enough to operate them continually. Nominally international, few Third World stations reach much beyond their immediate geographical neighbors. Third World clandestine broadcasts also have increased as political dissidents in exile, encouraged by neighboring nations, seek to reach listeners in their former homelands with attacks on the governments there.

By the 1980s the majority of the world's sovereign nations had international radio stations, but growth had slackened, and the largest stations were adding few languages or transmission hours, although regional conflicts in such places as Afghanistan, Central America, and the Middle East drew increased attention from leading international broadcasters and led to increased clandestine activity.

Purposes, programs, and audiences. Operators of international radio stations seek to influence public opinion, but for varying purposes. The first continuing international service, in the Netherlands, sought to remind Dutch listeners abroad of life in the homeland in order to strengthen morale and make them more effective spokespersons for the Dutch viewpoint. Many nations, especially those with colonies, have had similar services, and a few, including the USSR's Radio Rodina and the U.S.'s Armed Forces Radio and Television Service (AFRTS), still exist. Since U.S. military personnel are stationed in many foreign countries, English-speaking listeners there often have the opportunity to hear the AFRTS programming, most of which is from U.S. networks.

Most international services are financially supported and operated or supervised by governments. They seek to persuade listeners of their nation's goodwill, economic and military strength, rich CULTURE, and ideological leadership in order to increase trade, strengthen alliances, or gain new ideological converts. Religious stations usually attempt to convert listeners, strengthen the faith of believers, and also plead for funds. Commercial stations hope to entertain listeners so as to keep them tuned to and receptive to the ADVERTISING that pays the station's bills. Clandestine stations promote various political causes. Most stations broadcast far more positive material (usually about themselves) than they do negative material, although clandestine stations often emphasize the latter.

News and news-related programs (commentaries, features, editorials) take up the largest single share of program time on most government-supported stations. Popular music runs a fairly close second and predominates on international commercial stations (see MUSIC, POPULAR), although VOA, the BBC, and several other large stations feature disc-jockey-hosted jazz and pop music shows and encourage listener requests. Most international commercial stations devote little or no time to news, but the many stations operating under the aegis of France's SOFIRAD (Société Financière de Radio Diffusion), such as Radio Monte Carlo/Middle East, have developed sizable audiences for their newscasts in part because they are perceived as nongovernment broadcasters and thus freer of bias than most international stations.

Most government-supported stations employ relatively bias-free vocabulary in their newscasts, although item selection often is shaped by the country's prevailing IDEOLOGY. Commentaries, features, and editorials usually display more value-laden terminology. Most stations offer weekly listener "mailbags" in which listener inquiries about the broadcasting nation or source are answered. English is the most commonly used language, with Arabic, Spanish, French, Russian, and Kuoyu (Mandarin) also prominent. The Soviet Union, the United States, and the People's Republic of China all operate combinations of stations that broadcast fourteen hundred to two thousand hours per week in forty or more languages. Great Britain, the Federal Republic of Germany, the Democratic People's Republic of Korea, Albania, and Egypt all broadcast five hundred to eight hundred hours a week, most of them in thirty to forty languages.

Research data on audiences for international broadcasting are relatively scarce and simplistic. Many countries prefer to know nothing about their citizens' uses and perceptions of international broadcasting. But surveys give a fairly consistent picture of the audience, whose members tend to be relatively young, largely male, fairly well educated, of above-average income, and often with some foreign travel experience. Listener percentages are higher in countries with relatively few domestic media and/or with what listeners regard as media under tight government control; listening rates are thus low in western Europe, North America, and Japan, and high in eastern Europe and parts of Africa, the Middle East, and Asia. Listeners usually tune to three or four international stations with some regularity and listen for one to two hours per day. If the international station is available on medium wave, as are VOA, the BBC, Radio Moscow, and Radio Cairo, among others, its listenership usually increases dramatically.

Policy issues. The frequency SPECTRUM for international radio broadcasting becomes more crowded as more nations and groups enter the field or seek to expand. Most of the largest stations and some of the smaller ones have relay transmitters in foreign countries, especially in the Third World, to improve their chances of being received. All of this costs a great deal, and poorer nations simply cannot afford it.

The International Telecommunication Union (ITU), a United Nations agency, attempts to act as arbiter and to ensure that all nations wishing to broadcast internationally may do so, but much of the spectrum space in the shortwave bands has long been taken by the industrially developed nations. Thus there has been a struggle within the ITU between the "have" and "have not" nations over the just allocation of spectrum space. The ITU's World Administrative Radio Conferences of 1979 and 1984 made some progress toward meeting Third World demands, but the spectrum remained congested, reception tended to deteriorate, and those nations that could afford to sought to overpower competing signals by installing five-hundred- and one-thousand-kilowatt transmitters. The ITU and the United Nations have not sought to limit this superpower race, nor have they been able to prevent nations from jamming incoming international broadcasts. Broadcast content likewise has eluded all attempts at international regulation. Sovereign nations continue to decide how and what they will broadcast and jam, and cooperate with one another only when it is clearly in their self-interest. Some national governments, especially in Communist nations, consider certain international broadcasts to be "ideological pollution" akin to drugs and PORNOGRAPHY and feel perfectly justified in excluding them. *See also* NEW INTERNATIONAL INFORMATION ORDER.

The proliferation of communications satellites in the 1970s and 1980s made it easier for the largest stations to relay broadcasts to their overseas relay transmitters (*see* SATELLITE). Technical problems and equipment costs have limited direct in-home reception of satellite-transmitted international radio broadcasts, but further development of that technology is widely expected. The direct-broadcast satellite is seen by much of the Third World as a new instrument of superpower hegemony.

The problems connected with international radio have done little to discourage participants, and few international stations aside from clandestine operations have gone off the air since World War II. High initial investment and maintenance costs may find government officials and legislators looking for ways to economize, but few consider total elimination of such services. International radio allows access to audiences unreachable by any other medium, conveys news of developments quickly, and employs the special persuasive powers of the human voice. It is unlikely to vanish soon from the international arena.

Bibliography. Donald R. Browne, *International Radio Broadcasting,* New York, 1982; Bernard Bumpus and Barbara Skelt, *Seventy Years of International Broadcasting* (UNESCO Communication and Society Series, no. 14), Paris, 1984; Harwood L. Childs and John B. Whitton, eds., *Propaganda by Short Waves,* Princeton, N.J., 1942; Thomas Grandin, *The Political Use of the Radio* (Geneva Studies, Vol. 10, no. 3), Geneva, 1939, reprint (History of Broadcasting: Radio to Television Series) New York, 1971; Julian Hale, *Radio Power: Propaganda and International Broadcasting,* Philadelphia, 1976.

DONALD R. BROWNE

RATING SYSTEMS: RADIO AND TELEVISION

Commercial broadcasters generate revenues by selling advertisers access to the audiences won by their programming. Before a price can be established for ADVERTISING time on any series, whether on RADIO or television (*see* TELEVISION HISTORY), it is necessary to determine both the size and the composition of its audience. Thus research defines the broadcaster's "product" (the audience), and it is not surprising to find that studies of radio and television audiences have been part of the broadcasting scene from the start.

History

The broadcast measurement industry has seen many competitors and many different approaches through the years. Although individual radio broadcasters provided measurements of their audiences during the 1920s, in the United States the first independent and syndicated radio measurement company was the Co-operative Analysis of Broadcasting (CAB), founded by Archibald Crossley in 1930. Crossley used the telephone recall survey technique. In 1934 Claude Hooper entered the business, and his "Hooperating" dominated radio measurement for the next decade. In 1939 the British Broadcasting Corporation (BBC) introduced a "survey of listening" that employed a twenty-four-hour aided-recall technique. In 1942 A. C. Nielsen introduced the first direct measurement device, the Audimeter, which was attached to the radio and recorded the set's dial position on ticker-tape-like paper. Sydney Roslow began his Pulse service in 1941. Pulse used an aided-recall telephone technique and, in 1949, added the measurement of out-of-home listening because listeners in cars represented a growing portion of the radio audience. In-home audience measurement alone was no longer adequate.

The rapid DIFFUSION of television in the United States after World War II created a need for television audience measurement, which was provided from the inauguration of this new medium by many of the firms originally involved in radio measurement. Hooper was measuring television audiences in 1948, James Seiler founded the American Research Bureau in 1949, and A. C. Nielsen entered the market in 1950 with a television version of the Audimeter. The BBC audience measurement program was expanded to include television in 1952, and the independent commercial television stations in Great Britain began measuring television audiences in 1955. By the beginning of the 1960s most European countries had some form of radio and television audience measurement system.

Perhaps the most significant milestone in the history of U.S. broadcast audience measurement was the 1963 House of Representatives hearing chaired by Representative Oren Harris of Arkansas. This hearing challenged the rating services to defend the validity and reliability of their rating systems. As a result of this challenge the services increased the size of their samples and introduced stricter sampling procedures. An independent organization, the Broadcast Rating Council, was established to audit the rating services.

The era of overnight ratings began when Arbitron introduced the instantaneous meter in 1958, and Nielsen followed with its Storage Instantaneous Audimeter (SIA). Arbitron started to compete against Nielsen in the national arena but eventually conceded this market to Nielsen and concentrated on local markets. Nielsen soon cornered the national market with its Nielsen Television Index (NTI) service, although Nielsen and Arbitron continued to battle on the local television audience measurement front.

Procedures

Throughout the history of radio and television audience measurement a variety of methods have been tried. Early measurement services focused on the telephone. People were called either during the broadcast (the "coincidental") or on the day following the broadcast. Nielsen's Audimeter could not measure *who* in the household was listening and/or viewing. Arbitron's "diary" method proved to be the most effective for measuring who was listening or viewing.

As out-of-home radio listening became increasingly important, household measurement became less relevant, and the personal diary became the preferred measurement instrument. Arbitron selects its sample from a computer file of telephone households. In selected markets the sampling universe also includes unlisted telephone households, and special sampling procedures are employed to tap minority audiences. Respondents in the sample keep a seven-day personal diary. Each Arbitron survey lasts four weeks, with a different sample each week. The survey periods are January–February, April–May, July–August, and October–November. Major markets are surveyed four times per year; smaller markets are measured less frequently. Sample sizes range from 450 respondents in smaller markets to 3,000 in major markets. In all, Arbitron measures 201 radio markets.

RADAR, the network radio measurement service produced by Statistical Research, Inc., measures the audiences of the nation's radio networks through a telephone-based survey methodology. A random-digit dialing technique is used to include unlisted as well as listed households in the sample. One person per household is then designated as a respondent, who then provides one week of listening information in daily telephone interviews. There are two eight-week RADAR measurement periods per year, one in the fall and one in the spring. Data from the two most recent reports are published as a moving national average.

Television. Television measurement is accomplished by a combination of meters and diaries. Nielsen's national NTI service utilizes a panel of seventeen hundred metered households, supplemented by a separate diary sample of twenty-five hundred households that provides the essential "who is viewing" component. Each diary household keeps a diary for one week out of every three. The viewers-per-household (VPH) data from the diary household sample are combined with the metered household results to produce a biweekly NTI "pocketpiece" that reports the audiences of all network television programs. NTI also measures the audiences of the major cable services and nationally distributed syndicated programs. Meter-based household audience statistics are available for all fifty-two weeks of the year, but NTI pocketpieces combining household and individual viewing data are available for only forty-eight.

On the local level Arbitron and Nielsen rely predominantly on the diary. Meters have been introduced in major markets, and in these markets household audience estimates are available fifty-two weeks a year. However, in most markets metered measurement is not economically feasible, and diary-based surveys are employed. Each survey is four weeks in length. Major markets are surveyed seven times a year: in October, November, January, February, March, May, and July. Smaller markets are measured four times a year: in November, February, May, and July. These four surveys, when every market in the country is measured, are called the "sweeps" period. Broadcasters put their best programming on during these periods in order to attract the largest possible audiences in the surveys.

Nielsen provides reports in 205 designated market areas (DMAs), and Arbitron measures 211 areas of dominant influence (ADIs). Audience figures in both cases are provided for the metro area, the broader DMA or ADI, and a total survey area. Slight variations in definition and different statistical sources result in some variations between the DMA and ADI, although they basically parallel each other.

Key Measures

The key audience measures provided by both radio and television measurement services are the *rating* and the *share*. The rating equals the percentage of the given universe watching a particular television program or listening to a particular radio program. One percent of the given universe of households or persons equals one rating point. The share equals the percentage of the radio or television audience listening or viewing when a show is being broadcast that is listening to or viewing a given station. To calculate a share it is necessary to know the aggregate viewing or listening level. In radio this statistic is referred to as the PUR (persons using radio), and in television it is called HUT (homes using television) or PUT (persons using television). The share equals the rating for the program over the HUT or PUT, depending on whether one refers to the audience in terms of persons or households. Figure 1 illustrates these concepts.

There are slight variations in how television and radio ratings are calculated. Radio ratings are reported on an average-quarter-hour and cumulative basis. The average-quarter-hour rating is defined by Arbitron as the percentage of total viewers tuned to a station for at least five minutes during the average quarter-hour. The cumulative audience is the number of different listeners who tune to a station at different times of the day for at least five minutes.

The Nielsen NTI rating is based on the number of viewers who tune in a program during the average minute that it is on. This rating is called the average audience rating, and the total audience rating includes all viewers who watched at least one minute of the program. At the local level the rating is calculated somewhat differently. Included in the local rating are all viewers who tuned to a program for five minutes or more during an average quarter-hour. Therefore, the local rating would exclude those viewing for five minutes or less, whereas the network rating would include those viewers provided they viewed for at least one minute.

Services in Other Countries

The United States is only one of many countries with broadcast measurement services. Nielsen measures television audiences throughout the world. Although Arbitron confines its measurement to the United States, this does not mean that Nielsen is not challenged abroad. Audits of Great Britain (AGB) provides audience measurement services throughout Europe as well as in the Far East and Australia. In several countries metered services similar to the U.S. system are used. In the Federal Republic of Germany GFK and AGB's Teleskopie compete with meter-based systems. AGB in Italy, Secodip in France, Nielsen in Brazil and Japan, and Dentsu Advertising in Japan provide competitive television measurement services. These companies customize their services to fit local market conditions.

Because many countries have government-controlled radio and television systems supported by taxes or user fees, broadcast managers in those countries are less concerned with quantifying the audience than they are with measuring the audience's satisfaction with what it is viewing. Audience surveys are thus supplemented by *qualitative* viewer satisfaction scores. However, in any country in which advertisers look

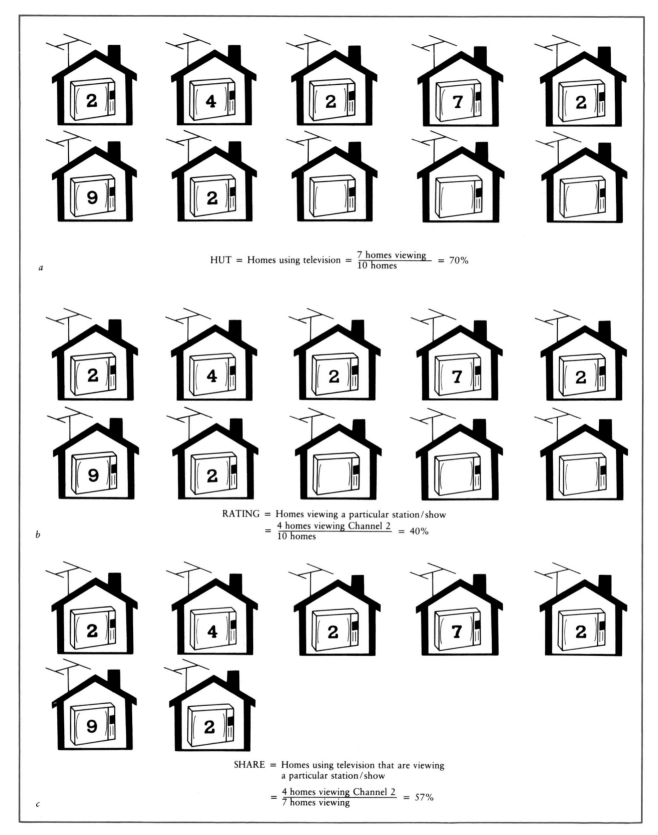

a

HUT = Homes using television = $\dfrac{7 \text{ homes viewing}}{10 \text{ homes}}$ = 70%

b

RATING = Homes viewing a particular station/show

= $\dfrac{4 \text{ homes viewing Channel 2}}{10 \text{ homes}}$ = 40%

c

SHARE = Homes using television that are viewing a particular station/show

= $\dfrac{4 \text{ homes viewing Channel 2}}{7 \text{ homes viewing}}$ = 57%

Figure 1. *(Rating Systems: Radio and Television)*   Key concepts in the measurement of audiences.

to audience research to provide estimates of the number of people viewing their COMMERCIALS, the rating remains the basic unit of audience measurement.

The People Meter

Rating services are still undecided about whether the meter or the diary is the best data collection method. Some believe that the meter provides the most accurate measure of household viewing because it requires no action on the part of the viewer, but the meter cannot confirm the presence of viewers watching the set; it only registers when the set is on and the channel tuned. The diary does record who is viewing but is dependent on the viewer's remembering—and accurately reporting—everything viewed. Experience has shown that survey participants fall short of perfection on both counts.

One solution to this industry problem is an electronic method that would record not only that the set is on but also who is watching. "People meters" have been developed by Nielsen in the United States and by AGB and others in Europe. A problem with people meters as they have developed so far is that they require active viewer participation, and this intrusive aspect can affect both viewing behavior and respondent cooperation in surveys. Experimentation continues in order to reduce the impact of these limitations on the efficacy of this all-electronic form of audience measurement.

Beyond Ratings

The BBC audience measurement system has from its inception provided data on audience satisfaction with what is being broadcast, and this type of qualitative measurement of television audiences has also been introduced to the United States. Other challenges taken up by research services have included measuring the use of videocassette recorders (VCRs) in both record and playback modes. As the VIDEO marketplace continues to be changed by innovations in electronics, the methods of measuring audiences will have to be continually adapted in the years ahead, and perhaps entirely new ones developed.

Bibliography. Hugh Malcolm Beville, *Audience Ratings: Radio, Television, and Cable*, Hillsdale, N.J., 1985; David F. Poltrack, *Television Marketing: Network, Local and Cable*, New York, 1982.

DAVID F. POLTRACK

READING

Most scholars would agree that the ability to write SPEECH down in a permanent, transportable form and to read it have affected both the growth of the mind and the growth of civilizations. But the nature of these effects is still open to debate. The effects of reading can be assessed from three different perspectives: (1) how reading functions in technological and nontechnological societies, (2) its effects on mental processes, and (3) its development in and out of SCHOOL.

Social Consequences of Literacy

Studies of reading in nontechnological societies report that reading serves primarily a *communicative* function and is highly personalized and dependent on the reader and writer sharing the same background (i.e., it is highly "contextualized"). By contrast the kind of LITERACY valued in contemporary industrialized societies requires general, abstract knowledge that will allow the reader to process texts that are complex and unfamiliar (i.e., "decontextualized").

Historically, literacy education was aimed at either a high level of literacy for a few or a low level of literacy for the masses. It has been suggested that to make the transition from a predominantly agricultural to an industrial society at least 40 percent of adults need to be literate (*see* DEVELOPMENT COMMUNICATION). For example, England reached that threshold in the eighteenth century, just before its Industrial Revolution. Politically, the ability to read well has been judged crucial for effective participation in democratic processes (*see* ELECTION; PUBLIC OPINION). From an economic perspective, some analysts contend that participation in a technological society requires a high (approximately twelfth-grade) reading level, necessary to read a sophisticated NEWSMAGAZINE, newspaper, and other print media. *See also* COMPUTER: IMPACT—IMPACT ON THE WORK FORCE.

Literacy has also been viewed as a potential force in leading people to a greater awareness of their role in society, a view held by Brazilian educator Paulo Freire. Literacy campaigns in Cuba, Nicaragua, and Sao Tome and Principe, among other places, have been organized according to Freire's ideas.

The term *cultural literacy* has been used to describe the knowledge shared by members of a literate society, needed for the decontextualized reading required in literate societies. (In the United States, for example, cultural literacy would include broad knowledge of the country's major historical figures, of major works of U.S. and English literature, and of basic civic and scientific knowledge.) Literate members of a culture share more than common knowledge. They also share the cognitive and interpretive skills necessary to derive from written materials simple and complex meanings, acquired from reading and writing in school and out of school, from reading classic and modern literature, and from the study of history, science, and other topics.

Cognition and Literacy

Soviet researcher LEV VYGOTSKY suggested that the skills needed for reading and writing that represent a situation explicitly (i.e., for reading and writing that are intelligible without a shared context between reader and writer) necessarily involve higher mental processes than face-to-face communication (*see* INTERACTION, FACE-TO-FACE). Studies by another Soviet scholar, ALEKSANDR LURIA, of newly literate Soviet peasants in the 1930s and by U.S. researchers Patricia M. Greenfield and Jerome S. Bruner of Wolof CHILDREN in Senegal found that literate people were capable of higher mental processing and more abstract reasoning. Other studies of the differences between spoken and written LANGUAGE also suggest that the process of producing and understanding written language requires greater use of abstract thought than does spoken language. In this regard Canadian researcher David R. Olson distinguishes between *utterance* and *text*. Utterance refers to the more informal oral language statements common in a personalized context. In texts, however, an author communicates with a reader not necessarily known to him or her through a more explicit and formalized language. Olson argues that the language of texts requires the autonomous and decontextualized representation of MEANING, not usually a part of the oral tradition (*see* ORAL CULTURE). The ability to abstract—which Olson argues comes from the use of written language—is said to underlie the achievements of Western culture.

U.S. researchers Sylvia Scribner and Michael Cole found that nonschooled literacy (in their case, of the Vai people in Liberia and Sierra Leone in West Africa) did not appear to produce cognitive changes (*see* COGNITION). Schooling, on the other hand, seemed to improve performance on a number of different cognitive and metacognitive tasks. Their suggestion is that it is schooling and not merely being able to read and write that is responsible for the growth of abstract thought. However, other explanations for the lack of cognitive effects of Vai literacy are possible: Olson's text-utterance distinction and Jeanne S. Chall's model of stages in reading development. Since the Vai use their own script primarily for highly contextualized functions (e.g., LETTER writing and personal recordkeeping) and not for the abstract functions that Olson ascribed to text, it may well be that in this case literacy does not influence higher cognitive tasks. Using Chall's stage-development scheme it is possible to hypothesize that Vai literacy reached a level that did not lead to the reading of unfamiliar, abstract texts, and thus the effects on cognitive functioning were minimal (see Table 1).

The relationship between reading and abstract thought is reciprocal: higher cognitive and linguistic abilities favor growth of reading skills, and vice versa. U.S. educator J. B. Carroll suggests that students' reading abilities can, with instruction, reach the levels of their cognitive and linguistic functioning, a rationale that has been used for nearly a century to define the condition of reading disability as a significant gap between reading achievement and cognitive and language achievement. Another approach to the relationship between cognition and reading is through analysis of mature reading comprehension. Cognitive scientists have developed models that detail the integration of reasoning into the process of reading comprehension, going back to U.S. researcher Edward L. Thorndike's statement that reading *is* reasoning. Researchers have also used knowledge of how a proficient reader comprehends in order to teach those skills to younger and/or less proficient readers.

The Development of Reading

The process of learning to read and the most effective way to initiate people—especially children—into reading continue to be of great interest to researchers, teachers, and parents. In beginning reading there is a long-standing debate between proponents of an initial emphasis on the "code" or on "meaning." Some have argued for a "whole language" or "global" approach to beginning reading instruction, placing reading in a functional and meaningful context right from the start. Others have argued—calling on research and theoretical evidence over the period from 1910 to 1980—that a "sound-symbol" or a "code-emphasis" approach to beginning reading instruction is more effective for both word identification and comprehension. Languages as diverse as English, Hebrew, German, and Chinese have been involved in this debate. Although research tends to indicate that greater attention to the code in the beginning leads to higher achievement in word recognition and comprehension (at least through the fourth year of school and possibly later), it has always been acknowledged that reading materials did and should use meaningful and interesting language and that comprehension has been and can be taught along with decoding skills. Two national reports published in the United States—*Becoming a Nation of Readers* (1985) and *What Works* (1986)—specifically recommended the direct teaching of phonics in the early grades based on the strength of available research evidence.

Another way to look at reading is from a developmental perspective. Chall proposed that reading progresses through six stages, each representing a qualitative advance yet dependent on the knowledge and skills acquired in the previous stages. Children develop many abilities and skills needed for learning

Table 1. Stages of Reading Development: An Outline of the Major Qualitative Characteristics and How They Are Acquired

Stage Designation	Grade Range (age)	Major Qualitative Characteristics and Masteries by End of Stage	How Acquired	Relationship of Reading to Listening
Stage 0: Prereading, "pseudo-reading"	Preschool (ages 6 months–6 years)	Child "pretends" to read, retells story when looking at pages of book previously read to him/her; names letters of alphabet; recognizes some signs; prints own name; plays with books, pencils, and paper.	Being read to by an adult (or older child) who responds to and warmly appreciates the child's interest in books and reading; being provided with books, paper, pencils, blocks, and letters.	Most can understand the children's picture books and stories read to them. They understand thousands of words they hear by age 6 but can read few if any of them.
Stage 1: Initial reading and decoding	Grade 1 & beginning Grade 2 (ages 6 & 7)	Child learns relation between letters and sounds and between printed and spoken words; child is able to read simple text containing high-frequency words and phonically regular words; uses skill and insight to "sound out" new one-syllable words.	Direct instruction in letter-sound relations (phonics) and practice in their use. Reading of simple stories using words with phonic elements taught and words of high frequency. Being read to on a level above what child can read independently to develop more advanced language patterns, knowledge of new words, and ideas.	The level of difficulty of language read by the child is much below the language understood when heard. At the end of Stage 1, most children can understand up to 4,000 or more words when heard but can read only about 600.
Stage 2: Confirmation and fluency	Grades 2 & 3 (ages 7 & 8)	Child reads simple, familiar stories and selections with increasing fluency. This is done by consolidating the basic decoding elements, sight vocabulary, and meaning context in the reading of familiar stories and selections.	Direct instruction in advanced decoding skills; wide reading (with instruction and independently) of familiar, interesting materials, which help promote fluent reading. Being read to at levels above their own independent reading level to develop language, vocabulary, and concepts.	At the end of Stage 2, about 3,000 words can be read and understood, and about 9,000 are known when heard. Listening is still more effective than reading.
Stage 3: Reading for learning the new *Phase A* *Phase B*	Grades 4–8 (ages 9–13) Intermediate, 4–6 Junior high school, 7–9	Reading is used to learn new ideas, to gain new knowledge, to experience new feelings, to learn new attitudes; generally from one viewpoint.	Reading and study of textbooks, reference works, trade books, newspapers, and magazines that contain new ideas and values, unfamiliar vocabulary and syntax; systematic study of words and reacting to the text through discussion, answering questions, writing, etc. Reading of increasingly more complex fiction, biography, nonfiction, and the like.	At beginning of Stage 3, listening comprehension of the same material is still more effective than reading comprehension. By the end of Stage 3, reading and listening are about equal; for those who read very well, reading may be more efficient.
Stage 4: Multiple viewpoints	High school, grades 10–12 (ages 15–17)	Reading widely from a broad range of complex materials, both expository and narrative, with a variety of viewpoints.	Wide reading and study of the physical, biological, and social sciences and the humanities; high-quality and popular literature; newspapers and magazines; systematic study of words and word parts.	Reading comprehension is better than listening comprehension of material of difficult content and readability. For poorer readers, listening comprehension may be equal to reading comprehension.
Stage 5: Construction and reconstruction	College and beyond (age 18+)	Reading is used for one's own needs and purposes (professional and personal); reading serves to integrate one's knowledge with that of others, to synthesize it, and to create new knowledge. It is rapid and efficient.	Wide reading of ever more difficult materials, reading beyond one's immediate needs; writing of papers, tests, essays, and other forms that call for integration of varied knowledge and points of view.	Reading is more efficient than listening.

From Jeanne S. Chall, *Stages of Reading Development*, New York, 1983, pp. 85–87.

to read before they receive formal reading instruction, including learning their native language (*see* LANGUAGE ACQUISITION), developing awareness of sounds in words, and learning the names of letters. At school the child's first task is to master the code—that is, to learn how to translate written language into an oral form. Once the code is mastered, fluency and automatic word recognition in context follow. Reading simple stories or books with rhyming or predictable patterns helps this process. Later stages involve using the already acquired skills to read unfamiliar, complex texts for purposes of learning from them, at first from a single viewpoint and eventually from a global perspective, melding read information with the reader's knowledge and experience to create new ideas.

Chall's stages represent a developmental continuum for individual children as well as differences in levels of literacy among societies or cultures. Thus the contextualized reading of the Vai is a kind of Stage 2 literacy, because the written word conveys information largely known by both reader and writer. Stage 2 literacy is not likely to have the cognitive consequences of Stage 3 literacy (i.e., using literacy to learn the new) or the cognitive consequences claimed by Olson for text (or decontextualized) literacy. Further, the kind of literacy required for the study of science and that required for political decisions need the critical comparisons of multiple viewpoints typical of reading at Stages 4 and 5.

U.S. researchers D. P. Resnick and Lauren B. Resnick have argued that mass literacy in the past was a Stage 2 literacy, meaning that large groups of people were able to read highly familiar materials and to read and write letters and simple notes. Attempts to provide universal Stage 3 literacy represent a more recent development, yet it can still be argued that even this higher level of literacy is not enough to have an informed populace in an increasingly complex world. Instead, the criterion for literacy that many have proposed for complex societies is at Stage 4, equivalent to a twelfth-grade reading level (see Table 2). Whether such a level can be achieved by (or provided for) most adults is an important question and a challenge for reading educators.

Table 2. Examples of Materials Accessible to Readers at Successive Stage Levels

Stage 1	"May I go?" said Fay. "May I please go with you?"[a]
Stage 2	Spring was coming to Tait Primary School. On the new highway big trucks went by the school all day.[b]
Stage 3A	She smoothed her hair behind her ear as she lowered her hand. I could see she was eyeing *beauty* and trying to figure out a way to write about being beautiful without sounding even more conceited than she already was.[c]
Stage 3B	Early in the history of the world, men found that they could not communicate well by using only sign language. In some way that cannot be traced with any certainty, they devised spoken language.[d]
Stage 4	No matter what phenomena he is interested in, the scientist employs two main tools—theory and empirical research. Theory employs reason, language, and logic to suggest possible, or predict probable, relationships among various data gathered from the concrete world of experience.[e]
Stage 5	One of the objections to the hypothesis that a satisfying after-effect of a mental connection works back upon it to strengthen it is that nobody has shown how this action does or could occur. It is the purpose of this article to show how a mechanism which is as possible psychologically as any of the mechanisms proposed to recount for facilitation, inhibition, fatigue, strengthening by repetition, or other forms of modification could enable such an after-effect to cause such a strengthening.[f]

[a] *American Book Primer*, p. 19.
[b] Ginn 720, Grade 2^2, p. 48.
[c] Ginn 720, Grade 5, p. 66.
[d] Book F: *New Practice Reader*, Graves et al., New York, 1962.
[e] A. B. Kathryn, "College Reading Skills," in *Modern Society*, 3d ed., ed. by John Biesanz and Mavis Biesanz, Englewood Cliffs, N.J., 1971.
[f] E. L. Thorndike, "Connectionism," *Psychological Review* 40 (1933): 434–490.

Source: Jeanne S. Chall, *Stages of Reading Development*, New York, 1983, p. 39.

Bibliography. Richard C. Anderson et al., *Becoming a Nation of Readers,* Washington, D.C., 1985; J. B. Carroll, "Developmental Parameters of Reading Comprehension," in *Cognition, Curriculum, and Comprehension,* ed. by John T. Guthrie, Newark, Del., 1977; Jeanne S. Chall, *Stages of Reading Development,* New York, 1983; John A. Downing, ed., *Comparative Reading: Cross-national Studies of Behavior and Processes in Reading and Writing,* New York, 1972; Paulo Freire, *Pedagogy of the Oppressed* (Pedagogía del oprimido), trans. by Myra Bergman Ramos, New York, 1970; Patricia Marks Greenfield and Jerome S. Bruner, "Culture and Cognitive Growth," *International Journal of Psychology* 1 (1966): 89–107; Shirley Brice Heath, "Being Literate in America: A Sociohistorical Perspective," in *Issues in Literacy: A Research Perspective* (Yearbook of the National Reading Conference, No. 34), ed. by J. A. Niles and R. V. Lalik, Rochester, N.Y., 1985; Aleksandr R. Luria, *Cognitive Development: Its Cultural and Social Foundations* (in Russian), trans. by Martin Lopez-Morillas and Lynn Solotaroff, Cambridge, Mass., 1976; David R. Olson, "From Utterance to Text: The Bias of Language in Speech and Writing," *Harvard Educational*

Review 47 (1977): 257–281; Charles A. Perfetti, *Reading Ability,* New York, 1985; Lauren B. Resnick and Phyllis A. Weaver, eds., *Theory and Practice of Early Reading,* 3 vols., Hillsdale, N.J., 1979–1980; Sylvia Scribner and Michael Cole, *The Psychology of Literacy,* Cambridge, Mass., 1981; U.S. Department of Education, *What Works: Research about Teaching and Learning,* Washington, D.C., 1986; Lev Semenovich Vygotsky, *Mind in Society,* ed. by Michael Cole, Cambridge, Mass., 1978.

JEANNE S. CHALL AND STEVEN A. STAHL

READING THEORY

The romantics and Victorians often valued literary works simply as a means of access to the minds and imaginations of their authors (*see* ROMANTICISM). In the early decades of the twentieth century this concern for the author yielded ground to a preoccupation with the work itself. T. S. Eliot, F. R. Leavis, I. A. RICHARDS, and the U.S. New Critics turned from authorial BIOGRAPHY and psychology to various theories of literary impersonality that grasped the literary text as an object in itself, as an autonomous, self-regulating organization of words that could not be reduced to the mind that produced it. It is only since the mid-1960s that literary theory has turned from both author and work to the indispensable role of the reader in the creation of literary MEANING and value. *See* AUTHORSHIP.

This new critical mode—variously called reception theory, reception aesthetics, or reader-response theory—regards a piece of WRITING as no more than a set of abstract marks that cue the reader into constructing a particular set of meanings. Meaning is seen less as an immanent property or quality of the written text than as a dynamic process of interaction between text and recipient. A BOOK is a physical object; a "text" is a process or construct based on, but not identical with, a set of material marks on a page. Many previous literary theories tended to view the reader merely as a passive receptacle into whom meaning could be poured; the act of INTERPRETATION was construed as an extraction, on the part of a reader, of some set of meanings that were already, so to speak, buried or secreted within the text itself. Reading theory challenges this empiricist notion of READING, viewing all meaning as the product of a complex collaboration between work and audience. The act of reading involves the continual construction of hypotheses, which are then ceaselessly modified, extended, or abandoned in the light of fresh textual evidence. Any literary work is intelligible only because the reader brings to it a set of what have been termed "pre-understandings," a frame of implicit prejudices, beliefs, and assumptions without which nothing in the work itself would be identifi-

able. A literary work cannot say everything about its subject, but leaves much to the reader's imagination; so reading theory conceives of the act of interpretation as a "concretization" of the text, a constant filling out of its gaps and connecting together of its various segments.

All readers are thoroughly historical beings, whose encounter with a literary work is shaped by their own inescapable social, cultural, and ideological situations. What happens in the act of reading is an encounter, or for some reading theorists a fusion, between the reader's own "historical horizon" and the alien "horizon" of the work itself. For this radical historicism there is never any possibility of knowing a work of the past "as it is": reading is ineluctably a relationship to a text born out of our own historical situation, not a simple reflection of some given object. It follows from this that the meaning of any literary work is highly variable, depending on the changing historical, aesthetic, and ideological circumstances in which it is received. The meaning (or value) of, say, one of Shakespeare's tragedies is not fixed and given for all time, but alters and develops as new generations come to absorb the work into their own very different concerns. Traditional criticism often conceives of our historical remoteness from a work of the past as a problem: how is criticism to leap the gap between the work and itself, abolishing the history that lies between them and understanding the work from the inside? For reading theory this is to overlook the truth that the literature of the past may come to be enriched and illuminated in fresh, unexpected ways by that intervening history. Literary meaning and value are always transitive, or *for* some particular reader, in some specific social conditions. Since such social and historical conditions vary widely, it no longer becomes possible to speak of *the* truth, meaning, or value of a literary work as an immanent quality that transcends the history of its reception.

Reading theorists are divided on the question of how much the reader contributes to the making of the literary text. Some, such as Polish critic Roman Ingarden and German critic Wolfgang Iser, imagine a kind of coauthorship between writer and reader, in which the reader is left free to construct the text in particular ways, but always within the constraining limits imposed by the author's own organization of it. More radical critics, notably French theorists like ROLAND BARTHES and MICHEL FOUCAULT, are suspicious of the whole notion of the author, viewing it as an unwarranted attempt to limit the possible range of meanings of a piece of writing. Barthes, accordingly, flamboyantly proclaims the "death of the author": we should see literary texts not as the fixed products of a single mind but as fields of free linguistic play, which readers may rewrite as they wish. This libertarian doctrine arises from the literature of modernism, which breaks with the classical realist conception of the text as equipped with a full, stable meaning that the reader has merely to dig out.

The U.S. critic Stanley Fish insists that everything in a piece of writing is a matter of reader interpretation, right down to the punctuation. The whole burden of literary activity is thus shifted dramatically onto the reader, who is continually bringing into existence the very work he or she appears to "receive." On this theory it becomes impossible, as Fish candidly recognizes, to answer the question, What is it that the reader is interpreting? (For the answer to this question also must consist in an interpretation on the part of the reader, and so on in a potentially infinite regress.) Fish does not believe, however, that his doctrine leads to interpretive anarchy, for the reason that readers are never isolated individuals capable of dreaming up any interpretation that pleases them, but always members of an interpretive community whose codes, conventions, and institutions will determine the kinds of interpretation they produce. What is doing the reading, then, on this model, is the interpretive community itself, of which any individual reader would seem little more than a passive representative. Fish's theory raises important questions of what it might mean to read "wrongly," of how far the work itself might be said to challenge or resist any particular reader's version of it, and of whether interpretive communities are to be seen as unified or conflictive.

Whatever the difficulties raised by reception theory, there is no doubt that it has considerably complicated and enriched our previous ideas about what was at stake in the apparently straightforward act of reading a piece of writing. To restore the reader to his or her properly active function involves transforming our understanding of literature as a whole.

See also IDEOLOGY; LITERARY CRITICISM.

Bibliography. Roland Barthes, *The Pleasure of the Text* (Le plaisir du texte), trans. by Richard Miller, London, 1976; Stanley Fish, *Is There a Text in This Class?* Cambridge, Mass., 1980; Michel Foucault, "What Is an Author?" in *Language, Counter-Memory, Practice: Selected Essays and Interviews* (in French), ed. by Donald F. Bouchard, trans. by D. F. Bouchard and Sherry Simon, Ithaca, N.Y., 1977; Roman Ingarden, *The Literary Work of Art* (Das literarische Kunstwerk), trans. by George G. Grabowicz, Evanston, Ill., 1973; Wolfgang Iser, *The Act of Reading: A Theory of Aesthetic Response* (Der Akt des Lesens), London and Baltimore, Md., 1978.

TERRY EAGLETON

REALISM

As the term has been used in the modern era, a belief in a reality outside the mind to which the writer or artist owes primary allegiance. LANGUAGE and images must reflect something outside the operations of the mind itself. The advent of realism as a literary and artistic value can be seen as a development of the scientific age from the late seventeenth century onward. The belief in an external world is a belief in a world of sensible particulars capable of being weighed and measured, analyzed, and put to use. Confidence in a scientifically perceivable and knowable reality was paralleled by a growing confidence in the ability to study and know humankind and to effect social change. From such confidence arose England's "Glorious Revolution" of 1688 and the American and French revolutions at the end of the eighteenth century. *See* DIDEROT, DENIS; LOCKE, JOHN.

Roots of realism. The first considerable body of artistic work to reflect the movement to realism is from seventeenth-century Holland, which took a leading role in social change. It early espoused Protestantism and republican ideals, and the wealth created by trade, COLONIZATION, and industry in its "Golden Age" was a capitalist, middle-class wealth. Holland also took a leading role in the new scientific developments in MATHEMATICS, optics, and astronomy. It produced an ART that did not depend on aristocratic patronage or the grand manner of execution but turned away from mythical or legendary subject matter toward the details of ordinary Dutch life. In the work of such painters as Rembrandt, Jan Vermeer, or Pieter de Hooch (Figure 1) we see a mimetic art created for a middle-class public, an art that does not accept the aristocratic assumptions of the grand style. The term *realism* was first used in France to describe the *vérité humaine,* or "human truth," of Rembrandt, and Dutch painting was to be an inspiration for much realism in a later period.

In literature the seventeenth century saw the establishment of what we have come to call realism in the European novel, although the term itself was not then used. The novel was a relatively new literary form that could take the existing physical and social world as its setting and could examine the behavior of human beings in contemporary social conditions. In England in particular, the new realistic novel accompanied a new MODE of dramatic representation. The THEATER underwent an important change, as the proscenium arch separated the audience from the actors, and dramatic characters became less symbolic and more representational (*see* DRAMA—HISTORY). In COMEDY especially, the actors performed the parts of recognizably modern character types before painted scenes representing the world outside the theater, the new buildings, streets, shops, and parks of London. In the novel, too, settings become increasingly recognizable, often urban places where characters neither angelic nor fiendish confront what seems not a fate but a series of problems. Other modes of writing that contributed to the new form include criminal BIOGRAPHY, Puritan written self-examination, and the personal LETTER, as well as drama and the old romance (*see* ROMANCE, THE). The art of eighteenth-century novelists like Pierre Marivaux in France and Daniel Defoe, Samuel Richardson, Henry Fielding (Figure 2), and Tobias Smollett in England appealed to a new, wider readership, and their works were sold in the marketplace, removed from the aristocratic tradition of patronage.

In LITERARY CRITICISM and controversy of the eighteenth century, discussions of the novel emphasize the change from the unreal and "improbable" constituents of the romance to the mundane and believable elements of the new forms of history. The realistic work deals with common and contemporary life and behavior; it does not use "high" style, and it never offends against probability. The realistic work is presumed to have an intrinsic aesthetic appeal; the belief that what is described or presented could actually exist is supposed to make the reader more likely to respond emotionally and pleasurably to the experiences presented. In his investigation of what he calls formal realism in *The Rise of the Novel* (1957), literary critic Ian Watt stresses the realistic story's attention to the scientifically probable in plot and structure, its respect for the realities of space and time, and its extensive use of characters neither noble nor historically significant. Characters are also given names that are not symbolic or openly descriptive (e.g., Mr. Greatheart, Mr. Badman) but credible, like the names of people we might meet (e.g., Tom Jones, Cécile Volanges).

Themes. The Enlightenment's belief in the value of such pictures of real life was an aspect of an ideological program that entailed deposing many religious and aristocratic works (broadly lumped under the heading of "romance") and denying their appeal. Claims for realism in art or literature reflected political aims, whether for the establishment of the republican rule of the middle class or for a wider extension of democracy. In art and literature alike, what might be called the age of high realism occurred in the nineteenth century, when the effects of the Industrial Revolution were most strongly felt. The period in which realism dominated the arts is customarily dated 1840–1880.

The center of realism in painting in the early nineteenth century was France; the realist movement rallied around the work of Gustave Courbet, and its rallying cry was Honoré Daumier's "il faut être de son temps" ("one must be of one's time"). Eugène Delacroix displayed in certain of his works the new realistic interests, as did Jean-François Millet, Gustave Doré, and later Edgar Degas and Édouard Manet. In England the major practitioners of realistic art were Edwin Landseer, John Everett Millais, and Ford Madox Brown, all of whom defied heroic history painting. Rembrandt was praised as the repre-

Figure 1. *(Realism)* Pieter de Hooch, *Courtyard of a House in Delft,* 1658. Reproduced by courtesy of the Trustees, The National Gallery, London.

Figure 2. *(Realism)* Illustration from *The History of Tom Jones: A Foundling,* after a drawing by Thomas Rowlandson, 1798. From *The Complete Works of Henry Fielding, Esq.,* New York: Croscup & Sterling Company, 1902, Book VII, p. 250.

sentative of the revolt against the *anciens*, those who regarded CLASSICISM, tradition, and authority as the fount of aesthetic values. Realistic artists chose as their subjects scenes of death and illness, labor, and the worlds of the middle class and poor (Figure 3). They emphasized painting in the open air (*plein-air*), making a virtue of getting away from the studio and painting nature and human beings in the particularity

Figure 3. *(Realism)* Jean-François Millet, *Potato Planters*, 1861–1862. Courtesy, Museum of Fine Arts, Boston. Gift of Quincy Adams Shaw through Quincy A. Shaw, Jr., and Mrs. Marian Shaw Haughton.

Figure 4. *(Realism)* John Everett Millais, *Lorenzo and Isabella*, 1849. National Museums and Galleries on Merseyside (Walker Art Gallery), Liverpool.

of a day. Human works and figures were fundamentally more important to the new realists than unhumanized nature.

Realism in its heyday affected literature as much as painting, and one of its chief theorists and major practitioners was Gustave Flaubert, who said, "The more Art develops, the more scientific it will be, just as science will become artistic." The realistic work might be characterized as one that acknowledges constraints—work, poverty, illness, time, change, death. It seems bravely to be investigating limitations, but with some lingering sense of the holy lurking in the external reality that is held up to the light. In England essayist John Ruskin was the chief prophet of realism in art and literature and novelist George Eliot one of its most eloquent practitioners. As Eliot explains in her moral appeal to us to understand her commonplace character Amos Barton: "You would gain unspeakably if you would learn with me to see some of the poetry and the pathos, the tragedy and the comedy lying in the experience of a human soul that looks out through dull grey eyes, and that speaks in a voice of quite ordinary tones."

The appeal of realism as a concept and a value in art lies ultimately in its moral claim that all human beings matter immensely. German critic Erich Auerbach traced our interest in this mode back to the Old Testament, with its heroes—so different from Greek heroes—engaged in "entangled and stratified human relations . . . ," living imperfect lives and experiencing psychological problems unknowable to Odysseus. Auerbach saw realism as essentially rhetorical: it must in the first place deny a hierarchy of styles, making what in classical terms would be a "low" subject (like fishermen or carpenters) into a "high" subject, or, rather, dispense with such notions altogether. He tended to see both late-RENAISSANCE practice and neoclassicism as aberrations, and the Western love of a humane and dynamic realism in its literature as the rule.

The common tendency to use *realistic* or *realism* as terms of unqualified approval has met periodic opposition. In the high noon of the nineteenth century's realist movement, realism could be identified as a kind of cynicism, reflecting an inclination to take the lowest and ugliest view of people and places. It was sometimes thought morally dangerous, encouraging gloom and pessimism, and often considered aesthetically destructive, as antipathetic to POETRY in general. Alfred, Lord Tennyson and Robert Browning, like T. S. Eliot and Ezra Pound after them, found in other cultures, in the past, and in tradition and legend material for poetry that discounted absolute realism, just as the Pre-Raphaelite painters whom Ruskin admired found an outlet in unrealistic subjects painted with great fidelity to detail (Figure 4). English critic C. S. Lewis distinguishes between "realism of content" (i.e., Watt's formal realism) and "realism of presentation," pointing out that all sorts of stories may make convincing use of credible detail without having to subscribe to realism of content and obey the rules of probability.

The decline of realism. According to U.S. scholar Wylie Sypher, "Realism is only a theory, not a style—an attitude, not a method." Or, as Watt says, realism is a convention. In the history of art we can see dogged and self-conscious realism exploding itself; the impressionists went faithfully to nature but included the nature of seeing, thus turning the concerns of painting to the subjective once more. Cubism and surrealism denied the old fidelity to external provable reality (Figure 5), and in literature James Joyce's *Ulysses,* among other works of the early twentieth century, broke through realism with a gigantic parody of realistic method.

At the popular level *realistic* is still a favorable term. Something realistic (a film or a novel) is "true-to-life" or "lifelike," as opposed to lifeless or, often, abstract or distorted. But the formal realism valued so highly since the eighteenth century proved a temporally contingent quality. And we misinterpret even the most "realistic" of literary forms—the novel—in its most "realistic" periods (e.g., the works of Victor Hugo and Charles Dickens) if we insist too much on its realism. Novelists have always incorporated many elements of the romance in their works, as well as exploring modes of stylistic play, imagistic presentation, textual or visual disruption, and surreal effects, just as the most realistic painters may have a vein of fantastic exuberance in their execution and may use symbolism or legend in their subject matter. Surrealism has often been called in as a new aesthetic value to redress the bony truths of realism. Modern novels are often fantastic and experimental, and deliberately break the laws regarding time and space. Vladimir Nabokov, Thomas Pynchon, Heinrich Böll, Gabriel García Márquez, and Italo Calvino are not hampered by the rules of probability.

Modern critics are less and less interested in realism. Since the end of the 1950s critical interest in the novel has focused on reader response (*see* READING THEORY) or on the work's psychological emblems, its location in a system of cultural signs and ambiguities (*see* STRUCTURALISM), or its richness of carnival play. Without wishing to rescind the moral and democratic feeling at the heart of realism's nineteenth-century appeal, the later twentieth century is more concerned with what is playful, and not with the formally and overtly coherent, finding its artistic vitality in mixed modes and unexpected reversals of formal expectations.

See also AESTHETICS; ROMANTICISM.

Bibliography. Erich Auerbach, *Mimesis: The Representation of Reality in Western Literature* (Mimesis: Dargestellte

Figure 5. *(Realism)* René Magritte, *The Listening Chamber*, 1953. Art Resource, New York.

Wirklichkeit in der abendländischen Literatur), Berlin, 1946; Damian Grant, *Realism*, London, 1970; C. S. Lewis, *An Experiment in Criticism*, Cambridge, 1961; Linda Nochlin, *Realism*, Harmondsworth, Eng., 1971; Clara Reeve, *The Progress of Romance*, Colchester, Eng., 1785; Wylie Sypher, *Rococo to Cubism in Art and Literature*, New York, 1960; Ian P. Watt, *The Rise of the Novel*, Berkeley, Calif., 1957, reprint 1974.

MARGARET ANNE DOODY

RECORDING. *See* SOUND RECORDING.

REFERENCE WORKS. *See* ENCYCLOPEDIA; LANGUAGE REFERENCE BOOK.

REITH, JOHN (1889–1971)

British broadcasting pioneer justifiably called the father of the BBC. When in 1922, at the dawn of RADIO broadcasting, John Charles Walsham Reith applied for the job of general manager of the BBC, the letters stood for British Broadcasting Company, a private concern being organized by a group of electrical companies. When on January 1, 1927, it was transformed by royal charter into a public corporation, the British Broadcasting Corporation, Reith became—and would remain until his retirement in 1938—one of the most influential men in Great Britain. Newly knighted, he was Sir John Reith, director-general.

Reith was a tall Scot of impressive presence. He had been manager of various firms of no great importance, including an engineering firm. Those who hired him expected efficient management but little more. They could scarcely foresee the authority with which he would assume his position and stamp his vision and austere standards on virtually all aspects of the BBC. He himself had a sense of mission and wrote in his diary that he was "properly grateful to God for His goodness in this matter." The task before him, as Reith saw it, was to carry into "the greatest possible number of homes everything that is best in every department of human knowledge, endeavour, or achievement." To use radio for diversion alone seemed to him a "prostitution" of its possibilities for service.

Reith's BBC had a MONOPOLY over radio broadcasting in Britain, which troubled some observers but was defended by Reith. Unified direction seemed to him a basic need, and for this the "brute force of monopoly" seemed essential. Such phrases worried his followers but reflected Reith's unflinching style of leadership. The very different radio system evolving in the United States, supported by ADVERTISING (*see also* SPONSOR), seemed to Reith and his associates a "chaos" unsuitable for Britain. In the course of a 1929 conversation with César Saerchinger, the first European representative of the Columbia Broadcasting System, Reith wondered how Americans could successfully "worship God and Mammon at the same time."

Under Reith the British radio audience grew rapidly and encompassed all social segments. Resistance to the license fees levied on set ownership to support the system was something less than had been expected. (Such resistance would develop later.) But criticism of elitist trends was heard. Reith was intent on broadcasting "the right English." The anonymous announcers developed a BBC style rather than personal styles. Dialects like Yorkshire and Cockney were confined to COMEDY. Language policies seemed to critics an aspect of class domination (*see* LANGUAGE IDEOLOGY). Announcers presenting evening music programs wore dinner jackets.

It was in news services that Reith's leadership provided a special strength. In 1927, over press opposition, Reith established the BBC's right to a journalistic role, for which he won remarkable independence. He generally supported the idea that opposing sides of controversial issues should be heard, which often annoyed government ministries. The government had vague contingency rights over broadcasting for use in emergencies. Reith's decisions on when to resist its intrusions proved important in establishing the BBC's degree of independence. He set a precedent during the 1926 general strike when Winston Churchill, then chancellor of the Exchequer, demanded that the cabinet should commandeer the BBC and use its facilities to quash the strike. Reith resisted the idea, as he would resist other demands—including one from the archbishop of Canterbury. Reith saw the BBC as inevitably a part of the Establishment but was determined not to yield its "independence of judgment."

In 1932 Reith began to make the BBC an international presence with broadcasts beamed to all parts of the world, at first in English only (not until 1938 in other languages). As world tensions increased, international radio (*see* RADIO, INTERNATIONAL) was becoming a cacophony of vituperative PROPAGANDA, which the BBC began to counter—not by retaliation but by restrained statement. Here the impersonal style of BBC news "readers," reporting without the resonances of promotion or indignation, proved remarkably effective, establishing wide trust among world listeners. This credibility may have been one of the most valuable legacies of the Reith years.

In the two years before Reith's 1938 retirement television seemed almost ready, and an experimental service was begun (*see* TELEVISION HISTORY). But the new medium did not imbue Reith with quite the fervor with which he had, years earlier, piloted the BBC into the radio age. In 1940, having withdrawn from the scene, he became Lord Reith of Stonehaven. In later years he was occasionally called on for other posts, such as head of the British Overseas Aircraft Corporation (BOAC) and of the Commonwealth Telecommunications Board.

See also RELIGIOUS BROADCASTING.

Figure 1. *(Reith, John)* *Sir John Reith*. Chalk drawing by Sir David Low. National Portrait Gallery, London.

Bibliography. Asa Briggs, *The BBC: The First Fifty Years,* New York, 1985; idem, *The History of Broadcasting in the United Kingdom,* 4 vols., London and New York, 1961–1979; Roger Milner, *Reith: The B.B.C. Years,* Edinburgh, 1983; John Reith, *The Reith Diaries,* ed. by Charles Stuart, London, 1975; César Saerchinger, *Hello America! Radio Adventures in Europe,* Boston, 1938.

HARTLEY S. SPATT

RELIGION

The major religions of the world have played a commanding role in cross-cultural communication either because their adherents were scattered across various areas, as in the case of the Jews (*see* DIAS-PORA; JUDAISM), or because they possessed an impulse to missionize, like the Buddhists in China and elsewhere. Within societies and cultural areas religions have often had a powerful effect on ways of exchanging and developing ideas. For example, the Brahmin class in India had the effect of monopolizing a form of sacred knowledge; and the use of Confucian texts in the examination system of imperial China left its mark on the whole literary and cultural field (*see* CONFUCIUS; EAST ASIA, ANCIENT). At a more restricted level ethnic religions, chiefly to be found in relatively small-scale societies, gave shape to the mythic lore and consciousness of the group.

The effects of WRITING were considerable in that it created the possibility of sacred texts, which became the focus of learning (*see* SCRIPTURE). Religious specialists credited with special knowledge became a common feature of traditions, though the mode in which they operated varied. Thus Brahmins had control of the (originally oral) tradition of sruti, or revelation, and those outside the upper three classes of the Hindu caste hierarchy were excluded from contact with the Vedic scriptures. The severe taboos surrounding transactions with Brahmins helped to preserve the esoteric character of divine knowledge. In the Christian traditions there developed a priesthood that also had special, though not exclusive, access to sacred knowledge, partly because in western Europe Latin became the specialized LANGUAGE of religion and learning even when people spoke various vernaculars (*see* MIDDLE AGES). In Judaism in its major formative period after the fall of Jerusalem in 70 C.E., the rabbis became important as highly trained interpreters of the Law, or Torah, and they became the means through which the Oral Torah was codified and developed. In Islam the main focus of INTERPRETATION of the tradition had to do with the Shari'a, or Law, and again there was need of a body of trained persons, an elite of jurisconsults (*see* ISLAM, CLASSICAL AND MEDIEVAL ERAS). In some respects Arabic became a sacred language, in the sense that only in Arabic is the Qur'an strictly speaking the Qur'an; translations are merely interpretations. For Arab cultures this did not present a barrier, but it has for the majority of Muslims, who live outside the heartlands of Islam. The Confucian classics, though not strictly sacred or revelatory texts, nevertheless have a complexity that required very skilled understanding, and the scholar-gentleman came to occupy a special role in the transmission of the tradition. Even in Buddhism, which was not supposed to be an esoteric religion, for the Buddha wished the teaching to be transmitted in the relevant vernacular languages, Pali (once a North Indian vernacular) came to be a sacred language for various Theravadin cultures (including Sri Lanka and Thailand), while the

great wing of Buddhism known as the Mahayana developed Sanskrit texts. In later Buddhism—for example, in Tibet—there were also trends toward an esoteric approach to learning.

Despite all this, it was certainly not the intention of the major traditions to restrict the transmission of their values and doctrines, unless social arrangements dictated it, as in Hindu India. This is especially obvious when the religions were consciously missionary in character—chiefly Christianity, Islam, and Buddhism. Even relatively nonmissionary systems such as Hinduism and Confucianism had an osmotic spread, permeating not only great cultural areas such as India and China but also beyond to Southeast Asia, Japan, and so on. If there were religious elites who dominated sacred learning, the logic was not so much to restrict the spread of ideas as to control it.

This was a major motive in the formation of canons. There was a multiplication, for instance, of supposed Christian texts in the second and third centuries, and to deal with heresies the Christian church set about forming a regular collection of approved scriptures. It was not always successful. The canon of Buddhist texts was supposedly fixed at councils after the death of the founder, but from the first century C.E. onward new Sanskrit texts were composed as were other texts in China, such as the famous Ch'an (Zen) classic, *The Platform Sutra*. Even the more conservatively oriented Theravadin scriptures added material in the interstices, filling out the barer bones of the earlier Buddhist records.

In theory many of the scriptures are considered to be communications directly or indirectly from beyond—from God or from the transcendental insight of the Buddha. It happens that the Buddha did not believe in a supreme God and did not take the sacramental rituals of the Brahmins seriously, so there was a certain openness about the mode of communication of the Transcendent to ordinary people. He was concerned, of course, about proper transmission, for this was the logic behind his founding of the Sangha order of monks and nuns. Among other things, the order was to preach the dharma (teaching). But among religions that had the sense of God and the sacred there was even greater concern to control the message, which was part of a sacred tradition embodied in a community. This tendency toward sacred control was reinforced in Western Christendom by the centralization of the church under the increasingly influential papacy. With the growth, through the Crusades, of the use of force to propagate the faith, the Inquisition had state assistance in suppressing heresy by physical means (*see* CRUSADES, THE). Because of the sacred character of the church it became easy to equate heresy with profanity, and so with the forces of the Antichrist. Thus differences of opinion were identified with rejection of the holy character of the sacraments and of the church.

Control over ideas. This ideological control was also something that concerned the Chinese emperors from time to time. In 213 B.C.E. the Ch'in emperor caused the burning of all books that could be used to attack the new regime—in fact all books, including the Confucian classics, that addressed higher values, philosophy, and religion (technical manuals on farming, divination, and the like were exempted). The burning was accompanied by a banning of the scholarly class. But later, and more generally, ideological control was exercised in alliance with and mostly in the name of the Confucian control. It was on this basis that eventually a modus vivendi was achieved among the Confucian, Taoist, and Buddhist traditions (although Buddhism continued to be persecuted sporadically). *See* BOOK; CENSORSHIP.

There were similar qualms in the West about how to treat non-Christian, and later non-Islamic, learning. In a way the position was reversed in the sense that in Christian Europe the old classical culture was viewed with some suspicion as being "pagan." For this reason the famous LIBRARY at Alexandria was burned by Christians in 391, and later with similar motives by Muslims in 642. The rediscovery of the classical past later on was, of course, a main reason for the RENAISSANCE of the fifteenth and sixteenth centuries, and there remained, even after the Reformation, tensions between the need for religious control and the desire to incorporate the best of secular or pagan knowledge into the fabric of Christian thought and life (and similarly with Islam).

The Reformation was spurred by various forces, including the increased use of the vernacular, such as the translations into English of the Bible by John Wycliffe. The invention of PRINTING gave a new impetus to the circulation of religious ideas and texts. The evolution, however, of a new alliance between church and state—for example, in England and Sweden—theoretically gave new possibilities of control. Thus entry into higher EDUCATION in Britain involved affirming the Anglican Thirty-nine Articles (keeping out Catholics, radical Reformers, and Jews). However, because many nineteenth-century European nationalist movements were dominated by liberals, the state tended to be halfhearted in enforcing religious conformity.

Dissemination of ideas. Though religions have in varying ways placed some restrictions on communication, they also have had, on the whole, a considerable concern for propagating the various aspects of the relevant faith. In doctrine there has been care regarding the question of true formulation, but the religions also became involved heavily in wider intellectual interests and some form of higher education for religious specialists—as with the training of *pan-*

ditas (learned persons) in the Hindu tradition, the establishment of Buddhist universities (above all, that at Nalanda in North India), Islamic universities such as al-Azhar in Cairo, and so on (*see* UNIVERSITY). Many of these forms of training went far beyond the religious interests of the tradition, but they were at least centered on the relevant faiths. Philosophy in Christian Europe, Islam, and India became a vital adjunct to religion, and Buddhist philosophy—for example, the critical approach of Nāgārjuna (ca. 100 C.E.)—itself became a way of reasoning held to lead toward the spiritual goal. The modes of formulating doctrines and the shape of the worldview became more sophisticated, as with the Neo-Confucian revival in China from the eleventh century on.

The mythic or narrative dimension of religion focused on the main events in the lives of founders, but it also came to incorporate a wealth of material that was important in reaching out to a wider, largely illiterate public (*see* LITERACY). Especially noteworthy here are the Jataka tales in Buddhism, which recount events in the previous lives of the Buddha and serve as illustrations of ethical behavior. In Christian Europe there also developed means of presenting stories in dramatic entertainment (the so-called mystery plays). The massive lore of Hindu life came to be expressed through the Puranas, a vast and intricate collection of myths. More important still were the great epics, the Mahabharata and the Ramayana, which formed the basis of dramatic presentations that traditionally entertained and molded the mores of Indian village life down the centuries (*see* MUSIC THEATER—ASIAN TRADITIONS). Now they also are used as the basis for the mythological dramas produced by the Indian film industry (*see* MYTHOLOGICAL FILM, ASIAN). In traditional China DRAMA was also integrated into religion through association with celebrations of the New Year, the cult of ancestors, and the like. On the other hand, Buddhism had a ban on monks or nuns watching drama or dance, and this inhibited the development of Buddhist drama. Much of the Jewish interpretation of the Bible concentrates on the complex stories contained in it, and the NARRATIVE dimension provides the main historical substance of Judaism, which through its CALENDAR commemorates some of the major events in the history of the Jewish people.

Religious traditions have typically also been concerned with more directly communicating ethical values. Sometimes these have been tightly integrated into a system of law, as in Judaism and Islam, and this involves the creation of a class of specialists to interpret the law. In Buddhism a strong emphasis in monks' sermons is morality, which is the strongest part of their educational effort in raising the standard of life of laypersons. As noted above, the Buddhist Jataka tales also have ethical implications. And

Christianity has evolved educational systems whose ethos is directed especially at ethical upbringing.

Varieties of rituals. At the heart of most religions is the practice of various rituals—from formal, as in the case of a Roman Catholic High Mass, to very informal, as in a meeting of the Society of Friends (*see* RITUAL). These may be supplemented by various modes of spiritual practice, such as meditation, prayer, and confession. This ritual-practical dimension of religion is a major means of communicating the substance of a faith (in fact the very word *communication* comes from the Latin term for the distribution and participation in the elements of the Eucharist or Lord's Supper or Communion). Because ritual performances involve more than the use of words they contain a symbolic side (reinforced also in many cases by religious ART).

SYMBOLISM is a strong way of conveying the meaning of the faith and has an impact greater than the abstractions of doctrine. It also often includes a picturesque element that has easy access to popular imagination. Thus pilgrimages to famous sacred places traditionally make a more tangible contribution to faith than mere words. The practice of pilgrimage is fairly central to Islam, the hajj to Mecca being a potent symbol of Islamic solidarity. It has also been important in Catholic and Orthodox Christianity, especially to the Holy Land. It is widespread in Buddhism—to Bodh Gaya, Sarnath, Kapilavastu, and Kusinagara, associated with major events in the Buddha's life—and also in Hinduism, especially to bathe in the sacred Ganges at Banaras. There is a traditional pattern of sacred mountains in Japan, which are foci of pilgrimages. These migrations helped with the circulation of ideas among adherents from widely different parts of the relevant area of the world. Their significance in some countries has declined (being replaced by that secular pilgrimage known as TOURISM), but elsewhere modern means of transport have increased the intensity of pilgrimage, especially with Islam and in the Indian subcontinent (*see* ISLAMIC WORLD, TWENTIETH CENTURY).

In some religious cultures the wandering holy person is an important phenomenon. This, for instance, contributed to the religious unity of India even when it was thoroughly divided politically, for the wanderer would journey to sacred sites all over India.

Of all the rituals, ultimately the most potent for the modern world may have been the sermon (*see* HOMILETICS). Preaching has a central place in much of Protestant Christianity, being in effect the most important sacrament. The preacher is supposed to convey the message of the Bible and behind that of God through his or her eloquence, and part of that conveying is the arousal of strong feelings of love, dedication, commitment, and so on. Protestant emphasis on the word has in recent times often been expressed, especially in the United States, by the use of the media—both RADIO (popularized rather spectacularly by Aimee Semple McPherson in southern California in the 1920s) and television, in which some preachers, such as Oral Roberts and Robert Schuller, have built up big audiences and prosperous organizations (*see* RELIGIOUS BROADCASTING). It happens that the free-enterprise aspect of media in the United States lends itself better to this extension of preaching than do the controlled systems in Great Britain and France and elsewhere in Europe.

The ritual aspect of religion thus has a certain polarity: at the one end are the nonverbal symbolisms of ritual action, and at the other is the highly verbalized ritual of preaching as a means of bringing the Ultimate to the people.

The object of much of such activity is the creation of feelings within people, and so it constitutes a kind of RHETORIC, which can result in powerful religious experiences. This is especially emphasized in that strand of religion often referred to as mysticism. Buddhist meditation, Christian monasticism, Hindu yoga, Sufi groups—all these may be vehicles for bringing about an inner experience of peace and insight. In turn these depth experiences have to be expressed and conveyed somehow through words and actions. On the one hand, there is a pervasive tradition in the mystical strand of the great religions that because the inner experience of the eternal is indescribable it is often conveyed best through silence. On the other hand, the sense of the presence of God, as in conversion experiences, often gives rise to enthusiastic utterance, including that strange form of speech known as glossolalia, or speaking in tongues. In the bhakti, or devotional wing of Hinduism, and in the Christian and Jewish traditions singing is associated with worship and the expression of such sentiments as joy and awe (*see* MUSIC PERFORMANCE; SONG).

Religious arts. The art of a religion is also a powerful means of communication. Thus the sublime smile of a Buddha figure may signify not just the relaxed peace and joy of one who has attained Enlightenment but also the sense that it is by a gesture—however minimal, like a smile—rather than by words that the truth is conveyed. But in an important sense the religious art of generations up to the modern era is often a substitute for writing. The story of the Buddha or Krishna is communicated in pictures; so are the stations of the cross in the Catholic tradition. The lighting of candles or incense sticks is a concrete means of expressing reverence, often in front of a picture or statue. The uses in the West of stained-glass windows, in Eastern Christendom of icons, in the Buddhist tradition of bas-reliefs, and so on, are powerful modes of educating the laity in the essentials of the narratives, and sometimes even of doctrines. Chinese Ch'an and Japanese Zen paintings, which contain large expanses of blankness, are means of showing in a minimalist way that we act by not acting and that the essence of things in this world is the void. *See* ICONOGRAPHY.

Religious art can create its own language—for instance, in mudras, the various gestures made by the hand in Buddha statues, each with a conventionally assigned meaning (e.g., that the Buddha is here teaching in an analytical way, or that he bids us leave fear behind). These mudras are part of the complex signals in a statue of the various motifs of the Buddha's life and doctrine. In the Hindu tradition, and to some extent among Buddhists and Jains as well, statues are conceived as themselves endowed with power, so they become sacramental incarnations of the holy and the locus of particular gods or supernatural beings. The study of such iconography is an important item in the understanding of religion.

However, some religions are icon-free—Islam and parts of Christianity (Calvinism in the old days, for instance, and still among some evangelical groups) and Judaism, which consider it wrong and inappropriate to depict God. God as spirit is beyond such representation, it is held, and depicting him may lead to the worship of the images themselves, or idolatry. Naturally, such religions have alternative means of expressing their attitudes toward the Ultimate. So Islamic ARCHITECTURE with its purity of form and its decoration (often with texts from the holy Qur'an) conveys something of the awe-inspiring otherness of the divine. In brief, differing religions hold different views about how best through the plastic arts to represent and express God as a holy being, or the unspeakable Ultimate of the Buddhist tradition.

Music is also a powerful means of communication because it has a natural affinity with differing emotions. In modern times especially, religions have taken an interest in the creation of hymns and music to encourage mass participation. Some already have their deeply inbuilt music—for instance, Islam with its chanting of the Qur'an. This, in an awe-inspiring and sacred way, most vividly encapsulates the revelation of God and is the real manifestation of the Islamic word. The Arabic-written Qur'an can be compared to a musical score, which though a guide to the music, is secondary to it. *See* MUSIC HISTORY.

Architecture also is a mode of conveying ideas. The soaring Gothic cathedral points to heaven. The massive towered Hindu temple is a holy mountain in stone around whose peaks and upper slope the gods gather (gods who are all ultimately varied representations of the one reality). By contrast the simplicity of the old Scottish kirk or a New England church reflects values of innerworldly asceticism, such as characterized much of the Reformation. The domed Orthodox church symbolizes the way heaven comes down to earth. In Moldavia (Romania) there are churches with frescoes painted on the outside, an evident mode of lay education in the myths and values of the faith. The shrine rooms of Buddhist temples are designed to confront the faithful with the greatness and serenity of Buddhahood at close range.

Missionary activities. Ultimately the most important symbols communicating the essence of religion are the people involved—the shaved monk, the village priest, the hermit, the wandering holy man, the preacher, the sober laypersons, and so on. This is also relevant to the way religions spread. Some of the great religions, notably Buddhism, Christianity, and Islam, have been highly successful missionary religions. Buddhism penetrated to virtually every country in Asia and left its imprint. Islam has large command over a huge crescent running across the middle of the world from West Africa to southeastern Indonesia. Though military conquest may have been one factor, as in Islam and colonial Christianity, more vital has been the presence of dedicated and holy people, such as Sufi mystics, Christian missionaries, and Buddhist monks.

Crossing cultural boundaries has presented challenges in communication and has subtly led to changes. Thus, for instance, the Chinese had to translate many technical and religious terms from Indian Buddhist practice and often chose terminology drawn from the Taoist tradition. This was a factor in the sinicization of Buddhism and the creation of original Chinese forms of Buddhism, such as Ch'an Buddhism, in which diverse cultural elements were creatively blended. The missionary efforts of Christianity led to the identification of many missionaries with the anticolonial struggles of the twentieth century and in turn with the effects of ecumenical cooperation overseas on the mother churches in the United States and Europe. But probably the deepest effect of Christian missionary activities was the invention of written modes for a host of languages hitherto only oral (*see* ORAL CULTURE). This has paved the way for new literatures.

The development of modern communications, along with increasing travel, means that there are new opportunities for diasporas, such as Sikhs living both in the Punjab and scattered not only through India but also in countries such as Great Britain and Canada. Minority Muslims in the United States, for instance, can readily maintain contact with Muslims abroad. These factors also lead to the more rapid cross-cultural spread of new religious movements, some of which are in any event old religions in new places, such as the Hare Krishna movement. Such cultural transmissions and emigrations give many of the world's cities a pluralist character, with religions from different cultural backgrounds living side by side and often in mutual interaction.

All this has reinforced some modern trends in religious education. Although the conservative branches of some traditional religions often reject critical scholarship and appear to have an interest in restricting the open inquiry of the young, since about 1970 concern has been evident in a number of countries to inform children of the variety of religions. It is a consequence of the modern separation of church and state that religion is increasingly a private option, and religious education is sometimes seen as a way to prepare the young for such a choice.

Bibliography. Redmond A. Burke, *What Is the Index?* Milwaukee, Wis., 1962; Trevor O. Ling, *A History of Religion East and West*, London, 1968; Albert C. Moore, *Iconography of Religions*, Philadelphia, 1977; Hans Schwartz, *Divine Communication: Word and Sacrament in Biblical, Historical and Contemporary Perspective*, Philadelphia, 1985; Ninian Smart and Richard Hecht, eds., *Sacred Texts of the World*, Blauvelt, N.Y., 1983.

NINIAN SMART

RELIGIOUS BROADCASTING

Broadcasts in the interest of religious values or practices have existed since the beginnings of RADIO broadcasting and have been a factor in all subsequent media developments, including television (*see* TELEVISION HISTORY), CABLE TELEVISION, VIDEO, and program distribution by SATELLITE. Virtually all media genres have been adapted to religious purposes. The impact has varied substantially from region to region, amid varying social and political circumstances.

Beginnings. The first surge of religious broadcasting took place in the United States and was initiated by the first licensed station, KDKA in Pittsburgh, Pennsylvania, which on January 2, 1921—less than two months after the station's debut—produced a remote broadcast from the local Calvary Episcopal Church. The idea of radio as an evangelistic tool inspired others. In 1924 KFUO ("Keep Forward, Upward, Onward") in Saint Louis, Missouri, working from the attic of the Lutheran Concordia Seminary, became the first station founded under religious auspices and was followed rapidly by others. By 1925 some sixty-three stations in the United States were owned by religious institutions. But the rise of commercial broadcasting (*see* SPONSOR) made radio frequencies increasingly valuable, and many churches were persuaded to sell out to commercial entrepre-

neurs, in many cases accepting a promise of free broadcast time as part of the transaction. By the 1930s the rash of church-owned stations had all but vanished. The broadcasting of Sunday services either from church premises or from station studios had become common.

Stations and networks—the National Broadcasting Company (NBC, formed 1926) and Columbia Broadcasting System (CBS, 1927)—faced a thorny problem as radio evangelism spread. Which churches, groups, or sects should or could be accommodated? Broadcasters encouraged the formation of local and regional councils of churches to help them cope with this issue. On the national level the Federal (later National) Council of the Churches of Christ represented more than a score of denominations. The councils tended to be dominated by the "mainline" Protestant denominations and ministers; groups and individual preachers not favored by the arrangements began to seek access by buying time on a commercial basis. At first CBS welcomed such purchases, selling network time to the Lutheran Missouri Synod as well as to the fiery Father Charles E. Coughlin of the Shrine of the Little Flower in Royal Oak, Michigan. But as Coughlin's broadcasts turned highly political and sometimes anti-Semitic, CBS adopted the NBC policy of refusing to sell time for religious purposes, instead apportioning a limited amount of free time to major Protestant, Catholic, and Jewish faith groups. Those bypassed or unsatisfied with their allotments focused increasingly on local coverage, free or purchased, and in some cases organized ad hoc hookups of stations via leased telephone lines. Many made over-the-air fund appeals to help them continue and expand their radio evangelism.

After World War II, with the rise of television, the U.S. networks emphasized a policy of "cooperative broadcasting." The major faith groups were invited to provide assistance to the networks in the production of weekly half-hour television series dedicated to religion, such as NBC's "Frontiers of Faith" and CBS's "Look Up and Live." The American Broadcasting Company (ABC, formed 1943, split off from NBC) was represented by "Directions." A wide diversity of groups maintained a presence on radio or television or both, by various arrangements. The Mormons were represented on network radio (first NBC, then CBS) by a nondoctrinal musical program, "Music and the Spoken Word," featuring the Tabernacle Choir, begun in 1929 and continuing more than a half century later. The Seventh-Day Adventists were represented by "The Voice of Prophecy," begun in 1930. In 1945 the Jewish Theological Seminary started "The Eternal Light," dramatizing aspects of Judaic culture and religion, offered weekly over NBC radio and occasionally produced for television. Some groups sought to extend their coverage through program SYNDICATION—the United Methodists with the film series "The Way," the Lutheran Missouri Synod with "This Is the Life." Many Catholic groups were program producers. Paulist Productions distributed an "Insight" series; the Franciscans syndicated radio dramas on the lives of saints and, later, a series of television spots. Commercial sponsorship became a factor: Texaco sponsored Monsignor Fulton J. Sheen in "Life Is Worth Living" (1952–1957), first on the short-lived Dumont Television Network, then on ABC Television. In 1968 the U.S. Catholic Conference established an Office of Radio and Television to represent it in all broadcasting matters.

In Europe the first religious broadcast took place in late December 1922 on BBC—the British Broadcasting Company (later Corporation). The Reverend John Mayo, Vicar of Whitechapel, London, spoke on the wonders of the new invention and what it could do for humanity. Within a year JOHN REITH, first director of the BBC, had developed an impressive advisory committee that included the archbishop of Canterbury, a staunch supporter who at first had the impression that listeners had to have their windows open to hear the wireless. In January 1924 the BBC broadcast a service from Saint Martin's-in-the-Fields, and audience response was so favorable that "outside broadcasts" of church services became a standard feature. At first these were not Sunday morning services; Reith was reluctant to broadcast anything on Sunday morning, let alone a church service, since he expected listeners to be in church. Nevertheless, a Sunday-morning service was broadcast in 1933, and this too became standard, along with religious talks and a daily fifteen-minute worship service.

With the coming of television the BBC experimented with various formats, including the popular "Songs of Praise," introduced in 1961. By the 1970s the BBC was taking the view that religious programming should be treated on its own merits and not be subject to special consideration. This gave rise to "Anno Domini" (later "Everyman"), a controversial and highly acclaimed DOCUMENTARY series dealing with moral and ethical issues worldwide. In 1976 a government report, the Annan Report, endorsed the idea that religious programs should not be solely Christian; subsequently broadcasts dealt occasionally with Islam and other great world faiths.

Trends worldwide. Elsewhere religious broadcasting has developed in various ways, always influenced by each country's distinctive religious and political makeup. The Federal Republic of Germany has had a wide diversity of programming on both national and local channels for Protestants and Catholics, with time also available to the Free Churches. Stations support substantial religious departments, and there is an elaborate advisory system. In Austria the broadcasting system allocates time mainly to Cath-

olics and Protestants, with several programs a year serving Old Catholics, Muslims, and Jews. Switzerland provides a wide range of formats and subjects under the auspices of the Reformed, Catholic, and Free Church groups. The German Democratic Republic provides a single Sunday-morning preaching program on radio plus six Saturday periods for television programs on "church" themes (no social commentary) and one or two live-worship services. Poland has no religious television; radio provides three programs a month for Catholics and one for the Protestant-Reformed-Orthodox group, all confined to pretaped programs. The USSR has no religious radio or television programs.

Until 1944 all religious broadcasting in Italy was Catholic, but subsequently regular programming was also provided for other groups, primarily Protestants and Jews. In the 1970s a proliferation of new stations, radio and television, in most cases operating on a commercial basis, attracted fundamentalist groups ready to purchase time. Radio Vatican has long run a twenty-four-hour international broadcasting service in a number of languages.

The state-operated broadcasting systems in the Scandinavian nations provide small percentages of their television and radio budgets and broadcast time for religious programs, again in cooperation with the representative church groups. The Church of Finland has its own radio pastors producing weekly programs, with the Finnish Broadcasting Company providing production services and transmission free of charge.

Outside North America and Europe the amount of religious broadcasting is smaller and varies considerably country by country. Africa presents sharp contrasts. In Ghana both Christian and Muslim groups have their own studio facilities and broadcast regularly through the Ghana Broadcasting Corporation. But the Ivory Coast allots no broadcast time to Protestants, who nevertheless manage to serve an Ivory Coast audience through broadcasts produced in Liberia and relayed by shortwave. In Burundi, which is more than half Catholic, the churches participate in the national Voice of the Revolution station. But in Ethiopia a station founded by Protestants was taken over in 1977 by the revolutionary government. In Kenya religious groups have maintained an extensive broadcasting program, including a training center and several recording studios, with the government providing time on the Voice of Kenya. *See* AFRICA, TWENTIETH CENTURY.

It is difficult to characterize religious broadcasting in the Muslim world because Islam presents a blend of religion and political, social, and economic IDEOLOGY. During periods of political crisis presidents Gamal Abdel Nasser and Anwar as-Sadat in Egypt and the Ayatollah Ruholla Khomeini in Iran assumed the unifying role of both imam (religious leader) and commander in chief. There is little distinction between religion and CULTURE, so while state-controlled radio and television regularly broadcast the call to prayer and give airtime to political-religious leaders, they do not provide time for religion in the Western sense. *See* ISLAMIC WORLD, TWENTIETH CENTURY.

There is a similar pattern in Japan, where Shinto is as much a cultural as a religious institution, as well as in predominantly Hindu nations such as India, where state broadcasting of the culture—music, DANCE, DRAMA—embraces religion, so that religious organizations are not accorded special programming. Asia, Africa, Latin America, and other parts of the Third World have this in common: religious broadcasting per se is the strongest where Western influence has been greatest, and religion on state-dominated stations varies according to the extent to which the nation has embraced Western technology and culture. *See* ASIA, TWENTIETH CENTURY; LATIN AMERICA, TWENTIETH CENTURY.

Three organizations specialize in coordinating religious broadcasting and other communication activities internationally. The World Association for Christian Communication, headquartered in London, works with churches and other groups in sixty countries. UNDA (Latin for "wave") is an international Catholic organization serving Catholic broadcasters on every continent. The Lutheran World Federation maintains its Communication Office in Geneva to coordinate the work of Lutheran churches around the world.

Technology and outreach. When shortwave radio became a reliable means of long-distance communication, Christian missionary groups soon grasped its potential. On Christmas Day, 1931, the World Radio Missionary Fellowship went on the air in Quito, Ecuador, with station HCJB, then a carbon microphone in a wooden box, a 250-watt transmitter in a sheep shed, and an antenna wire strung between two eucalyptus poles. Since then HCJB has grown to ten studios, twelve transmitters, twenty-eight antennas supported by fifty towers, and a staff of two hundred North Americans, broadcasting twenty-four hours a day in thirteen languages and reaching virtually every corner of the globe. HCJB is but one of a half-dozen large shortwave evangelistic efforts. The Far East Broadcasting Company, with offices in thirteen countries, broadcasts in ninety languages and dialects for a total of about eight thousand hours per month. Trans World Radio, established in 1952, claims to reach a listening area that includes 80 percent of the world's population; it broadcasts from sites in Monte Carlo, the Netherlands Antilles, Guam, Swaziland, and Sri Lanka, and from Evangelisum Rundfunk (its branch in the Federal Republic of Germany), and it also uses purchased time on Radio

Cyprus. Seventh-Day Adventists support programming on more than thirty-nine hundred radio, television, and cable outlets in ninety countries. *See* RADIO, INTERNATIONAL.

A development with many international as well as national ramifications is the so-called electronic church, a movement that began, like religious broadcasting itself, in the United States. Making maximum use of new technologies, it is at the same time an extension of the tent revivalism characteristic of earlier decades in the United States. In the 1950s Billy Graham brought television cameras and sophisticated ADVERTISING techniques to his evangelical mass meetings and, with the help of WILLIAM RANDOLPH HEARST's newspapers, became an overnight celebrity. Radio evangelist Oral Roberts moved to television, offering to heal people in their homes if they would lay their hands on the television set. In the 1960s Rex Humbard built the first church designed for television, and a decade later Pat Robertson perfected a ninety-minute religious format that closely resembled popular commercial host-show programs. Via satellite, his programs were fed to some fifty-five hundred cable systems by the Christian Broadcasting Network (CBN), reaching a large audience that included many outside the United States. The impact of the electronic church was significant because of the right-wing political ties of many of its preachers. Religion was more openly being politicized, even as many politicians were using religious appeals.

The National Religious Broadcasters (NRB), established in 1944 with the encouragement of the National Association of Evangelicals to "fight for the right of churches to continue to buy air time," grew into a coalition of some one thousand radio stations (including campus stations), ninety-two television stations, and more than five hundred production companies and distributors related to electronic evangelism. When the NRB lobbied for deregulation of broadcasting, mainline churches complained that the electronic evangelists had become captives of commercial broadcasting and its values and that their emphasis on purchase of time played into the hands of commercial broadcasting and drove religious diversity off the air. During the 1970s the number of stations carrying mainstream denominational religious programs dropped by more than half, as stations sold time to electronic church operations in preference to carrying free network or local programs.

Meanwhile the challenge of the new technologies has influenced religious groups of all sorts, new or old. In the United States the Southern Baptists have created a program network (ACTS) that combines satellite, conventional television stations, cable systems, and low-power television stations. The Mormon church has two-way interactive satellite interconnection with its temples. The Catholic church has a satellite system interconnecting its major dioceses. Clearly, as new forms of broadcast communications emerge, their use by religious groups will not be far behind.

See also CITIZEN ACCESS; HOMILETICS; RELIGION; SCRIPTURE. For religious expression in other media *see* ARCHITECTURE; ART; MUSIC HISTORY; POETRY; SCULPTURE.

Bibliography. William F. Fore, *Television and Religion: The Shaping of Faith, Values, and Culture,* Minneapolis, Minn., 1987; George Gerbner, Larry Gross, et al., *Religion in Television,* Philadelphia, 1984; Jeffrey K. Hadden and Charles E. Swann, *Prime Time Preachers: The Rising Power of Televangelism,* Reading, Mass., 1981; Peter G. Horsfield, *Religious Television: The Experience in America,* New York and London, 1984; Paul A. Soukup, *Communication and Theology: Introduction and Review of the Literature,* London, 1983.

WILLIAM F. FORE

RENAISSANCE

A term first used in the nineteenth century to characterize the complex of changes in western Europe during the period 1350–1600 that supplanted many of the institutions and goals of the CULTURE of the MIDDLE AGES. The terms *Middle Ages* and *Renaissance* ("rebirth") reflect a bias, strongly promoted in the latter era, that the one true culture was that of classical antiquity (Greek and Roman), that it had been lost in the period 400–1300, and that it was brought again to life by the rediscovery and reevaluation of the monuments, writings, and LANGUAGE of the ancients. *See* HELLENIC WORLD; ROMAN EMPIRE.

Renaissance ideals were sustained and in part formulated by the emergence of capitalism as an economic system. Capitalism, as practiced in urban-centered trade, industry, and banking, created a middle class that fostered kinds of ART and technology quite different from those sponsored by the aristocracy of the feudal era. Middle-class aspirations also encouraged an increased concern with human affairs and with the individual personality as compared with the more theocentric focus of the Middle Ages.

Humanism. Much of the character of the Renaissance was imparted by an intellectual movement that became known as humanism. Humanism was not the generalized interest in the welfare of human beings that the term later suggested but a scholarly devotion to the learning and languages of classical antiquity, especially in the fields of history, moral philosophy, RHETORIC, and POETRY—fields that in modern times came to be called the humanities. Humanism played a major role at the start of the Renaissance in shaping the political principles of the newly empowered bourgeoisie, and humanists found key roles in republican governments, duchies, and the administration of the church. Humanists in the universities (*see* UNIVERSITY) joined in opposition to the traditional and dominant organization of learning known as scholasticism, in which the key disciplines were theology, natural philosophy (science), MATHEMATICS, music, logic, law, and medicine. Scholastics tended to retain the upper hand in university EDUCATION, but the humanist reform of secondary education left an indelible mark. Humanism was ushered in by the fourteenth-century Italian poet

Figure 1. *(Renaissance)* School of Piero della Francesca, *Ideal City.* Mid-fifteenth century. Ducal Palace, Urbino. Alinari/Art Resource, New York.

and essayist Petrarch, who pointed the way to the treasures of ancient Roman literature, writing in a Latin and a Tuscan Italian that revived the elegance of style of the great Roman writers and providing an intimate image of his own personality.

Humanists took the lead in the rediscovery and editing of the classical Greek and Latin manuscripts that had been forgotten in monastic and secular libraries throughout the Middle Ages (*see* LIBRARY—HISTORY). They collaborated with the first PRINTING houses from the 1470s on to bring ancient learning and literature to a wide audience. They wrote original work inspired by ancient authors, the most influential examples being theoretical or practical treatises and essays like Leon Battista Alberti's books on painting and ARCHITECTURE and Niccolò Machiavelli's *Il principe* (The Prince, 1513). The discovery and publication of scientific texts stimulated the scientific revolution of the later Renaissance, and theologian-humanists like Desiderius Erasmus and MARTIN LUTHER produced scholarly revisions of SCRIPTURE

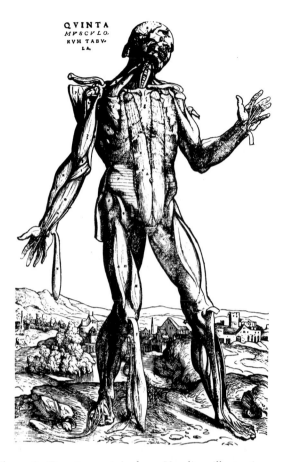

Figure 3. *(Renaissance)* Andreas Vesalius, illustration from *De Humani Corporis Fabrica*. Basel, 1543. Engraving.

and the writings of the church fathers that radically altered the path of theological studies. The classical interests of the humanist movement and Renaissance culture in general have been wrongly accused of being antireligious; humanist scholarship provided the intellectual underpinnings both for the establishment of Protestantism and for the reform of the Roman Catholic church.

The arts. Artists and their patrons shared the fascination of the humanists with the remains of classical antiquity. This is most apparent in architecture, in which, after 1420 in Italy, there appeared colonnades carrying round arches, ancient orders, masonry domes, and other characteristically Roman features. A system of proportions based on the human body differentiated classical from medieval architecture, and Renaissance designers not only returned to that approach but also developed a more subtle system integrated with the consonances of musical theory (*see* MUSIC THEORIES).

Proportions, particularly as applied to the human body, also interested figural artists, who studied and imitated the remains of ancient SCULPTURE. A math-

Figure 2. *(Renaissance)* Leonardo da Vinci, studies of water eddies, ca. 1510. Ink drawing no. 12660, verso. Windsor Castle, Royal Library. © Her Majesty Queen Elizabeth II.

ematical perspective system for painters based on medieval optical treatises was developed by Alberti and the sculptor-architect Filippo Brunelleschi; it profoundly affected the organization of paintings throughout the Renaissance, favoring symmetrical composition with a central viewing point and a box-like space.

But not all of Renaissance art was oriented to the study of its ancient antecedents and mathematical concepts. In fifteenth-century Italy a vigorous lyrical naturalism emerged out of the international court style, and in northern Europe, particularly in Flanders, painters like Jan van Eyck and Rogier van der Weyden developed a style of oil painting (the medium of the early Italians was mostly tempera) of meticulous mimetic detail and jewellike richness of surface.

By the early sixteenth century a fully developed Renaissance style, known as High Renaissance or classic Renaissance, had grown in grandeur to challenge its ancient models and was employed by leaders of the state and church in order to express their power and to display their discrimination. Artists such as Raphael, Titian, and Michelangelo were sought out by Western rulers, and their work profoundly influenced the art of subsequent centuries. For the first time artists were acclaimed for their individual styles and were accorded a prestigious position in society.

The same was true with music. Contemporary with the classic moment in art, medieval polyphony, long focused on abstract approaches to musical structure, gave way in part to a closer expressive and mimetic relationship between music and text, both sacred and secular. The increased patronage of music by both popes and princes furthered the careers of several great Renaissance composers, including Josquin des Prez, Orlando di Lasso, and Giovanni Pierluigi da Palestrina. In secular music the madrigal, normally set to contemporary Italian poetic texts, became the representative Renaissance form; its counterpart in sacred music was the Latin motet. *See* MUSIC HISTORY; SONG.

Science and technology. Renaissance science, departing from the medieval emphasis on abstract the-

Figure 4. *(Renaissance)* Jacopo Sansovino, Library of San Marco, Venice, begun 1536. Alinari/Art Resource, New York.

ory, progressed primarily in the descriptive disciplines, such as botany, zoology, anatomy, and CARTOGRAPHY. Three accomplishments of Italian Renaissance art aided the contribution of graphic artists to scientific endeavor: the control of proportion, the rationalization of sight through painters' perspective, and the projection of relief through the reproduction of effects of light and shadow (chiaroscuro). Artists wanted to reproduce nature as accurately as possible, but they also believed that the technical achievement of accuracy should serve an ideal vision. The notebooks of Leonardo da Vinci are an extraordinary record of the workings of a voracious empirical mind that touched on all aspects of Renaissance scientific and technological investigation, but Leonardo never organized his observations into functioning theoretical principles.

Advances in mapmaking and navigation spurred the Renaissance rulers to exploit the riches of Asia by finding direct sea routes that would avoid the long and dangerous trade caravans across the deserts to the Levant. In the late fifteenth century Portuguese ships rounded the southern tip of Africa, proving that there were no fabled terrors south of the equator, and the Spanish rulers sent an Italian sailor, Christopher Columbus, westward to find India, with well-known results. The consequent influx of gold from the New World accelerated the decline in Italian maritime power and cultural preeminence. *See* EXPLORATION.

The major scientific issue of the later Renaissance was posed in the field of astronomy by the Polish scholar Nicolaus Copernicus, a theoretician rather than an observer, who placed the sun rather than the earth at the center of the universe. The conflict of this hypothesis with church dogma, and incidentally with human pride, propelled it into the foreground of international attention, especially after Galileo Galilei, the first great modern scientist, took up the defense of the heliocentric theory at the cost of his freedom.

Perhaps the most important Renaissance contribution to technology was the development of printing in Germany, principally by JOHANNES GUTENBERG and Peter Schöffer, in the mid-fifteenth century. By the 1470s there were publishing houses throughout Europe capable of printing in Greek and Hebrew as well as in Latin and the vernaculars. Humanists collaborated with publishers by discovering and editing manuscripts of the basic writings of the Western tradition. New literary and expository writings exerted great influence and, from the 1520s on, played a particularly important role in the growing struggle between the Roman Catholic church and Protestantism.

From almost the earliest moment, books were illustrated with woodcuts (*see* BOOK). Woodblocks of the same height as the metal letters could easily and inexpensively be put into the printing frame, and to readers accustomed to illuminated manuscript books it seemed the natural thing to do. It also seemed natural to the designers to imitate manuscript paintings. Color printing was used from an early date, and in many incunabula (books printed before 1500) the illustrations were colored by hand to make the imitation more convincing. The chief purpose was to give printed books the status of handwritten ones, and both the style and the content were echoes of the manuscript culture. *See* PUBLISHING—HISTORY OF PUBLISHING.

It took a long time before illustrations were fully accepted as an independent and irreplaceable form of communication. Not until the 1530s—more than sixty years after the appearance of the first books with pictures—were scientific, technological, and architectural texts produced in which illustrations effectively instructed. Andreas Vesalius's *De Humani Corporis Fabrica* of 1543 is the best-known example.

Artists began making reproducible prints shortly after the first books were produced. Most early prints were engravings on copper. Woodcuts seemed too crude until Albrecht Dürer, in the 1490s, showed

Figure 5. *(Renaissance)* Andrea del Verrocchio, *Bartolomeo Colleoni*, ca. 1483–1488. Campo dei Santi Giovanni e Paolo, Venice. Alinari/Art Resource, New York.

Figure 6. *(Renaissance)* Albrecht Dürer, *The Cannon,* 1518. Etching on iron. The Metropolitan Museum of Art, New York, Fletcher Fund, 1919. (19.73.111)

how they too could serve artistic ends. He also made the first significant etching, on iron, but this technique then lay dormant for decades. *See* GRAPHIC REPRODUCTION.

The subject of Dürer's etching, a mobile cannon, wielded more temporal power than any prince portrayed by that artist. Its use by the armies of Charles VIII of France in 1494–1495 facilitated the conquest of Italy, and the experience of Charles and his successors in pursuing their Italian claims accelerated the progress of the Renaissance in France. The mobile cannon also radically changed the form of fortifications: the medieval brick walls stretching between tall square towers gave way to low stone walls with bastions designed to facilitate the movement of defensive artillery; the new shape of these walls affected the way Renaissance cities developed.

Politics. Prior to the age of mobile artillery, war retained something of the choreographic character of chivalrous combat, as when the small Italian states of the fifteenth century hired the armies of condottieri to fight other mercenaries. But the wars of the sixteenth century were waged to extend nations and to defend RELIGION, and these wars were deadly serious.

The formation of the nation-state was one of the primary achievements of the Renaissance. In the sixteenth century, especially in England, France, and the Holy Roman Empire (which at its height under Emperor Charles V included most of central Europe, Spain, and the Netherlands), rulers brought the divisive power of the high nobility under central control to create the great political units of the modern era. But Italy, which had been the generator of Renaissance culture, remained fragmented into many city-states and duchies and became the political pawn of the powerful new nations. The twilight of the Renaissance and the dawn of the era known to students of the arts as baroque and to historians as the Age of Absolutism were linked to these changes.

Bibliography. Hans Baron, *The Crisis of the Early Italian Renaissance,* Princeton, N.J., 1955, reprint 1966; Creighton Gilbert, *History of Renaissance Art,* New York, 1973; Marie Boas Hall, *The Scientific Renaissance, 1450–1630,* New York, 1962; William M. Ivins, *Prints and Visual Communication,* London, 1953, reprint Cambridge, Mass.,

1969; Paul O. Kristeller, *Renaissance Thought: Its Classical, Scholastic, and Humanist Strains*, New York, 1961, reprint 1965; Paolo Rossi, *Philosophy, Technology and the Arts in the Early Modern Era* (I filosofi e le macchine), trans. by Salvator Attansio, New York, 1970.

JAMES S. ACKERMAN

RENOIR, JEAN (1894–1979)

French filmmaker. Jean Renoir, the second son of the famed impressionist painter Pierre-Auguste Renoir, shared with his father a love of nature and a zest for life. During World War I he served in the French cavalry and air force and was twice wounded. After the war he married his father's model, Andrée Heuschling, and in 1924 he launched his career in MOTION PICTURES. His wife (under the name Catherine Hessling) starred in many of his silent films, most of which had limited success.

In the 1930s, with the coming of sound, Renoir became perhaps the key figure in French cinema. More fully than any others, his films captured the mood of the nation, from an anarchic revolt against bourgeois values, as in *Boudu sauvé des eaux* (Boudu Saved from Drowning, 1932), to commitment to social causes (including a film made specifically for the French Communist party) to an ultimate paralysis and disillusion, as in *La règle du jeu* (The Rules of the Game, 1939). His two masterpieces of the period were *La grande illusion* (Grand Illusion, 1937), an international success that explored national loyalties and class affinities in a World War I setting, and *La règle du jeu*, a bitter comedy about class tensions that was not appreciated until after World War II.

Renoir spent World War II in the United States but found it difficult to adapt his spontaneous and improvisatory style to the HOLLYWOOD studio system; still, he directed films there throughout the 1940s. With *The River* (1951), made in color in India, Renoir regained his artistic freedom and recaptured the quality of his prewar films, as well as prompting a young Indian artist, Satyajit Ray, who had assisted him on location, to embark on his own filmmaking career. Renoir's later films of the 1950s were colorful evocations of past eras featuring international STARS like Anna Magnani and Ingrid Bergman. The young critics who founded the film magazine *Cahiers du cinéma* and who created the NEW WAVE FILM movement that transformed French cinema at the end of the 1950s recognized his inspiration, and Renoir returned the compliment by dedicating to them his autobiography, *My Life and My Films* (1974). In 1975 Renoir received an honorary Academy Award for his cumulative work, and in 1977 he was inducted as an officer of the French Legion of Honor.

Figure 1. *(Renoir, Jean)* Jean Renoir. National Film Archive, London.

Renoir was a master of literary adaptation, especially in his films of Émile Zola's novels *Nana* (1926) and *La bête humaine* (The Human Beast, 1938). The world of the THEATER served him frequently as a metaphor, via both amateur theatricals (*La grande illusion*, *La règle du jeu*) and spectacular evocations (*The Golden Coach*, 1952; *French Cancan*, 1954). Nature in all its varied aspects also played a prominent part in Renoir's work, whether lyrical, as in *Une partie de campagne* (A Day in the Country, 1936), cruel (*The Southerner*, 1945), or life-giving (*The River*).

François Truffaut, his disciple, identified an all-encompassing sympathy for the human species as Renoir's "trade secret," quoting words spoken by Renoir himself as a performer in *La règle du jeu*: "You see, in this world, there is one awful thing, and that is that everyone has his reasons." But perhaps critic André Bazin has best summed up Renoir's special qualities. It seemed to Bazin that Renoir, through his use of depth-of-field CINEMATOGRAPHY, kept audiences constantly aware of his characters' complex interrelationships with all aspects of their environment and that this resulted in the most intimate knowledge of their inner life. One could observe and caress the surface and, through the surface, touch the soul:

In Renoir's films acquaintances are made through love, and love passes through the epidermis of the world. The suppleness, the mobility, the vital richness of form in his direction, result from the care and the joy he takes in draping his films in the simple cloak of reality.

Bibliography. Roy Armes, *French Cinema*, New York, 1985; André Bazin, *Jean Renoir* (in French), ed. with an intro. by François Truffaut, trans. by W. W. Halsey and W. H. Simon, New York, 1973; Raymond Durgnat, *Jean Renoir*, Berkeley, Calif., 1974; Jean Mitry, *Histoire du cinéma*, 5 vols., Paris, 1967–1980; Jean Renoir, *My Life and My Films* (in French), trans. by Norman Denny, New York, 1974.

SHELDON MEYER

REPRESENTATION, PICTORIAL AND PHOTOGRAPHIC

At the center of the idea of representation is the idea of one thing standing for another. If we leave the idea this general, then we might say that when the thing that stands for another is itself a picture this is an example of pictorial representation, and if the picture is a photograph it is an example of photographic representation. A task of the theory of representation is to formulate any significant distinction between pictorial representations and other representations, and to formulate a distinction between photographic representations and other kinds of pictorial representations, if there is one.

Representation in General

Examples of things that represent other things are extremely varied. The following, for instance, are probably too different from one another to be comprehended by any useful theory.

1. The name *John F. Kennedy* represents John F. Kennedy.
2. Leonardo da Vinci's painting *Mona Lisa* represents some particular woman.
3. A street map of Chicago represents, among other things, the interstate highway system just west of downtown Chicago.
4. An electrocardiogram represents certain aspects of the electrical situation in the vicinity of someone's heart.
5. A red piece of litmus paper represents the acidity of some liquid.
6. A photograph of Mount Vesuvius represents Vesuvius erupting.
7. A finish-line photograph represents the outcome of a horse race.
8. An attorney represents a client during a court proceeding.
9. John F. Kennedy represented the people of Massachusetts in the U.S. Senate.
10. The riderless horse in John F. Kennedy's funeral procession represented John F. Kennedy, the assassinated president.
11. Various actors have represented John F. Kennedy in plays and movies.
12. The character Shylock in William Shakespeare's play *The Merchant of Venice* represents Jews in general.

These examples show that construing *represents* as more or less a synonym for *stands for* is to construe the sense of the term *represents* too widely. The element that varies in these examples is the relation between the first thing and the second when the first represents the second. Representation itself is undoubtedly a relation, a connection between two things, but the connection can be achieved in markedly different ways.

In examples 8 and 9, the relation is one of political or legal representation, and it has to do with one person acting in place of or on behalf of others. Example 10 is a kind of "symbolic" representation, as is example 12, although of a somewhat different kind. Example 11 is representation of the kind sometimes called impersonation. Examples 8 through 12 are interesting and legitimate examples of representation in the most general sense but will not be discussed here.

In examples 1 through 7, all except example 1 involve a representation that is itself a picture or something like a picture, and all seven have in common certain logical features. In example 1 the connection between a name and what it represents seems utterly "conventional," while in examples 2 through 7 the first thing seems connected to what it stands for by a kind of "natural" relation. The natural relation in examples 2 and 3 seems to be the relation of resemblance; that is, the first thing represents the second by looking like it. In examples 4, 5, and 7 the natural relation seems to be causation; the first thing represents the second by being a causal consequence of it. Example 6 is special because it seems that the photograph is linked to what it pictures by both resemblance and causation. Except for the case of photographs, most interest in representations is centered on cases in which the link between a representation and what it represents is not causal.

Pictorial Representation

A name stands for a person and may be said to represent that person. A picture of the same person also represents that person. What is the difference between the name and the picture? There is nothing in the name itself that could indicate whose name it is, and for this reason one might say that the connection between the name and the person is entirely arbitrary. It is only by knowing that the name belongs to the person that an observer could connect the two. From the picture, however, an observer can discover whose picture it is. This is a real difference between names and pictures, but it is not yet formulated precisely enough because there are representational words that do allow an observer to infer what the words stand for. Suppose there is a man named Fred standing in the doorway. From the word *Fred* an observer can infer nothing about the person (except, perhaps, that the person is male, because Fred is conventionally a male name). From a picture an observer can tell that the person is standing in the doorway, that he is a man, and various specific features of his appearance. But consider the description "the tall man with blond hair and blue eyes who is standing in the doorway." Certainly one can infer some very definite features of the thing represented by those words. The words have a connection with the man that is not entirely arbitrary. Indeed, one might discover from the words just those features of the represented person that can be discovered from his picture. Then what is the difference between words and pictures when the words are not names but are genuine descriptions?

There are three principal theses about the nature of pictorial representation. The first takes pictorial representation to be essentially a matter of resemblance; the second supposes it to be a matter of substitution, in which the representation is a kind of surrogate for the thing represented; and the third insists that pictorial representation is essentially the same as representation by words or any other items that stand for things, the difference being only a matter of the kind of system in which the standing-for occurs.

Pictorial representation as a kind of resemblance. The difference between pictures and words, we may suppose, is that a picture is the kind of representation that resembles what it stands for, and therefore an observer knows that whatever is represented by the picture will look like the picture. The observer also knows from descriptive words what the represented thing will look like, but not because of any natural relation of resemblance: the words do not look like what they stand for.

If a pictorial representation is the kind of representation that looks like what it represents, then what remain to be explained are (1) what it means for one thing to look like another, especially when one of the things (the picture) is two-dimensional and at least in that regard seems not much at all like the thing it represents, which typically is three-dimensional; (2) how a pictorial representation is to be understood as such if it happens not to stand for anything; and (3) why the relation of pictorial representation is asymmetrical—that is, why the picture typically represents what is depicted and not the other way around, this being a problem if resemblance is all there is to pictorial representation because the picture and what it depicts seem clearly to resemble each other.

1. The idea that a representation is essentially a simulacrum is at least as old as PLATO and ARISTOTLE. In their writing free use is made of the term *mimesis,* usually translated as "imitation" and occasionally as "representation." In the *Poetics* Aristotle asserts that a tragedy is an imitation of a human action, assuming evidently that it will not be difficult to extrapolate the idea of imitation from cases of statuary, for instance, in which the statue may be said to imitate the person it stands for, to the more abstract case in which a drama may be said to imitate an action. An element of this conception is contained in the word *represent* and its etymological suggestion that a representation re-presents the thing it stands for. The representation may be more or less complete with regard to the number of features it displays. In example 2, for instance, the painting is relatively full, presenting in considerable detail the face it shows. Example 3 is different; it is more abstracted and presents only structural, relational details. In example 2, a painting of a woman, the part of the painting corresponding to the woman's hair is of a particular color and thereby indicates that the represented woman's hair is of that very color. In example 3, however, the part of the map corresponding to a highway is colored black, and this does not indicate anything about the color of the highway represented. The map is a representation that has abstracted virtually all the features of what is represented except those of distance and direction (*see* GRAPHICS; MAP PROJECTION).

The thesis that pictorial representation is a matter of resemblance has only recently been called into serious question. Its proponents have included Leon Battista Alberti, Joshua Reynolds, and John Ruskin. Since the time of Alberti most theoretical proponents of the resemblance thesis have relied heavily on some theory of perspective in pictures as a way of giving content to the idea that pictorial representations look like what they depict. In fact, perspectival pictures have been taken to be exactly that: two-dimensional objects that look like three-dimensional arrays. This assumption involves a number of problematic prior assumptions concerning the behavior of the eye when it is directed at a two-dimensional surface as opposed to being directed at a three-dimensional vista. Research has begun into the nature of the human visual system that may well determine whether these assumptions are tenable.

The central problem is to explain what it is for the

representation to look like what it represents. The two things do not look like one another in every respect, and in some salient respects they are quite different. For instance, the picture is probably of a considerably different size; a picture with a total area of six square feet might represent Chicago, an area thousands of times greater. The colors of the picture may well be different from those of the object. And equally troublesome is the fact that what is seen by an observer is markedly different if the observer moves during the observation. Then what does it mean to say that the picture looks like its object? Perhaps the best answer this theory can give is that the conception of resemblance is a "primitive" conception—the kind of conception we accept readily enough in mathematical and scientific theories—that is not itself defined but is conveyed in examples. The theory might also observe that it is exceedingly difficult and perhaps impossible to define the relation of resemblance in general, and so it is no particular liability of the theory that it invokes this relation in explaining pictorial representation.

2. Suppose that what makes a picture represent a particular horse is that the picture resembles the horse. Then what are we to say of a pictorial representation of an object that does not exist, say, a unicorn? It cannot be its resemblance to a unicorn that makes the picture a picture of a unicorn, because there is no unicorn that the picture could resemble. Indeed, many of us have learned what unicorns look like from pictures, and we could not have done that if we first needed to know what a unicorn looked like in order to realize that the pictures were of unicorns. This conundrum, which is one part of the general logical problem of understanding fictional references, besets all theories of pictorial representation, but it seems especially acute in the case of the resemblance theory.

3. It sounds awkward to say that whenever one thing resembles another, the other resembles the one, which is to say that resemblance is a symmetrical relation; but it is difficult to quarrel with this assertion. If it is granted, then whenever a pictorial representation of a face resembles some particular face, the face also resembles the picture. Then why is it that the picture represents the face and not also the other way around? The obvious answer, which leads to the core of the resemblance theory, is that when two things resemble one another in whatever respects are relevant, if one is a pictorial representation and the other is not, then the picture represents the other thing but the other thing does not represent the picture. This answer is unassailable, but it assumes that we already know what it is for something to be a picture. The resemblance theory must thus be supplemented by a theory of what it is for something to be a picture, for it is only when we know in advance that something is a picture that we can proceed to learn what it pictorially represents.

Pictorial representation as a kind of substitution. This theory has been advanced mostly in the form of schematic suggestions made by Ernst Gombrich, but it has origins in ancient Greece and also in the Bible. Aristotle's idea is that in at least some cases of mimesis the imitation can produce in an observer certain effects like those that would be caused by the original. Thus a tragedy, an imitation of an action, produces in its audience feelings closely related to those that the action itself would produce were the audience to witness it. The biblical injunction against idolatry is far from clear, but part of its concern seems to be that those who make representations of God are in danger of coming to use the representations as substitutes for God. One kind of idolator undertakes to worship the idol, thereby treating it as only God should be treated.

Gombrich's idea is that what he calls "the roots" of representation are to be found in the biological and psychological mechanisms observable in children and animals. In his celebrated discussion of children and their hobbyhorses Gombrich notes that the hobbyhorse is used by a child in place of a real horse and thus in some sense stands for a horse. What matters, according to Gombrich, is not that the hobbyhorse look like a horse (which it does not) but that it be capable of being used as the child would use a horse (which it is). It is the connection between riding the hobbyhorse and riding a real horse that makes the hobbyhorse acceptable to the child.

In later discussions Gombrich extends this idea of substitution, asserting that pictorial representations in general support the same kinds of reactions as would be provoked by what they depict. These reactions have to do mostly with the psychology of vision and not with actions like the child's riding, but the idea remains that the representation is a surrogate for the original and is in some sense used as the original might be.

This daring, imaginative theory has done much to stimulate recent work in the theory of pictorial representation, partly by loosening the grip of the idea of resemblance. The theory respects the intuitive sense of *represent* as meaning to re-present, but it understands that what is being presented is not the visual appearance of an original but a kind of functional substitute for the original. In doing this it promises to supply a more substantial content for the conception of resemblance. It is not yet clear, however, that the substitution theory is free of the problems of the representation theory. Those problems threaten even the example of the child's hobbyhorse, in which we were freed of the need to formulate any resemblance between the hobbyhorse and real horses because all that mattered was the blunt fact that both the hobbyhorse and a real horse could be ridden. Riding a hobbyhorse, however, is not exactly the same as riding a real horse. It is *like* riding a real horse, one might say, and surely that is correct; but now we have the problem of explaining how riding a hobbyhorse resembles riding a real horse, and this is reminiscent of the old problem of resemblance. If it is easier to explain the resemblance of riding a hobbyhorse to riding a real horse than it is to explain the visual resemblance of a hobbyhorse to a real horse, then the substitution theory may have a considerable advantage over the resemblance theory. If not, then although it is a welcome augmentation of our understanding of pictorial representation, it cannot simply replace the resemblance theory.

Pictorial representation as denotation. This is the most recent of the three theories, owing its development largely to Nelson Goodman. This theory forsakes the use of any conception of resemblance as any part of the explanation of pictorial representation. It insists, instead, that pictorial representations denote their objects just as words denote what they stand for. Examples 1 and 2 are exactly the same, in this theory, with regard to the relation between the representation and the thing represented. This relation, denotation, is understood in this theory, as it is typically in theories in logic (*see* SYMBOLIC LOGIC) and MATHEMATICS, as a primitive notion, and it is not defined. The sense of the notion is assumed to be conveyed clearly in examples like these: the relation of the symbol *1* to the number one, the relation of the word *Chicago* to the city of Chicago, the relation of the word *woman* to any particular woman.

The central tenet of this theory is that when one thing stands for another in the way that a pictorial representation stands for a thing, the representation denotes the thing it stands for. This denotation is exactly the same relation as the one between any symbol and what it denotes. Thus the name *John F. Kennedy* denotes that man, and the painting *Mona Lisa* denotes the particular woman pictured in the painting.

The critical task of the theory is to explain the difference between the kind of denoting symbol that is a word or group of words and the kind of denoting symbol that is a picture. One might expect the theory to say that pictorial denoting symbols resemble the things they stand for, but it is a special aim of this theory to avoid using the idea of resemblance. It declares instead that the difference is to be found in the systems in which these denoting symbols occur. There is no intrinsic difference between a word and a picture, and there is no significant logical difference between the ways they relate to what they stand for. The difference is a systemic one. In any denotational

system symbols are associated with the things they stand for. This association is achieved by means of rules of correlation or correspondence, and once one knows these rules and is thereby equipped to use the system, one can determine what object, if any, a symbol denotes. The rules of correlation differ from system to system, and so therefore do the methods used to determine what a given symbol denotes. Goodman characterizes the logic of symbol systems in terms appropriate to discussing the characteristics of formal, logical systems.

The difference that distinguishes merely denotational systems from those whose denoting symbols can be said to represent what they denote has to do with how it is determined just what symbol is present. The physical, observable symbols we encounter are in fact inscriptions of symbols, according to Goodman, just as "woman" and "woman" are two different inscriptions of the same symbol (the word *woman*). The question is whether every alteration in a given inscription is logically significant in that symbol's system. The following example roughly explains the point.

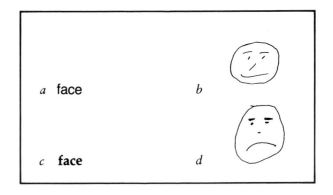

In this example (*a*) is an inscription of a word, (*b*) is an inscription of a pictorial symbol, and (*c*) is an alteration of (*a*), with various lines changed; (*d*) is a similar alteration of (*b*); (*c*) still inscribes the same word as (*a*)—the alterations were not enough to change the syntax of the inscription. However, according to this theory, (*d*) is an inscription of a different symbol from that inscribed by (*b*). It is a characteristic of the kind of system (*b*) and (*d*) belong to that every alteration is symbolically significant. Because (*d*) inscribes a different symbol from (*b*), (*d*) may well denote something different. It remains true, however, that the relation of (*b*) and (*d*) to whatever they may denote is exactly the same as the relation of (*a*) and (*c*) to faces.

According to Goodman's theory, pictures of the

kind to which we are accustomed belong to what he calls "the traditional Western system of representation," and it is a characteristic of inscriptions in that system that, as with (b) and (d), every difference makes a difference. This explains why we find ourselves often attending with greater efforts at discrimination to pictures than to words in order to determine just what they stand for; and this explanation requires no reliance whatever on the idea that the picture looks like what it represents. A consequence of this theory is that symbols like the street map in example 3 are not regarded as true representations because the systems in which they achieve their denotations are systems in which different symbol inscriptions can inscribe the same symbol.

The theory of pictorial representation as denotation, unlike the resemblance and substitution theories, does not take a pictorial representation to be any kind of intimate, intrinsic re-presentation of the object it represents. The representation need not resemble its object, nor need it function in any way as a surrogate for the object.

Perspective is understood by this theory in terms of the correlation rules that link denoting symbols to their objects. The resemblance theory takes perspective to be a technique for making one thing look like another. The denotation theory takes perspective to be rather like a CODE that links coded messages to their uncoded contents. Imagine a picture showing two oranges of equal size, one farther away than the other. Perspectival technique requires that one painted orange, the one nearer the viewer, be larger than the other. The resemblance theory explains this by noting that this will make the picture look like a pair of equal-sized oranges, one farther away than the other. The denotation theory says that in fact the picture is just like the sentence "There are two equal-sized oranges in front of you but at different distances." Once one has learned the rules that correlate words with their objects, one will correlate the sentence with a pair of oranges. Similarly, once one has learned the rules of perspective one will correlate this picture with a pair of oranges.

One of the considerable achievements of the denotation theory is that from the outset it addresses a central phenomenon in pictorial representation, the phenomenon of one thing standing for another. It construes this in terms of the relation of denotation, a well-understood relation and one that we make good use of in many formal theories as well as in ordinary situations of naming.

A major dissatisfaction with the denotation theory has been its neglect of the idea of resemblance. For centuries artists, critics, and observers have spoken of pictorial representations in terms of resemblance, noting greater or lesser similarity in various pictures.

The denotation theory tells us that we are in fact applying the rules of pictorial representation in order to infer what a pictured person will look like. But almost none of us can say what any of these rules are.

The denotation theory has a reply to this, and the success of the theory may depend on how compelling it can make this reply. It says that we deal with the words of our LANGUAGE regularly, determining what those words refer to and how accurate they are, without being able to formulate the rules governing how we do this. We do this habitually, and the relevant habits are acquired as we gain more experience with the particular symbol system that is our native language. It is just the same with the symbol systems of pictorial representation. Our experience of pictures from those systems is just as thoroughgoing as our experience of language, and it too leads to the development of habits. These habits, which guide our comprehension of words and pictures, are the products of experiential learning, and it is irrelevant whether we can formulate rules that describe these habits.

Photographic Representation

Theories of PHOTOGRAPHY in general, and of photographic representation in particular, are of recent origin and prominence, in part because photography is a relatively new representational art and in part because it has proved peculiarly resistant to theoretical understanding that goes beyond the sheer technical aspects of photographic production. Two kinds of theories have emerged. The first treats photographs as essentially like any other pictures and hence as pictorial representations to be understood however one chooses to understand pictorial representation in general. The other treats photographs as images of a peculiar kind, peculiar because of their close causal connection with what they picture.

The pictorial conception. Theories emphasizing this conception tend to regard photographs as pictures that happen to be made with the use of a camera and the attendant photochemical paraphernalia of the darkroom but that function as representations independently of these facts concerning their production. It may or may not be true that these representations have an intimate causal connection with what they depict, but the logic of a photograph's representationality is independent of that connection. Thus it might be the case that in the production of a particular photograph the camera was trained on some object x, but what in fact the photograph represents will be determined without regard to any prior reference to x. It is possible that the photograph will represent something besides x, say y. The determination of what the photograph represents will be settled by one's theory of pictorial representation, and there is no conceptual reason why one should not be free to make use of a resemblance theory, a substitution theory, a denotation theory, or any other supportable theory to show that the photograph represents y and not x. Proponents of the pictorial theory do not rely on the natural relation of causation and so may wish to avoid the natural relation of resemblance as well.

Particular problems for pictorial theories of photography are created by newspaper photographs, television pictures, and other photographic images made of discrete units of color and illumination. A theory like Goodman's regards pictorial representations as essentially unique and unreplicatable because the logic of their systems requires that every alteration in a symbol inscription, including those undetectable by an observer, is significant. Dot-matrix pictures can be duplicated precisely. A denotation theory of pictorial representation that incorporates a pictorial conception of photographs should perhaps treat these dot-matrix pictures as nonphotographic, regarding them as more like maps and words than as pictorial representations.

The causal conception. Theories that emphasize the causal origin of photographs vary considerably, but all consider photographs to stand in a special relation to their objects, a relation not exhibited by other kinds of pictures. The basic idea, shared to some extent by Rudolf Arnheim, André Bazin, and Stanley Cavell, is that when a photograph pictures an object the object is causally responsible for the photograph. The causal efficacy of the object in securing its own representation must be understood, if it is to be plausible, in terms of the object's emission or reflection of the light that exposed the photographic film.

Although theories of this kind emphasize the causal connection, they typically assume that a resemblance relation will result from the causal relation. This assumption makes statements like example 7 troublesome. A finish-line photograph indicates the order in which the horses crossed the finish line, precisely because of the causal connection between that photograph and the actual race; but in fact the photograph does not resemble the race, at least not in the sense of looking like anything that transpired during the race. A similar problem for the theory arises in example 6 if we suppose the photograph to be so inept that it does not look at all like Mount Vesuvius. Thus it seems likely that no theory of photographic representation will be altogether satisfying unless it blends elements of the pictorial conception and elements of the causal conception.

See also PERCEPTION—STILL AND MOVING PICTURES; VISUAL IMAGE.

Bibliography. Leon Battista Alberti, *De Pictura,* and *De Statua* (On Painting, and On Sculpture), ed. and trans. from the Latin by Cecil Grayson, London, 1972; Rudolf Arnheim, *New Essays in the Psychology of Art,* Berkeley, Calif., 1986; André Bazin, *What Is Cinema?* (Qu'est-ce que le cinéma?), 2 vols., Berkeley, Calif., 1967, 1971; Stanley Cavell, *The World Viewed: Reflections on the Ontology of Film,* enl. ed., Cambridge, Mass., 1979; Ernst H. Gombrich, *Meditations on a Hobby Horse,* 4th ed., Chicago, 1985; Nelson Goodman, *Languages of Art,* 2d ed., Indianapolis, Ind., 1976; W. J. T. Mitchell, *Iconology: Image, Text, Ideology,* Chicago and London, 1986; Kendall L. Walton, "Pictures and Make-Believe," *Philosophical Review* 82 (1973): 283–319; idem, "Transparent Pictures: On the Nature of Photographic Realism," *Critical Inquiry* 11 (1984): 246–277.

TED COHEN

REVOLUTION

All nations are subject to periodic revolts. On rare occasions those revolts result in social revolutions, which are societywide events in which regimes representing ruling elites are overthrown by force through the action of opposition groups. Part of the revolutionary process is the communication of solidarity among the revolutionaries and the villainization of the ruling elite.

Social revolutions are complex phenomena, involving numerous groups having both common and contradictory interests among themselves. In the English Revolution of 1640–1649, for example, opposition to the throne included Protestant sects, certain elements of the gentry, London merchants, yeomanry, small merchants, urban poor, and peasants. Thus central to the revolutionary process is the destruction of barriers to communication among the various groups struggling against the regime.

In a stable society authoritative communication is mostly from the elites to the governed. Within a revolutionary situation collective grievances and symbols of resistance are communicated from the dominated to the dominators, so that one aspect of the revolutionary process is the democratization of communication. During the American Revolution the banner of a snake composed of the thirteen colonies with the caption "Don't tread on me!" signified the concept of strength in unity and the resistance of the colonies to English rule. Other symbols of resistance from various social movements and revolutions are the raised clenched fist (adopted by socialist workers in Europe, also used in the United States in the protests of the 1960s), the hammer and sickle (representing the unity of industrial and agricultural labor) of the Russian Revolution, and bare-breasted Liberty carrying the tricolor and a rifle from the French Revolution.

Figure 1. *(Revolution)* François Rude, *Le départ des volontiers en 1792 (La Marseillaise)*, Arc de Triomphe, Paris, 1833–1836. Lauros-Giraudon/Art Resource, New York.

In revolution formerly isolated groups begin communicating across what formerly seemed "natural" barriers, facilitating innovations in the communicative process. This was evident in the Iranian Revolution (1979–1980). Western-oriented, technically trained middle-class Iranians created a market for cassette tape recorders, which were subsequently used by the mullahs (Islamic clergy) to record and circulate the revolutionary messages of the then-exiled Ayatollah Khomeini and by the masses to record gunshots from confrontations with the shah's Javidan Guards, playing them through loudspeakers to confuse the guards in subsequent demonstrations (*see* DEMONSTRATION).

Much behavior of dissident groups is directed at dramatizing messages to the authorities and to nonparticipants. The famed Boston Tea Party of the Sons of Liberty in the American Revolution was a form of street THEATER. In the French Revolution the storming of the Bastille was a surprisingly bloodless affair, but its symbolic significance was much more powerful than its strategic importance. The "long march" of Mao Zedong has symbolized the arduous efforts of the revolutionary forces in the Chinese Revolution. Similarly the sacking of the U.S. embassy by Iranian university students symbolized the anti-imperialism of the Iranian Revolution. Such acts of dissidence have a tremendous impact on the consciousness of the populace, often being celebrated for centuries thereafter.

The destruction of the barriers to communication also leads to a sense of collective solidarity among the dissidents, uniting them under a set of common symbols. The unifying symbols serve to reinforce a sense of common suffering and mutuality of interests among the revolutionary groups. Thus in the English Revolution the Quakers dressed in simple dark CLOTHING and soldiers shaved their heads to distinguish themselves from the elaborate trappings of the nobility and the crown.

Revolutionary visions. Within dissident groups there develops a vision of an alternative society to the present one. That utopian vision (*see* UTOPIAS) is communicated among dissidents through a variety of media: books, pamphlets, posters, speeches, music, plays, films, and so forth. The *Communist Manifesto* of KARL MARX and Friedrich Engels was written as a PAMPHLET during the revolution of 1848. Not only did it provide a concise critique of capitalist social relations, but it also presented a program for the evolution to a Communist society.

It is the promulgation of the vision of an alternative that allows for the radical critique of domination that exists in contemporary society. Thus the writings of Gerrard Winstanley gave the Levellers of the English Revolution a critique of agrarian feudal relations. Critiques of the regime and contemporary society

are maintained in iconic as well as symbolic form. For example, the Nicaraguan Sandinistas have made a shrine out of a building in which a blood bank was housed that was owned and operated by the Somozas, who sold the blood to the United States. The building is a reminder to the Nicaraguans of the parasitic hold the Somozas had on the country.

The solidarity of dissident collectives is communicated through the use of common symbols, pageantry, and mass gatherings. In the Iranian Revolution dissident groups adopted fundamentalist Islam in resistance to the Western-oriented regime of the shah. Women increasingly wore the traditional female dress of the chador, and Islamic holidays were celebrated with fervor in mass gatherings in the streets in contradiction to orders by the shah. Within those mass gatherings religious icons and large pictures of Khomeini were carried. Young men courted martyrdom by confronting the defenders of the regime, shouting revolutionary slogans at them and lifting their shirts as an invitation to death. With each killing a forty-day mourning period, complete with mass processions, would be required, which would induce similar behavior. Not only was dissident solidarity communicated to the regime, but provocations by self-assured revolutionaries were made. By adopting the symbols of Islam the revolutionaries made the regime appear to be the violator of a sacred heritage.

Within a revolution part of the process is the conceptualization of "new humans," who are seen as the next step in the evolution of the human species. They are more intelligent and virtuous than the flawed characters of contemporary society. New norms and ideals of behavior are communicated. Thus within the English Revolution nonconformist clergy perceived the revolution as the triumph of the virtues of the Protestant ethic of hard work, sobriety, and rational living as opposed to the conspicuous consumption of the nobility and the court. Likewise within the French Revolution the image of the Citizen of Republican Virtue was promulgated. In the Russian Revolution there emerged the ideal of the "New Socialist Man," who was without the vices of capitalist alienation. He was a "comrade": a friend, a fellow worker, a true socialist, and a fighter for the ideals of socialism. Such images were present in the Cuban Revolution as well. In each case ideals of new humanity were valorized in heroic art and immortalized in literature.

After the revolution. Once the regime is overthrown, slogans and symbols emerge that reflect the euphoric aspirations. In the Chinese Revolution of 1925–1949 Mao's famous slogan "Let a thousand flowers bloom" reflected the sense of liberation. Major cities experienced a surge in free speech as reflected in the huge wall posters displayed in public places. In the Iranian Revolution the Islamic Revolutionary Guards placed roses in the barrels of their rifles, symbolizing the beginning of a new order. Khomeini's slogan "Neither East nor West" expressed the newly felt cultural pride of the Iranians in throwing off the cultural imperialism of the West and casting a suspicious eye toward the USSR of the East. In Russia after the October Revolution there emerged the notion of "people's art" to celebrate the revolution among artists. V. I. Lenin proposed the creation of monumental PROPAGANDA. Statues of the heroes of the revolution and large-scale memorials were built throughout the country despite the lack of facilities and materials. Additionally, mass street performances and demonstrations were held in celebration. All ART was subject to popular discussion and dispute. Socialist realism emerged as the official style of art because it reflected popular taste.

With the old order overthrown, revolutionaries herald the dawning of a new age. They develop new forms of address, nomenclature, and modes of expression. Thus in the French Revolution persons referred to each other as "Citizen." Streets and cities are renamed (e.g., St. Petersburg became Leningrad, and Saigon became Ho Chi Minh City). The capital of the newly independent United States of America was named after the leader of the revolution. The French Revolution resulted in the institution of a new CALENDAR, which was discarded in Year III of the revolution, during the Thermidor counterrevolution. New anthems are sung in praise of the new regime. In France the national anthem became the "Marseillaise." After the revolution the national anthem of the USSR became the "Internationale."

Consolidation and counterrevolution. Once revolutionaries take over the state, they must turn to the issue of the consolidation of power. Most theorists of revolution understand that in the wake of a revolution there is a period of reaction, in which contending parties jockey for position and power within the newly formed state. This is usually a period of political instability in which warring factions claim to be the true inheritors of the revolution and are likely to depict each other as counterrevolutionaries. Thus revolutionary symbols become associated with new purposes, not those of revolt but of consolidation and a return to law and order—or "counterrevolution." Usually the counterrevolution is bloodier than the revolution itself.

A striking example of the process, with symbols harnessed alternately to both revolutionary and counterrevolutionary ends, has been Iran. Symbols of the revolution—the Qur'an, the sword, images of Imam Khomeini—became symbols of state. The new constitution was averred to be the incarnation of Islamic law. Symbols of the Western influence associated with the shah's regime were either destroyed or appropriated; monuments built by the shah were renamed. Although within the revolution a spate of feminism erupted among the educated, it too was declared evidence of Western corruption and was rooted out. Western jeans were declared subversive for women, and the chador was pronounced the only acceptable feminine wear in public. The dominance of Islamic symbols made it extremely difficult to criticize the regime without being accused of impiety and blasphemy. In Western revolutions symbols of rebellion have likewise turned into symbols of state building, legitimacy, counterrebellion.

Thus in a revolution, communication patterns democratize, symbols change, and language alters to reflect new social relations and aspirations. Symbolic revolt accompanies political revolt, as old symbols take on new meanings and new symbols emerge and are in turn transformed in the revolutionary process.

Bibliography. Daniel A. Foss and Ralph Larkin, *Beyond Revolution: A New Theory of Social Movements,* South Hadley, Mass., 1986; Christopher Hill, *The World Turned Upside Down,* Harmondsworth, Eng., 1970; George Rude, *The Crowd in History: A Study of Disturbances in France and England, 1730–1848,* New York, 1964.

RALPH W. LARKIN

RHETORIC

The study and teaching of practical, usually persuasive, communication. Behind the concept lies the hypothesis that the influence and significance of communication depend on the methods chosen in conceiving, composing, and presenting messages. The kinds of methods considered rhetorical have varied radically across the centuries.

As a concept and term, rhetoric originated in southern Europe in the fifth century B.C.E. and has been present continuously in Western thought. The term derives from the Greek *rhētorikē,* which survives in many modern languages, as in *rhétorique* (French), *rhetórica* (Spanish), and *Rhetorik* (German).

Early Theory and Practice

Earliest works on rhetoric came from traveling teachers called Sophists. These works included compilations of significant literary passages and cogent quotations; handbooks on the pleading of legal cases by writers like Corax and Tisias, fifth century B.C.E. Sicilians; and admired orations such as Gorgias's *Encomium of Helen.* More philosophical works from the fourth century B.C.E. included Isocrates' *Against the Sophists,* a rationale for learning statecraft through rhetorical practice and the study of models; PLATO's

Gorgias and *Phaedrus;* and ARISTOTLE's *Rhetoric,* the most comprehensive treatment of the subject in antiquity. Plato's and Aristotle's views of rhetoric exemplify a continuing dispute over the legitimacy of rhetorical theory, practice, and pedagogy. Plato saw popular discourse as generally superficial and often deceitful. Ideal rhetoric, he said, should express philosophical distinctions, preferably through dialectical questioning and answering but in any event through exposition by speakers with full philosophical understanding of their subjects and unerring knowledge of what hearers need to know. Aristotle's mature view held that rhetoric is the "faculty of observing in any given case the available means of persuasion." Rhetoric, said Aristotle, is an indispensable instrument for creating and sustaining human sociality within a *polis.* He contended that there is an art of rhetoric because systematic principles of invention, arrangement, style, and presentation are observable, and they govern the influence of discourse. Conflicts between the Platonic, idealist view of communication and Aristotelian functionalist views have marked the history of rhetoric from classical to modern times. *See also* HELLENIC WORLD.

Roman culture inherited primarily Isocratean and Platonic interpretations of rhetoric. Strategies of oratorical practice, especially legal pleading, received closest attention from the two great Latin writers on the subject: CICERO and Quintilian. From the fall of the Roman Republic to the fall of the Western ROMAN EMPIRE, study of rhetoric as speech composition and delivery formed the core of Roman education; but as imperial control of public institutions grew, display rather than practical social influence came to dominate rhetorical study and practice. In consequence, historians have called the imperial period the Second Sophistic.

Toward the end of the imperial period Aurelius Augustinus (St. Augustine, 354–430), a professional teacher of sophistic rhetoric, was converted to Christianity and thereupon developed a highly original but significantly Platonic and Ciceronian theory of sacred rhetoric: HOMILETICS. His major works on this subject were *De magistro* (The Teacher) and *De doctrina Christiana* (On Christian Doctrine). In St. Augustine's theory God was the source of ultimate knowledge, and human communication was the conversion of thoughts and feelings into shared sign systems according to principles of religious exegesis and Ciceronian stylistic practices (*see also* SIGN SYSTEM).

Following the fall of the Roman Empire in the West, most classical works on rhetoric were either lost or went unnoticed. It was mainly on a few works by St. Augustine and Cicero that understanding of communication had to be rebuilt once secular scholarship and administrative and commercial activities required attention to ordinary discourse. Inherited

theory, however, was primarily theory of stylistics, and the frame of reference was theological. In consequence, until at least the fifteenth century study of rhetoric remained predominantly study of style, with some developments in philology. This trend was reinforced in the sixteenth and seventeenth centuries by pedagogical redefinitions of the liberal arts, promulgated especially by French philosopher and logician Petrus Ramus (1515–1572). Defining rhetoric as the study of style and presentation, he considered all other aspects of communication to be the domain of logic.

An alternative but not immediately successful claim was developed by George Campbell (1719–1796) in his *The Philosophy of Rhetoric,* originally published in 1776 and republished in more than forty editions and reprints in English between 1776 and 1963. Campbell, a Scottish theologian, drew selectively on the entire body of classical and later thought about rhetoric, but he grounded his analysis in the philosophical and psychological premises of British philosophers Francis Bacon, JOHN LOCKE, and especially David Hume. Campbell called rhetoric "the grand art of communication," asserting that it was an intellectual discipline founded in and justified by "the new science of the human mind." For the first time since Aristotle, theory of rhetoric was fused with a comprehensive psychology. Campbell's project, however, was far less influential than the unoriginal and essentially stylistic *Lectures on Rhetoric and Belles Lettres* (1783) by Scottish rhetorician Hugh Blair, which appeared in scores of editions in the eighteenth and nineteenth centuries—in English, French, Italian, Russian, and Spanish. Also important was *English Composition and Rhetoric* (1866), by Scottish philosopher and psychologist Alexander Bain, who said the concerns of rhetoric were correctness, polish, and elegance. His book became a model for textbooks on writing in England and the United States.

Early Modern Trends

It is not surprising that identification of rhetoric with verbal style dominated modern British and European thinking until very recently, although classical scholars, especially in Germany, were actively collecting, editing, and commenting on ancient Greek and Latin rhetorical texts. In the United States students of composition began to show interest in broader dimensions of rhetoric in the early decades of the twentieth century. Charles Sears Baldwin's essay, "Rhetoric," in Paul Monroe's *Cyclopedia of Education* (1914), and Baldwin's later books, such as *Ancient Rhetoric and Poetic, Interpreted from Representative Works* (1924), were parts of his program to revive classical conceptions of the intellectual problems associated with composition and presentation. At the same time, students of oral communication were putting forward theories of communicative behavior based on current psychological theories. Reflecting a WILLIAM JAMES influence, James A. Winans gave a pragmatic interpretation of speaking in his *Public Speaking* (1915/1917); and Charles H. Woolbert, in works published between 1917 and 1922, provided behavioristic accounts of speaking and writing based on theories of psychologist John Watson. Rising interest in SEMANTICS was reflected in such works as Charles K. Ogden and I. A. RICHARDS's *The Meaning of Meaning* (1923) and Richards's *The Philosophy of Rhetoric* (1936).

World War II and After

World War II marked a historic turning point in rhetorical studies. International concern with PROPAGANDA and PERSUASION stimulated ever wider multidisciplinary attention to all aspects of rhetorical processes.

Intensive psychological study of persuasive processes during wartime led to such postwar experimental studies as those sponsored by the Yale Institute of Human Relations under the direction of CARL HOVLAND. Two landmark works, both by Hovland and others, were *Communication and Persuasion* (1953) and *The Order of Presentation in Persuasion* (1957). Comparable research was carried out by social scientists from psychology, sociology, speech communication, mass communication, human relations, and other specialties. Since 1950 these inquiries have focused on interrelations among forms of communication, media, topics, communicative situations, and predispositions of audiences.

Reassessments of how science, communication, and values are interrelated led philosophically inclined scholars to explore the natures of philosophical and scientific argumentation. British philosopher Stephen Toulmin's *The Uses of Argument* (1958) continues to influence theory of argument. Chaim Perelman and L. Olbrechts-Tyteca, in Belgium, addressed the same subject in 1958 in their *La nouvelle rhétorique: Traité de l'argumentation* (English translation, 1969). These and other writers asserted that Cartesian assumptions and formal logic cannot explain argumentation as generally practiced. Perelman and Olbrechts-Tyteca specifically derived their explanations from classical theories of rhetoric and dialectic and from analyses of the structures of everyday argument. Mario Untersteiner's *The Sophists,* published in 1948 in Italian and in English in 1953, also reflected renewed interest in informal argument, as did Maurice Natanson and Henry W. Johnstone, Jr., in *Philosophy, Rhetoric, and Argumentation* (1965). Similar interests led to European and American rediscovery of Italian philosopher Giambattista Vico

(1668–1744) and the importance he gave to rhetorical theory in his long-neglected *The New Science* (English translation, 1970).

A different thrust in rhetorical studies emerged in LITERARY CRITICISM following World War II: verbal behavior was interpreted as symbolic action. The philosophical background for this view came from Ernst Cassirer in Germany, especially his *The Philosophy of Symbolic Forms* (1923–1929 in German; English translation, 1957), and Susanne K. Langer, *Philosophy in a New Key* (1942), in the United States. Crucial works relating rhetoric to literary criticism were the writings of philosopher KENNETH BURKE. Burke redefined rhetoric as symbolic inducement to an act or attitude. He proposed "dramatistic" rather than "scientistic" approaches to symbolic works. By "dramatistic" he sought to emphasize the active, rather than the reactive, nature of symbolic processing. Burke's fundamental theoretical and critical stance was first articulated in *The Philosophy of Literary Form* (1941; reissued in slightly revised form, 1957). His symbolic action theory now informs a number of research programs in social psychology, literary criticism, philosophy of science, and rhetorical theory and criticism. Central premises of Burke's view are (1) humans are by nature symbol-making and symbol-using beings; (2) use of symbols is inevitably selective, therefore always rhetorical ("dramatistic") action toward self and others by an "actor"; and (3) selection and use of symbols are always accomplished from some perspective—"terministic screens" are adopted, through which we view and represent ideas or feelings.

Burke's conception of rhetoric is, at its base, Aristotelian, though vastly broadened. Other returns to the classical tradition have also appeared. In *The Ethics of Rhetoric* (1953) and in his textbooks on English composition, Richard M. Weaver sought to reinstate the Platonic program for rhetorical study and practice. In other textbooks on oral and written composition in the United States various authors sought to resuscitate such classical concepts and practices as use of topics (*topoi*) when discovering what could be said (*inventio*), evaluation of figures of speech for their psychological rather than ornamental force, and analysis of discourse as informal reasoning rather than as formally logical argument. *Classical Rhetoric for the Modern Student* (1965), by Edward P. J. Corbett, was a landmark textbook of this kind because it reinjected classical concepts and practices into a pedagogy of writing that had for nearly two centuries displaced these considerations in favor of stylistic and/or formally logical precepts.

For the most part, traditional rhetoric focused on concerns of speakers and writers and minimally on how practical discourse is perceived and processed by recipients. Speaker-listener and writer-reader relationships tended to be portrayed as relationships of hunter and hunted. In the 1950s and after, interdisciplinary inquiry fostered the concept that communication is a transaction between and among mutually involved, active, autonomously but interdependently choosing persons. Philosophers, rhetoricians, psychologists, sociologists, critics, and teachers of oral and written composition have increasingly focused on rhetorical phenomena as interactions among symbolizers, symbolic formulations, predispositions of creators and perceivers, implicitly or explicitly articulated propositions, and the milieus in which communication that is actually or apparently intended to influence occurs. Many scholars have argued that no enterprise that includes intentional transactions can be entirely nonpersuasive or nonrhetorical. It does not follow that all consideration of communication is consideration of rhetoric. Many communicative phenomena are impersonal and therefore not marked by persuasive intentions, such as interactions of electronic systems, much communicational "noise," genetic directiveness, or unconscious signaling among animals or humans (see ANIMAL COMMUNICATION).

The most radical departure from traditional thinking about rhetoric has been attribution of epistemic significance to the theory and practice of rhetoric. Broadly stated, contemporary claims for an epistemic status for rhetoric allege that human conceptions are very frequently or always articulated symbolically and that few or no human realities can exist apart from their selective, self-persuasive formulations. Such formulations, it is claimed, are always created from a human, situated point of view and are formed for some purpose that seems potentially satisfying for the formulator alone or for some audience. In its strongest form this epistemic claim alleges that humans cannot know without strategically, hence rhetorically, acting toward and upon their elemental perceptions.

Epistemic claims for rhetoric have been made from markedly different premises. In his *Rhetoric as Philosophy: The Humanistic Tradition* (1980) and other works, Ernesto Grassi has followed Vico in contending that discovery must precede any "logical" formulation, and that this antecedent "noticing" occurs by virtue of selective, humanizing, rhetorical actions toward phenomena of awareness. In the United States classicist and philosopher Richard McKeon has argued from a Ciceronian point of view in numerous books and essays published between 1957 and 1980 that knowledge can enter personal and social life only through rhetorical construction. Drawing on Burke and Cassirer and on neurophysiological resources, Richard B. Gregg in *Symbolic Inducement and Knowing* (1984) accepts Burke's definition of rhetoric as symbolic inducement and expands the concept of rhetoric to include all processes by which we are induced, lured, invited, goaded, and enticed to "know" that which we take to be "knowledge." Other scholars have discussed the relationships between formulating selectively, or rhetorically, and coming to know, making less sweeping claims for the epistemic status of rhetoric than those just cited. In general, however, all of those who make epistemic claims for rhetoric have been moved to do so by a belief that when humans give form to knowledge they do so selectively and purposefully, hence rhetorically, rather than as a process of achieving some literal representation of reality.

Consideration of the relationships between rhetorical activity and epistemology has brought a rapprochement among rhetorical, philosophical, literary, and scientific studies. With or without using the term rhetoric, much critical study of scientific discourse, literature, politics, anthropology, and other human behavior now addresses the question, What happens socially and epistemologically when a notion is symbolically formed? To this extent the study of rhetoric has ceased to be a discipline or a single art and has become the study of all the arts, techniques, or rhetorics available to humans who must make situated choices among symbolic systems and among the options available within a given system used in a particular situation. Aristotle's original definition might be revised to read: Rhetoric is the art of discovering, using, and evaluating the available and the actually used symbolic means of inducing in any given case.

The concept of rhetoric as a subject of study and practice has been so far extended beyond the traditional arenas of speaking and writing that some have argued that acculturation to the forms and practices of organizations, social groups, sciences, technologies, subcultures, and cultures is significantly rhetorical learning. Such learning, it is said, involves learning what is communicatively appropriate to particular bodies of content in particular kinds of situations. In principle, however, the original impetus for the study of rhetoric remains: to discover the available means of communication so that practice can be rendered more effective and sociality can be created, maintained, and understood.

See also COMMUNICATION, PHILOSOPHIES OF; FORENSICS; MODELS OF COMMUNICATION; ORATORY; PUBLIC SPEAKING.

Bibliography. Carroll C. Arnold and John Waite Bowers, eds., *Handbook of Rhetorical and Communication Theory*, Boston, 1984; Kenneth Burke, *A Grammar of Motives and a Rhetoric of Motives*, Cleveland, Ohio, 1962; Cicero, *De oratore*, trans. by E. W. Sutton, Cambridge, Mass., 1948; Samuel Ijsseling, *Rhetoric and Philosophy in Conflict*, The Hague, 1976; George Kennedy, *The Art of Persuasion in Greece*, Princeton, N.J., 1963; idem, *The Art of Rhetoric* *in the Roman World*, Princeton, N.J., 1972; James J. Murphy, *Rhetoric in the Middle Ages*, Berkeley, Calif., 1974; Walter J. Ong, *Ramus: Method and the Decay of Dialogue*, Cambridge, Mass., 1958; Brian Vickers, ed., *Rhetoric Revalued*, Binghamton, N.Y., 1982.

CARROLL C. ARNOLD

RICHARDS, I. A. (1893–1979)

British literary critic and educator. First a fellow of Magdalene College and university lecturer at Cambridge and later a professor at Harvard, Ivor Armstrong Richards is considered by some to have virtually launched the modern TEACHING of literature in the English-speaking world and to have been the founder of modern LITERARY CRITICISM in English. In the course of his prolific career (he wrote or coauthored more than sixty books) Richards moved from the study of LANGUAGE and literary INTERPRETATION to research on EDUCATION. His work was informed throughout by two unifying concerns: a desire to effect a mediation between the arts and science and a passionate interest in the general processes of human communication.

Richards's first books were coauthored (*Foundations of Aesthetics* in 1922 with C. K. Ogden and James Woods, and *The Meaning of Meaning* in 1923 with C. K. Ogden) and revealed interests in the nature of artistic experience and in SEMANTICS that would be lifelong. Two of the next volumes that Richards wrote on his own—*Principles of Literary Criticism* (1924) and *Practical Criticism* (1929)—had the most transforming effect on later literary criticism and pedagogy. Literary studies in the English-speaking world in the opening decades of the twentieth century tended to be impressionistic, antiquarian (e.g., focused on classical or linguistic origins), or historical in the most literal sense (e.g., emphasizing knowledge of historical or social backgrounds rather than of texts themselves) and were decidedly overshadowed both in the intellectual world and in the general society by the rapidly developing fields of the sciences. In formulating a coherent theory of criticism and clearly defining basic terms for aesthetic experience (and in effect resuming and refining the project of Richards's great predecessor in English criticism, Samuel Taylor Coleridge), *Principles of Literary Criticism* and *Practical Criticism* gave to English literary study a solid conceptual and methodological framework that it had previously lacked. Especially in *Practical Criticism*—with his experimental registering of his students' unmediated responses to a sequence of unfamiliar poems, then his systematic analysis of those data and his formulation of numbered sets of criteria for poetic interpretation based on it—Richards did much to give literary study more of the shape of a "science."

Richards's theory of ART as "the supreme form of the communicative activity" was rooted in nineteenth-century ROMANTICISM, but he found additional footing for the theory in the new discipline of psychology. Richards turned teachers and scholars away from the notion of literature as a static and finished entity toward a conception of literature as the communication of dynamic experience from author to reader, one that could in turn inculcate finer communicative ability in readers as well. The corollary of Richards's vision of literature as communication was close and ideally unbiased reading of individual texts, and he in effect created the school of close reading of primary sources, the New Criticism, which dominated literary studies in English for decades thereafter. When the U.S. poet and critic John Crowe Ransom published *The New Criticism* in 1941, he hailed Richards as a founding figure.

Richards's later work turned more toward educational reform and the propagation of the system of Basic English first formulated by C. K. Ogden in the 1920s. (Moving to Harvard in the 1940s, Richards chose to be located at the School of Education rather than in the English Department.) But here too, in works like *Basic English and Its Uses* (1943) and *Design for Escape: World Education through Modern Media* (1968), Richards's long-standing interests in language and in an accommodation between literature and science were manifest. Toward the end of his career Richards turned to the writing of POETRY and comic plays. He also lived long enough to see the New Criticism come under attack from "newer" schools, primarily the Marxists and structuralists (*see* AUTHORSHIP; MARXIST THEORIES OF COMMUNICATION; STRUCTURALISM).

JOSEPH CADY

RIDDLE

In general usage, an act of playful communication in which a party poses a witty question to a respondent who is obligated to offer an apt reply. Folklorists commonly distinguish between a larger class of traditional questions designed to confuse or test a respondent and the riddle per se. The riddle per se is felt to require (1) an (at least) implied question-and-answer structure, (2) a solution reachable through information contained in the question, (3) a basis in the general cultural knowledge of performer and respondents (shared language, worldview, and/or tropes), and (4) a slot within a particular tradition and PERFORMANCE context.

The riddle is one of the oldest and most culturally widespread of FOLKLORE genres. Examples have been found in Greek, Latin, Hebrew, and Sanskrit traditions. One of the most notable examples from antiquity is the Riddle of the Sphinx, which is the story of the half-woman, half-animal who would fly to the walls of the citadel of Thebes and ask a riddle of the young men there: "What is it that goes on four legs in the morning, two at midday, and three in the evening?" When the young men could not answer correctly, she ate them. After Creon's son Haemon had been eaten by the Sphinx, Creon promised the kingdom and the hand of Laius's widow, Jocasta, to anyone who could answer the riddle. A young stranger passing through the city, Oedipus, correctly answered, "Man, who crawls in infancy, walks upright in his prime, and leans on a cane in old age," thereby causing the Sphinx to kill herself and also, incidentally, fulfilling the prophecy of the oracle of Delphi that Oedipus would kill his father and marry his mother.

Cultural contexts. Riddles evolve from common features of the group's environment. Linguistic environments are particularly influential. For example, the common English riddle, "What is black and white and red (read) all over? *Newspaper,*" works only because in English the adjective *red* and the verb *read* (in its past-participle form) sound alike. Similarly, the following riddle depends on linguistic features of Spanish for its wit:

> Cual es el animal que lleva la hembra en la barba? *El chivo.*
>
> What animal carries its female in his beard? *A goat.* (Feminine *chiva* also means "goatee.")

When literacy is shared by interactants, riddles such as the following become possible:

> The beginning of every end,
> The end of every place,
> The beginning of eternity,
> The end of time and space.
> What is it? *E.*

Each culture, moreover, builds its riddles on common practices and objects, as indicated in the Yoruba riddle, "A dark black ram goes to the river; it turns white. *Soap,*" which alludes to the fact that the Yoruba's native soap is black but produces white lather. Note also the metaphorical features of the riddle, in that the soap is compared to a ram. The means of creating wit here differ from the preceding English and Spanish examples, which exploit linguistic features only.

Riddles, in turn, contribute to the maintenance of those cultures from which they draw their material. Among contemporary U.S. society, riddling commonly serves as entertainment, although some investigators underscore the importance of riddling to children's cognitive development (*see* CHILDREN; LANGUAGE ACQUISITION). In a wide spectrum of cultures riddles also function to manage social conflict, teach rules of conduct, and conceptualize the environment for adults as well as children. For example,

among the Venda of Africa children's riddles are introductions to the ritual formulas that both teach neophytes proper behavior and act as verbal tokens of their preparation for rites of passage.

Other verbal puzzles. Distinct from the riddle per se is the *neck riddle,* so called because its teller's neck is saved from death if hearers cannot guess the answer. Consider, for example:

> Under gravel I travel
> On green leaves I stand,
> Riding a colt that never was born
> And holding the bridle in my hand.

Although this enigma, like all neck riddles, employs an interrogative structure and was reportedly posed to respondents, two features distinguish it from a genuine riddle. First, the information required in order to respond is uniquely the knowledge of the riddler. The question alludes to the facts, which are known only to the poser, that he rode a mount that had been a foal taken from its mother's womb before birth. He put leaves in his shoes to muffle his footsteps, camouflaged himself with leaves, and put gravel on top of his shoes. Moreover, like other neck riddles, this example was embedded in a narrative as an episode describing the riddler's escape from death by virtue of creating a riddle that would-be executioners could not solve—a violation of the dialogic features of genuine riddles.

Queer-word riddles are a kind of substitution riddle, in which nonsense words are substituted for some of the words in a description of an action taking place. There is often no relationship between the queer words and their referents. For example:

I went up fumble grumbles, looked out the hazel fazel. There I saw old squibbly squabbly eating up all the little denin pipes.
I went up a ladder in the barn, looked out a window, and saw a pig eating some ducks.

Another type of verbal enigma, the *wisdom question,* calls for a response based on the recall of specialized rather than general cultural knowledge. The clues for solutions are not contained in direct questions, such as "What was the first operation in the Bible? *The removal of Adam's rib to create Eve.*" There is no display of wit in such puzzles; answers require the recall of memorized facts from particular fields, such as baseball, literature, or the Bible.

Joking questions merely parody the riddle form to permit the delivery of a comic punch line. Unlike a riddle, a joking question is insoluble and calls for a conditioned and virtually immediate capitulation by the respondent, as in the following exchange:

> POSER: Where does a 500-pound gorilla sit?
> RESPONDENT: I don't know.
> POSER: Anywhere he wants.

Catches and joking questions share the features of insolubility and comic intent. *Catches* are questions framed in such a manner that what appears to be the appropriate response compromises the respondent. To the catch, "What do virgins eat for breakfast?" the response, conditioned by exposure to joking questions, is generally, "I don't know." As an apparent confession of sexual activity, this response characteristically embarrasses the adolescent female to whom the question is commonly directed.

Riddles and other verbal enigmas draw on the established interrogative patterns of the groups in which they arise. Yet, in the majority of cases, the conventions for responding to interrogatives are turned, temporarily, to confusing purposes. Particularly in riddling, "normal" responses are rendered inadequate. Special strategies are developed that call forth unexpected connections between phenomena. Thus, the process of riddling disorients respondents. When the logic of the fit between question and answer at last becomes apparent, the conventional foundations of group perceptions are only rarely actually broken down. Along the way, however, disorientation leads to a reexamination of the culture's cognitive orders, language, and tropes.

See also HUMOR; SPEAKING, ETHNOGRAPHY OF; SPEECH PLAY.

Bibliography. Roger D. Abrahams, *Between the Living and the Dead,* Helsinki, 1980; Donn V. Hart, *Riddles in Filipino Folklore,* Syracuse, N.Y., 1964; John Holmes McDowell, *Children's Riddling,* Bloomington, Ind., 1979; William J. Pepicello and Thomas A. Green, *The Language of Riddles,* Columbus, Ohio, 1984; Robert Petsch, *Neue Beitrage zur Kenntnis des Volksrätsels, Palaestra IV,* Berlin, 1899; Charles T. Scott, *Persian and Arabic Riddles,* Bloomington, Ind., 1965; Archer Taylor, *English Riddles from Oral Tradition,* Berkeley, Calif., 1951.

THOMAS A. GREEN

RITUAL

May be defined as the PERFORMANCE of more or less invariant sequences of formal acts and utterances not encoded by the performers. Many would argue that ritual is not simply one of many modes of communication available to humans but *the* one that has made other sorts of human communication possible, particularly those resting on LANGUAGE.

Although popular understanding tends to associate ritual with the concerns or practice of RELIGION, a fundamental aspect of the definition offered here is that it does not stipulate ritual's subject matter. Ritual is understood to be a form or structure, that is, a number of features or characteristics in a more or less fixed relationship to one another. Events conforming to this definition occur outside religious contexts. Psychiatrists, for instance, have used the terms ritual and ceremony to refer both to the pathological behavior of obsessive-compulsives and to the healthy but stereotyped interactions between parents and children. In fact, usage does not have to be confined to the human species. Ethologists use the term to designate stereotypic displays through which members of a very large number of species communicate with their conspecifics (e.g., the courtship rituals of great-crested grebes or fiddler crabs). (*See* ANIMAL COMMUNICATION; ANIMAL SIGNALS; ETHOLOGY.)

A second feature noted in the definition is performance. If there is no performance, there is no ritual; performance itself is an aspect of that which is performed. The medium is part of the message; more precisely, it is a metamessage about whatever is encoded in the ritual.

Third, the definition stipulates that the sequences of formal acts and utterances constituting ritual are not absolutely invariant but only more or less so. This stipulation not only allows for imperfection in performance but also recognizes that some variation will likely be present within any liturgical order (ritual) no matter how punctilious its performance must be. For example, certain Melanesian rituals call for offerings of pigs by hosts to guests, but the number of pigs given may vary. Among the Maring of Papua New Guinea men pledge to assist groups other than their own in future rounds of warfare by dancing at their festivals. There is a specified place in these rituals for such dancing, but the sizes of visiting contingents differ. Most significant and fundamental, the individual always has the choice of whether or not to participate in a ritual. *See also* FESTIVAL.

Kinds of Messages Transmitted in Ritual

That there are variant and invariant aspects of ritual implies that two classes of messages are being transmitted. First are the apparently changeless messages signified by the invariant order of the ritual's canon. These are concerned with the enduring aspects of the social and cosmological order. Second are messages carried by whatever variation the ritual allows or requires: giving away twenty pigs or thirty. These are concerned with the immediate states of the performers, expressing, among other things, the current relationship of the performers to the invariant order that the canon encodes. Such informational aspects of the ritual transmission of these self-referential messages as the features of ritual that may vary, the digital representation of analogic processes, and the material representation of abstractions will not be discussed here.

Figure 1. *(Ritual)* Tarahumara Easter ritual, Mexico: procession to the village cemetery. Ava Vargas/Anthro-Photo.

The relationship of SIGN to signified in each of these two classes of messages may be different. That which is signified by the invariant canon is not confined to the here and now, may not be material, and, as in the case of transcendent deities, might not even be thought to exist within the space-time continuum. Since these significata are not present in their entirety, their signification requires the use of symbols, in the sense meant by philosopher CHARLES S. PEIRCE, symbols being signs related "only by law" (convention) to that which they signify. Words are the quintessential symbols in this usage.

In contrast, the states of the performers signaled by variations in performance exist in the here and now. As such, the relationship of the sign to the signified need not be symbolic in Peirce's sense, and often it is not. It may be indexical. An index in Peirce's usage is a sign that is "really affected by" its referent; a dark cloud, for instance, is an index of rain. A gift of thirty pigs by a host to a guest in a Melanesian ritual feast does not *symbolize* the host's great worth or influence; it *indicates* it, as a gift of ten pigs would not. It may even be claimed that

dancing at someone else's festival does not symbolize a man's pledge to fight but is rather an index of that pledge, or something like it, because the dancing is, in John L. Austin's sense, performative. That is, the dancing brings the pledge into being and therefore cannot help but indicate it.

The indexical nature of the signs referring to current states of transmitters is of considerable importance. Indexical communication is relatively free from a vice inherent in the symbolic relation. When signs are freed from what they signify, as is the case when the symbolic relation between sign and signified prevails, lying is, if not for the first time made possible, at least enormously facilitated. It is much more difficult to lie indexically. This is not to claim Maring dancers always honor their pledges or even that they were sincere when they made them. It is simply to say that they made them. What leads the hosts to feel confident—to the extent that they do—that visiting dancers will honor their pledges is the association of those pledges with messages intrinsic to the invariant canon, a matter to be discussed later.

It has just been asserted that the self-referential

message relies for its significance, and in some cases for its acceptability, on the canonical. It is conversely the case that the canonical message carried by ritual in turn depends on the self-referential. Indeed, there is a self-referential message present in all ritual without which the canon would be devoid of force or significance. Ritual, in sum, is not simply a collection of messages and metamessages but a complex form of communication in which the two sorts of messages are mutually dependent.

The Necessity for Performance

A ritual is an order of *acts* and *utterances* and as such is enlivened or realized only when those acts are performed and those utterances voiced. This relationship of the act of performance to that which is being performed—that it brings it into being or realizes it or makes it real—cannot help but specify as well the relationship of the performers to that which they are performing. They are not merely transmitting messages they find encoded in the canon. They are participating in—that is, becoming part of—the order to which their own bodies and breath give life.

To *perform* a liturgical order, which is by definition a relatively invariant sequence of acts and utterances encoded by someone other than the performers themselves, is perforce to *conform* to that order. As such, authority or directive is intrinsic to liturgical order. But participation suggests something more binding than whatever is connoted by terms like authority and conformity. Communication entails transmitters, receivers, and messages, but in ritual performances transmitters are always among the most important receivers of their own messages; there is a partial fusion of transmitter and receiver. A further fusion that occurs during ritual is that the transmitter-receiver becomes one with the message being transmitted and received. In conforming to the order that comes alive in performance, the performer becomes a part of it for the time being. Because this is the case, for performers to reject whatever is encoded in the canons that they are performing while they are performing them seems to me to be a contradiction in terms, and thus impossible. This is to say that by performing a ritual the performers accept, and indicate to themselves and others that they accept, whatever is encoded in the canons of the liturgical order that they are performing. This message of acceptance is the indexical message—or metamessage—intrinsic to all ritual, the message without which canonical messages are devoid of force. It is not a trivial message, because humans have the choice, at least logically, of participating or not. It follows, incidentally, that myth and ritual are not the same, despite the claims of some scholars. Myth itself, as a form, does not specify the relationship of those who tell it or read it or hear it to the content of the myth. *See also* FOLKTALE.

Figure 2. *(Ritual)* Albrecht Dürer, *The Triumphal Procession of Emperor Maximilian* (detail), 1526. Marburg/Art Resource, New York.

Figure 3. *(Ritual)* A renowned warrior and his pig, Highland New Guinea. Irven DeVore/Anthro-Photo.

This message of acceptance, however, is not synonymous with belief. Belief is an inward state, knowable subjectively if at all. Acceptance, in contrast, is a public act visible to both witnesses and the performers themselves. Acceptance is thus a fundamental social act forming the basis for public social orders as unknowable and volatile belief cannot. Acceptance not only is not belief; it does not even imply belief. Although the act of participation may make the private beliefs of individuals congruent with their public acts, this does not always happen. Participants may have their doubts, but doubt does not vitiate the acceptance. Some theologians even suggest that acceptance may be more profound than belief, for in the act of participation performers may transcend their doubts by accepting in defiance of them.

To say that acceptance is intrinsic to performance is not to claim that the performer will abide by whatever rules or norms he or she has accepted. A man may pilfer from the poor box on his way out of church to keep an assignation with his neighbor's wife after participating in a liturgy in which he has recited the Ten Commandments, and all this without making his acceptance less binding. Liturgical performance establishes conventions—understandings, rules, norms—in accordance with which behavior is supposed to proceed; it does not control that behavior directly. Participation in a ritual in which a prohibition against adultery is enunciated might not keep a man from committing adultery, but it does establish for him a rule that he has accepted. Acceptance entails obligation, and whether or not he abides by it he has obligated himself to do so.

This is not an insignificant point. Some conventions, such as linguistic conventions, may be simple products of usage. In other cases, however, usage is full of vagary and violation. As such, usage is not itself capable of establishing convention. Societies must establish conventions in ways that protect them from the erosion of ordinary usage. Ritual does so, and in this respect it may be without equivalents. Rules promulgated by decree may also be protected from the erosion of usage by the power of the promulgator, but their promulgation does not entail acceptance.

To establish a convention—a publicly recognized rule or understanding stipulable in language and open to modification through language—is to specify it, communicate it, and accept it. If acceptance entails obligation, it follows that ritual invests whatever conventions it represents with morality, for breach of obligation is always and everywhere regarded as immoral. Indeed, it may be argued that breach of obligation, in contrast to such specific acts as homicide, is the fundamental immoral act. Homicide is not always and everywhere immoral; it is killing someone whom there is an obligation not to kill that is immoral.

In sum, ritual *embodies* social contract. As such, it is the fundamental social act upon which human society is founded.

Features of Ritual

Rituals include both words and acts. Differences in the communicative capacities of words on the one hand and acts, substances, and objects on the other will not be discussed here. Another problem is, however, raised by the discussion of acceptance, social contract, and morality. It was earlier noted that in ritual the transmitter, receiver, and message become fused in the participant, but nothing was said about the nature of the participant. Given the possibility of disconformity or even conflict between public acts and private processes of the performer as accepting agent, this is highly problematic.

It may be suggested that the use of the body defines the self of the performer for himself or herself and for others. In kneeling, for instance, the performer is not merely sending a message of submission in ephemeral words. The use of the body *indicates* that the subordinated self is neither a fabrication of insubstantial words nor some insubstantial essence or soul that cannot be located in time or space. It is his or her visible present living substance that the performer "puts on the line" or that "stands up (or kneels down) to be counted." *See also* BODY MOVEMENT.

Reliance upon both word and act in ritual has further significance. By drawing themselves into the formal postures to which canonical words give symbolic value, the performers give bodily form to the symbols they represent. They give substance to symbols as the symbols give them form. The canonical and indexical come together in the *substance* of the *formal* posture.

Another important feature of ritual is its invariance. It is from its invariance that sanctity is derived. Sanctity is to be understood in communicational terms as a property of certain discourse, particularly that of ritual, rather than of the objects of that discourse. Thus it is the creedal assertion of Christ's divinity and not Christ himself that is sacred. That Christ may be divine is another matter. Sanctity, to put it differently, is a possible property of discourse in which objects may be represented as possessing divine qualities.

In corpora of religious discourse, sanctity inheres in and flows from a certain class of expressions that may be called ultimate sacred postulates. "There is no God but the One God, and Muḥammad is his prophet" is an example. Such expressions are peculiar. Because their significata are typically devoid of materiality, they are in their nature objectively unverifiable and empirically unfalsifiable. They also seem to be impervious to logical assault. Although they are often mysterious, barely comprehensible, or even self-contradictory (e.g., the divine as both one and three), they are taken to be unquestionable.

The unquestionable quality of these expressions is of the essence. Sanctity may be defined as the quality of unquestionableness imputed by congregations to expressions that are in their nature absolutely unfalsifiable and objectively unverifiable.

The unquestionableness of these "ultimate sacred postulates," it may be argued, following U.S. anthropologist Anthony F. C. Wallace, derives from the invariance of their expression in ritual. Information, in information theoretical terms, is that which reduces uncertainty among possible alternatives. If a sequence of acts and utterances is fixed, its performance cannot reduce uncertainty among alternatives because there are no alternatives. Hence, to the extent that a canon is invariant it is devoid of information. But, Wallace observed, information is not synonymous with MEANING, and the meaning of a canon's informationlessness is the certainty of its contents.

This certainty is one of the grounds of sanctity's unquestionableness. Earlier it was argued that performances conforming to invariant canons constitute acceptance of whatever those canons encode. Acceptance may be construed as an agreement not to question, another aspect of unquestionableness. In sum, the notion of the sacred is implicit in ritual's invariance.

While sanctity has its apparent source in ultimate sacred postulates, which are typically without material referents, it flows to other sentences that do have material or social referents and that may be directly implicated in the regulation of society, sentences such as "Henry is by Grace of God King," "I swear to tell the truth," "Thou shalt not kill," "Honor thy father and thy mother." In its flow the generalized unquestionableness of the sacred is transformed into more specific qualities—truth, reliability, correctness, propriety, morality—thus sanctifying, *which is to say certifying*, the messages in terms of which and by which social life proceeds. The pledges that the Maring signify by dancing are sanctified by their association in ritual with ultimate sacred postulates. Sanctity, in sum, underwrites the discourse on which human social life generally is based.

As the notion of the sacred springs out of ritual's invariance, so, British anthropologist Maurice Bloch has argued, may the notion of the divine. The words spoken by ritual's performers are not their own words. Their origin is immemorial. Words imply speakers, and immemorial, invariant words imply first speakers who existed in time immemorial, at the beginning of time or even before time began.

Religious Experience

As important as liturgical invariance may be, language and the human way of life must be founded on more than formal acceptance and tricks in INFORMATION THEORY. We have been concerned thus far with sanctification and the sacred, but the sacred is only the discursive component of a more inclusive phenomenon that may be called "The Holy." The other aspect of "the Holy," which, following Rudolph Otto, we may call "the Numinous," is its nondiscursive, experiential aspect. Numinous experience is frequently (but not always) invoked in rituals. The social conditions called "communitas" and "effervescence" are among its manifestations, and the intimate, nonverbal modes of communication called "communion" and "communing" may be numinously charged.

In an essay on communication we are not concerned with numinous (or "religious") experience per se but rather with its epistemic qualities, particularly

Figure 4. *(Ritual)* The faithful pray before the Wailing Wall in Jerusalem. United Nations photo 149159/ John Isaac (sm).

as they relate to messages encoded in language. It is important to note in this regard that those who have had such experiences report them to be deeply or even ultimately meaningful but that their meanings seem to be beyond discursive grasp. Their ineffable meaning is not so much a matter of signification as itself a directly experienced state of consciousness or even "being."

Such experiences do have sensible physiological components. Being directly felt, emotionally and physically as well as cognitively, they seem always to be powerfully convincing—not merely accepted formally or represented as certain but experienced as absolutely undeniable. When such experiences occur in the presence of ultimate sacred postulates or representations thereof, those postulates seem to become their source and their subjects. This is to say that in ritual, ultimate sacred postulates may be predicated with the quality of the undeniable by the numinous experience of the worshiper. Thus, in ritual, messages encoded in language, in which a symbolic relation prevails between sign and signified, are grasped by immediate experience. To put it a little differently, messages in which the signified is conveyed through symbols are grounded in that which seems directly known through the senses. This is the third ground of unquestionableness forged in ritual.

The characteristics of the sacred and the numinous are the inverse of each other. The sacred is discursive, but its significata are not material, and therefore it is unfalsifiable. The numinous is immediately material but nondiscursive, and therefore it is not merely unfalsifiable but undeniable. Ultimate sacred postulates thus come to partake of the immediately known and undeniable quality of numinous experience. That this is logically unsound is beside the point, inasmuch as the association is not one that is intellectually conceived but directly experienced.

In their union in ritual, then, the most abstract and distant of conceptions are bound to the most immediate and substantial of experiences. A remarkable spectacle is revealed to us at the end: the unfalsifiable supported by the undeniable yields the unquestionable, which transforms the dubious, arbitrary, and conventional into the correct, the necessary, and the natural. This operation makes possible institutions based on language and thus makes language itself possible. Inasmuch as humanity is defined as such by its possession of language and by language it may be claimed that this structure is the foundation on which the human way of life stands, and it is realized in ritual.

See also SEMIOTICS; SIGN SYSTEM.

Bibliography. J. L. Austin, *How to Do Things with Words*, 2d ed., ed. by J. O. Urmson and Marina Sbisa, Cambridge, Mass., 1975; Gregory Bateson, *Steps to an Ecology of*

Mind, New York, 1972; Maurice Bloch, "Symbols, Song, Dance and Features of Articulation," *European Journal of Sociology* (Archives Européenes de Sociologie) 15 (1974): 55–81; Clifford Geertz, *The Interpretation of Cultures,* New York, 1973; Charles Sanders Peirce, *Elements of Logic, Vol. 2, Collected Papers of Charles Sanders Peirce,* ed. by Charles Hartshorne and Paul Weiss, Cambridge, Mass., 1931–1960; Roy A. Rappaport, "The Obvious Aspects of Ritual," in *Ecology, Meaning, and Religion,* Richmond, Calif., 1979; John R. Searle, *Speech Acts,* Cambridge, 1969; Anthony F. C. Wallace, *Religion: An Anthropological View,* New York, 1966.

ROY A. RAPPAPORT

ROMAN EMPIRE

The civil wars plaguing the Roman Republic from about 50 B.C.E. on precipitated its collapse and led in the following decades to concentration of power in the hands of a single man, Augustus Caesar. The advent of empire under his rule created an immediate need to organize communications over territory that extended from Spain to Syria. Augustus exploited existing structures while also introducing bold new initiatives, many of which remained in place throughout the centuries of the Roman Empire—some until the sack of Rome in 410 C.E.

Imperial Communications

The imperial government employed many forms of communication. A wide range of techniques, including public celebrations, monuments, written accounts and speeches, COINS, ARCHITECTURE, and careful recordkeeping, all served to consolidate, legitimize, and preserve the emperor's sovereignty.

Public image. While Augustus and his circle of trusted advisers sought to control the circulation of ideas and information to reinforce the emperor's dominance of Roman society, they also took pains to make it appear that there had been no fundamental break with the traditions of the Republic. For example, under the Republic the celebration of a military triumph, with its long RITUAL procession, its display of foreign captives and plunder to the crowds that thronged the route, and the construction of commemorative temples and public buildings, had offered members of the senatorial aristocracy, Rome's political elite, their most conspicuous opportunity to enhance their prestige. Augustus put an end to this by claiming the right to celebrate military triumphs as an exclusively imperial prerogative. Successful generals were forced to settle for mere "triumphal decorations," which the emperor himself bestowed, and their statues were erected not in the Roman Forum—the civic and religious communications cen-

ter of the Republic—but in a new forum built by Augustus and dominated by symbolism associated with his victories. The messages were clear: a physical shift away from the Republican civic center to the emperor's newly constructed spaces, and a shift in focus away from numerous senatorial generals to Augustus himself. Later emperors—Vespasian, Domitian, Nerva, Trajan, Septimius Severus—followed Augustan precedent and sought visual legitimization of their reigns by constructing lavishly decorated forums of their own (see Figure 1).

Augustus left instructions that the written account of his own accomplishments, addressed to the Roman people, be inscribed on bronze tablets and set up in front of his mammoth mausoleum in the heart of Rome. While this document had some literary precedent in senatorial funeral addresses and magistrates' statements of accounts, nothing so grandiose and elaborate had ever before appeared in Rome or had ever been circulated so widely. In this document Augustus prides himself on having restored notable public monuments in Rome "without inscribing my own name on any of these." What Augustus does not say is that during his reign the initiation of all public building activity in Rome, as well as most other monumental forms of expression, became the exclusive prerogative of the emperor. Under Augustus's successors, leading senators in Rome found their opportunities for self-glorification ever more restricted: portrait statues and inscriptions appear most often in their private residences, at family tombs outside the city, or—at still greater remove from Rome—in the public spaces in the Italian and provincial cities and towns where they had connections.

To give sharper definition to the emperor's public image, the visual arts were pressed into service. Sculpted reliefs on the "altar of peace," near the northern gate of the city, represented the emperor, his family, and state officials marching in solemn religious procession into a new golden age of peace (see Figure 2). Coins, minted in Rome and controlled by the emperor, were circulated throughout the empire; they portray Augustus with idealized classicizing features, and accompanying legends and ICONOGRAPHY present him as the savior of citizens' lives (see Figure 3). Later emperors also used coins for these purposes (see Figure 4). The public appearances of emperors, and the physical settings in which these occurred, were staged performances, carefully arranged for maximum impact. The sight of an emperor in his conspicuous tribunal at crowded spectacles and games, located in theaters and amphitheaters, made these far more than popular entertainments, just as imperial portraits on coins and statues functioned as far more than artistic creations.

The domestic architecture of the emperors conveyed its own distinctive messages. For his principal

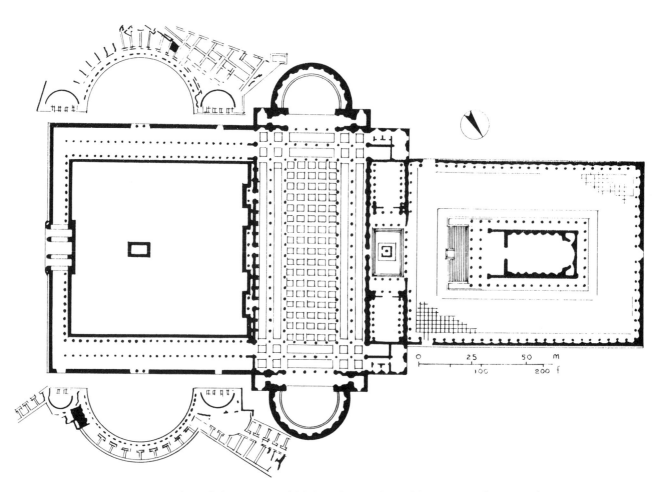

Figure 1. *(Roman Empire)* Plan of the Forum of Trajan, Rome. From Trewin Copplestone, ed., *World Architecture: An Illustrated History,* London: Hamlyn, 1963, p. 61, fig. 154.

Figure 2. *(Roman Empire)* Imperial Procession, from the frieze of the *Ara Pacis Augustae,* ca. 13–9 B.C.E. Marble relief. Alinari/Art Resource, New York.

Figure 3. *(Roman Empire)* Gold aureus ca. 8 B.C.E. Lyons. Obverse; Augustus Divi. F. Laureate head of Augustus to right. Reproduced by courtesy of the Trustees of The British Museum.

Figure 4. *(Roman Empire)* Silver eight-denarius piece. Obverse; Imp. Caes. Domit. Aug. Germ. P.M. Tr. Pot. V. Laureate head of Domitian to right. Reproduced by courtesy of the Trustees of The British Museum.

residence, Augustus selected a modest house on the Palatine hill, in an area favored earlier by Republican aristocrats for their private dwellings, but also near precincts replete with religious associations. However, he rapidly expanded the original residence to include richly painted public halls for formal audiences, a library, and a banqueting hall, all part of a precinct that included a new temple consecrated to his own special protective deity, the god Apollo. By the time of Domitian, nearly a century later, virtually the entire hill had been converted to imperial residence, incorporating parks and gardens.

Letters and archives. In a classic ancient description of the duties and functions of Roman emperors, the author lays special emphasis on the importance of words and letters (*see* LETTER), and on a ruler's need, therefore, to possess the virtue of eloquence: he must make speeches before the senate and address the people at public meetings; he must promulgate official edicts; he must "send letters to all parts of the globe." Emperors wrote their own private letters; they dictated official ones to others, adding a "subscription" in their own hand before the imperial seal was affixed. The growing importance of the role of assistants and advisers in this process is signaled by the creation of three distinct posts in the imperial secretariat, with their titles reflecting their different functions (*ab epistulis, a studiis, a libellis*).

Letters were normally written with reed pen and ink on papyrus (*see* WRITING MATERIALS). Pages were pasted together (so also with books) to make a roll, which was tied with thread and then sealed. More informal notes for delivery to persons in closer range were often scratched with a stylus on folding tablets coated with wax, and recipients could erase the original message, using the same tablets for their replies (see Figure 5).

Increasingly, the records of letters and transactions were preserved in imperial ARCHIVES. In the first century, the standard word for imperial archives,

commentarii, applied especially to records of trials, kept under strict imperial control. Later, the correspondence between the emperor Trajan and his legate in Bithynia presents a broader category of *commentarii*—records of imperial decisions, pronouncements, and acts of favor; other *commentarii* contained records of grants of Roman citizenship to individuals (representing several thousands of entries by the mid-third century); a fourth category concerned the aqueducts of Rome, recording grants of imperial permission to tap the public water system for private use. Finally, *commentarii* registering lands assigned in colonies by the emperor, or bestowed as an act of generosity, were preserved together with surveyors' plans and drawings.

The Extent of Literacy

Roman cities, unquestionably, were full of things to read; we know of booksellers' stalls and of a trade in secondhand books. Outside of Rome, it was standard practice for the Roman senate to send copies of its major enactments to municipalities and colonies in Italy and the provinces, and to instruct local officials and provincial governors to "see to it that the decree is put up in the most frequented place possible." But what proportion of the inhabitants was able to read them? The subject is controversial, and the related set of questions, as to how the Greeks and Romans actually used written communications, is complex.

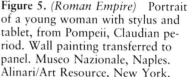

Figure 5. *(Roman Empire)* Portrait of a young woman with stylus and tablet, from Pompeii, Claudian period. Wall painting transferred to panel. Museo Nazionale, Naples. Alinari/Art Resource, New York.

One group of scholars holds that LITERACY, by which we mean the ability to write a simple message with understanding, together with the implied ability to read with some fluency, extended to between 60 percent and 80 percent of the population. However, such a figure seems seriously exaggerated. It is true that widespread literacy might be suggested by the eight thousand surviving graffiti from Pompeii, scratched or painted on walls, and ranging from the obscene to the literary (see Figure 6). Many examples in both Greek and Latin are known also from Rome, as are official notices that warned against messing up walls with graffiti, and examples from other locations prove that enthusiastic sightseers, then as now, could not be deterred from scribbling at the famous tourist sites. However, the status, sex, and occupations of the graffiti writers are scarcely ever specified, so that it is hazardous to argue from them about the identity of the writers or how representative they were of the public.

It is also true that public and private libraries proliferated under the empire. Augustus gave decisive impulse to the future of such facilities in Rome by building two libraries, each containing separate sections for Greek and Latin books. By the fourth century there were twenty-nine in Rome alone, while eminent citizens of towns in Italy, Asia Minor, Greece, North Africa, and Egypt built and endowed libraries as personal benefactions. However, the existence of libraries is no guarantee of extensive literacy: at Rome, permission to use them had to be secured from an imperial official, which was difficult even for members of the emperor's inner circle. As regards city libraries, they are better evidence for the literary interests of the donor than for the extent of literacy in towns.

Other distinctive cultural, social, and economic conditions of imperial society together suggest a much lower rate of functional literacy. First, high literary culture—authors, recitors, readers, and collectors and circulators of books—did not penetrate far beyond the wealthy elite, which can hardly have amounted to much more than .25 percent (150,000) of the 60 million inhabitants of the empire in the second century. In a world of scribes and copyists rather than of printers, there existed no technology capable of producing vast numbers of books, newspapers, or documents. Second, since the majority of the population lived outside cities, access to teachers and school instruction, which were distinctly urban phenomena, was meager for most rural inhabitants. A third factor is the limited need, by those who controlled the labor force in this preindustrial society, for literate slaves or employees. One writer on agriculture notes that even the managers of substantial productive estates "need not read and write so long as they have good memories"; and frequently itinerant scribes fulfilled the needs of citizens, including high officials, who were themselves semi- or barely literate. On balance, a full-scale study of imperial literacy seems destined to reach somber conclusions. Using the definition adopted here, a provisional estimate of three million to six million functional literates throughout the empire—between 5 percent and 10 percent of the population—seems most realistic.

Geographical Factors in Travel and Communication

The size and scope of the empire both encouraged and hindered travel and communication. The geographical and cultural distances were enormous, but the imperial organization of this large area made it possible to improve roads and administrative networks and to construct relatively efficient communications systems.

The emperor and the organization of space. A number of Augustan initiatives reveal a new conception of Rome's relationship to the world it dominated, and a concern for the communications systems that would bind the capital more closely to its satellite cities, both in Italy and beyond. For example,

his division of Rome into numbered regions and named neighborhoods was a scheme quickly adopted by the major imperial port cities in Italy, Puteoli, and Ostia. In addition, he organized Italy into eleven regions. The network of Roman roadways converged, conceptually at least, in Rome, as Augustus solemnly and symbolically affirmed by placing in the forum a "golden milestone," a monument that probably listed the names of the principal cities of Italy along with their distances in Roman miles from the walls of Rome. His conception of Rome's mastery of space had even wider geographical horizons, as is proved by his great project to draw and display in the heart of Rome a sculpted monumental map of the entire world—which meant, in essence, the Mediterranean world.

A logical complement to the foregoing initiatives was the systematic improvement and development of the main arteries of traffic on both land and sea. By the reign of Diocletian (285–316), Roman emperors had constructed fifty-three thousand miles of roads, a network that linked Rome with the most distant provinces and frontiers (see Figure 7). Military engineers, demonstrating remarkable accuracy in surveying, kept road alignments straight in open country, and in broken country kept to high ground, avoiding narrow valleys. Augustus repaired most of the major paved roads of Italy at his own expense. By the time of Trajan (98–117) a road one thousand miles long ran from Holland along the Rhine and Danube to Tomi, via Vienna and Belgrade; under Claudius, Vespasian, and Trajan the early links to Lyons were extended to the Atlantic Ocean, the

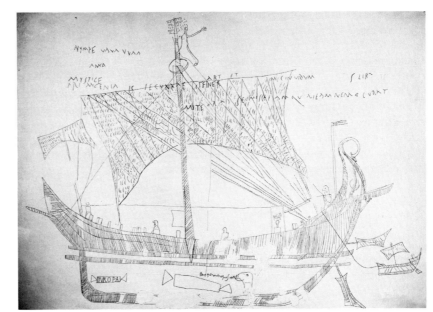

Figure 6. *(Roman Empire)* Graffiti from Pompeii. Courtesy of the Soprintendenza Archeologica di Pompei.

Figure 7. *(Roman Empire)* The Appian way, in the Campanian countryside. Construction began in 312 B.C.E. SEF/Art Resource, New York.

English Channel, and the North Sea. In North Africa roadways ran inland from Carthage and south to connect the desert trade with ports, and, eventually, a coast road twenty-eight hundred miles in length extended from Tangiers to Alexandria. Cylindrical milestones six feet high listed the names of the emperors who built or repaired the road, together with distances from Rome (on trunk roads in Italy) or from the district capital (in the provinces).

While detachments of imperial troops stationed along the roadways helped to keep these safe from highwaymen, the safety of the seas from pirates was secured by the imperial fleets (see Figure 8). In the first case the chief concern of the emperor was to protect the transport of military supplies; in the second the primary motive was the economic need of feeding the capital. As early as the Augustan Age, the emperor can be seen mobilizing resources, in exceptional circumstances, to produce prodigious maritime giants: two vessels that transported Egyptian obelisks to Rome had a capacity of more than three thousand tons, and one of them was at least three hundred feet in length.

To expedite official and especially military dispatches, Augustus adapted the courier system that he found in Egypt and fashioned a service in which each messenger himself went the entire route. The new system, which enabled couriers to be privately interrogated and their papers more swiftly delivered, depended on changes of horses and fresh carriages being kept always in readiness at relay stations, which

were 6 to 16 miles apart. Grooms and wheelwrights were provided, as well as inns every 20 to 25 miles for overnight stops. Couriers traveled roughly 50 miles a day, but urgent messages could be transmitted much more quickly. News of the revolt of the Rhine army reached Rome from over the Alps (and in midwinter) in nine days, a rate of more than 150 miles per day. As the system developed the couriers appointed were increasingly army scouts. Every user of the service had to possess an official pass, entitling its bearer to the use of state-maintained facilities; these passes were normally signed by the emperor, but governors of provinces also could issue a limited number in their names. Since all users of this system had to know exactly where inns and changing stations were situated, hand lists were available, indicating the locations and distances between stopping places along any given route, and sometimes information about the range of services offered. A thirteenth-century copy of one of these third-century "itineraries" has survived, the so-called Peutinger Table (see Figure 9). An elongated piece of parchment thirteen inches wide and twenty-two feet long, it presents a highly schematized road map of the Roman world from Britain to the mouth of the Ganges; the map shows the major routes, names cities and major towns, indicates distances between these in Roman miles, and suggests, by means of pictorial symbols not unlike those of modern guidebooks, the grades of facilities available for couriers and other travelers at each stopping place (*see* CARTOGRAPHY).

Speed of communications. Emperors reached their subjects mostly by the spoken word: everything from lost-property notices to daily news bulletins and governmental edicts was read or proclaimed by criers in Rome's most frequented public spaces, where they vied for attention with itinerant vendors, each peddler possessing his or her own distinctive cry. Communication of news over wide distances, however, presented formidable problems. The Egyptian scribe who prepared a draft of the news of Nero's accession learned of the event thirty-five days after it took place in Rome; other papyri reveal that in Middle and Lower Egypt the emperor Trajan was still thought to be alive four months after his death. A reasonably sophisticated communications system operated in the army. The arrangement of forts on the frontiers was based on information about enemy forces that was passed to the rear lines by signals, so as to permit troops to concentrate at threatened points; signal torches from watchtowers along the Danube under Trajan seem to have spelled out messages by semaphore (*see* SIGN SYSTEM).

Except through the courier system, land travel was very slow (thirty-five Roman miles per day being thought a remarkably good speed), and the fre-

Figure 8. *(Roman Empire)* Roman sailing ships. Gliptoteca Ny-Carlsberg, Copenhagen. Alinari/Art Resource, New York.

Figure 9. *(Roman Empire)* A copy of the Peutinger Table. Detail from *Peutingeriana Tabula Itineraria, Vindobonae, Ex Typographia Trattneriana,* 1753. Courtesy of the Library of Congress.

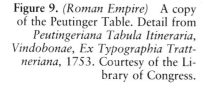

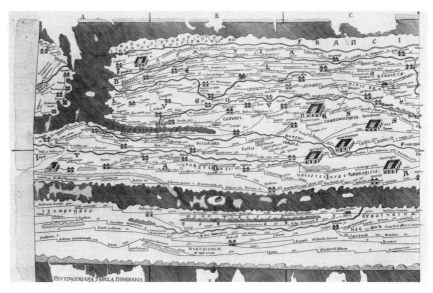

quently tardy delivery of even the most urgent official news underlines the backwardness of much of Roman imperial technology. Long-distance travel by horseback was slowed by the absence of stirrups, of fastened iron horseshoes, and by the lack of proper saddles. For the land transport of goods, the draft horse was usually passed over for lack of a satisfactory harness, and preference given instead to the ox and mule—slower animals with less traction power. As for the sea, the Romans were slow to develop the use of the lateen sail; because of the Mediterranean winds, long voyages remained notoriously insecure and restricted to the period between April and October. Long-distance vessels were almost exclusively cargo ships, and carried passengers only incidentally.

Travelers

During the first two centuries of imperial peace, travel over wide expanses of territory was unquestionably easier than it had ever been before, or than it would be again until the nineteenth century. Moreover, Greco-Roman cultural unity assured that if travelers spoke both Greek and Latin, they would be understood wherever they went. Private individuals traveled for trade, health, pleasure, and piety or to gain and impart knowledge. Nor was all voyaging the exclusive prerogative of the rich. Roman soldiers engraved their names on the pyramids, and sailors assigned to Italy from the economically backward regions of the empire sent letters home to their families in Egypt and elsewhere; military service moved persons of low status across wide distances. There were also the wandering Cynics and beggar priests, for whom poverty was no bar to travel; indeed such men, social dropouts and critics, were a significant feature of later antiquity. Thus, in the course of a journey, one could expect to move along roads busy with government officials, traders, pilgrims, the sick, letter carriers, sightseers, runaway slaves, fugitives, prisoners, athletes, artisans, teachers, and troops. Who did not travel? Most peasants, except for herdsmen, and in general women, until pilgrimages became more common.

Private traders covered impressive distances, reinforcing the cultural links between eastern and western regions of the empire: the rich Gallic shipper who moved Spanish oil from Baetica both to Gaul and to Rome, or the Syrian who carried wares to Lyons, or the merchant from Asia Minor who boasted on his tombstone in Phrygia (Turkey) that he had rounded the southern tip of Greece seventy-two times on voyages to Italy. The incredible dispersion of North African pottery in Italy and throughout the Mediterranean from the outset of the second century points also to sophisticated organization of private trading ventures over wide distances; while the fact that slaves, freedmen, and other humble "front men" could legally be entrusted to supervise business on their masters' behalf suggests something of the socially heterogeneous character of those on the road. Indeed, the sight of a slave traveling alone or with a few others must have been common; otherwise, it is difficult to understand how fugitive slaves found it so easy to remain inconspicuous, especially in large cities.

It was primarily the rich who could afford to travel for reasons of health or pleasure. Medical authorities who advocated long sea voyages—for instance, from Italy to Egypt—to cure tuberculosis were prescribing for the wealthy elite, the same persons who frequented numerous famous spas and mineral springs in Italy and Sicily. But a more motley group of invalids, including the freeborn poor, made the trek to one or another of the many sanctuaries of Asclepius, the god of healing. The most famous of these were in Epidaurus (Greece), the Aegean island of Cos, and at Pergamum in Asia Minor. For the wealthy, travel for pleasure amidst the trappings of luxury became an established part of the pattern of life. Roman senators routinely maintained more than one private villa, in Italy and near the cities of their origin in the provinces, as well as comfortable establishments in the suburbs of Rome. Various indicators, moreover, suggest that persons other than the rich could indulge themselves in pleasurable travel. Inns, mules, and carriages were available for hire in all but the most remote places; means of conveyance could be hired in one city and left at the gate of the next; and the existence of guides and guidebooks at the most famous sites, as well as a brisk trade in souvenirs and reproductions of works of art, all point to the development of widespread TOURISM on a far from primitive scale, with people of moderate fortune the mainstays of the market.

The ease of physical mobility facilitated the spread of cults, most conspicuously that of Christianity. From the itineraries that can be recovered from the book of Acts alone, it has been calculated that the apostle Paul traveled nearly ten thousand miles during his reported career. He is only the most famous of those who traveled specifically to spread the Christian mission; many others are known from passages in the New Testament, especially natives of the eastern lands who had migrated to Rome in order to live and work. The more dynamic of pagan cults, such as that of Isis, were carried to Italy by traders and immigrants; they clustered in the most cosmopolitan urban centers such as Rome and the major port cities. There the new foreign settlers found neighbors from the same country already established, and sanctuaries for their native Syrian and Egyptian gods in full operation.

With the arrival of the uncertainties of the third century—barbarians threatening the armies at the frontiers, severe economic crisis in the city and countryside—prosperity declined, the roads again became unsafe, and Greco-Roman cultural unity, which had been facilitated by the improved patterns of communication connecting eastern and western cities, was fragmented. City life declined as town dwellers, increasingly burdened by taxation, gravitated for protection toward the landed estates of the powerful. The upper classes continued to travel, however. After Rome's conversion to Christianity, one new aspect was the professional moving about of the clergy, to church councils and elsewhere; a second was pilgrimages by the rich to the Holy Land, birthplaces of the new RELIGION. With the conversion of Constantine, we find petitions being brought to him from representatives of the Carthaginian and Alexandrian churches, and the emperor's judgments and replies once again being slowed by the limitations imposed by distance and the difficulties and delays of travel—limitations that had always separated the Roman emperor from the vast majority of his subjects.

See also HELLENIC WORLD; MIDDLE AGES.

Bibliography. J. P. V. D. Balsdon, *Life and Leisure in Ancient Rome*, New York, 1969; Lionel Casson, *Travel in the Ancient World*, London and Toronto, 1974; R. Chevallier, *Roman Roads* (Les voies romaines), trans. by N. H. Field, Berkeley, Calif., 1976; John H. D'Arms, *Commerce and Social Standing in Ancient Rome*, Cambridge, Mass., 1981; Werner Eck, "Senatorial Self-Representation: Developments in the Augustan Period," in *Caesar Augustus, Seven Aspects*, ed. by Fergus Millar and Erich Segal, Oxford, 1984; Moses I. Finley, *The Ancient Economy*, Berkeley, Calif., 1973; Ludwig Friedlander, *Roman Life and Manners under the Early Empire* (in German), 4 vols., London, 1907–1913, reprint New York, 1979; Peter Garnsey, Keith Hopkins, and C. R. Whittaker, eds., *Trade in the Ancient Economy*, Berkeley, Calif., 1983; N. G. L. Hammond and H. H. Scullard, eds., *The Oxford Classical Dictionary*, 2d ed., Oxford, 1970 (s.vv. "archives," "books," "itineraries," "letters," "libraries," etc.); W. V. Harris, "Literacy and Epigraphy I," *Zeitschrift für Papyrologie und Epigraphik 52* (1983): 87–111; Ramsay MacMullen, *Roman Social Relations, 50 B.C. to A.D. 284*, New Haven, Conn., 1974; Wayne A. Meeks, *The First Urban Christians: The Social World of the Apostle Paul*, New Haven, Conn., 1983; Fergus Millar, *The Emperor in the Roman World, 31 B.C.–A.D. 337*, Ithaca, N.Y., 1977; Fergus Millar and Erich Segal, eds., *Caesar Augustus, Seven Aspects*, Oxford, 1984; Michael I. Rostovtzeff, *The Social and Economic History of the Roman Empire*, 2d ed., rev. by P. M. Fraser, 2 vols., Oxford, 1957; Nigel Sitwell, *Roman Roads of Europe*, New York, 1981; Zvi Yavetz, "The Res Gestae and Augustus' Public Image," in *Caesar Augustus, Seven Aspects*, ed. by Fergus Millar and Erich Segal, Oxford, 1984.

JOHN H. D'ARMS

ROMANCE, THE

Many different literary forms have been called romances, including courtly or chivalric tales from the MIDDLE AGES and stories of heroic exploits and exotic adventures from many periods and countries. In modern popular FICTION, however, the term *romance* describes a NARRATIVE that traces the course of a woman's courtship and successful marriage. Romances are a female GENRE; they are read primarily by women, and most are written by women. Many novels contain love stories, but only when the love plot provides both the narrative's shape and its primary conflict is the work considered a romance. Although many romances take place in the past—eighteenth-century gothic romances set in the medieval period or twentieth-century novels set in the Victorian age—romances dramatize issues and dilemmas that are contemporary to the female audiences of their own time. *See* LITERATURE, POPULAR.

With few exceptions, popular romances are ephemeral literature, novels that are read widely when they are published and then go out of print a short time later. Most are issued in inexpensive editions that are bought or borrowed, read, and thrown away. Catalogs of circulating libraries (*see* LIBRARY) in the nineteenth century list various types of romances among the offerings; romance fiction also was issued in series of nineteenth-century dime novels and other inexpensive paperback formats. The ro-

mance genre has been especially prominent in periods when female roles were either changing rapidly or under apparent stress or imperatives to change. For much of its history the genre has been dominated by British writers, with authors in other countries copying successful models produced in Britain.

The popular romance began in the eighteenth century and developed in tandem with the novel itself. Increasing levels of EDUCATION and LITERACY, which accompanied the expansion of the middle class, generated an audience of readers eager for entertainment. By the mid-nineteenth century many genres of popular fiction had emerged, each appealing to various segments of the audience for light fiction. The romance, and indeed much popular fiction in general, developed as an amusement for middle-class women who had the LEISURE to read for entertainment. Romance conventions influenced other popular genres, notably the sentimental gothic novel popular in the early nineteenth century. While the pure romance created suspense by placing impediments of FAMILY, geography, social status, or misunderstanding between the potential lovers, the sentimental gothic novel—such as Ann Radcliffe's *The Mysteries of Udolpho* (1794)—used nefarious plots or pseudo-occult effects to separate the couple and threaten their relationship. Although most romances end in a happy marriage, some do not. When the heroine does not follow the accepted norms of female behavior, particularly if she is sexually promiscuous or domineering, the story—as in Kathleen Winsor's *Forever Amber* (1944)—may end in her defeat or humiliation. Novels that do not follow the strict conventions of the genre, like Margaret Mitchell's *Gone with the Wind* (1936), may attract a male audience as well as a durable readership.

In the eighteenth century, as the novel developed as a literary form, romance conventions were central to many fictional narratives. Samuel Richardson's stories of seduction, *Pamela* (1741) and *Clarissa Harlowe* (1747), offered models for the plethora of popular romances read by women in the ensuing century. Both Richardson novels drew upon the increasing social concern with female chastity and supported the value of virginity before marriage that had become so important to the future prospects of middle-class women. Susanna Haswell Rowson's *Charlotte Temple* (1791) suggested that a woman who failed to remain chaste would inevitably suffer. As other writers followed Richardson's example, the popular romance was born. Serious writers in the century after Richardson, notably Jane Austen and Charlotte Brontë, also explored the social implications of female dependence on marriage, using the romance as a vehicle for social criticism as well as entertainment. The romance as a popular genre is characterized by a narrower emphasis on the emo-

ROMANCE NUEVO, EN QUE SE DECLARA Y DA CUENTA, como estando cautivo un cristiano, natural de la ciudad de Valencia, en la ciudad de Constantinopla, en el palacio del gran Turco, se enamoró de él la hija de dicho Rey: dase cuenta como con sus persuasiones la redujo á nuestra santa Fe, bautizándola; y como despues murieron mártires. Con todo lo demas que verá el curioso lector.

Figure 1. (Romance, The) "New romance, where it is declared and account is given, of how while captive a Christian, a native of the city of Valencia, in the city of Constantinople, at the palace of the great Turk, the daughter of the said King fell in love with him: account is given of how with his persuasions he reduced her to our Faith, baptizing her; and how later they died as martyrs. With everything else that the curious reader will see." From E. R. Cepeda, Romancero impreso en Cataluña (Imprenta de B. Pla y Viuda Pla, 1770–1865), Tomo III (Facsímiles) LII–XCIV. Madrid: José Porrúa Turanzas S.A., 1984, p. 449.

tional, behavioral, and individual aspects of courtship and marriage, thereby supporting common social assumptions—for example, that the female imperative to marry makes courtship a contest between women and men, that romantic love should lead to marriage, and that individuals are responsible for their own fates.

From the beginning, romances have mirrored and exploited the social dilemmas of women in their culture. With few options open to eighteenth- and nineteenth-century women, many were preoccupied with marriage and the status and roles it could confer upon or deny them. Because romances charted the course of successful courtship, drawing on the conflicts and tensions felt by many women in their own lives, the novels attracted readers confronted with the limited options of marriage or single dependency. In the twentieth century the genre responded to the confusions and conflicting expectations of women readers who felt dislocated by rapid social change (see FOTONOVELA).

Female chastity became a less central concern in the romance novel as options for women began to widen. Popular romances in the Victorian period—for example, Maria Susanna Cummins's *The Lamplighter* (1854) and Augusta Jane Evans Wilson's *St. Elmo* (1867)—linked traditional notions about female sexuality with support for a broader range of women's social functions. Courtship and marriage frequently provided a stage for the heroine's performance of the domestic roles of nurturing, managing a home, and serving as the moral center of the family.

Victorian-era romances posited a world in which men and women inhabited distinctly separate spheres. Both potential marriage partners profited by the successful conclusion of a romance: men gained emotional and domestic support, and women gained economic security and the opportunity to participate in socially sanctioned female activities. Although some romance heroines of the time aspired to individual achievement, their primary concerns remained domestic, and their success was defined in terms of their roles as lovers and wives.

Romances continued to reflect conservative notions of femininity until the decades following World War II. In the 1950s and 1960s romances were among the most active and lucrative areas of fiction publishing (see PUBLISHING—PUBLISHING INDUSTRY). Three subgenres dominated the field: the modern gothic romance of Eleanor Burford Hibbert (Victoria Holt) and Mary Stewart; the historical romance of Georgette Heyer, Barbara Cartland, and Anya Seton; and, to a lesser extent, the simple romance of the Canadian-based Harlequin Enterprises and other paperback houses. These variations continued many traditions of earlier books, particularly in assumptions of male dominance in relationships and insistence upon female chastity as a requirement for a successful courtship and marriage.

With the resurgence of the feminist movement around 1970, both traditional female roles and the romance genre underwent significant alterations. Initially changes in romance formulas represented responses by authors and publishers to the widely publicized "sexual revolution"; novels began to include longer and less euphemistic portrayals of sexual encounters and to loosen the restrictions on premarital sex for heroines. Writers such as Kathleen Woodiwiss and Rosemary Rogers sold millions of copies of historical romances in which heroines had multiple sexual encounters. Toward the end of the decade even the most conservative romances became more overtly sexual in content.

The increasing popularity of these newer formulas led to intense competition for readership. Predicting an expanded market for romances, U.S. publishers designed and issued new romance series, or lines, to undermine Harlequin's domination of the market. To lure readers away from older formulas and encourage an expanded audience, editors and publishers urged authors to liberalize the limits of acceptable sexual and social behavior for heroines, to portray more egalitarian relationships between heroine and hero, to find new settings and new problems that reflected contemporary social mores and issues, and to feature heroines with interests beyond marriage and family. These changes, however, did not alter what many saw as the genre's essential support of traditional beliefs about the significance and rewards of successful courtship and marriage for women, even when the heroines were not portrayed as dependent on men for economic security and social status.

The simple romance, which adheres strictly to the courtship and marriage plot and is told primarily from a female perspective, is only rarely found in films or television programs. The audiences for the film and electronic media are more heterogeneous than those for popular fiction, and media production expenses must be offset by appealing to a larger audience than that needed to make a paperback book profitable. Some essential conventions of romance novels do not work well in film or television. The novels' reliance on a female perspective is difficult to achieve on film and may not appeal to a male audience. The focus on emotional aspects of romance is not easily dramatized, because these aspects frequently develop through the heroine's long internal monologues. The virtual requirement that there be a new hero and heroine for each story works against television's typical series structure. Television's closest analogy to the popular romance, the SOAP OPERA, shares many of the same preoccupations but differs significantly from the romance genre in structure. Soap opera narratives focus on domestic and love relationships and are concerned with sexual and romantic relationships, but their plots are more open-ended and dramatize more relationships among more characters. Those romance formulas that include adventure and outside agencies as impediments to love are, however, sometimes to be found in film and

Figure 2. *(Romance, The)* Cover of a Harlequin Romance, 1982. Courtesy of Harlequin Enterprises Limited, Ontario, Canada.

television. Some ALFRED HITCHCOCK films (both his 1940 adaptation of Daphne du Maurier's *Rebecca* and his 1946 *Notorious,* for example) bear close similarities to the conventions and point of view of romance fiction. Some novels with more heterogeneous audiences (like *Gone with the Wind*) also have been successfully adapted to film. More frequently, however, romance conventions appear in films as elements of a larger narrative.

Like novels in other formulas of popular fiction, romances are rarely classed with conventional best-sellers and are infrequently reviewed, although they may be tremendous commercial successes and are often translated into many different languages. The genre has been the subject of much controversy, with some critics assuming that romances encourage women readers to passively accept their status and others defending them as an appropriate entertainment form for women who feel that traditional female roles are fulfilling and valuable. Despite such arguments, however, the romance genre has proved itself to be both enduring and flexible in appealing to its changing audience over time.

See also FEMINIST THEORIES OF COMMUNICATION.

Bibliography. Nina Baym, *Woman's Fiction: A Guide to Novels by and about Women in America 1820–1870,* Ithaca, N.Y., 1978; Sandra M. Gilbert and Susan Gubar, *The Madwoman in the Attic: The Woman Writer and the Nineteenth-Century Literary Imagination,* New Haven, Conn., 1979; Mary Kelley, *Private Woman, Public Stage: Literary Domesticity in Nineteenth-Century America,* New York, 1984; Tania Modleski, *Loving with a Vengeance: Mass-Produced Fantasies for Women,* Hamden, Conn., 1982; Kay Mussell, *Fantasy and Reconciliation: Contemporary Formulas of Women's Romance Fiction,* Westport, Conn., 1984; Janice A. Radway, *Reading the Romance: Women, Patriarchy, and Popular Literature,* Chapel Hill, N.C., 1984.

KAY MUSSELL

ROMANTICISM

A term that first appeared in the second half of the eighteenth century and was used to refer to European literature from the MIDDLE AGES to the RENAISSANCE.

The word *romantick,* as it was often spelled, was derived from the medieval form of the romance (*see* ROMANCE, THE). Romantick literature was a result of the Enlightenment, which believed that since such literature emerged from specific environmental and historical circumstances it was as valid as the literature of the classic tradition, which had emerged in the same way (*see* CLASSICISM). The attributes of romantick literature were judged to be alternative and antithetical to those of the classic tradition, which by the mid-eighteenth century had been dominant in Europe for several centuries. Romantick meant uncontrolled and fantastically imaginative, as opposed to controlled and rational. The classic depended on a widely accepted cultural norm; the romantick emphasized individual sensibility. The late Enlightenment CULTURE of sensibility is best understood as one of emotional liability, in contrast to the emotionally static culture of classicism. Romantick was rapidly expanded to include painting, landscape, and FICTION, as well as POETRY. The Gothic novel was an exemplar of this "romantick culture," as was the "classic style" of Austrian composers Franz Joseph Haydn and Wolfgang Amadeus Mozart.

Romanticism emerged as a new cultural epoch in the 1790s, in response to the French Revolution, the

Figure 1. *(Romanticism)* Théodore Géricault, *Raft of the Medusa,* 1818–1819. Louvre, Paris. Alinari/Art Resource, New York.

Figure 2. *(Romanticism)* Louis Edward Fournier, *The Funeral of Shelley: The Last Rite at Viareggio,* 1889. National Museums and Galleries on Merseyside (Walker Art Gallery), Liverpool.

Revolutionary Terror, and the ensuing militarism and imperialistic expansion that culminated in the oppressive and bureaucratic Napoleonic empire. A few Europeans judged that the Revolution, in bringing about the opposite of its purported aims of liberty, equality, and fraternity, proved the failure of the Enlightenment and thus of European culture. They also saw that if European culture had failed there was no longer any public or general source from which the value of an individual could be derived. Thus the romantics of the 1790s and after saw as their primary task the creation of a new culture.

Romanticism as a Cultural Movement

Romanticism retained two central ideas from the Enlightenment romantick: the possibility of a culture not merely alternative to but actually transcending the regnant culture, and the need for individuals to create that culture from their own resources of imagination and personality. For the new romantic only the self could create value, both of the individual and of life itself.

That *romanticism* came to designate those emergent writers and artists of the very late eighteenth and early nineteenth centuries was a historical accident. Whether the term was used in approval or disapproval, it was based on the recognition that those known as romantics were proposing a culture that would be an alternative to and would transcend the dominant culture of Europe by solving the problems that had invalidated it.

This gives a clue to understanding the great variety of ways in which the terms *romanticism* and *romantic* have been used. To those who did not believe that the traditional culture of Europe had been fatally compromised, romanticism was simply engaged in a fantastic, destructive, and perhaps insane endeavor. To those who believed the opposite, romanticism was heroic, creative, and culturally redemptive. Hence

Figure 3. *(Romanticism)* Eugène Delacroix, *Paganini,* ca. 1832. The Phillips Collection, Washington, D.C.

the exaltation of the artist and poet, the essentially creative individual (*see* AUTHORSHIP). For one side romantic individuality was aberrant and to be condemned; for the other it was the only source of cultural hope.

Thus in popular usage *romantic* has come to mean any behavior or set of judgments that violates the dominant cultural conventions. To those who believe

Figure 4. *(Romanticism)* John Constable, *Weymouth Bay*, 1816. Reproduced by courtesy of the Trustees, The National Gallery, London.

Figure 5. *(Romanticism)* George Stubbs, *Lion Attacking a Horse*, 1770. Yale University Art Gallery, New Haven, Conn. Gift of the Yale University Art Gallery Associates.

that there is no alternative to the established culture and its ideologies (*see* IDEOLOGY), *romanticism* and *romantic* are terms of scorn ascribed to those who endeavor fruitlessly to achieve such an alternative. To those convinced that there must be an alternative to a culture whose failure and destructiveness are evident, these are terms of approbation. It would be schematic but nevertheless illuminating to say that the antiromantic believes that the individual exists

for the sake of the culture, one's task being to maintain it; but to the romantic, culture exists not merely for the sake of the individual but also to support the individual's need to transcend that culture. In extreme forms the first position can easily become a reactionary conservatism, while the second can degenerate into a facile redemptionism or even a belief in REVOLUTION for its own sake.

Because of the almost impossible burden it places

on the individual and the need to achieve cultural innovation, romanticism is much too various to be defined in terms of its attributes or the kinds of ART and thought the romantics actually produced. For example, medievalism was thought to be an attribute of romantic ARCHITECTURE until classicism was recognized to be just as important. The aim in both cases was not revivalism but to uncover architecture's roots. The romantics' wish to transcend the existing culture led them automatically to analyze it. Analysis took the place of traditional synthesis, but since to see the world synthetically is metaphysics, romanticism became antimetaphysical. Thus from the beginning, and in its consequences up to the present, romanticism has been engaged in an analytic dismantling of the superstructure of Western culture. In the mid-twentieth century, philosophy rejected metaphysics as a merely linguistic phenomenon; later, deconstructionism proposed that analysis can show the incoherence in any linguistic construct. Romanticism sees synthetic coherence as a matter of will rather than reason.

Romantic Themes

If this antimetaphysical position can be taken as the reductive foundation of romanticism, it has its own superstructure of related themes to be discerned not only in literature and every kind of verbal speculation but also in the other arts and in the lives of the romantics themselves. The first of these themes is alienation, which results from the conviction that one's culture has failed. Alienation can be expressed in the form of sickness: melancholia, despair, and suicide were all common themes in the works and lives of early nineteenth-century romantics. The effort to escape from that depression took the form first of satirical or ironic attacks on the failed culture and its various modes of cultural vandalism, and second of a realization that attack is not enough,

Figure 6. *(Romanticism)*   Caspar David Friedrich, *Winter Landscape with Church*, 1811. Inv. Nr. 4737. Museum für Kunst und Kulturgeschichte der Stadt Dortmund.

that the failed culture must be transcended. In the 1820s and 1830s the effort to transcend it was symbolized in the figure of the virtuoso, that person who carried art or thought past what had previously been possible. The hero of this period was Niccolò Paganini, the awe-inspiring violinist.

Closely related to alienation and antimetaphysical cultural analysis were two other romantic themes that spread throughout Western culture. These were historicism and REALISM, which are two sides of a coin. One explanation of historicism may be found in the philosophy of G. W. F. Hegel. By the end of the eighteenth century the incoherence of the Enlightenment had become apparent. On the one hand, it was believed that human beings are a product of nature and can therefore know nature both in the form of environment and in the form of individual personality and mind. On the other hand, Immanuel Kant demonstrated that one can know nature only in terms of one's own interests, and therefore one cannot know nature in itself at all. Hegel demonstrated that knowledge of reality is not a property of the individual mind, as Kant had proposed, but that the individual mind is itself a product of human history, of *Geist*, as he called it—that is, of culture in the anthropological sense of learned behavior. Our grasp of the world is the result of the dialectical interaction of the categories of thinking (that is, of LANGUAGE) and the data of the senses. That interaction is unstable and historical. This was the source of U.S. pragmatism, which was concerned with the question of exactly how innovation occurs historically. An analytic examination of European cultural history or even a small part of it, as in the novels of Walter Scott, reveals not only the sources of present thinking but also an alternative MODE of thinking. History proves that cultural transcendence is possible, and in the historical novel both author and reader can enter a different culture. *See* HISTORIOGRAPHY.

Realism, which has appeared in romantic works from the start, depends on taking a historical attitude toward one's present. Just as historicism is an uncovering of what had been forgotten, so realism is an uncovering of what the prevailing culture has ignored. It is analogous to science, which advances only if experimentation uncovers data that current theories cannot account for. Thus realism brings to public attention factors and attributes of current life that the official explanations of that life—its regnant ideologies—cannot explain and therefore ignore. Literary realism has continued in its romantic function up to the present. Moreover, the fantastic (even wildly fantastic) release of the imagination, a persistent romantic tradition, is best understood as psychological realism. As empirical realism challenges regnant ideologies, so psychological realism challenges and undermines the reason and releases both

the will and the unconscious mind. Religious revivalism and innovation—often derived from non-European cultures—and mysticism come under this heading.

There is widespread disagreement about when the romantic period ended, theories positing the 1820s and 1830s to later in the nineteenth or even the twentieth century. Thus some see the emergence of modernism in the first decade of the twentieth century not as a break with romanticism but as a fulfillment of it, as perhaps the first true romanticism. Since cultural innovation is romanticism's aim, it can be argued that genuine and significant innovation is still in the romantic tradition, and that romanticism has not only not ended but is more powerful than ever.

Bibliography. Michael G. Cooke, *The Romantic Will*, New Haven, Conn., 1976; Frederick Garber, *The Autonomy of the Self from Richardson to Huysmans*, Princeton, N.J., 1982; Morse Peckham, *Beyond the Tragic Vision: The Quest for Identity in the Nineteenth Century*, New York, 1962; Charles Rosen and Henri Zerner, *Romanticism and Realism: The Mythology of Nineteenth-Century Art*, New York, 1984; Peter L. Thorslev, *Romantic Contraries: Freedom versus Destiny*, New Haven, Conn., 1984; Geoffrey Thurley, *The Romantic Predicament*, New York and London, 1983.

MORSE PECKHAM

ROPER, ELMO (1900–1971)

U.S. political pollster who pioneered accurate and selective studies of PUBLIC OPINION. Born in Hebron, Nebraska, and educated at the University of Minnesota and the University of Edinburgh, Elmo Roper showed little indication of his future fame as a pollster when he first sold retail and wholesale merchandise. Becoming increasingly interested in consumer preferences and sales management, he joined two partners to form a market consulting firm in 1933. His unusual method was to forecast sales by using carefully prepared questionnaires in interviewing subjects who were selected to represent the general census. He was so successful and so accurate in using smaller samples and higher quality control in an era characterized by large, unselective sampling that in 1935 he was engaged to write a regular public opinion column in HENRY LUCE's *Fortune* magazine, a feature that continued for fifteen years.

For the 1936 presidential ELECTION Roper created a four-point attitude scale, permitting him to quantify mixed responses. Unlike rival pollster GEORGE GALLUP, who used a two-point scale, Roper was able to detect shades of gray in complex voter responses. While the notoriously incorrect POLL of *The Literary Digest* forecast Alfred Landon as the victor by 19 percent, Roper, like Gallup and Archibald Crossley, correctly forecast Franklin D. Roosevelt as the winner, but Roper outstripped rival pollsters in accuracy, coming to within 1 percent of the actual vote. Using the same methods in the 1940 and 1944 elections Roper again proved accurate, with errors as small as one-fifth of a percent.

However, in the 1948 presidential election Thomas Dewey was so far ahead that neither Roper nor his rivals undertook a final poll. Harry S. Truman's upset victory embarrassed all the pollsters and led to a Social Science Research Council inquiry. The exposed weaknesses of rigid forecasts based on quota sampling showed the need for more finely tuned techniques. The results were a change to probability sampling and a greater awareness of shifts in voter thinking as campaigns progress.

Like Gallup, Roper retained a lifelong interest in perfecting polling techniques and in educating people about polls. Besides his column in *Fortune* Roper wrote articles for *Public Opinion Quarterly* and other magazines.

HEYWARD EHRLICH

RUMOR

An unverified report that may turn out to be either true or false; or, the process by which such a report is carried forward and diffused. Rumors are often assumed to spread primarily by word of mouth, but in an era of electronic communication the mass media not infrequently forge crucial links in rumor transmission, amplifying and speeding up the effects of rumor in ways inconceivable when their DIFFUSION depended solely on word of mouth. Terry Ann Knopf, in her study of rumor, argued that the U.S. news media have often played a significant role in race riots by their transmittal of rumors that later proved to be unfounded.

Although the content of rumors is infinitely variable, certain themes tend to reappear—for example, rumors of mass poisoning in wartime. Several researchers have attempted to develop standard classifications of rumors. The best known is probably that of Robert Knapp, who studied more than one thousand rumors collected in 1942 by the Massachusetts Committee on Public Safety and sorted them into three broad categories: "pipe dreams" (wish-fulfillment rumors), "bogies" (expressive of fears and anxieties), and "wedge drivers" (aggression rumors).

It is useful to distinguish between the origins of rumors and the functions they serve. Although most research has focused on rumors that appear to arise spontaneously, it should be pointed out that rumors can be powerful PROPAGANDA weapons and have often been used that way—for example, by governments, especially in wartime, or by political partisans,

to enhance the fortunes of one political candidate at the expense of another. Though the origins of such rumors have generally been concealed to increase their acceptance by the intended audience, they are later shown to have been deliberately created and planted. By contrast, the origins of most rumors, like those of folktales and legends, are often shrouded in obscurity (*see* FOLKTALE).

Functions of rumors. Though the origins of many rumors may be obscure, the functions they serve are easier to discern and can be grouped into two main categories: instrumental and expressive. Writers on rumor have tended to emphasize the instrumental set of functions. Rumors serve to provide information in situations that demand action but are inadequately defined—for example, a battle or a natural disaster such as a flood or an earthquake. Tamotsu Shibutani, in his now classic study of rumor, has labeled this function "improvised news." Rumors arise in situations of uncertainty and threat, when authoritative information is in short supply. Gordon W. Allport and Leo Postman hypothesized that the amount of rumor in circulation was a multiplicative function of the importance of the issue and the ambiguity surrounding it, and Shibutani argued that rumors arise in any situation in which the demand for news exceeds its authoritative supply, as under conditions of CENSORSHIP or crisis. Experimental studies by Ralph Rosnow and Gary Fine have demonstrated that rumors are spread more often under conditions of ambiguity and by subjects high in anxiety. The function of rumor is to reduce uncertainty and thereby diminish the sense of threat, though if a rumor turns out to be false and the actions taken on the basis of it incorrect, the price paid for reducing uncertainty may well be high. In situations of uncertainty, rumor serves as a coping mechanism, though not necessarily an adaptive one. People listen to such rumors because of a need for information; they transmit them because supplying a scarce commodity enhances their status.

Providing information under conditions of uncertainty and threat is only one of the functions served by rumor. Rumors can also serve to rouse a group to action and justify its behavior, as in a race riot or revolt. For example, the U.S. National Advisory Commission on Civil Disorders estimated in 1968 that rumors had significantly increased tension or disorder in two-thirds of the incidents studied. It is this second, justifying function of rumor that has been labeled expressive. Expressive rumors, like instrumental ones, may reduce unease by permitting a group to take action against some perceived threat, but that threat is often another racial, religious, or ethnic group, and the actions taken may prove violent.

Transmission of rumors. Rumor, as a process of communication, can be seen to involve variables that also affect other communication processes, including such factors as source credibility, selective PERCEPTION (see SELECTIVE RECEPTION), recall (and forgetting). However, there has been little systematic study of their application to rumor.

Probably the best-known experimental studies of rumor transmission are those of Allport and Postman, in which subjects were asked to transmit, one at a time, information they had received either from a previous subject or from the experimenter. On the basis of a large number of such experiments, Allport and Postman described three basic distorting processes. The first of these is called *leveling,* elimination of some details. The second is called *sharpening,* selective emphasis on a limited number of details. The third was called *assimilation,* a tendency to change some details to produce a more coherent whole, or one fitting better with the knowledge and past experience of the transmitter. Sometimes this tendency was found to produce elaboration rather than selective omission of detail. Such findings have been replicated by other investigators and have practical implications. Eyewitness TESTIMONY in a legal context, for example, while often regarded as reliable, may involve distortions closely paralleling those in rumor transmission. Outside the laboratory the transmission of rumor is undoubtedly more complex than the research experiments suggest.

It is reasonable to suppose that accuracy in transmission will vary as a function of many factors, including the salience of the rumor to the individual. The term *accuracy* is itself variable in meaning. Omitting some details and emphasizing others may at times convey meaning accurately. One systematic investigation of newspaper accuracy in the reporting of six specific crises found that the general impression conveyed by media accounts was accurate but that the newspapers erred in the reporting of numerous details, usually because an authoritative source was not available or had not been consulted.

One well-known instance of a media-generated rumor involved a 1938 CBS radio broadcast titled "The War of the Worlds," about an invasion from Mars. It was broadcast from New York and featured ORSON WELLES. Freely adapted from a novel by H. G. Wells, the play had the Martians landing in nearby New Jersey, and it included fictional news bulletins appropriate to the plot. More than 6 million people were later estimated to have heard the broadcast; of these, 28 percent were found to have thought, at least temporarily, that the events were real. Most of the listeners were soon reassured, but many rushed from their homes and spread the word to others. Some people reported that they had seen the Martians. Observers later concluded that the Munich crisis of the previous month, when the possibility of world war seemed to hang in the balance, had contributed

to the panic and the credence given to the rumors.

Almost forty years later a fictitious radio report of a disaster at a nuclear power station at Barsebäck in southern Sweden was widely described by the media as having caused a similar panic among listeners who mistook it for a current news report. Although a subsequent investigation indicated that these media reports were themselves largely fictional—inaccurate rumors transmitted by newspapers and television stations on the basis of faulty early reports—a widespread impression of panic caused by the radio broadcast persisted.

An early study of rumors about the state of Joseph Stalin's health, as reported in Paris newspapers, found that the newspapers tended to print rumors congenial to their political attitudes, and Rosnow has argued that by presenting rumors alongside hard news newspapers and electronic media enhance the credibility of the former. The potential for subtle influence, witting as well as unwitting, is clear.

Most rumors die a natural death, either because the situation is resolved or because interest wanes. At times of crisis authorities sometimes attempt to stop a rumor by issuing denials; they run a risk of giving it further currency. The success of the suppression effort may depend on the level of trust that exists in a community and the credibility of the official source issuing denials and "authoritative" information.

Rumors are thus one kind of information always being generated and communicated within a social group. Certain conditions (e.g., social crises and natural disasters) intensify the production of rumors; others (e.g., emotional arousal) contribute to the distortion of the content; still others (e.g., publication by the mass media) multiply the range and speed of their spread. Whereas psychologists have tended to view rumors as distortions of reality, designed to meet a variety of individual needs, sociologists have tended to emphasize the social context of rumors as well as their problem-solving functions. Both perspectives are useful for understanding how rumors emerge and spread and what role they play in social life.

See also GOSSIP.

Bibliography. Gordon W. Allport and Leo J. Postman, *The Psychology of Rumor,* New York, 1947, reprint 1965; Hadley Cantril, Hazel Gaudet, and Herta Herzog, *The Invasion from Mars,* Princeton, N.J., 1947; Terry Ann Knopf, *Rumors, Race, and Riots,* New Brunswick, N.J., 1975; Ralph L. Rosnow and Gary Alan Fine, *Rumor and Gossip: The Social Psychology of Hearsay,* New York, 1976; Tamotsu Shibutani, *Improvised News: A Sociological Study of Rumor,* New York, 1966; Ralph H. Turner and Lewis M. Killian, *Collective Behavior,* Englewood Cliffs, N.J., 1957.

ELEANOR SINGER

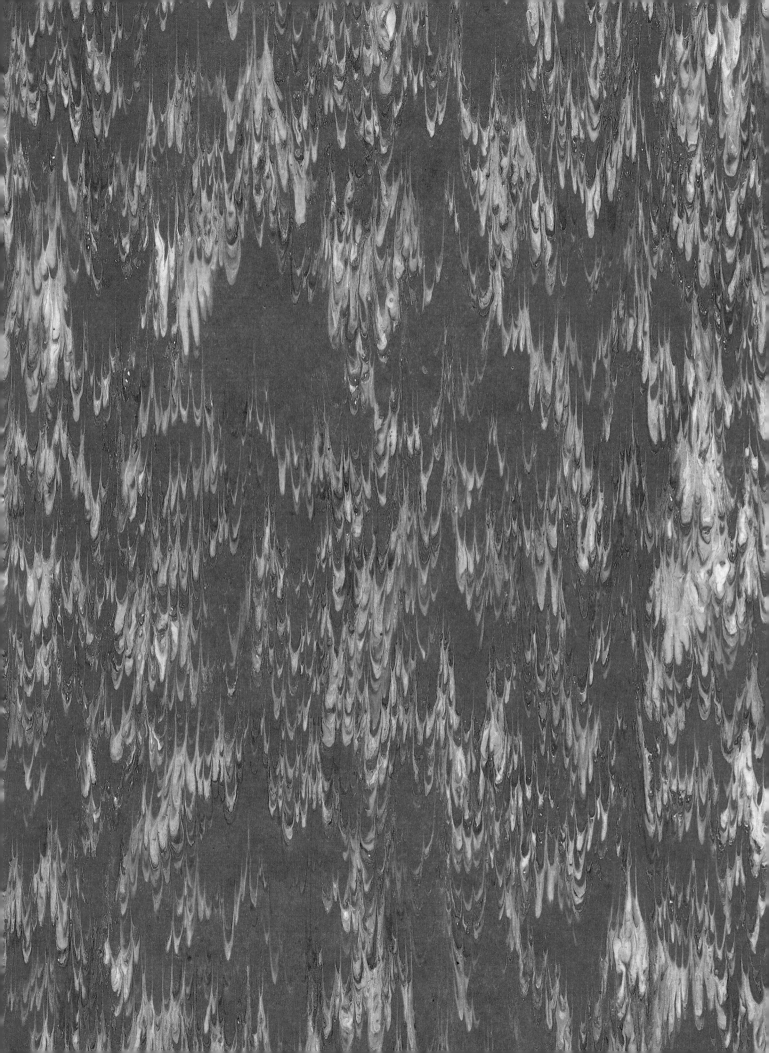